Ethics and Weapons of ...
Religious and Secular Perspectives

This volume offers a unique perspective on the discussion of weapons of mass destruction (WMD) by broadening the terms of the debate to include both secular and religious viewpoints not normally considered. Contributors represent the following diverse ethical traditions: Buddhism, Christianity, Confucianism, feminism, Hinduism, Islam, Judaism, liberalism, natural law, pacifism, and realism. The two introductory chapters outline the technical aspects of WMD and international agreements for controlling WMD. A concluding essay compares the different ethical traditions.

All the authors address the same set of moral issues, creating a dialogue both within and across traditions. The debate structure is particularly useful and appealing for pedagogical purposes. The introductory essays on the technical and legal aspects of WMD could easily be used to introduce the subject to students.

By far the most comprehensive survey of moral perspectives on WMD, this volume should be of particular interest to professionals and students in political science, philosophy, religious studies, and international law.

Sohail H. Hashmi is Alumnae Foundation Associate Professor of International Relations at Mount Holyoke College.

Steven P. Lee is Professor of Philosophy at Hobart and William Smith Colleges.

The Ethikon Series in Comparative Ethics

The Ethikon Series publishes studies on ethical issues of current importance. By bringing scholars representing a diversity of moral viewpoints into structured dialogue, the series aims to broaden the scope of ethical discourse and to identify commonalities and differences among alternative views.

TITLES IN THE SERIES

Brian Barry and Robert E. Goodin, eds., *Free Movement: Ethical Issues in the Transnational Migration of People and Money*

Chris Brown, ed., *Political Restructuring in Europe: Ethical Perspectives*

Terry Nardin, ed., *The Ethics of War and Peace: Religious and Secular Perspectives*

David R. Mapel and Terry Nardin, eds., *International Society: Diverse Ethical Perspectives*

David Miller and Sohail H. Hashmi, eds., *Boundaries and Justice: Diverse Ethical Perspectives*

Simone Chambers and Will Kymlicka, eds., *Alternative Conceptions of Civil Society*

Nancy L. Rosenblum and Robert Post, eds., *Civil Society and Government*

Sohail H. Hashmi, ed., Foreword by Jack Miles, *Islamic Political Ethics: Civil Society, Pluralism, and Conflict*

Richard Madsen and Tracy B. Strong, eds., *The Many and the One: Religious and Secular Perspectives on Ethical Pluralism in the Modern World*

Margaret Moore and Allen Buchanan, eds., *States, Nations, and Borders: The Ethics of Making Boundaries*

Sohail H. Hashmi and Steven P. Lee, eds., *Ethics and Weapons of Mass Destruction: Religious and Secular Perspectives*

Ethics and Weapons of Mass Destruction

Religious and Secular Perspectives

Edited by

SOHAIL H. HASHMI
Mount Holyoke College

STEVEN P. LEE
Hobart and William Smith Colleges

PUBLISHED BY THE PRESS SYNDICATE OF THE UNIVERSITY OF CAMBRIDGE
The Pitt Building, Trumpington Street, Cambridge, United Kingdom

CAMBRIDGE UNIVERSITY PRESS
The Edinburgh Building, Cambridge CB2 2RU, UK
40 West 20th Street, New York, NY 10011-4211, USA
477 Williamstown Road, Port Melbourne, VIC 3207, Australia
Ruiz de Alarcón 13, 28014 Madrid, Spain
Dock House, The Waterfront, Cape Town 8001, South Africa

http://www.cambridge.org

First published 2004

Printed in the United States of America

Typeface ITC New Baskerville 10/12 pt.   *System* LaTeX 2$_\varepsilon$ [TB]

A catalog record for this book is available from the British Library.

Library of Congress Cataloging in Publication Data

Ethics and weapons of mass destruction : religious and secular perspectives / edited by
Sohail H. Hashmi and Steven P. Lee.
p.   cm. – (The ethikon series in comparative ethics)
Includes bibliographical references and index.
ISBN 0-521-83671-9 – ISBN 0-521-54526-9 (pbk.)
1. Nuclear warfare – Moral and ethical aspects.   2. Weapons of mass destruction – Moral and
ethical aspects.   I. Hashmi, Sohail H., 1962–   II. Lee, Steven.   III. Series.
BL65.A85E84   2004
172'.42 – dc22   2003064631

ISBN 0 521 83671 9 hardback
ISBN 0 521 54526 9 paperback

Contents

Tables and Figures

TABLES

FIGURE

Acknowledgments

This book is the result of a dialogue project organized by the Ethikon Institute in collaboration with Mount Holyoke College. The trustees of the Ethikon Institute join with Philip Valera, president, and Carole Pateman, series editor, in thanking all who contributed to the success of this project.

We are especially indebted to Mount Holyoke College, the W. Alton Jones Foundation, Joan Palevsky, the Sidney Stern Memorial Trust, and the Ahmanson Foundation for their generous financial support.

Special thanks are due to Donal O'Shea, dean of faculty, and to Eva Paus and Karen Remmler, directors of the Weissman Center for Leadership at Mount Holyoke College, for all their assistance in making the Mount Holyoke conference possible. Without the hard work of Linda Fernandes and the staff of the International Relations Program at Mount Holyoke, the colloquium would not have run as smoothly or proven as beneficial to the participants as it did. Thanks are also due to Michael Klare, director of the Five College Peace and World Security Studies Program, for his early encouragement of this project.

In addition to the authors' contributions, the project and its results were greatly enhanced by the active participation of other dialogue partners: Gavin T. Colvert, Vincent A. Ferraro, Kavita Khory, Kurt Mills, Will Oxtoby, and Jon W. Western. We are particularly indebted to Sohail Hashmi and Steven Lee for taking on the challenging task of editing this book.

We note with sadness that two of the contributors, Julia Ching and Paul Szasz, did not live to see this project to fruition. Their essays here are among the last completed in two long, distinguished, and prolific careers.

Finally, we wish to express our thanks to Terence Moore of Cambridge University Press for his encouragement, valuable guidance, and support.

ABOUT THE SPONSORS FOR THIS VOLUME

THE ETHIKON INSTITUTE, a nonprofit organization, is concerned with the social implications of ethical pluralism. Its dialogue-publication projects are designed to explore a diversity of moral outlooks, secular and religious, and to clarify areas of consensus and divergence among them. By encouraging a systematic exchange of ideas, the institute aims to advance the prospects for agreement and to facilitate the peaceful accommodation of irreducible differences. The Ethikon Institute takes no position on issues that may divide its participants, serving not as an arbiter but as a neutral forum for the cooperative exploration of diverse and sometimes opposing views.

THE HARRIET L. AND PAUL M. WEISSMAN CENTER FOR LEADERSHIP at Mount Holyoke College promotes educational activities and events that enhance students' understanding of the pressing problems of our times and that provide opportunities for engaged citizenship. Through classroom activities, conferences, and symposia, it seeks to engage the college community, on and off campus, in discussions about feasible solutions.

Abbreviations

ABM	antiballistic missile
BW	biological warfare
BWC	Biological Weapons Convention
CBW	chemical and biological warfare
CTBT	Comprehensive Test Ban Treaty
CW	chemical warfare
CWC	Chemical Weapons Convention
IAEA	International Atomic Energy Agency
JAB	*jus ad bellum*
JIB	*jus in bello*
JWP	just war pacifism
JWT	just war theory
MAD	mutual assured destruction
NBC	nuclear, biological, and chemical weapons
NMD	National Missile Defense
NNWS	nonnuclear weapon state
NPT	Nonproliferation Treaty
NWNP	no way nuclear pacifists
NWS	nuclear weapon state
PGM	precision-guided munitions
PTBT	Partial Test Ban Treaty
SALT	Strategic Arms Limitation Treaty
START	Strategic Arms Reduction Treaty
WMD	weapons of mass destruction

Ethics and Weapons of Mass Destruction

Religious and Secular Perspectives

Introduction

Sohail H. Hashmi and Steven P. Lee

The term "weapons of mass destruction" (WMD) entered popular parlance some fifty years ago. By convention, though not always without controversy, it has been understood to include not only nuclear weapons – the weapon of mass destruction par excellence – but also biological and chemical weapons. If indeed the last two types are included in the category of WMD, then ethical debates on such weapons date back much further in time, to the late nineteenth century, when chemical weapons became enough of a concern to European states that they moved to delegitimize them even before they were fully developed.[1] Yet attention to the ethics of WMD as a category of weapons distinct from others has been extremely sparse, whether it is among policy makers, the media, or scholars – that is, until recently. The September 11, 2001, terrorist attacks on the United States demonstrated quite clearly the vulnerability of even the most powerful states to large-scale death and destruction perpetrated by a group of committed insurgents. The weapons employed on that day were unconventional weapons of the crudest sort: box cutters and civilian airplanes. After the attacks, however, no one can remain complacent that future terrorism will not involve chemical, biological, or nuclear weapons. The George W. Bush administration argues that the prevention of such an event requires preemptive action, not just against nonstate actors, such as the al-Qaʻida network, but also against alleged state sponsors of terrorism, the regime of Saddam Hussein in Iraq being the first target. The terrorists' war on America and the American war on terrorism have propelled questions about the nature and morality of weapons of mass destruction and about the morality of different means to control their proliferation out of specialized seminars and books into the forefront of public discourse around the world.

This book began to take shape several months before WMD acquired the central place in policy debates that they now occupy. Our challenge has been to keep up with the rapid pace of international developments. Still, we are confident that the two objectives with which this book was conceived are as timely today as when we began, and that they will remain so for many years to come. First, we have sought to broaden the range of *participants* in the ethical debates on WMD. We begin by canvassing ethical perspectives familiar to Western readers, the traditional voices heard in discussions of military policy, namely, realism, natural law theory, liberalism, and Christianity. We then bring into the conversation voices not often heard in Western discussions, specifically, Buddhism, Confucianism, Hinduism, Islam, and Judaism. Finally, we consider the critical perspectives offered by feminism and pacifism.

Second, we have sought to update and broaden the *content* of the ethical discourse on WMD. The end of the cold war requires the reevaluation of many moral issues pertaining to nuclear weapons in light of the dramatic changes in the international system. The ethics of biological and chemical weapons has been largely ignored, in part due to the cold war emphasis on nuclear weapons. The ethical discussion needs to extend beyond nuclear weapons to include chemical and biological weapons.

APPROACH

The comparative method we have used in this volume is to bring scholars from a broad range of ethical traditions, both religious and secular, into structured conversation on a defined set of moral concerns created by WMD. The search for moral truths on as complex a subject as the development, deployment, threat to use, and actual use in war of such weapons is inherently multifaceted. One supposition of a comparative approach is that no one ethical tradition or perspective is likely to have all the pieces. Consistent with other volumes in the Ethikon Series, we have sought to realize the comparative approach by asking our authors to address a set of six specific questions, in the belief that comparison can best be achieved by having the contributors address the same set of topics. We have included a comparative essay at the end, which seeks to make the similarities and differences among the authors more explicit. In addition, we begin the volume with two essays that provide some of the background necessary for the study, an essay on the nature of WMD and an essay on the way WMD have been treated in international law.

Another justification for a comparative approach is that, historically, the traditions themselves have developed as much through interaction with other perspectives as through internal revisions.[2] Our ethical understanding of practical issues can be expanded, refined, qualified, and, in general, improved by an effort to engage the insights of ethical perspectives other than the one in which we are situated. A comparative approach allows us to identify hidden assumptions behind a particular tradition's discourse, assumptions whose validity is questioned only when examined in light of other discourses, other ways of looking at the problem.[3] Alternatively, the process of comparison may allow us to discover an overlapping consensus on the issue in question among different perspectives.

At the same time, caution needs to be observed in applying a comparative approach. A comparative approach can be misleading because it may suggest that the traditions are more sharply drawn and more in conflict than is in fact the case.[4] When we divide human thinking into a set of traditions, we invite a clear characterization of each of them, and this may tend to ignore the fluidity of the development of human thought. There may be more overlap and blurred borders than the divisions suggest. In addition, the divisions may tend to suppress conflicts within traditions, and the conflicts within traditions may be as important for our thinking about an issue as the differences among them. We have tried to minimize these dangers by including two chapters for each tradition, one that provides a broad overview of moral reasoning on six basic questions relating to WMD and a second that focuses on alternative understandings or controversial points within the tradition.

The traditional debate on the ethics of military policy in the West, the debate with which our readers are probably most familiar, is that among proponents of the ethical perspectives of realism, natural law, liberalism, and Christianity. Realism, which would be seen by many of its proponents as well as its critics as more an antiethical than an ethical tradition, poses the traditional challenge to efforts to think about military matters in moral terms. In international relations, all there is, and perhaps all there should be, is self-interest. The other three traditions have in different ways taken up the challenge posed by realism, seeking to show that war by its nature is or should be a morally limited enterprise. Much of the thinking in these traditions has focused on just war theory, a systematic effort to set limits on when it is acceptable to go to war and what it is acceptable to do in war.

To complement the traditional debate, we have included perspectives drawn from the Buddhist, Confucian, Hindu, Islamic, and Jewish traditions. Exponents of two of these traditions, Hinduism and Islam, have been quite vocal in appealing to them to justify state policies regarding WMD. For example, during India's and Pakistan's flurry of nuclear testing in 1998, various Hindu militants proclaimed the end of Gandhian pacifism, while Islamic groups in Pakistan paraded cardboard missiles with the words "Islamic bomb" scrawled down their side.[5] Jewish intellectuals and organizations in the United States have been outspoken about many aspects of American nuclear policy, but as both Reuven Kimelman and Joseph David write, a societal consensus exists in Israel that its weapons of mass destruction are off-limits to public discourse. Thus, we find very limited application of Jewish ethics to Israel's WMD arsenal.[6] Buddhists have preferred to act on a more international rather than state-specific level, commenting on broad concerns relating to WMD through various religious associations. Because of the official communist ideology of the People's Republic of China, Confucianism has not figured prominently in whatever little public information we have of that country's security discussions. Confucian ethics on most issues relating to international relations has been elaborated mainly by individual scholars living outside China.

None of these traditions has a record of ethical discourse on WMD as sustained or systematic as that found in the perspectives in the traditional debate. Each is a relatively recent and sometimes reluctant participant in the conversation. All of the writers on these traditions acknowledge that their challenge is as much to construct moral positions on the questions of this book as it is to describe well-articulated existing positions. Nevertheless, all would agree that each of the traditions has sufficient moral resources to respond to WMD in a manner that is not contrived or arbitrary. Donald Swearer, for example, argues for what he calls an ethics of retrieval.[7] Instead of placing the ethics of the traditions beyond history, we should, he argues, seek to find it in norms formulated in a time different from our own prescriptions that can be applied today. There is an important difference between a tradition's lacking resources to handle a new problem and its simply having untapped resources that would do the job. In either case, the resources may appear to be lacking, as they perhaps were regarding nuclear weapons to many Christians at the onset of the cold war. But we cannot assume a lack from the appearance of a lack. It is our job, in carrying out this comparative study of the ethics of WMD, to prospect for those untapped resources, while keeping open the possibility that they may in fact be lacking.

Finally, serving as a counterpoint to the other perspectives, we include the critical standpoints of pacifism and feminism. Pacifism and feminism tend to call into question assumptions the other perspectives take for granted, including the very moral relevance of the distinction between conventional weapons and WMD.

MORAL ISSUES

Now we consider the second of the objectives mentioned above, our effort to update and expand the moral discussion of WMD.

Human beings have moralized about war and the means to conduct it for millennia. All major world civilizations have evolved traditions of moral inquiry that reflect on similar concerns: When is war a legitimate option? Who are legitimate targets? What weapons may be used to attack and possibly kill them? Ethical evaluations of WMD are naturally grounded in the answers that the traditions have provided to these questions. What the traditions have to say about the morality of war in general will be the basis – adequate or inadequate – for what the traditions imply about the ethics of WMD. Thus, the first of the six questions the authors were asked to address is: What are the general norms that govern the use of weapons in the conduct of war, and what are the sources from which the tradition derives these norms?[8]

But the advent of particularly lethal forms of weaponry during the past two hundred years strains to the limit the familiar patterns of moral reflection. Are WMD, in a moral sense, so different from conventional weapons that the traditions may have little or nothing relevant to say about their acceptability? Michael Walzer suggests as much with respect to nuclear weapons: "Nuclear weapons explode the theory of just war. They are the first of mankind's technological innovations that are simply not encompassable within the familiar moral world."9

And yet throughout the long years of the cold war, nuclear weapons and, to a lesser extent, chemical and biological weapons were in fact the subject of moral analysis. The cold war debates pitted the consequentialist arguments of realists and others who defended U.S. and NATO strategic doctrine against critics drawn from various ethical perspectives, including natural law deontologists and liberal social contract theorists and utilitarians influenced by just war criteria. These positions in turn were subjected to more fundamental criticism of the "war system," first by pacifists influenced by secular as well as Christian or Jewish ethics and second, during the 1970s and 1980s, by feminists. None of these ethical perspectives offered a single view on the difficult moral issues raised by nuclear deterrence, as evinced, for example, by the disagreements among Christian proponents of outright disarmament and Christian defenders of deterrence.10 And almost always, even those who argued for evaluating WMD according to the familiar categories of just grounds (*jus ad bellum*) and just means (*jus in bello*) did so guardedly and with appeals to the coercive power of necessity.11

The end of the cold war shifted public discussion in the United States and Western Europe away from the morality of superpower nuclear strategy to the dilemmas of controlling WMD proliferation. Some developments during the 1990s provided hope that the nonproliferation regime might be gaining strength: Both China and France acceded to the Nuclear Nonproliferation Treaty in 1992, and the treaty was renewed indefinitely in 1995 following its twenty-five-year review; several important nuclear-threshold states renounced their nuclear weapon option, including Argentina, Brazil, and South Africa; the Chemical Weapons Convention entered into force in 1997 following its ratification by the requisite sixty-five states. Yet there have also been a number of developments in the opposite direction, most importantly the nuclear tests conducted by India and Pakistan in May 1998 and the subsequent testing by both countries of ballistic missiles that have progressively increased the range and reduced the time required to deliver nuclear payloads to their targets. Two other states, Iran and North Korea, are known to have active research programs that could lead to the production of nuclear weapons. In addition, at least eleven countries are believed to have ongoing research programs or existing stockpiles of both chemical and biological weapons.12 Finally, the rise of international terrorist networks and the prospect of "loose nukes" or poorly protected radioactive, chemical, or biological agents created by the collapse of the Soviet Union raise serious concerns about WMD in the hands of nonstate actors.

All of these developments underscore the truly global nature of WMD proliferation and the need for global responses if we are to deal effectively with it. The cold war ethical discourse seems in light of today's concerns to be too circumscribed in terms of its participants (limited largely to American and West European policy makers and ethicists) and its scope (limited largely to nuclear deterrence). This book is a step, we hope, toward broadening the parameters of the cold war debates.

All of the core issues involved in the superpower standoff during the cold war are still salient: the morality of developing nuclear weapons and the diversion of resources to "nonusable" weapons, a deterrence strategy that relies primarily on the explicit or implicit threat of nuclear war, the possibility that a conventional war might quickly escalate into a nuclear war, the threat of rogue elements in the military using nuclear weapons without proper authority, and the fear of WMD falling into the hands of nonstate actors who cannot be deterred by threats of retaliation in kind. What is different in the twenty-first century is that these concerns have moved from the superpower level to the regional level. Regional conflicts, where belligerents are not separated by thousands of miles, where there is a long history of conventional wars, and where checks on the unauthorized use of nuclear weapons are not fully developed, pose greater risks for the escalation of wars to the nuclear level. In addition, the threat posed by chemical and biological weapons needs to be given much more attention than it received during the cold war. Such weapons are far easier and cheaper to manufacture than nuclear weapons, and they may well be the WMD of first resort by states and terrorist groups. We must also consider the morality of multilateral and unilateral preemptive action to disarm or to prevent the acquisition of WMD by so-called rogue states. The first consideration here must be the criteria by which some states are permitted to maintain WMD while others are denied them.

Five of the six questions we have asked our authors to address seek to elicit their traditions' perspectives on these and other old and new concerns raised by WMD. First, is there any circumstance under which it is morally permissible for any agent to use weapons of mass destruction in war? Second, is the development or deployment of weapons of mass destruction for the sake of deterrence a licit option? We pose here the familiar question: Is one justified in threatening to do something that one considers evil to do? Third, with respect to proliferation, if some nations possess weapons of mass destruction (either licitly or illicitly), is it proper to deny such possession to others? Fourth, is WMD disarmament a moral imperative, morally objectionable, or morally neutral? Does the answer to this question differ for universal versus unilateral, voluntary versus forcible disarmament? And finally, we asked what, if any, policy options the ethical traditions advocate given the moral positions they espouse. For example, what attitudes do the traditions' spokespersons express on current or proposed international agreements, such as the Chemical Weapons Convention, the Biological Weapons Convention, the Nonproliferation Treaty, and the Comprehensive Test Ban Treaty? If they find them objectionable, what concrete policy alternatives do they prefer?

RELEVANCE

Before we can address the moral issues raised by weapons of mass destruction, we need to consider briefly two questions having to do with relevance: the relevance of the very category "weapons of mass destruction" and the relevance of ethics to public policy on the development and use of such weapons.

When Albert Einstein and Bertrand Russell, among others, used the phrase "weapons of mass destruction" in the Pugwash Manifesto, issued on July 9, 1955, they had in mind nuclear weapons. In Chapters 1 and 2 below, Susan Martin and Paul Szasz discuss some historical and legal reasons that the label "weapons of mass destruction" came to be applied also to biological and chemical weapons, and only these three classes of weapons.[13] But, as Martin, Szasz, and others suggest, the label may not be descriptively accurate.[14] From the perspective of this book, the interesting question is whether – given the qualitative differences among them – there is a morally relevant reason to consider all three classes of weapons together and to distinguish them from "conventional" weapons.

Two questions arise: First, should all nuclear, chemical, and biological weapons be included in the category of WMD? Is the category, as conventionally understood, too broad? Second, should other kinds of weapons be included in the category as well? Is the category, as conventionally understood, too narrow? In discussing these two questions, we will find that a third arises: What counts as "mass destruction"?

On the suggestion that the conventional understanding of WMD is too broad, consider first chemical weapons. Martin points out that they are the least destructive of the three classes of WMD.[15] Their harmful effects depend on environmental factors such as atmospheric conditions, and people can protect themselves from their effects with proper clothing and breathing apparatus. Moreover, some chemical weapons may be designed only to incapacitate temporarily, thereby serving a military purpose without causing long-term destruction.[16] Some of these points may be made as well about biological weapons. Active measures may be taken to minimize the threat from biological weapons, including inoculation against the most likely threats and rapid quarantining of the affected population.

So, why put chemical and biological weapons into the category of WMD? Nuclear weapons are so manifestly more destructive that chemical and biological weapons seem out of place in the same category. A single label encompassing all three weapon types seems too broad.

One response is that some chemical and biological weapons, if used effectively and under the proper environmental circumstances, would probably kill or maim on a level close to that of a small fission bomb. Moreover, the effects of the initial strike would be felt by people who were not present or even born at the time, through transmission, genetic mutation, and environmental pollution.[17] So, even though chemical and biological weapons may not be comparable to nuclear weapons in the rate and extent of damage that they can immediately cause, they are, in some cases at least, descriptively closer to nuclear weapons in the *total* damage they have the potential of causing *over time* than they are to conventional weapons.

In addition, including nonlethal forms of biological and chemical weapons in the WMD category, despite that crucial point of dissimilarity, serves valuable pragmatic purposes and may be justified morally on those grounds. If some chemical and biological weapons can cause mass destruction, then we have good reason to develop practical policies that avoid their development and use. Such policies may be more effective if they ban all chemical or biological weapons, rather than seek to draw complicated distinctions among different types of them. As we know, in all areas of social life, a simple rule is easier to understand and enforce than a complicated one. A complicated rule may be difficult to understand, and it can generate borderline cases and encourage legalistic challenges on the part of those whose intention is to skirt the rule. There is practical value in rules that draw clear and bright lines of weapon prohibition, even when the result may be to ban some weapons that are, considered in themselves, no more objectionable than conventional weapons. Some of the authors in this volume make this point about WMD. Here then we have a pragmatic argument against the charge that the conventional category of WMD is too broad. The justification for including nonlethal forms of chemical and biological weapons in the category of WMD is that doing so facilitates simple rules and clear line drawing in our arms control and disarmament policies.

The second question is whether the traditional understanding of WMD is too narrow. Does it exclude weapons that it should include? Many conventional weapons also have the capacity to bring about mass destruction. One only needs to recall that the conventional bombings of several German and Japanese cities in World War II caused casualties greater than those resulting from the atomic bombings of Hiroshima or Nagasaki. Carol Cohn and Sara Ruddick point out that, given their ubiquity, small arms – perhaps the most typical conventional weapon – have had devastating consequences in the fabric of society, especially on the lives of women, in many parts of the world, bringing about mass destruction of their own.[18] The perpetrators of genocide in Rwanda killed hundreds of thousands with machetes. And Duane Cady suggests that given the extensive civilian harm and deaths caused by economic sanctions, such as those imposed on Iraq in the 1990s, such sanctions could themselves be seen as a weapon that causes mass destruction.[19]

Given these facts, why limit the members of the class of WMD to nuclear, chemical, and biological weapons? If the label were extended to include all weapons (and possibly even instruments not designed to be weapons) that have the potential for causing mass destruction, the distinction between WMD and conventional weapons would be largely or completely lost. As the Rwandan example sadly shows, even agricultural implements can be used to cause mass destruction. Perhaps the distinction should be lost. As the pacifist and feminist authors in this volume argue, if all weapons can cause mass destruction, there is no use in classifying some weapons as "conventional" and others as WMD.

If we grant that conventional weapons and methods of war can also cause mass destruction, is there any morally relevant way to distinguish WMD from them? One way is to focus not on *how many* are killed or on *how* they are killed, but on *who* are killed. This raises our third question: What counts as mass destruction? This is a question raised, explicitly or implicitly, by many of the authors in this volume. In just war theory, as well as in most non-Western traditions, who is killed is morally crucial. According to the principle of discrimination, soldiers may be killed in battle, but civilians are not to be attacked. What distinguishes WMD from conventional weapons is the special relationship WMD have to civilian deaths. In the case of nuclear weapons, the explosive effects are so great that almost anywhere they would be used they would kill many civilians, even if that were not the purpose of their use. This is reinforced by the strong probability that in any likely nuclear war, many nuclear weapons would be used. In general, then, it is close to impossible to use nuclear weapons without killing many civilians. In addition, the secondary effects of nuclear weapons, such as radiation and environmental damage, would severely affect civilians.

Consider now chemical and biological weapons. Neither kind is very effective in military terms.[20] Chemical weapons were originally used (in World War I) in a discriminate way. But they were not very effective militarily even then, and, as Martin writes, whatever effectiveness they had depended on the element of surprise.[21] Their general lack of military effectiveness results from their dependence on atmospheric conditions and the ability of the opponent to protect against them. As for biological weapons, Martin notes, the delayed onset of the effects of their use generally makes them militarily ineffective in battle. The battle may be long over before any symptoms take the soldiers out of action. In addition, like chemical weapons, their use is also dependent on various environmental factors. While chemical and biological weapons are not very effective militarily, they can do great damage to civilians.[22] This means that they are more likely to be used against civilians than against military forces, and if they were used against military forces, the greater harm is likely to be done to civilians who are relatively unprotected and unprepared to respond.

Thus, the use of nuclear, chemical, or biological weapons would almost necessarily involve many civilian deaths. Although the use of conventional weapons may involve many civilian deaths, this is not necessarily so. Conventional weapons can be used with military effectiveness in ways that discriminate between combatants and civilians. As a result, suggest some of the authors, we may say that WMD are necessarily or inherently indiscriminate, while conventional weapons are not. This is a morally relevant difference to justify the distinction between WMD and conventional weapons. In light of this, it might be better to refer to nuclear, chemical, and biological weapons not as weapons of mass destruction, but rather as *weapons of indiscriminate destruction*, for this better captures their moral distinctiveness.

This approach provides a fuller answer to the first question as well, in that it helps to explain why the conventional WMD category is not too broad. Nuclear weapons and most biological and chemical weapons are inherently indiscriminate, and this provides a basis for considering them together as a moral category. Inherent indiscriminateness becomes, from the perspective of moral relevance, both a necessary and a sufficient condition for regarding nuclear weapons and most biological and chemical weapons as WMD. We may add to this the pragmatic argument discussed above: Even nonlethal chemical and biological agents may be regarded as WMD because of the moral value of clear line drawing in policies of control and prohibition. Putting all these points together gives us this definition:

Weapons of mass destruction are those classes of weapons most of whose members have the characteristic of being, when used in war, inherently indiscriminate, meaning that their use, with whatever intention, would almost certainly result in the deaths of many civilians.

This definition gives us the WMD category as conventionally understood, that is, one that includes all nuclear, chemical, and biological weapons.[23] Because inherent indiscriminateness is a morally important feature, the conclusion is that the traditional category of WMD defines a group of weapons that require special moral attention.

But there is another basis on which to challenge the claim that biological and chemical weapons should be included along with nuclear weapons in the WMD category. There are morally relevant differences between nuclear weapons, on the one hand, and biological and chemical weapons, on the other, despite their shared feature of inherent indiscriminateness. Nuclear weapons have a special moral property that the other two do not have. When used for deterrence, nuclear weapons can lead to what has come to be called mutual assured destruction (MAD), and this has special moral importance.[24]

MAD is a state in which two opponents with nuclear weapons are able to threaten each other with complete annihilation, meaning not mere military defeat but societal destruction. A nuclear attack can produce so much damage to people and infrastructure that the society being attacked ceases to be a functioning whole. MAD is, of course, an idea familiar from the cold war nuclear standoff between the United States and the Soviet Union, but it is a property of nuclear arsenals, and so survives the demise of the cold war. For example, India and Pakistan may currently be in a situation of MAD.

MAD is morally special because it creates moral paradox, a situation in which contradictory moral claims are both apparently true. On the one hand is the moral principle that, if it is morally wrong to use a weapon in war, then it is morally wrong to threaten to use the weapon. Because nuclear weapons are inherently indiscriminate, it is morally wrong to use them in war. It thus follows from the principle that it is also morally wrong to threaten to use them, that is, to practice nuclear deterrence. But on the other hand is the moral principle that a state cannot be morally prohibited from doing what is necessary for its survival. Practicing nuclear deterrence when one's opponent is threatening nuclear attack is the only way to ensure the state's survival. It follows that when one's opponent is threatening nuclear attack, practicing nuclear deterrence cannot be morally wrong.[25] This is the moral paradox: Nuclear deterrence can be both morally wrong and not morally wrong. The paradox does not arise for chemical or biological weapons because they cannot be used to threaten societal destruction.

But this point of moral difference between nuclear weapons and other WMD does not undercut the moral importance of inherent indiscriminateness, which they share. The moral similarity of nuclear, biological, and chemical weapons remains as a justification for considering them as a group and leaves them worthy of moral study in their distinctiveness from conventional weapons, even though such a study does not exhaust what it is morally important to say about nuclear weapons.

There remains a question that may be on the minds of many readers at this point: Is there any practical significance to moral debates about WMD? What impact does ethics have on decisions to acquire or use weapons of mass destruction? A response to this question of the efficacy of morality in public policy may be given on two levels: analytical and normative.

First, it is clear that WMD have been subjected to moral evaluations of various sorts since their invention. These evaluations have been proffered not just by philosophers and theologians but by politicians and statesmen who make the decisions on proliferation or nonproliferation of WMD. Indeed, the language of morality is ubiquitous in the political world. Statesmen rarely claim that they do what they do simply because they *can* do it; they justify their actions as those they *ought* to do to protect their own citizens or other people, to defend or propagate cherished values, and to punish or bring to justice wrongdoers. Even nonstate actors, including those who rely on terrorism as their mode of operation, regularly invoke moral justifications, such as self-defense, necessity, or divine command. It is the job of moral philosophers to analyze these moral arguments, to explore the broader ethical contexts in which they are made, and to assess their cogency. This task itself would be sufficient to merit a book on ethics and weapons of mass destruction.

Moreover, the moral arguments made by politicians are often more than simply rationalizations for policies adopted on self-interested or other non-moral grounds. A growing literature on constructivism in the study of international relations argues that national security policies are the product of both material interests and socially constructed or culturally determined norms.[26] Norms not only constrain state behavior, but also shape the identities of states as international actors. These identities in turn determine how states perceive their security environments and conceive their material interests. Constructivists acknowledge that ethical traditions, both religious and secular, are among the most powerful sources for norms.[27]

Ethical concerns factor into policy decisions in a number of ways: by directly informing elite decision making, by influencing counterelites who then pressure elites, and by shaping the political culture in which elites and counterelites act, thereby narrowing the options available to them. For example, during the cold war, philosophers and theologians played a quite public and self-consciously policy-oriented role. When the U.S. Conference of Catholic Bishops issued their pastoral letter, *The Challenge of Peace*, in 1983, their avowed goal was "to encourage a public attitude which sets stringent limits on the kind of actions our own government and other governments will take on nuclear policy."[28] Concerned by the policies of the Reagan administration, the bishops sought to alter or to constrain the government's policies by shaping the political culture in which the government acted or by influencing opposition leaders. At the same time, conservative Christian organizations mobilized to lobby on behalf of government policies. Some of their leaders had forged personal relationships with President Reagan that afforded them direct access to him. The extent to which such religious advocacy influenced American nuclear policy remains controversial and yet to be fully documented.[29]

We may also cite examples from other cultural contexts, where the linkage between ethical perceptions and political action seems more clearly drawn. In Chapter 3, Scott Sagan recounts the Islamic Republic of Iran's reluctance to retaliate with chemical weapons during the Iran-Iraq War, even after repeated and devastating Iraqi chemical attacks against Iranian troops.[30] In Chapter 17, Sohail Hashmi reports on Iran's dramatic policy change regarding its nuclear development program immediately after the fall of the shah.[31] The ethical understanding of the new Iranian elites, informed by Islamic values, directly contributed to their policy decisions. In Chapter 16, Kanti Bajpai outlines the main points of Hindutva, an ideological reading of Indian history that emphasizes Hindu defenselessness against foreign aggressors. This understanding of the past informs a political culture shared by large numbers of Hindus in India and abroad that then influences the policies they espouse. Hindutva underlies the politics of the BJP government, which came to power in India in 1998, including its attitude toward military preparedness. "This is an ethics," Bajpai concludes, "if a hard-bitten one."[32]

All of our authors would agree that the role ethics play in public policy remains indeterminate and requires much more careful empirical study. The growing interest in normative issues among social scientists will lead, we hope, to greater clarity on this question. In the meantime, on the basis of the available evidence, we can assert the proposition that ethics *do* influence policy outcomes. The burden of proof, it seems to us, is equally, if not more, on those who would deny that ethics matter.

The normative question is: *Should* ethics play a role in decision making? With respect to weapons of mass destruction, only the most hardened moral skeptics among us may assert the possibility or the value of a completely amoral approach to policy decisions. For most of us, any weapon that gives human beings the power to kill large numbers of our species, to inflict harm on unborn generations, and to threaten the continuation of our human civilization intuitively begs the deepest moral questioning. It is as impossible to divorce morality from WMD as it is to suspend moral judgment from torture or genocide. The types of moral reasoning we employ and the ethical conclusions we draw depend on a host of variables, including our ethical presuppositions, the types of questions we ask, and the relative value we assign to different goods. The chapters in this book demonstrate the different ways people evaluate the morality of weapons of mass destruction. But they all agree that the enterprise is inescapable.

Notes

1. Richard M. Price, *The Chemical Weapons Taboo* (Ithaca, N.Y., and London: Cornell University Press, 1997), 31. See also Paul Szasz's discussion in Chapter 2 below, under "Chemical and Biological Weapons," of the pre–World War I international agreements banning the use of "poison or poisoned weapons" and "asphyxiating or deleterious gases."

2. Examples of this interaction and mutual influence can be seen in the way Christian thinkers have adopted natural law arguments (see Nigel Biggar, introduction to Chapter 9) or in the way Confucianism was changed as a result of its interactions with Buddhism (see Philip Ivanhoe, introduction to Chapter 14).

3. This point is made forcefully by Carol Cohn and Sara Ruddick in Chapter 21 below, and echoed by several other contributors.

4. C. A. J. Coady elaborates on this point in the introduction to Chapter 5.

5. See Katherine Young, introduction to Chapter 15, and Sohail Hashmi, Chapter 17, under "Proliferation."

6. See Reuven Kimelman, Chapter 19, under "The Israeli Situation: Nuclear Weapons," and Joseph David, Chapter 20, under "Mass Destruction and Lessons of the Holocaust."

7. Donald Swearer, Chapter 12, under "Taking Stock of a Dilemma."

8. For more detailed analyses of how most of the ethical traditions discussed in this volume have handled the ethics of war generally, see the previous volume in the Ethikon Series: Terry Nardin, ed., *The Ethics of War and Peace: Religious and Secular Perspectives* (Princeton, N.J.: Princeton University Press, 1996).

9. Michael Walzer, *Just and Unjust Wars* (New York: Basic Books, 1977), 282.

10. See Nigel Biggar's discussion in Chapter 9.

11. A classic example comes from the Pastoral Letter on War and Peace issued by the U.S. Catholic bishops in May 1983: "These considerations of concrete elements of nuclear deterrence policy, made in light of John Paul II's evaluation, but applying it through our own prudential judgments, lead us to a strictly conditioned moral acceptance of nuclear deterrence." National Conference of Catholic Bishops, *The Challenge of Peace: God's Promise and Our Response* (Washington, D.C.: United States Catholic Conference, 1983), 79.

12. These are China, Egypt, India, Iran, Israel, Libya, North Korea, Pakistan, Russia, Sudan, and Syria. Joseph Cirincione et al., *Deadly Arsenals: Tracking Weapons of Mass Destruction* (Washington, D.C.: Carnegie Endowment for International Peace, 2002), 17.

13. On this issue, see also Nina Tannenwald, *The Nuclear Taboo: The United States and the Non-Use of Nuclear Weapons since 1945* (New York: Cambridge University Press, forthcoming).

14. Two pointed critiques of the "weapons of mass destruction" category are Wolfgang Panofsky, "Dismantling the Concept of 'Weapons of Mass Destruction,'" *Arms Control Today* 28:3 (April 1998): 3–8; and Gregg Easterbrook, "Term Limits: The Meaninglessness of 'WMD,'" *New Republic* (October 7, 2002): 22–5.

15. Susan Martin, Chapter 1, under "Chemical Weapons."

16. An interesting moral implication of this is discussed by Nigel Biggar, citing a point of Paul Ramsey's (see Chapter 9, under "Use of Weapons of Mass Destruction"). It could be that if such a reliable chemical weapon were developed, killing in war might generally no longer be morally permissible. Killing in war is permitted, as in the case of killing in self-defense, only because there is no reliable nonlethal way of stopping the attack. But such a chemical weapon would provide such a way.

17. See Sohail Hashmi's discussion in Chapter 17, under "Use in War," of the lasting genetic and environmental damage caused by the Iraqi chemical weapons attack on Halabja.

18. Carol Cohn and Sara Ruddick, Chapter 21, under "Sources and Principles."

19. Duane Cady, Chapter 24, under "Peace and the Old (Violent) World Order."

20. Nuclear weapons are also not militarily effective, but for a different reason. In a situation where adversaries both possess nuclear weapons, any use of them is likely to elicit retaliation, which would bring such destruction to the side that struck first that any military advantage the strike might have brought in isolation would be far outweighed by the harm the resulting nuclear war would bring to that side.

21. Susan Martin, Chapter 1, under "Chemical Weapons."

22. In speaking here of the harm that chemical and biological weapons do to civilians, we are excluding the incapacitating agents mentioned earlier, which do little long-term harm to anyone and are included in the category of WMD for pragmatic reasons.

23. Some of the authors suggest that cluster bombs and land mines should be included in the category of WMD, and they seem to fit our definition. For, like nuclear, biological, and chemical weapons, these munitions seem to have extensive civilian destruction as an almost necessary consequence of their use. But their tendency to cause civilian deaths is largely a consequence of their design. They could, it seems, be designed so as largely to eliminate civilian casualties (e.g., both could be designed to disarm automatically after a certain period of time), whereas the civilian effects of WMD seem much more intractable to engineering.

24. In Chapter 4, under "Deterrence," Susan Martin suggests that this form of deterrence, mutual assured destruction, may also be possible with biological weapons. If opponents each possessed sufficient quantities of especially virulent biological agents, they might each have the capacity to destroy the other's society.

25. This is the idea behind Michael Walzer's doctrine of supreme emergency, discussed in Henry Shue's essay, Chapter 7 below.

26. These issues are discussed in the essay by Scott Sagan, Chapter 3 below, under "Sources and Principles."

27. A useful introduction to constructivism, particularly relevant to the subject of this book, is Peter J. Katzenstein, ed., *The Culture of National Security: Norms and Identity in World Politics* (New York: Columbia University Press, 1996). For a critique, see Michael C. Desch, "Culture Clash: Assessing the Importance of Ideas in Security Studies," *International Security* 23:1 (Summer 1998): 141–70.

28. U.S. Catholic Bishops, *Challenge of Peace*, 60.

29. For example, George Weigel argues that the Catholic bishops' pastoral letter was as much influenced by American political culture as it influenced American policies. George Weigel, "The Bishops' Pastoral Letter and American Political Culture: Who Was Influencing Whom?" in *Peace in a Nuclear Age: The Bishops' Pastoral Letter in Perspective*, ed. Charles J. Reid, Jr. (Washington, D.C.: Catholic University of America Press, 1986), 171–89. Janice Love, "From Pacifism to Apocalyptic Visions: Religious Perspectives on Nuclear Deterrence," in *After the Cold War: Questioning the Morality of Nuclear Deterrence*, ed. Charles W. Kegley, Jr., and Kenneth L. Schwab (Boulder, Colo.: Westview Press, 1991), 157–76, concludes that no conclusive answer can be given to the question of what impact religious lobbying had on Reagan-era policies and that the issue requires more careful investigation.

30. Scott Sagan, Chapter 3, under "Iran and Chemical Weapons."

31. Sohail Hashmi, Chapter 17, under "Disarmament."

32. Kanti Bajpai, Chapter 16, under "Political Hinduism, History, and Nuclear Weapons."

1

Weapons of Mass Destruction

A Brief Overview

Susan B. Martin

The phrase "weapons of mass destruction" was first used in a communiqué issued by American President Harry Truman, British Prime Minister Clement Attlee, and Canadian Prime Minister Mackenzie King on November 15, 1945.[1] In a "Declaration on Atomic Bomb," they proposed the establishment of a commission under the United Nations that would investigate ways of eliminating the destructive use of atomic energy while promoting its "widest use for industrial and humanitarian purposes."[2] They urged the commission to make four specific proposals, including a proposal "for the elimination from national armaments of atomic weapons and of all other major weapons adaptable to mass destruction."[3]

According to Vannevar Bush, who claims to have authored the phrase, it was intended to cover biological as well as nuclear weapons.[4] The phrase was repeated in a resolution of the UN General Assembly on January 24, 1946, which called for the elimination of all weapons "adaptable to mass destruction," and a General Assembly resolution on December 14, 1946, referred to the elimination of "all other major weapons adaptable now or in the future to mass destruction."[5] In 1947 the UN Commission for Conventional Armaments addressed the definition of weapons of mass destruction in an effort to distinguish WMD from conventional weapons and thus define the scope of their mandate. The definition finally accepted in 1948 stated that weapons of mass destruction "included atomic explosive weapons, radioactive material weapons, lethal chemical and biological weapons, and any weapons developed in the future which have characteristics comparable in destructive effect to those of the atomic bomb or other weapons mentioned above."[6] Various challenges to this definition had been made. For example, the representatives of the United Kingdom and Australia questioned the use of "lethal" to modify chemical and biological weapons; the Ukrainian delegate defined "weapons of mass destruction as weapons directed primarily against peaceful populations and weapons not of defense but of aggression"; and the Soviet delegate argued that the proposed definition was too restrictive. According to the Stockholm International Peace Research Institute (SIPRI), he argued that "the Germans has [*sic*] used weapons other than atomic, with mass destructive effect on population and cities far from the field of battle," and he suggested that it was ill-advised to try to distinguish between and to develop separate regulations for weapons of mass destruction versus conventional weapons.[7] In response, the British delegate "stated that 'V' weapons would definitely fall within the category of conventional armaments since their destructive effect, statistically considered, had not been large. The number of persons killed by the 14,000 'V' weapons dropped on England was 56,000, or four persons per weapon."[8]

Despite the objections of the USSR, which voted against the definition of weapons of mass destruction adopted by the UN Commission for Conventional Armaments, the equation of "weapons of mass destruction" with nuclear, biological, and chemical weapons gained currency in international forums. The link among these weapons was also reinforced by the declaration of the Federal Republic of Germany that it would not "manufacture in its territory any atomic weapons, chemical weapons or biological weapons."[9]

In the immediate postwar years, chemical and biological weapons received little attention, despite a warning from the UN secretary-general in 1948 that the problems posed by these weapons were being overshadowed by atomic weapons.[10] This began to change with allegations that the United States used chemical and biological weapons in the Korean and Vietnam Wars, and in the late 1960s the Eighteen-Nation Committee on Disarmament began to address chemical and biological weapons.[11] Because biological weapons were seen as having little or no military utility, an agreement on them was expected to be easier to reach than an agreement on chemical weapons, and it was decided to address biological and chemical weapons in separate negotiations. These negotiations eventually produced the Biological Weapons Convention (BWC), which entered into force in 1975, and the Chemical Weapons Convention (CWC), which entered into force in 1997.[12] Overall, however, nuclear weapons continued to overshadow chemical and biological weapons.

With the end of the cold war and the joint effort by Russia and the United States to dramatically reduce their nuclear arsenals, attention has shifted to "weapons of mass destruction" as a whole and to biological and chemical weapons in particular. Indeed, the proliferation of weapons of mass destruction has been identified as one of the main threats to the national security of the United States.[13] One explanation for this new emphasis on weapons of mass destruction is the possible need of smaller states to use "asymmetric strategies" to counter the United States's overwhelming conventional military strength. "Asymmetric strategies" refers to strategies that employ non-reciprocal means to counter a threat. While a symmetric strategy would, for example, counter a nuclear threat with a nuclear threat and a conventional threat with a conventional threat, an asymmetric strategy might counter a conventional threat with a terrorist or WMD threat. Other possible reasons for the new focus on chemical and biological weapons include the rise of apocalyptic terrorist groups that may be more likely to use weapons of mass destruction and the American military's need for a threat to justify its budgets. Whatever the reason for this new attention to chemical and biological as well as nuclear weapons, it raises anew the question of the ethics surrounding nuclear weapons and other types of weapons of mass destruction.[14]

This new attention to "weapons of mass destruction" also requires us to revisit the logic of grouping chemical, biological, and nuclear weapons together under that label. What, if anything, distinguishes these weapons from other weapons used in war? Is it simply their destructive power? Or is there something different about how these weapons are used?

This in turn raises a series of questions about ethics and weapons of mass destruction. What, exactly, do we find ethically troubling about these weapons? Is it simply their destructive power? Or is there something inherently unethical about the use of poison (chemical weapons), disease (biological weapons), and/or radiation (nuclear weapons)? Perhaps it is the long-term or indiscriminate effects of at least some of these weapons that bothers us.[15] Or is it less the weapons themselves than the uses to which the weapons are put (e.g., deterrence) that is problematic? If the latter, then perhaps the real problem is the delivery vehicles (missiles and long-range bombers) that allow these weapons to attack cities from long distances that are the root of the problem. But does this mean that the use of these weapons is acceptable if they are confined to combatants? What if, in the case of chemical and biological weapons, harassing or incapacitating agents are used to cause temporary effects instead of death?

Depending on the exact reasons for ethical opposition to these weapons, we may need to revisit the distinction made between weapons of mass destruction, on the one hand, and conventional weapons, on the other. For example, if it is destructiveness per se that we find troubling, then we may need to discuss fuel-air explosives. Fuel-air explosives are conventional bombs that disperse and then ignite an aerosol cloud of fuel, generating tremendous blast effects comparable to that produced by tactical nuclear weapons. If it is the effects of WMD on civilians that trouble us most, then we may also need to address land mines and cluster bombs. Cluster bombs contain hundreds or thousands of submunitions that are spread over a wide area when the bomb explodes. Because not all of these submunitions explode on release, cluster bombs create an unexploded ordnance problem in the areas where they are used, posing a threat to civilians when the battle has moved on.

To facilitate the discussion of ethics and weapons of mass destruction that occurs in the following chapters, I present a brief analysis of nuclear, biological, and chemical weapons. For each weapon type I briefly review its history of use, the types of weapons and their most salient characteristics, the destructive capability of the weapons, important recent developments, and specific ethical questions about the weapons that have been raised.

NUCLEAR WEAPONS

Nuclear weapons came about as a result of developments in physics and of what was thought at the time to be a wartime race between the Allies and the Germans to harness nuclear energy for military purposes. The United States was the first nation to develop the atomic bomb, and it dropped one bomb each on Hiroshima and Nagasaki at the end of World War II. The amount of damage and the number of civilian deaths caused by the atomic bombing of Hiroshima and Nagasaki were not new: Between 1939 and 1945, some 51,509 British civilians died as a result of conventional attacks by German bombers and rockets, and approximately 50,000 citizens of Hamburg died in the course of a week's worth of conventional bombing in July and August 1943. As many as 539,000 German civilians may have died as a result of aerial bombardment during World War II. While a single plane carrying one atomic bomb killed about 68,000 people and injured another 76,000 in Hiroshima, Allied incendiary raids on Dresden killed between 130,000 and 200,000 people with 1,400 aircraft sorties over two days. In addition, U.S. Army Air Force "fire raids" on Japan caused an estimated 100,000 deaths in Tokyo on one night in March 1945 – approximately the same number of immediate deaths that occurred as a result of the atomic attacks on Hiroshima and Nagasaki.[16] These figures emphasize that what was new about the atomic bombs used against Japan was not the absolute amount of destruction that was done, but the relative speed with which the destruction was inflicted.[17]

The demonstrated power of atomic weapons meant that the American monopoly would not last long; the USSR acquired the atomic bomb in 1949, Great Britain in 1952, France in 1960, and China in 1964. In addition, efforts to create more powerful weapons were made, and the United States acquired the hydrogen bomb in 1952, followed by the Soviet Union in 1953, Great Britain in 1957, China in 1967, and France in 1968.[18] Israel is thought to have had a handful of nuclear weapons by 1967; India carried out a peaceful nuclear explosion in 1974 and another series of tests – which were matched by Pakistan – in 1998.[19] South Africa built six atomic bombs and stored them disassembled from 1980 to 1989, when their nuclear weapons program was curtailed; South Africa reports that the bombs were destroyed in 1991.

The identification of possible proliferators is difficult and controversial.[20] Two states – Iran and North Korea – top the list of states thought to be seeking nuclear weapons today.[21] Ten other states have had past nuclear weapons programs and/or have the current potential to develop nuclear weapons: Algeria, Argentina, Brazil, Germany, Japan, Libya, Romania, South Korea, Sweden, and Taiwan.[22] Of the three types of weapons of mass destruction, nuclear weapons are the most difficult to acquire. They require the most scientific knowledge, the most financial resources, and the most difficult-to-acquire materials.[23]

Nuclear weapons, and in particular the emergence of a world with more than one nuclear power, was seen by many to change drastically the nature of international politics. For example, Bernard Brodie wrote in 1946, "Thus far the chief purpose of our military establishment has been to win wars. From now on its chief purpose must be to avert them. It can have almost no other useful purpose."[24] This emphasis on the prevention or deterrence of war among nuclear states came about as a result of two characteristics of nuclear weapons: their destructive power and the inability to defend against nuclear attack.

Deterrence involves using a threat of punishment to stop someone from doing something. For a deterrent threat to be effective, the threat must promise to do more harm and thus impose more costs than the benefits that would be gained through the action to be deterred.[25] Although we typically think of war as a battle between the offense and the defense, deterrence (or the threat of punishment) has always been involved. Before the age of planes and missiles that could penetrate an enemy's airspace, the threat of punishment was tightly linked to what happened on the battlefield. One could impose punishment only after defeating an enemy's military forces on the battlefield, although the threat of greater or lesser punishment to come could be used to influence the enemy's willingness to surrender. With the advent of airplanes and missiles, it became possible to inflict punishment – to attack an enemy's population and homeland – before the struggle on the battlefield had been decided (or even begun).

Missiles that could attack targets anywhere on the globe made pure deterrent strategies – strategies that were not linked to the defeat of the enemy's forces – possible.[26] Nuclear weapons made them practical, because a state with nuclear-armed missiles could threaten any other state with unimaginable destruction, regardless of the results of any clash between their armed forces.[27] Because the destructive power of nuclear weapons is so great, the threat of a nuclear attack is thought to outweigh any possible gains for which an aggressor may hope. While advocates of nuclear deterrence acknowledge that deterrence is not guaranteed and that there is always some possibility of nuclear use, they generally see the prevention of war among nuclear states (and the loss of lives that such wars would entail) as outweighing the losses involved in a minor nuclear exchange. There are, of course, many challenges to this view; as the following chapters suggest, many object to nuclear weapons and to the policy of deterrence on ethical grounds.

In addition to strategic nuclear weapons, other kinds of nuclear weapons have also been developed. Tactical or battlefield nuclear weapons are sometimes thought of as smaller yield nuclear weapons that have less destructive power. However, this is a misconception. As Harald Müller and Annette Schaper point out, "tactical" nuclear weapons are distinguished from "strategic" nuclear weapons by their range, with strategic weapons defined as intercontinental weapons that were capable of reaching the territory of the United States.[28]

Tactical weapons were first developed by the United States as an "asymmetric strategy" to compensate for NATO's conventional inferiority vis-à-vis the USSR. When the Soviet Union responded by deploying tactical nuclear weapons of its own, the presence of battlefield nuclear weapons in Europe became a way of underlining the inevitability of any conventional conflict there escalating to the nuclear level. Russia's strategy today mirrors NATO's strategy during the cold war: It is relying on tactical nuclear weapons (as well as a policy of first use of nuclear weapons in the case of "large-scale aggression utilizing conventional weapons in situations critical to the national security of the Russian Federation") to counter American conventional superiority.[29]

It is not clear that tactical nuclear weapons differ from strategic nuclear weapons in ways that are important for a discussion of ethics and WMD. While tactical nuclear weapons may sometimes contain less destructive power than today's strategic nuclear weapons, their destructive power is still immense. "Little Boy," the bomb dropped on Hiroshima, had a yield of 15–16 kilotons, "Fat Man," the bomb dropped on Nagasaki, a yield of 21 kilotons, while current tactical nuclear weapons can have yields ranging from one to several hundred kilotons.[30] It is also not clear that the effects of these "battlefield" nuclear weapons would be confined to combatants, although this depends on how isolated the battlefield is from civilian life.

CHEMICAL WEAPONS

Chemical agents can be defined as "poisons that incapacitate, injure or kill through their toxic effects on the skin, eyes, lungs, blood, nerves or other organs"; chemical warfare refers to the wartime use of such agents against enemy targets (human, animal, or plant).[31] As these definitions make clear, not all chemical weapons are intended to kill; chemical weapons include the use of harassing and incapacitating agents (see Table 1.1).

Chemical weapons were first used in modern warfare in World War I. The first chemical agents used were irritant gases in 1914.[32] Lethal chemical weapons were also employed, beginning with the German use of chlorine gas against the French at Ypres in April 1915. This was an attempt to break through the stabilized front that was paralyzing the war. While the attack was successful in the narrow sense that Allied defenses were breached, the Germans were unable to consolidate and exploit their advantage.[33] Once the British acquired the ability to retaliate (September 25, 1915) and both

TABLE 1.1. *Examples of Chemical Warfare Agents*[a]

Name	Type of agent	Mechanism	Time for onset of effects	Military function[b]
3-Quinuclidinyl benzilate (BZ)	Psychochemical	Causes mental disturbance	Delayed	Incapacitating
Adamsite (DM)	Vomiting agent	Vomiting, also irritation of eyes and respiratory system	Rapid	Harassing
Botulinum toxin	Toxin	Neuromuscular paralysis	Variable (hours or days)	Lethal
Hydrogen cyanide	Blood agent	Interferes with all respiration	Rapid (a few seconds or minutes)	Lethal
LSD	Psychochemical	Causes mental disturbance	Slight delay in onset of symptoms	Incapacitating
Ortho-chlorobenzylidene malononitrile (CS), chloroacetophenone (CN), etc.	Tear gas	Irritation of eyes, respiratory tract, may cause nausea and headache	Immediate	Harassing
Phosgene	Choking agent	Damages lungs	Immediate to more than three hours	Lethal
Staphylococcus	Toxin	Severe nausea, vomiting, and diarrhea	Two to four hours after ingestion, though can also be inhaled	Incapacitating
Sulfur mustard	Blister agent	Cell poison	Blistering of eyes, lung, and skin delayed hours to days; eye effects more rapid	Lethal

| Tabun (GA), sarin (GB), soman (GD) | Nerve agent G | Interferes with transmission of nerve impulses | Very rapid by inhalation (a few seconds) | Lethal |
| VX | Nerve agent V | Interferes with transmission of nerve impulses | Very rapid by inhalation (a few seconds); relatively rapid through skin (a few minutes to a few hours) | Lethal |

[a] Adapted from the United Nations, Report of the Secretary General, Department of Political and Security Council Affairs, "Table 2: General Characteristics of Lethal Chemical Agents," in *Chemical and Bacteriological (Biological) Weapons and the Effects of Their Possible Use* (New York: United Nations, 1969), 29 and 28–37; with additional information drawn from *Biological and Chemical Warfare Threat*, rev. ed. (Washington, D.C.: U.S. Government Printing Office, 1999), 28–30 and Appendix F, "Chemical Warfare Agents," 35; and SIPRI, "Table 1.1, Toxic Chemicals That Have Been Developed into CW Agents," "Table 2.1, Military Classification of CBW Agents," and "Table 2.5, Estimates of the Relative Potencies of CB and Non-CB Weapons," in *The Problem of Chemical and Biological Warfare*, vol. 2: *CB Weapons Today* (New York: Humanities Press, 1975), 33–35, 122, and 134.

[b] The UN discussion does not distinguish between harassing and incapacitating agents. It explains that "lethal chemical agents kill in relatively small doses, and as a rule the amount that causes death is only slightly greater than that which causes incapacitation. Death may occasionally be caused by high doses of presumed incapacitating agents, and conversely, minor effects could be caused by low doses of lethal agents.... Incapacitating chemicals, like tear gas and certain psychochemicals, produce in normal healthy people a temporary, reversible disability with few, if any, permanent effects.... They are called incapacitating because the ratio between the lethal and incapacitating doses is very high" (UN, Report of the Secretary-General, 28 and 34). Harassing agents (e.g., tear gas) have brief effects, as opposed to incapacitating agents that have effects that last for hours or days and generally cause nonfatal casualties. See SIPRI, *CB Weapons Today*, 35; Brian Beckett, *Weapons of Tomorrow* (New York: Plenum Press, 1983), 137. Note that depending on how they are used, even harassing agents can have lethal effects. See the discussion of the use of tear gas in the Vietnam War by John Cookson and Judith Nottingham, *A Survey of Chemical and Biological Warfare* (London: Sheed and Ward, 1969), 14–26. The dangers of using "nonlethal" chemical weapons is also illustrated by the use of a gas by Russian Special Forces troops on October 26, 2002, in an attempt to rescue people held hostage by Chechen militants in a Moscow theater. Over one hundred people died as a result of exposure to the gas, which was identified by the Russian Health Ministry as a powerful form of the opioid drug fentanyl.

sides acquired protective equipment, gas was relegated to a supporting role while at the same time its use expanded.[34] The Germans then introduced mustard gas in 1917, and the number of casualties attributed to chemical warfare rose dramatically.[35] Debates about the effectiveness of chemical weapons in World War I continue to this day, although it is generally accepted that gas did not resolve the stalemate on the battlefield. Surprise was seen as key to a successful chemical weapons attack, and the most important effects of chemical weapons were their psychological effects and the attrition that they caused.[36]

Ethical questions about the use of chemical weapons were raised after World War I, with some arguing that chemical weapons were more humane than conventional weapons.[37] This argument was largely based on the ability of chemical weapons to cause casualties but not death; Augustin Prentiss argues, "The use of chemicals in the World War played a large part in reducing the percentage of deaths from battle injuries."[38] Edward Spiers adds that "generally, gas caused less suffering than wounds from other weapons" and that "although some casualties would suffer for the rest of their lives from war gassing, many more would make a relatively quick recovery and at least emerge from the experience with their body and limbs intact."[39]

During World War II chemical weapons were not used in the main military theaters, although Japan did make some use of chemical weapons against China, and Germany used gas in the concentration camps.[40] At the end of World War I, the Allies had begun to plan for major air attacks combining high explosive bombs with gas attacks launched against German cities, but the war ended before these attacks could be carried out.[41] The possibility of escalation to this kind of attack helps to explain why chemical weapons were not used by the Allies or by Germany in World War II. In addition, German use of chemical weapons was discouraged by the emphasis in German strategy on quick movement (the Blitzkrieg, for example); once it lost air superiority, the vulnerability of its cities gave Germany no incentive to initiate the use of chemical weapons. Hitler is also said to have opposed chemical operations because of his experience with gas in World War I. Initiation of chemical warfare by the Allies was evidently discouraged by their belief that the use of chemical weapons in one theater of the war would mean the use of chemical weapons in all theaters. Once Germany was defeated and the use of chemical weapons could be confined to the Pacific theater, the Allies considered using chemical weapons to lessen casualties in the invasion of Japan. However, the decision to use the atomic bomb precluded any decision about the use of chemical weapons.[42]

Nerve gas, which is both more toxic and easier to use than other chemical agents, was invented during World War II by the Germans. A lethal respiratory dose of tabun, sarin, or soman is believed to cause death in one to ten minutes. Compared with this, a lethal dose of phosgene, the most toxic respiratory-effect chemical warfare agent previously available, takes four to twenty-four hours to kill. Blood agents such as hydrogen cyanide are quick-acting but are effective only if delivered in large, concentrated doses. The nerve gases thus combined the efficiency of mustard gas with the rapidity of action of the blood gases and made chemical war techniques more feasible for fast moving, land-warfare operations. Nerve gas was first used by Iraq during the Iran-Iraq War.

Allegations that chemical weapons have been used have often been made in the years since World War II. In addition to the Iran-Iraq War, other generally accepted cases of chemical weapons use include their use by Egypt in Yemen (1963–67); by the United States in Indo-China (1961–70; the United States acknowledges use of irritants and antiplant agents, but the use of casualty agents is alleged by both sides); and by Iraq against the Kurds (1987–88). No widespread use of chemical weapons was made during the Persian Gulf War, despite Iraq's previously demonstrated capability and willingness to use these weapons.[43]

Even with the advent of nerve agents, chemical weapons do not approach the destructive power of nuclear weapons[44] (see Table 1.2). In addition to causing fewer deaths and injuries than would be caused by an attack with a similar amount of nuclear material, chemical weapons lack the blast effects that cause physical destruction.[45] Chemical weapons also differ from nuclear weapons in that the effects of chemical attack are highly dependent on the presence of defenses and on various environmental conditions (e.g., temperature, wind speed, terrain). Despite this, chemical weapons have been seen as playing a useful role on the battlefield, and Thomas McNaugher notes that chemical attacks on cities could be quite effective.[46] He argues that the walls and buildings in cities may prevent the dispersion of chemical agents once they are released, and that "given the correct weather conditions, a deadly cloud of gas might form, the urban equivalent of what was called 'pancaking' in World War I. These arguments suggest that chemical weapons may be more destructive and thus more like nuclear weapons, when used against cities than when used tactically." Despite this, he argues that "the difference between chemical and nuclear destructiveness probably remains substantial."[47]

While chemical weapons are the least destructive of the three types of WMD, they are also the easiest to acquire. The scientific knowledge required is basic, little specialized equipment is required, specialized materials (e.g., precursor chemicals) are much more widely available than the materials needed for nuclear weapons, and they are relatively cheap to produce.[48] Randall Forsberg et al. report that "a sophisticated production facility to make militarily significant quantities of one class of nerve agents might cost $30–50 million, although dispensing with modern waste-handling facilities might cut the cost in half."[49] In 2001, the United States identified Iraq, Libya, North Korea, and Syria as states with chemical weapons programs

TABLE 1.2. *Comparative Effects of Chemical, Biological, and Nuclear Weapons*[a]

Source	Type of attack	Conventional	Chemical	Biological	Nuclear
U.S. Congress, Office of Technology Assessment[b]	Scud-like missile with maximum payload of 2,000 kg, with neither best- nor worst-case weather conditions	N/A	Area in which 50–100 percent of unprotected population would receive fatal doses: 0.22 km² / Approximate number of deaths: 600–2,000 (300 kg of sarin nerve gas)	Area in which 50–100 percent of unprotected population would receive fatal doses: 10 km² / Approximate number of deaths: 30,000–100,000 (30 kg of anthrax spores)	Area in which 50–100 percent of unprotected population would receive fatal doses: 190 km² / Approximate number of deaths: 570,000–1,900,000 (hydrogen bomb, 1.0 megaton TNT equivalent)
Fetter[c]	Attack by a missile warhead, without civil defense	Dead: 5 Injured: 13 (1 tonne of high explosive)	Dead: 200–3,000 Injured: 200–3,000 (300 kg of sarin)	Dead: 20,000–80,000 (30 kg of anthrax spores)	Dead: 40,000 Injured: 40,000 (20 kilotons)
	Attack by a missile warhead, with civil defense	Dead: 2 Injured: 6 (1 tonne of high explosive)	Dead: 20–300 Injured: 20–300 (300 kg of sarin)	Dead: 2,000–8,000 (30 kg of anthrax spores)	Dead: 20,000 Injured: 20,000 (20 kilotons)
SIPRI[d]	A 5–6 ton bombload dropped by a single aircraft (urban area target)	Area over which 50 percent casualties (half of these fatalities) can be expected: 22 hectares (High explosive)	Area over which 50 percent casualties (half of these fatalities) can be expected: 75 hectares (VX)	Area over which 50 percent casualties can be expected: 0–5,000 hectares (No BW agent specified)	Area over which 50 percent *immediate* casualties can be expected: 200,000 hectares (Fusion bomb, 10 megaton airburst)

| UN[e] | Attack by single strategic bomber on totally unprotected population | N/A | Area affected: up to 60 km² Maximum effect on humans: 50 percent deaths (15 tons of nerve gas) | Area affected: up to 100,000 km² Maximum effect on humans: 50 percent morbidity; 25 percent deaths if no medical intervention (10 tons of BW agent) | Area affected: up to 300 km² Maximum effect on humans: 90 percent deaths (1 megaton) |

[a] Adapted from, with reference to original sources: Malcolm Dando, *Biological Warfare in the 21st Century* (London: Brassey's, 1994). 5.

[b] U.S. Congress, Office of Technology Assessment, "Figure 2-1: Comparative Lethal Areas of Chemical, Biological, and Nuclear Weapons: Missile Delivery on an Overcast Day or Night, with Moderate Wind (Neither Best nor Worst Case)," in *Proliferation of Weapons of Mass Destruction: Assessing the Risks*, OTA-ISC-559 (Washington, D.C.: U.S. Government Printing Office, August 1993). 53. Estimates of fatalities assume 3,000–10,000 unprotected people/km². Note that the approximate number of deaths from a chemical warhead filled with sarin was originally reported as 60–200. The figure here reflects a correction made by Gerald Epstein, project director for the Office of Technology Assessment (OTA) series on proliferation of weapons of mass destruction, in a posting to a list-serve (cbw-sipri@sipri.se) on January 24, 2003.

[c] Steve Fetter, "Table 6: A Comparison of the Casualties Produced by Nuclear, Chemical, Biological, and High-Explosive Warheads," from "Ballistic Missiles and Weapons of Mass Destruction," *International Security* 16:1 (September 1991): 27. He assumes "a missile with a throw weight of 1 tonne aimed at a large city with an average population density of 30 per hectare. Assumes that civil defenses reduce casualties from conventional and nuclear explosions by a factor of two, and casualties from chemical and biological weapons by a factor of ten."

[d] SIPRI, "Table 2.5: Estimates of the Relative Potencies of CB and Non-CB Weapons," in *The Problem of Chemical and Biological Warfare*, vol. 2: *CB Weapons Today* (New York: Humanities Press, 1975). 134.

[e] United Nations, Report of the Secretary General, Department of Political and Security Council Affairs, "Table 5: Comparative Estimates of Disabling Effects of Hypothetical Attacks on Totally Unprotected Populations Using a Nuclear, Chemical, or Bacteriological (Biological) Weapon That Could be Carried by a Single Strategic Bomber," in *Chemical and Bacteriological (Biological) Weapons and the Effects of Their Possible Use* (New York: United Nations, 1969). 44.

that have not signed the CWC.[50] If we include those countries that have acknowledged chemical weapons programs under the CWC, that have had past programs, that have been suspected of seeking chemical weapons, or that have the industrial prerequisites for chemical weapons, the number of possible chemical weapons states is estimated at around forty.[51]

BIOLOGICAL WEAPONS

Biological warfare[52] refers to the wartime use against an enemy of agents causing disease or death in humans, animals, or plants following multiplication within the target organism.[53] Biological agents are disease-causing microorganisms, such as bacteria (e.g., anthrax, cholera), rickettsiae (e.g., Rocky Mountain spotted fever), and viruses (e.g., smallpox, yellow fever). Biological agents have a range of characteristics that affect their suitability for military use and the probable results of a biological attack. For example, whether or not disease would spread from the point of attack is determined by its infectiousness and its contagiousness. Infectiousness refers to the "relative ease with which [the disease] is transmitted to other hosts."[54] A disease that can be transmitted by air and by water is more infectious than a disease that can be spread by air only. "Contagiousness" is a subtype of "infectious"; the contagiousness of an agent refers to whether the disease is transmitted by direct physical contact. A droplet-spread disease can be spread by sneezing, coughing, or talking; such diseases are more likely to spread beyond the immediate target (and thus are more infectious) than is a contagious disease spread only by direct contact (e.g., gonorrhea).[55] Biological agents vary greatly in this regard. Some, like smallpox, spread rapidly from human to human, posing the danger of epidemics; others can be transported by animals or insects and can therefore be spread far from the area originally attacked; still others, like anthrax, pose little epidemic threat because there is little or no chance of secondary infection[56] (see Table 1.3).

Biological agents can also be incapacitating or lethal; "incapacitating agents are those which, in natural outbreaks, cause illness but rarely death."[57] Another important characteristic of biological agents is their required incubation period. Biological agents are living organisms that multiply within their host; the incubation period refers to the multiplication phase that occurs before symptoms of the disease appear. The delayed effect of biological weapons is one of the reasons they have been seen as having little military utility on the battlefield. In addition, like chemical weapons, the effects of a biological attack are dependent on environmental factors such as the weather, the terrain, and the presence of possible nonhuman carriers of the disease.[58]

As with the use of chemical weapons (poison), the idea of using disease (mankind's common enemy) as a method of warfare is something that many find morally repugnant. Thus, a report by the UN secretary-general comments that "the idea that bacteriological (biological) weapons could deliberately be used to spread disease generates a sense of horror."[59] Developments in biotechnology raise the possibility of other horrifying options, including genetic weapons and biological agents that could be targeted at specific ethnic groups.[60] Such weapons do not exist today but may in the future. As Malcolm Dando explains, while it is becoming increasingly possible to identify genetic differences among ethnic groups, it is not yet clear how "to target the genetic differences in order to produce a damaging effect." He warns, however, that "while it can be hoped that ethnically specific weapons will never become a reality, it would be foolish to imagine that they are an impossibility or that incredibly precise targeting might not become available."[61]

Unlike chemical weapons, there are no generally recognized examples of the widespread use of biological weapons in modern warfare.[62] All the participants in World War II except Germany developed biological weapons. Japan's biological weapons program was the most extensive.[63] It undertook the development of offensive biological weapons as early as 1931, experimented with these weapons on POWs, undertook field trials in at least eleven Chinese cities, and used these weapons against China and the Soviet Union.[64] Much of the Japanese use was ad hoc and/or experimental in nature, and problems with dissemination prevented any large-scale use of biological weapons.

Since World War II, various allegations of biological weapons use have been made.[65] However, none of these allegations has been fully authenticated, in part because it has never been possible to culture organisms directly from the alleged means of dissemination.[66] This does not guarantee that biological weapons have never been used, because it can be difficult to detect their use. This difficulty grows over time, and the longer the period between the report of an alleged biological warfare incident and its investigation, the more difficult it is to gather conclusive evidence. However, unnatural outbreaks of disease have several characteristics that differentiate them from natural outbreaks of disease, and this means that any large-scale use of biological weapons is likely to be detected.[67] This also means that the oft-discussed possibility of a covert biological attack that goes undetected because it is mistaken for a natural outbreak of disease is unlikely.

Research on biological weapons continues. While the United States unilaterally discontinued its offensive biological weapons program in 1969, it continues with defensive research allowed under the BWC, and the line between offensive and defensive research is difficult to draw.[68] The Soviets also signed the BWC but continued a secret offensive biological weapons program. Despite an accident at one of their facilities that caused an outbreak of anthrax at Sverdlovsk, that program remained hidden until revealed by defectors from the Soviet Union. While the offensive biological weapons

TABLE 1.3. *Possible Biological Warfare Agents*[a]

Agent (type)	Infectivity and incubation period	Risk of person-to-person spread	Lethality and availability of chemotherapy[b]	Known weaponization?[c]
Anthrax (bacterial)	Moderate to high, 1–6 days	Negligible	For inhalation anthrax: 80–100 percent lethal; antibiotic treatment effective before release of toxins	Yes: Soviet Union, Iraq, United States
Brucellosis, also known as undulant fever (bacterial)	High, 1–60 days	Extremely low	Less than 25 percent; antibiotic treatment available	Yes: United States
Cholera (bacterial)	Low, 1–5 days	High	10–80 percent; antibiotic treatment available	
Dysentery (bacterial)	High, 1–4 days	High	2–20 percent; antibiotic treatment available	
Eastern equine encephalitis (viral)	High, 5–15 days	Negligible	Greater than 60 percent; No antibiotic therapy	
Ebola				Possibly: USSR
Lasa fever				Possibly: USSR
Marburg (viral)		High		Yes: USSR
Monkey pox				Possibly: USSR
Plague (bacterial)	High, 1–10 days	High	30–100 percent; antibiotic treatment when given early is moderately effective	Researched: United States and USSR
Psittacosis (rickettsial)	High, 4–15 days	Moderately high	10–100 percent; antibiotic treatment available	
Q fever (rickettsial)	High, 2–21 days	Negligible	0–4 percent; antibiotic treatment available	

Smallpox (viral)	High, 7–16 days	Extremely high	Up to 35 percent; no antibiotic therapy but vaccine can be effective if admitted shortly after exposure	Yes: USSR
Tularemia, also known as rabbit fever (bacterial)	High, 1–10 days	Negligible	0–60 percent; antibiotic treatment available	Yes: United States
Typhoid (bacterial)	Moderately high, 7–21 days	Moderately high	4–20 percent; antibiotic treatment available	
VEE (viral)	High, 1–5 days	Negligible	Less than 2 percent; no specific antibiotic therapy available	Yes: United States
Yellow fever (viral)	High, 3–6 days	None; requires vector	4–100 percent; no specific antibiotic therapy available	Yes: United States

[a] Susan B. Martin, "The Role of Biological Weapons in International Politics: The Real Military Revolution," *Journal of Strategic Studies* 25:1 (2002), 67–68. This table was compiled from a variety of sources. When differing estimates for infectiousness, incubation period, and lethality were given, I took the extreme figures from each end. The figures given thus represent the widest range of estimates. Sources used were: "Table 1, Characteristics and Symptoms of Some Anti-Human Biological Agents," posted as part of the Chemical and Biological Weapons Nonproliferation Project at the Henry L. Stimson Center, at http://www.stimson.org/cbw; United Nations, Report of the Secretary General, Department of Political and Security Council Affairs, "Annex IV: Some Biological Agents Used to Attack Man," in *Chemical and Bacteriological (Biological) Weapons and the Effects of Their Possible Use* (New York: United Nations, 1969), 92–93; "Examples of Biological Warfare Agents," in *The Biological and Chemical Warfare Threat*, rev. ed. (Washington, D.C.: U.S. Government Printing Office, 1999), 2; SIPRI, "Table 1.2, Pathogenic Micro-organisms Studied as Potential BW Agents," "Table 1.3, Estimated Potencies of Selected CBW Agents," and "Table 2.3, BW Agents Standardized during the US Biological Weapons Program," in *The Problem of Chemical and Biological Warfare*, vol. 2: *CB Weapons Today* (New York: Humanities Press, 1975), 38–41, 42, and 128–29; W. Seth Carus, "Table I: Characteristics of Biological Agents," in "The Poor Man's Atomic Bomb?" *Biological Weapons in the Middle East*, Policy Paper no. 23 (Washington, D.C.: Washington Institute for Near East Policy, 1991), 68–69; Anthony H. Cordesman, "Table 7: Key Biological Agents Likely to be Used in the Third World," in *Weapons of Mass Destruction in the Middle East* (London: Brassey's, 1991), 80; Ken Alibek with Stephen Handelman, *Biohazard* (New York: Random House, 1999).

[b] The figures for lethality are for lethality without medical treatment.

[c] Note that this indicates simply whether a particular agent has been weaponized by a state at any time; it should not be taken as an indication that the agent composes part of a state's current arsenal.

program was canceled by Mikhail Gorbachev in 1990 and again by Boris Yeltsin in 1992, it has been alleged that the program continues.[69]

The destructive power of biological weapons is much greater than that of chemical weapons and can compare to the effect of small nuclear weapons (see Table 1.2). As Steve Fetter explains, "Kilogram for kilogram, anthrax produces lethal concentrations over an area about one thousand times larger than does sarin; warhead for warhead, roughly one hundred times larger."[70] Biological weapons also pose a greater proliferation risk than do nuclear weapons. In 2001, the United States identified China, Iran, Iraq, Libya, North Korea, Pakistan, Russia, and Syria as states that may have offensive biological weapons programs; it stated that India's research is confined to research on biological warfare defense.[71] If we include those states that have had past programs, have been suspected of seeking biological weapons, or have the underlying capabilities necessary to produce biological weapons, the number of possible biological weapons states increases to approximately twenty-five.[72]

Biological weapons are much less expensive than nuclear weapons, use more readily available materials, and are less technologically demanding. Forsberg et al. estimate that "an industrial fermentation plant suitable for conversion to BTW [biological and toxin warfare] agent production could be built for about $10 million."[73] As with chemical agents, much of the necessary scientific knowledge is in the open literature, and much of the necessary equipment has civilian applications. In addition, many biological agents can be found in the wild. But this does not mean that biological weapons that can kill large numbers of people are easy to make; designing a munition that can effectively release a biological agent without killing it is particularly difficult. Japan discovered this during the Second World War.[74]

The spate of anthrax letters sent in the wake of the September 11 attacks in the United States also makes clear that very low-tech biological attacks are possible. While such attacks do not create mass destruction and death, they have been effective in creating panic and disruption. They also underscore how little we know about biological weapons. For example, the minimum number of anthrax spores to which a person has to be exposed in order to become infected is not known, and knowledge both of how to treat anthrax and of the dangers posed by different kinds of contact with anthrax-contaminated objects has evolved over the course of the attacks.[75]

CONCLUSION

Grouping nuclear, biological, and chemical weapons under the label "weapons of mass destruction" obscures important differences among these three types of weapons. One of the clearest differences among these three weapons types is their destructive power, with nuclear weapons the most destructive, chemical weapons the least, and biological weapons falling somewhere in between. Nuclear weapons are so destructive that there seems to be little possibility of using them either solely against combatants or in a proportionate manner. But the same is not necessarily true for biological and chemical weapons.

As experience in both World War I and the Iran-Iraq War makes clear, it is possible to limit a chemical attack to an attack on combatants.[76] However, the effects of a chemical weapons attack depend on the characteristics of the agent (e.g., lethal or incapacitating, persistence) as well as on the method of attack and various environmental factors. With biological weapons it is also theoretically possible to limit an attack to one on combatants. While this again depends on the agent used, a nonpersistent, noncontagious agent (lethal or incapacitating) could be targeted against enemy troops alone.[77] However, because biological agents are living organisms that interact with their environment and that can evolve in unpredictable ways, it is impossible to predict with certainty the effects of a biological attack.

Unless we find something inherently unethical about nuclear, biological, and chemical weapons, all of this suggests that it may not be very useful to discuss the ethics of weapons of mass destruction as a group. To the extent that it is particular uses and particular effects of weapons that we find objectionable, we may find it necessary to distinguish among nuclear, chemical, and biological weapons and, indeed, perhaps even among various chemical and biological agents. It may also be necessary to expand our focus to include at least some conventional weapons.

Notes

1. William Safire, "On Language: Weapons of Mass Destruction," *New York Times*, April 19, 1998, sec. 6, p. 22, Lexis-Nexis Online. Note that according to Safire, some people trace the phrase "weapons of mass destruction" to the Russian term *oruzhiye massovovo porazheniya*, a phrase that "originally referred to any heavy attack from the air."

2. See "The President's News Conference Following the Signing of a Joint Declaration on Atomic Energy," November 15, 1945, available at http:www.trumanlibrary. org/trumanpapers/pppus/1945/191.htm (April 1, 2003), especially point 7 of the declaration.

3. Ibid., point 7c of the declaration.

4. Safire, "On Language: Weapons of Mass Destruction." Much of the declaration is focused on the tension between exploiting the peaceful benefits of new scientific research and avoiding their use as "means of destruction." This suggests that the phrase of "all other major weapons adaptable to mass destruction" may have been left vague in an attempt to cover "future advances in scientific knowledge." See "The President's News Conference Following the Signing of a Joint Declaration on Atomic Energy." See also Nina Tannenwald, *The Nuclear Taboo: The United States and the Non-Use of Nuclear Weapons since 1945* (Cambridge: Cambridge

University Press, forthcoming), chap. 4; Vannevar Bush, *Pieces of the Action* (New York: William Morrow, 1970), 297–98.

5. Stockholm International Peace Research Institute (SIPRI), *The Problem of Chemical and Biological Warfare*, vol. 4: *CB Disarmament Negotiations, 1920–1970* (New York: Humanities Press, 1971), 193; Jozef Goldblat and Thomas Bernauer, *The Third Review of the Biological Weapons Convention: Issues and Proposals*, UNIDIR Research Paper no. 9, April 1991 (New York: United Nations, 1991), 1 and n.1. The phrase was also used when the Baruch Plan was presented to the United Nations Atomic Energy Commission. See Tannenwald, *Nuclear Taboo*, chap. 4.

6. SIPRI, *CB Disarmament Negotiations*, 194, see also 221–22; see also Goldblat and Bernauer, *Third Review of the Biological Weapons Convention*, 1; Tannenwald, *Nuclear Taboo*, chap. 4.

7. SIPRI, *CB Disarmament Negotiations*, 194.

8. Ibid., 194–95.

9. Ibid., 224–26. The declaration helped to ease the Federal Republic of Germany's membership in the Western European Union and NATO and was later incorporated into the Brussels Treaty.

10. Ibid., 195.

11. After World War II, arms control efforts focused on "general and complete" disarmament. When that proved unworkable, the focus shifted to more limited objectives. In the nuclear realm, this produced the Partial Test Ban Treaty in 1963 and the Nonproliferation Treaty in 1968.

12. The preamble to the BWC includes biological and chemical weapons as weapons of mass destruction. It reads in part: "Convinced of the importance and urgency of eliminating from the arsenals of states, through effective measures, such damaging weapons of mass destruction as those using chemical or bacteriological (biological) weapons. . . ." See Goldblat and Bernauer, "Appendix 2: Text of the BW Convention," in *Third Review of the Biological Weapons Convention*, 32. The convention does not provide a specific definition of WMD or, for that matter, of biological weapons.

13. For example, biological weapons have been identified as "the last major threat to a deployed [American] force" by George Friel, the commanding general of the U.S. Chemical and Biological Defense Agency. Quoted by Erhard Geissler, "Biological Weapon and Arms Control Developments," in *SIPRI Yearbook 1994: Armaments and Disarmament* (Oxford: Oxford University Press, 1994), 714.

14. Previous discussions of ethics have focused either on war in general or on nuclear deterrence in particular. See, for example, Geoffrey Goodwin, ed., *Ethics and Nuclear Deterrence* (London: Croom Helm, 1982); Terry Nardin, ed., *The Ethics of War and Peace: Religious and Secular Perspectives* (Princeton, N.J.: Princeton University Press, 1996); Joseph S. Nye, Jr., *Nuclear Ethics* (New York: Free Press, 1986); Barrie Paskins and Michael Dockrill, *The Ethics of War* (Minneapolis: University of Minnesota Press, 1979); Bruce M. Russett, "Ethical Dilemmas of Nuclear Deterrence," *International Security* 8:4 (Spring 1984): 36–54; Michael Walzer, *Just and Unjust Wars* (New York: Basic Books, 1977).

15. Forsberg et al. argue that "what distinguishes weapons of mass destruction from conventional weapons are the large-scale and indiscriminate nature of the effects of the former, particularly against civilians." Randall Forsberg et al., *Nonproliferation Primer* (Cambridge: MIT Press, 1995), 14.

16. These figures are taken from Ian F. W. Beckett, "Total War," in *Warfare in the Twentieth Century*, ed. Colin McInnes and G. D. Sheffield (Boston: Unwin Hyman, 1988), 9; and from U.S. Congress, Office of Technology Assessment (OTA), *Proliferation of Weapons of Mass Destruction: Assessing the Risks*, OTA-ISC-559 (Washington, D.C.: U.S. Government Printing Office, August 1993), 46. Note that Beckett gives the figure of 51,509 for British civilian deaths as a result of conventional attacks by German bombers and rockets, while earlier I quoted the British delegate to the UN Commission for Conventional Armaments as claiming that 56,000 people had died as a result of the "V" rocket attacks (see n. 8 above). No further information on these statistics is provided. Whether the difference in the figures is due to a difference between "civilian" and "British" deaths, whether it is a result of different estimates of the number of deaths, or whether it is a reflection of the difficulties of compiling accurate statistics in wartime conditions is not clear.

17. Also new was the lasting health and environmental damage caused by the use of atomic bombs.

18. While 23,000–80,000 deaths might be expected from an atomic bomb (12.5 kiloton TNT-equivalent, about the size of that dropped on Hiroshima), somewhere between 570,000 and 1,900,000 might be caused by a hydrogen bomb (1.0 megaton TNT equivalent). See Forsberg et al., *Nonproliferation Primer*, fig. 1, p. 16.

19. It is unclear whether India, Pakistan, or Israel possess thermonuclear weapons. India claims to have tested successfully a thermonuclear device on May 11, 1998, although this has been questioned by U.S. analysts. Pakistan claims to have the ability to build a thermonuclear bomb. Some reports conclude that Israel possesses thermonuclear bombs. On India, see Office of the Secretary of Defense, *Proliferation: Threat and Response* (January 2001), 23, at http://www.defenselink.mil (November 3, 2001); Federation of American Scientists, "WMD Around the World: India's Nuclear Weapons," at http://www.fas.org/nuke/guide/india/nuke/index.html (April 1, 2203). On Pakistan, see Office of the Secretary of Defense, *Proliferation: Threat and Response*, 27. On Israel, see Warner D. Farr, LTC, U.S. Army, "The Third Temple's Holy of Holies: Israel's Nuclear Weapons," Counterproliferation Papers Future Warfare Series No. 2, USAF Counterproliferation Center, Air War College, Air University, Maxwell Air Force Base, Alabama, September 1999, available at http://www.au.af.mil/au/awc/awcgate/cpc-pubs/farr.html.

20. See Susan B. Martin, "Incentives to Proliferate: Variance across Chemical, Biological and Nuclear Weapons," paper presented at the Annual Meeting of the American Political Science Association, Washington, D.C., September 2000.

21. The George W. Bush administration has focused on North Korea, Iran, and, until the overthrow of Saddam Hussein in 2003, on Iraq. See U.S. Department of State, International Information Programs, "U.S. Warns of Nations Seeking Weapons of Mass Destruction," April 16, 2002, available at http://usinfo.state.gov/topical/pol/terror/02041607.htm (November 11, 2003). For previous lists of suspect states, see Office of the Secretary of Defense, *Proliferation: Threat and Response*; U.S. Congress, OTA, *Proliferation*, 13.

22. Three former Soviet republics, Ukraine, Kazakhstan, and Belarus, are also former nuclear weapon states.

23. For a useful overview and comparison of the steps involved in the acquisition of nuclear, chemical, and biological weapons, see Forsberg et al., *Nonproliferation Primer*, 39–64. In terms of costs, Forsberg et al. estimate that the Iraqis spent about $10 billion on their nuclear program before the Gulf War. See ibid., 22.

24. Bernard Brodie, "Implications for Military Policy," in *The Absolute Weapon*, ed. Bernard Brodie (New York: Harcourt, Brace, 1946), 76.

25. A more complete definition would also take into account the probability that the threat will be carried out and the probability that the aggression will succeed.

26. Even with bombers some clash of military forces is involved, as the enemy could launch fighters to intercept bombers.

27. Missile defense reconnects deterrent strategies with war-fighting strategies. If missile defenses are employed, deterrence will have to rely on a mixed strategy once again: A state employing a deterrent strategy will have to demonstrate the ability to overcome the other side's defenses in addition to the ability to inflict overwhelming punishment.

28. See Harald Müller and Annette Schaper, "Tactical Nuclear Weapons: Definitions, Types, Missions Risks, and Options for Control – A European Perspective," in *Tactical Nuclear Weapons: Options for Control*, UNIDIR/2000/20 (Geneva: United Nations Institute for Disarmament Research, 2000), 22–26. As Müller and Schaper point out, the distinction between "tactical" and "strategic" as applied to nuclear weapons is thus quite different from the distinction between "tactical" and "strategic" made in classical military thought.

29. The quote is from "Russia's Military Doctrine," *Arms Control Today*, May 2000, ProQuest Direct. See also Nikolai Sokov, "Nuclear Weapons and Russia's Economic Crisis," *Policy Memo Series, Memo #43*, Program on New Approaches to Russian Security, November 1998, at http://www.csis.org/ruseura/ponars/policymemos/pm_0043.pdf (April 1, 2003); William Potter and Nikolai Sokov, "Tactical Nuclear Weapons: The Nature of the Problem," *CNS Reports* (Monterey: Center for Nonproliferation Studies), at http://cns.miis.edu/pubs/reports/tnw_nat.htm (September 12, 2001).

30. The smallest nuclear warhead on a U.S. ballistic missile has a yield of 100 kilotons.

31. Forsberg et al., *Nonproliferation Primer*, 13. Chemical agents also include toxins – poisons that are produced by bacteria, plants, and animals – although toxins are sometimes classified as biological agents because they are produced by living organisms. The key to classifying a particular agent as a chemical weapon is the mechanism through which it does damage. Napalm, for example, is not usually considered a chemical weapon because it is an incendiary substance that exercises its effect through fire and the subsequent loss of air and visibility. See United Nations, Report of the Secretary General, Department of Political and Security Council Affairs, *Chemical and Bacteriological (Biological) Weapons and the Effects of Their Possible Use* (New York: United Nations, 1969), 6, see also 5; John Cookson and Judith Nottingham, *A Survey of Chemical and Biological Warfare* (London: Sheed and Ward, 1969), 181.

32. It is not clear which state was the first to use chemical weapons. SIPRI reports that they were used first by the Germans against the French at Neuve-Chapelle, but they also note that there is a possibility that this was in response to the use of chemicals by the French. SIPRI, *The Problem of Chemical and Biological Warfare*,

vol. 1: *The Rise of CB Weapons* (New York: Humanities Press, 1971), 131–32 and 27–28; see also Edward M. Spiers, *Chemical Warfare* (Urbana: University of Illinois Press, 1986), 14; Valerie Adams, *Chemical Warfare, Chemical Disarmament* (Bloomington: Indiana University Press, 1990), 27.

33. Frederic J. Brown, *Chemical Warfare: A Study in Restraints* (Princeton, N.J.: Princeton University Press, 1968), 3–4; SIPRI, *The Rise of CB Weapons*, 29–31, 134; Spiers, *Chemical Warfare*, 15–16; Hugh D. Crone, *Banning Chemical Weapons* (Cambridge: Cambridge University Press, 1992), 16.

34. Brown, *Chemical Warfare*, 10.

35. Unlike previous chemical warfare agents that were nonpersistent and were dangerous only if breathed into the lungs, mustard gas is a persistent agent that was also absorbed through the skin. See Brown, *Chemical Warfare*, 11–12; Spiers, *Chemical Warfare*, 25–26; Adams, *Chemical Warfare, Chemical Disarmament*, 35–36; Crone, *Banning Chemical Weapons*, 18; Victor A. Utgoff, *The Challenge of Chemical Weapons* (New York: St. Martin's Press, 1991), 6–7. Note that a casualty "is any loss of personnel which reduces the effective fighting strength of a military unit," not a person "who is either killed in action on the field of battle or who *died* from the effects of battle wounds." See Augustin M. Prentiss, *Chemicals in War* (New York: McGraw-Hill, 1937), 649–50. Adams notes that while the introduction of mustard increased the number of gas casualties, "the mortality rate among mustard casualties was much lower than for other lethal gases, averaging around 1 or 2 percent." Adams, *Chemical Warfare, Chemical Disarmament*, 35.

36. Spiers, *Chemical Warfare*, 14–16, 26 ff.; Prentiss, *Chemicals in War*, 647–84; Adams, *Chemical Warfare, Chemical Disarmament*, 39–44.

37. Spiers, *Chemical Warfare*, 30–33.

38. Prentiss, *Chemicals in War*, 653; see 649–55 passim. See also Col. H. L. Gilchrist, *A Comparative Study of World War Casualties* (Washington, D.C.: U.S. Government Printing Office, 1928).

39. Spiers, *Chemical Warfare*, 31; see Robert Harris and Jeremy Paxman, *A Higher Form of Killing* (New York: Hill and Wang, 1982), 35–36, for a dissenting view. It is important to note that there are problems with the data on World War I casualties, including casualties from gas. See Spiers, *Chemical Warfare*, 32; Adams, *Chemical Warfare, Chemical Disarmament*, 25; Harris and Paxman, *Higher Form of Killing*, 34–35.

40. Italy also used chemical weapons in Ethiopia during the 1930s. The first uses of chemical weapons by the Japanese are reported to have been experimental in nature. The Japanese evidently estimated that the Chinese were unable to retaliate on the battlefield and that there was little chance of retaliation by China's allies. Later on in the conflict the Japanese used chemical weapons to drive out Chinese forces hidden in tunnels, to defend perimeters, and to contaminate areas through which Chinese troops would have to travel. No international response other than a rhetorical one was made to this use of chemical weapons: After receiving reports in mid-1942 about the use of chemical weapons against the Chinese, Roosevelt threatened retaliation; the Japanese ignored that warning, no action was taken, and subsequent retaliatory threats were also ignored. Japanese use of chemical weapons against the Allies is said to have been deterred by the U.S. ability to hit the Japanese homeland and the lack of civilian

defensive preparations. See John Ellis van Courtland Moon, "Chemical Weapons and Deterrence: The World War II Experience," *International Security* 8:4 (Spring 1984): 3–35; Adams, *Chemical Warfare, Chemical Disarmament*, 66–69.

41. Moon, "Chemical Weapons and Deterrence," 5; Adams, *Chemical Warfare, Chemical Disarmament*, 38.

42. See Moon, "Chemical Weapons and Deterrence"; Brown, *Chemical Warfare*; Utgoff, *Challenge of Chemical Weapons*, 27–68; Adams, *Chemical Warfare, Chemical Disarmament*, 56–70.

43. Possible explanations for this lack of use range from Coalition defensive measures to the retaliatory threats made by the Bush administration to the lack of a threat to Saddam Hussein's regime that would have justified the use of these weapons. The "Gulf War syndrome" suffered by many veterans of the Persian Gulf War suggests to some that limited use of chemical weapons may have been made, although others suggest that these symptoms are due to a variety of other factors, including the vaccinations received by Coalition troops, the burning of the oil wells, and the possible release of agents during Coalition attacks on Iraqi chemical and biological warfare facilities.

44. See Steve Fetter, "Ballistic Missiles and Weapons of Mass Destruction," *International Security* 16:1 (Summer 1991): 5–42; U.S. Congress, Office of Technology Assessment, "Figure 2-1, Comparing Lethal Areas of Chemical, Biological and Nuclear Weapons" and "Figure 2-2, Comparing Lethal Areas of Chemical and Biological Weapons," in *Proliferation of Weapons of Mass Destruction: Assessing the Risks*, OTA-ISC-559 (Washington, D.C.: U.S. Government Printing Office, August 1993), 53 and 55; SIPRI, "Table 2.5: Estimates of the Relative Potencies of CB and Non-CB Weapons," in *The Problem of Chemical and Biological Warfare*, vol. 2: *CB Weapons Today* (New York: Humanities Press, 1975), 134.

45. See SIPRI, *CB Weapons Today*, 131–32; note that this "advantage" is shared with biological weapons.

46. On the battlefield, chemical weapons may serve as a force multiplier, particularly against "human wave" attacks; as a means of forcing enemy troops from concealed or enclosed positions; as a defense against ambush; to disorient attacking forces and break contact with superior enemy forces; and as a tactical deterrent, to deter the use of chemical weapons by the other side. Incapacitants and harassing agents are thought to be useful in situations where enemy troops are intermingled with civilian populations.

47. Thomas L. McNaugher, "Ballistic Missiles and Chemical Weapons: The Legacy of the Iran-Iraq War," *International Security* 15:2 (Fall 1990): 30.

48. Both the CWC and export control efforts such as those of the Australia Group attempt to control the materials needed to manufacture chemical weapons. Such efforts are easier with nuclear weapons than they are with either chemical or biological weapons, because of the broader commercial applications of many of the technologies, equipment, and materials associated with chemical and biological weapons. In short, the "dual-use problem" is much greater with chemical and biological weapons than it is with nuclear weapons.

49. Forsberg et al., *Nonproliferation Primer*, 52.

50. Office of the Secretary of Defense, *Proliferation: Threat and Response*.

51. This number includes Belarus, Kazakhstan, and Ukraine.

52. For a fuller treatment of biological weapons, see Susan B. Martin, "The Role of Biological Weapons in International Politics: The Real Military Revolution," *Journal of Strategic Studies* 25:1 (March 2002): 63–98.

53. Note that while some definitions of biological agents include toxins because they are poisons produced by living things (bacteria, plants, and animals), I find it more useful to classify toxins as chemical agents because toxins act more like chemical agents than they do like biological agents. On the definition of biological weapons, see Brian Beckett, *Weapons of Tomorrow* (New York: Plenum Press, 1983), 11; Nicholas A. Sims, *The Diplomacy of Biological Disarmament* (New York: St. Martin's Press, 1988), esp. 17–18 and 295–98; SIPRI, *CB Disarmament Negotiations*; SIPRI, *SIPRI Yearbook 1972: World Armaments and Disarmament* (New York: Humanities Press, 1972), 502; UN, Report of the Secretary General, 5; World Health Organization, *Health Aspects of Chemical and Biological Weapons: Report of a WHO Group of Consultants* (Geneva: World Health Organization, 1970), 12.

54. John M. Last, ed., *A Dictionary of Epidemiology* (New York: Oxford University Press, 1983), 51.

55. Ibid., 22. See also Paul Smith, "Archaic Medical Terms: A Resource for Genealogists and Historians," October 10, 2001, at http://www.paul_smith. doctors.org.uk (October 13, 2001); "Glossary of Epidemiology Terms," *CDC*'s *Reproductive Health Information Source*, National Center for Chronic Disease Prevention and Health Promotion, at http://www.cdc.gov/nccdphp/ drh/epi_gloss.htm (October 13, 2001). Note that infectiousness differs from infectivity, which is an "agent capability that embodies [the] capability to enter, survive, and multiply in the host." The more infective an agent is, the more potent it is, so that a smaller amount of the agent is necessary to produce disease. Last, *Dictionary of Epidemiology*, 51.

56. Donald Ainslie Henderson, Director of the World Health Organization's Smallpox Eradication Unit from 1966 to 1971, argues, "The way air travel is now, about six weeks would be enough time to seed cases [of smallpox] around the world. Dropping an atomic bomb could cause casualties in a specific area, but dropping smallpox could engulf the world." Quoted in Richard Preston, "The Demon in the Freezer," *New Yorker* 75:1 (July 12, 1999): 52. Note that others disagree, arguing that smallpox could be contained rather quickly. See Ken Alibek with Stephen Handelman, *Biohazard* (New York: Random House, 1999), 113; WHO, *Health Aspects of Chemical and Biological Weapons*, 70. Anthrax is probably the most discussed biological agent today. If inhaled and untreated, anthrax kills almost everyone exposed to it. It cannot be passed from person to person, but anthrax spores are so indestructible that they can permanently infect the area in which they have been used. Anthrax is thus an agent that is likely to have effects on noncombatants.

57. UN, Report of the Secretary General, 16.

58. See Martin, "The Role of Biological Weapons"; Beckett, *Weapons of Tomorrow*, 114–15. For a discussion on how scientific developments may influence the development of both new biological agents and defenses against biological warfare, see the SIPRI study: Erhard Geissler, ed., *Biological and Toxin Weapons Today* (Oxford: Oxford University Press, 1986).

59. UN, Report of the Secretary General, 87; see also Leonard A. Cole, *The Eleventh Plague* (New York: W. H. Freeman, 1997).

60. See Malcolm Dando, "Appendix 13a: Benefits and Threats of Developments in Biotechnology and Genetic Engineering," in *SIPRI Yearbook 1999: Armaments, Disarmament and International Security* (Oxford: Oxford University Press, 1999), at http://projects.sipri.se/ cbw/cbw-new.html (July 4, 2000); Charles Piller and Keith R. Yamamoto, *Gene Wars: Military Control over the New Genetic Technologies* (New York: Beech Tree Books, 1988); Steven M. Block, "Living Nightmares: Biological Threats Enabled by Molecular Biology," in *The New Terror: Facing the Threat of Biological and Chemical Weapons*, ed. Sidney D. Drell, Abraham D. Sofaer, and George D. Wilson (Stanford, Calif.: Hoover Institution Press, 1999), 39–75; Robert P. Kadlec and Alan P. Zelicoff, "Implications of the Biotechnology Revolution for Weapons Development and Arms Control," in *Biological Warfare: Modern Offense and Defense*, ed. Raymond A. Zilinskas (Boulder, Colo.: Lynne Rienner, 2000), 11–26.

61. Dando, "Benefits and Threats of Developments in Biotechnology and Genetic Engineering," 14–15.

62. There was an attempt by the British to spread smallpox to the American Indians during the eighteenth-century French and Indian Wars through the gift of blankets from a smallpox hospital. However, it is not clear that this attempt was successful; it is difficult to isolate the effect of the blankets from the natural spread of the disease. See Erhard Geissler, introduction to *Biological and Toxin Weapons Today*, 8; George W. Christopher, Theodore J. Cieslak, Julie A. Pavlin, and Edward M. Eitzen, Jr., "Biological Warfare: A Historical Perspective," *Journal of the American Medical Association* 278:5 (August 6, 1997): 412; SIPRI, *The Rise of CB Weapons*, 215.

63. On the history of biological weapons, see Erhard Geissler and John Ellis van Courtland Moon, eds., *Biological and Toxin Weapons: Research, Development and Use from the Middle Ages to 1945*, SIPRI Chemical and Biological Warfare Studies, no. 18 (Oxford: Oxford University Press, 1999); Christopher et al., "Biological Warfare: A Historical Perspective," 413. Despite the fact that Hitler issued an order forbidding the development of biological weapons, some research took place in Germany and there were some allegations that the Germans may have engaged in a primitive form of biological warfare. See SIPRI, *The Rise of CB Weapons*, 223; Cookson and Nottingham, *Survey of Chemical and Biological Warfare*, 55; Alibek, *Biohazard*, 33–34. On the Japanese biological weapons program, see Christopher et al., "Biological Warfare: A Historical Perspective"; Thomas Stock, Maria Haug, and Patricia Radler, "Chemical and Biological Weapon Developments and Arms Control," in *SIPRI Yearbook 1996: Armaments, Disarmament and International Security* (Oxford: Oxford University Press, 1996); Yuki Tanaka, *Hidden Horrors: Japanese War Crimes in World War II* (Boulder, Colo.: Westview, 1996); Peter Williams and David Wallace, *Unit 731: Japan's Secret Biological Warfare in World War II* (New York: Free Press, 1989); Sheldon H. Harris, *Factories of Death: Japanese Biological Warfare 1932–1945 and the American Cover-up* (New York: Routledge, 1994); and Arvo T. Thompson, "Report on Japanese Biological Warfare (BW) Activities," Frederick, Md.: Camp Detrick Army Service Forces, May 31, 1946.

64. Christopher et al., "Biological Warfare: A Historical Perspective," 413, report that "at least 10,000 persons died as a result of experimental infection or execution following experimentation during the Japanese program between 1932 and 1945." Stock et al., "Chemical and Biological Weapon Developments and Arms Control," 687–88, state that Japanese experiments using biological weapons "killed at least 3,000 people from China, Korea, Mongolia and Russia," although "the exact number of deaths may have been ten times greater."

65. For more information on alleged uses of biological (and chemical) weapons, see SIPRI, *The Rise of CB Weapons*, which provides information on allegations of the use of CBW up to 1968, and the *SIPRI Yearbook* series, begun in 1972, which provides information on CBW allegations that occur in the following years.

66. See SIPRI, *The Rise of CB Weapons* and the *SIPRI Yearbook* series.

67. Mark L. Wheelis, "Investigating Suspicious Outbreaks of Disease," in *Biological Warfare: Modern Offense and Defense*, ed. Raymond A. Zilinskas (Boulder, Colo.: Lynne Rienner, 2000), 105–17.

68. See Judith Miller, "When Is Bomb Not a Bomb? Germ Experts Confront the United States," *New York Times on the Web*, September 5, 2001, at http://nytimes.com (September 12, 2001); Judith Miller, Stephen Engelberg, and William J. Broad, "U.S. Germ Warfare Research Pushes Treaty Limits," *New York Times*, September 4, 2001, Lexis-Nexis (September 12, 2001); Elisa D. Harris, "Research Not to Be Hidden," *New York Times*, September 6, 2001, Lexis-Nexis (September 12, 2001).

69. "Concerns Renewed about Russia's Bio Weapons Program," *CBW Chronicle* 2:4 (May 1998), at http://www.stimson.org/cwc/new.htm. For an account of the Soviet program by one of its top scientists, see Alibek, *Biohazard*.

70. Fetter, "Ballistic Missiles and Weapons of Mass Destruction," 26.

71. Office of the Secretary of Defense, *Proliferation: Threat and Response*.

72. This number includes Belarus, Kazakhstan, and Ukraine.

73. Forsberg et al., *Nonproliferation Primer*, 59.

74. The difficulties involved in producing biological weapons may be especially problematic for terrorist groups. On the possible use of chemical, biological, and nuclear weapons by terrorists, see Jonathan B. Tucker, "Chemical and Biological Terrorism: How Real a Threat?" *Current History* 99:636 (April 2000): 149–50; David C. Rapoport, "Terrorism and Weapons of the Apocalypse," *National Security Studies Quarterly* 5:3 (Summer 1999): 49–67; Jonathan B. Tucker, ed., *Toxic Terror: Assessing Terrorist Use of Chemical and Biological Weapons* (Cambridge: MIT Press, 2001); Richard A. Falkenrath, Robert D. Newman, and Bradley A. Thayer, eds., *America's Achilles Heel: Nuclear, Biological, and Chemical Terrorism and Covert Attack* (Cambridge: MIT Press, 2000); Jean Pascal Zanders, Edvard Karlsson, Lena Melin, Erik Näslund, and Lennart Thaning, "Appendix 9a: Risk Assessment of Terrorism with Chemical and Biological Weapons," in *SIPRI Yearbook 2000: Armaments, Disarmament and International Security* (Oxford: Oxford University Press, 2000), at http://projects.sipri.se/cbw/research/cbw-yearbook.htm (October 15, 2001).

75. For example, see William J. Broad, Stephen Engelberg, Judith Miller, and Sheryl Gay Stolberg, "Excruciating Lessons in the Ways of a Disease," *New York Times on the Web*, October 31, 2001, at http://nytimes.com (November 4, 2001); Daniel

Zwerdling, "Amount of Anthrax Spores Needed to Make People Sick," *National Public Radio*, October 30, 2001, Lexis-Nexis Online. For more information on biological terrorism, see Thomas V. Inglesby et al., "Anthrax as a Biological Weapon: Medical and Public Health Management," *JAMA* 281:18 (May 12, 1999):1735–1963; as well as *Emerging Infectious Diseases* 5:4 (July–August 1999), at http://www.cdc.gov/ncidod/EID/ eid.htm (this is a special issue devoted to biological terrorism).

76. It is important to note that we may reject the use of these weapons even if their use can be limited to combatants. Richard Price notes that "the unique aspect of the emergent CW norm at the Hague conference of 1899 is that it did not . . . simply ban particular uses of such shells (e.g., against civilians) while implicitly conferring legitimacy upon their use against soldiers in the field. Rather, the Hague declaration took the form of a more absolute prohibition in that any kind of first use of such weapons was to be regarded as unacceptable." See Richard Price, "A Genealogy of the Chemical Weapons Taboo," *International Organization* 49:1 (Winter 1995): 90.

77. But not all agents are of this type; as reported by the UN secretary-general, "Certain chemical and bacteriological (biological) agents are potentially un-confined in their effects, both in space and time, and . . . their large-scale use could conceivably have deleterious and irreversible effects on the balance of nature." See UN, Report of the Secretary General, 87.

2

The International Law Concerning Weapons
of Mass Destruction

Paul C. Szasz

In the post–World War II period, extensive negotiations have taken place concerning arms control and disarmament, for the most part under the auspices of the United Nations General Assembly, at least as far as world-wide arrangements are concerned. The greatest part of these negotiations has focused on nuclear weapons, less often on chemical or biological weapons, and relatively infrequently on other types of arms (see Table 2.1).

Although not defined formally in any legal instrument, nuclear, chemical, and biological weapons have come to be known collectively as "weapons of mass destruction"[1] in contrast to the others, called "conventional weapons." The former term evidently reflects the fact that these weapons can cause destruction (in the case of nuclear weapons) and death (in the case of all three types) on a massive scale. These weapons also have the characteristic that, even if not used in large quantities, they tend to be indiscriminate, in particular in affecting civilians even more than military personnel, as the latter are more likely to use protective gear. Of course, this is not necessarily so: A nuclear weapon used against a warship at sea will probably kill or injure only military personnel. By contrast, most conventional weapons, when properly used, permit discrimination among targets – though land mines often do not, as a result of which treaties have recently been concluded to ban[2] or severely restrict them.[3] On the other hand, the events of September 11, 2001, indicate that massive destruction and indiscriminate killing can also be accomplished by conventional means involving the use of only the most primitive weapons.

This study deals first with chemical and biological weapons, the attempts to control which have long been intertwined, and then separately with nuclear weapons.[4] Although this chapter discusses how international law regulates these supremely dangerous devices, it should be noted that to the extent that states could not agree on legal prohibitions or restrictions, resort is sometimes had to the language of ethics, such as appeals to the "conscience of mankind."[5]

TABLE 2.1. *Major International Agreements on Weapons of Mass Destruction*

To prevent the spread of nuclear weapons

Antarctic Treaty, 1959[a]   **45 states**[b]
Bans any military uses of Antarctica and specifically prohibits nuclear
tests and storage of nuclear wastes on the continent.

Outer Space Treaty, 1967   **129 states**
Bans nuclear weapons in earth orbit and their stationing in outer
space.

Latin American Nuclear-Weapon-Free Zone Treaty (Treaty of   **33 states**
Tlatelolco), 1967
Bans testing, possession, and deployment of nuclear weapons in Latin
America and the Caribbean and requires safeguards on facilities.

Nonproliferation Treaty, 1968   **188 states**
Bans transfer of nuclear weapons or weapons technology to
nonnuclear weapon states. Requires safeguards on their nuclear
facilities. Commits nuclear weapon states to negotiations to halt the
arms race. Commits nonnuclear states not to acquire nuclear
weapons. Promotes peaceful uses of nuclear energy. Renewed
indefinitely in 1995.

Seabed Treaty, 1971   **115 states**
Bans nuclear weapons on the seabed beyond a twelve-mile coastal
limit.

South Pacific Nuclear-Weapon-Free Zone Treaty (Treaty of   **13 states**
Rarotonga), 1985
Bans testing, acquisition, and stationing of nuclear weapons in the
South Pacific. Requests five nuclear weapon states to sign a protocol
banning use or threat of nuclear weapons and nuclear testing.

Southeast Asia Nuclear-Weapon-Free Zone Treaty (Treaty of   **10 states**
Bangkok), 1995
Bans the development, stockpiling, testing, and acquisition of nuclear
weapons in Southeast Asia.

African Nuclear-Weapon-Free Zone Treaty (Treaty of Pelindaba), 1996 **51 states**
Bans research, manufacture, acquisition, and stockpiling of nuclear
weapons in Africa. Not yet in force.

To limit nuclear testing

Partial Test Ban Treaty, 1963   **135 states**
Bans nuclear explosions in the atmosphere, outer space, or
underwater.

Threshold Test Ban Treaty, 1974   **U.S.-USSR**
Bans underground tests having a yield above 150 kilotons.

Peaceful Nuclear Explosions Treaty, 1976   **U.S.-USSR**

Bans underground nuclear explosions for "peaceful purposes" having a yield above 150 kilotons; bans "group explosions" having a yield above 1.5 megatons.

Comprehensive Test Ban Treaty, 1996   **170 states**

Bans all nuclear explosions, including underground tests. Not yet in force.

To limit nuclear weapons

ABM Treaty (SALT I) and Protocol, 1972, 1974   **U.S.-USSR**

Limits antiballistic missile systems to one deployment site on each side. Bans nationwide antiballistic missile system and development, testing, or deployment of sea-based, air-based, or space-based ABM systems. President George W. Bush announced U.S. intention to withdraw from ABM Treaty in December 2001.

SALT I Interim Agreement, 1972   **U.S.-USSR**

Froze the number of strategic ballistic missile launchers for five years; extended by parties until 1986 when President Ronald Reagan dropped U.S. commitment.

SALT II, 1979   **U.S.-USSR**

Limited number of strategic nuclear delivery vehicles and multiple-warhead launchers; was not ratified, but its limits were adhered to until 1986 when President Reagan dropped U.S. commitment. Superseded by START in 1991.

INF Treaty, 1987   **U.S.-USSR**

Eliminates American and Soviet ground-launched missiles of intermediate and shorter ranges (300 to 3,500 miles). Requires dismantling within three years; extensive verification provisions.

START I and Protocol, 1991, 1992   **5 states**

Reduces number of deployed U.S. and former Soviet strategic nuclear warheads by approximately one-third; Lisbon Protocol makes Russia, Belarus, Ukraine, and Kazakhstan responsible for carrying out former USSR treaty obligations.

START II, 1993   **U.S.-Russia**

Reduces the number of deployed U.S. and Russian strategic nuclear warheads to 3,000–3,500 each by year 2003, extended by a 1997 protocol to the year 2007; bans multiple-warhead land-based missiles. Russia declared treaty to be nullified in June 2002 because of U.S. withdrawal from the ABM Treaty. Effectively superseded by SORT.

(continued)

TABLE 2.2 *(continued)*

Strategic Offensive Reductions Treaty (SORT), 2002   U.S.-Russia
Reduces and limits the number of strategic nuclear warheads to
1,700–2,200 each by year 2012. Not yet in force.

To prohibit development and use of chemical and biological weapons

Geneva Protocol, 1925   134 states
Bans the use in war of asphyxiating, poisonous, or other gases, and
of bacteriological methods of warfare.

Biological and Toxin Weapons Convention, 1972   167 states
Bans the development, production, and stockpiling of biological
and toxin weapons; requires the destruction of stocks; lacks
verification mechanism.

Chemical Weapons Destruction Agreement, 1990   U.S.-Russia
Requires parties to reduce chemical weapons stocks to maximum of
5,000 tons by the year 2002. Destruction schedule seriously
delayed.

Chemical Weapons Convention, 1993   180 states
Bans the use, production, development, and stockpiling of
chemical weapons. Requires the destruction of all chemical
weapons stockpiles within 10–15 years of the treaty's entry into
force, which occurred in 1997.

---

[a] Date indicates year agreements were opened for signature (multilateral agreements) or
signed (bilateral agreements).
[b] Number of states indicates signatories as of the year 2003.
Sources: Ruth Leger Sivard et al., *World Military and Social Expenditures 1996*, 16th ed. (Leesburg,
Va.: WMSE Publications, 1996), 29; *SIPRI Yearbook 2003: World Armaments, Disarmament and
International Security* (Oxford: Oxford University Press, 2003), 765–88.

SOURCES OF INTERNATIONAL LAW ON WMD

International law is not made by international lawyers, though they may
assist in the process, just as national laws are not made by lawyers but by
legislators, some of whom may happen to be lawyers. International law is
made by governments, some democratic, some not, directly by the negotiation and conclusion of treaties or by acting so as to establish customary law or indirectly through intergovernmental organizations that create
soft law.

In making international law, governments pursue their own long- and
short-term interests. Ethical considerations may influence this process, particularly to the extent that democratic governments are pressured by certain
constituencies – as is also the case in the making of national laws. But, generally speaking, it cannot be said that such considerations are prominent or

even overt in any international or domestic legislative process, though over time law does tend to reflect the most important values of the community that creates it. To determine to what extent this is so is the task not of lawyers but of those who study and maybe formulate the applicable ethical yardsticks.

International law is created by states (i.e., by governments) to govern themselves and their interactions. As in other subjects of international law, that concerning weapons of mass destruction is derived from many sources.

Treaty Law

International treaties (which may also be called conventions, agreements, protocols, charters, constitutions, articles of agreement, statutes, memoranda of understanding, and so on) are agreements principally between sovereign states that are governed by international law. In modern times, treaties have become the principal source of international law, and multilateral treaties (i.e., treaties with more than two parties) to which most states are or are expected to become parties can be considered to constitute international legislation. There are hundreds of such treaties, and more are being negotiated and concluded each year, for the most part under the auspices of international organizations; many are of a world-wide scope, while others are regional or subregional. However, unlike national legislation, treaties do not apply to all potential entities within their geographical scope, but only to the states that have ratified them. Even those may be able to make "reservations" by which they modify certain of the provisions of the treaty with respect to themselves. The result is that treaty law is less a seamless web and often more a ragged blanket, with some states (the nonparties) not bound at all, and others bound subject to various exceptions. It should also be noted that treaties do not enter into force until they have secured a sufficient number of ratifications (a number specified in the treaty itself), which in some instances may take many years or may not occur at all. Most treaties are subject to denunciation, whereby a state can withdraw from the treaty upon giving appropriate notice and fulfilling any other conditions set out in the treaty for such a step.

Modern multilateral treaties often create some mechanism for supervision and review, sometimes to be carried out by the international organization that sponsored the negotiation of the treaty and sometimes by a special organization or quasi-organization established by the treaty itself. At the minimum, provision is made for periodic meetings of the parties – in the case of arms control treaties, normally every five years – to review the operation of the treaty and compliance therewith and perhaps to consider changing or supplementing it.

Finally, although most obligations established by treaties run only between their parties, affecting third parties only incidentally, certain treaties, particularly environmental and arms control ones, create obligations that explicitly or implicitly benefit all states. These are referred to as *erga omnes* obligations.

Customary Law

International customary law comes into being by the actual practice of states, based on their understanding of what is legally required of them (referred to as *opinio juris*). Unlike treaty law, which is "black letter" – that is, based on a written text – customary law is unwritten though its terms may be derived from diplomatic correspondence, judicial decisions, or academic writings. By its nature, therefore, there is generally far less certainty about whether a given rule of customary law actually exists and what its precise terms are than there is about treaty law. To determine whether a rule exists, it is necessary to examine the actual practice of states, which may consist of real "actions,"[6] of diplomatic protests, of positions assumed in international organizations, or even of inaction when action might normally be warranted.[7] It is also sometimes necessary to determine whether the action was motivated by a sense of legal obligation or by some other factor: courtesy, for example, the desire to gain some advantage, or in reaction to outside pressures.

Nevertheless, customary law is important for several reasons; until the advent of modern multilateral legislative treaties, customary law was in effect the only international law in existence and it still governs those, steadily fewer, areas that are not covered by treaties. More important, customary law, unlike treaty law, binds all states without their having taken any explicit steps (such as ratification) to become bound, with the exception of "persistent objectors" that from the beginning have taken the public position that they would not be bound by the norm in question. Indeed, some customary rules acquire the status of peremptory norms from which no deviation is permitted, by treaty or otherwise. These are referred to as *jus cogens*.

General Principles of Law

The relatively few legal principles that appear to constitute part of the law of essentially all states – such as the general condemnation of poisoning – are also considered to constitute part of binding international law.

Unilateral Undertakings

Especially in the field of nuclear weapons, unilateral undertakings by states play an important role. Declarations setting out such undertakings may be considered as binding as long as they are in effect. The question therefore arises as to the circumstances under which the undertakings they contain can be terminated. If these are from the beginning limited in time, there is no difficulty about their automatic termination, but it would probably not be legal to terminate them sooner. If no limit is stated, they can presumably be terminated at any time, provided proper notice is given, unless the declarations were made explicitly or implicitly to induce other states to take certain actions, which these have then taken in reliance thereon. In the latter case, the declarations might be considered part of treaty arrangements, to which the normal rules of treaty law apply.[8]

Other Manifestations of International Law

Aside from norms embodied in binding hard law, there are others that are not legally binding but that are still expected to be observed. These are called "soft law"; though that may appear an oxymoron, in fact most soft law norms are actually complied with. To the extent that they are observed and a state practice develops, these norms may harden into customary international law or they may be codified into treaty law. The following paragraphs describe some of the principal manifestations of this type of international quasi-law.

Nonbinding Agreements. Sometimes states enter into agreements that constitute political undertakings of their governments, but which they do not wish to be legally binding. For example, the Helsinki Accords of 1975, and the many subsequent agreements concluded by means of the Helsinki Process through the Conference on (and later the Organization for) Security and Cooperation in Europe, include a number of statements concerning arms control and limitations in Europe. Other examples of nonbinding agreements are the voluntary but coordinated adherence to as yet unratified treaties, as occurred in the case of the U.S.-USSR START II agreement setting equal ceilings for the strategic nuclear weapons of the two parties, to be achieved by staged reductions.[9] Even though such instruments are not binding, the respective governments may agree to implement them voluntarily.

Resolutions of International Organizations. Generally speaking, resolutions of international organizations constitute at best recommendations to their members without any implied legal force. There are exceptions, however. For example, certain solemn resolutions of the UN General Assembly adopted after extensive negotiations and by general agreement or consensus and in any event without any explicit opposition do carry a certain expectation of compliance that is normally realized.[10] In the arms control field there are, among the thousand-odd resolutions that have been adopted, only a few that are both normative in form and that were adopted without significant opposition – so that this form of soft law plays at best a minor role in the present context.

The UN Security Council is, however, empowered to adopt decisions binding on states if it determines that there exists a threat to the peace.[11] Although for over five decades the council used this power only when it required that sanctions be imposed on a state in connection with particular, disruptive behavior, in the wake of the September 11, 2001, attacks against the United States, it adopted a resolution commanding all states to take specified actions against terrorism.[12] So far, the council has not – though it presumably could – taken similar action to prohibit or to restrict any weapon of mass destruction that it might well determine to constitute a threat to the peace.

International Regulations. Certain international organizations, such as the International Atomic Energy Agency, issue norms in the form of regulations to be observed by states. Their legal force depends on the legal basis on which they are promulgated. Normally, that basis is a treaty, either the constitution of the organization itself or some other agreement that delegates certain rule-making functions to the organization. The legal force of the regulation then depends on what that treaty specifies.

Judicial Decisions. In international law, judicial decisions do not create *stare decisis*, that is, an international common law that is to be generally observed. Judgments of courts are binding only between the parties to the dispute in question,[13] and advisory opinions (as the term suggests) are not binding even on the entity that requested them, unless that entity has provided (by an internal rule or an agreement) that the opinion would be considered as binding. That having been said, it is also true that international courts (like national ones) endeavor to maintain a consistency of jurisprudence so that having once decided a point of principle, they will normally maintain that point and even cite the previous decision as support for the new one. Furthermore, because of the respect enjoyed by the World Court, its decisions concerning points of international law are generally followed by other courts and by arbitral tribunals, as well as by other international actors, such as governments and international organizations. As there is no compulsion to do so, one may consider such judicial decisions as constituting at least soft law.

Scholarly Studies. Aside from courts, findings or proposals as to the content of international law (the interpretation of treaties, the existence and contents of customary law, the force of given types of soft law) may be made by individual scholars or by scholarly groups, as well as by officially convened bodies of international jurists (such as the UN's International Law Commission ILC). Though their findings and proposals have no legal force, they may be considered sufficiently authoritative that in fact they are followed by governments, by international organizations, and even, cautiously, by courts.[14]

International Criminal Law

The concept that certain actions are inherently evil and should be punishable by any state without necessarily any connection with the accused person, the victim, or the place of commission has long existed. These are sometimes called "universal crimes," and those who commit them are characterized as *hostes humani generis* – enemies of all humanity. However, it has been only in recent years that international criminal law has been seriously developed, because classically international law applied only to states.

Numerous existing treaties and several under active consideration criminalize certain actions by individuals. The normal requirement of such treaties is that the parties are obliged to make such actions criminal under their domestic laws, that they will either prosecute accused perpetrators or extradite them to another party that wishes to prosecute, and that they will cooperate with each other in furthering such criminal proceedings. In addition, recently a number of international criminal tribunals have been established or proposed, each with jurisdiction over certain defined crimes. Among the rules such tribunals observe is that the official position of accused persons (e.g., as head of state or of government) does not relieve them of criminal responsibility or mitigate punishment, that superiors are responsible for the criminal acts of subordinates of which the former knew or had reason to know, and that obedience to superior orders does not relieve criminal responsibility but may be considered in mitigation of punishment.

The Rome Statute of the International Criminal Court (ICC) entered into force on July 1, 2002. The ICC will operate as the first permanent forum for trying individuals accused of genocide, crimes against humanity, war crimes, and the as-of-yet undefined crime of aggression. As discussed below, the Rome Statute may be interpreted in such a way as to allow prosecuting individuals who employ weapons of mass destruction under certain circumstances.

CHEMICAL AND BIOLOGICAL WEAPONS

In 1874, fifteen European states seeking agreement on the laws and customs of war adopted the Brussels Declaration, which, had it entered into force, would have banned the use of poisons or poisoned weapons.[15]

The first treaty concluded in this area was the 1899 Hague Declaration IV.2 Concerning Asphyxiating Gases.[16] By this agreement, the contracting parties agreed not to use, in wars between them, "projectiles the sole object of which is the diffusion of asphyxiating or deleterious gases."

The 1907 Hague Conference adopted Hague Convention IV Respecting the Laws and Customs of War on Land,[17] which is still considered to be in force – indeed, to have attained the status of customary law binding on all states. Annexed to that convention were the Regulations Respecting the Laws and Customs of War on Land, article 23(a) of which forbids the employment of "poison or poisoned weapons."

The 1925 Geneva Protocol

World War I saw the first (and fortunately last) large-scale use of various poison gases, which were particularly effective in the trench warfare that characterized that conflict. The victims for the most part were military personnel, many of whom were killed; more suffered with injured lungs all their lives.

The universal revulsion that followed led to the adoption in 1925 of the so-called Geneva Protocol,[18] which entered into force in 1928 and was formally titled "Protocol for the Prohibition of the Use in War of Asphyxiating, Poisonous or Other Gases, and of Bacteriological Methods of Warfare." That brief treaty recalled that "the use in war of asphyxiating, poisonous and other gases, and of all analogous liquids, materials or devices" had already been "justly condemned by the general opinion of the civilized world" and had been prohibited by previous treaties. Desiring that "this prohibition shall be universally accepted as a part of International Law, binding alike the conscience and practice of nations," the parties agreed that they would accept these prohibitions "as between themselves" and extend them also to bacteriological methods of warfare.

It should be noted that the Geneva Protocol did not completely ban the use of the indicated weapons, but merely prohibited their use in war between the parties. Moreover, many of the ratifying states did so with reservations to the effect that the treaty would not apply in respect of any other party that violated the prohibition. In practice, this meant that for those states the treaty prohibited only first use against another party.

Whatever the limitations of the Geneva Protocol might be, the fact is that in World War II there was almost no use of poison gases or of bacteriological weapons. Whether this was due to the legal prohibition or to the conclusion of all warring parties that such weapons could not be effectively employed in that conflict is open to debate.

Soon after the war, however, extensive research commenced in a number of countries for far more potent weapons of both types. These developments led to extensive debates as to the interpretation of the scope of the 1925 treaty in the light of later technological developments. In 1969 the UN General Assembly attempted to resolve these questions by a resolution[19] that first of all declared that the Geneva Protocol expressed "generally accepted principles of international law" (i.e., its prohibitions had become customary law binding not only on the 135 parties but even on nonparties) and that it applied to "any chemical agents of warfare . . . which might be employed because of their direct toxic effects on man, animals or plants"[20] and to "any biological agents of warfare . . . which are intended to cause disease or death in man, animals or plants, and which depend for their effects on their ability to multiply in the person, animal or plant attacked." The reason for replacing the term "bacteriological" used in the 1925 protocol with "biological" was the discovery of viruses, rickettsiae, and other agents that have the ability to multiply in a host. Recent developments have led to the conclusion that the prohibitions of the Geneva Protocol apply not only to international conflicts but also to internal ones, such as civil wars or rebellions.[21]

The Geneva Protocol, as was characteristic of pre–World War II treaties, did not provide for any procedure for supervision; presumably, it was deemed sufficient that any violation would become immediately apparent to the party injured thereby. In 1989 the General Assembly tried to retrofit an essentially voluntary control mechanism by directing the UN secretary-general to establish a mechanism whereby experts would investigate any charges of violations of the protocol or other relevant rules of customary international law, at the request of a UN member.[22] This mechanism was used to investigate reciprocal charges by Iran and Iraq in the war between them during the 1980s.

The Biological Weapons Convention

Because the Geneva Protocol prohibited only the *use* of the proscribed weapons under narrowly circumscribed circumstances, it was considered desirable, especially after World War II, to broaden the prohibition to include even the possession of such weapons. Impetus was given by a 1969 report of the UN secretary-general entitled *Chemical and Bacteriological (Biological) Weapons and the Effects of Their Possible Use*[23] and a 1970 World Health Organization report, *Health Aspects of Chemical and Biological Weapons*.[24] Though some states initially wanted to prohibit all the weapons covered by the Geneva Protocol, it proved easier to negotiate an agreement concerning just biological weapons, because it was then considered that such a treaty would not require a verification scheme (or perhaps that such a scheme for these weapons would not be practicable), while one for chemical weapons would be essential and feasible. Consequently, in 1972, the Convention on the Prohibition of the Development, Production and Stockpiling of Bacteriological (Biological) and Toxin Weapons and on Their Destruction (the Biological Weapons Convention, or BWC)[25] was concluded. It entered into force in 1975.

The BWC prohibits, aside from the actions indicated by its title, the acquisition by any other means or the retention of toxins and microbial or other biological agents. It also outlaws the possession of weapons and other equipment or means of delivery designed to use the prohibited items for hostile purposes or in armed conflict. The convention does not explicitly prohibit the use of such weapons, perhaps because it relied for that prohibition on the Geneva Protocol and the customary international law that the General Assembly had recognized in 1969, or more likely because it was considered that if parties were prohibited from acquiring and possessing such weapons and were obliged to destroy any that they may have had, they could not possibly use them. Unlike the Geneva Protocol, which prohibited use only against other (complying) parties, the BWC in effect precludes any use against anyone – thus constituting an *erga omnes* obligation. In effect, it entirely outlaws such weapons, but necessarily only for the parties to the convention. Thus, any retaliation (retorsion) in kind is precluded, whether against a party or against a nonparty.

The convention contains only a vague control mechanism: A party suspecting a violation by another party may complain to the UN Security Council. The latter may then investigate the complaint, and all parties agree to cooperate with such an investigation. This provision has never been applied, even though there had always been suspicions about Soviet compliance – and in recent years it was disclosed that the USSR had indeed maintained a massive biological weapons program.[26] However, demands for the establishment of a genuine monitoring regime have become more insistent, particularly after the Chemical Weapons Convention was concluded. These demands have been discussed at the quinquennial review conferences of the BWC parties, and in recent years these have established a working group that has evolved a protocol to the convention based largely on the verification regime of the CWC,[27] which would thus require the establishment of a new international organization to implement the protocol. It had been hoped that the negotiations would be concluded at a session of the working group during the summer of 2001 and that the text would be adopted at a meeting of the BWC parties later in the year. Because the U.S. administration indicated earlier that year that it considered the proposed protocol "fatally flawed," it seems unlikely that such an instrument will be concluded in the near future. Yet, in the post-September 11 climate, the United States appears once more to be reconsidering its attitude.

The Chemical Weapons Convention

After the conclusion of the BWC, it took another twenty-one years for agreement to be reached in 1993 on the Convention on the Prohibition of the Development, Production, Stockpiling and Use of Chemical Weapons and on Their Destruction (the Chemical Weapons Convention, or CWC).[28] It entered into force in 1997. This lengthy incubation stage was almost entirely due to the difficulty in agreeing on an inspection regime that would, on the one hand, be strict enough to satisfy the parties that none of the others was committing any significant violations and, on the other, would not be unduly intrusive on national sovereignty.

Unlike the BWC, the CWC explicitly prohibits the use of the proscribed weapons. In any event, because of the illegality of any possession, acquisition, and holding of chemical weapons, this convention also creates an *erga omnes* obligation and thus also precludes any retaliation in kind. The difficult issue of the treatment of temporarily incapacitating chemicals, called "riot control agents," was resolved by allowing their continued use for domestic law enforcement but not as a "method of warfare" (which the United States, but not all states, interpret as permitting some battlefield uses, such as for saving lives).

The bulk of the CWC (plus a lengthy "Verification Annex" and a "Confidentiality Annex") sets out an elaborate control regime. That regime is in part based on the safeguards system of the International Atomic Energy Agency but also takes into account the shortcomings that had become apparent in the operation of that system, in particular those disclosed as a result of the post–Gulf War inspections in Iraq. To implement that regime, the CWC, unlike the Geneva Protocol or the BWC, establishes an organization: the Organization for the Prohibition of Chemical Weapons. OPCW has further elaborated the control provisions and has proceeded to carry these out, including national inspections. Although no substantive violations of the CWC have been detected or suspected, many parties (including the United States) have not been fully cooperative in making the required reports and in facilitating inspections.[29]

Prohibitions on Individuals

Neither the Geneva Protocol nor the BWC contains any provisions concerning the responsibility of individuals. All the prohibitions and obligations under these instruments are addressed solely to the state parties.

By contrast, the CWC requires the parties to prohibit natural and legal persons anywhere in their territory or under their jurisdiction, or possessing their nationality, from undertaking any activity prohibited to states under the convention (e.g., the production, possession, or use of chemical weapons) and to criminalize any such activities under national law.[30] The protocol being developed to add a monitoring regime to the BWC would contain similar provisions.[31]

The Statute of the International Criminal Tribunal for the Former Yugoslavia (ICTY) gives the tribunal jurisdiction over violations of the laws or customs of war, including "employment of poisonous weapons."[32]

The 1998 Rome Statute of the International Criminal Court gives jurisdiction to the court over individuals who commit "war crimes," which are defined as including *inter alia* "serious violations of the laws and customs applicable to international armed conflict, within the established framework of international law." Among these violations are the following: "employing poison or poisoned weapons" and "employing asphyxiating, poisonous or other gases, and all analogous liquids, materials or devices."[33] However, these crimes are not enumerated among those applicable to internal conflicts.[34]

NUCLEAR WEAPONS

The 1945 San Francisco Conference on the United Nations was adjourned and the UN Charter was signed some weeks before the first nuclear explosions. Consequently, the charter does not address the issues of nuclear weapons at all. By contrast, the first part of the first session of the General Assembly, which met in London in January–February 1946, was very much preoccupied with these issues and its very first resolution established a Commission to Deal with the Problems Raised by the Discovery of Atomic Energy.[35] That commission was charged to make specific proposals, among other things, "for control of atomic energy to the extent necessary to ensure its use only for peaceful purposes" and "for the elimination from national armaments of atomic weapons and all other major weapons adaptable to mass destruction."[36]

Thus, from the very beginning, the United Nations strove to delegitimize any military uses of nuclear energy or, in any event, any nuclear weapon.[37] It largely failed in that endeavor, for relatively rapidly five and later on a few other states developed nuclear weapons, and two states placed many thousands into their arsenals to implement successive strategies such as "massive retaliation" (when one of these states had many more such weapons that could reach the other's territory), "deterrence," "counterforce," "countervailing," and, finally, "mutual assured destruction"[38] (the aptly named MAD doctrine). On the other hand, no military use has been made of any of these weapons in a period of over five decades marked by many wars, conflicts, and acute tensions.

For convenience, one can divide the efforts concerning the military uses of nuclear energy into two categories, which will be dealt with seriatim in this study: measures seeking to limit and control the production, testing, and deployment of nuclear weapons (collectively referred to as "arms control") and efforts to forbid them altogether (referred to as "disarmament") – as chemical and biological weapons have been banned.

Control and Limitation of Nuclear Weapons

Nuclear Testing. As more and more types of nuclear weapons, first of the fission (the A-bomb) and later of the fusion (the H- or thermonuclear bomb) variety, were developed by the initial five nuclear powers (which, by coincidence, were the five permanent members of the Security Council), a veritable orgy of testing by means of explosions took place – originally for the most part in the atmosphere. Aside from dangerously polluting their immediate environment, these explosions soon put a large burden of radioactive particles into the atmosphere, which gradually reached earth and were soon detectable in practically all living beings, including humans.

Objections to this pollution rapidly led to considerable pressures to forbid nuclear testing. These pressures were expressed both internationally in the policies of most of the nonnuclear powers and domestically in at least the three democratic possessors of nuclear weapons. Initially, efforts were made to ban all testing, but this proposal faltered on the difficulty of making sure that no state cheated by conducting subterranean tests that either could not be detected from a distance at all or could not be reliably distinguished from other disturbances, such as earthquakes.

In 1963, this Gordian knot was cut by dividing the problem and for the nonce banning only all atmospheric nuclear tests. This eliminated the environmentally most objectionable tests and could readily be monitored, while permitting the continuation of subterranean nuclear testing that at that time could not be adequately monitored. Consequently, the Treaty Banning Nuclear Weapons Tests in the Atmosphere, in Outer Space and Under Water,[39] or, as it is more commonly known, the Partial Test Ban Treaty (PTBT), was concluded.

As provided in the PTBT and as required by continuing political pressures, negotiations continued on a treaty that would also forbid underground testing. The reasons for this concern were that even subterranean tests have environmental consequences and that any tests help to develop nuclear weapons. It was hoped that if all tests were banned, this would inhibit additional states from acquiring untestable nuclear weapons (thus reducing "horizontal proliferation") while also hindering the established nuclear powers in developing new types of weapons ("vertical proliferation"). The principal obstacle was, as from the beginning, the difficulty in designing adequate means of monitoring. Gradually, this obstacle diminished: More sensitive measuring devices were developed and the objections to on-site observations (still considered essential to verify conclusions reached by external monitoring) diminished because of the extensive experience with International Atomic Energy Agency (IAEA) monitoring and the successful negotiation of the 1993 CWC, as well as by the collapse of the paranoid Soviet system. Finally, in 1996, the Comprehensive Test Ban Treaty (CTBT) was adopted by the General Assembly – though with provisions that made it unlikely that the treaty would enter into force in the near future, if ever.[40] However, a Preparatory Commission was established, which, aside from formulating the documentation for the coming into force of the treaty and the establishment of the Comprehensive Test Ban Treaty Organization (CTBTO), is actually setting up much of the network of monitoring stations that are foreseen by the CTBT.

From time to time during this process one or more of the nuclear powers declared moratoria on further testing, usually for the ostensible purpose

of advancing negotiations. Some of these actions were taken entirely unilaterally, and some were coordinated with other powers; some were expressly limited in time, while others were continued until some specified
event happened, for example, testing by another power. Several bilateral
treaties were concluded between the United States and the USSR restricting
testing,[41] thus helping to improve the atmosphere for further negotiations.
Currently, a moratorium is being observed pending the entry into force of
the CTBT.

Demilitarized or Nuclear-Weapon-Free Zones. One means of limiting nuclear
weapons has been the designation of particular areas or environments in
which the deployment or use of nuclear weapons is forbidden. In some
instances, this limitation was the principal objective of the exercise, while in
others it was merely incidental to the establishment of a particular protective
regime.

The 1959 Antarctic Treaty[42] forbids all military activities in the Antarctic,
including the testing of any sort of weapons (article I.1). It also forbids all
nuclear explosions on the continent (article V.1).

In 1967 the Treaty on Principles Governing the Activities of States in the
Exploration and Use of Outer Space, including the Moon and Other Celestial Bodies[43] (the Outer Space Treaty), was opened for signature. Article IV.1
provides that: "States Parties to the Treaty undertake not to place in orbit
around the earth any objects carrying nuclear weapons or any other kinds
of weapons of mass destruction, install such weapons on celestial bodies, or
station such weapons in outer space in any other manner." In 1979, there
followed the Agreement Governing the Activities of States on the Moon and
Other Celestial Bodies[44] (the Moon Treaty), article 3.3 of which provides
that: "States Parties shall not place in orbit around or any other trajectory
to or around the moon objects carrying nuclear weapons or any other kinds
of weapons of mass destruction or place or use such weapons on or in the
moon."

In 1971 came the Treaty on the Prohibition of the Emplacement of Nuclear Weapons and Other Weapons of Mass Destruction on the Seabed and
the Ocean Floor and in the Subsoil Thereof[45] (the Seabed Treaty).

Over the years, "nuclear-weapon-free zones" have been established for
Latin America and the Caribbean, the South Pacific, Southeast Asia, and
Africa. Treaties concerning other regions are under consideration, and one
for Central Asia is being negotiated. Following guidelines established by the
General Assembly,[46] the relevant treaties prohibit any of the parties from
testing, using, manufacturing, producing, or otherwise acquiring nuclear
weapons, and provide for the IAEA to apply its safeguards to monitor compliance. In a protocol to such treaties, all the nuclear powers undertake
not to contribute in any way to violations of the obligations of the parties

to the treaty and not to use or to threaten to use nuclear weapons against the parties. If any nonregional powers have territories within the region, they undertake in another protocol that these will also comply with the obligations of the parties.

In 1998, Mongolia declared its nuclear-weapon-free status,[47] so far the only state to have done so.

Nuclear Organizations and Nuclear Safeguards. In the mid-1950s, three organizations were established to further the peaceful uses of nuclear energy: the International Atomic Energy Agency (IAEA), the European Atomic Energy Commission (Euratom), and the European Nuclear Energy Agency (ENEA, now NEA). Though none of these organizations required the parties to renounce nuclear weapons, each provided that nuclear materials, equipment, or facilities that were supplied to them for peaceful uses should not be used for nuclear weapons, and each established a control system to monitor compliance with this undertaking. Currently, the NEA control system is inoperative, as all of its members are covered by Euratom and/or IAEA safeguards. The Euratom controls are operated in conjunction with those of the IAEA, as all Euratom members are parties to the Nonproliferation Treaty (NPT) and thus subject to its safeguards provisions.

The IAEA originally operated its safeguards system solely to ensure that assistance it had granted or arranged was not used for any military purpose and more importantly to take over the control functions that suppliers under bilateral nuclear agreements had reserved for themselves vis-à-vis the recipients. However, since NPT entered into force, the principal function of IAEA safeguards has become the control of compliance with that treaty. It also carries out the control functions foreseen for it in the several regional nuclear-free-zone treaties. After the Gulf War, it carried out, at the direction of the Security Council, inspections and the destruction of Iraq's illegal nuclear weapons facilities.[48]

The IAEA's safeguards are informally supplemented by several agreements among nuclear suppliers, whereby these decide what types of materials should trigger reports to the agency when supplied to nonnuclear weapon states.[49]

The Nonproliferation Treaty (NPT). In 1968, the Treaty on the Nonproliferation of Nuclear Weapons[50] was concluded. In a unique arrangement, NPT divides its parties into two categories, with radically different obligations. Each nonnuclear weapon state (NNWS) party undertakes not to receive from anyone any nuclear weapons or other nuclear explosive devices, not to manufacture or otherwise acquire such weapons or devices, and not to seek assistance in such manufacture (article II). The nuclear weapon states (NWSs) are the five states that had exploded a nuclear weapon or device before January 1, 1967 (article IX.3), namely, China, France, the United Kingdom, the USSR (now the Russian Federation), and the United States.[51] They undertake not to transfer nuclear weapons or explosive devices to any other state and not to assist any NNWS in manufacturing or otherwise acquiring such weapons or devices (articles I and II). Furthermore, each NNWS undertakes to accept IAEA safeguards on all its peaceful nuclear activities (article III), for which the agency developed a special safeguards system.

To induce the NNWSs to become parties to NPT, the NWSs had to make certain concessions. In particular, they had to agree – at least in principle – to achieve at the earliest possible date "the cessation of the nuclear arms race and to undertake effective measures in the direction of nuclear disarmament," to "seek to achieve the discontinuance of all test explosions of nuclear weapons for all time and to continue negotiations to that end," and "to facilitate the cessation of the manufacture of nuclear weapons, the liquidation of all . . . existing stockpiles, and the elimination from national arsenals of nuclear weapons and the means for their delivery pursuant to a Treaty on general and complete disarmament under strict and effective international controls" (preamble). More particularly, the NPT parties undertook "to pursue negotiations in good faith on effective measures relating to cessation of the nuclear arms race at an early date and to nuclear disarmament, and on a treaty on general and complete disarmament under strict and effective international controls" (article VI). When implemented, this would eliminate the anomalous distinction between the two categories of parties by restoring equality among them by making them all NNWSs.

Even though the NNWS parties have largely lived up to their obligations under NPT, as annually certified by the IAEA, the NWSs have not complied at all with their disarmament-related obligations. As a result, the quinquennial Review Conferences for NPT have been extremely contentious and several times were unable to agree on any consensus report. This was also true of the 1995 Review and Extension Conference, at which the parties had to decide whether to extend NPT indefinitely (article X.2). Though consensus was reached on the extension, the NWSs were forced to reaffirm their commitment to pursue in good faith negotiations toward nuclear disarmament and to agree to making rapid progress on negotiating a comprehensive test ban treaty[52] – and probably not coincidentally, the CTBT was finally concluded a year later. Otherwise, however, there is no apparent progress toward nuclear disarmament – even after the World Court in an advisory opinion unanimously concluded that there is an obligation to pursue such negotiations in good faith and bring them to a conclusion, and the General Assembly specifically endorsed this plea. At the 2000 NPT Review Conference, the NWSs made an unequivocal undertaking to accomplish a total elimination of their nuclear arsenals leading to nuclear disarmament, which would finally fulfill the obligation they had assumed three decades earlier in the NPT.[53] Although the United States and USSR/Russia have agreed on and implemented several substantial reductions of their nuclear arsenals, both of them still retain many thousands of nuclear weapons. Thus, their efforts have not been considered as a move toward genuine nuclear disarmament.

NPT contains a withdrawal provision whereby any party may "in exercising its national sovereignty" withdraw from the treaty "if it decides that extraordinary events, relating to the subject matter of this treaty, have jeopardized the supreme interests of its country," by giving three months' notice to the other parties and the UN Security Council (article X.1).[54] [So far, only North Korea has utilized this provision. On January 10, 2003, it announced that it was withdrawing from the NPT, citing the escalating confrontation with the United States. Ten years earlier it had announced a similar intention to withdraw when the IAEA found it in violation of the treaty, but on the last day of the notice period it was persuaded not to do so. – Eds.]

Other Approaches to Nuclear Arms Reduction. With the end of the cold war and the inability or unwillingness of the nuclear powers to negotiate seriously toward nuclear disarmament, other suggestions have been made to achieve at least some multilaterally assured reduction in nuclear armaments. These proposals include a ban on the production of nuclear weapons materials (principally plutonium and highly enriched uranium)[55] and the transfer of excess stocks of these materials to the IAEA or at least their placement under its controls. So far, not much progress has been made in these directions.

Unilateral Undertakings Concerning Nuclear Weapons. From time to time, one or more of the nuclear weapon states have made various undertakings, individually or collectively, that they would: (1) come to the assistance of any NNWS that was attacked by nuclear weapons (referred to as "positive security assurances"),[56] (2) not use nuclear weapons against any NNWS, unless it was allied with a NWS (referred to as "negative security assurances"), and (3) not be the first to use nuclear weapons in a conflict. These undertakings were generally made to induce NNWSs to become parties to NPT or to reduce pressures on the NWSs to comply with their own commitments under NPT.

The Prohibition of Nuclear Weapons

Directly Applicable Legal Instruments. There are no treaties that directly address, positively or negatively, the legality of nuclear weapons. The closest is the NPT, which as explained above calls for negotiations for the elimination of such weapons. The CTBT contains similar sentiments in its preamble, but no provision requiring such negotiations.

The UN General Assembly has adopted a number of resolutions directly relevant to the issue of legality. All these were adopted by considerable majorities, but over the objection of at least some of the nuclear powers.

In 1961, the assembly adopted a Declaration on the Prohibition of the Use of Nuclear and Thermo-Nuclear Weapons,[57] whose initial operative paragraph asserts that:

(a) The use of nuclear and thermo-nuclear weapons is contrary to the spirit, letter and aims of the United Nations and, as such, is a direct violation of the Charter of the United Nations;

(b) The use of nuclear and thermo-nuclear weapons would exceed even the scope of war and cause indiscriminate suffering and destruction to mankind and civilization and, as such, is contrary to the rules of international law and to the laws of humanity;

(c) The use of nuclear and thermo-nuclear weapons is a war directed not against an enemy or enemies alone but also against mankind in general ...;

(d) Any State using nuclear and thermo-nuclear weapons is to be considered as violating the Charter of the United Nations, as acting contrary to the laws of humanity and as committing a crime against mankind and civilization.

Twenty years later the assembly adopted a Declaration on the Prevention of Nuclear Catastrophe,[58] in which it solemnly proclaimed that:

1. States and statesmen that resort first to the use of nuclear weapons will be committing the gravest crime against humanity;

2. There will never be any justification or pardon for statesmen who would take the decision to be the first to use nuclear weapons;

3. Any doctrines allowing the first use of nuclear weapons and any actions pushing the world towards a catastrophe are incompatible with human moral standards and the lofty ideals of the United Nations.

Two years thereafter the assembly adopted a resolution on Condemnation of Nuclear War[59] in which it:

1. *Resolutely, unconditionally and for all time condemns* nuclear war as being contrary to human conscience and reason, as the most monstrous crime against peoples and as a violation of the foremost human right – the right to life; and

2. *Condemns* the formulation, propounding, dissemination and propaganda of political and military doctrines and concepts intended to provide "legitimacy" for the first use of nuclear weapons and in general to justify the "admissibility" of unleashing nuclear war.

In recent years, the General Assembly has annually adopted resolutions calling for the negotiation of a convention "prohibiting the use or threat of use of nuclear weapons under any circumstances."[60]

Indirectly Relevant Legal Instruments. Some guidance as to the legitimacy under international law of nuclear weapons may be sought in the fields of humanitarian and of environmental law.

A basic principle of humanitarian law, set out in particular in the 1949 Fourth Geneva Convention (for the Protection of Civilians), which is generally accepted as now constituting generally binding customary law, and also in the 1977 Protocol I to the 1949 Conventions, is that every care must be taken to protect noncombatant civilians and not to use weapons indiscriminately so that civilians might be injured. Protocol I also forbids the wanton destruction of the environment.

Furthermore, attention should be paid to the so-called Martens Clause: "Until a more complete code of the laws of war has been issued . . . the inhabitants and the belligerents remain under the protection and the rule of the principles of the law of nations, as they result from the usages established among civilized peoples, from the laws of humanity, and the dictates of the public conscience." This statement first appeared in the preamble to the 1907 Hague Convention (IV) Respecting the Laws and Customs of War on Land[61] and has since been incorporated into other legal instruments and may be considered as constituting customary law. Thus, until there is an explicit regulation on the use of nuclear weapons, the general "laws of humanity" and "public conscience" must be taken into account in deciding on the legitimacy of such use.

In the field of environmental law, there are numerous treaties that require the parties to protect specified environments, such as Antarctica, the high seas, and certain fragile ecosystems. Undoubtedly, the use of nuclear weapons would not be compatible with these undertakings. The question, however, is whether these treaties, which are intended to regulate normal circumstances, were meant to apply to and limit the parties in the case of armed conflicts.

The Advisory Opinion of the World Court. In 1993, the World Health Assembly (WHA) addressed a request for an advisory opinion to the International Court of Justice (ICJ, or the World Court) with respect to the following question: "In view of the health and environmental effects, would the use of nuclear weapons by a State in war or other armed conflict be a breach of its obligation under international law, including the WHO [World Health Organization] Constitution?"[62] The next year the UN General Assembly addressed the following question to the court: "Is the threat or use of nuclear weapons in any circumstance permitted under international law?"[63]

The court consolidated the proceedings relating to these two requests. After receiving written observations and oral comments from an unprecedented number of states, it issued its advisory opinion on July 8, 1996. It rejected the request from the WHA for technical reasons,[64] though thereby at least implying that the use of nuclear weapons was not contrary to the WHO Constitution. However, in response to the request from the General

Assembly it examined at length all relevant considerations, in particular the instruments referred to immediately above, and replied to the question as follows:[65]

A. Unanimously,

    There is in neither customary nor conventional international law any specific authorization on the threat or use of nuclear weapons;

B. By eleven votes to three,

    There is in neither customary nor conventional international law any comprehensive and universal prohibition of the threat or use of nuclear weapons as such;

C. Unanimously,

    A threat or use of force by means of nuclear weapons that is contrary to article 2, paragraph 4, of the United Nations Charter and that fails to meet all the requirements of article 51, is unlawful;

D. Unanimously,

    A threat or use of nuclear weapons should also be compatible with the requirements of international law applicable in armed conflict, particularly with those of the principles and rules of international humanitarian law, as well as with specific obligations under treaties and other undertakings which expressly deal with nuclear weapons;

E. By seven votes to seven, by the President's casting vote,

    It follows from the above-mentioned requirements that the threat or use of nuclear weapons would generally be contrary to the rules of international law applicable to armed conflict, and in particular the principles and laws of humanitarian law;

    However, in view of the current state of international law, and of the elements of fact at its disposal, the Court cannot conclude definitively whether the threat or use of nuclear weapons would be lawful or unlawful in an extreme circumstance of self-defence, in which the very survival of a State would be at stake;

F. Unanimously,

    There exists an obligation to pursue in good faith and bring to a conclusion negotiations leading to nuclear disarmament in all its aspects under strict and effective international control.

The General Assembly, by a split vote, expressed its appreciation to the World Court for responding to the assembly's request, took note of the advisory opinion, and underlined the unanimous conclusion expressed in the final paragraph concerning the obligation of good faith negotiations toward nuclear disarmament.[66] It did not, however, as it customarily does, explicitly accept the opinion, presumably because the crucial part (paragraph E) was too controversial.

Prohibitions on Individuals

Because for a long time it was not deemed feasible for any individual to possess and use a nuclear weapon, no relevant prohibition against individuals was deemed necessary or adopted.[67] In 1980, the IAEA-sponsored Convention on the Physical Protection of Nuclear Material[68] was concluded, dealing with such materials in international transport. Except for some IAEA recommendations, however, there is no international legal instrument dealing with the domestic protection of nuclear materials or even nuclear weapons from theft or other misuse.

After heated debate in Rome, the ICC was not given jurisdiction over war crimes involving nuclear weapons. However, the UN General Assembly, through an ad hoc committee, has been pursuing for some years the conclusion of a treaty for the suppression of acts of nuclear terrorism.[69]

NEW TYPES OF WMD

Although the UN Commission for Conventional Armament foresaw in 1948 that additional types of weapons of mass destruction might be developed in the future,[70] such a broadening of the WMD category has not in fact yet occurred. The commission specifically referred to the possible development of radiological weapons, that is, weapons designed to spread radioactive material by means of a conventional, not nuclear explosion. But disputes continue on whether radiological weapons should be classified as weapons of mass destruction. Recent events have of course increased concerns that terrorists unable to obtain real nuclear weapons might resort to spreading radioactive materials by means of a conventional explosion (a so-called dirty bomb). The General Assembly has from time to time adopted resolutions urging that measures be taken to prevent the emergence of new types of weapons of mass destruction.[71]

MISSILES

Over the years a number of bilateral treaties (United States–USSR)[72] and restricted multilateral arrangements[73] have been concluded, and even more proposed, for limits on the deployments of various types of missiles and prohibiting assistance to other states in such deployment, particularly of intercontinental ballistic missiles (ICBMs). There are also references to means of delivery in the NPT and the BWC. Most of these instruments explicitly or implicitly dealt with missiles carrying nuclear weapons, because the use of such missiles with conventional explosives, rather than with some type of weapon of mass destruction, would clearly be uneconomic (balancing the cost of the missile against the damage it might cause) and strategically ineffective.

SUMMARY AND CONCLUSION

It follows from the above that the use of either chemical or biological weapons is illegal under customary international law and under the indicated treaties. This also means that any retaliation (retorsion) in kind to a chemical or biological attack is prohibited. Furthermore, the parties to the Chemical Weapons and Biological Weapons Conventions (a great majority of states) are under an obligation not to manufacture or to possess such weapons and to destroy any that they may have.

The situation as to the threat or use of nuclear weapons is not so clear, as indicated in the recent advisory opinion of the World Court. However, it appears that the circumstances under which such weapons might legitimately be used are very narrowly circumscribed, especially by the need to strictly observe international humanitarian law. In any event, any first use of such weapons would almost surely be illegitimate, as would any retaliatory use not strictly limited to the extent of the attack it was countering or that violates any of the other international rules as to the threat or use of force. On the other hand, the nuclear weapon states have undertaken, with Security Council endorsement, to come to the defense of nonnuclear weapon states subjected to nuclear attack.

Notes

1. The term comes from an early report of the UN Commission for Conventional Armaments (S/C.3/30 of August 13, 1948), in which the commission indicated the types of weapons with which they would not deal, namely: "atomic explosive weapons, radio active material weapons, lethal chemical and biological weapons, and any other weapons developed in the future which have characteristics comparable in destructive effect to those of the atomic bomb or other weapons mentioned above."

2. The 1997 Convention on the Prohibition of the Use, Stockpiling, Production and Transfer of Anti-Personnel Mines and on their Destruction (Oslo/Ottawa Landmines Convention). *International Legal Materials* 36:6 (1997): 1509.

3. Protocol on Prohibitions or Restrictions on the Use of Mines, Booby-Traps and Other Devices (Protocol II), in either its original 1980 and even more in its amended 1996 form, to the 1980 Convention on Prohibitions or Restrictions on the Use of Certain Conventional Weapons Which May Be Deemed to Be Excessively Injurious or to Have Indiscriminate Effects. For both, see Jozef Goldblat, *Arms Control: A Guide to Negotiations and Agreements* (Oslo: International Peace Research Institute; London: Sage, 1994), 482. Most of the agreements and texts referred to in this chapter are reproduced in that volume. An updated second edition is also now available: Jozef Goldblat, *Arms Control: The New Guide to Negotiations and Agreements* (Oslo: International Peace Research Institute; London: Sage, 2002). Citations of Goldblat below refer to the first edition.

4. It should be noted that some of the treaties that deal primarily with limitations on nuclear weapons also deal, incidentally, with all "other weapons of mass destruction." See, for example, the Outer Space Treaty (preamble), the Moon Treaty (art. 3), and the Seabed Treaty (art. 1).

5. One example is found in the preamble to the Biological Weapons Convention. See Goldblat, *Arms Control,* 370.

6. Sometimes a state's official statements are contradicted by its actions. For example, although torture is still widely used, no government today will admit that it employs it. The practice of torture is either denied or explained as an illegal aberration whose perpetrators are to be duly punished. Consequently, since torture is no longer practiced under any assertion that international law sanctions it, while the contrary is uniformly asserted, it can be claimed that the prohibition of torture has become customary international law – indeed, possibly a *jus cogens* rule from which states are not allowed to deviate.

7. For example, the fact that no state protested the Soviet satellite Sputnik's overflight of its territory established the international legal principle (soon codified in the UN General Assembly's Declaration on the Peaceful Uses of Outer Space and somewhat later in the Outer Space Treaty [see note 43 below]) that space, like the high seas but unlike the airspace over national territory, belongs to the international community and not to any state. On the other hand, the fact that no nuclear weapons have been used since the end of World War II does not prove that their use has become prohibited by customary law, because the abstention from use by those who could do so has never been based on a sense of legal restraint but on considerations such as fear of retaliation or concern about public reaction.

8. It should be noted that the UN General Assembly is proposing to establish the principle of irreversibility to apply to "nuclear disarmament, nuclear and other related arms control and reduction measures." See UNGA Resolution 55/33 R of November 20, 2000, para. 3(d).

9. Goldblat, *Arms Control,* 697.

10. The best example of such a resolution is that adopting the 1948 Universal Declaration of Human Rights (UDHR), compliance with which has been so widespread (though sometimes more in statements than in action) that it is generally accepted that the UDHR has surmounted its status as soft law and has become customary international law – aside from also having been codified in the two 1966 International Covenants.

11. See UN Charter, art. 39.

12. Security Council Resolution 1373 (2001) of September 28, 2001.

13. See ICJ Statute, art. 59.

14. ICJ Statute, art. 38.1(d).

15. See Goldblat, *Arms Control,* 188.

16. Ibid., 256.

17. Ibid., 257.

18. Ibid., 277. The title "Protocol" reflects the fact that this treaty was signed as an adjunct to the 1925 Convention for the Supervision of the International Trade in Arms and Ammunition and in Implements of War, which itself never entered into force.

19. UNGA Resolution 2603 A (XXIIV) of December 16, 1969.

20. The United States, one of the three states that voted against the 1969 resolution, for a long time favored a narrow interpretation of the Geneva Protocol, holding that antiplant materials (such as Agent Orange) were not covered. In 1975, at the end of the Vietnam War, the United States renounced the first use of herbicides in war, except for use within U.S. bases and around their immediate defensive perimeters.

21. See the ICTY Appeals Chamber decision on the *Tadic* Jurisdictional Motion, Case No. IT-94-1-AR72, October 2, 1995, note 8 and related text, reproduced in *International Legal Materials* 35:1 (1996): 69. However, that decision was taken before the adoption in 1998 of the Rome Statute of the ICC (see note 33 below), which did not include in that court's jurisdiction the use of poisoned weapons or poisonous gases in internal conflicts.
22. UNGA Resolution 44/115 B of December 15, 1989.
23. UN Publication Sales No. E.69.I.24.
24. WHO Publication (Geneva 1970).
25. Goldblat, *Arms Control*, 370.
26. After the Gulf War, the Security Council required Iraq to accept extremely intrusive UN and IAEA inspections (Resolution 687 [1991] of April 3, 1991, part C), which revealed ongoing programs to produce biological, chemical, and nuclear weapons.
27. Procedural Report of the Ad Hoc Group of the States Parties to the Convention on the Prohibition of the Development, Production and Stockpiling of Bacteriological (Biological) and Toxin Weapons and on Their Destruction (UN doc. BWC/AD HOC GROUP/56, May 18, 2001).
28. Goldblat, *Arms Control*, 711.
29. The United States is the only state to make a reservation to the CWC, to the effect that samples collected in the United States may not be transferred out of the country – a condition it would probably find unacceptable if insisted on by other parties. See *Multilateral Treaties Deposited with the Secretary-General: Status as at December 31, 2000* (UN doc. ST/LEG/SER.E/19), vol. II, p. 316.
30. Article VII.1 of the CWC.
31. See draft referred to in note 27 above, article X.1.
32. For an interpretation of this clause (article 3[a]) as also applying to internal conflicts, see note 21 above.
33. ICC Statute, article 8(b)(xvii) and (xviii). See *International Legal Materials* 37:5 (1998), 1002. In a hotly controverted decision, the conference refused to add nuclear weapons to this list.
34. ICC Statute, article 8(c) and (e).
35. UNGA Resolution 1 (I) of January 24, 1946.
36. Ibid., paras. 5(b) and (c).
37. The IAEA statute prohibits the use of agency assistance "for any military purpose," thus also covering uses such as the propulsion of warships. NPT, on the other hand, prohibits to nonnuclear weapon parties only "nuclear weapons" and "other nuclear explosive devices," thus banning even peaceful nuclear explosions, which the IAEA Statute does not prohibit and which the agency at one time expected to further.
38. The United States considered that to inflict "unacceptable damage" on the Soviet Union it would have to destroy 25 percent of its population and 70 percent of its industrial capacity. Goldblat, *Arms Control*, 53.
39. Ibid., 318.
40. Article XIV.1 of the CTBT provides that it is to enter into force only if ratified by the forty-four states listed in an annex to the treaty. These states were the ones that the IAEA had listed in 1995 and 1996 as possessing nuclear power or certain research reactors. As these states include India, which originally firmly

declared that it would never become a party, a formidable obstacle appeared to exist from the beginning. Although India's stance has eased somewhat since it carried out its own test explosions in 1998, in 1999 the U.S. Senate declined to ratify the CTBT, and later both Presidents Clinton and Bush declared that they would not resubmit it to the Senate, thus creating another impediment.

41. The 1974 Threshold Test Ban Treaty (Goldblat, *Arms Control*, 391), and the 1976 Peaceful Nuclear Explosions Treaty (ibid., 409).

42. Goldblat, *Arms Control*, 309.

43. Ibid., 322.

44. Ibid., 467.

45. Ibid., 349.

46. UNGA Resolution 3472 B(XXX) of December 11, 1975. These guidelines have recently been updated by the UN Disarmament Commission (UN doc. A/54/42, Annex I).

47. The General Assembly welcomed this development (Resolutions 53/77 D of December 4, 1998, and 55/33 S of November 20, 2000), and the five nuclear powers made a joint statement of negative as well as qualified positive security assurances for Mongolia (UN doc. A/C.1/55/PV.6, October 5, 2000, pp. 4–5).

48. See note 26 above.

49. In particular, the London Nuclear Suppliers Group (NSG) and the NPT Exporters Committee (Zangger Committee), in Goldblat, *Arms Control*, 86–88.

50. Ibid., 343.

51. The fact that India and Pakistan, which are not NPT parties, exploded nuclear devices in 1998 does not therefore make them NWSs within the meaning of NPT. This accounts for the two countries' reluctance to join NPT.

52. UN doc. NPT/CONF.1995/32 (Part I), Decision 3 and Decision 2, paras. 3 and 4(a). Reproduced in *International Legal Materials* 34:4 (1995): 967–73.

53. UN doc. NPT/CONF.2000/28, vol. I, p. 14.

54. See, however, UNGA Resolution 55/33 R of November 20, 2000, referred to in note 8 above.

55. See, e.g., UNGA Resolution 55/33 R of November 20, 2000, para. 3(b).

56. Security Council Resolution 255 (1968), adopted on June 19, 1968, "welcomes the intention expressed by certain States that they will provide or support immediate assistance, in accordance with the Charter, to any non-nuclear-weapon State Party to the Treaty on the Non-Proliferation of Nuclear Weapons that is a victim of an act or an object of a threat of aggression in which nuclear weapons are used." The Soviet Union, United Kingdom, and United States supported this resolution. Security Council Resolution 984 (1995), approved by all five nuclear weapon states on April 11, 1995, elaborates further the assistance that nonnuclear weapon states may expect. In response to a request from a state attacked or threatened by a nuclear weapon state, the Security Council members would help to settle the dispute and to restore international peace and security, as well as take "appropriate" measures, individually or collectively, for technical, medical, scientific, or humanitarian assistance. In addition, "appropriate" measures might be taken by the Security Council to assure compensation from the aggressor for loss, damage, or injury sustained as a result of the aggression.

57. UNGA Resolution 1653(XVI) of November 24, 1961, para. 1(a).

58. UNGA Resolution 36/100 of December 9, 1981.

59. UNGA Resolution 38/75 of December 15, 1983.
60. E.g., UNGA Resolution 55/34 G of November 20, 2000, adopted by 109 votes for, 43 against, and 16 abstentions, with the Western nuclear powers against and China and Russia abstaining.
61. Goldblat, *Arms Control*, 257.
62. World Health Assembly Resolution 46/40 of May 14, 1993.
63. UNGA Resolution 49/75 K of December 15, 1994.
64. Legality of the Use by a State of Nuclear Weapons in Armed Conflict, Advisory Opinion, *I.C.J. Reports* (1996), 66.
65. Legality of the Threat or Use of Nuclear Weapons, Advisory Opinion, *I.C.J. Reports* (1996), 226.
66. UNGA Resolution 51/45 M of December 10, 1996. The General Assembly has since annually repeated this demand (e.g., Resolution 55/33 X of November 20, 2000).
67. See, however, paras. 1 and 2 of the 1981 General Assembly Declaration on the Prevention of Nuclear Catastrophe (note 58 above).
68. Goldblat, *Arms Control*, 473.
69. See, e.g., UNGA Resolution 54/110 of December 9, 1999, para. 12. The principal obstacle to the treaty appears to be the question of whether "state terrorism" should be included.
70. See note 1 above.
71. E.g., UNGA Resolutions 3479 (XXX) of December 11, 1975, and 54/44 of December 1, 1999.
72. The 1972 SALT I Interim Agreement, the 1979 SALT II Agreements, the 1987 INF Treaty, the 1991 START I Treaty, and the 1993 START II Treaty. See Goldblat, *Arms Control*, 385, 457, 518, 591, and 697, respectively.
73. In particular, the Missile Technology Control Regime concluded in 1987 by seven countries. See ibid., 89.

PART ONE

THE ORIGINAL DEBATE

3

Realist Perspectives on Ethical Norms and Weapons of Mass Destruction

Scott D. Sagan

What role do ethics play in statesmen's decisions about the acquisition and use of nuclear, chemical, and biological weapons? Most realists would write an exceedingly short paper – indeed, perhaps a one-word telegram – on this topic: "None." Real statesmen do not follow ethical norms. Power considerations and the rules of prudence, not ethical concerns, govern international life. In the modern world, as in the ancient world, the strong do what they can and the weak do what they must.

I have considerable, but by no means complete, sympathy for this position. This chapter therefore presents an analytic description of the standard realist position, assesses current debates about its accuracy, and provides the beginnings of an alternative realist vision. I argue that some, though by no means all, statesmen do follow ethical norms in their weapons policies and that realists must take this fact into account, while not losing their focus on the highly competitive nature of international politics. In the modern world, the strong may not want to do what they can, for excessively aggressive behavior will force the weak to develop their own weapons of mass destruction. This result would be neither in the interest of the great powers, including the United States, nor, I believe, in the broader interests of the global community.

SOURCES AND PRINCIPLES

Realists trace their intellectual roots back to the classical writings of Thucydides, Hobbes, and Clausewitz, and these philosophers' views about the "necessities of war" are often mirrored in the writings of modern neorealists.[1] Both Thucydides and Hobbes maintain that war is natural and unavoidable in the state of nature and therefore men must be perpetually aggressive in defending their interests: "It is a general and necessary law of nature to rule wherever one can," the Athenian generals tell the Melians before they conquer Melos, kill its men, and enslave its women and children.[2] Clausewitz began his treatise *On War* by similarly noting that competition in war forces all states to use the maximum degree of force available:

Force, to counter opposing force, equips itself with the inventions of art and science. Attached to force are certain self-imposed, imperceptible limitations hardly worth mentioning, known as international law and conventions, but they scarcely weaken it. . . . The maximum use of force is in no way incompatible with the simultaneous use of the intellect. If one side uses force without compunction, undeterred by the bloodshed it involves, while the other side refrains, the first will gain the upper hand.[3]

Modern neorealists hold similar views, derived from their two theoretical assumptions: Leaders of states behave in a highly rational manner and the international system is anarchic in nature.[4] Without any world government to enforce agreements, norms, or laws, states must do whatever is necessary to enhance their ability to survive. Ethical concerns can have little influence in this vision of a dog-eat-dog international system. In George Bernard Shaw's *Pygmalion*, when Alfred Doolittle offers his daughter Eliza to Henry Higgins for fifty pounds, he is queried, "Have you no morals, man?" "Can't afford them, Governor," he answers.[5] For modern neorealists, anarchy makes all state leaders as impoverished as Doolittle. "States in anarchy cannot afford to be moral," argue Robert Art and Kenneth Waltz:

The preconditions for morality are absent in international politics. Every state, as a consequence, has to be prepared to do what is necessary for its interests as it defines them. Anarchy is a realm where all can, and many do, play "dirty pool." . . . Strategic interdependence and the absence of morality mean that each state, if it wishes to be effective, must be prepared to play according to the rules set by the "dirtiest" player.[6]

Realists advocate balance of power policies – *realpolitik* – because they see no other means to protect the state in an effective manner. A state's life in the anarchic international system will be nasty and brutish, but it need not be short, if its leaders prepare for war and use military force in a cold and calculating manner to protect themselves from current and potential enemies. There is therefore a long tradition among realists in arguing that amoral *realpolitik* behavior is both strategically wise and morally preferred to its alternatives, because it is necessary to maintain even a modicum of peace and stability in a harsh world of rival states.[7]

The major debates about ethics in the international relations (IR) literature in political science today, however, are less normative than empirical in nature. Modern political scientists have been less concerned about identifying the best norms and principles by which international politics should be governed than they are in determining what role, if any, ethical norms actually do play in statesmen's decisions. The neorealist vision that ethics play little role in decision making concerning the use of force has recently been challenged by "neocultural" scholars, who argue that cultural norms – widely held beliefs within a community about what behavior is legitimate, appropriate, and natural – have a strong impact on international political decisions. These scholars have argued that there is a growing moral norm against developing chemical, biological, and nuclear weapons and that an international taboo against the use of weapons of mass destruction has had a strong impact on state leaders' decisions in crises and war.[8]

This chapter focuses primarily on the empirical question of how much influence, if any, ethical concerns have on statesmen's policies regarding weapons of mass destruction. It also is a first step toward a different and, I think, more realistic realist perspective on the issue of ethics and weapons of mass destruction. I argue that the neoculturalists are correct to argue that ethical norms sometimes do have an important impact on real states and real statesmen. I also argue, however, that a realist perspective is correct in that the impact of such norms cannot be understood outside the context of power relations in the anarchic and competitive international system.

Toward an Alternative Realist Vision

Four arguments are central to this effort to develop a revised realist perspective. The first concerns ethics and selection effects in a highly competitive international system. Statesmen who are strongly influenced by moral considerations are likely to promote policies concerning weapons of mass destruction that are considerably different from those followed by statesmen who are concerned only with cold considerations of their state's parochial and material national security interests. If it is true that some, *but only some,* state leaders are influenced by ethical norms, however, more ruthless states are likely to take advantage of such leaders. States in the international system should therefore be conceived as acting like firms in the market. Some will and some will not behave according to the logic of *realpolitik* and profit maximizing logic, but those that do not will suffer in the competition.[9]

The second argument could be called the "balance of ethics principle." Statesmen who focus only on the balance of power and ignore moral considerations altogether can create great fear and opposition among other statesmen who do place high value on moral principles. They will be seen as the leaders of greedy states, unable to cooperate with allies, too willing to break treaties whenever it suits them, and unable to settle for anything less than hegemony over others. A political leader who sees absolutely no place for ethics and cooperation in international life is therefore going to create a self-fulfilling prophecy. John Mearsheimer has advocated a radical brand of realism, which he labels "offensive realism": "A state's ultimate goal is to be the hegemon in the system.... Survival mandates aggressive behavior."[10] But such radical realists forget that the word "offensive" has two meanings – aggressive and obnoxious – and if some statesmen do seek a modicum of moral behavior, then excessive *realpolitik* behavior by others will encourage these statesmen to fight harder, to develop their own more destructive weaponry, and to create counterbalancing coalitions against the more offensive power. I argue that wise realist statesmen should therefore temper or shape their *realpolitik* behavior to take into account how other leaders view the ethical or unethical nature of their actions.

In short, realist statesmen should keep one eye on the balance of power to protect the state in the immediate term and one eye on the balance of ethics in order to minimize others' hostility over the long run. This perspective would not be entirely surprising to classical realists. After all, Thucydides's description of the Athenians' brutal behavior toward the weak Melian colony was a tragic vision. The stronger Athenians certainly did what they could against the Melians. But Thucydides noted that the Athenians eventually lost the Peloponnesian War as their power and hubris led to imprudent behavior and counterbalancing by other city-states.

Third, realist principles can lead to considerable restraint with respect to weapons of mass destruction. Restrained policies that appear to some scholars to be caused by ethical considerations or taboo-like behavior are often actually the calculated pursuit of long-term national security interests. This is the case when the nonuse of such weapons is due to a fear that an adversary would take your military action as a precedent or excuse to do something that you do not want to see happen in the future. There is an important analytic difference between cases in which you are refraining from an act because you think it is wrong versus refraining from an act because you fear that if you do it, others eventually will do it, too, as a direct or indirect consequence of your action. The first is a strong form of an ethical taboo; the latter is more like a rule of prudence. The distinction is important because taboos are not likely to be overturned by a single violation (indeed, they may be reinforced). But this is not necessarily the case when it comes to precedents. When the restraint is based more on fear of setting precedents, it should be called a tradition of nonuse, but not a taboo. Using nuclear or other weapons of mass destruction under such circumstances could set a new precedent and hence greatly increase the likelihood of future use. In short, traditions may be more fragile than taboos.

The fourth argument concerns the relationship between power and ethics in determining arms control agreements and regimes. Ethical norms may indeed matter in international politics, but the norms that matter most are the ones that are supportive of, and therefore are supported by, the most powerful actors. As is discussed below, the most important international rules and regimes that concern weapons of mass destruction are the ones that have been promulgated by the United States and other great powers. This does not mean that the array of arms control agreements that form the major institutionalized norms concerning weapons of mass destruction are unimportant or unproductive. Realism reminds us, however, that states will behave in a hypocritical manner with respect to arms control regimes when leaders feel they are not in their state's interests. An alternative realist perspective would add that to be most effective over the long term, even strong powers must craft their policies to take into account the ethical concerns of other actors, including the weak.

UTILIZATION: TABOO OR NOT TABOO?

One of the most important puzzles of both the cold war and post–cold war eras is how to explain the fact that nuclear weapons have not been used in war since the attacks on Hiroshima and Nagasaki in 1945. Is the fifty-year tradition of nonuse of nuclear weapons best explained by the logic of deterrence or the nuclear taboo? How do realists explain the use and nonuse of nuclear weapons?

President Harry Truman's "decision" to drop two atomic bombs on Hiroshima and Nagasaki in August 1945 is not at all puzzling from a realist perspective.[11] States would be expected to use whatever effective weapons they have at their disposal in wars, especially in major conflicts in which restraints imposed by the need to reach potential compromise settlements have been abandoned. By 1945, the government's policy of unconditional surrender as the U.S. war aim in the Pacific was strongly entrenched and enjoyed wide public support. Moreover, given the ongoing incendiary bombing of Japanese cities, U.S. decision makers did not even see themselves as crossing an ethical threshold. They did not anticipate significant public opposition within the United States to the use of the atomic bomb. (And they were right: In a November 1945 poll, only 4.5 percent of the U.S. public opposed the dropping of the bombs, while 22.7 percent thought that the U.S. "should have quickly used many more of the bombs before Japan had a chance to surrender."[12]) There was certainly no fear of retaliation in kind, or even retaliation of any kind. Moreover, what appeared shocking to revisionist historians – that U.S. statesmen might have considered the dropping of the bombs on Japan to have beneficial "bonus" effects on the emerging conflict with the Soviet Union – would appear natural and predictable to most realists. With all these factors favoring immediate use of the atomic bomb, the case appears to be overdetermined.

Given the twin belief in statesmen's rationality and in the effectiveness of balances of power, it is not surprising that modern realists have viewed *mutual possession* of nuclear weapons as a force for peace and stability, rather than as a force for war.[13] Realists would therefore offer a simple explanation – the balance of terror – for the nonuse of nuclear weapons by the Soviet Union and the United States during the height of the cold war. Both cold war rivals developed large and secure (i.e., survivable) nuclear arsenals to ensure that they could retaliate massively after an attack by the other. Both developed nuclear doctrines that emphasized a mix of counterforce targeting (attacking nuclear forces to limit damage in the event of war, to confound enemy war plans, and to add credibility to limited first nuclear weapons use threats) and countervalue targeting (attacking population centers deliberately to maximize punishment as retribution after a first strike). Both sides targeted the other's senior leadership in the nations' capitals and military bases, with some hope that this might limit damage through "decapitation" in the event of war and with more serious expectations that such "counterleadership" threats would deter even the most ruthless, self-interested capitalist or communist leader.[14]

Preventive War

There is a more specific nuclear puzzle, however, that is more difficult to explain from a realist perspective. First, why did nuclear weapons states not launch a preventive war to prevent their adversaries from developing a nuclear capability that can threaten the utter destruction of their nation? A *preventive* war is an attack deliberately initiated or deliberately provoked in peacetime due to the belief that long-term military trends favor an adversary and that it is therefore better to conduct war now, rather than at a later date.[15] Preventive war is considered illegitimate, for a number of related reasons, in most ethical traditions.[16] First, a state, like an individual under domestic law, must be guilty of an aggressive act, rather than just presumed likely to commit one, in order to justify punishment. Second, it is difficult to predict the future intentions of states, which may change dramatically over time, and thus it is difficult to know with much certainty whether a preventive war today is necessary to prevent aggression in the future. If preventive war is deemed acceptable, it could encourage leaders to go to war whenever they saw potential enemies on the horizon. (General Thomas Powers, General Curtis LeMay's successor at Strategic Air Command, once commented that the United States received its "first strategic warning" of the impending Soviet attack in 1848 when Marx and Engels published *The Communist Manifesto*.[17])

Since realists argue that statesmen should do whatever is necessary to protect the security and survival of the state and should not be influenced by moral norms, how can they explain why statesmen have so rarely engaged in preventive wars when facing an adversary acquiring nuclear weapons? Scholars must be very careful when interpreting documents that report on government officials discussing preventive war or other acts widely considered to be of questionable legitimacy, for there is often a "realist bias" in international security discourse. By this I mean that in much of daily life (and much of public political discourse) individuals mask arguments promoting self-interest in broader moral terms. "We need to do this because it is the right thing to do." But in security affairs decision making, leaders are expected to be tough, cold-minded realists. This encourages statesmen and soldiers in private to mask moral arguments with reference to more "justifiable" national security interests. Leaders are therefore more likely to argue not that the government should refrain from doing something because it would be wrong, but rather that the government should refrain from doing something because it won't be effective or others will think it is wrong.

Even with that cautionary note, I think the evidence from the most serious "close call" to a preventive nuclear strike in U.S. nuclear history suggests that President Dwight Eisenhower rejected recommendations for a preventive war against the Soviet Union in the early 1950s primarily for realist reasons. During the Truman administration, there was some discussion of a preventive atomic war, but the United States lacked the nuclear weapons capability to win quickly and decisively in what was then expected to become a long and drawn-out conventional war of attrition with the Soviet Union. In the early 1950s, however, U.S. capabilities had grown to the point where senior military officials began to advise the president that a preventive war against the Soviets was advisable.[18] Eisenhower confided to Secretary of State John Foster Dulles in September 1953 that he believed a preventive attack on the USSR might be necessary and justified. In the near future, he argued:

[The U.S.] would have to be constantly ready, on an instantaneous basis, to inflict greater loss upon the enemy than he could reasonably hope to inflict upon us. This would be a deterrent – but if the contest to maintain this relative position should have to continue indefinitely, the cost would either drive us to war – or into some form of dictatorial government. In such circumstances, we would be forced to consider whether or not our duty to future generations did not require us to *initiate* war at the most propitious time that we could designate.[19]

Despite these considerations, Eisenhower rejected the concept of preventive nuclear war in 1954. The president could have been influenced primarily by normative constraints, by fears of domestic or allied nations' opposition, or by more realist concerns about the costs of any preventive war. The evidence suggests that his primary reasons were realist in nature, not due to ethical concerns that preventive war would be illegitimate. First, one should note his view on the effectiveness of nuclear deterrence indicated in the comment to Dulles quoted above. Second, Eisenhower was not convinced that the United States had the military power or political will, even after a "successful" nuclear first strike, to eliminate security threats over the long term. At a National Security Council briefing on nuclear war in March 1954, for example, "The President pointed out that . . . the colossal job of occupying the territories of the defeated enemy would be far beyond the resources of the United States at the conclusion of this war."[20] Finally, although domestic political considerations may have played some role in Eisenhower's reluctance to order a preventive attack, he showed little moral inhibition against planning to use nuclear weapons first and massively if the Soviet Union attacked the United States or NATO even with conventional forces: "We are *not* going to provoke war, and that is why we have got to be patient. If war comes, the other fellow must have started it. Otherwise, we would not be in a position to use the nuclear weapon. And we have to be in a position to use that weapon if we are to preserve our institutions and win the victory in war."[21]

What about other cases of potential preventive attacks to thwart nuclear proliferation? Two points should be briefly noted. First, as realists would predict, there have been a number of preventive attacks to stop nuclear and missile proliferation, although they were conventional bombing raids or covert operations, rather than nuclear weapon strikes. The Israelis used covert operations to slow down the Egyptian missile programs, which they feared could be used to deliver nuclear weapons, in the 1960s.[22] Israel also destroyed the Iraqi nuclear reactor at Osiraq in 1981, the most clear-cut case of an unprovoked preventive attack to reduce proliferation dangers.[23] The 1991 and 2003 wars against Iraq can also be seen, at least in part, as preventive wars by the United States to stop Saddam Hussein's regime from eventually acquiring nuclear weapons.[24]

Second, realists would correctly stress that in the case of a potential preventive war against China, fear of Soviet intervention constrained American considerations in the early 1960s, and then fear of American intervention limited Russian planning in 1969. In both cases, the potential attacking nuclear power sought military support – or at least a firm commitment of neutrality – from the other nuclear power before attacking China. In neither case, however, did the potential attacker get reassurances on that score and thus could not rule out military responses from the other side.[25] In short, a form of extended nuclear deterrence also helped to prevent preventive war against third parties during the cold war.

DETERRENCE, SELF-DETERRENCE, AND PRECEDENT SETTING

How far does the writ of deterrence run according to realist logic? While realists have argued that mutual deterrence, through the threat of unacceptable retaliation, was both necessary and effective during the cold war, there is a more puzzling set of cases of nuclear nonuse when the United States faced a weaker power that did not possess nuclear weapons. These cases include North Korea in the 1950s, Vietnam in the 1960s, and Iraq in the 1990s. This phenomenon has been labeled by John Lewis Gaddis as "self-deterrence."[26] Self-deterrence is a confusing term, however, because there are many different reasons why state leaders may decide not to use nuclear weapons against nonnuclear states. First, there could be fear of setting a precedent whereby others would be more likely to use nuclear weapons in the future. Second, there could be a paucity of appropriate targets or a shortfall in nuclear weapons capabilities at the time. Third, there could be pressures from important allies or public opinion. Fourth, it is possible that the decision was made because senior political authorities believed that such nuclear strikes would be morally wrong.[27] Only the third and fourth causes of nuclear restraint could be accurately seen as "self-deterrence" produced by ethical norms or a nuclear taboo. I illustrate the distinction between deterrence and self-deterrence – between realist explanations and neoculturalist explanations – by examining the most recent case of American nonuse of nuclear weapons in a major war against a nonnuclear adversary. The case also raises dilemmas about how to best deter the use of chemical and biological weapons.

The Nonuse of Nuclear Weapons in the Gulf War

What was U.S. policy with respect to nuclear weapons use and threats during the Persian Gulf War in 1991? What threats did senior U.S. officials make during Operation Desert Storm, and what was their intent? We now know, from numerous officials' memoirs, that the senior U.S. leaders had decided they would not use nuclear weapons even in response to an Iraqi use of chemical weapons, but nevertheless cautiously planted some seeds of doubt in the mind of Saddam Hussein for the sake of deterrence. As President George Bush and National Security Advisor Brent Scowcroft note in their joint memoirs:

What if Iraq used chemical weapons? We had discussed this at our December 24 meeting at Camp David and had ruled out our own use of them, but if Iraq resorted to them, we would say our reaction would depend on circumstances and that we would hold Iraqi divisional commanders responsible and bring them to justice for war crimes. No one advanced the notion of using nuclear weapons, and the President rejected it even in retaliation for chemical and biological attacks. We deliberately avoided spoken or unspoken threats to use them on the grounds that it is bad practice to threaten something you have no intention of carrying out. Publicly, we left the matter ambiguous. There was no point in undermining the deterrence it might be offering.[28]

Secretary of State James Baker later recalled that, at a meeting with Iraq's foreign minister Tariq Aziz, he nevertheless "deliberately left the impression that the use of chemical or biological agents by Iraq could invite tactical nuclear retaliation."[29] Baker has argued that the U.S. nuclear threat successfully deterred Saddam from using Iraqi chemical and biological weapons.[30] Many government officials and scholars have uncritically accepted this position.[31] An important debate on this issue, however, revolves around whether it was the ambiguous U.S. nuclear threats or the more explicit threat to march to Baghdad and overthrow Saddam Hussein's regime that deterred Iraqi use of their chemical and biological weapons.[32]

Far less attention has been paid to explaining the "dog that didn't bark": Why didn't the United States use nuclear weapons against Iraqi troops during the 1991 Gulf War? The Gulf War presented a tactical situation where most of the conditions for legitimate nuclear use under just war theory – just cause, discrimination, proportionality – may have been present. Tactical and strategic considerations may also have favored nuclear weapons use. Low-yield nuclear warheads were available in the theater of combat, and with Iraqi forces dug into desert field positions, the potential for a discriminate tactical nuclear attack with virtually no collateral damage to civilian populations was possible. Baghdad was isolated politically, and there was, in contrast to earlier cases such as the Korean and Vietnam Wars, no fear of other states retaliating with their nuclear weapons in response to a U.S. nuclear first use against Iraq. Anticipated American and allied casualties might have been significantly reduced if conventional attacks could be avoided. Under these conditions, U.S. leaders' reluctance to brandish the nuclear arsenal is the puzzle that needs to be explained.

Nina Tannenwald's detailed study makes the strongest case for a nuclear taboo being the main cause of the nuclear restraint displayed by American leaders during the Gulf War.[33] One unnamed White House official is quoted saying that U.S. nuclear use was "so far-fetched" that it never came up in high-level discussions. When asked about tactical nuclear weapons use, the White House chief of staff, John Sununu, replied that "we just don't do things like that." A senior military officer states that tactical nuclear weapons use "is simply beyond the pale. General Colin Powell, then Chairman of the Joint Chiefs of Staff, responded to a request for a study of nuclear options by Secretary of Defense Richard Cheney by arguing: 'Let's not even think about nukes. You know we are not going to let that genie loose.'" When Joint Chiefs of Staff officers developed a military plan with many tactical weapons being used in the desert battlefield, Powell had the plan destroyed after showing it to Cheney. Tannenwald concludes:

These kinds of convictions, which go well beyond arguments from utility to those of identity and community, involve a deeper discourse of "civilization." They illustrate a constitutive effect of the taboo, showing how the taboo works in deeper, more fundamental ways. By the time of the Gulf War – in contrast to 1945 – Americans had come to see use of nuclear weapons as contrary to their perceptions of themselves.[34]

The evidence gathered by Tannenwald clearly does point to a growing conviction among many American political and military leaders that use of nuclear weapons by the United States is "inappropriate." My reading of the Gulf War case, however, differs from Tannenwald's interpretation. Longer term material factors, especially concerns that U.S. nuclear use in this conflict would harm Washington's nonproliferation efforts by encouraging other states to acquire nuclear weapons in the future, appear to have been critical.

Consider the analogy that Powell used to describe his reluctance to plan for the use of nuclear weapons: "We're not going to let that genie loose."[35] This implies not that nuclear use was morally wrong or unthinkable, but that it was undesirable. It also implies that even if the immediate effects might be positive, the long-term effects were highly uncertain and uncontrollable and potentially disastrous. Powell reports that the secret study of potential nuclear attacks against Iraqi forces "unnerved" him: "To do serious damage to just one Iraqi division in the desert would require a considerable number of small tactical nuclear weapons.... If I had any doubts before about the *practicality* of nukes on the field of battle, this report clinched it."[36] The lack of moral language here is noteworthy, especially in contrast to his discussion of following the "warrior's code" of not killing unnecessarily in his memoirs. Powell displayed concern about reducing civilian collateral damage and unnecessary Iraqi military casualties throughout the Gulf War, but interestingly these were not the concerns expressed when arguing for U.S. nuclear restraint.

A second example comes from a postwar interview with General Charles Horner, the commander of the bombing campaign against Iraq. Horner's explanation for not using nuclear weapons is focused on influencing future proliferation decisions:

> People have asked me did I ever think about using nuclear weapons.... you could use nuclear weapons but for what targets? The nuclear weapon's only good against cities, it's not any good against troops in the desert, I mean it takes too many of 'em.... One of the major lessons of Desert Storm is the fact that it's about the new world, it's not about the Cold War world, it's about how useless nuclear weapons are except to people who have no conscience, and one of the principal targets that we had was the nuclear weapons capability of Iraq, the counter proliferation effort that's going to characterize operations in the future.... [It is about] India and Pakistan having nuclear weapons – this is the new warfare, the counter proliferation war against nuclear weapons and weapons of mass destruction.[37]

These quotes suggest that the desire to reinforce the "tradition of nonuse" rather than a nuclear taboo may have been the driving factor in the U.S. decision not to use nuclear weapons in the Gulf War. This realist interpretation leads to a different assessment of the future of U.S. nuclear restraint. If nonuse against such nonnuclear enemies is due less to an internalized nuclear taboo and more to concerns about precedent setting, then U.S. restraint may not hold if a so-called rogue state gets nuclear weapons and uses them first, even in self-defense. As is discussed in the conclusion, this perspective also raises concerns about current U.S. policy to threaten nuclear retaliation in response to other states' chemical or biological weapons attacks.

PROLIFERATION: CAUSES AND CONSEQUENCES

What are the central causes of nuclear, chemical, and biological weapons proliferation? With respect to nuclear weapons, realists have a clear and simple answer: States will seek to develop nuclear weapons when they face a significant military threat to their security that cannot be met through alternative means; if they do not face such threats, they will be willing to remain nonnuclear states.[38] Realists therefore envision the history of nuclear proliferation as a kind of strategic chain reaction. Every time one state develops nuclear weapons to balance against its main rival, it also creates a nuclear threat to another state in the region, which then has to initiate its own nuclear weapons program to maintain its national security. The United States developed the atomic bomb, fearing that Nazi Germany was about to develop one. After August 1945, the Soviet Union developed the bomb because the U.S. attacks on Japan demonstrated that nuclear weapons were technically possible, and the emerging cold war meant that a Soviet bomb was a strategic imperative. Britain and France apparently built nuclear weapons because of the growing Soviet nuclear arsenal and the resulting reduction in the credibility of the U.S. nuclear guarantee to NATO allies. China developed the bomb primarily because Beijing was threatened with possible nuclear attack by the United States at the end of the Korean War and during the Taiwan Straits crises. After China developed the bomb in 1964, India, which had just fought a war with China in 1962, was bound to follow suit. After the Indian test in 1974, the nascent Pakistani nuclear weapons program had to move forward. Facing a recently hostile neighbor with both a nuclear weapons capability and conventional military superiority, it was inevitable that the government in Islamabad would seek to produce a nuclear weapon as quickly as possible.

This standard realist view thus minimizes the role of other factors that can restrain (and sometimes encourage) nuclear weapons procurement, such as ethical norms, domestic political interests, and concerns about global prestige or opprobrium.[39] Instead, most realists maintain that if a state does not acquire nuclear weapons, it must be due to one of three reasons. First, the state may lack the technical capability to build the bomb, a condition that continues to exist in the poorest parts of the developing world. Second, some states that could build nuclear weapons do not do so because they have a nuclear guarantee from an allied nuclear state that it will respond to any attack on its ally. This explains the limited proliferation within NATO and Japan's nonnuclear status. Finally, realists argue that some states have struck an implicit bargain under the Nonproliferation Treaty (NPT) that they will not get nuclear weapons in exchange for a guarantee that their neighbors will also not get them. Under this vision, the NPT is seen as an institution permitting nonnuclear states to overcome a collective action problem. Nonnuclear states in the NPT would prefer to become the only nuclear weapons power in their region, but since that is an unlikely outcome if one state develops a nuclear arsenal, each is willing to refrain from proliferation if, and only if, its neighbors remain nonnuclear.

Realists have written far less on the spread of chemical and biological weapons, but a similar logic would apply.[40] Nonnuclear states that perceive severe threats to their security are likely to develop chemical or biological weapons despite legal or moral inhibitions. Chemical and biological weapons are often called a "poor man's nuclear weapon" because they are easier and cheaper to develop, though they are generally far less effective (with a major exception being made for some virulent biological agents). Although most states have agreed not to build chemical or biological weapons under the rules of the Chemical Weapons Convention (CWC) and Biological Weapons Convention (BWC), realists would predict that weaker states would be tempted to cheat on the agreements they have signed. This prediction is supported by reports that at least seven nonnuclear states – Iran, Iraq (prior to the U.S.-led invasion in 2003), Libya, North Korea, South Korea, Syria, and Taiwan – are suspected of hiding chemical weapons and/or biological weapons stockpiles or production facilities.[41]

Proliferation Optimists and Pessimists

Given common realist arguments about the necessity for maintaining balances of power, it is not surprising that many realists argue that further proliferation of weapons of mass destruction is inevitable. The major powers today will seek to stem the tide, for it hurts their relative power position, but they are highly unlikely to meet complete success. What is more surprising, at first glance, is that many realists do not worry too much about the consequences of proliferation. These so-called proliferation optimists assume that all states, regardless of their internal characteristics, behave in similar, essentially rational ways. Since a mutual exchange of nuclear weapons would produce disaster for both the initial attacker and the state that retaliates, new nuclear powers are likely to be highly cautious and constrained in their use of their new arsenals. For many realists, a prescription for maintaining a balance of power has turned into a faith in the stability of the nuclear balance of terror. Kenneth Waltz's essays arguing that "more [proliferation] may be better" are the most influential work among the proliferation optimists. Waltz concludes:

The likelihood of war decreases as deterrent and defensive capabilities increase. Nuclear weapons make wars hard to start. These statements hold true for small as well as big powers. Because they do, the gradual spread of nuclear weapons is more to be welcomed than feared.[42]

This view is by no means universally shared. Critics have maintained that Waltz is unrealistically optimistic in minimizing four critical dangers.[43] First, rational states may well be deterred from engaging in preventive wars during early stages of a nuclear arms race. But in many states nuclear weapons are controlled by military organizations, not by statesmen. Military officers are biased in favor of offensive doctrines and preventive wars because they believe war is inevitable in the long term. This leads them to favor decisive operations and preventive strikes when their nation is ahead in an arms race and the perceived adversary is catching up. Preventive wars are therefore more likely between new nuclear powers where strict civilian control of the military does not exist.

Second, Waltz assumes that it is easy to build survivable deterrent forces. This may not be the case if a new proliferating state's military is not competent in maintaining the secrecy and security of their nuclear arsenal's locations and operations. Third, proliferation pessimists are concerned that the danger of accidental nuclear war – caused by false warnings, unauthorized use, or technical accidents – will increase in new nuclear states. Finally, critics note that the danger of terrorist theft of nuclear weapons will rise as the technology spreads to new nuclear states that either harbor terrorist organizations or have sympathizers of terrorist organizations within their governments.

In short, proliferation pessimists, unlike traditional neorealists, do look inside the state, arguing that different kinds of regimes and military organizations will produce different kinds of nuclear policies. Not all new nuclear states are likely to be able to maintain the degree of nuclear stability created over time by the United States and Soviet Union during the cold war. The proliferation pessimists do, however, still hold the neorealist view that selection effects occur in the competitive international system. Many new proliferators will be able to control nuclear weapons well, but others will not, and those less competent states will suffer the consequences. Unfortunately, the physical and political consequences of any nuclear weapons use by smaller powers may not be limited to those powers themselves.

DISARMAMENT: CAUSES AND CONSEQUENCES

Realists have a clear position on complete nuclear disarmament. They are opposed to it. If there were no world government capable of verifying and enforcing strict disarmament, any state would be tempted to cheat or to develop nuclear weapons quickly in a serious crisis. The first state to get nuclear weapons in such a crisis would not be deterred from using them by the threat of retaliation. Thus, realists argue, nuclear disarmament would ironically increase the likelihood that nuclear weapons would someday be used.[44] This has been called the "instability of small numbers" problem and helps to explain why realists have traditionally focused far more attention on incremental arms control measures than on complete disarmament efforts.

It is by no means clear, however, that all political leaders have shared this logic. Indeed, there are at least two cases – Iran with respect to chemical weapons and Japan with nuclear weapons – in which ethical considerations appear to have led to abstinence. These cases may be exceptions to the neorealist rule that states will develop whatever weapons they can to protect themselves. Iran and Japan may also, however, be prime examples of the realist idea of the selection mechanism: If states do not follow realist principles in crises, they will suffer severe consequences, as other more ruthless states will take advantage of them.

Iran and Chemical Weapons

When Ayatollah Khomeini created the Islamic Republic of Iran in 1979, he and the ruling mullahs inherited the shah's secret nuclear weapons research program, but the research facilities and power reactor programs quickly fell into disrepair as senior scientists left the country in large numbers and Western governments tightened exports controls over technology and nuclear materials.[45] In 1979, Iran had no dedicated chemical weapons program, having signed the Geneva Protocol outlawing the development or use of such weapons. Despite the outbreak of the war with Iraq in 1980, the Khomeini regime made little effort to revitalize what it considered an "idolatrous" nuclear program, canceling ongoing equipment orders with European firms.[46] Neither did it begin large-scale chemical or biological weapons programs. In 1982, when Saddam Hussein initiated the battlefield use of chemical weapons against Iranian soldiers and revolutionary guards, Iran was unable to respond in kind with chemical weapons or to threaten to escalate the conflict with other weapons of mass destruction.

Despite the Iraqi use of chemical weapons, Ayatollah Khomeini opposed Iran's acquisition or use of chemical weapons on grounds that this would violate the Qur'an's injunctions against polluting the atmosphere, even during a holy war. He reportedly issued a fatwa, or religious edict, outlawing the use of chemical weapons.[47] Khomeini was both the spiritual leader and commander-in-chief of the Islamic Republic of Iran and his ethically driven position held as state policy until 1987, when he relented and approved the use of chemical weapons in retaliation against Iraq.[48]

The results of Khomeini's refusal to prepare for or to permit retaliation in kind to Iraq's chemical attacks were devastating. Estimates of Iranian casualties from repeated Iraqi chemical strikes during the war range from 45,000 to 100,000 soldiers and revolutionary guards. The CIA reportedly argued that the Iraqi use of chemicals was a decisive factor in driving a reluctant government in Tehran to the negotiating table.[49] As realists would also predict, however, the Iraqi chemical attacks eventually pushed Iran to reverse its position. In 1998, Speaker of the Parliament Hashemi Rafsanjani drew the following lessons from Iran's experience during the war with Iraq:

With regard to chemical, bacteriological, and radiological weapons training, it was made very clear during the war that these weapons are very decisive. It was also made very clear that the moral teachings of the world are not very effective when war reaches a serious stage. . . . We should fully equip ourselves in the defensive and offensive use of chemical, bacteriological, and radiological weapons.[50]

Japan and Nuclear Weapons

Japanese nuclear policy is the most prominent example of the disavowal of nuclear weapons that neoculturalist scholars interpret as being determined by ethical norms. For over thirty years, Tokyo has declared that it follows the so-called three nonnuclear principles: not to make nuclear weapons, not to possess them, and not to bring them into Japan. Peter Katzenstein maintains that without the "nuclear allergy" that comes from Japan's moral opposition to nuclear weapons, the Tokyo government would have developed nuclear weapons long ago. The institutionalization of these ethical and cultural norms into government policy, Katzenstein argues, "places great obstacles in the path of those who want to make Japan a normal country, with a normal military force and normal levels of military spending."[51]

Realists question this interpretation of Japan's nuclear policy, placing more emphasis on the U.S. nuclear guarantee to Japan. They cite evidence that Japan has deliberately created, through its basic technological prowess and its nuclear energy program, a capability to break out of its unarmed position rapidly if the United States withdrew its military support.[52] Moreover, realists note that during the North Korean nuclear crisis of 1993–94, senior government spokesmen hinted that Tokyo might change policies.[53] Realists therefore suggest that if North Korea develops a nuclear arsenal in the future and the U.S. nuclear guarantee is withdrawn in response, then Tokyo would quickly make its latent nuclear weapons capability a real one, which is permissible under the NPT's three-month escape clause.[54]

We cannot know today whether neorealism or neoculturalism would be proven correct in the event that the United States pulled its nuclear umbrella away from Japan. But my realist compass points to the likely outcome if Japanese officials did follow their moral nonnuclear principles and refrained from building a nuclear arsenal to counter a nuclear North Korea. Tokyo would be forced to change its foreign policy radically under the pressure of coercive threats. A historical analogy is relevant, since Japan did practice an unusual form of self-restraint with respect to advanced weaponry once before: In the early eighteenth century, the Japanese outlawed firearms and returned to the use of swords throughout their society. The reasons, as explained by Noel Perrin, were both geopolitical and cultural in nature: geopolitical because once their wars with Korea were over at the end of the seventeenth century, Japanese leaders did not fear conquest by their neighbors; cultural, in that swords, not guns, held symbolic value for the samurai classes (since others were forbidden to own swords), were considered more honorable to use, and were more aesthetically pleasing. This condition continued for over a hundred years, until a defenseless Japan was forced to open up to the outside world by the U.S. fleet. "The samurai of Japan were never willing to make this distinction between what is beautiful and what is useful," Perrin concludes, adding, "at least until they met Admiral Perry."[55]

CONCRETE OPTIONS: ARMS CONTROL REGIMES
AND MILITARY DOCTRINES

A realist perspective should maintain that ethical norms matter, but that power shapes which norms are influential in world politics. An example is the norm against assassination of leaders. It is not surprising from a realist perspective that the strongest powers in the international system, from the Romans in their day to the United States today, have been the instigators of international norms that discourage political assassination since they have other military means to defeat adversaries.[56] Realism reminds us that the strong usually make the rules, but also that the strong often flaunt them. The United States clearly targeted Muammar Qaddafi's tent in response to Libyan supported terrorist attacks in 1984 and repeatedly targeted Saddam Hussein's underground command bunkers during the 1991 Gulf War and the 2003 Iraq War.[57] But Washington officials were quick to announce that these were strikes on national "command and control" facilities, not illegal and immoral assassination attempts.

Realism helps to explain why the United States (and other nuclear powers) so strongly supported the creation of the Chemical Weapons Convention (CWC) and the Biological Weapons Convention (BWC). Treaties that outlaw the use and possession of the "poor man's nuclear weapons" clearly favor strong states that have nuclear forces and stronger conventional forces. From most ethical perspectives, it would appear wrong or at least ironic that the possession and potential use of the most harmful and least discriminate of WMD (nuclear weapons) have not been unequivocally outlawed, while the use and possession of the generally less harmful and more discriminate weapons (chemical and most biological weapons) are banned by international law. Such an outcome is understandable, however, in light of the interests of the most powerful actors in the international system.

In a world in which many states could acquire nuclear, chemical, and biological weapons, however, the governments of strong states would be well advised to pay more heed to the perspectives and interests of weaker states. It is here that radical realism can easily misguide the statesmen. The United States is by far the most powerful actor in the international system since the end of the cold war, and the U.S. government has been tempted to abandon many arms control agreements and constraints on U.S. nuclear policy on the grounds that they are no longer necessary to protect American interests.

Four examples stand out. First, the Comprehensive Test Ban Treaty (CTBT) was originally championed by the U.S. government in an effort to increase the constraints on the testing programs of other current and future nuclear powers, albeit at the cost of placing similar constraints on the U.S. testing program. Given that the United States has conducted more nuclear weapons tests than all other nuclear powers combined, this seemed like a very good deal to previous American administrations, Democratic and Republican alike. The Bush administration, nevertheless, has opposed the CTBT and refused to push for ratification on the grounds that this would hamper nuclear weapons development and the reliability of the American stockpile.[58] If the United States tests nuclear weapons, other states will surely restart their testing and development programs, ultimately leading to a world of more nuclear weapon states.

Second, similar arguments can be made about the Nonproliferation Treaty. In the NPT, the nonnuclear weapon states agreed not to acquire nuclear weapons (article 2) and the nuclear weapon states pledged to work in good faith toward the eventual elimination of nuclear weapons (article 6). The U.S. government, however, has done little to convince others that these article 6 commitments are taken seriously, a source of great debate at every NPT review conference. This too is problematic from a long-term perspective. For if the U.S. refusal to contemplate nuclear disarmament encourages other states to abandon the NPT, it will again lead toward a world of widespread nuclear proliferation. Maintaining a small nuclear arsenal may well be in the ultimate interests of the United States, but having signed an agreement that it will work in good faith toward disarmament, its government officials should not signal bad faith by ridiculing advocates of nuclear disarmament, as they have often done in the past.

A third example is the Anti-Ballistic Missile (ABM) Treaty. The attraction of building a national missile shield appears obvious at first. "Wouldn't it be better to protect the American people than to avenge them?" Ronald Reagan often asked when promoting his Star Wars plan.[59] Yet despite the lure of perfect missile defenses, the U.S. government did not built them because of uncertainty about their effectiveness and because all cold war studies showed that enemy countermeasures would be cheaper than our planned defenses. Republican and Democratic presidents therefore reluctantly accepted nuclear deterrence and agreed under the ABM Treaty not to deploy missile defenses.

What has changed? Technological advances in sensors, kill vehicles, and computer integration systems made the basic task – which once seemed impossible to all but the most committed Star Wars advocates – appear more promising.[60] What has not changed, however, is the basic political problem of countermeasures and secondary reactions. The Chinese are likely to react to U.S. missile defense deployments by deploying more nuclear weapons and advanced missiles. The Indian government will be as disturbed by the Chinese offensive buildup as the Chinese government will be by a U.S. defensive buildup and is likely to increase both the size and alert levels of its arsenal. Pakistan is likely to respond to a future Indian nuclear buildup by increasing the size and alert status of its own nuclear-armed bombers and missile arsenal. If U.S. missile defenses exacerbate the problems of proliferation elsewhere in the world in this way, the end result could be a reduction, not increase, in U.S. and global security.

Finally, the George W. Bush administration has maintained a nuclear policy of "calculated ambiguity," threatening possible nuclear retaliation in response to chemical or biological weapons. This strategy may well reduce the likelihood of the United States being attacked by states with such weapons of mass destruction. But unless this doctrine works 100 percent of the time in the future, it also increases the likelihood that the U.S. president would feel compelled to use nuclear weapons after a chemical or biological weapons attack because he would feel that the nation's reputation of acting on its deterrent threats was at stake.[61] The use of U.S. nuclear weapons, however, would encourage many other states to abandon their ethical inhibitions against developing nuclear weapons and thus would eventually increase the likelihood of future nuclear wars.

The tradition of nuclear nonuse is fragile. If it is in the U.S. interest and the global interest to maintain that tradition, it would be prudent for the U.S. government to abandon threats to respond with nuclear weapons except in response to a nuclear attack. A really strong state should not always do what it can with weapons of mass destruction.

Notes

1. On the classical roots of modern realism, see Benjamin Frankel, ed., "The Roots of Realism," *Security Studies* 5:2 (Special Issue, Winter 1995/96); Kenneth N. Waltz, *Man, the State, and War* (New York: Columbia University Press, 1959); and Laurie M. Johnson Bagby, "The Use and Abuse of Thucydides in International Relations," *International Organization* 48:1 (Winter 1994): 131–53.

2. Thucydides, *History of the Peloponnesian War* (Baltimore, Md.: Penguin, 1974), 404.

3. Carl von Clausewitz, *On War* (Princeton, N.J.: Princeton University Press, 1976), 75–76.

4. The seminal text of neorealism remains Kenneth N. Waltz, *Theory of International Politics* (New York: McGraw-Hill, 1979). See also Kenneth N. Waltz, "The Origins of War in Neorealist Theory," in *The Origin and Prevention of Major Wars*, ed. Robert I. Rotberg and Theodore K. Rabb (New York: Cambridge University Press, 1988), 39–52; and Robert O. Keohane, ed., *Neorealism and Its Critics* (New York: Columbia University Press, 1986).

5. George Bernard Shaw, *Pygmalion*, Act II, lines 245–55.

6. Robert J. Art and Kenneth N. Waltz, "Technology, Strategy, and the Uses of Force," in *The Use of Force*, 2nd ed., ed. Art and Waltz (Lanham, Md.: University Press of America, 1983), 6–7.

7. See Robert W. Tucker, "Morality and Deterrence," in *Nuclear Deterrence: Ethics and Strategy*, ed. Russell Hardin, John J. Mearsheimer, Gerald Dworkin, and Robert E. Goodwin (Chicago: University of Chicago Press, 1985), 53–70; Joel H. Rosenthal, *Righteous Realists: Political Realism, Responsible Power, and American Culture in the Nuclear Age* (Baton Rouge: Louisiana State University Press, 1991); and Michael Joseph Smith, *Realist Thought from Weber to Kissinger* (Baton Rouge: Louisiana State University Press, 1986).

8. Richard M. Price, *The Chemical Weapons Taboo* (Ithaca, N.Y.: Cornell University Press, 1997); Nina Tannenwald, *The Nuclear Taboo: The United States and the Non-Use of Nuclear Weapons since 1945* (New York: Cambridge University Press, forthcoming); Dana P. Eyre and Mark C. Suchman, "Status, Norms, and the Proliferation of Conventional Weapons," and Richard Price and Nina Tannenwald, "Norms and Deterrence: The Nuclear and Chemical Weapons Taboos," both in *The Culture of National Security: Norms and Identity in World Politics*, ed. Peter J. Katzenstein (New York: Columbia University Press, 1996), 79–113 and 114–52; and Peter J. Katzenstein, *Cultural Norms and National Security: Police and Military in Postwar Japan* (Ithaca, N.Y.: Cornell University Press, 1996).

9. See Kenneth N. Waltz, *Theory of International Politics* (Reading, Mass.: Addison Wesley, 1979), 118; Scott D. Sagan, "More Will Be Worse," in Scott D. Sagan and Kenneth N. Waltz, *The Spread of Nuclear Weapons: A Debate Renewed* (New York: W. W. Norton, 2003), 84.

10. John J. Mearsheimer, *The Tragedy of Great Power Politics* (New York: W. W. Norton, 2001).

11. Indeed, the incentives and momentum for using the atomic bomb were so great that there was no single "decision" point. Most of the officials privy to the secret simply assumed that the atomic bomb would be used whenever it was physically ready. See Barton J. Bernstein, "Understanding the Atomic Bomb and the Japanese Surrender: Missed Opportunities, Little-Known Near Disasters, and Modern Memory," *Diplomatic History* 19:2 (Spring 1995): 227–74.

12. Paul Boyer, *By the Bomb's Early Light* (New York: Pantheon, 1985), 183.

13. Waltz, "Origins of War in Neorealist Theory," 49 and 51; and Mearsheimer, *Tragedy of Great Power Politics*, 128–30 and 224–32.

14. On cold war nuclear doctrines, see Scott D. Sagan, *Moving Targets: Nuclear Strategy and National Security* (Princeton, N.J.: Princeton University Press, 1989); and Desmond Ball and Jeffrey Richelson, eds., *Strategic Nuclear Targeting* (Ithaca, N.Y.: Cornell University Press, 1986).

15. Jack S. Levy, "Declining Power and the Preventive Motivation for War," *World Politics* 40:1 (October 1987): 82–107.

16. Jeff McMahan, "Realism, Morality, and War," in *The Ethics of War and Peace: Religious and Secular Perspectives*, ed. Terry Nardin (Princeton, N.J.: Princeton University Press, 1996), 84–86.

17. U.S. Congress, House Appropriations Committee Hearing, Department of Defense Appropriations for 1960, 86th Congress, 1st session, pt. 2, p. 376.

18. See Scott D. Sagan, "The Origins of Military Doctrine and Command and Control Systems," in *Planning the Unthinkable*, ed. Peter R. Lavoy, Scott D. Sagan, and James J. Wirtz (Ithaca, N.Y.: Cornell University Press, 2000), 16–46; and Marc Trachtenberg, "A 'Wasting Asset': American Strategy and the Shifting Nuclear Balance, 1949–1954," *International Security* 13:3 (Winter 1988–89): 5–49.

19. Memorandum by the President to the Secretary of State, September 8, 1953, *Foreign Relations of the United States, 1952–1954*, vol. 2, National Security Affairs, pt. 1, p. 461 (emphasis in original).

20. Memorandum of Discussion of NSC meeting, March 4, 1954, *Foreign Relations of the United States, 1952–1954*, p. 636.

21. Memorandum of Discussion, December 3, 1954, *Foreign Relations of the United States, 1952–1954*, pp. 804–6.

22. Stewart Steven, *The Spymasters of Israel* (New York: Macmillan, 1980), 139–48.

23. Shai Feldman, "The Bombing of Osiraq – Revisited," *International Security* 7:2 (Fall 1982): 114–42.

24. Avigdor Haselkorn, *The Continuing Storm: Iraq, Poisonous Weapons and Deterrence* (New Haven, Conn.: Yale University Press, 1999).

25. William Burr and Jeffrey T. Richelson, "Whether to 'Strangle the Baby in the Cradle': The United States and the Chinese Nuclear Program, 1960–64," *International Security* 25:3 (Winter 2000–2001): 54–99; Gordon H. Chang, *Friends and Enemies: The United States, China, and the Soviet Union* (Stanford, Calif.: Stanford University Press, 1990), 228–52; Scott D. Sagan, "Correspondence: Proliferation, Pessimism and Emerging Nuclear Powers," *International Security* 22:2 (Fall 1997): 194–97.

26. John Lewis Gaddis, "The Origins of Self-Deterrence: The United States and the Nonuse of Nuclear Weapons, 1945–1958," in Gaddis, *The Long Peace: Inquiries into the History of the Cold War* (New York: Oxford University Press, 1987), 104–46.

27. In *The Long Peace*, Gaddis himself stresses the second and third factors as producing nuclear restraint in his analysis of the Korean War and the Taiwan Straits crises during the cold war.

28. George Bush and Brent Scowcroft, *A World Transformed* (New York: Knopf, 1998), 463. See also Colin L. Powell with Joseph Perisco, *My American Journey: An Autobiography* (New York: Random House, 1995), 486.

29. James A. Baker III with Thomas M. DeFrank, *The Politics of Diplomacy: Revolution, War, and Peace, 1989–1992* (New York: G. P. Putnam's Sons, 1995), 359.

30. Ibid.

31. Daniel Byman, Kenneth Pollack, and Matthew Waxman, "Coercing Saddam Hussein: Lessons from the Past," *Survival* 40:3 (Fall 1998): 132; Leonard A. Cole, *The Eleventh Plague* (New York: W. H. Freeman, 1997), 127; Steven Erlanger, "U.S. Set to Give Up Arms Inspections for Curbing Iraq," *New York Times*, November 8, 1998, sec. 1, p. 1; and Lawrence Freedman and Efraim Karsh, "How Kuwait Was Won: Strategy in the Gulf War," *International Security* 16:2 (Fall 1991): 26, n. 72.

32. For examinations of the effects of the Gulf War threats, see William M. Arkin, "Calculated Ambiguity: Nuclear Weapons in the Gulf War," *Washington Quarterly* 19:4 (Autumn 1996): 3–18; Haselkorn, *Continuing Storm*, 51–85; Barry R. Posen, "U.S. Security Policy in a Nuclear-Armed World, or: What If Iraq Had Had Nuclear Weapons?" *Security Studies* 6:3 (Spring 1997): 1–31; and Scott D. Sagan, "The Commitment Trap," *International Security* 24:4 (Spring 2000): 85–115.

33. Tannenwald, *Nuclear Taboo*, ms. pp. 324–68. See also McGeorge Bundy, "Nuclear Weapons and the Gulf War," *Foreign Affairs* 70:4 (Fall 1991): 83–94; and Thomas Schelling, "The Role of Nuclear Weapons," in *The Turning Point: The Gulf War and U.S. Military Strategy*, ed. L. Benjamin Ederington and Michael J. Mazarr (Boulder, Colo.: Westview, 1994), 105–15.

34. Tannenwald, *Nuclear Taboo*, ms. p. 342. The quotes are from pp. 328, 332–33, and 341.

35. Powell, *My American Journey*, 472.

36. Ibid., 472–73 (emphasis added).

37. http://www.pbs.org/wgbh/pages/frontline/gulf/oral/horner/2.html (November 29, 2001).

38. Bradley A. Thayer, "The Causes of Nuclear Proliferation and the Utility of the Nuclear Nonproliferation Regime," *Security Studies* 4:3 (Spring 1995): 463–519; Benjamin Frankel, "The Brooding Shadow: Systemic Incentives and Nuclear Weapons Proliferation," and Richard K. Betts, "Paranoids, Pygmies, Pariahs, and Nonproliferation Revisited," both in "The Proliferation Puzzle," ed. Zachary S. Davis and Benjamin Frankel, special issue of *Security Studies* 2:3/4 (Spring/Summer 1993): 37–38, 100–24.

39. Scott D. Sagan, "Why Do States Build Nuclear Weapons?" in *The Coming Crisis: Nuclear Proliferation, U.S. Interests, and World Order*, ed. Victor Utgoff (Cambridge: MIT Press, 2000), 17–50.

40. Susan B. Martin, "The Role of Biological Weapons in International Politics," *Journal of Strategic Studies* 25:1 (March 2002): 63–98.

41. For more information, see the Center for Defense Information chemical and biological weapons fact sheet at http://www.cdi.org/issues/cbw/factsheet.html.

42. Waltz, "More May Be Better," in Sagan and Waltz, *The Spread of Nuclear Weapons*, 45. For similar arguments, see John J. Mearsheimer, "Back to the Future: Instability in Europe after the Cold War," *International Security* 15:1 (Summer 1990): 5–56; and David J. Karl, "Proliferation Pessimism and Emerging Nuclear Powers," *International Security* 21:3 (Winter 1996–97): 87–119.

43. The paragraph is based on Sagan, "More Will Be Worse," in Sagan and Waltz, *The Spread of Nuclear Weapons*.

44. See Thomas C. Schelling, *Arms and Influence* (New Haven, Conn.: Yale University Press, 1966), 248–51.

45. See Leonard S. Spector, *Going Nuclear* (Cambridge, Mass.: Ballinger, 1987), 45–57.

46. See Sohail Hashmi, Chapter 17 of this volume, under "Disarmament"; and Yoav Yitzhak Schlesinger, "Fumes of Faith: Iranian Chemical Weapons Use in the Iran-Iraq War," undergraduate honors thesis, Stanford University, Center for International Security and Cooperation, 2001.

47. See Gregory Giles, "The Islamic Republic of Iran and Unconventional Weapons," in Lavoy et al., eds., *Planning the Unthinkable*, 82–83.

48. Ibid.; for further details, see Schlesinger, "Fumes of Faith."

49. Giles, "Iran and Unconventional Weapons," 83 n. 15, and Martin Walker, "Iraq's Use of Chemical Arms Main Source of U.S. Fears," *The Guardian* (London), January 6, 1989, p. 1, as cited in Javed Ali, "Chemical Weapons and the Iran-Iraq War," *The Non-Proliferation Review* 8:1 (Spring 2001): 52 n. 72.

50. Giles, "Iran and Unconventional Weapons," 84.

51. Katzenstein, *Cultural Norms and National Security*, 148–51. See also Thomas U. Berger, *The Cultures of Antimilitarism: National Security in Germany and Japan* (Baltimore, Md.: Johns Hopkins University Press, 1998).

52. "The Capability to Develop Nuclear Weapons Should Be Kept: Ministry of Foreign Affairs Secret Document in 1969," *Mainichi*, August 1, 1994, p. 41; quoted in Selig S. Harrison, "Japan and Nuclear Weapons," in *Japan's Nuclear Future*, ed. Selig S. Harrison (Washington, D.C.: Carnegie Endowment for International Peace, 1996), 9.

53. Sam Jameson, "Foreign Minister Says Japan Will Need Nuclear Arms If North Korea Threatens," *Los Angeles Times*, July 29, 1993, p. 4; originally cited in Harrison, "Japan and Nuclear Weapons," 29; David E. Sanger, "In Face-Saving

Reverse, Japan Disavows Any Nuclear-Arms Expertise," *New York Times*, June 22, 1994, p. 10.

54. See Kenneth N. Waltz, "The Emerging Structure of International Politics," *International Security* 18:2 (Fall 1993): 67; and Matake Kamiya, "Will Japan Go Nuclear? Myth and Reality," *Asia-Pacific Review* 2:2 (Autumn/Winter 1995): 5–19.

55. Noel Perrin, *Giving Up the Gun: Japan's Reversion to the Sword, 1543–1879* (Boston: David R. Godine, 1979), 32–80, quote at 41.

56. Ward Thomas, "Norms and Security: The Case of International Assassination," *International Security* 25:1 (Summer 2000): 105–33.

57. David C. Martin and John Walcott, *Best Laid Plans* (New York: Harper & Row, 1988), 286–88; Rick Atkinson, *Crusade: The Untold Story of the Persian Gulf War* (Boston: Houghton Mifflin, 1993), 272–74; Michael R. Gordon and General Bernard E. Trainor, *The Generals' War: The Inside Story of the Conflict in the Gulf* (Boston: Little, Brown, 1995), 86–88.

58. See "The Comprehensive Test Ban Treaty: Next Steps," proceedings of conference at Center for International Security and Cooperation (CISAC), Stanford University (July 19, 2000).

59. Francis Fitzgerald, *Way Out There in the Blue* (New York: Simon and Schuster, 2000), 203.

60. See Dean Wilkening, *Ballistic Missile Defense and Strategic Stability*, Adelphi Paper 334 (Oxford: IISS, May 2000).

61. On this issue, see Scott D. Sagan, "The Commitment Trap," and Susan B. Martin and Scott D. Sagan, "Correspondence: Responding to Chemical and Biological Threats," *International Security* 25:4 (Spring 2001): 193–98.

4

Realism and Weapons of Mass Destruction

A Consequentialist Analysis

Susan B. Martin

Most of the chapters in this volume examine how to apply centuries-old religious or secular ethical perspectives to the relatively new issue of weapons of mass destruction. For a realist, the challenge is different – it is to take realist analyses of WMD and determine whether and how ethics fit into those analyses. In this chapter, I present realism's argument for a consequentialist form of moral reasoning in international politics. In particular, I examine the contribution that a particular strain of realism, structural realism, can make to such a consequentialist argument. I illustrate this through a structural realist analysis of weapons of mass destruction, explaining how structural realism understands these weapons and the consequences that follow from them. The aim of this chapter is thus to demonstrate the contribution that realism, especially the structural realist theory of Kenneth Waltz, can make to an ethical analysis of weapons of mass destruction.[1]

Drawing on the work of Lea Brilmayer, I argue that realism mandates a consequentialist instead of a deontological approach to international politics.[2] Actions or outcomes are judged to be ethical or unethical on the basis of their consequences, not on the basis of whether they comply with abstract moral principles. In addition, a realist analysis of international politics must begin with "the world as it is." Thus, for realism, the first step of any analysis of WMD is to understand the characteristics of weapons of mass destruction and their consequences – the effect of these weapons on international politics. Such an analysis provides a basis for understanding international political developments, for policy prescriptions, and even for ethical analysis. However, an ethical analysis of WMD has to move beyond a realist analysis: It has to identify and justify the standards used to evaluate consequences, and then apply those standards to the issues surrounding weapons of mass destruction.

The purpose of this chapter is thus not to provide an ethical analysis of weapons of mass destruction per se but to prepare the groundwork for a consequentialist analysis of WMD by presenting structural realism's understanding of these weapons and of the consequences that follow from them. Before proceeding, however, two points require clarification: first, how my argument relates to that of Scott Sagan in the preceding chapter, and second, how realism approaches issues of morality and ethics generally.

Sagan examines the issue of ethics and realist analyses of WMD by focusing on how realism understands the role of ethics in foreign policy: Do ethical norms constrain the behavior of states and statesmen, and if so, how? He argues that "statesmen do follow ethical norms in their weapons policies," largely because of the negative consequences of not doing so.[3] Sagan and I thus agree that realism contributes to a discussion of the ethics of international politics through a focus on the consequences of possible international behavior. However, while he focuses on foreign policy behavior – whether state leaders act according to some set of normative beliefs – I focus on how the theory of realism, especially structural realism, contributes to a consequentialist analysis of WMD.

REALISM AND MORALITY

While the role of ethics and morality in the tradition of realism has been examined before, neorealism is usually left out of these analyses.[4] The goal of realism as an analytic theory is to understand and to explain international politics. Classical realist theorists, such as E. H. Carr, Hans Morgenthau, and George Kennan, combine assumptions about the actors in international politics (states and state leaders) with assumptions about the international environment. Morality often enters their analyses through the assumptions they make about human nature; Morgenthau, for example, assumes that "all human beings seek power," and this assumption informs his conclusion that "international politics is of necessity power politics."[5] In reaction to classical realists, Kenneth Waltz argues that much of international politics, in particular, recurrent patterns of international outcomes such as the formation of balances of power or the outbreak of war, can be explained by a focus on the structure of the international system.[6] In Waltz's structural realist theory, presented in *Theory of International Politics*, states are identified as the main actors in international politics, and only a minimal assumption about their nature – that states want to survive – is made.[7] It is the structure of the international system, characterized by anarchy and the distribution of power (the number of great powers), that are the main explanatory variables in structural realism. Because it sheds the assumptions about human nature that led previous realists into a discussion of morality, and because it aims to be an objective, scientific theory that explains international politics, structural realism has been regarded as having little or nothing to contribute to a discussion of ethics and international relations.[8]

I want to suggest that structural realism can contribute to a discussion of ethics in international affairs in at least three ways. First, both classical and neorealist analysts have warned of the dangers of morality in international politics. The international system is composed of equal, sovereign states with no international authority above them to enforce laws or to create a community in which common norms evolve.[9] Instead, each state decides for itself what actions it should take, and each state is responsible for its own survival. The introduction of morality in the anarchic international system can be dangerous, especially when a state assumes that its particular moral and ethical views are or should be universal. For example, a state may put its survival in jeopardy when it assumes that other states share its moral beliefs and then takes or refrains from actions on the basis of those beliefs. A state that refrains from fighting wars because it believes that the taking of human life is immoral is likely to soon find itself conquered by another state. As Patricia Wrightson explains, for realists, "to put moral considerations before political survival or order is to lose both."[10] Another danger that follows from the assumption of universal moral beliefs is the proliferation of wars of "good versus evil." International disputes cast in terms of moral differences tend to escalate as those differences are used to justify the destruction of "evil" and lead to demands of unconditional surrender.[11]

Second, Brilmayer argues that realism mandates a consequentialist as opposed to a deontological approach to questions of ethics and international politics. She focuses on a strand of thought that she labels "realist morality" and explains that "realist morality is based on the proposition that in situations of anarchy – international affairs being one such situation – the consequences of one's actions should be given higher moral priority than the moral attractiveness of the means that one employs."[12] The necessity of consequentialist as opposed to deontological reasoning follows from the anarchic structure of the international system – the fact that in the international arena, others "may not comply with [or even share our] legal and moral norms... and that there is no effective power for enforcing those moral rules."[13]

But if we are to judge actions as ethical or unethical on the basis of their consequences, we need a good understanding of the consequences that are likely to follow from a particular action. This is where the theory of structural realism is important. Structural realism contributes to a consequentialist analysis through its attempt to explain exactly how the anarchic structure of the international system impacts international politics. Structural realism's analysis extends beyond a discussion of the lack of shared norms and the lack of an effective power to enforce norms and agreements.[14] It argues that the anarchic structure of the international system also constrains states to be concerned with relative power, because it is a state's power relative to other states that determines its ability to carry out its preferred policies and, ultimately, its ability to survive.[15]

Structural realism also suggests that the anarchic structure of the international system means that there is a disjuncture between state behavior – what states intend – and the international outcomes that result. The classic example is of the security dilemma and, in particular, of an arms race that results from the purely defensive actions taken by states.[16] Take two states, each of which arms itself in order to defend against possible attacks. Each state knows that it acquired arms for defensive purposes only, but it is less sure about the intentions of the other state. Because the other state may use the arms it has acquired for offensive purposes, each state feels the need to respond by acquiring more arms to defend itself. The cycle repeats and an arms race results, as each state seeks to protect itself against the possible aggressive intentions of the other state. Neither state intended to threaten the other state; neither state wanted an arms race. Each state sought only to defend itself. But because the anarchic structure of the international system means that war is always possible and that each state must protect itself against possible threats or risk annihilation, each state was compelled to react to the acquisition of arms by the other. The states' policies were intended to be nonprovocative and to provide self-defense, but the international outcome that resulted from those policies was an arms race.

Thus, structural realism's understanding of the anarchic structure of the international system and the way in which it causes a disjuncture between intentions and outcomes means that if one is to choose an action based on its consequences, a good understanding of structural effects is necessary. To the extent, then, that the anarchic character of the international system mandates consequentialist as opposed to deontological reasoning and to the extent that structural realism correctly captures the dynamics of international politics, structural realism is a necessary part of an ethical analysis of international politics.

The final way that ethics are involved in structural realism is the same way that ethics are involved in any sort of policy prescription. When a structural realist analysis moves from an explanation of structural effects to recommendations or prescriptions for state policy, it moves from "is" to "ought," and that movement entails a normative choice about what the goals of state policy should be. Structural realism itself does not make specific policy prescriptions, leaving the choice of particular ends to the policy maker or analyst in question.

Thus, structural realism does not (and does not claim to) provide, in and of itself, a complete ethical analysis of international politics. Such an analysis involves identifying the ends or consequences by which outcomes should be judged. Structural realism claims only to help illuminate the consequences that will follow from certain actions in international politics; whether those consequences are "positive" or "negative," whether those consequences should be promoted or discouraged, is outside the scope of the theory.

Some may object that structural realist theory does entail normative judgments, in its focus on stability and peace. This focus is especially apparent in the discussion of bipolar versus multipolar systems.[17] However, structural realism's focus on stability and peace arises from the analysis of the effect of a change in the distribution of power (from multipolarity to bipolarity) on international politics.[18] The distribution of power is one of the main explanatory variables in structural realism, and two areas in which a change in the distribution of power has important effects are the stability and peacefulness of the system. Structural realist theory suggests that bipolar systems are more peaceful but less stable than multipolar systems.[19] Whether bipolar systems are therefore to be preferred over multipolar systems, or vice versa, is a normative judgment that the theory itself does not address. While Waltz makes his personal preference for bipolarity clear, it is possible to disagree with him on normative (and other) grounds.[20]

A REALIST ANALYSIS OF WEAPONS OF MASS DESTRUCTION

In international politics, the "world as it is" is characterized by the existence of independent, more or less sovereign states that are insecure because there is no overarching authority to control or limit their actions (i.e., anarchy). The "world as it is" is also characterized by the existence of weapons of mass destruction. Realism thus takes the existence of weapons of mass destruction for granted; once these weapons have been invented and are physically possible, they must be taken into account by states seeking to survive. Returning to a world where weapons of mass destruction do not exist is not possible. Even if all existing weapons were destroyed, so long as the knowledge of how to make them exists, states must take into account the possibility that some state at some time will acquire them.[21]

One of the most important consequences of anarchy is the insecurity it produces. Anarchy results in insecurity because there is no central authority to prevent any state from using the resources at its disposal to attack or harm another state. The constant possibility of war means that states, assumed at a minimum to want to survive, are constrained to safeguard their security at all times.

One way of understanding how weapons of mass destruction affect international politics, then, is to ask how they influence the way in which states pursue security. Realists come up with different answers to this question, in large part because of differences in their understanding of the characteristics of weapons of mass destruction.[22] Some realists, who can be grouped under the heading of "nuclear revolution theorists," argue that nuclear weapons have transformed the way that states pursue security by making "pure" deterrent strategies possible.[23] Deterrence is defined as an attempt to stop someone from doing something by threatening or frightening him or her. For a deterrent threat to be effective, the threat must promise to do more harm and thus impose more costs than the benefits that would be gained through the action to be deterred.[24] The destructive power of nuclear weapons is thought to make them the ideal strategic deterrent weapon, because nuclear weapons can do enough damage to outweigh any possible gains for which an aggressor may hope.[25] A second-strike nuclear force – one that can absorb a nuclear attack and retain the ability to launch a retaliatory strike – provides its possessor with the ability to deter attacks on its vital interests. Nuclear weapons are thus understood to promote peace and stability among those who possess them.[26]

Nuclear revolution theorists thus argue that nuclear weapons make it more difficult to use force for aggressive purposes, encourage prudence and caution, make it difficult to overestimate the benefits of aggression, and discourage arms races and thereby help to avoid the tensions and conflicts that arise from such races.[27] Nuclear deterrence thus enhances state security. Again, realism itself does not justify these effects as positive or negative, although nuclear revolution theorists do tend to see these effects as positive. It is possible, however, to accept these effects and argue that they are negative; for instance, one might argue that nuclear deterrence helps to preserve an unjust status quo in the international system.

The nuclear revolution school's understanding of nuclear weapons is not universally accepted, even among realists. For example, some scholars argue that nuclear weapons do not differ significantly from conventional or other types of weapons. During the cold war, these scholars focused on the question of how the United States could deter a Soviet attack and argued that deterrence of the Soviet Union required the ability to fight and win a nuclear war.[28]

While realist scholars have given less attention to chemical and biological weapons, they would approach the analysis of these weapons in the same manner. No moral distinctions between types of weapons are drawn. Only when we understand the international political consequences of WMD can we make judgments about appropriate policies or about the moral legitimacy or illegitimacy of these weapons. And for structural realism, to understand the role that these weapons will play in international politics, we must understand how they affect the ability of states to pursue security and survival.

When one examines the arguments presented by the nuclear revolution school about deterrence, it becomes clear that biological weapons share many of the characteristics that make nuclear weapons effective deterrent weapons.[29] States that face severe security threats but cannot acquire nuclear weapons may thus seek biological weapons as a strategic deterrent. (Note that the ability of biological weapons to serve as a strategic deterrent provides another answer to Sagan's puzzle concerning why the United States did not use nuclear weapons in the Gulf War.)[30]

Chemical weapons, in contrast, are primarily tactical, not strategic weapons – they simply do not have the destructive power required for strategic deterrence. They do have some battlefield utility, but this is usually outweighed by the availability of chemical warfare defenses and the disadvantages of using chemical weapons against a state that can retaliate in kind. Chemical weapons thus have little military utility and do not have much effect on a state's security.[31]

The Use of WMD in War

The question of whether it is morally permissible to use WMD is not addressed by structural realism. It sees the use of weapons as governed primarily by the desire of insecure states to survive and by the utility of using or refraining from the use of the weapon in question. Normative concerns that conflict with survival take second place. As Waltz explains in the case of nuclear weapons, "Deterrent policies derive from structural theory, which emphasizes that the units of an international-political system must tend to their own security as best they can. The means available for doing so shape the policies of states and, when nuclear weapons become available, lead them in fact to take deterrent stances."[32] Like nuclear weapons, biological weapons are useful primarily for deterrence, and the same structural imperatives that lead nuclear states to adopt deterrent stances will lead biological states to do the same.

In the case of chemical weapons, realism would explain their use or nonuse by the perceived utility of these weapons; in particular, the use of chemical weapons is most likely against targets that cannot retaliate and that do not possess chemical defenses. For example, during World War II, attitudes toward chemical warfare (CW) changed as conditions on the battlefield shifted. John Ellis van Courtland Moon argues that one can identify four distinct phases in the chemical weapons policies of the Allies. In the first phase, from September 3, 1939, to December 7, 1941, neither side had an incentive to initiate chemical warfare. The use of chemical weapons was discouraged by the fact that the cities of both sides were easy targets, by Germany's belief that it could win without using chemical weapons, and by each side's belief that the other side was better prepared for chemical warfare than it itself was. This was followed by a transitional second phase, from 1941 to 1942, when the Japanese attack on Pearl Harbor broadened the war and created the need for an Allied policy on the use of chemical weapons. This led to a third phase, a period of global CW deterrence that lasted from 1943 to 1944. During this period, the Allies were persuaded that initiation of chemical warfare in one theater of war would lead to its use in other areas. The Allies also sought to deter the Axis powers from using chemical weapons by arguing that the use of chemical weapons against any of the Allies would be considered an attack on all of them. Finally, in 1945 (the fourth period), there was an erosion of deterrence. Once Germany was defeated and the use of chemical weapons could be confined to the Pacific theater, the Allies considered initiating chemical warfare in order to lessen casualties in the invasion of Japan. No final decision on the use of chemical weapons was taken because the atomic attacks on Hiroshima and Nagasaki brought the war to an end.[33]

Structural realism draws distinctions among weapons (e.g., nuclear, biological, or chemical weapons or incendiary bombs) based on their international political consequences. To the extent that the utilities of nuclear, biological, chemical, advanced conventional, and conventional weapons differ, structural realism would expect states to use those weapons in different ways.

Structural realism does not make moral judgments about the use of WMD, although it can help us to understand the international political consequences of the use or nonuse of these weapons. An ethical analysis would then require a standard by which to judge those consequences.

Deterrence

Some realists argue that the consequences of nuclear deterrence are positive, in that they discourage the major use of force among nuclear-armed states, discourage arms races, and so on. Whether this holds true for biological and chemical weapons depends on the characteristics of those weapons; some research suggests that biological weapons could be used, like nuclear weapons, for strategic deterrence, while chemical weapons are much less suited for that role. Again, whether one judges deterrence as ethical depends on one's understanding of the consequences of deterrent policies as well as on an evaluation of those consequences. For example, in evaluating the consequences of nuclear deterrence, one has to weigh the likelihood and costs of accidental nuclear use against the probability and benefits of successful deterrence. Even if one accepts that nuclear deterrence discourages not just nuclear but also major conventional wars among nuclear states, one still faces a choice between no nuclear deterrence and the increased possibility of more conventional wars versus a decreased possibility of war but an increased risk that nuclear weapons will be used. A similar question arises with regard to biological deterrence: Is it ethical to risk the use of biological weapons in order to discourage the use of force? These are questions that realism itself does not answer.

Proliferation

Structural realism argues that as long as weapons of mass destruction are useful for deterrence, defense, or offense, states will pursue them. Strong proponents of the nuclear revolution school argue that the slow spread of nuclear weapons and deterrent strategies will lead to a spread of the positive effects of nuclear deterrence, for example, a decrease in the likelihood of war and an increase in stability. Thus, structural realism does not see anything unique about the current nuclear powers that justifies denying nuclear weapons to other states.[34] Other realists disagree, and oppose the spread of nuclear weapons to other states. This disagreement may be based on a different understanding of the role of nuclear weapons in international politics. For example, while Waltz argues that it is relatively easy for a state to acquire and control a nuclear force designed for deterrence, Sagan argues that it can be quite difficult. For Sagan, the spread of nuclear weapons will result in an increased likelihood of both nuclear accidents and deliberate nuclear use.[35]

Even if one agrees with Waltz that nuclear deterrent forces are easy to establish and maintain and that nuclear deterrence promotes peace and stability, it is possible to oppose the spread of nuclear weapons. If one is concerned with maximizing the extent to which the United States and other major powers can act abroad, for example, the spread of nuclear weapons would be viewed in a negative light.

Disarmament

Structural realism does not have a position on the morality of disarmament. It suggests that because the structure of the international system constrains states to seek security, complete disarmament is unlikely so long as weapons of mass destruction have utility. The nuclear revolution school suggests that, in the case of nuclear weapons, complete disarmament could have the consequence of making the world safe for conventional, major power war. Again, whether these consequences are positive or negative depends on judgments that have to be made outside the theory. Structural realism does acknowledge some room for arms control in addressing the tensions created by the weapons themselves, in addressing some aspects of the security dilemma, and in encouraging the nonacquisition of destabilizing technologies and weapons. The ABM Treaty is the obvious example here because it limited the deployment of potentially destabilizing antimissile defenses during the cold war.

Concrete Options

Structural realists explain states' interest in controlling, limiting, and even eliminating WMD by reference to the interests of the major powers and the utility of the weapons. Thus, the Chemical Weapons Convention (CWC) is possible not because chemical weapons are morally objectionable but because there is a general consensus that the advantages of chemical weapons are outweighed by their disadvantages. However, the CWC will not become universal so long as some states believe that chemical weapons can be used successfully to resolve problems that they face.

Similarly, the Biological Weapons Convention (BWC) can be explained by the realization of the nuclear powers that biological weapons would provide other states with a cheap and relatively easy way to counter their nuclear forces. Once the United States realized that its security was diminished and not enhanced by the existence of biological weapons, it renounced those weapons and began to support a disarmament agreement. In the case of the Soviet Union, research and production of biological weapons continued even after the BWC went into effect. The Soviet program was driven partly by the belief that the United States was also violating the treaty and partly by the conviction that biological weapons would be useful in the Soviet Union's conflict with the United States.[36]

A structural realist analysis of the Nuclear Nonproliferation Treaty (NPT) emphasizes that the treaty serves the interests of the major powers by helping them to safeguard their monopoly on nuclear weapons. It would also acknowledge that the NPT helps to avoid security-dilemma dynamics among nonnuclear states.

CONCLUSION

Structural realism is a theory of international politics, and as such its analysis of weapons of mass destruction begins with the nature of the international system. Because states are constrained by anarchy to safeguard their own security, structural realism analyzes weapons of mass destruction by examining the characteristics of the weapons and their impact on state security. In particular, it examines whether these weapons enhance peace and stability by making it easier for states to protect themselves or whether they make conflict and war more likely by decreasing the security of states.

Structural realism does not directly address the ethics of weapons of mass destruction. It shares with other realist approaches to international politics a concern about the potential dangers of morality in international affairs. It also shares with other realist approaches a preference for a consequentialist approach to questions of ethics in international politics, because the application of deontological principles will often have unintended and perhaps disastrous results. Further, structural realism contributes to such a consequentialist analysis through its illumination of how the structure of the international system influences international politics.

There are at least three main ways to criticize this approach to the question of the ethics of weapons of mass destruction. One is to disagree with realism's preference for a consequentialist as opposed to a deontological approach. This can be done by arguing either that realism's understanding of anarchy is flawed or that despite realism's correct understanding of anarchy, deontological principles should still be applied to international behavior.[37]

Second, one can disagree with the structural realist understanding of the effects of anarchy as well as with its understanding of the "world as it is," and in particular with its understanding of weapons of mass destruction. There are fierce disagreements among those who consider themselves realists over weapons of mass destruction. For example, while the nuclear revolution school believes that nuclear weapons are purely deterrent weapons and as such only a finite number of these weapons is needed to protect a state's security, "other avowed realists (Paul Nitze or Ernest Lefever) urged unstinting attention to the precise nuclear balance."[38]

Finally, even if one agrees with realism's understanding of anarchy and the preference for a consequentialist approach that follows, and even if one accepts structural realism's account of weapons of mass destruction and their role in international politics, one can disagree with the judgments made about the consequences of weapons of mass destruction. Even if we accept that biological and nuclear weapons discourage the use of force, for example, the effects of their use may be so horrible that any policies that increase the risk of their use may be judged unacceptable.

Notes

1. Realism is a tradition whose roots can be traced back through Machiavelli to Thucydides. Modern realism is usually divided into classical realism and neo-realism. Classical realist theories recognize the importance of anarchy but also incorporate individual and state characteristics in their explanations of international outcomes. In contrast to classical realism, neorealist theories focus on the effects of anarchy and the distribution of power in the international system; examples of neorealist theorists include Kenneth Waltz and Robert Gilpin. "Structural realism" refers to a subset of neorealist theory, particularly to the theory presented by Kenneth Waltz in *Theory of International Politics* (New York: Random House, 1979). It is important to note that structural realism does not claim that structure explains everything about international politics; it recognizes that when explaining particular policies or events, as opposed to general patterns of international outcomes, factors from the state and individual level of analysis need to be included.

2. Lea Brilmayer, "Realism Revisited: The Moral Priority of Means and Ends in Anarchy," in *Global Justice*, Nomos 41, ed. Ian Shapiro and Lea Brilmayer (New York: New York University Press, 1999), 192–215. I draw heavily on Brilmayer's analysis of realism as consequentialist, although I disagree with her dismissal of neorealism. Brilmayer dismisses neorealism from her analysis because it "focuses on a supposedly objective analysis" of international politics and because it "professes a lack of interest in normative questions" (p. 194). But such an objective analysis is exactly what is required if we are to understand the consequences of actions in international politics, and just because the theory itself does not address moral questions does not mean that we cannot make use of the theory's contribution in discussions of moral issues.

3. See Scott Sagan, Chapter 3 above, in the introduction.

4. See, for example, Jack Donnelly, "Morality and Foreign Policy," in *Realism and International Relations* (Cambridge: Cambridge University Press, 2000), 161–92; Jeff McMahan, "Realism, Morality, and War," in *The Ethics of War and Peace*, ed. Terry Nardin (Princeton, N.J.: Princeton University Press, 1996), 78–92; David

R. Mapel, "Realism and the Ethics of War and Peace," in ibid., 54–77; Patricia Stein Wrightson, "Morality, Realism, and Foreign Affairs: A Normative Realist Approach," in *Roots of Realism*, ed. Benjamin Frankel (London: Frank Cass, 1996), 354–86.

5. Hans J. Morgenthau, *Politics among Nations*, 5th ed. rev. (New York: Alfred A. Knopf, 1978), 38, 266, and 36–38 passim.

6. See Kenneth N. Waltz, *Man, the State and War* (New York: Columbia University Press, 1959); Waltz, *Theory of International Politics*.

7. Waltz, *Theory of International Politics*, 91–92; see also 134.

8. See Wrightson, "Morality, Realism, and Foreign Affairs," 377; Steven Forde, "International Realism and the Science of Politics: Thucydides, Machiavelli, and Neorealism," *International Studies Quarterly* 39 (1995): 143; Brilmayer, "Realism Revisited," 194.

9. See Scott Sagan in Chapter 3 above. Realists typically argue that norms in international politics cannot be separated from relative power. If a norm is broken by a sufficiently powerful state, not only is that norm weakened or even overturned, but the states that adhere to the norm may be eliminated. Since the international realm is anarchic, there is no international authority to prevent or sanction such norm breaking. In other words, the existence of norms depends on the self-interest of the most powerful states.

10. See Wrightson, "Morality, Realism, and Foreign Affairs," 356. Indeed, realism has often defined itself in opposition to idealism, largely because realists argue that acting on deontological principles in international politics can lead to disastrous results.

11. Ibid.; see also Waltz, *Theory of International Politics*, 205; and Donnelly, "Morality and Foreign Policy," 166, who argues that realism takes "a valuable caution against moralistic excess" and inflates it "into an unsound general rule of statecraft."

12. Brilmayer, "Realism Revisited," 198.

13. Ibid., 204–5.

14. Indeed, it is often neoliberal analyses of international politics that emphasize the lack of enforcement power in the anarchic international system. See Kenneth A, Oye, ed., *Cooperation under Anarchy* (Princeton, N.J.: Princeton University Press, 1986); David A. Baldwin, ed., *Neorealism and Neoliberalism: The Contemporary Debate* (New York: Columbia University Press, 1993).

15. Note that the theory of structural realism uses three characteristics to define political structures: the ordering principle (anarchy or hierarchy), the differentiation of the units, and the distribution of capabilities across units. See Waltz, *Theory of International Politics*, 88–101. For a discussion of how anarchy impacts international politics, see ibid., 102–16.

16. On the security dilemma, see John Herz, "Idealist Internationalism and the Security Dilemma," *World Politics* 2:2 (January 1950): 157–80; and Robert Jervis, "Cooperation under the Security Dilemma," *World Politics* 30:3 (1978): 167–214.

17. As becomes clear below, this concern with peace and stability also features in neorealist analyses of nuclear weapons.

18. Bipolar international systems have two major powers; multipolar systems have three or more great powers. Unipolar systems with one great power are also possible.

19. Stability refers to the maintenance of the same polarity, while peacefulness refers to the (relative) lack of major power war. Waltz's arguments concerning the relation among stability, peace, and polarity can be found in Kenneth N. Waltz, "The Emerging Structure of International Politics," *International Security* 18:2 (Fall 1993): 44–79; *Theory of International Politics*; and "The Stability of a Bipolar World," *Daedalus* 93:3 (Summer 1964): 881–909. Other analysts have come to different conclusions about this relation. See, for example, Karl W. Deutsch and J. David Singer, "Multipolar Systems and International Stability," *World Politics* 16:3 (1964): 390–406.

20. Randall Schweller argues that structural realism has a "status-quo bias" that leads to misleading arguments about international politics, and Robert Cox has argued that it has taken an ideological form "abstracted from the real historical framework imposed by the Cold War" and imposed it on international relations past, present, and future. See Randall L. Schweller, "Neorealism's Status-Quo Bias: What Security Dilemma?" in *Realism: Restatements and Renewal*, ed. Benjamin Frankel (London: Frank Cass, 1996), 90–121; Robert W. Cox, "Social Forces, States and World Orders: Beyond International Relations Theory," in *Neorealism and Its Critics*, ed. Robert O. Keohane (New York: Columbia University Press, 1986), 204–54.

21. Thus, Morgenthau argues that the effect of nuclear disarmament "would be the limited and primitive character of war when it *begins*; armaments races would simply be postponed to the beginning of hostilities instead of preceding and culminating in it." Morgenthau, *Politics among Nations*, 412, emphasis added.

22. For useful discussions of the different perspectives, see Charles Glaser, "Why Do Strategists Disagree about the Requirements of Strategic Nuclear Deterrence?" in *Nuclear Arguments: Understanding the Strategic Nuclear Arms and Arms Control Debates*, ed. Lynn Eden and Steven E. Miller (Ithaca, N.Y.: Cornell University Press, 1989), 109–72; Charles L. Glaser, *Analyzing Strategic Nuclear Policy* (Princeton, N.J.: Princeton University Press, 1990); James Denardo, "A Primer on Cold War Nuclear Debate," in *The Amateur Strategist* (Cambridge: Cambridge University Press, 1995), 18–42; Steve Miller, ed., *Strategy and Nuclear Deterrence* (Princeton, N.J.: Princeton University Press, 1984); Robert Jervis, "What Deters? The Ability to Inflict Mass Destruction," in *American Defense Policy*, 5th ed., ed. John F. Reichart and Steven R. Strum (Baltimore, Md.: Johns Hopkins University Press, 1982), 161–70; Colin S. Gray, "What Deters? The Ability to Wage Nuclear War," in ibid., 171–87; Benjamin S. Lambeth, "What Deters? An Assessment of the Soviet View," in ibid., 188–98.

23. The costs or punishment that can be imposed by the victor on the vanquished are always a deterrent to war, but before nuclear weapons such punishment came only after victory on the battlefield had been achieved. With nuclear weapons, punishment becomes the first and only stage of war.

24. A more complete definition would also take into account the probability that the threat will be carried out and the probability that the aggression will succeed.

25. Note that the other characteristics of nuclear weapons also encourage deterrent strategies. The inability to defend against a nuclear attack, the irrelevance of relative force size, the speed with which nuclear weapons cause destruction, and the clarity of the costs inflicted by a nuclear attack all reinforce deterrence.

26. See, for example, Robert Jervis, *The Meaning of the Nuclear Revolution* (Ithaca, N.Y.: Cornell University Press 1989); Kenneth N. Waltz, "Nuclear Myths and Political Realities," *American Political Science Review* 84:3 (September 1990): 731–45.

27. Arms races are discouraged because only an absolute number of nuclear weapons are needed for an effective deterrent policy; relative force size does not matter, so one state's increase in the size of its forces does not decrease the effectiveness of other states' nuclear deterrent policies. Note that this logic holds only in a world without missile defense. In a world with missile defense, the size of a country's forces relative to its adversary's missile defense system does matter.

28. See, for example, Colin S. Gray, "Nuclear Strategy: The Case for a Theory of Victory," *International Security* 4:1 (Summer 1979): 54–87.

29. See Susan B. Martin, "The Role of Biological Weapons in International Politics: The Real Military Revolution," *Journal of Strategic Studies* 25:1 (March 2002): 63–98.

30. See Scott Sagan, Chapter 3 above, under "The Nonuse of Nuclear Weapons in the Gulf War." While the United States was well prepared to deal with Iraqi chemical weapons, it was not adequately prepared to deal with the Iraqi use of biological weapons. How exactly Iraq planned to use its biological weapons is not known. A CIA document on Iraq's BW program, posted on the GULFLINK website, states that "Baghdad would consider using biological weapons under certain extreme circumstances, probably as a retaliatory option for unconventional attack or as a weapon of last resort to save the regime from falling" and that "Baghdad is most likely to use biological weapons in a strategic role as a terror weapon against military and civilian targets. It is less likely [to use] biological weapons in tactical situations against opposing ground forces" at http://www.gulklink.osd.mil/declassdocs/cia/19960702/070296_cia_73883_73883_01.html (November 25, 2003). Scott Ritter suggests that Iraq acquired biological weapons for their deterrent capability, while UNSCOM reported to the Security Council that "Iraq's intentions with regard to the operational use of biological and chemical weapons have been subject to conflicting presentations by Iraqi authorities.... On the one side, it was explained that the biological and chemical weapons were seen by Iraq as a useful means to counter a numerically superior force; on the other hand, they were presented as a means of last resort for retaliation in case of a nuclear attack on Baghdad." Scott Ritter, *Endgame: Solving the Iraq Problem Once and for All* (New York: Simon and Schuster, 1999), 92; UN Security Council document S/1195/864, October 11, 1995, p. 28, at http://www.un.org/Depts/unscom/sres95-864.htm (June 21, 1999).

31. See my discussion of chemical weapons in Chapter 1 above.

32. Kenneth N. Waltz, "Waltz Responds to Sagan," in Scott D. Sagan and Kenneth N. Waltz, *The Spread of Nuclear Weapons: A Debate* (New York: W. W. Norton, 1995), 112.

33. John Ellis van Courtland Moon, "Chemical Weapons and Deterrence: The World War II Experience," *International Security* 8:4 (Spring 1984): 3–35.

34. See Kenneth N. Waltz, "More May Be Better," in Sagan and Waltz, *Spread of Nuclear Weapons*, 13.

35. See Scott D. Sagan, "More Will Be Worse," in ibid., 47–91.

36. On the Soviet biological weapons program, see Ken Alibek with Stephen Handelman, *Biohazard* (New York: Random House, 1999).

37. Alternative understandings of anarchy include Hedley Bull, *The Anarchical Society* (New York: Columbia University Press, 1977); Alexander Wendt, "Anarchy Is What States Make of It: The Social Construction of Power Politics," *International Organization* 46:2 (Spring 1992): 391–425. Feminist scholars have also challenged the realist understanding of anarchy; see, for example, V. Spike Peterson, "Rereading Public and Private: The Dichotomy That Is Not One," *SAIS Review* 20:2 (Summer/Fall 2000): 11–29. As noted above, Donnelly argues that while realism has valid concerns about the role of morality in international affairs, it takes those concerns too far. See Donnelly, "Morality and Foreign Policy," 166.

38. Michael Joseph Smith, *Realist Thought from Weber to Kissinger* (Baton Rouge: Louisiana State University Press, 1986), 232.

5

Natural Law and Weapons of Mass Destruction

C. A. J. Coady

The ethical tradition of natural law is often viewed rather narrowly as that part of Roman Catholic moral teaching not reliant on revelation. But this sort of proprietary identification casts too sectarian a light on its value.[1] I shall treat the tradition as a much broader church. It will thus encompass some theorists whose inclusion might surprise, but I do not propose a treatment that is so generous as to remove any sense that there is something distinctive covered by the heading "natural law." The recognition that natural law is, like all traditions, a family of theories, insights, and ideas need not drive us into thinking of it as too extended a family.[2] We should not, for instance, see it as equivalent to all theories that reject relativism, conventionalism, and positivism in law or ethics. These really have too little in common to form even a loose tradition.[3]

Perhaps the best way forward is to specify some traits that have been common to a number of theories historically associated with the idea that understanding morality is a matter of grasping something about the underlying rationality of the universe with respect to the place of human beings (or rational agents) in it. This "something" is discovered in reality rather than constructed by human will, but it reveals that the good for agents is a matter of acting well in accord with nature. In this sense, it reveals moral facts, but these are more like recipes for constructing a good life than an inventory of abstract states of affairs.

This idea can be seen at work in embryonic form in Aristotle, perhaps Plato, certainly the Stoics, Cicero, Aquinas, and various late medieval and early modern developers of his thought such as Vitoria and Suarez, then in Grotius, Hobbes, Locke, and various Thomists in the nineteenth and twentieth centuries, the most publicly accessible and influential of whom was probably Jacques Maritain.[4] Most recently, the tradition has included the nonholy trinity of John Finnis, Joseph Boyle, and Germain Grisez.[5] There are also some aspects of Chinese philosophical ethics that have similarities to natural law approaches.[6] All these thinkers have a very different approach to ethics than that characteristic of intuitionists or Kantians or utilitarians, though of course there are overlapping concerns and doctrines. There are also important, sometimes striking, differences within the tradition as I have described it. (Indeed, there are striking disagreements between exponents of the tradition even in the more restricted interpretation that connects it closely with Catholic teaching – a point noted by Boyle.[7]) My placing of Hobbes within it will dismay some, and he is, in several respects, an atypical natural law theorist, but the dismay seems to me largely a product of misunderstandings about his ethics. I say more on this below.

The traits I would invoke are the following:

1. An emphasis on the basic rationality of ethics.
2. An emphasis on the centrality of human nature to our grasp of morality.
3. A distinction between enacted ("positive") law and natural law (basic morality) that gives natural law a superior position but regards the positive law as ideally informed by morality.
4. A background theological perspective in which natural law is part of the divine reason that sustains the universe.

It will be seen from this list that the tradition regards morality as involving practical dictates and principles that are grounded in the kind of being who is to act. It thus involves a sort of fusion of the affective and the cognitive in that the flourishing of human beings is the background to moral endeavor. This is quite well captured in Aquinas's famous statement of the basis of natural law in the *Summa theologia*. Aquinas argues that just as being is the first thing that confronts the understanding broadly considered, so good is the first thing that falls under the apprehension of practical reason where an agent acts for an end under the aspect of good. The first principle of practical reason therefore is that good is universally desired, and hence "the first precept" of law is that good is to be pursued and done, and evil is to be avoided. Aquinas continues:

All other precepts of the natural law are based upon this, so that whatever the practical reason actually apprehends as man's good belongs to the precepts of the natural law as something to be done or avoided.

Since, however, good has the nature of an end, and evil the nature of a contrary, hence it is that all those things to which man has a natural inclination are naturally apprehended by reason as being good, and consequently as objects of pursuit, and their contraries as evil, and objects of avoidance. Therefore the order of the precepts of the natural law is according to the order of natural inclinations.[8]

There are several notable features of this account. One is that the beginnings of the story are at a high level of generality; the first principle of natural law is the abstract requirement that good is to be pursued and evil avoided. The further, more concrete precepts of the natural law are geared toward certain fundamental "inclinations" of human nature, and some of these we share with other orders of the world. Even here, the natural law operates at a fairly high level of generality. At one level, as Aquinas goes on to say, there is the norm of self-preservation (shared with all beings); at the next (shared with all animals) there is the good of sexual intercourse and the education of offspring. Then there are the goods proper to humans according their nature as rational beings, namely knowing the truth about God and the need to live in society. Specifically, this involves shunning ignorance and avoiding offense to those among whom one has to live and "other such things regarding the above inclination." It is worth noting how casual Aquinas is about spelling out the "dictates" of natural law. He seems to think the important thing is to give a general orientation from which people can derive their own specific injunctions by reasoning. This is a long way from some modern-day natural lawyers who think that quite specific and binding injunctions can be drawn from biological observations about the natural function of human organs, such as the sexual organs. Aquinas does have something to say about such matters as masturbation and homosexuality under the heading of "unnatural vices," but this is somewhat removed from the perspective of natural law.[9] It is also worth noting that Aquinas's approach to natural law is, in one important respect, pluralistic. This contrasts with Hobbes, for where Hobbes has only one basic precept of natural law, Aquinas lists several and treats the list as open-ended. Hobbes insists, with Aquinas, on the centrality of self-preservation, but where Aquinas goes on to list the further animal and rational goods, Hobbes tries to get everything out of the one imperative.[10]

The natural law tradition is universalistic, in the sense that it seeks to ground morality on features common to human nature, but this is not to deny that morality is also circumstantial in that its dictates must pay heed to context and empirical realities. This insight allows a role for local history, community tradition, and a variety of ways that human imagination may structure institutions to embody universal values. There is, therefore, room for the law of nations, local positive and customary law, as well as the morality that follows conventions of all sorts. But the universalism of the tradition does mean that there tends to be a certain cosmopolitan perspective hostile to narrow extremes of nationalist and communitarian moralities. It is not surprising that natural law theorists were founders of modern international law and that the thought of Jacques Maritain was influential in the thinking of many of those involved in drawing up the UN Charter. More recently, natural law thinkers such as John Finnis, Joseph Boyle, and Germain Grisez have been prominent opponents of nuclear deterrence, and Finnis has argued that the tradition should support further moves toward a form of world government.[11]

Before turning to problems for the natural law ethic, there is an important comparative point to be made about the relationships between natural law theories and other traditions. The emphasis on different traditions, the exploration of which is rightly encouraged by the Ethikon Institute, can have the undesirable side-effect of suggesting incompatibility where it need not exist. Some intellectuals, and some forms of inquiry, are so dominated by the quest for generality that they treat intellectual history as a form of warfare in which neatly distinguished schools or "-isms" contend for supremacy. There is no doubt some truth in this – there is plenty of combat in the world of the intellect – but the concentration on -isms and their representatives can make us see contrasts and exclusions in the wrong places. The field of international relations and international ethics is particularly prone to this temptation (or is it a disease?). Books and articles bristle with oppositions among liberal internationalism, realism, natural law, positivism, and so on. These oppositions certainly have some point, but they obscure many compatibilities and similarities, and they can make for lazy thinking. Consider the opposition between natural law and the social contract tradition loosely associated with liberalism. The fact is that it is perfectly possible to be committed to both natural law and social contract (and indeed, liberalism). Indeed, such commitment is not only possible in theory, but fairly common in reality.[12] Not only do Hobbes and Locke employ a social contract, but many of the Renaissance Thomists espoused something very close to social contract thinking. Admittedly, they could not consistently believe in natural law and hold that *all* morality was a matter of social agreement, but most social contract theorists don't believe this anyway. In the work of Suarez and Molina, in particular, it is clear that they envisage political rule as arising from the contrivance of human beings aware of the difficulties of living in a state of nature.[13] In the matter of liberalism more generally, there are many ways in which a natural law position could be developed that gives a pre-eminent moral role to freedom and a major place to political liberty. Locke is merely one thinker who combines natural law and liberalism. It is a peculiarity of some contemporary thought that it insists on landing liberalism with an underpinning of either moral skepticism or moral voluntarism.[14]

CRITICISMS OF NATURAL LAW

Critics of natural law raise numerous objections. We cannot canvass all of them, but the following are commonly urged. They concentrate on three features of the theory: nature, application, and nonpluralism.

The first is that the idea of human nature cannot play the central role assigned to it in the tradition. Contemporary thought is less enamored of essences and fixed natures than the classical and medieval world-views. Our picture of the world tends to be more dynamic and fluid than that which fostered the growth of natural law theory. In particular, human nature is more adaptable and plastic than the ancients ever imagined, and we are more conscious of our self-creative capacities than were our intellectual predecessors. Hence, the idea of human nature is a poor guide to the nature of morality.

The human and natural worlds are, no doubt, less dominated by essences and substantial forms than medieval thinkers supposed, but the objection needs to rely on more than this observation. Sometimes critics of the natural law tradition seem to deny that there is any such thing as "human nature" or any other sort of nature, but both biology and ecology refute this. Moreover, the modern conquest of nature does not provide a uniformly optimistic narrative. It is increasingly recognized that there are alarming drawbacks to the striving for transformation. There are many thinkers, not particularly linked to the natural law tradition, who would see the limitations imposed by nature as less dismissible and contingent than often imagined. Of course, these remarks merely gesture at a huge debate, and I would not want to provide unqualified support to any luddite revulsions from technology that have arisen as a reaction to dawning realization of the negative aspects of technological triumphalism.

Another criticism of the natural law tradition arises from the difficulty in moving from the general prescriptions of the theory (the level of what Aquinas calls "inclinations" or, as we might more perspicuously say in English, basic needs)[15] to the detailed answers to concrete moral problems. Call this "the application problem." The problem is Janus-faced. On the one hand, the theory tends to be either too mechanically precise, and its verdicts therefore unbelievable, or, on the other hand, it tends to be compatible with too many specific and conflicting conclusions, and therefore unhelpful. The former problem is illustrated by the invocation of natural law on behalf of various improbable conclusions in the area of sexual ethics.[16] The second problem is that once one returns to the moral theoretical high ground, the tradition seems to tell us only that our morality has to give a special priority to human nature and its basic needs. This leaves room for all sorts of conclusions in particular cases. It is, however, unclear that this is a serious objection to the theory. Something similar is also true of utilitarianism, Kantianism, and many other moral theories. Utility in different hands commands many different things, as the development of so many forms of utilitarianism attests. And Kant was sure that the categorical imperative directly forbade suicide, promise breaking, and lying in all circumstances, but few of his many followers think the same.[17] Indeed, this sort of uncertainty and contestability is arguably a condition that a moral theory should meet, given only that it orients our thinking in a distinctive fashion.

A final objection to the tradition concerns its apparent assumption that consideration of human nature will yield a unitary conception of the ends of life. Against this it is urged, most eloquently by Sir Isaiah Berlin, that human flourishing is essentially diverse and the ends of life potentially conflicting and disharmonious. Berlin sees his "value pluralism" as presenting a challenge to all (or most) traditional moral theories, and he also wants to distance it from any form of relativism and maintain support for the objectivity of moral thinking.[18]

There are problems in understanding this objection and evaluating its force. For one thing, if it cuts against all or most prior moral theories, then it is at least not a specific objection to natural law. For another, Berlin has difficulty mounting his case without falling into relativism; indeed, some of his supporters have cheerfully toppled into its dubious embrace. So John Gray has taken Berlin's pluralism in the direction of cultural relativism and Bernard Williams has ventured on the path of a complex subjectivism.[19] Given the difficulties of relativism, the pluralism objection will be less telling if it must cohabit with it. But even if an untainted version of pluralism can be plausibly sustained, it is at least unclear how much it would conflict with the natural law outlook. This is because the natural law tradition is capable of treating human nature more flexibly than the objection supposes. The idea that human flourishing may take many different forms is a harmless, indeed platitudinous, observation at some levels. It can hardly be imagined that Aristotle, Aquinas, or Locke would be disturbed by the idea that some find a fulfilling life in musical pursuits and others in farming, and that many farmers would find the concert life depressing and most musicians would be miserable on the farm. There are, no doubt, more challenging versions of pluralism, but the problem is that it tends to present as a mixed bag of the truistic and the highly contentious. Neither the practice of farming nor that of musicianship blatantly flies in the face of fundamental human goods, but the practice of the assassin, no matter how lucrative and enjoyable its practitioners find it, clearly does. We need more clarity about what pluralism is claiming, but at least it poses a question to natural law about how much diversity of human flourishing it can allow.

A final point about the scope of natural law concerns its capacity to handle issues having to do with the environment and nonhuman animals. Many contemporary theorists call for a new, nonhuman-centered ethic that will allow a value to the environment not dependent in any way on human needs. There is much that is challenging, and a good deal that is unclear about this demand. But at least it can be said that the natural law tradition can allow for the importance to fundamental human needs of harmony with nature. Indeed, it may be no part of human flourishing that human beings should adopt an attitude of dominance toward the rest of the world. Hubris is a human vice.

NATURAL LAW AND WARFARE

The tradition of natural law has had significant formative effects on the development of just war theory, as well as international law and more recently humanitarian law. Natural law theorists such as Vitoria, Suarez, and Grotius were founders of modern international law and were especially influential in the elaboration of just war theory as an ethical basis for the international law of warfare.[20] A typical approach to the linking of natural law with the ethical control of war can be seen from the following quotations from Suarez. In discussing wars of self-defense, he thinks it sufficient to claim that "the right of self-defense is natural and necessary."[21] In defense of a right to wage even aggressive war, he gives as the reason "that such a war is often necessary to a state, in order to ward off acts of injustice and hold enemies in check. Nor would it be possible, without these wars, for states to be maintained in peace. Hence this kind of warfare is allowed by natural law...."[22] The question of justifying aggressive war is, and remains, a difficult one, and the debate about it has recently received lively stimulus from the problem posed by armed humanitarian intervention. A lot turns, as Suarez realized, on the definitions of defense and aggression. But whether he is right or wrong is not my present concern. His discussion recalls the objection that appeals to natural law are too indeterminate to settle difficulties of this sort out of hand. But they may usefully point in the direction that further debate should proceed. In the present instance, this would lead to further questions about the nature and "necessity" of the state, the difficulties of determining and dealing violently with injustice outside one's own state borders, and the degree that this contributes to peace.[23]

In the matter of warfare, and more specifically the problems posed by what are called "weapons of mass destruction" (WMD), the natural law approach is to identify the rationally defensible good, if any, served by war and to advance further discussion in that light. This involves a concern for the morally legitimate grounds for going to war (commonly called the *jus ad bellum*, or JAB) and the moral constraints on how the war is fought (the *jus in bello*, or JIB). The latter is the primary focus for WMD, since, as we see below, they raise the issue of weaponry and legitimate targets in the context of justice. The most relevant principles of the JIB are the principles of discrimination and of proportionality.

Locke's discussion of the state of nature and his contrast of it with the state of war illustrates the relevance of natural law to issues of justice and war. Unlike Hobbes, Locke sees the state of nature as quite different from the state of war. The state of nature is basically peaceable under the laws of nature, though it suffers many inconveniences because of the lack of a "common superior" to decide disputes. The state of war, however, arises from the violent aggression of some against others and licenses violent response to the point of destruction of the attacker. This is related to the fact that anyone has the right to punish any offense against the law of nature in a state of nature.[24] But what is perfectly clear from Locke's discussion in those chapters and in the chapter on conquest is that there are moral limits to what can be done and to whom by the right of war. Locke's emphasis on the importance of defending the innocent and preserving innocent life is pronounced. It is perfectly clear that legitimate violence should be directed against perpetrators (whom he characterizes as "beasts of prey," like the lion or the wolf) and not those who have no part in the offense. So he says in chapter XV that a conqueror with a just cause "gets no power" over those among the enemy populace who are innocent of waging the war. As Locke puts it: "They ought not to be charged as guilty of the violence and injustice that is committed in an unjust war any farther than they actually abet it."[25] Locke is actually discussing the postwar entitlements of a conqueror rather than the limits on how he wages the war, but his comments apply naturally to the latter and are clearly in the tradition of just war thinking. This licenses violence only against those perpetrating the injustice that makes the war legitimate in the first place. Hence this is the point of the JIB principle of discrimination, which restricts our right to kill to those who are perpetrating the evil that legitimately calls forth the violent response. As Vitoria, in similar spirit to Locke, had earlier put it: "The foundation of the just war is the injury inflicted upon one by the enemy, as shown above; but an innocent person has done you no harm."[26]

The case is somewhat different with Hobbes. His construction of natural law on the very narrow basis of self-preservation alone, combined with his very restricted understanding of justice, lead to his breaking with the just war tradition. But contrary to popular belief, Hobbes is not an amoralist about war. Famously, he says: "Where there is no common power, there is no law: where no law, no injustice. Force and fraud, are in war the two cardinal virtues."[27] This attitude has helped to provide intellectual support for various forms of "realism" about international politics and war in particular. But Hobbes has his own pale version of the morality appropriate to war, as indeed do many contemporary realists, often in spite of their own professions to the contrary. He thinks that reason and natural law have their parts to play in answering questions about when to go to war and how to wage it. This is not the place to discuss the consistency or the detail of Hobbes's position; it suffices to note that he thinks that the sovereign should exercise care in any resort to war (especially with regard to the overriding value of peace and security) and that cruelty should be avoided and requirements of honor met.[28] This mirroring of just war theory is reductive: The fulsome shape of the JAB appears in the thin form of "providence" (or as we might say, prudent foresight), and the demanding conditions of the JIB reflect as the (largely unspecified) requirements of honor.

WEAPONS OF MASS DESTRUCTION

Since there is usually a tremendous amount of destruction in war, whatever weapons are used, it may seem that the concentration on specific weapons as "weapons of mass destruction" is peculiar. Is the machine gun a weapon of mass destruction since its use enabled the efficient and rapid killing and injuring of vastly more people than previous weapons? Is the airplane, especially the bomber? These are not normally viewed with the disapproval reserved to WMD. Why not? There seem to be two reasons. First, these weapons are not in themselves geared to the idea of mass destruction, though that has indeed proved to be a common employment. The machine gun could be used in certain circumstances simply to encompass the death of a small number of people more certainly than less rapid-firing weapons. Second, and more important, one crucial problem about WMD is not primarily that concerning the number but rather the type of people killed. One thing morally problematic about WMD is that they either inherently fail to discriminate between legitimate and nonlegitimate targets or are believed to have this defect. They are (or are believed to be) such that their normal use will rain death and destruction on the just and unjust, on civilians and troops, on hospitals and military installations alike. Nuclear weapons fit into this category, as do certain chemical and biological agents.

The point about employment serves to highlight both connections and disconnections between WMD and conventional weapons. Both types of weapon can be immoral in the same way, namely, by violating the principle of discrimination. The fire-bombing of Tokyo and the destruction of Dresden are good examples of conventional attacks that stand under similar moral condemnation as the use of nuclear weapons. Indeed, in their immediate effects, these were comparable to the nuclear bombings of Hiroshima and Nagasaki. Yet conventional bombing need not be as indiscriminate as this, whereas it seems inherent in the idea of a WMD that it is geared to violation of the principle of discrimination. Of course, there are rare circumstances in which a case can be made for the standard WMD being used ethically – a low radiation-yielding nuclear bomb against an armed enemy fleet in a remote ocean location or a poisonous chemical agent against an individual like Hitler who is in charge of waging an unjust war. It may even be that some weapons conventionally classed as WMD, though they can be used to violate the principle of discrimination, do not have an inherent tendency to do so. To this I return below.

Much anxiety is directed to the threat posed by access to chemical and biological weapons on the part of individuals and small groups, and certainly any such use, were it to be effective, would constitute a dangerous form of terrorism. Nonetheless, the fear of WMD terrorism can downplay the fact that the use of these weapons by nonstate actors has so far been very rare (and not very successful); by far the greatest damage done by way of mass destruction of civilian (and military) populations has been done by states. Witness the use of poison gas in World War I, the nuclear devastation of Hiroshima and Nagasaki by the United States, and the gassing of Iranians by Iraqi forces in the Iran-Iraq War. (It should be remarked that the Iraqi weapons of mass destruction are estimated to have killed only 6,000 as against the U.S. slaughter of around 200,000, mostly Japanese civilians, in the atomic raids of World War II.) Moreover, conventional weapons – bombs, rockets, and mines – have been used by powerful states in precisely the way that WMD operate, namely, to kill and maim large numbers of civilians.

It is true that states are not entirely excluded from the discussion, since there is a deal of anxiety about WMD proliferation. But this anxiety is principally directed to so-called rogue states that have not yet been accepted into the club of the righteous mass destroyers. Many of the "rogue" states are indeed dictatorial and oppressive, yet Western powers have supported them politically and supplied them with arms and armament technology in the past (witness Iraq and Pakistan) and have devoutly supported or ignored the nuclear arming of Israel. Furthermore, by a number of criteria, there is much that is "roguish" about the behavior of the major Western states. If ethics is our concern, then this partiality about illegitimate use of weapons needs to be dispelled.

Of course, it has been argued that the "taboo" against chemical weapons, in particular, has a large element of irrationality in it since some chemical weapons need not be indiscriminate and are less devastating in their effect than many conventional weapons. It is true that the use of poison gas in World War I was heavily concentrated on attacking troops, not civilians, and that various proposals to use gas against civilian populations came to nothing. Even so, it is estimated that at least 5,000 civilians suffered from the effects of the military use of poison gas and over a hundred were killed.[29] This "inevitable spillover" (as one authority called it) may nevertheless be within the limits of unintended "collateral damage" given the massive damage to troops that was its primary objective.[30]

I do not intend adjudicating here on the claim that some common candidates for WMD status do not violate the discrimination principle. But the possibility that this is so leads to other reasons for concern with WMD. One of these harks back to Hobbes's prohibition on unnecessary cruelty. There is the idea that some weapons are morally obnoxious whether they violate discrimination or not. This certainly responds to reactions that people have often had to the development of new weapons, especially where they involve any element of dramatic suffering. But it may be responded that this "gut feeling" is misleading and even sentimental. Most deaths and injuries in war are ghastly and involve cruel suffering, even when they are inflicted "conventionally," for example, by rifle, bayonet, mortar, cannon, or bomb. It may be replied that such weapons are not intended to create extreme suffering, though that is sometimes their effect, but even if this is so, it seems less adequate as a response to the use of napalm and flame-throwers.

One thing the issue of cruelty opens up is the relevance of another condition of the just war tradition concerning the JIB, and that is proportionality. Whether some weapon is cruel depends partly on whether its use is really necessary to achieve an objective not out of kilter with the suffering caused.

On behalf of flame-throwers, for instance, it might be argued that they *can* be used legitimately when enemy troops cannot be removed in other ways from bunkers, caves, or dugouts without great loss of life to one's own troops or without damaging delay to other significant strategic objectives. This is on the assumption that there are serious military reasons for removing them. In other circumstances, their use, even against combatants, is immoral because it is disproportionate.[31]

The idea of proportionality comes into play not only in explication of cruelty but with regard to mass destruction itself. I argued that a primary issue in concern for WMD was their propensity to kill the wrong people rather than their tendency to kill large numbers. But it remains true that weapons whose purpose, or most likely use, is to kill very large numbers of people immediately raise an issue of proportionality, even if the people killed are otherwise legitimate targets. Most of the killing in World War I was that of soldiers in battle, so noncombatant immunity was mostly not an issue; nonetheless, the sheer numbers killed posed an acute problem, fully appreciated only after the war, because it raised the question of whether the war goals, and the means of pursuing them, could possibly justify such losses. It also pointed to the often neglected issue of the consequences for the civilian population and the future of the warring societies of such loss of life. If there were weapons (such as nuclear or certain biological weapons) that guaranteed such outcomes, even when used solely against armies, this would challenge their use.

There is an important issue involving both discrimination and proportionality that is pretty much neglected in the just war tradition, though I think the tradition has the resources to deal with it. This is the matter of war and the environment. If one thinks that morality requires a concern for the natural environment and for at least some animal life that is independent of other human interests, then one will regard environmental destruction by bombing or poisoning as raising an acute moral issue of wrongful targeting. But even if one's valuation of the environment is more instrumentally concerned with human welfare, a powerful case can be made against the various forms of devastation that much modern weaponry visits on the natural world. The consequences of such destruction for future human beings, in no sense guilty of the wrongs that licensed the war in the first place, are often horrendous in terms of death, maiming, nutrition, disease, and life-style.

DETERRENCE

Then there is the question of deterrence. Here the issue for WMD generally is mostly a generalization of the debate about nuclear deterrence. There is first the complex factual question about the effectiveness of such weapons as deterrents. This is a much muddier issue than often supposed since the possession of WMD sometimes seems to inhibit attack and sometimes doesn't.

Indeed, sometimes it can increase the tensions and misunderstandings that all too often lead to war. As to the ethical questions around deterrence, the nuclear debate has familiarized us with a nest of problems here. Some of these concern the *consequences* of such policies and include the massive dangers of deterrence failure as well as the dangers of escalation from conventional to nuclear war that are inherent in the possession of nuclear weapons. The natural law tradition is concerned with these, as indeed are most moral traditions, since prudence is a central virtue, and a proper concern for consequences should be a part of any moral outlook. The flaw in utilitarianism, and other forms of consequentialism, is not that they worry about consequences, but that they worry about nothing else.

Aside from consequences, however, there are two other sources of concern about deterrence that arise from its very nature. The first is a matter of the relation between the outcome of the deterrence and the attitude that is required to sustain it. I will be brief about this because I have written extensively about it elsewhere.[32] The nuclear deterrent has been sustained by a (conditional) determination to violate massively the principle of discrimination. This staunch intention is shared by Western and non-Western powers. It is a profoundly immoral commitment that has, I believe, had a corrupting effect on political life in the last fifty-odd years. The immorality of the nuclear threat is sometimes concealed by the idea that it is all somehow a bluff (at least by "us") so that there is really no intention to use the weapons, but, with Henry Shue in Chapter 7 below, I consider this a self-comforting delusion.

The second consists in the fact that deterrence is a strategy of fear creation. Sometimes, of course, one needs to arouse fear for purposes of protection against those bent on damage, but, as pacifists rightly point out, the generation of fear is a profoundly ambiguous exercise. This is so for several reasons. One is that the purposes for which the fear is created are inherently open to different interpretations; the deterrer is given to thinking that his purposes are benign, but it would be naive to think that this is how others must interpret his threats and armed displays. The more powerful, and the more indiscriminate, the displays and threats, the more likely their targets are to think them aggressive rather than defensive and to take steps to protect themselves. This is one of the causes of escalation (and proliferation), but even if the targets do not respond in kind, the deterrent stance, especially when it becomes permanent posture, tends to have a poisonous effect on political relations. The deterrer finds increasing dangers abroad that require the expansion of military might and the strengthening of an overkill deterrent capacity. Fear itself fuels the creation of further fear. An international order of fear inherits all the problems of a domestic government of fear. In particular, the climate of dominating fear is not a long-term recipe for the creation of genuine peace. For peace is more than mere stability if less than divine harmony. It requires a certain level of amicable dispositions that are dissipated by an atmosphere of fear. Peace is an ideal that has always played a role in just war thinking, though its significance has sometimes been submerged by the more legalistic conditions, and sometimes bellicose subject matter, of the tradition. Not only is peace broadly preferable to war (so that war must be a "last resort," as one of the conditions of the JAB puts it), but the point of waging a just war, as Augustine insisted, is to establish peace.[33]

PROLIFERATION

Opposition to proliferation of WMD has an air of paradox about it because those most concerned to denounce the prospect of the spread of ownership of these weapons are often those who already have them in some form and are prepared to use them in extremis. The paradox arises from the fact that if there are good arguments for the United States, for instance, to have nuclear weapons for deterrence or even use, then why aren't these also good arguments for any nation with defense needs? If nuclear deterrence was so good for world stability, then why shouldn't its benefits be spread around, as the neo-realist Kenneth Waltz once notoriously argued?[34]

The paradox can be resolved by pointing out that "we" are somehow special, either because we are specially imperiled or exceptionally good. The former is hardly plausible since many states can persuasively argue that they face more serious dangers from other states than either the United States or Russia does (whatever problems they have with terrorism). As for the latter, our conviction that we are "holier than they" is likely to be viewed differently by them. Indeed, in the case of the United States the argument is particularly hard to run, since it is one of the few nations that have actually used WMD to devastating effect. Many Americans are so convinced of their nation's unique moral status that they find the failure of the rest of the world to accord it moral superiority baffling. This was the burden of many comments by the U.S. leadership in the wake of the dreadful terrorist attacks of September 11, 2001. President Bush expressed amazement at the misunderstanding that led to people hating America: "Like most Americans," he said, "I just can't believe it because I know how good we are."[35] This was reflected in much of the quasi-religious political rhetoric evoked in Washington by the attack: "good versus evil," "coalitions of the good," "crusade," "operation infinite justice," and so on. Those beyond American shores (and many within) are right to view this picture with incredulity, since good and evil, and much in between, are more evenly distributed among people and nations than this rhetoric suggests.

Pointing this out is liable to provoke the accusation that one is committed to the dreaded "moral equality" thesis whereby all states must be treated as equally good. But this is a red herring. The point is not that all nations weigh equally in the moral scales, but that none is immune from moral and intellectual faults. One of the good things stressed by realist thinkers is precisely that moralistic stances in foreign affairs are invariably directed outward and often blind nations to their own sins. In the context of proliferation, this makes the provision of moral and legal exemptions to oneself an impediment to dealing with it.

But in spite of this, WMD proliferation is a bad thing. The more states that engage in the deterrent game with these weapons, the more the risks that they will be used with consequences that are likely to be not only immoral but disastrously so. No doubt the existing WMD states are in bad faith denouncing proliferation while keeping many of their WMD, but this does not mean that the spread of such weapons and deterrent strategies is thereby made more acceptable. In some ways, the problem is like that of global pollution. The wealthy polluters are in no position to point the finger at the poorer countries that increase pollution as they drive toward development, but increased pollution is still a bad idea. In the case of proliferation a serious contribution to stemming it would be for the existing WMD powers to abandon these weapons. To their credit, some steps along this path have been taken, as indicated in Chapter 2 of this volume. This brings us to the topic of disarmament.

DISARMAMENT

On my interpretation of natural law and the just war tradition, the right to war represents a certain concession to the vagaries of the human condition and the uncertainties of the international order. The tradition emphasizes the priority of peace and places strong restrictions on resort to war. Hence, it favors efforts to remove the likelihood of war, and where disarmament measures help that removal, they should be supported. It seems very plausible that universal WMD disarmament and renunciation fit this bill. World opinion has been behind this for some time, as evidenced by the various treaties discussed in Chapter 2.

One intellectual obstacle to this development is the possibility that some weapons usually classed as WMD need not violate nor inherently tend to violate the JIB. A reasonable response to this worry is to insist that it makes more prudential sense to ban classes of weapon than to pick and choose among them. There is a familiar insight here that lies behind many legal prohibitions (and indeed provides much of the impulse toward such moral theories as rule-utilitarianism). So, in Australia, when there are heat waves, authorities will often declare "a day of total fire-ban" prohibiting the lighting of any fires in the open. This applies to every class of person and to every fire, even though very experienced country folk may be perfectly capable of keeping a small fire under control. The danger of allowing exemptions is too great. Similarly with the WMD ban; given the awful prospects of many of these weapons for violating discrimination and fueling further technological development in the same direction, it makes sense to put a stop to the whole class, even if some claims to membership are more a matter of appearance than reality. This is especially so when there exists already a degree of international respect for such a ban and where we may anticipate reasonable prospects of enforcing it.

Another objection to WMD disarmament is that it may distract attention from the need for more general disarmament, just as a concern for the horror of WMD damage may obscure the horrible effects of conventional war. This point is characteristically made by pacifists and is urged by Robert Holmes in Chapter 23 below. I am sympathetic to the concern, but the risk is surely worth taking. Moreover, there is the contrary prospect that reduction in WMD armaments will produce a momentum in favor of more general disarmament proposals and antiwar attitudes. There is a tendency in pacifist thinking to all-or-nothing solutions, but incremental measures are often more realistic and may encourage a developing pace in disarmament.

Similar considerations apply to the stark opposition between proponents of multilateral and unilateral disarmament. The debate is largely a product of the cold war and reflects some of the gross simplifications of that conflict. The options are not really between the totally multinational or totally unilateral but between judicious resorts to various combinations of both. Some unilateral measures can safely be adopted that may prompt more multilateral ones, and agreements between some powers can precede general acceptance by all nations. Similar points could be made about inspection regimes. No agreement will be perfect, but this should not impede commitment to steps along the road to a more peaceful world.

CONCRETE ACTION

A major problem with disarmament measures is the disproportion of military and political power in the international order. It is not surprising that weak, unstable states that have, or think they have, good reason to fear their neighbors or remote but influential powers are anxious to obtain or keep weapons that are thought to give them some kind of military leverage. This is one of the things that fuels proliferation. Another is the status symbol effect of possessing what are regarded as superweapons. Add to these the unwillingness of the powerful states to abandon nuclear weapons and to drag their heels over chemical and biological weapons, and you have a potent recipe for deadlock.

Against this background, there are two scenarios that need to be considered for future action on WMD. The first is one that was discussed at the workshop from which this book has emerged, was supported by several participants, and is gaining favor in many quarters in the West. This is basically the strategy of reviving imperialism or, as some put it, *pax Americana.* The idea is that the United States (with or without its allies) should more overtly embrace a hegemonic role in the world and should use military might to invade "rogue states" and either replace them with client regimes or run them as colonies. A scenario of this sort has emerged at the top levels of U.S. policy formation in the wake of the terrorist attacks on the World Trade Center and the Pentagon and the counterattack on Afghanistan. It is the governing motif of the attack on Iraq and has been made explicit with the espousal of the policy of "regime change."

This strategy is likely to compound the international imbalance that feeds the drive to procure and keep WMD and may well trigger more international terrorist attacks (with or without WMD). The reactions to such U.S. domination by the powers that lie outside the new Raj (such as Russia, China, and India) are not pleasant to contemplate. The strategy is also likely to inherit all the follies and crimes that went with old-fashioned imperialism. The fact that U.S. meddling in the affairs of Central and South America through the twentieth century was almost uniformly disastrous for the peoples and politics of those regions should give grounds for suspicion of the new strategy. Nor is one's confidence in any such policy increased by the absurd perceptions (mentioned earlier) that American political leaders entertain of themselves and their state as paragons of goodness. Reprising some version of Kipling's "white man's burden" is hardly an appetizing prospect for the new century:

> Take up the White Man's burden –
> Send forth the best ye breed –
> Go, bind your sons to exile
> To serve your captives' need;
> To wait in heavy harness
> On fluttered folk and wild –
> Your new-caught, sullen peoples,
> Half-devil and half-child.
> (Rudyard Kipling, "The White Man's Burden")

The second scenario is the internationalist one aimed at cooperation and at resort to law rather than mayhem. There is certainly a leadership role here for the United States, but it is one of moral and political initiative rather than crushing power. Here the one superpower has an ambiguous record. On the positive side, the U.S. government or its citizens have often sponsored moves aimed at gaining international cooperation via legal instruments to achieve a more secure, peaceful, and fair international order. But, on the negative side, the U.S. government has then often failed to ratify or to endorse the collaborative outcomes of these initiatives. The record of successive U.S. governments on the ratification of international treaties and conventions is simply wretched. The United States remains one of only two states to refuse ratification of the Convention on the Rights of the Child (the other is Somalia, which basically doesn't have a government). Although it ratified the Biological Weapons Convention of 1972, it has rejected the International Criminal Court, the establishment of which it originally supported and which could be a significant factor in dealing with terrorists and perpetrators of atrocities in war. It has also refused to ratify the Comprehensive Test Ban Treaty. There are indeed flaws in all of these and in the many others that the United States has rejected, but all efforts at international cooperation involve compromise, and the official American position too often amounts to the demand for cooperation on only American terms. The criminal court rejection, for example, is based on the idea that the court should have jurisdiction over other nationalities, but it is unacceptable for the court to have jurisdiction over Americans. As one senior U.S. army official explained to me: "We're the good guys!" This rejection of universality is perverse to the point of arrogance.

There is no certainty that the second scenario will be successful in reducing or eliminating the dependency on WMD, but, for the most part, we do not live in a world of certainties. It is probable that the cooperative path is one that offers more hope for the future, since it is all too likely that the domination scenario will create such animosities, fears, and countermeasures as are likely to negate its short-term achievements. This is not to deny that U.S. military power may on occasion be appropriate in dealing with the problem of WMD. Rather, it is to emphasize the primacy of the second scenario and to locate such uses within that framework.

CONCLUSION

Unlike the religious traditions discussed in this book, the natural law tradition is primarily philosophical. Religious traditions impinge directly on human practice, though often ambiguously, but it is commonly thought that abstract philosophical moral theories have no impact on people's behavior and indeed that this is particularly true of the international order. These claims are presented as empirical observations, but they are often the product of philosophical theory, notably that of realism (see Chapters 3 and 4 above). Realists have a split mind on ethics. On the one hand, they often claim that morality and moral theory have no influence on international politics, which is dominated by power and national interest, and on the other they worry that moral thinking has an undue influence on international relations, since it should be governed by considerations of national interest alone. Leaving realist confusions aside, the plain fact is that philosophical theorizing about morality has always had profound, though complex, effects on human practice. Sometimes these effects are direct, as when utilitarian philosophers had a role in shaping legal changes in nineteenth-century

Britain and India.[36] More often they are indirect, as when people base their behavior on outlooks that embody philosophical theories they may never have heard of. Much popular debate about the alleged distinctiveness of "Asian values," for instance, relies implicitly on the philosophical theory of cultural relativism.

Of course, moral edicts, whatever their source, cannot guarantee obedience, but they form part of the complex mix of reason and passion that guide human behavior. They have been factors in the largely successful battle against slavery, the partly successful emancipation of women, and the struggle against racism, not to mention the framing of democratic constitutions. In the case of natural law, the tradition has been influential on Christian attitudes to war (see Chapter 9), on the development of international law and human rights law, and, increasingly in our day, via just war theory, on Western military codes. Much of this influence is ambiguous in various ways, but its significance is undeniable. In the matter of WMD, this ancient tradition still speaks to our present anxieties.

Notes

1. This identification is even to be found in so thoughtful a representative of the tradition (and of Catholic moral thinking) as Joseph Boyle. Boyle construes the most representative figures of the tradition as comprising "scholastic moral philosophers and theologians, particularly within Catholicism since the time of Aquinas," and he emphasizes a close connection between "Catholic moral and social teaching and the natural law tradition." But this emphasis is both too exclusive and too inclusive. It is too exclusive because the ancient pagan Stoics and Cicero deserve inclusion, as does the Protestant Hugo Grotius, the Anglican Richard Hooker, the heterodox Thomas Hobbes, and the enlightened John Locke. It is too inclusive because there are major figures who have contributed to the formation of Catholic moral teaching who are outside the natural law tradition, most notably St. Augustine and his followers. See Joseph Boyle, "Natural Law and International Ethics," in *Traditions of International Ethics*, ed. Terry Nardin and David Mapel (Cambridge: Cambridge University Press, 1991), 112.

2. Distaste for this is partly what moves Boyle to his more restricted view of the tradition.

3. But Boyle surely thinks too tightly of tradition when he speaks of the need for "a shared intellectual tradition" to have "a common commitment to a set of moral and political views and to a set of analytical strategies." Boyle, "Natural Law and International Ethics," 112.

4. Jacques Maritain, *The Rights of Man and Natural Law*, trans. D. C. Anson (New York: Gordian Press, 1971).

5. John Finnis, Joseph M. Boyle, Jr., and Germain Grisez, *Nuclear Deterrence, Morality and Realism* (Oxford: Clarendon; New York: Oxford University Press, 1987).

6. *Mencius* (Shandong: Shandong Youyi Press, 1993), 3.6, p. 130.

7. Boyle, "Natural Law and International Ethics," 115.

8. Thomas Aquinas, *Summa theologica*, IIa, IIae, q. 94, a. 2, ed. and trans. Fathers of the English Dominican Province (New York: Benziger Brothers, 1947), 1009–10.

9. Thomas Aquinas, *Summa theologiae*, IIa, IIae, q. 154, a. 11, ed. and trans. Thomas Gilby (Cambridge: Blackfiars, 1967), vol. 43, pp. 243–47. The reference to the "unnatural" simply picks up a traditional categorization of these supposed vices, and not a particularly clear one. Aquinas makes no serious recourse to the governing ideas of natural law in his discussion of these vices. This is just as well, since it is an outcome of his discussion that masturbation is a more serious sin than incest or rape!

10. Thomas Hobbes, *Leviathan*, ed. E. Curley (Indianapolis: Hackett, 1994), chap. 14, sec. 1 p. 79.

11. See John Finnis, "The Ethics of War and Peace in the Catholic Natural Law Tradition," in *The Ethics of War and Peace: Religious and Secular Perspectives*, ed. Terry Nardin (Princeton, N.J.: Princeton University Press, 1996), 21–24. For the joint critique of nuclear deterrence, see Finnis et al., *Nuclear Deterrence, Morality and Realism.*

12. Similar things could be said about the likely compatibility of natural law and virtue ethics, though we do not have the space to explore this here. Suffice to note that significant figures in the natural law tradition, such as Aquinas and Aristotle, gave a central place to the virtues in their ethical theory.

13. See Quentin Skinner, *The Foundations of Modern Political Thought* (Cambridge: Cambridge University Press, 1978), vol. 2, chap. 5, esp. pp. 153–66.

14. That this insistence was also a feature of the opposition of the modern papacy to liberalism, encapsulated in an extreme form in the acerbic oddities of Pius IX's "Syllabus of Errors," compounds the confusion.

15. For the needs emphasis, see David Wiggins, *Needs, Values, Truth: Essays in the Philosophy of David Wiggins*, Aristotelian Society Series, vol. 6 (Oxford: Blackwell, 1987), 14–16; and Peter Geach, *The Virtues* (Cambridge: Cambridge University Press, 1977), chap. 1, pp. 1–19.

16. So we find several "natural law" arguments against contraception propounded by Catholic conservative thinkers that are drawn from the alleged natural purposes of the sexual organs or of sexuality more broadly understood. This is not the place to review these arguments, but I believe they fail largely because of their narrow, biological focus. Important as procreation is as a human good, it has to be seen in the light of broad human realities and needs. For an influential version of this line of argument, see "Humanae vitae," in *The Papal Encyclicals*, comp. Claudia Carlen (Ann Arbor: Pierian, 1990), 5, no. 277: 223–36.

17. Immanuel Kant, *Metaphysical Foundations of Morals*, in *The Philosophy of Kant: Immanuel Kant's Moral and Political Writings*, ed. C. J. Friedrich (New York: Modern Library, 1949), 168–87.

18. Isaiah Berlin, "The Pursuit of the Ideal," in *The Proper Study of Mankind: An Anthology of Essays*, ed. H. Hardy and R. Hausheer (London: Chatto and Windus, 1997), 9–16.

19. John Gray, *Isaiah Berlin* (London: Harper Collins, 1995); and Bernard Williams, *Ethics and the Limits of Philosophy* (London: Fontana, 1985).

20. Francisco de Vitoria, *Political Writings*, ed. A. Pagden and J. Lawrance, Cambridge Texts in the History of Political Thought, series ed. R. Guess and Q. Skinner (Cambridge: Cambridge University Press, 1991); Francisco Suarez, S.J., *Selections from Three Works of Francisco Suarez, S.J.*, trans. G. L. Williams, A. Brown, and J. Waldron, vol. 2 of the Classics of International Law, series ed. J. B. Scott (Oxford: Clarendon; London: Humphrey Milford, 1944); Hugo Grotius, *De jure belli ac pacis libri tres (On the Law of War and Peace)*, vol. 2, trans. F. W. Kelsey (Oxford: Clarendon; London: Humphrey Milford, 1925).

21. Suarez, *Selections from Three Works*, 802.

22. Ibid., 803.

23. This also indicates that the oppositions among pacifism, just war thinking, and realism are not as stark as usually supposed. For a good discussion of points of connection between these, see A. J. Coates, *The Ethics of War* (New York: Manchester University Press, 1997).

24. John Locke, *Two Treatises of Government*, ed. P. Laslett (New York: Mentor, 1960), treatise 2, chap. 3, sec. 16, p. 319.

25. Locke, *Two Treatises*, 435.

26. Vitoria, *Political Writings*, 314–15. This emphasis is very strong in the major just war theorists, but it is easy to lose sight of it when they are discussing international law. Grotius, for instance, lists various awful things, including killing the innocent, that are done by "right of war" when they can be done "with impunity." But later he "retraces" his steps to make it clear that most of these are unjust according to reason and natural law.

27. Hobbes, *Leviathan*, 78.

28. Thomas Hobbes, *The Elements of Law: Natural and Politic*, 2nd ed., ed. Ferdinand Tonnies (London: Cass, 1984), pt. 1, chap. 19, sec. 2, p. 101. As Hobbes puts it: "Though there be in war no law, the breach whereof is injury, yet there are those laws, the breach whereof is dishonour. In one word, therefore, the only law of actions in war is honour; and the right of war providence."

29. Richard M. Price, *The Chemical Weapons Taboo* (Ithaca, N.Y.: Cornell University Press), 62.

30. Ibid.

31. This is not the place to explore the many complexities in the idea of proportionality employed in just war theory. For the points made here we must rely on the evident intuitive sense that it makes.

32. See, especially, C. A. J. Coady, "Escaping from the Bomb," in *Nuclear Deterrence and Moral Restraint*, ed. Henry Shue (Cambridge: Cambridge University Press, 1989); and "Deterrent Intentions Revisited," *Ethics* 99 (October 1988): 98–108.

33. On Augustine's account of peace, see C. A. J. Coady and Jeff Ross, "St. Augustine and the Ideal of Peace," *American Catholic Philosophical Quarterly*, special issue on the Philosophy of St. Augustine, 74:1 (2000): 153–61.

34. See, for example, Kenneth Waltz, "More May Be Better," in Scott D. Sagan and Kenneth N. Waltz, *The Spread of Nuclear Weapons: A Debate* (New York and London: W. W. Norton, 1995); and "Nuclear Myths and Political Realities," in *The Use of*

Force: Military Power and International Politics, ed. Robert J. Art and Kenneth N. Waltz (Lanham, Md.: University Press of America, 1993).

35. *The Weekend Australian,* October 12–13, 2001.
36. For the influence of Bentham and the two Mills, especially James, on the law and administrative policy of British India, see Eric Stokes, *The English Utilitarians and India* (Oxford: Clarendon, 1959).

6

War and Indeterminacy in Natural Law Thinking

John Langan, S.J.

The preceding chapter by C. A. J. Coady is instructive on a variety of intellectual issues and impressive in its readiness to present moral conclusions that make serious demands on contemporary Western societies and their political leaders. In what follows, I do not attempt a detailed criticism of his paper, in which I find little to disagree with. In particular, I welcome his presentation of natural law in a way that acknowledges its significant departures from a deductive model of ethical reasoning (despite the deductivist language that Aquinas employs in a number of key places).[1] Rather, I want to focus on making two points, one about natural law and one about warfare; these points will, I think, give us an alternative reading of the place of natural law arguments and a different approach to making moral judgments about weapons of mass destruction. The points turn on the large element of indeterminacy in natural law arguments.

The first point is about natural law. We need to direct our attention to something that is not well articulated in Aquinas's account of natural law and that actually seems to be repudiated in Hobbes's approach to natural law. This is the role of institutions in specifying the application of moral principles and in providing us with a reasonable expectation that actions taken in accordance with these moral principles will be broadly intelligible within a culture and will enable us to appraise agents in ways that converge toward an agreement of judgments.[2] In the famous passage from the *Summa theologiae*, I–II, 94, 2, which Coady cites at some length, there is a persistent and significant gap between the natural inclinations that Thomas classifies on three levels and that he correlates with different types of goods and the actions with respect to those inclinations that he is prepared to endorse or condemn.

For example, how does one go from a natural inclination to the sexual union of male and female to the condemnation of various forms of sexual activity not falling within the scope of monogamous marriage? When Thomas, for instance, refers to a natural inclination to sexual intercourse between male and female, it is plausible to think that this excludes homosexuality and masturbation as well as bestiality (if we add a species restriction). Taken by itself, the natural inclination would not seem to offer much guidance on the morality of divorce or on choices between monogamy and polygamy, or between marital intercourse and adultery, since in all of these the natural inclination to heterosexual intercourse can be satisfied. To reach his conclusions on these matters, views that are common in medieval and modern Christianity, Aquinas has to rely on further considerations about the good of the offspring of sexual union. The affirmation of the natural inclination does, however, seem to provide a basis for rejecting celibacy, which was a constitutive element in a religious way of life that was highly esteemed in thirteenth-century Europe and was chosen by Thomas himself. Of course, one can argue that the fact or the reality of the natural inclination (in this case, the inclination to sexual intercourse between male and female) does not establish a moral obligation to act according to that inclination. One can argue for a looser sort of connection, for example, an obligation not to act or choose against the good that corresponds to the natural inclination. This is the preferred line for Germain Grisez, John Finnis, and their followers.[3] Aquinas himself takes the line of arguing that the obligation corresponding to the natural inclination falls on the community (*multitudo*) and not on the individual.[4] But the essential point is that I would insist on is that the existence of the natural inclination is not by itself sufficient to establish specific moral obligations holding across cultural and institutional contexts.

My own view is that the argument for such obligations requires reference to one or more social institutions that will specify our roles and responsibilities with regard to the natural inclination and its corresponding good. With regard to the natural inclination to sexual union, the central institution would be marriage as conceived in the Western Christian tradition and given legal recognition in most European societies. Aquinas does not argue for this so much as he assumes it while he goes on to offer more specific moral conclusions. The institution of marriage was not particularly controversial in Aquinas's time, and he may well not have felt that it stood in need of detailed justification or evaluation. His system certainly allows for lines of argument that would attempt to justify the institution on the basis of the natural inclination and the corresponding good. But, unlike most social philosophers since Hobbes, he is not ready to explore a systematically critical or constructivist view of social institutions on the basis of which he could affirm the way in which social institutions shape our movement from intending the good to choosing among the available actions having the potential to realize that good. Nor does he explore the possibility that there are serious moral objections to the dominant pattern of social institutions and to the expectations they generate.

An interesting example of the way in which he excludes this set of possibilities is his treatment of the report deriving from Julius Caesar that the Germans did not consider theft to be wrong.[5] This he presents as the Germans' failure to recognize a moral obligation, and he traces it to previous moral failures on their part; he does not examine the possibility that they might have had a different institution of property than the one recognized by the Romans and taken into the Western legal tradition.

One way, however, of defending Thomas's critical remarks about the Germans is close to the surface of what he says and is of continuing relevance. It is to argue that the institutions governing property, sexual activity, and social life are not to be accepted as givens but are to be criticized in the light of whether they respect or protect the basic goods that correspond to the natural inclinations. Thus, one can argue on natural law grounds against penal policies denying conjugal visits to prisoners and against restrictions on free inquiry impeding our natural inclination to learn the truth about God. Such laws and regulations prevent the fulfillment of natural inclinations. It is obvious, however, that both for Thomas and for those who work within the natural law tradition, creating impediments between a natural inclination and its fulfillment does not conclusively establish the wrongness of an act; otherwise, such institutions as capital punishment and rationing of health care would be ruled out a priori.

According a significant place to the assessment of institutions and their role in making moral principles more determinate will, of course, complicate natural law arguments. But this may not be a bad thing, since the neglect of such considerations has produced serious embarrassments for the natural law tradition. Thus, the failure of many natural law thinkers to cast a critical eye on the institution of slavery is an embarrassment to any contemporary effort to commend the natural law tradition as well as the Catholic moral tradition with which it is so tightly intertwined.[6] Acknowledging the place of social institutions and their normative implications would give a historicizing cast to natural law thinking. It would in many cases bring the tradition closer to the actual practice of those natural law thinkers who were intent on resolving particular cases and who, in doing so, had to accept the limitations and opportunities that the consideration of particulars brings with it.[7]

But you may wonder what all this talk of institutions, particularly such fundamental institutions as marriage and the family, the state and the military, the legal system and the complex of practices that constitute the concept of property and the basis of economic life, has to do with weapons of mass destruction. Here we need to remember two points: one systematic and one historical. The systematic point is that the natural law argument about the morality of war does not proceed simply from an affirmation of the good of life and continued existence to the establishment of a norm forbidding actions that involve the taking of human life. Such a way of proceeding would have an attractive simplicity, but it would point to an overly broad pacifist conclusion, which would not be acceptable to Aquinas or to the Western Catholic tradition that he is articulating. Well before we can consider the moral standing of weapons of mass destruction, we have to acknowledge the role of political and military institutions in legitimating the killing of other persons.

Historically, of course, these weapons originate from the practice of warfare as conducted by modern states. Just war thinking, which in its classic presentations originates within the natural law tradition, presupposes an institutional framework of political units that can meet the criterion of "proper authority."[8] The just war tradition's requirements of probability of success and proportionality are in accordance with the natural law requirement that norms, if they are to achieve the status of law, must be for the common good.[9]

The focus in most contemporary natural law and just war discussions about the use and possession of weapons of mass destruction has been on the problem of discriminate use. Natural law theory affirmed the good of life corresponding to the natural inclination to continue in existence, even while it allowed for the taking of life in certain types of situations, of which it recognized three: self-defense, capital punishment, and just war.[10] In this tradition, warfare, if it is to be just, must be limited; in particular, it must observe the distinction between combatant and noncombatant, soldier and civilian. Weapons of mass destruction are commonly thought to present an extremely grave threat to the values protected by this distinction, especially the value of innocent life. Even under war conditions, the natural law tradition forbids the taking of the lives of innocent human beings, though the doctrine of double effect allows for the indirect killing of some persons under specified conditions.[11]

"Weapons of mass destruction" is a term that focuses our attention in the first place on the results of using certain types of weapons rather than on the technology used in the weapon. For the natural law tradition, it is the loss of innocent life as a result of using certain weapons that is the heart of the moral problem, not the nature of the destructive agent. There is no logical or physical necessity that nuclear, biological, and chemical weapons actually be used as weapons of mass destruction or that they be used in a way that violates the distinction between combatants and noncombatants. In World War I, for instance, poison gas was used against soldiers in the front line and not against civilians. There is also the possibility that what are commonly called conventional weapons can be used in such a way that they become weapons of mass destruction, as, for instance, in the firebombing of Hamburg, Dresden, and Tokyo, which involved massive violations of noncombatant immunity. Commercial aircraft and chemical fertilizers, which are not weapons in any ordinary sense, can be used to murder innocent civilians, as the inhabitants of New York City and Oklahoma City can testify. But what stirs concern in the general public and in many intelligent observers of international affairs is the great likelihood that nuclear, biological, and chemical weapons will be used in ways that will actually produce mass destruction and that will violate the principle of discrimination. The scale and design of the weapons and their delivery systems often make it clear that such indiscriminate use or the threat of such use is precisely the point.

Weapons of mass destruction and, more specifically, nuclear weapons have a paradoxical relationship to the practice of war.[12] On the one side, they are simply a stage in the technology of war in the modern age. They extend the range and scale of destruction in conflicts waged by states contending for supremacy and anxious to defend themselves and their interests. In a series of stages moving from the mass mobilization of the Napoleonic armies through the industrialization of warfare in the American Civil War to the wars of attrition and destruction waged by the great powers in the twentieth century, war became total. The growth of air power during World War II rendered large stretches of belligerent countries or even entire countries (Britain, Germany, Japan) vulnerable to devastating attack even when the nearest armies were hundreds of miles away. In the period after World War II, this line of development came to a peak with the introduction of hydrogen bombs and intercontinental missiles.

But the system of mutual assured destruction that ensued produced a dramatic change, in which adversarial relations had to be included within frameworks of negotiation and cooperation. States with nuclear arsenals had more firepower than they could ever reasonably use; states with nuclear adversaries faced the prospect of annihilation; states with nuclear weapons and nonnuclear adversaries faced the prospect of lasting stigma if they used their nuclear weapons. Long-standing correlations between institutions exercising power (states) and the instruments of military power (weapons) could no longer be relied on. The United States in Vietnam and the Soviet Union in Afghanistan both discovered the irrelevance of weapons of mass destruction to the military projects they had undertaken. Both suffered from their inability to translate overwhelming firepower into effective local power at acceptable political costs. War, which in the beginning of the twentieth century had been seen by various imperialists and social Darwinists as a test of national capability and will, had become a game that the most powerful states dared not play against each other. Deterrence came to replace both offense and defense, with regard to both nuclear and chemical weapons.

During the same century, the decline of imperial ambitions and the reliance of a wide range of political movements on guerrilla warfare, terrorism, and the techniques of armed insurgency in order to establish political independence on a local or national basis combined to create situations in which warfare would be limited, even though it often did not respect noncombatant immunity. Political issues of the highest importance (the establishment of new states, the settlement of boundaries, the end of empires, the adoption of new economic regimes) would be resolved not by the application of the greatest force but by a complex combination of force locally applied and persuasion of local and international audiences.

The outlines of this story are, of course, quite familiar. But we should not think that the current outcome of the story is in all respects irreversible. There clearly are important political leaders and movements in American political life that would like to replace nuclear deterrence not with abolition of nuclear weapons but with a form of nuclear defense in which missiles and nuclear weapons would not serve as weapons of mass destruction. This is justified by its proponents as a means of responding to the threat posed by "rogue states," that is, states that, it is claimed, are not deterrable by established weapons systems. Whether such weapons could provide an effective or reliable replacement for regimes of deterrence is highly questionable. But if they had a reasonable prospect of success, they would enable dominant powers to assert their will in situations where they might otherwise be deterred by the threat of weapons of mass destruction to be used by terrorists or rogue states.

To put my point in concise form, it is not correct to assume that the relationship between nuclear weapons and other weapons of mass destruction and their institutional and political context will remain constant. If this point is joined with the previous point about the necessity of including institutional factors in arguments that proceed from general principles affirmed in the natural law tradition to conclusions about particular cases and policies, then it seems that we should not expect to arrive at a stable consensus in applying natural law principles when fundamental institutional factors are subject to change. This is not merely with regard to particular cases calling for decisions, but also with regard to general norms and policies. The arguments that many of us used to justify the system of nuclear deterrence in the cold war cannot be assumed to continue to hold good in the face of fundamental political and technological changes. A parallel conclusion will hold for many of the arguments used in criticizing nuclear deterrence.

Notes

1. For an early statement of difficulties with a deductivist interpretation of Aquinas's ethical theory, see John Langan, "Beatitude and Moral Law in Thomas Aquinas," *Journal of Religious Ethics* 5 (1977): 183–95.
2. The appeal to the state of nature in *Leviathan* brings us back to a situation that is prior to the formation of contracts and the elaboration of social institutions that depend on consent.
3. See John Finnis, *Natural Law and Natural Rights* (Oxford: Clarendon, 1980), 118–25.
4. Thomas Aquinas, *Summa theologiae*, II, 152 *ad* 1.
5. Ibid., I–II, 94, 4c, where he attributes their error on this matter to bad customs or a bad disposition of nature.
6. See, for instance, John Noonan, "Development in Moral Doctrine," *Theological Studies* 54 (1993): 664–67.

7. For overviews of casuistical thinking within the natural law tradition, see Stephen Toulmin and Albert R. Jonsen, *The Abuse of Casuistry: A History of Moral Reasoning* (Berkeley: University of California Press, 1988); and James F. Keenan, S.J., and Thomas Shannon, eds., *The Context of Casuistry* (Washington, D.C.: Georgetown University Press, 1995).

8. In discussing just war thinking, I have in mind two major but significantly different recent contributions to that tradition. The first, which has focused a great deal of the recent public discussion, is *The Challenge of Peace* (1983), the pastoral letter of the U.S. Catholic bishops, which illustrates the way in which natural law thinking is commonly, but not necessarily, embedded within a religious tradition, in this case, Roman Catholicism. The second work is Michael Walzer, *Just and Unjust Wars* (New York: Basic Books, 1973). Walzer proposes a form of just war thinking that is based on human rights rather than on natural law.

9. Aquinas, *Summa theologiae*, I–II, 90, 2.

10. Aquinas discusses capital punishment in ibid., II–II, 62, 2; self-defense in ibid., 64, 7 (which is also the most important exposition of the principle of "double effect"); and just war in ibid., II–II, 40, 1 (where he lays down the requirements of proper authority, just cause, and right intention, which must be met if a war is to be justified).

11. See Michael Walzer, *Just and Unjust Wars*, 3rd ed. (New York: Basic Books, 2000), 151–59.

12. This line of reflection was first articulated in Bernard Brodie et al., *The Absolute Weapon: Atomic Power and World Order* (New York: Harcourt, 1946).

7

Liberalism

The Impossibility of Justifying Weapons of Mass Destruction

Henry Shue

> Supreme emergency has become a permanent condition. Deterrence is a way of coping with that condition, and though it is a bad way, there may well be no other that is practical in a world of sovereign and suspicious states.
> Michael Walzer, *Just and Unjust Wars.*[1]

> Deterrence itself, for all its criminality, falls or may fall for the moment under the standard of necessity. But as with terror bombing, so here with the threat of terrorism: supreme emergency is never a stable position. The realm of necessity is subject to historical change. And, what is more important, we are under an obligation to seize upon opportunities of escape, even to take risks for the sake of such opportunities.
> Ibid.[2]

It is my purpose to side with the Michael Walzer who urges taking risks to bring about historical change in what is necessary and against the Michael Walzer who settles for coping, however reluctantly, with a supposedly permanent supreme emergency that is claimed to excuse the criminality of threats of mass destruction with nuclear weapons. In the process I hope to demonstrate the failure of one of the most comprehensive attempts to justify nuclear deterrence – and thus a reliance on the most highly developed weapons of mass destruction – in a manner consistent with liberalism.

LIBERALISM AND WEAPONS OF MASS DESTRUCTION

A ringing phrase used by Winston Churchill in a memo just before Christmas 1939 to advocate "laying successively a series of small minefields in Norwegian territorial waters at the two or three suitable points on the coast, which will force the ships carrying ore to Germany to quit territorial waters and come onto the high seas," an initiative that Churchill himself later misleadingly described in his history as "simple and bloodless," has now transmogrified into a moral excuse for threatening mass destruction.[3]

Churchill gave his proposal to force commercial ships into international waters, where they could be attacked by the British navy, by means of mining Norwegian territorial waters, which he realized might precipitate a German attack on Norway or Sweden (the source of the iron ore), extremely broad justifications:

We are fighting to re-establish the reign of law and to protect the liberties of small countries. Our defeat would mean an age of barbaric violence, and would be fatal, not only to ourselves, but to the independent life of every small country in Europe.... We have a right, and indeed are bound in duty, to abrogate for a space some of the conventions of the very laws we seek to consolidate and reaffirm. Small nations must not tie our hands when we are fighting for their rights and freedom. The letter of the law must not in supreme emergency obstruct those who are charged with its protection and enforcement.[4]

Thanks to Michael Walzer's masterful and influential treatment, the Churchillian plea of "supreme emergency" has been transformed into a consideration so powerful that in *The Law of Peoples* in 1999, John Rawls, arguably the most influential recent proponent of liberalism, invokes "the supreme emergency exemption" as a now well-established element of the doctrine of just war and goes on to claim that the conception of a supreme emergency distinguishes the liberal doctrine of just war from the Christian natural law doctrine, asserting that "political liberalism allows the supreme emergency exemption," while the Catholic doctrine of double effect does not (since some attacks on noncombatants would be excused by supreme emergency, but not by double effect).[5] Since Rawls himself, however, provides nothing to justify his "supreme emergency exemption" and offers little to explain how it could possibly even be compatible with liberalism – much less provide a distinguishing feature of liberalism – it is valuable to return to the original notion of a supreme emergency, as developed by Walzer around Churchill's phrase, and then to consider the attempt, also initiated by Walzer, to transform it into an excuse for nuclear threats that would at least be acceptable to liberals.

"Weapons of mass destruction" are weapons that kill extremely large numbers of human beings in one fell swoop. Liberalism, in all its varieties, is a family of doctrines that agree that the unit of ultimate value is the individual human being. Consequently, it is abundantly clear why any attempted justification of any weapon of mass destruction should pose a monumental, if not insurmountable, problem for liberalism. How is a doctrine according to which individual persons are in some sense the ultimate end to justify a means that slaughters individual persons in great numbers? Actually, the challenge for individualism is more daunting yet. The two fundamental norms governing the use of weapons, adapted by liberalism from the just war tradition that is centuries older than liberalism, are discrimination, or noncombatant immunity, and proportionality.[6] While the principle of proportionality can be given a "consequentialist" interpretation according to which the end of winning a war can justify means that involve a certain amount of death and destruction, the principle of discrimination has traditionally been understood mainly in an "internalist" manner prohibiting any intentional killing of civilians as a means to any end.[7] Rawls takes himself, I gather, to be adopting a reconstruction of liberalism on this point, relying on reasoning provided earlier by Walzer. Any such reconstruction, however, is at best rowing upstream against a very strong current of respect for individual life.

Because, according to liberalism, an individual person is an ultimate end – the final locus of value – a person deserves a kind of respect that is entirely incompatible with that person's being used merely as a means to any ordinary end. Respect for persons is certainly incompatible with a person's being intentionally killed as a means to any ordinary end. In fact, it is not easy for a liberal to justify killing combatants, much less noncombatants, although the usual rationale is some variant on the idea that a combatant is a person who is engaged in attempting to inflict harm on other persons and may therefore be harmed – and if necessary, killed – in order to protect the persons the combatant would otherwise harm. It is difficult enough to state this rationale in a manner that does not amount to saying simply that the combatant's death may be inflicted as a means to protecting the life of the combatant's intended victim. Normally, it is suggested that the combatant, by being a threat to other persons, has forfeited, or waived, his or her own right not to be killed. Be that as it may, it is extremely difficult to see how liberalism could possibly permit weapons that are called "weapons of mass destruction" precisely because they are indiscriminate. Biological, chemical, and nuclear weapons may kill any person in their path, making no discrimination whatsoever on the basis of the distinction between combatant and noncombatant or any other distinction. For the victims of the weapon who are engaged in no harm to any person, how can being killed so indiscriminately not constitute, at a minimum, a failure to respect the value of their lives?

The only significant theoretical discussions of weapons of mass destruction within liberalism focus entirely on nuclear weapons, saying nothing important about biological or chemical weapons. Unfortunately, I cannot remedy that failure here. Indeed, it is an enormous mystery, as Richard Price has demonstrated, how liberals can confidently assume that biological and chemical weapons are so intolerably immoral that their very production and possession ought to be illegal, while insisting that the production and possession of nuclear weapons, and the system of nuclear deterrence that relies on possessing and threatening to use nuclear weapons, is not only perfectly legal but is, for some strategists reasoning at highly abstract levels, a brilliant breakthrough in war prevention.[8]

Although I sometimes employ the now popular term "weapons of mass destruction," and I certainly believe that biological and chemical weapons are as fully unjustifiable as, I argue here, nuclear weapons are, I do not believe that very much can usefully be said about all these weapons lumped together beyond the obvious fact that the use of weapons of any of the three kinds grossly violates the principle of noncombatant immunity.[9] The reason is that while all three kinds kill indiscriminately if actually used, the alleged excuses for having them nevertheless are quite different. One must not look merely at the physical effects of weapons but must examine the political and military dynamics of their possession or use and the resultant moral excuses offered for using or having them. In particular, no one, to my knowledge, has ever claimed that a balance of terror resting on biological or chemical weapons could provide stable mutual deterrence, while this claim is constantly and standardly made to excuse nuclear weapons. Because the excuses for having these respective three kinds of indiscriminate weapons are different, the arguments against them must be different as well and must speak directly to the disparate excuses and underlying social dynamics. Different excuses require different critiques. Here I can deal seriously with only one excuse for one type of weapon of mass destruction – the one that liberals are most inclined to rely on.

Liberals tend to comfort themselves with the easy thought that "we" can be trusted to handle our weapons of mass destruction – which happen to be nuclear – responsibly, while "they" cannot be trusted to handle theirs – which often happen to be biological and chemical – responsibly. The possibilities that, at the current stage of the various technologies, nuclear weapons themselves are more destructive, less discriminate, and less proportional to any conceivable end or that the stability of deterrence resting on nuclear weapons was never severely tested during the cold war and remains purely a matter of blind faith in abstract theory is simply passed over. My own view is that the liberal position is wildly inconsistent between biological and chemical weapons, on the one hand, and nuclear weapons, on the other, and is merely the incoherent product of a political inability to face up to the immorality of the particular kind of weapons of mass destruction, nuclear ones, that the states of some liberal societies have blundered into relying on.[10] Here I argue that this inconsistency ought to be resolved by condemning nuclear weapons, not by accepting biological or chemical weapons. I am wrong, however, about the nuclear weapons if John Rawls is correct in assuming that Michael Walzer has carved out an exception to the general liberal rule, specifying a circumstance in which some weapons of mass destruction – nuclear ones – may permissibly be used. The attempt to justify this exception for retaining a weapon of mass destruction is the heart of the matter today.

USE AND SUPREME EMERGENCY

In part four of *Just and Unjust Wars*, "Dilemmas of War," Walzer wrestles with the most fundamental kind of moral conflict, conflict between means and end – between, in the instance of war, the moral imperative to fight well whenever one fights, especially to avoid the slaughter of the innocent that must concern any liberal (and not liberals only, of course), and the moral imperative to win in the case in which it is actually true that "defeat would mean an age of barbaric violence." Between (1) a doctrine of the sliding scale that undermines the moral importance of limited means and (2) a doctrine of absolutism about moral limits on means that fails to appreciate that in some instances morality itself requires victory, emerges (3) Walzer's notion of a supreme emergency as part of an argument from extremity that, by stopping one step short of absolutism, as Walzer measures it, makes victory possible when victory is morally required, while restraining the means of war unless and until restraint would bring a defeat for . . . what? That will be the most difficult question: What precisely must be at risk in order for there to be a supreme emergency? But first we need quickly to locate the conception of supreme emergency in the overall argument.

One of Walzer's most important contributions is the demonstration that what he denominates the sliding scale is a betrayal of the core of just war. The doctrine of the sliding scale promotes the adjustment of the moral limits on the means of war in proportion to the degree of moral importance attached to the end of victory in the war for one's own side – "a sliding scale: *the more justice, the more right.*"[11] And "the greater the justice of my cause, the more rules I can violate for the sake of the cause – though some rules are always inviolable."[12] The final clause importantly complicates the meaning of the sliding scale. On Walzer's transcription of the doctrine – he is formulating it in order to attack it – the scale slides but not all the way. Even on the doctrine of the sliding scale, the breaking of the rules stops when "inviolable" rules are reached. Walzer's version might be called the limited sliding scale; the purer, which is to say more simplistic, version – the unlimited sliding scale – would simply allow the more rules of war to be violated, the greater the moral importance of victory in the war being fought, period.

Although it is a large topic, which need not be pursued here, I would say, for what it's worth, that Walzer is correct to adopt the messier formulation of the limited sliding scale. While abstract theorists tend to want us to "make up our minds" between consequentialist and internalist modes of reasoning, it is theoretical tidiness, not faithfulness to reality, that is at stake for them. And here, as he characteristically does, Walzer stays true to ordinary ways of thinking. The puritanical and the priggish never give an inch, and the calculating can never find anything sacred. Many decent people, however, are willing to shave a bit off the corners if the stakes are high – and a bit more if the stakes are even higher – but "there's a limit." This is the limited sliding scale, which, I would conjecture, is often the only sensible way to behave. Walzer's important point is that whatever the case in other arenas, this natural tendency to use a limited sliding scale is not reflected in the principles of just war (and for good reason). The *jus in bello*, especially the requirement to take due care in order to avoid injuring or killing noncombatants, is equally strict however great the justice of one's cause, in normal instances.[13]

One surprising result of Walzer's formulation of the doctrine of the sliding scale in the limited version is that although in ordinary cases the limited sliding scale is much more permissive than Walzer's own doctrine of extremity centered on the conception of supreme emergency, in extreme cases – the ones that Walzer himself would judge to be supreme emergencies – the limited sliding scale could be more demanding than Walzer's view. This depends on whether it is the limiting inviolable rules, as they are understood on the sliding scale, that the conception of supreme emergency justifies violating. We cannot tell because we are not told which rules the limited sliding scale takes to be the inviolable ones.

Thus, one moral extreme would be the pure sliding scale: bit-by-bit erosion of moral limits on means of warfare, indefinitely extended. Significantly more restrictive is the limited sliding scale, which Walzer – correctly, I think – takes to be one of the two main views ordinarily in contention. The other main contender is the opposite extreme from the pure sliding scale, which Walzer calls "moral absolutism": "the rules of war are a series of categorical and unqualified prohibitions . . . that . . . can never rightly be violated even in order to defeat aggression. . . . *Fiat justicia ruat coelum*, do justice even if the heavens fall. . . ."[14] The attachment of the clause "even in order to defeat aggression" is odd, because in the era of the United Nations Charter no war is justified in being fought at all unless it is a war of defense against aggression. To allow the limits on the means of warfare to be relaxed whenever necessary to defeat aggression would be to allow them to be relaxed whenever a war satisfying contemporary *jus ad bellum*, that is, consisting of defense against aggression, might otherwise be lost. That would leave no role at all for *jus in bello* except to restrain the means used by aggressors and the means used by defenders who were not seriously threatened with defeat.

Nevertheless, the main point is clear: Moral absolutism requires that the moral limits on the means of fighting always be observed, whatever the consequences. Walzer's own view, the argument from extremity, is then readily introduced as "just short of absolutism . . . do justice unless the heavens are (really) about to fall."[15] Even so, not all limits are relaxed. Walzer is explicit about the limits that, for the argument from extremity, are not relaxed: "the only restraints upon military action are [then] those of usefulness and proportionality."[16] Clearly, the critical limit that is relaxed is noncombatant immunity!

Supreme emergency, as we shall soon see below, is then the paradigm case of extremity, or necessity. Before probing into the conception of supreme emergency, I would like to locate it further by quoting Walzer's summary of the possible positions on the relation between the morality of means and the morality of ends:

1. the war convention [noncombatant immunity] is simply set aside (derided as "asinine ethics") under the pressure of utilitarian argument [simple abandonment of limits on means];
2. the convention yields slowly to the moral urgency of the cause: the rights of the righteous are enhanced, and those of their enemies devalued [limited sliding scale];
3. the convention holds and rights are strictly respected, whatever the consequences [moral absolutism]; and
4. the convention is overridden, but only in the face of an imminent catastrophe [argument from extremity].[17]

Only such an imminent catastrophe qualifies as a supreme emergency. Plainly, one necessary condition of a supreme emergency is *imminence* of the threatened catastrophe.[18]

Walzer points out that in December 1939 when Churchill declared a "supreme emergency" the British were in fact far from facing imminent catastrophe; in attempting to keep iron ore out of the hands of Germany at this point before Allied armies had fought a single battle, "they were not thinking of avoiding defeat but (like the Germans in 1914) of winning a quick victory."[19] Thus, Walzer rightly notes that this strategic application of the argument from extremity is completely inappropriate, but he believes that the argument itself can be compelling when applied to appropriate circumstances. I too am willing to concede that Churchill's remarks contain the elements of compelling arguments applicable to two narrow kinds of case, both quite unlike the actual situation in December 1939. Yet the argument I see does not include all that Walzer saw and that has become famous and influential, on Rawls among many others. Consequently, I would like first to formulate what I take to be the most compelling argument and then examine Walzer's arguments, explaining why I think one of them overreaches.

General Threat to Principled Society

In the language of Churchill's memo to the British cabinet, one finds several cheap debating tricks and the elements of two importantly different kinds of arguments, one kind that I find more compelling and one kind that Walzer finds more compelling and then elaborates into two versions, only one of which I think liberals can accept. Both general kinds are introduced in the first sentence quoted.[20] If one emphasizes "to protect the liberties of small countries," one can build one or the other version of Walzer's species of argument. If one emphasizes "to re-establish the reign of law," one can construct the other, with which I now begin.

The most compelling form of argument available against the view Walzer calls moral absolutism is that the survival of the values that animate and give significance to a body of principle or law may in exceptional cases depend on the reluctant, regretful, and temporary violation of some of the constituent principles or laws. One must be suspicious of "temporary." Churchill writes of the duty "to abrogate for a space some of the conventions of the very laws we seek to consolidate and reaffirm." This is one of Churchill's slippery tricks. As Walzer perceptively notes, talk of temporary abrogation "is a euphemism. Since human life is at stake, the abrogation is not temporary, unless Churchill plans to raise the dead after the war is over."[21] It would have been more honest for Churchill to call his proposed violation of Norway's neutrality rights a violation. Nevertheless, although one misunderstands the nature of rights if one attempts to engage in a "utilitarianism of rights," that is, regularly violating some rights as a means to maximizing the fulfillment of rights overall, it is still the case that if *in fact* a system of rights – or Churchill's stated concern, "the reign of law" – will not survive unless some rights are violated, or some laws are broken, the very value and significance of the rights or laws that ordinarily compel one not to violate the rights, or break the laws, may become in those extraordinary circumstances reasons for violation or breaking, reluctantly, regretfully, and temporarily.

Any defender of unvarying respect for rights or compliance with law will, I think, generally do better to deny the premise rather than to reject the inference, as the Walzerian "absolutist" does. This becomes a central part of my argument later: The defender of respect and compliance is wiser not to challenge the validity of the inference but to ask how often the premise is true, and what supports the contention that this is one of those rare instances when it is. If *in fact* the reign of law will survive only if we selectively and briefly break some of the laws, then I agree with Churchill that we not only may but ought to break those laws: "...have a right, indeed are bound in duty...." Once again, putting it as "the letter of the law must not in supreme emergency obstruct those who are charged with its protection and enforcement" is Churchillian sophistry. We are not discussing violating only the letter of the law. We are talking about violating the law, period – in Churchill's case, violating the neutrality of Norway in such a way as to invite a German invasion of Norway in which Norwegians would die.[22]

Still, beneath Churchill's unnecessary debater's stratagems is a valid argument, provided that one is willing to consider the consequences of one's actions for the survival and effectiveness of the whole system of rights and laws (and thus is not an "absolutist" by Walzer's definition). But how often is it, if ever, that the reign of law will survive only if we break laws? How often will a system of rights survive only if we violate rights? Many a terrorist seems to have assured himself that only through terror can one stop terror, but when has this ever actually been true? The practical implication, of course, is that since supposed short-cuts are almost always highly tempting, and especially if they promise to save lives and funds, we need to consider long and hard whether apparent cases of the application of the premise are real cases.

Unfortunately, there has been at least one case in which the premise was true: the Nazis. I believe that the human spirit is indomitable, and I cannot deny that it is conceivable that civilization would have recovered even from a Nazi victory. But that would have been a risk too great to run, and I see no reason to reject Churchill's claim that Allied defeat in World War II would have led to "an age of barbaric violence" and no reason to deny Walzer's assessment: "Nazism was an ultimate threat to everything decent in our lives, an ideology and a practice of domination so murderous, so degrading even to those who might survive, that the consequences of its final victory were literally beyond calculation, immeasurably awful. We see it – and I don't use the phrase lightly – as evil objectified in the world, and in a form so potent and apparent that there could never have been anything to do but fight against it."[23] Consequently, I agree that people would have had to do what it actually took to win against at least the Nazis.

Tragically, this did not include much of what was in fact done, as Walzer himself has eloquently argued. It did not include the atomic bombing of Nagasaki, the atomic bombing of Hiroshima, or the fire-bombing of Tokyo and other Japanese cities, none of which had anything to do with defeating the Nazis. Nor did it include the brutal Allied bombing of German cities, which not only slaughtered noncombatants but probably extended the war by stiffening German morale and wasting airpower that could have been used instead in militarily effective ways, thus reducing the death toll among combatants and noncombatants on both sides. Invoking the very notion of supreme emergency, Walzer condemns all but the earliest bombing: "For the truth is that the supreme emergency passed long before the British bombing reached its crescendo. The greater number by far of the German civilians killed by terror bombing were killed without moral (and probably also without military) reason."[24] That the "strategic" bombing in Europe was indeed militarily misguided, and colossally so, has now been convincingly shown by Robert A. Pape.[25]

Thus, Walzer himself not only condemns as too early the violation of Norwegian territorial waters recommended by Churchill's initial use of the phrase "supreme emergency," but also condemns as too late, and thus unnecessary and grossly excessive, the attempted aerial terrorization of German noncombatants. I would guess that it gives Walzer some pause that even in the war to which it is most compellingly appropriate, the argument from extremity, invoking supreme emergency, was more abused than accurately used. Practical thinkers must regret that even their most carefully formulated principles can be misapplied. Still, one should not perhaps reject a sound, narrow argument itself simply because opportunists will employ it inappropriately, unless the temptation to do so appears irresistible.

On this first reading of the Churchillian argument, minus the sophistry, then, a supreme emergency is a supreme *moral* emergency in the form of a threat to principled society. The "imminent catastrophe," in Walzer's phrase,[26] would be a moral catastrophe, such as the indefinite eclipse of the reign of law or the descent from civilization into "an age of barbaric violence," in Churchill's terms.[27] The threat in such a supreme emergency is a threat to the moral fabric of the life of at least a large portion of humanity – a threat to principled social life in general.[28] But a great temptation exists to allow the conception of supreme emergency to widen to include all of what I will call a *national* emergency.

Plainly, a supreme moral emergency may de facto coincide with one or more national emergencies. If Nazi Germany embodied evil in the form of barbarity and the destruction of the reign of law, while Britain, France, the Soviet Union, the United States, Canada, and the other Allies were the only force capable of blocking that destruction, then defeat by the Nazis of Britain, France, the Soviet Union, the United States, Canada, and the other Allies would in fact have been a supreme moral emergency as well as a set of national emergencies for each nation listed.[29] Without our pursuing further here the factual question of whether World War II in Europe is a case of the conjunction of supreme moral and national emergencies, we can see at least that such a conjunction is in principle possible. Moral and national emergencies would coincide whenever the survival of specific nations was essential for the survival of the threatened ideal through being militarily essential to blocking the ideal's destruction. Obviously, one does well to ask how often such conjunctions occur; I am simply conceding that the conjunction is possible, and assuming that it occurred in World War II, in order to move on to the point I want to emphasize.

This point is that normally no such conjunction in fact occurs. In the normal case, the defeat of a single nation, or even the defeat of an alliance, would not constitute the destruction of any moral ideal, such as the reign of law or civilized society. Certainly, I mean neither to minimize the destructiveness and indeed horror of war nor to ignore the great significance for a society of military defeat, especially if defeat is followed by military occupation. Yet precisely as it is rare for a nation on one side of a conflict to embody evil to the extent that Nazi Germany did, it is rare for any party to any conflict to be an essential bulwark for a moral ideal in any manner that would entail that the military defeat of that nation would lead to, or even seriously threaten to lead to, the annihilation of that moral ideal. Fortunately, ideals survive the destruction of particular embodiments of them. Britain, France, Russia, and Spain, for example, have all won and lost various wars through the centuries of their history, but none of these defeats has, to my knowledge, led to the destruction of any moral ideals. Defeats of France and Spain, for example, have not led to the end of French or Spanish culture, much less to the end of civilization itself. Of course, the actual victor in a European conflict was never a totalitarian, genocidal state determined utterly to transform the conquered society. The point is, quite simply, that while one can grant that victory by Nazi Germany would have been a supreme *moral* emergency, that is the rarest exception. Otherwise terrible conflicts, rife with death and destruction of great significance, involve no such civilizational stakes.

The crucial point for present purposes is one that I hope is fairly plain: One must preserve a firm conception of what might paradoxically be called a (terrible but) "normal war" in order to preserve, by contrast, a sharp conception of a supreme moral emergency. In a supreme moral emergency, the heart and soul of *jus in bello*, noncombatant immunity, may be violated. The issue concerning supreme emergency is not when a nation is entitled to fight by all just means (the general answer: whenever it, while innocent of inflicting severe harm, is attacked); the issue is when, if ever, a nation is entitled to fight by means that include even attack on the innocent, if those attacks would be, as Walzer always requires, useful and proportional.[30] While we should perhaps be prepared to entertain this suspension of noncombatant immunity for the narrowest range of cases – and while that range should perhaps include in addition to the Nazis other regimes of civilizational annihilation, such as European colonizers in the Americas – it is vital to maintain a tight conceptual firewall between those morally exceptional cases of supreme *moral* emergency and (terrible but) "normal war." Otherwise, any potential national defeat might be misconstrued as a supreme moral emergency, and noncombatant immunity would be widely undermined, except in the cases in which its violation promised little or no advantage. Wars are almost never unimportant, and defeat is never insignificant. But too many people who ought to know better are at present inclined to see "the clash of civilizations" all around. "Ethnic cleansers" routinely describe their atrocities as unavoidable in the defense of civilization, religion, and culture; their depredations of course go far beyond the violation of noncombatant immunity, constrained by utility and proportionality, which is the most that Walzer would allow even in a genuine supreme emergency. Nevertheless, supreme emergency, with "supreme" too liberally construed, is a profound threat to just war: Every serious case threatens to become an exceptional case, and the limits threaten never to apply in any instance in which they would make a difference. The conception of supreme emergency is a conception of an exception to one of the most important moral limits embodied in civilization – an "exemption," as Rawls calls it. Such an exception or exemption must be buttressed with heavy restraints against expansion lest it become the fatal leak that releases the torrent that bursts the dam.

Two Threats to Specific Nations or Communities

On the first account of supreme emergency sketched above, the threat that creates a supreme emergency is barbaric ruthlessness, and what are threatened are the general moral structures underlying civilized society, such as the rule of law itself. Principled society itself is threatened by a supreme moral emergency. "The liberties of small countries" are threatened as well, but their danger reflects the underlying lawlessness and unprincipled exertion of sheer force that is the core of the supreme moral emergency.

Actually, for Walzer, *national* emergencies may come in either of two forms, which I will from now on call the *physical* and the *political* interpretations of national emergency, although these mere labels communicate very little by themselves. These forms constitute yet a second and a third account of what, for Walzer, must be threatened in order for a supreme emergency to exist, although he does not always distinguish them from each other. Treating the *physical* national emergency as a supreme emergency strikes me as compatible with a liberal justification; treating the *political* national emergency as supreme seems less clearly so. In both cases, what is threatened is a community, not a moral structure. Although any normal political community is one – perhaps unique – embodiment of a moral structure, moral structures can survive the destruction of at least some of their embodiments.

Well aware himself of the danger that supreme emergency will be interpreted too broadly, Walzer has tried to define the cases of supreme emergency narrowly. Far from countenancing just any potential national defeat as a supreme emergency, he sometimes restricts it, in part of what I take to be his definitive discussion, to "enslavement or extermination" – "where an entire people are enslaved or massacred."[31] This is what I am calling the physical interpretation of a national community: A supreme emergency exists whenever a national community faces the imminent danger of extermination or enslavement. This provides a second clear criterion of a supreme emergency. It is different from the first criterion: the imminent danger of the elimination of a moral ideal or of the destruction of a civilizational structure (like the rule of law). In the case of the Nazis, both criteria were abundantly satisfied: The Nazis aimed at destroying moral ideals and physically eliminating communities. Yet the two are conceptually separable. If communities A, B, C, and D each embodied fundamentally the same civilization and moral ideals but consisted of different ethnic groups, and a genocidal adversary set out to exterminate only community A, because it hated that particular ethnic group, Walzer's second criterion using the physical interpretation of a community would be satisfied. This would constitute a supreme emergency for community A, in spite of the fact that even if community A were the victim of a thorough genocide, its moral ideals and form of civilization would live on in communities B, C, and D.

Now, as I have indicated already and emphasize again below, I believe that in fact attacks on noncombatants, even if in rare instances somehow morally excusable, are almost always at best diversions of resources and therefore lack military utility and, even worse, usually are counterproductive by stiffening resistance and fanning hatred. Nevertheless, I am willing to grant

Walzer's inference: If *in fact* a physical community will not survive physically, but will be enslaved or exterminated unless its defenders violate noncombatant immunity, and if *in fact* it is likely to survive if noncombatants are killed in proportional numbers, the defenders may be excused for violations of discrimination with such (improbable) utility and proportionality. I hasten to add that it would be far, far better if enough of the rest of us intervened to defend them and to defeat their attackers without violation of noncombatant immunity by them or us. If we fail to come to their aid through such a genuinely humanitarian intervention, their violations of the principle would fall, in a very real sense, partly on us for leaving them with no alternative way to save themselves.

How can this be defended? Is the defense compatible with liberalism? While I am as uncomfortable as Walzer is with moral arguments being "a matter of arithmetic,"[32] when numbers are the only difference, numbers tell. Liberalism is committed to the individual person being the ultimate moral unit. In the hypothetical under consideration, many innocents will be slaughtered or enslaved in the nation being subjected to genocide unless – and I continue to insist that I find this factually implausible – a significantly smaller number of innocents on the side of the aggressor are killed during the defense, which will, as a result of this breach of noncombatant immunity, be successful. If there were such a case, in fact, I believe that saving the lives of many innocents threatened with genocide would excuse taking a smaller number of lives on the aggressor's side, provided there actually was no alternative.[33] I think it may be compatible with understanding individual persons to be the ultimate moral units to take the lives of a small number in order to save the lives of a much larger number in the specific circumstance of an attempted genocide or enslavement (not, of course, in general), when this is the only possible salvation for the larger number.[34] But I grant that it is disturbingly difficult to see why this is not an instance of using the deaths of some, who have to no degree forfeited their rights, as a means to the end of avoiding the deaths of others. One possibility is that there is a shade of difference between two formulations of the fundamental liberal principle – (1) treat every person as having ultimate moral value and (2) never treat any person only as a means – and that such a desperate measure satisfies (1) while violating (2). One would then have to decide on the essence of liberalism before deciding on the compatibility of the desperate measure; this is beyond me, at least here.

The most guilty parties, by my reckoning, are the genocidal aggressors. The second most guilty parties are the capable bystanders – "us" – who could have come to the aid of the intended victims and enabled them to defend themselves while abiding by noncombatant immunity. The bystanders share in the moral responsibility for the breach of immunity by the desperate intended victims, because the bystanders are causally responsible, along with the aggressors, for the intended victims' situation being as desperate as it is. The third most guilty, and excusable, are those threatened victims with only the choice between submitting to genocide or enslavement and fighting an extremely dirty but successful war of self-defense against annihilation.

In other parts of the very same discussion, Walzer slides, it seems to me, to a different version of the threat to community, which I am referring to as the *political* interpretation of national emergency. Here I see no justification, liberal or otherwise, for treating this national emergency as a supreme emergency. Consider the following two comments about political communities in contrast with individual persons, which in Walzer's text are separated by the brief consideration of "arithmetic" to which I have just responded:

It is not usually said of individuals in domestic society that they necessarily will or that they morally can strike out at innocent people, even in the supreme emergency of self-defense. They can only attack their attackers. But communities, in emergencies, seem to have different and larger prerogatives. I am not sure that I can account for the difference, without ascribing to communal life a kind of transcendence that I don't believe it to have.

It is possible to live in a world where individuals are sometimes murdered, but a world where entire peoples are enslaved or massacred is literally unbearable. For the survival and freedom of political communities – whose members share a way of life, developed by their ancestors, to be passed on to their children – are the highest values of international society.[35]

The intellectual struggle in these passages is palpable and admirable. Here, for one thing, is a theorist with deep liberal instincts fighting mightily against any presupposition of "communal transcendence" incompatible with retaining individual persons as the units of ultimate moral concern, while emphasizing that those individuals are deeply social and flourish only in communities (as any plausible liberalism must).[36] For liberalism, communities matter not in themselves but to their individual members, whose shared, but not transcended, way of life they embody. If political communities are the highest values of international society because of the value of those communities to the individual persons who constitute them, all is well (and liberal). The worry is: What is meant by "communities, in emergencies, seem to have different and larger prerogatives" than individuals do? Which prerogatives, and why? What is the difference that needs accounting for? Does this open the door for something other than the massacre or enslavement of large groups of persons to count as a supreme emergency? I fear that it does and that this would constitute an insupportable widening of the category.

Let me be as clear as possible about the kind of widening of the category of supreme emergency that concerns liberals. Some wars are mostly over power, wealth, and territory – the adversaries may not even have any important disagreements at any level that can sensibly be characterized as the level of principle. By contrast, other wars are understood as – whatever they are motivated by – wars over religion, political ideology, or culture. These wars are sometimes over "a way of life, developed by their ancestors, to be passed on to their children." Suppose a Protestant power threatens to defeat a Catholic power, or vice versa. And suppose that we have every reason to believe that the victorious Protestants will burn down the Catholic churches, monasteries, and convents and murder priests, nuns, and monks who resist. We expect that they will ban the practice of Catholicism and make some variety of Protestantism a requirement for citizenship. This will be a tragic and murderous violation of the Catholics' right of freedom of conscience, and if we represent, say, NATO, we might well consider intervening on the side of the persecuted Catholics. If the stakes are not high enough for us to risk becoming combatants, they are certainly not high enough to excuse anyone for killing noncombatants. But if the victors will kill only those who resist and will not massacre or enslave the general population, I believe that whoever fights them, whether it is the Catholics alone or the Catholics with assistance from NATO, should honor the immunity of noncombatants. The rest of us should perhaps contribute additional combatants to defend against the aggression, but we should not acknowledge that anyone would be excused for attacking noncombatants. In other words, as terrible an aggression as I have described, it does not seem to me to qualify as a supreme emergency, as it would if the victors were going to massacre every Catholic or if this were their first step on the road to eliminating all Catholics from the face of the earth. I hope that Walzer would agree, because if one classifies all wars of religion, ideology, or culture as cases of supreme national emergency, one eliminates the restraint of noncombatant immunity from a large portion of contemporary conflict.

Similarly, any victory over a democratic nation by an authoritarian nation might end the "reign of law" within that specific nation for as long as the conquest held. The secure enjoyment by this political community of its way of life, including the rule of law, might be ended. This would be another unlawful and outrageously unjust aggression, and it should be resisted by all just means (and perhaps, again, the rest of us should assist in the defense). But this aggression need not threaten the end of the "reign of law" as such and should not, I think, qualify as a supreme emergency. The defeat of a single nation, as distinguished from the extermination or enslavement of its people, does not, as terrible as it is, constitute the eradication of any moral ideal.

If the threat of the simple defeat of a political community – the political version of a national emergency – were to count as a third kind of supreme emergency, it would be difficult to see where to draw any line between supreme emergency and the national emergency faced by the losing side in most wars. Any defeat in which the losses are not primarily material would then threaten to become understood as the destruction of a way of life. But if most people survive, so may their way of life; and their children or grandchildren may be able to restore their traditions. The only firm and relevant line I can see for the threat to nations or other communities is the line at "enslavement or extermination." Otherwise, "supreme emergency" degenerates into "do whatever it takes to win," which is the betrayal of just war (and the last thing that Walzer himself could possibly wish).

Further, I see no way to excuse the killing of innocent persons in defense of a political community, where that political community is interpreted as something other than the persons who constitute it (have constituted it and will constitute it – the historical succession of individuals), without granting ultimate moral significance to some entity other than individual persons, in a way that is clearly incompatible with liberalism.

By What Means?

I have made a sustained effort to carve out a narrow niche – strictly speaking, two niches: moral and physical national – for "supreme emergency," a niche into which it can be firmly locked in order to prevent it from leaking out and eroding the heart of just war: noncombatant immunity. The most direct inference would be: If the only way to assure the long-term survival of the practice of honoring a principle is to violate that very principle in an isolated instance in order to defeat the principle's worst enemy, one not only may but must violate it. The inference at the heart of the argument from the threat to principled society – the supreme moral emergency – is more complex: If the only way to assure the long-term survival of the practice of honoring principles at all is to violate a fundamental principle (such as the immunity of noncombatants) in an isolated instance in order to defeat a ruthless enemy of principled conduct as such, one not only may but must violate the principle. Even so, one may, according to Walzer, violate it only within the restraints of "usefulness and proportionality." Consequently, this restriction to useful and proportional violations belongs firmly at the end of any full statement of the position. I do not see in the name of what one could refuse in principle so to act in such a case, if indeed there again arise any such cases.

And that, I have insisted, is the real rub for the notion of supreme emergency: If it is formulated narrowly enough not to threaten to undermine the entire edifice of just war, will it ever again apply, as it did to the Nazis? Its weak spot is not, I believe, the validity of the inference but the applicability of its premise. I simply leave the question: What is it that is prohibited by the principle of the immunity of noncombatants that (1) the argument from extremity, centered on supreme emergency narrowly construed, would excuse if it were proportional, and that (2) would actually be militarily useful by contributing significantly to victory?

DETERRENCE

I am not aware of any "strategy" resting on the notion that although using biological or chemical weapons would be indiscriminate, possessing them can provide stable deterrence, but this assertion is constantly made in support of the "strategy" of continuing to possess some number of nuclear weapons of mass destruction. However, the maintenance of a system of nuclear deterrence cannot be fit, I now suggest, into any reasonable conception of a supreme emergency. Having examined Walzer's conception in some detail, we can fairly quickly indicate superficially why it does not provide the excuse he invokes for maintaining devices for mass destruction, although space here permits hardly the beginning of a serious discussion of the complexities of the differences between actual use and threatened use on which discussions of deterrence turn.[37]

The "classic" threat to use nuclear devices was a threat to exterminate the people on the other side. The comparative advantage, to put it perversely, of weapons of mass destruction, such as nuclear devices, is the disproportionate damage to which any limited initial uses of relatively small devices may escalate. It is of course true that the smallest nuclear devices need do no more damage than conventional weapons, but no advantage would lie in threatening to use only them. The advantage – the terror – lies in the high risk that damage comparable to the damage done by conventional weapons will escalate, spiraling out of control to incomparable damage. Walzer brilliantly cut through Paul Ramsey's monumental, intricate, but obfuscatory employment of the doctrine of double effect to defend nuclear threats:

The entire burden of Ramsey's argument falls on the idea of death by indirection.... Its standing is undermined here by the fact that Ramsey relies so heavily on the deaths he supposedly doesn't intend.... Surely anyone designing such a strategy must accept moral responsibility for the effects on which he is so radically dependent.[38]

To me this seems dead on: The effects that one's strategy relies on in order to work are its intended effects in the only sense of "intention" morally relevant to the conduct of war. As Walzer further noted, "all their [the defenders'] arguments depend upon the ultimate wickedness of counter-city strikes."[39] There would be no military point in making a nuclear threat that could definitely not escalate; one could threaten the same damage with conventional weapons and not recklessly run the risk of nuclear retaliation. Hence, that (mythical) kind of proportionate nuclear threat would be unjustified for a quite different reason, namely, reckless pointlessness.[40]

Two sides locked into a "balance of terror," like the United States and the Soviet Union during the cold war, were mutually threatening each other with extermination. Whatever might conceivably be said in defense of an-extermination-for-an-extermination as somehow parallel to an-eye-for-an-eye, which does not seem to me to be worth discussion, is most certainly not open to adoption by a liberal believing that individual persons are the units of ultimate moral concern. Such a contention about putatively just retaliation at the collective level has no similarity whatsoever with the conception of supreme emergency. Supreme emergency excuses violation of the principle of noncombatant immunity when danger is imminent and violations have "usefulness and proportionality." Walzer's original argument from extremity does not say: If you are threatened with extermination, you may be excused for exterminating the general population of the threatening society. The original Walzerian argument says: If you are imminently threatened with extermination, you may be excused for the reluctant, regretful, and temporary violation of the noncombatant immunity of individual persons to the extent useful (which I read as: necessary) and proportional. Any planned incineration of metropolises, such as the "strategy" of mutual assured destruction, does not qualify, because, as we see in the next section, that long-contemplated slaughter is not the unavoidably only available response in the face of imminent disaster. We have had the time, if we had had the will and the vision, to have arranged other responses that would have defused the situation.

De-alerting

The mystery for me, indeed, is how Walzer could have thought the conception of supreme emergency could possibly have helped to excuse our continuing nuclear threats for a very long time. The fundamental error was: "Supreme emergency has become a permanent condition."[41] On the contrary, each side had (and has) the choice between trying to maintain and trying to escape from the balance of terror. That the capabilities of any large force of nuclear weapons, like those of either the United States or the former Soviet Union, threaten physical extermination is clear, so our situation was for a time a case of the physical version of the threat to national communities. Walzer was explicit that he did not see what I have above called a threat to principled society – the moral supreme emergency – but a threat to a specific community, although what he described was the political version (which a liberal cannot accept), not the physical version, of the national threat:

Deterrence theory doesn't depend upon a view of Stalinism as a great evil (though that is a highly plausible view) in the same way that my argument about terror bombing depended upon an assertion about the evils of Nazism. It requires only that we see appeasement or surrender to involve a loss of values central to our existence as an independent nation-state.[42]

For the reasons given earlier, it is the threat to the lives of individual human beings from weapons of mass destruction that a liberal should find compelling, not the loss of political independence for a nation-state. This is the only justification for the killing of innocents based on a threat to a nation compatible with liberalism.

The further crucial question for the applicability of the argument from extremity, then, was and is: Is the threat – whatever the target of the threat – imminent? And the answer is that the national policies chosen, not some inextricable natural reality, determine whether physical destruction remains imminent, as, I would grant, it now still is. Only a permanently poor policy of reliance on weapons of mass destruction creates a permanent (physical national) supreme emergency. This explains both what was mistaken in Walzer's argument then and an urgent concrete option that ought to be implemented now. One of the unforgivably monumental failures of the Clinton administration was not even taking U.S. nuclear forces off alert status in spite of the earlier collapse of the Soviet Union. This constitutes mind-numbing recklessness and seems to reflect the characteristic Clinton inability to command the military. The Bush administration similarly shows no sign of eliminating the totally unjustified high level of alert of U.S. nuclear forces and appears to indulge the extraordinary illusion that the balance of nuclear terror can be ended only through the unilateral pursuit of ballistic missile defenses.[43] Steven Lee years ago demonstrated that matters would be even more highly dangerous than they are now if missile defenses were ever actually to work.[44] And the only grounds for believing missile defenses can ever possibly work are Pentagon tests so artificial (in, for example, the absence of multiple decoys) as to constitute patent scientific fraud. Successful or unsuccessful, missile defenses are in the current situation an appallingly bad idea that can, at best, only make matters worse.

So nuclear extermination continues to be more nearly imminent than there is any reason, apart from lack of leadership by the Clinton administration and misguided leadership by the Bush administration, for it to be. Nuclear forces are catastrophic accidents waiting to happen, yet more out of control in Russia than in the United States, but on the edge of disaster partly as a matter of conscious policy concerning alert status in the United States. What I understand to be the high likelihood of inadvertent nuclear exchanges – still today, now – is one of multiple reasons why I think we ought, first, immediately to de-alert, and then rapidly reduce nuclear forces while eliminating all strategic plans that include them. But this is another way of saying that I believe nuclear devices are supremely dangerous and for that very reason ought to be eliminated. Therefore, I cannot deny that they pose an imminent threat of extermination. Yet the primary threat is less that the United States will choose to exterminate the Russians or that the Russians (or someone else) will choose to exterminate the United States than that the whole crazy system will be kept long enough to go haywire through accident and/or inadvertence. In short, we still face an imminent threat of extermination, and the system of nuclear deterrence is the source of the problem, not the solution to it. The imminence of the threat is the best single argument for moving rapidly to dismantle the nuclear devices. In no way is it an argument for keeping them and continuing to rely on them, as current U.S. national policy does.

Walzer's position faces a kind of dilemma: If deterrence works well enough to keep, it works well enough to have given the world the opportunity to escape it – what Jonathan Schell has aptly called a "gift of time."[45] If the situation is so much less dangerous now than I think it still is – if nuclear deterrence could be shown, not merely assumed, actually to have worked during the cold war – this would appear to be the time "to seize upon opportunities of escape, even to take risks for the sake of such opportunities." And if, as I suspect, nuclear deterrence cannot work well when most severely tested, any attempt to maintain deterrence is itself much the greater danger, especially if combined with the current general complacency based on a tendentious superficial interpretation of the cold war. The world should ditch the nuclear variant of weapons of mass destruction as promptly as possible. It seems to me only a matter of time before cities burn, if not in Europe or North America, then in China, India, Pakistan, or the Middle East. All of humanity should turn back from the most serious wrong turn in the history of weapons technology. So perhaps Walzer and I can agree about what to do: Get rid of it – he because he thinks it is safe to, and I because I think it is dangerous not to. Our difference may be in our understanding of the urgency for action and, consequently, the level of risk it is in our interest to run to rid ourselves of this awful threat.

CONCLUSION

In any case, Walzer, of all people, would not want to keep nuclear deterrence only because it worked, even if it did, irrespective of what it committed us to do in order to save ourselves. How could he have believed that nuclear deterrence involves anything with "usefulness and proportionality"? Apparently, he believed that during the cold war both sides were bluffing. Here is his clearest statement: "The strategy works [!] because it is easy. Indeed, it is easy in a double sense: not only don't we do anything to other people, we also don't believe that we will ever have to do anything. The secret of nuclear deterrence is that it is a kind of bluff." Sadly, I believe that this was wishful thinking. I believe that in fact both the United States and the then USSR were fully committed to retaliating and would in fact have retaliated against what they perceived to be a nuclear attack, which might well have been some inadvertent event. I agree with Walzer that this would have been only to "drag our enemies after us into the abyss,"[46] but we have all kinds of evidence that we would have done exactly that. And that in the future India, Pakistan, and China would too.

Walzer seems to me to have had inordinate faith that rationality would prevail in the kind of severe crisis in which retaliation was the policy for which everyone in control of nuclear devices had trained all their careers. Earlier in the book he says: "Though nuclear deterrence rests only on threats, and the acts threatened are of such a nature that moral men and women might well refuse at the final moment to carry them out, no one is prepared in advance to admit to inhibitions."[47] But men and women with any inhibitions are carefully weeded out of units that control nuclear devices, and those who stay in are tested and tested in order to be sure that they will implement attack orders as given. And in the chapter on nuclear deterrence, he writes: "We strain for credibility, but what we are putatively planning and intending remains incredible."[48] But both the planning and the intending were deadly serious and utterly real. And completely unjustifiable: The best argument I know for having kept a weapon of mass destruction – Walzer's – fails.

Our fundamental disagreement is factual: Walzer believed in 1977 that we were pretending to be ready to kill millions; I believe that we were then, and still are, ready to kill millions as long as we think that we are retaliating against something appropriately terrible done to us. If Walzer is correct about the nature of nuclear deterrence, it is morally superior even to strategic bombing, since no innocents will actually be killed. If I am correct, we have only to wait for the bluff of a nuclear power to be called, or to seem to be called, for unprecedented slaughter to begin. I see no way a liberal (or any other sane person) could willingly accept continuing indefinitely to run this risk.

Notes

1. Michael Walzer, *Just and Unjust Wars: A Moral Argument with Historical Illustrations*, 3rd ed. (1977; New York: Basic Books, 2000), 274.
2. P. 283.
3. Winston S. Churchill, *The Second World War: The Gathering Storm*, bk. II, "The Twilight War," chap. 9, "Scandinavia, Finland" (Boston: Houghton Mifflin, 1948), 544. The operation would not have been unprecedented: "We had laid a minefield across the three-mile limit in Norwegian territorial waters in 1918, with the approval and co-operation of the United States" (p. 533). This proposal and its supporting arguments are insightfully analyzed by Walzer, *Just and Unjust Wars*, 242–50.
4. Churchill, *Gathering Storm*, 547. Quoted by Walzer, *Just and Unjust Wars*, 245.
5. John Rawls, *The Law of Peoples with "The Idea of Public Reason Revisited"* (Cambridge: Harvard University Press, 1999), 98–99 and 103–5.
6. See Henry Shue, "War," in *Oxford Handbook of Practical Ethics*, ed. Hugh LaFollette (New York and Oxford: Oxford University Press, 2003), 734–61.
7. For the suggestion that proportionality and discrimination, respectively, embody "consequentialist" and "deontological" reasoning, see A. J. Coates, *The Ethics of War* (New York and Manchester: Manchester University Press, 1997), 241. I adopt

the term "internalist," in preference to "deontological," following C. A. J. Coady, "Escaping from the Bomb: Immoral Deterrence and the Problem of Extrication," in *Nuclear Deterrence and Moral Restraint: Critical Choices for American Strategy*, ed. Henry Shue (Cambridge and New York: Cambridge University Press, 1989), 163–225. See also Chapter 5 by Coady in this book.

8. Richard M. Price, *The Chemical Weapons Taboo* (Ithaca, N.Y., and London: Cornell University Press, 1997). On whether nuclear weapons of mass destruction are actually legal, see Charles J. Moxley, Jr., *Nuclear Weapons and International Law in the Post Cold War World* (Lanham, Md., and Oxford: Austin & Winfield, 2000), esp. chap. 3, "The ICJ's Nuclear Weapons Advisory Opinion"; and Paul Szasz's discussion in Chapter 2 above, under "Nuclear Weapons."

9. For more detailed discussion, see Peter R. Lavoy, Scott D. Sagan, and James J. Wirtz, eds., *Planning the Unthinkable: How New Powers Will Use Nuclear, Biological, and Chemical Weapons* (Ithaca, N.Y., and London: Cornell University Press, 2000).

10. Henry Shue, "Having It Both Ways: The Gradual Wrong Turn in American Strategy," in Shue, ed., *Nuclear Deterrence and Moral Restraint*, 13–49; compare the reply by David Lewis, "Finite Counterforce," 51–114.

11. Walzer, *Just and Unjust Wars*, 229 (emphasis in original).

12. Ibid.

13. The reformulation of the immunity of noncombatants from a prohibition turning on esoteric issues about intention to a positive requirement of behavior reflecting due care is, I believe, a monumentally important contribution of Walzer's reading of *jus in bello* – see Walzer, *Just and Unjust Wars*, 153–56. I have previously noted it too briefly in Henry Shue, "Eroding Sovereignty," in *The Morality of Nationalism*, ed. Robert McKim and Jeff McMahan (New York and Oxford: Oxford University Press, 1997), 352. If taken seriously, Walzer's reformulation has powerful implications for policies such as NATO's bombing of Kosovo in 1999 and the U.S. bombing of Afghanistan in 2001–2.

14. Walzer, *Just and Unjust Wars*, 230.

15. Ibid., 231. Walzer here also labels this "the utilitarianism of extremity." The point of the label is clear: One does not engage in balancing generally – that is what the adherent of the sliding scale does – but one does balance at the extreme, most notably, in a supreme emergency. It is noteworthy that the adherent of the doctrine of the sliding scale is "utilitarian" – that is, balances means and ends – everywhere except the extreme, while the adherent of the argument from extremity is "utilitarian" – balances means and ends – only at the extreme. The two views are in this respect mirror images of each other. The moral absolutist, then, simply never engages in moral balancing and always obeys the rules.

16. Ibid. That utility and proportionality remain in force is critical below in the discussion of nuclear deterrence, since we have no evidence that deterrence works and abundant evidence that its threat is disproportional.

17. Ibid., 231–32.

18. Ibid., 255.

19. Ibid., 248.

20. I have almost no interest in Churchill's true intentions, if there is any such thing. I take him to have been trying to ram a policy through the cabinet more or less any way he could. I am simply foraging through his prose looking for potential

elements of arguments. The version of supreme emergency that has become influential and matters is not Churchill's but Walzer's.

21. Walzer, *Just and Unjust Wars*, 247. Walzer means the Norwegian and Swedish dead during the German attack in response to the British mines in the territorial waters of a neutral Norway.

22. "We have more to gain than to lose by a German attack on Norway" (Churchill, *Gathering Storm*, 546). As Walzer observes, "One immediately wants to ask whether the Norwegians had more to gain than to lose" (*Just and Unjust Wars*, 244).

23. Walzer, *Just and Unjust Wars*, 253.

24. Ibid., 261. Walzer considers the genuine supreme emergency to have lasted for the two years after the defeat of France in the summer of 1940 (p. 255).

25. Robert A. Pape, *Bombing to Win: Air Power and Coercion in War* (Ithaca, N.Y.: Cornell University Press, 1996), chap. 8, "Germany, 1942–1945." Pape argues powerfully that "strategic" bombing has never contributed to a military victory anywhere at any time and has always diverted air resources from militarily more useful employments. For a response to his critique, see Karl Mueller, "Denial, Punishment, and the Future of Air Power," *Security Studies* 7 (1998): 182–228.

26. Walzer, *Just and Unjust Wars*, 232.

27. Churchill, *Gathering Storm*, 547.

28. It would seem to me to place the threshold too high to require that the threat be literally global. Would triumphant Nazis have dominated literally every society on earth? I don't know, but it seems bad enough that they would have thrown one entire continent into barbarity.

29. I assume that while the argument takes the Nazis to be the embodiment of evil, it does not take the Allies to be the embodiment of good – only to be a force strong enough to defeat the significantly greater evil. This seems highly relevant to the "war on terrorism": From the extent of evil on one side, nothing follows about the extent of goodness on the other.

30. Walzer, *Just and Unjust Wars*, 231.

31. Ibid., 254.

32. Ibid.

33. The principle of proportionality is notoriously vague. Would it even be justified to kill a larger number of innocents on the aggressor's side to save a smaller number of innocents on the side attacked? Not if an innocent is an innocent – that is, not if each innocent counts for one, irrespective of whether he or she lives within an aggressor state. I have struggled with some of the ambiguities of proportionality in Shue, "War," in LaFollette, ed., *Oxford Handbook of Practical Ethics*, 747–52.

34. If this view is incompatible with the doctrine of double effect, understood as being centrally about intentions, but is indeed compatible with liberalism, the contrast between double effect and liberalism quoted from Rawls at the beginning is to this extent correctly drawn.

35. Walzer, *Just and Unjust Wars*, 254.

36. This, among many other things, makes the frequent characterization of Walzer's overall position as "communitarian" heavily one-sided and seriously misleading.

I do not make the opposite but equally simplistic claim that "he is a liberal"; like any interesting views, Walzer's are complicatedly rich.

37. Far and away the best analysis of both the dynamics and the morality of deterrence using nuclear devices is Steven Lee, *Morality, Prudence, and Nuclear Weapons* (Cambridge and New York: Cambridge University Press, 1993).

38. Walzer, *Just and Unjust Wars*, 280.

39. Ibid., 283.

40. See Shue, "Having It Both Ways."

41. Walzer, *Just and Unjust Wars*, 274.

42. Ibid., 273.

43. See Center for Defense Information, *National Missile Defense: What Does It All Mean?* (Washington, D.C.: Center for Defense Information, 2000); and Peter Van Ness, "Star Wars All Over Again," *Asian Perspective* 25 (2001): 227–38.

44. Steven Lee, "Morality, the SDI, and Limited Nuclear War," in Shue, ed., *Nuclear Deterrence and Moral Restraint*, 381–416.

45. Compare Jonathan Schell, *The Gift of Time: The Case for Abolishing Nuclear Weapons Now* (New York: Henry Holt, 1998). Schell thinks we have earned the gift not through making deterrence work but only by having been lucky.

46. Walzer, *Just and Unjust Wars*, 275.

47. Ibid., 214 n.

48. Ibid., 282.

8

A Liberal Perspective on Deterrence and Proliferation of Weapons of Mass Destruction

Michael Walzer

I did not expect to be the focus of Henry Shue's argument about what liberalism does or doesn't permit with regard to weapons of mass destruction. I suppose that the argument of *Just and Unjust Wars* is in some sense a liberal argument, though it relies so heavily on Catholic theory and Jewish anxiety that perhaps it isn't best read as Shue has read it. Until very recently, liberal political theorists took little interest in war; they were concerned with domestic society (which was represented as an escape from war) and then with international cooperation. The effort to outlaw war among states as it had been outlawed among individuals strikes me as the typical liberal response to the threat of aggression: Treat war as a crime, and deal with it by summoning the global police. The continuing relevance of just war theory is a consequence of the failure (so far, at least) of this liberal project.

So Shue's reading of just war as a liberal doctrine strikes me as a reconstructive effort. But I think that it is a good effort, picking up important features of the doctrine, not only in my version of it. And he reads my version with wonderful sympathy and generosity – more than I can muster on my own behalf after all these years. I doubt that I can rise to his challenge, which focuses in careful detail on the idea of "supreme emergency" and denies its relevance to questions of deterrence. Given that focus, Shue doesn't address several other questions raised in this book, which, I confess, I would rather write about, not only because I am uncomfortable with my deterrence argument, but also because the other issues (which I take up below) seem to me more pressing.

I am uncomfortable with my (qualified) defense of deterrence in part for the reasons that Shue gives: The argument sits uneasily with the previous account of "supreme emergency." And yet I can't now construct a better argument. Shue quotes me as saying that deterrence theory doesn't depend on a view of Stalinism as a great evil, comparable to Nazism. Of course, I thought then and still think that "great evil" is a plausible description of Stalinist Russia, indeed, the right description. By the time Reagan used the term, it no longer applied, but the fear of an evil regime surely figured, and figured legitimately, in the background of the argument for deploying nuclear weapons when they were originally deployed. Still, in the aftermath of World War II, Stalinism was not the same kind of threat that Nazism had been at the beginning of the war. The danger now was not the triumph of evil but the erosion of decency through fear, appeasement, and retreat. This certainly did not justify breaking through the moral barrier of noncombatant immunity. But then deterrence did not involve breaking through the barrier; it required, or seemed to require, only that we threaten to do that. If the danger was less, so was the response. It was nonetheless an immoral response (because a threat to act immorally is also an immoral act). I argued, some twenty years later, that the best way to think about this response was not to deny its immorality but to treat it as a special case of supreme emergency, where the emergency was ongoing ("permanent" was definitely not the right word). I still can't think of a better way to account for deterrence, and Shue doesn't offer an alternative political/military strategy for me to consider. In the absence of an alternative, I can say only this: We would probably not be disagreeing in this way, in a book on centrally important military questions, written and edited freely, with no arguments ruled out, if the United States had not deterred the Soviet Union in the 1950s. Is that freedom worth the risks that Shue describes? I am honestly not sure.

But I also argued in the 1970s that we were bound to seek a way out of the emergency, and it is clear that we have failed to do that with anything like the urgency required. So it may be that the force of Shue's challenge lies mostly in the past, and that we agree about what must be done today. Nuclear weapons were developed to deter Nazi Germany and deployed to deter Stalinist Russia. They are not being used for any comparable purpose right now. So I think, as he does, that it is time to stand down, to look for ways of disengaging from the system of nuclear deterrence. And I also think, as I assume he does, that if disengagement is to have even a chance of working, it must begin with unilateral moves by the United States, given its strategic position, the size of its arsenal, and so on.

Standing down will, however, be a complicated business, in part for reasons having to do with democratic politics. Though he doesn't develop the argument at length here, Shue is committed to a double denial of the effectiveness of deterrence: It doesn't work (or it doesn't work with sufficient certainty), and, moreover, it is terribly dangerous. In good liberal fashion, he does not rely entirely on its immorality in opposing it. We have more to fear from deterrence itself, he argues, from the threat of mass destruction and the military personnel trained and committed to carry it out, than from whatever is being deterred. But I am struck by the fact that this argument is, at least in part, unpersuasive even to those ordinary liberals who hate and fear war and every year oppose or struggle to reduce the military budget. Consider the current debate about the nuclear shield. Opponents of the shield, most of whom are probably liberals, claim that it will produce great instability – as if the (relative) stability of the current system is obvious to all. And the reason for the projected instability is that if the shield were successful, one great power, the United States, would be immune from retaliation to its own first strikes, which is to say, it would be undeterred. One can't argue in this fashion without being a friend of deterrence. It is still possible, and legitimate, to worry about accidents, but this fear of an undeterred superpower should put in perspective the arguments of the 1950s. Even now, it seems to make sense to say that we are less afraid when there is mutual deterrence than we would be without it. And if ordinary American liberals are worried about a unilateral escape from deterrence, they would probably also be worried about, and opposed to, a unilateral withdrawal from it.

But one can be an opponent of unilateral escape, such as the shield would allow, and still hope for a mutual stand-down – and still advocate American moves toward a stand-down, whether these are immediately reciprocated or not. These moves should include a reduction of weapon stockpiles, a lowering of the level of combat readiness, a shift in aiming policy, and so on. That is probably a good liberal position, but not a position only for liberals.

Is this the most important argument that we need to have today? In fact, in practice, the United States is not going to give up its own weapons of mass destruction if everyone else in the world is busy acquiring them. Why not? Wouldn't it be a good thing if one country, especially a big and powerful country, set a moral example? Again, the political answer (but doesn't it also have moral force?) is that ordinary people, not only those in America, would feel more threatened, at risk, exposed, in a world of extensive proliferation and U.S. disarmament than they do today. Maybe that is wrong; one would have to weigh the reduced (but not eliminated) risk of accident against the new risk of undeterred attack. I don't know how to do that. But I think I do know that the only policy likely to win democratic support is a cautious stand-down, testing the response of the others, whoever the others are, at regular intervals.

In any case, there will be no end to deterrence, it will never be phased out entirely, unless and until some effective way is found to block proliferation. So the most immediately important questions seem to me to be these:

1. Can states that already have weapons of mass destruction deny them to other states? More specifically, and more practically, can they follow a policy of selective denial?
2. Can these states use (conventional) military force to make the denial effective?

Shue doesn't address these questions, though he does argue strongly and persuasively for the military intervention of "the rest of us" to deal with the cases that meet his own account of supreme emergency. I wonder if proliferation at some point, or at many points, won't constitute an emergency at least of this sort: that it would justify military action (within the limits of *jus in bello*) by states not immediately involved or threatened. But I am not sure that I can point to an identifiably liberal argument on this issue. There is an older doctrine – one can find it in John Stuart Mill – that advocates or at least defends the use of force by enlightened liberal states for the sake of civilized, that is, mostly, liberal values. That doctrine has been in disfavor for a fairly long time; the particular forceful actions that it either inspired or rationalized were rarely enlightened. Nonetheless, both with regard to humanitarian intervention and with regard to proliferation, it seems to me that we cannot avoid thinking again about the moral inequality of states.

Thus a possible liberal answer to (1) is "yes," so long as the states that already have weapons of mass destruction are committed – let's say, actively committed – to getting rid of them. And this is so long as the selectivity is focused on states that are widely believed to be likely first-users, states that are not interested, or not primarily interested, in deterrence. I don't think that it is inconsistent to argue, on the one hand, that states already involved in the system of mutual deterrence should commit themselves to dismantle it and, on the other hand, that states newly possessed of weapons of mass destruction should commit themselves to the very system that needs to be dismantled. First things first. We live in stages.

And a possible liberal answer to (2) is also "yes" – so long as the states that are attacked with conventional weapons are widely and plausibly believed to be "rogue" or "failed" states. These designations are obviously matters of judgment and open to contestation. But we can bring evidence to bear, and the evidence suggests that there are some states that would probably be unwilling to constrain their deployment of weapons of mass destruction or who would be incapable (because of their internal instability) of guaranteeing the constraints. Worse than this, there are some states that are actually ready to use these weapons or, worse again, have recently used them. Here again I draw on the internationalist and interventionist aspects of liberal thought, and I don't want to do so naively. I fully recognize that Vietnam was in this sense a liberal war; I also believe that it was an unjust war. But internationalist interventions are not necessarily unjust.

Consider an example: The United States intervened in Iraq (before the 2003 war) claiming not only a right but an obligation to prevent Iraq from acquiring or developing weapons of mass destruction. We also claimed that other countries were obligated, if not to help us, then at least not to help Iraq. And if they did help Iraq, as some apparently did, we claimed (though we didn't always exercise) rights of enforcement against them. Given the character of the Iraqi regime and the character of the American regime, these seem to me defensible liberal claims. They received UN sanction, though of a somewhat ambiguous sort; I am not sure that the claims depend on that, though UN votes do provide some evidence of what I called "wide and plausible" beliefs about the character of the Iraqi regime under

Saddam Hussein. This might be a useful case to focus on in thinking about a liberal world order and the enforcement mechanisms (economic sanctions, inspections, no-fly zones) available within it. What are the rights and obligations of states committed to liberal values in the face of states that oppose and threaten those values – and then seek to acquire weapons of mass destruction?

A good many liberal writers in both Europe and America assumed that there was an easy response to states of the second sort (given that you couldn't just call the police): not military action by a single state or a coalition of states, but the imposition of economic sanctions. According to some accounts, however, the human costs of the blockade of Iraq were greater than the costs of the 1991 Gulf War up to the moment when President Bush called it off – and greater, probably, than the costs of an extended Gulf War, aimed at bringing down the regime in Baghdad, would have been. Under certain conditions, economic blockade may be a weapon of mass destruction, and war a more limited response.

I am unsure what role the UN and international law can play in stopping the development of frighteningly dangerous weapons by frighteningly dangerous states. Agents of the UN, acting under the aegis of international law, could certainly make a liberal world order more effective if they intervened strongly to prevent proliferation of this sort. But what if they didn't? It seems to me that if a "rogue" state is about to acquire nuclear, biological, or chemical weapons, and if the UN refuses to conduct or support action against it (because of regional rivalries, say, or the use of the great power veto), that cannot settle the matter. Nor does it settle the matter if an armed response would violate standing international law. The moral/political questions are independent of the legal questions, and the possible legitimacy of unilateral action (subject to all the necessary calculations of prudence and proportionality) survives any multilateral refusal to act. But, I admit, the better liberal position is to appeal to international institutions and to the rule of law, whenever possible, even if the appeal requires extensive and convoluted interpretive efforts. It is probably a good thing – it is certainly the liberal way – at least to make the effort.

9

Christianity and Weapons of Mass Destruction

Nigel Biggar

It cannot be said that earliest Christianity was pacifist. Certainly, Christians were criticized in the second century A.D. for abstaining from military service,[1] and there is no record of any Christian author of the period approving of participation in battle. However, since Christians were subject to intermittent persecution by the state until the early fourth century, it is difficult to say whether their military abstinence was a result of moral principle or political alienation. And while in the third and fourth centuries some theologians expressly condemned military service on the part of Christians,[2] this in itself could be taken to suggest a Christian presence in the army; and other evidence indicates that such a presence was growing from the end of the second century onward.

Following the conversion of the emperor Constantine in A.D. 312, and Christianity's subsequent toleration and gradual privileging, Christian participation in public office increased – and with it the need to reckon with the (tragic) necessity of using force to maintain the good of public peace and to assert the good of justice. Augustine (354–430), bishop of Hippo in North Africa, was one of the earliest to develop a rationale for the Christian use of force,[3] and it is mainly from him that the Christian theory of "just war" stems. Scattered in Augustine's writings are the three primary conditions of *jus ad bellum* (justice in embarking on war) that medieval thought would later systematize, and which Thomas Aquinas (c. 1225–74) would famously present: It must be undertaken on the authority of the ruler of a sovereign political entity; its cause must be just; and those undertaking it must do so with the right intention.[4]

The canon lawyers and theologians of the Middle Ages did more, however, than merely organize occasional fragments of thought about the justice of war into a coherent body of doctrine; they also developed it in two main respects. First, they extended what counts as a just cause. For Augustine, this could only be an injury perpetrated against an innocent neighbor, not against oneself, since Christians are bound to prefer the life of an aggressive neighbor to their own.[5] In developing his theory of natural law, however, Aquinas argued that *self*-defense is right, because all beings "naturally" seek their own preservation.[6] Behind this opaque and questionable appeal to the "natural" lies a covert and more intelligible invocation of the Judeo-Christian understanding of the goodness of creation:[7] All God's creatures are intrinsically valuable; I am a creature; therefore I am valuable; therefore I should show due care for myself – including that of self-defense against unjust aggression.

In light of Scott Sagan's identification of "the ethical" with altruism and his sharp differentiation of it from "the prudential" (in Chapter 3 above), it is important to note that Aquinas sets just war doctrine in the larger ethical framework of eudaimonism,[8] according to which the pursuit of one's own well-being (*eudaimonia* in Greek) – whether as an individual or a national community – is the ultimate rationale for any morally right action. Clearly, this understands morality differently from Kantian altruism. At the same time, it is not a form of Hobbesian "realism," because it does not narrow down well-being or self-interest simply to self-preservation[9] but understands it to include just conduct toward others. Accordingly, just war doctrine assumes that it is the duty of a national government to pursue what is in the interests of its people (including their security), provided that it understands those interests with sufficient breadth and therefore pursues them fairly and generously.

The second significant development in just war theory during the medieval period was the articulation of one of the criteria of *jus in bello* (justice in the waging of war), namely, noncombatant immunity or "discrimination."

The fifteenth and sixteenth centuries A.D. saw further advances. The stipulation of *jus ad bellum* that the cause must be just was refined by Francisco de Vitoria (c. 1485–1546) so as to exclude difference in religion.[10] To this and the other categorical conditions were added several prudential ones: that the use of force should be a last resort, that it should be proportionate to the evil remedied, and that it should enjoy the prospect of success. These considerations are "prudential" in that they are concerned to avoid causing unnecessary evil effects. They do not, however, render just war doctrine consequentialist or utilitarian, first, because they do not involve any pseudo-calculation of maximal good effects, and second, because such attention as they pay to consequences is conditional on certain categorical stipulations (about just cause and right intention) having been met.

Finally, during this period, *jus in bello* was further specified by a requirement that the means of waging war be proportionate to its end.

Fatefully, Europe ignored Vitoria's denial of the justice of war to advance the cause of a particular religion and dissolved into the best part of a hundred years of intermittent bloodshed between Catholic and Protestant from 1562 to 1648. Toward the end of this period the Dutch theologian and jurist Hugo Grotius (1583–1646) published *De iure belli ac pacis* (On the law of war and peace, 1625), in which he reworked the just war tradition so as, in effect, to reinforce Vitoria's repudiation of religious war. This he did, inter alia, by restricting just cause to self-defense and by recasting the justification of war in legal, rather than moral, terms. Through Grotius, it is commonly agreed, just war doctrine entered the discourse of international law, although the extent to which he is responsible for its secularization remains a moot point.[11]

This brief outline of the premodern history of Christian thinking about war is sufficient to show the tradition's complexity.[12] It includes both pacifist and just war elements, and although the latter has predominated since the fourth century A.D., the former has persisted to the present day – where it finds notable expression, for example, in the thought of John Howard Yoder (1927–97) and Stanley Hauerwas.[13] Since the Christian pacifist verdict on the military or deterrent use of weapons of mass destruction is absolute (*any* use, as with that of all other lethal weapons, is wrong), and since Robert Holmes and Duane Cady treat pacifism at length later in this volume, I will not dwell here long. Suffice it to say, in terms that muddy the too clear waters of Holmes's distinctions, that Christian pacifism can be at once principled, pragmatic, and "philosophical."[14] It can be principled in that Jesus's combination of faith in the providence of God and repudiation of violent means is taken as normative. It can be pragmatic in that the fundamental rationale of this norm is that faithful nonviolence is, by the providence of almighty God, the best way to achieve ultimate peace. And it can be "philosophical" in the sense that it repudiates war as "irrational" – that is, as a means to peace that is less than optimal in the light of the vindication of the unjustly crucified Jesus by the power of God in raising him from the dead.

Before we proceed to discuss Christian views of weapons of mass destruction simply in terms of just war theory, one further qualification needs to be made. There is no clear boundary between Christian doctrines of just war and secularized ones; both discourses share much moral language and many principles. At certain points, however, we should expect their different metaphysics or "grand narratives" to issue in different analyses and conclusions – different conceptions of what is "rational." So, in the hope of letting the distinctively Christian shape of Christian just war doctrine emerge, in what follows we concentrate on moral theological sources.

MORAL SOURCES AND PRINCIPLES

The two moral principles of just war that bear directly on the issue in hand are those that govern *jus in bello*: discrimination and proportionality. The first precludes the intentional killing of "innocents." The second requires the damage caused by the belligerent means to be "proportionate" to its end. Both presuppose three principles of *jus ad bellum*: just cause, authorization by the sovereign, and right intention. Indeed, they are entailed by the last of these.[15] In going to war, according to Christian doctrine, we may not intend to wreak vengeance on the enemy.[16] We may intend only to stop the aggression and restore a just peace. *If* this is our intention, we will cause only such damage as may reasonably be thought necessary to achieve these ends. Disproportionate damage, deliberately inflicted, indicates that our intention is otherwise.[17] Accordingly, and more specifically, we may target only those who are responsible for the aggression and who offer resistance to the restoration of a just peace. The deliberate killing of anyone other than these – that is, of the innocent – indicates that the taking of revenge, rather than the doing of justice, is our actual end.

In the course of Christian thought about these matters, the definition of "innocent" has been tightened. For Augustine, the "innocent" were those not guilty of unjust aggression. The problem with this moral concept of innocence, however, is that guilt is difficult enough to ascribe with any precision in a peacetime law court; and in the midst of battle it is virtually impossible. In practice, then, Augustine's concept tends to amount to the collective guilt of the enemy population, with the exception of the two categories of women and children, whose innocence he, along with his classical Roman inheritance, presumed.[18] Although adumbrations of a significant qualification of Augustine's position are discernible in the medieval period,[19] it was not until the sixteenth century that this became explicit. It was then that Vitoria argued for a distinction between an objective violation of right and subjective guilt – that the one does not necessarily imply the other[20] – and effectively equated guilt and innocence with the bearing or nonbearing of arms.[21] Here, "innocence" exchanges its moral sense for a behavioral one: The innocent are those who are *innocens*, that is, "nonharming" or "noncombatant." Accordingly, its embrace expands beyond women and children to include agricultural laborers and other peaceable civilians, foreign sojourners, clerics, and members of religious orders.[22]

This change in the definition of the "innocent" marks a shift in the concept of the justice that war properly intends. This now has less to do with punishing those who are morally culpable for the original injury than with stopping and reversing the injury itself.[23] Or to put the point in terms that are currently fashionable, it is less retributive and more restorative.[24] Although I cannot point to evidence of them in Vitoria's own writings, there are two reasons why such a reconception of justice suits the Christian point of view. The first is anthropological: Human beings are creatures with finite powers, and our capacity to discern and weigh guilt and innocence is as limited as our ability to make the punishment fit the crime. Human justice is unavoidably crude, as Augustine poignantly recognized: "What of those judgements passed by men on their fellow-men, which cannot be dispensed with [?] . . . How pitiable, how lamentable do we find them! For indeed those who pronounce judgement cannot see into the consciences of those on whom they pronounce it."[25] The point here is not that human efforts at doing justice are futile but that there are times when to attempt retribution is to take an excessive risk of perpetrating fresh injury. And besides, there is more to justice than retribution.

The second reason why one should expect Christians to be inclined to favor a restorative concept of justice is that the themes of compassion for wrongdoers, mercy and forgiveness toward them, and reconciliation with them were recurrent in the life and teaching of Jesus and are therefore prominent in the New Testament.[26] These do not exclude the notion of retribution, but at least they qualify – and arguably subordinate – it.

If Christian tradition has come, in time of war, to presume the innocence of all who are not actively engaged in perpetrating unjust aggression, it has also come to admit that not all killing of innocents is morally wrong. Such killing has been deemed permissible, provided that it is "unintended." This brings us to the controversial doctrine of double effect, which was adumbrated by Aquinas in his treatise on self-defense.[27] Here he distinguishes between the intended effect of a single act and its unintentional or accidental effect, arguing that only the first determines its moral quality. He then proceeds to argue that, when acting in a private capacity, it is morally permissible to kill an aggressor only on condition that one's intention is to save one's own life, and that the aggressor's death is necessary for ("proportionate to") this end. However, Aquinas allows an exception to this rule in cases where the agent is acting with public authorization (for example, as a soldier). Here he may intend to kill an aggressor, provided that he "refers" this to – is motivated by – the public good.[28] Vitoria was the first to employ the Thomistic principle of double effect in discussing *jus in bello*, holding that only the killing of the innocent by "primary intent" is immoral.[29] Since then, as we shall see below, the principle has been the subject of much elaboration and controversy.

The conditions of discrimination and proportionality for *jus in bello* are the moral principles by which Christian thought bears most directly on the morality of the uses of weapons of mass destruction. Others bear indirectly. Of these we have already mentioned the *jus ad bellum* principle of right intention, which the *jus in bello* principles presuppose. More indirectly still, and through right intention, bears the principle of the motive of love. From its beginnings, the Christian doctrine of just war has justified itself in terms of love. For Augustine, the use of force is justifiable only insofar as it is motivated by love for the neighbor – as enjoined by the second part of Jesus's summary of the Law[30] – and not by any "private passion." Augustine had two kinds of neighbor in mind: first, the innocent individual or political community whose injury constitutes just cause;[31] but also the enemy, who might benefit from punishment.[32] To these, as indicated above, Aquinas added responsible love for oneself.

Beyond moral principles, there are also theological beliefs that shape Christian just war theory. We have already mentioned the concept of the creatureliness of human being, with its implication of the limitations of human justice. Another implication is the limitation of human responsibility for the good of the world. Whatever its ascetic tendencies and other-worldly hopes, orthodox or mainstream Christianity has consistently endorsed the ancient Jewish affirmation of the goodness of the world of time and space and the value of human investment in it – for example, in the traditional Christian emphasis on the high importance of procreation.[33] However, if humans carry serious responsibility for the fate of the world, theirs is only the *finite* responsibility of creatures. What this means is that they are responsible for defending or promoting worldly, secular goods – such as national self-determination or liberal democracy – only insofar as they *may;* that is, within moral limits, and not at all costs. As Augustine put it, the primary political calling of the Christian is to serve justice, not to command secular success.[34] For this doctrine's inspiration, one need look no further than the earthly fate of Christianity's Founder.

To some extent, of course, Christianity's modest view of human responsibility results from its sensitivity to the limits of human power. Nevertheless, it is structured as much by hope as it is by humility. Orthodox Christians believe that God is supremely good, powerful, and wise; that he intends the salvation of his human creatures; that his Incarnation in Jesus shows this salvation to involve the world's transformation, not its abandonment; and that the Resurrection of the crucified Jesus gives ground to the hope that the fragility and failure of human efforts to promote the world's good will not be the last word. This hope inclines Christians to regard any failure as provisional and to scan the horizon for fresh signs of success, perhaps in unexpected forms.

USE OF WEAPONS OF MASS DESTRUCTION

Before we address the question of Christian just war theory's evaluation of the use of weapons of mass destruction, we must analyze the terms in which it is posed. First of all, the "use" under consideration here is of the military (i.e., defensive or aggressive), not deterrent, kind. Discussion of the latter is reserved for the next section. Second, just war theory does not object to "mass" destruction as such (although it will lament it), but only to that which is indiscriminate and disproportionate. Obviously, there will be destruction that is so massive as to fall foul of these two criteria, but there are degrees of massiveness, and certain kinds of mass destruction might meet the requirements of just war. Third, there may be weapons whose destructive force is so great as to make any military use of them necessarily indiscriminate and disproportionate. In other cases, however, whether a weapon observes the limits of just war will depend not just on its intrinsic properties, but also on the particular military uses for which it is intended and the circumstances in which these intentions are realized.

For the sake of simplicity, our discussion of weapons and uses that are massively destructive will proceed in terms of kinds of weapon. First, there are nuclear weapons in their several species – strategic, theater, and tactical. The main difference among these species lies in their range: Strategic weapons are aimed at targets deep inside enemy territory; theater weapons, at targets supporting enemy forces in battle; and tactical weapons, at targets in battle. Insofar as the use of tactical or theater weapons against the enemy might endanger one's own forces, their destructive capability is likely to be less than that of strategic weapons.

What differentiates all nuclear weapons *by nature* from conventional ones is the damage they cause by radiation. This characteristic feature also differentiates them *morally* because the effect of radiation is both difficult to control (it can spread beyond the battlefield and into areas where civilians are resident) and enduring (it can cause genetic defects in successive and entirely innocent generations, and it can make territory both uninhabitable and unproductive for very long periods). Therefore, by their nature nuclear weapons are more likely to press against the limits of discrimination and proportionality than conventional ones.[35]

Certainly, during the cold war the targeting of strategic nuclear weapons on centers of population was widely condemned by Christian ethicists. Against those who invoked the principle of double effect to argue that the massive destruction of noncombatants would be a side-effect of a right intention to defend civilization and democracy, the response was rightly given that, to be sincere, subjective intention must *actually govern* objective action. If the intention is not to include the wanton slaughter of noncombatants, then at least that slaughter cannot be a *means* to the end of defending civilization – whether through demoralizing the enemy populace or blackmailing the enemy government. If the killing of noncombatants is not an intended means, then the target will be of direct military significance. If this military target is the *genuine* target, then the force used against it will be no more than is necessary to destroy *it*; and if there is a realistic way of destroying it that could involve fewer civilian casualties, that will be chosen instead. And even then, if it is foreseeable that the efficient destruction of a military target is likely to involve civilian deaths as an unwanted side-effect, those deaths must still be "proportionate" – that is, the military target must be sufficiently important to warrant them, and the damage done to noncombatants by way of their deaths or the destruction of their living environment must not jeopardize the just and stable peace for which the war as a whole, and this engagement in particular, is being fought.

The germ of an exception to this absolute prohibition can be found, however, in the thought of Paul Ramsey.[36] Ramsey dissented from the official Roman Catholic prohibition of the intentional killing of the innocent *in any circumstances*. He argued that the principle of double effect, with its distinction between direct and indirect effects, is properly an expression of love for the neighbor and is subordinate to it. Whereas in most cases the intentional killing of the innocent offends against love, there are some cases where love requires it – for example, the case of pregnancy where both mother and fetus are bound to die, but where the intentional killing of the fetus would save the mother's life. Here, Ramsey argues, the doomed fetus must be presumed charitable and therefore unwilling to cling on to its right to (rapidly diminishing) life at the expense of killing its maternal neighbor.[37] Ramsey does go on to deny that this exception to the rule against the intentional killing of the innocent can be used to justify the intentional killing of noncombatants (e.g., by "area bombing") in order to defend civilized values. The reason he gives is that the exception holds only when the innocent are already moribund and when their deaths are certain to save others' lives – whereas in modern war the breaching of the rule would probably result in large-scale noncombatant deaths on *both* sides.[38] Nevertheless, by implication Ramsey concedes that the intentional killing of noncombatants could be proportionate under certain conditions – conditions that are more susceptible of being met in the present, post–cold war situation.

What Ramsey concedes only by implication, however, is baldly affirmed by James Turner Johnson, who, dropping Ramsey's first condition, writes that "in the last resort, foreseeable yet unavoidable harm to non-combatants in a battle area may be allowed in order to protect non-combatants in other geographic areas who would otherwise be put at menace or to protect values of equal or greater weight than harm to innocent persons by the use of indiscriminate means of war."[39]

If just war doctrine affords some minority support for certain intentional use of nuclear weapons against population centers, it offers justification of their use against military targets more readily. Nevertheless, during the cold war the dangers of escalation from "limited" use to full-scale nuclear exchange were widely reckoned so grave as to rule out even any "counterforce" use of nuclear weapons at the level of theater or battlefield[40] – although, again, Ramsey appears to have thought otherwise.[41] However, beyond the tensions and global polarities of the cold war, counterforce use against nonnuclear powers is far less likely to result in a major nuclear confrontation. Accordingly, for example, the use of low-yield nuclear weapons by the United States against Iraq might have been justifiable if they alone had been capable of penetrating deep, fortified bunkers and destroying by heat blast the chemical and bacteriological weapons contained in them; if the latter had threatened indiscriminate lethal harm to population centers; if there had been good reasons to suppose that they were about to be used; and if the bunkers had been in sparsely populated desert locations.[42] Even so, any decision to breach the international taboo against the military use of nuclear weapons, which has been universally observed since 1945, should be made only with the utmost reluctance, in the very last resort, and with the greatest trepidation – because once one state has dared to cross the nuclear threshold and survived, others will surely consider following.[43] For that reason every conceivable effort must be made to avoid arriving at a situation where the use of nuclear weapons of any kind might be justified – and that effort should include the development of "conventional" weapons to render that use unnecessary.

The second kind of weapon commonly associated with mass destruction comprises those that use chemical and bacteriological agents. Paul Ramsey, however, argues that "too many have too quickly slapped the notation 'immoral' upon any such weapons," overlooking the fact of nonlethal, noncontagious, incapacitating gases.[44] Following Ramsey, James Turner Johnson points out that these weapons could be unusually proportionate, insofar as their effect is to incapacitate, rather than kill, the enemy:

Where the alternative is to disable a soldier by shooting him, incinerating him with napalm, or irradiating him, an incapacitating gas with temporary effect, followed by the imprisonment of the enemy force, would seem to be more in line with the just war principle . . . of inflicting the least harm necessary to prevent the enemy from accomplishing his own goals.[45]

Moreover, it is not clear that the lasting effects of these weapons are more terrible than those of gun or artillery fire: "a veteran with lungs scarred by mustard gas might seem relatively whole by comparison with one who had lost one or more limbs to shellfire or machine gun bullets."[46] The main problem with chemical and bacteriological weapons, according to Johnson, is the difficulty of limiting their effects to combatants. However, he himself points out that in World War I gas warfare was conducted on well-defined battlefields from which noncombatants were far removed; and he remains open to the possibility that technological developments might yet allow greater control over the effects of this kind of weapon.[47] Ramsey alludes to just such a development, when he writes that

[i]nstead of using violent means to seal a border against infiltration and which if effective reduce an attacker's residual life expectancy from, say, fifty years to fifty minutes, *it is possible to lay down a cloud within a three mile limit this side of the border which will stick there and not be blown away* and which will increase his chances of going to sleep or becoming dizzy from, say, 2% to 98%.[48]

For Ramsey the decisive objection to the use of even temporarily incapacitating chemical weapons lies in "the disproportionate and uncontrollable consequences" likely to follow any breach of the convention against their use – namely, the

danger of escalation through a number of unconventional weapons systems which have in common only the fact that they are gaseous or micro-biological. . . . There is the danger that war would move rapidly through the class names, chemical and biological, the lethal as well as the non-lethal; and that these weapons might be directed at mass casualties sooner than weapons we are used to.[49]

In addition to "unconventional" weapons whose massive destructive capability is commonly supposed to be intrinsic, there are also "conventional" weapons that can be so used as to achieve massive destruction. In particular, what I have in mind here is the use of incendiary and other conventional bombs in the "strategic/area bombing" of German cities during World War II. Some have argued that this was justified either as an unintended side-effect or as a necessary means of defending civilization against barbarism. For example, William Temple, archbishop of Canterbury for most of the war, initially held that civilian deaths were permissible, provided simply that they were not intended. Later, becoming straightforwardly utilitarian, Temple argued that noncombatants may be intentionally targeted, not out of vengeance, but because the citizens of any modern state bear responsibility for the latter's actions, and, besides, the "total" nature of modern war virtually erases the distinction between combatants and civilians anyway.[50] Others – most notably, John C. Ford, S.J.[51] – have used a properly rigorous concept of the principle of double effect to suggest a negative judgment on area bombing.[52] As Ford implies, for an intention actually to be right, it must find expression in corresponding objectives. That is, if I really do not intend to kill civilians, then my target will be military and I will take steps to avoid or minimize civilian casualties; and if such casualties are probable, I will accept them only if the military target's destruction is proportionately important and is likely to yield the hoped-for benefits, and only if there is no other way of achieving it. Oliver O'Donovan puts the point succinctly: "The intention of an act is implied in the structure of the act, and not in some moment of psychological clarity in the actor."[53]

NUCLEAR DETERRENCE

Christian views of the morality of the deterrent use of weapons or strategies of mass destruction run right across the gamut of options. Paul Ramsey, of whom it has been said that his work on this topic is the "*Ursprung* from which subsequent efforts in Christian ethics have explicitly or implicitly taken their cues" and that "the power and precision of [his] argument is virtually without parallel among Christian ethicists today,"[54] offers a case for the moral justification of nuclear deterrence. Countercity targeting he rules out absolutely, because it infringes the prohibition of the intentional killing of noncombatants, even as a means to a greater good.[55] Counterforce targeting, on the other hand, Ramsey believes may be put to deterrent use. The argument he makes for this is notoriously ambiguous. Richard Miller speaks of Ramsey's application of the rule of double effect in this context as "gymnastic,"[56] and David Attwood writes that the epigram with which Ramsey summarizes his position is "alarmingly recalcitrant to careful analysis."[57] The epigram is this: "A threat of something disproportionate is not necessarily a disproportionate threat."[58] This could mean several things. It could mean that it is permissible to threaten to perform an act of disproportionate destruction, provided that what is intended is not the actualizing of the threat, but only deterrence.[59] However, as early as 1965, Ramsey showed considerable sympathy for the objection that such a policy of bluff would involve a government "authoritatively leading its own subjects into a gravely sinful consent,"[60] and in 1982 he confirmed that that argument had been decisive in leading him to withdraw his support from the policy.[61] David Attwood offers another, more coherent interpretation: What Ramsey meant is that the destruction permissibly threatened is only *apparently* disproportionate. The point here is that, apart from reference to a particular set of circumstances, it is impossible to determine whether something is or is not proportionate; and that it is permissible to exploit this indeterminacy for deterrent purposes.[62] Such a reading echoes another of Ramsey's arguments: that the very possession of nuclear weapons capable of being used against population centers constitutes a deterrent, because "[n]o matter how often we declare, and quite sincerely declare, that our targets are an enemy's forces, he can never be quite *certain* that in the fury or in the fog of war his cities may not be destroyed."[63] Implicit here is a further distinction that needs to be brought to the surface: not just between actual and apparent disproportion, but also between proportionality from one's own point of view and that from the enemy's. There may be significant dissymmetry here. From my viewpoint, a use of tactical nuclear weapons against your invading forces could be proportionate (if it seriously diminishes your capacity for aggression, with minimal collateral damage and without serious risk of escalation). From yours, however, the proportionality of my nuclear response is uncertain, making the risk of provoking it disproportionate. In the light of this last distinction, Ramsey's Delphic summary of his position could be rendered more intelligibly thus: "A threat of something disproportionate for the enemy to provoke is not necessarily a disproportionate threat for us to make." This reading has the advantages both of being plausible and of not requiring Ramsey to affirm something he expressly repudiated (a policy of bluff). It therefore makes the best sense of him, although not necessarily being the sense that he intended.

In contrast to Ramsey, the deliberations of the U.S. National Conference of Catholic Bishops in its 1983 pastoral letter, *The Challenge of Peace*, turn on the grave dangers of escalation:

A number of expert witnesses advise us that commanders operating under conditions of battle probably would not be able to exercise strict control; the number of weapons used would rapidly increase, the targets would be expanded beyond the military, and the level of civilian casualties would rise enormously.... Their testimony and the consequences involved in this problem lead us to conclude that the danger of escalation is so great that it would be morally unjustifiable to initiate nuclear war in any form.[64]

Accordingly, the bishops enjoin that nonnuclear attacks must be resisted by other than nuclear means.[65] The risks of transgressing the political, psychological, and moral barrier maintained since 1945 are just too great to warrant the initiation of nuclear war.[66] As for the "limited" or proportionate use of nuclear weapons *in response to a nuclear attack*, the bishops do not categorically rule it out, but they express extreme skepticism about its limits in practice:

Would leaders have sufficient information to know what is happening in a nuclear exchange? Would they be able under the conditions of stress, time pressures, and fragmentary information to make the extraordinarily precise decision needed to keep the exchange limited if this were technically possible? Would military commanders be able, in the midst of the destruction and confusion of a nuclear exchange, to maintain a policy of "discriminate targeting"? . . . Given the accidents we know about in peacetime conditions, what assurances are there that computer errors could be avoided in the midst of a nuclear exchange? Would not the casualties, even in a war defined as limited by strategists, still run in the millions? How "limited" would be the long-term effects of radiation, famine, social fragmentation, and economic dislocation?[67]

In this way, the bishops cast considerable doubt on whether it is possible even for a discriminate, counterforce use of nuclear weapons to remain proportionate; and they imply extreme skepticism about the morality of a deterrent policy that intends such use. They do not consider whether it would be permissible to *pretend* such an intention (i.e., to bluff), because it is quite clear to them that U.S. policy (in 1983) is deadly serious: "In our consultations, administration officials readily admitted that, while they hoped any nuclear exchange could be kept limited, they were prepared to retaliate in a massive way if necessary."[68] In the end, the bishops opt for "a strictly conditioned moral acceptance of nuclear deterrence."[69] The main conditions that they stipulate are these: that a policy claiming to be based on the prevention of the use of nuclear weapons by others desist from planning for prolonged nuclear warfare or for "victory" (i.e., seeking a "war-fighting capability"); that it abandon any quest for nuclear superiority; and that it be used as a step on the way toward progressive disarmament.[70]

The 1982 report of the Church of England's Board for Social Responsibility, *The Church and the Bomb*, shares with *The Challenge of Peace* extreme skepticism about the possibility in practice of maintaining a "firebreak" between different levels of weapon (conventional, tactical nuclear, theater nuclear, strategic nuclear)[71] and therefore of preventing escalation and keeping war limited and proportionate.[72] The report is explicit in its use of a "thick" concept of right intention, which integrates it with the choice of proportionate means. If one's declared intention not to kill noncombatants is genuine, it will find objective expression in measures taken to minimize collateral damage: "One must be prepared to go to great lengths to avoid harming [civilians] and make great sacrifices to that end."[73] Unlike *The Challenge of Peace*, however, *The Church and the Bomb* judges that the high risk of escalation and so of disproportion between destructive effects and peaceful goals renders immoral even the defensive use of nuclear weapons.[74] Accordingly, it takes a harder (and more consistent) line on nuclear deterrence. Since this involves a conditional threat to do something that is in itself immoral, it involves sinful consent to act immorally: "Sin is completed in act but begins in consent, and the consent to act immorally, even though the act never be performed, is already sinful."[75] But what if this intention is only pretended – that is, a bluff? The report's answer is basically the same as Ramsey's, though more developed. In order to work, a policy of bluff would have to prevent the enemy from discovering its real intention never to realize the threat. That is, knowledge of the truth would have to be kept secret to the highest echelons of the political and military leadership. This raises two problems, one practical and one moral. The first is that of how the policy's maintenance and secrecy could be ensured across changes of government and general staff. The second is that, while the intentions of those party to the secret would be upright, those of personnel in lower echelons would not be: Theirs would be a sinful intention to use immoral means, when commanded to do so. And indeed, insofar as these would be required by their superiors to consent to such an intention, culpability for encouraging their moral corruption could ultimately be traced to the highest echelons.[76]

The same arguments against a policy of bluff appear in *Nuclear Deterrence, Morality, and Realism*[77] by John Finnis, Joseph Boyle, and Germain Grisez. Described by one reviewer as "an impressive construction whose sheer analytical rigour and attention to detail marks it out from the great majority of contributions to the subject,"[78] this book evaluates nuclear deterrent policies and possibilities toward the end of the cold war in the mid-1980s. Finnis and his colleagues reckon that, notwithstanding its technical eschewal of countercity targeting,[79] American policy toward the Soviet Union necessarily threatened massive civilian casualties, in order to retain its credibility as a deterrent. Since the Soviets were unequivocal about responding to counterforce use of tactical nuclear weapons with countercity attacks, the United States and NATO could hope only to deter such attacks and prevent escalation by threatening retaliation that would wreak unacceptable collateral damage (in the course of hitting military targets).[80] Since this damage was essential to the threat, it was an intended means rather than an accepted side-effect. The threat itself, therefore, was immoral. Unlike the American Catholic bishops and the Church of England's working party, Finnis et al. do not make the principle of proportionality (and so the probability of escalation) central to their argument.[81] This is because the principle of discrimination is quite sufficient, in their eyes, to decide the case.

But, putting current policy aside, could not an effective threat be made without being intended? As already indicated, the authors of *Nuclear Deterrence* find a policy of bluff both impracticable and immoral. What, then, about deterrence through the ambiguities of "mere possession"? Here they argue that the maintenance and constant refurbishment and updating of the deterrent system would amount to a threat, albeit nonverbal, to wreak immoral destruction.[82] Robert Song correctly points out that a *perceived* threat need not be an *intended* threat.[83] However, if this distinction is not to rest on a policy of bluff, the deterrent nation would have to publicly (and sincerely) renounce any such threat while maintaining and developing the system that appears to pose it. Finnis and his colleagues dismiss this possibility on two grounds: First, the enemy could test the renunciation and become sufficiently confident to dare to exploit it; and second, it would be too schizophrenic a policy, making it impossible to explain convincingly to military personnel and taxpayers the purpose, respectively, of their training and their fiscal support.[84]

Finally, Finnis et al. consider whether a genuinely pure counterforce strategy could be developed. They reckon not. Such a strategy would have to be a war-winning, and not merely a war-fighting one; because if defeat cannot be avoided, then there can be no reason to begin or to continue a nuclear exchange.[85] There are two main kinds of war-winning counterforce capabilities: "a virtually disarming ... and extremely reliable" first-strike force and "an almost impregnable" strategic defense system.[86] In neither case, judge Finnis and company, is the hope of development realistic.[87] On the one hand, it would be impossible to attain such technological superiority as to guarantee the complete effectiveness of a first strike against the enemy's weapons systems; and any effectiveness that is less than complete would expose the attacker to catastrophic retaliatory damage. Further, possession of a first-strike capability would create a situation of "crisis instability," in which the enemy would be severely tempted to preempt an attack.[88] On the other hand, it is equally doubtful that such technological superiority could be attained as to guarantee a perfect capability to intercept all the adversary's offensive nuclear weapons. And it is equally likely that the attempt to create such a system of strategic defense would aggravate the arms race and foster "crisis instability."[89] And besides, even if it were possible, the development of pure counterforce war-winning capabilities would take time, during which an immoral system, threatening the deaths of millions of noncombatants, would have to be maintained.[90]

Like Finnis and his colleagues, and unlike his mentor, Paul Ramsey, Oliver O'Donovan judges the strategy of nuclear deterrence to be morally indefensible; but the reasons he gives reach beyond the criteria of just war theory to draw on an astute theological critique of modernity. O'Donovan identifies nuclear deterrence as the mature expression of a modern project of pursuing absolute peace by deliberately enhancing the disproportion between the costs of war and its rewards.[91] "Disproportion is not an accident of modern deterrence," he claims; "it is the principle on which it is thought."[92] The story he tells of the birth and growth of this project seems plausible, although the historical connections between its various moments are more asserted than demonstrated. It begins with war-weariness in the late eighteenth and early nineteenth centuries, becomes articulate in the philosophy of Kant and the theology of Schleiermacher, gains expression in the theories of war espoused by von Clausewitz, Francis Lieber, and Tolstoy's Prince Andrei, and finds its first twentieth-century military incarnation in the concept of the strategic air strike.[93] To O'Donovan, the deliberate throwing off of moral constraints on the conduct of war is the result of a greedy impatience with the pursuit of proximate justice and a titanic aspiration "for the seat of divinity and the exercise of omnipotence" – in other words, a manifestation of original sin.[94]

Human pretense to superhuman control vitiates the strategy of nuclear deterrence at two points. First, adopting a Hobbesian reduction of human motivation to the single point of the fear of extinction, it supposes a quasi-mechanical predictability about human actions and reactions that is quite unrealistic.[95] Second, drawing on the technological bent of the modern mentality, it claims that the deterrent state's pacific intent can transcend its disproportionate threat as a master transcends his tool.[96] Such transcendence is sometimes made to take the form of a bluff. O'Donovan denies, however, that a state is capable of practicing mental reservation, arguing that the secret resolutions of an inner cabinet of government comprise a conspiracy rather than state policy and implying that such private plans are unlikely to be able to withstand the juggernaut of "the enormous programmed machinery of national and international crisis-management in circumstances of great public panic."[97] Alternatively, the state is supposed to transcend its disproportionate threat not by bluffing but by postponing a decision about whether it will or will not actualize its hypothetical plan of nuclear attack. Come the day of crisis, however, the absence of any decisive plan of action will constitute a vacuum into which the hypothetical plan is inevitably drawn. "By degrees," O'Donovan shrewdly predicts, "the hypothetical intention becomes the actual intention."[98]

PROLIFERATION OF WEAPONS OF MASS DESTRUCTION

During the cold war, nuclear conflagration between the superpowers was avoided by a balance of nuclear threats. As *The Church and the Bomb* puts it, "The proliferation of nuclear technology to an increasing number of states introduces a new element of substantial uncertainty into the nuclear balance."[99] Finnis and his colleagues specify this concern:

The system of mutual deterrence has worked up to now under relatively favourable conditions: the confrontation has been between only two superpowers, and the experiences of these two nations have provided their leaders with good reasons for restraint. This success may well encourage the development of nuclear deterrents by nations with vastly more difficult security problems, and with leaderships and political cultures less inclined to restraint by their historical experiences.[100]

James Turner Johnson, on the other hand, entertains the notion that the "horizontal" proliferation of nuclear weapons might actually advance the cause of multilateral renunciation. He argues that the banning of gas warfare by the Washington Treaty of 1922 and the 1925 Protocol was achieved not because of horror at its indiscriminate and enduring effects, but because of the difficulty of controlling its use, the ease and cheapness with which it can be produced by any power – no matter how immature or irresponsible its leadership – and the near impossibility of an effective defense against it. He notes that these three characteristics now apply to nuclear weapons as well – the second, thanks to horizontal proliferation – and considers the inference that this might actually aid arms control. In the end, however, he judges the argument to be "seriously flawed." One reason is that the world today is far more fragmented than it was in the 1920s:

Proliferation in 1922 and 1925, as applied to chemical and bacteriological weapons, meant possession or potential possession by a handful of powers with governments and traditions of government at least apparently stable enough to ensure compliance. Today, even aside from the obvious problem of an atomic bomb in the hands of a Qaddafi, there is the matter of international terrorism and the justifiable fear that nuclear proliferation will result in the use or threat of a nuclear weapon by a terrorist group for its own ends.[101]

So what is to be done? The Church of England working party observes that the nonnuclear signatories of the Nonproliferation Treaty (NPT) of 1968 agreed to forego nuclear weapons on an undertaking of the nuclear weapons powers to "take speedy and effective steps toward . . . nuclear disarmament."[102] It also argues that "the justifications for possession [of nuclear weapons] which continue to be used by existing nuclear powers . . . are capable of indefinite repetition,"[103] implying that unless the nuclear parties to the treaty fulfill their side of the agreement, the other parties will have equal reason to set about acquiring nuclear armaments. Accordingly, it urges the nuclear signatories to meet their obligations "in the hope of putting new life" into the treaty.[104]

The Challenge of Peace makes the same exhortation, noting in addition that the NPT's multinational controls have been gradually relaxed by states exporting fissionable materials for the production of energy and calling on the United States and other nuclear exporting states to "make clear its determination to uphold the spirit as well as the letter of the treaty."[105]

While agreeing with the complaint that the current effect of the NPT is "discriminatory"[106] in that it denies nuclear weapons to the many while a few retain them, Sydney Bailey argues that nonnuclear weapons states derive advantages from the treaty – "if that were not so, more than 120 of them would not have ratified it."[107] What these advantages are Bailey himself does not explain, but it is reasonable to suppose that, in spite of its failure so far to move the main nuclear powers to disarm, the NPT has created or confirmed regional nuclear weapons-free zones, thereby relieving many states of the burdens of competing in a local nuclear arms race.

Concern about proliferation, however, can no longer restrict its thinking to ways of breathing new life into the NPT. This is because, with the dissolution of the Soviet Union, the problem threatens to develop a new dimension over which the NPT has no effective jurisdiction: namely, the possession of nuclear weapons by bodies that are not states. This is an especially dangerous development because such bodies would be less encumbered than most states by the constraint of political accountability, would stand outside the conventions of international diplomacy, would probably be more unstable because of susceptibility to internal fissures, and would therefore be far more difficult to treat with and to monitor. Here the rationale of the *jus ad bellum* stipulation that war be launched only by a legitimate authority comes into sharp focus.

NUCLEAR DISARMAMENT

At one end of the spectrum of Christian views about disarmament is James Turner Johnson, who places his faith in the system of balanced strategic nuclear deterrents and asks only for the greatest possible lowering of the level of balance. He treats as unproblematic the claim that the strategic deterrent system is designed to ensure the nonuse of nuclear weapons and could have no other rational use. Indeed, it has already brought about a remarkably effective de facto ban, "and whether a *de jure* ban ever comes into being or not, it is this disutility that stands as the strongest barrier against nuclear war."[108] He admits that this does not remove "the grave moral problem" of the immorality of counterpopulation targeting, but argues that "so long as war remains possible – that is, so long as the eschaton [the divine fulfillment of history] is not yet here – moral purposes may sometimes best be achieved by not entirely savory means." In other words, the threat of indiscriminate or disproportionate destruction is "the lesser evil."[109]

The American Catholic bishops are far less complacent. In their eyes, the deterrent system is too precarious to live with; and, besides, they aspire to a peace that is not just the absence of war.[110] While they refuse to support a policy of unilateral disarmament, the bishops urge the need to take calculated risks in venturing "independent initiatives" in arms control and reduction, which are designed to elicit reciprocity.[111]

Likewise, the Church of England working party judges that, at the level of the opposing military alliances, disarmament must be multilateral, since anything else would be dangerously destabilizing.[112] Nevertheless, they too see scope for unilateral action within an overall multilateral approach. In particular, what they have in mind is Britain's renunciation of its independent nuclear deterrent, partly to reinvigorate the Nonproliferation Treaty "by showing that at least one of the nuclear powers is prepared to take its obligations under this instrument seriously" and partly to eliminate the destabilizing effect of yet another center of decision making about the use of nuclear weapons.[113]

In contrast, Finnis and company express an unusual – and excessive[114] – pessimism about the prospects of multilateral disarmament:

[M]utual disarmament is far less in prospect than it was at the beginning of the nuclear era, for all the talk, the initiatives, and the agencies for promoting it. Each side's project of maintaining and enhancing nuclear deterrence has proved to be a step – or, more accurately, a continuous walk – *away* from mutual disarmament.... [T]he history of the nuclear era offers no ground for considering mutual disarmament a realistic prospect in the foreseeable future.[115]

However, even if the prospects were better, that could not justify maintaining a nuclear deterrent as an interim measure. The deterrent is simply immoral: "To maintain the deterrent pending mutual disarmament, or even as a spur to mutual disarmament, is to maintain the murderous intent which the deterrent involves."[116] Accordingly, it must be abandoned unilaterally and without delay: "Morality's demands do not wait."[117] Finnis et al. are under no illusions about the probable consequences of what they advocate. They recognize that (at the time of writing) unilateral disarmament by the West would probably issue in unconditional capitulation to the USSR.[118] They do not welcome this: They are well aware of the evils of the Soviet system and of the (relative) moral superiority of the West.[119] Nevertheless, for all its Christian provenance, the West is not to be confused with the Kingdom of God – not even *in nuce*. That Kingdom is not of this world and will be achieved not by human Progress, but by divine Providence.[120] Certainly, humans have responsibility to defend and promote "goods" or dimensions of human flourishing, but theirs is the limited responsibility of creatures to do what they *may*, not all that they *can*.[121] Besides, most important of all the goods they should promote is "the heavenly community," which they do primarily by shaping themselves and their relationships through adopting pure intentions and thus making morally right choices:[122] "[I]n one's choices, moral rightness is more important than any other worldly good."[123] It is for this reason – this *religious* reason – that Finnis and his colleagues argue that "[n]o matter how great the good at stake, if an evil means is required to serve it, one should say, simply, I cannot." They continue:

> The old saying about right and the heavens came from a world-view in which the heavens were not expected ever to fall. As Christians, we believe (and as people acquainted with modern physics, we expect) that they will eventually fall. Yet we also hope that the end of this physical universe, like the death of each human person, will not be the end. As he will raise each person, God will raise up the universe: there will be new heavens and a new earth. Meanwhile, neither Soviet domination of the world nor a nuclear holocaust need be considered the falling of the heavens. But either would be a great catastrophe, and faced with any human catastrophe, the Christian is to say: We look for the resurrection, and everlasting life.[124]

Oliver O'Donovan agrees with Finnis and company that the nuclear deterrent is immoral and should be dismantled, but he reckons sheer unilateral disarmament to be imprudent. On the one hand, the West has nothing good to lose by letting go of its nuclear deterrent. In O'Donovan's eyes, it has failed on all counts: It has not persuaded the world of the folly of (all) war;[125] it has stymied attempts to remedy injustice – and to sterilize the seeds of strife – by proportionate means;[126] it has created stability in Europe at the nuclear level at the price of instability elsewhere at the subnuclear one;[127] it has exacerbated the arms race;[128] and it has subverted liberal values by according Western civilization the status of an ultimate value (or, in Finnis's words, identifying it with the Kingdom of God), thereby embracing a form of political totalitarianism.[129] As for vulnerability to nuclear blackmail, O'Donovan argues that that would be no greater without a nuclear deterrent than with one. First of all, it would make no sense for an expansionist enemy to use nuclear weapons against territories that he intended to occupy: "Badly contaminated territories are not controllable."[130] Second, the threat of a strategic nuclear strike in response to a conventional or tactical nuclear attack already obtains with the deterrent. All that would be different without one would be the capacity to wreak nuclear revenge – to no political, and therefore moral, purpose.[131] Third, a strategic strike might be threatened to prevent opposition to limited expansion – for example, by the Warsaw Pact into West Berlin. But there is good reason to doubt the effectiveness of the nuclear deterrent in fending this off, since NATO would be unlikely to risk full nuclear exchange to stop such an incursion.[132]

So, according to O'Donovan, the West has nothing to lose by being without its nuclear deterrent. It does, however, have something to lose if it disarms without at the same time bolstering its conventional and battlefield nuclear weapons. This is because dangerous instability would arise if it were to be bereft of its capacity to retaliate against an enemy attack; and one way of doing that without launching strategic nuclear weapons would be to mount an invasion of the enemy's own territory – an invasion that the enemy could not counter with nuclear force except by contaminating his own land. However, any move to bolster conventional forces would itself be destabilizing, unless the enemy understood its rationale and trusted its motivation. For this reason – *pace* Finnis et al. – O'Donovan holds that disarmament should be attempted first on a bilateral basis and, only if that fails, on a unilateral one.[133]

SOME CURRENT ISSUES

We turn now, and finally, to consider what the Christian tradition has to say about current international law and policies concerning the military use of discriminate chemical weapons, the military and deterrent uses of nuclear weapons, and the American construction of a national system of defense against missile attack. Since Christian reflection on these matters appears to have taken a holiday since the end of the cold war, I must now go beyond critical reportage of what the tradition *has* said and venture an opinion on what I think it *should* say.

Regarding the present ban on the use and development of chemical and biological weapons, the Christian just war tradition first of all points out that temporarily incapacitating gases would actually be morally preferable to lethal or permanently damaging weapons, provided that the geographical scope of their effects could be sufficiently controlled. It seems, however, that the kind of precise control envisaged by Ramsey[134] is not yet feasible. Moreover, unless international law can be made to discriminate between different kinds of chemical and biological weapons, the controlled use of even nonlethal gases would be imprudent, since it could seriously weaken the authority of the general ban on the use of far less benign and discriminating kinds (e.g., those carrying bacteriological agents).

At the moment, the military use of nuclear weapons is not *absolutely* repudiated by international law.[135] Should it be? The answer to this question depends on whether (with Paul Ramsey) one can envisage a situation where the use of nuclear weapons would be discriminate and proportionate. Paul Szasz mentions one candidate: the use of a nuclear weapon against a warship at sea.[136] We have mentioned another: the first use of low-yield nuclear weapons in an attack on desert bunkers housing chemical or biological missiles. But then arises the question, Would not even such limited uses stand in grave risk of stimulating escalation? Most of the Christian answers to this question tend toward the affirmative, but they all assume a cold war context. What about the risk of escalation now? As argued above, beyond the context of tense superpower rivalry, this is much reduced, at least as regards use against a nonnuclear power. Whereas it is conceivable that the USSR would have threatened the use of nuclear weapons to defend Iraq against American attack, it is significant that Russia stayed its nuclear hand in the war of 2003, as it had done when NATO bombed Slavic Serbia in 1999. Even so, there would have to be very strong reason indeed to breach the de facto international taboo on the use of nuclear weapons in general: The threat to be countered would have to be very grave, and no other effective means of meeting it should be available.

What about deterrent use? Clearly, deterrence by means of countercity targeting or the threat of disproportionate collateral damage caused by counterforce use are both ruled out, morally speaking. May one deliberately threaten damage that is objectively immoral, without intending to carry it out? The arguments against the unrealism, impracticability, and immorality of the nuclear bluff are cogent. Therefore, in that the current nuclear deterrent threatens disproportionate damage, it should be dismantled.

This is not to say, however, that *no* nuclear deterrent should ever replace it. One that threatens collateral damage that it would be proportionate for a defender to wreak, but disproportionate for an attacker to risk, would be morally permissible. Certainly, whether it *would* be proportionate for a defender to wreak certain damage depends partly on the risk of escalation. Still, since it cannot be said that this risk will always be high in every conceivable situation, the Christian tradition does not rule all nuclear counterforce deterrence as illicit.

What, then, about replacing the nuclear deterrent with a comprehensive system of defense against nuclear attack, such as the Strategic Defense Initiative (SDI) with which the Reagan administration experimented, or the National Missile Defense (NMD) project on which the administration of George W. Bush is currently embarked? Whether NMD is feasible – technologically, financially, and politically – we have yet to see. Should its feasibility turn out to be highly improbable, it would be foolish – and therefore immoral – to pursue it. Let us suppose otherwise, however, and consider the moral objections that have been raised against a practicable system.

One of these is that NMD would be "destabilizing."[137] This invites reflection, of course, on the kind of stability that would be disturbed. Insofar as it is the "peace" that rests on the threat of massively disproportionate retaliation, Christian ethics would welcome its prudent unsettling. But would not NMD be imprudent, because, by making the United States invulnerable to retaliation, it would heighten the vulnerability of enemy states to American attack, and so intensify international insecurity? The answer is both "no" and a qualified "yes." No, because the current size of Russia's strategic nuclear forces is such that they could still overwhelm a limited NMD.[138] No, because there is strong evidence that China does not fear an American first strike: In April 2001, China's top arms control official, Sha Zukang, reportedly "made plain that China's fear was not that the United States would launch a surprise attack. . . ."[139] The answer is "yes," however, in that other states – say, an equivalent to Saddam Hussein's Iraq on the verge of using chemical and biological weapons – would indeed be vulnerable to American attack. But is it not good that such states should be – and feel – insecure?

There is another kind of instability that NMD would introduce. China's strategic nuclear forces are much more limited than Russia's[140] and could be neutralized by a defensive system.[141] While China does not fear a nuclear first strike, what it does fear is that the undermining of its deterrent will give the United States much more room for unilateral military activity and therefore a significant diplomatic edge in East Asian affairs. Indeed, there is evidence that it is this, rather than immunity from the reckless acts of "rogue" states,[142] that a system of missile defense is mainly designed to achieve.[143] So NMD could well "destabilize" relations between the United States and China, in the sense that it would give the former greater scope for engaging in – or at least threatening to engage in – military action in pursuit of political goals in East Asia. However, insofar as the "aggressive" military action feared by China includes the kind that was displayed in Kosovo and the kind that might be displayed in defense of Taiwan[144] – kinds that are, arguably, just – Christian ethics finds no ground for condemnation in "instability" of this sort.

A second moral objection raised against NMD is that it will trigger an arms race. What, in Christian eyes, would be objectionable about this? Not the development of weaponry as such; for if wars can be just, then weapons of some kind are needed to fight them, and the more effective and discriminate these are, the better. What would be objectionable would be the spending of vast resources on both sides to maintain a situation where mutual total destruction is assured or just to maintain a situation of stalemate at an unnecessarily high level of armament. What would also be objectionable is the heightening of mutual insecurity and suspicion in circumstances that might issue in actual nuclear conflict.

Would NMD stimulate an arms race that involves these features? If the defensive system were sufficiently comprehensive, it could undermine the basic concept of the 1972 Anti-Ballistic Missile Treaty, which is that the bilateral reduction of strategic weaponry is rational so long as both Russia and the United States remain vulnerable to "assured destruction." For that reason, one of the pillars of the ABM Treaty is the ban on nationwide defenses against strategic missiles. It may be that an agreement will be reached to limit NMD so as to maintain American vulnerability to the Russian deterrent. If not, Russia might seek to develop the capability to overwhelm the defensive system by reequipping its intercontinental ballistic missiles (ICBMs) with multiple warheads.[145] Nevertheless, there is broad agreement among experts that, even if the United States proceeds with NMD, Russia will continue to abide by arms control and disarmament agreements and to negotiate further ones – because it cannot afford, financially, to do otherwise.[146]

What about China? It seems very unlikely that it would respond to the development of NMD with a massive buildup of its minimal strategic nuclear capability, because it would be starting from a very low base, and such a policy would entail very heavy financial burdens. Besides, China's chief arms control expert has publicly declared that, instead of engaging in a costly arms race, China would take the relatively cheaper option of developing the capability of disabling the vulnerable radar network and communication nodes of the American defensive system.[147]

It seems clear enough, then, that if America's pursuit of a system of missile defense does provoke Russian rearmament or Chinese military development, it will not amount to an arms race of cold war proportions. And while it will heighten certain international tensions, it will not do so in such a way as to bring the world to the brink of nuclear war.

My conclusion, therefore, is that, as things stand, Christian just war theory supports the project of NMD – but with one important caveat. Effective defense against nuclear attack should not be pursued as a final, technical solution to the problem of national insecurity. Insecurity, whether collective or individual, is a fact of human existence that may be managed wisely or foolishly, but must be lived with. Human security in history can never be other than more or less precarious; and sinful attempts to transcend this creaturely limitation only tempt nemesis. Those who would build a system of NMD, therefore, should bear in mind the fate of the Maginot Line, and be careful to pursue national security with equal vigor on other fronts, too. Hearts should not be so set on missile defense, for example, that the urgent task of keeping ex-Soviet plutonium and highly enriched uranium out of the hands of terrorist groups is neglected.[148] And faith in the construction of a shield against nuclear attack should not be allowed to relax diplomatic efforts to reach agreements with the so-called rogue states, against whose putative aggression the defensive system is partly directed.[149] Just because a state does not conduct itself according to the "realist" canons of Hobbesian "rationality" and is motivated as much by self-respect, honor, and resentment of historic injustice as by self-preservation, it should not be dismissed too quickly as beyond the pale of dialogue. This is not to say, with liberal sentimentality, that there are no real barbarians in the world – only that we are obliged always to hope that we have not found one.

ADDENDUM: THE VIEW FROM THIS SIDE
OF SEPTEMBER 11, 2001

The terrorist attacks on New York and Washington on September 11, 2001, have changed much about how the United States in particular and the West in general view the conditions of their security. What light do the attacks and their aftermath throw on my concluding remarks immediately above? I discern two points. First of all, they serve to underline the caveat that NMD can be no panacea. Some have gone so far as to argue that the attacks have rendered it irrelevant.[150] This is an exaggeration. It is clearer now than before that some so hate the West and its most powerful representative, the United

States, that, were they ever to possess the capability of launching a nuclear missile against it, they would do so – regardless of the consequences. A defensive shield, therefore, would not be redundant. But it certainly will not be sufficient. And other strategies for bolstering security might reasonably have greater claim on limited resources.

As for always hoping that those with whom we have to deal are not barbarians, beyond the pale of some kind of rational dialogue – what does this mean in relation to the perpetrators of the atrocities of September 11? It seems that in Usama bin Ladin we have found a barbarian, one with whom negotiation is impossible, because his hatred of us has grown so overripe that he intends nothing less than our total destruction. In what sense, then, should we continue to hope that he will turn out to be otherwise? In the sense that we are willing to entertain the possibility that, though his ill-disciplined resentment has festered out of all proportion, not all of its roots are simply malevolent and irrational. It may be that the policies of American and other Western governments regarding the Middle East have perpetrated, or at least perpetuated, injustices that well deserve a measure of resentment, and that these policies should be revised accordingly. This is not to admit that the West is as responsible for the woes of Muslims as Bin Ladin and his supporters believe it to be. But it is to be willing to admit that his unbridled anger is not without traces of truth to which we are answerable. On reflection, my original formulation did not quite hit the mark. It is not that we are obliged to hope naively against all the evidence that we are not dealing with a barbarian; rather, we must be careful to heed the elements of truth that lie buried in the rank growth of falsehood that stands before us. To put the point concretely: NMD is not enough, nor is a purely military "War against Terrorism." Attention also needs to be paid to the resentments that feed Muslim terrorism and to the American and other Western policies that help to feed those resentments.

Notes

1. By the pagan philosopher, Celsus, in his *Alethes Logos* (c. A.D. 178).
2. E.g., Tertullian (c. A.D. 160–c. 225), Origen (c. A.D. 185–c. 254), and Lactantius (c. A.D. 240–c. 320).
3. See Augustine, *City of God*, XIX.6; *Quaestiones in heptateuchum*, 6.10; *Letters* 138 (to Marcellinus) and 189 (to Boniface).
4. *Summa theologiae*, IIaIIae, Q.40. Although medieval just war theory is best known through Aquinas, who provides "an easily accessible window" onto it, he was in fact only one of many who contributed to its development during this period. However, "while the influence of the canonists overshadowed Thomas's thought on war during his own time, by the dawn of the modern period, theorists like Vitoria and Suarez looked no further than Thomas for the authoritative statement of justified resort to armed force." James Turner Johnson, *Morality and Contemporary Warfare* (New Haven, Conn., and London: Yale University Press, 1999), 45.

5. Augustine, *De libero arbitrio*, bk. I, ch. 5.11–13.
6. *Summa theologiae*, IIaIIae, Q.64, a.7.
7. See the first creation story in the book of Genesis in the Hebrew Scriptures (the Christian Old Testament), chap. 1 (e.g., "And God saw everything that he had made, and behold it was very good").
8. Aristotle is generally regarded as the classical exponent of eudaimonism.
9. As Anthony Coady points out in his introductory comments in Chapter 5 above, "Aquinas's approach to natural law is, in one important respect, pluralistic. This contrasts with Hobbes, for where Hobbes has only one basic precept of natural law, Aquinas lists several and treats the list as open-ended. Hobbes insists, with Aquinas, on the centrality of self-preservation, but where Aquinas goes on to list the further animal and rational goods, Hobbes tries to get everything out of the one imperative."
10. Francisco de Vitoria, *On the Law of War*, Q.1, a.3.
11. For a recent argument that Grotius's political thought belongs to the tradition of Christian theology, see Oliver O'Donovan and Joan Lockwood O'Donovan, *From Irenaeus to Grotius: A Sourcebook in Christian Political Thought, 100–1625* (Grand Rapids, Mich.: Eerdmans, 1999), 787–92.
12. This complexity becomes intensified in Chapter 10 below, when Martin Cook turns our bewildered attention to contemporary Protestant apocalypticism.
13. See John Howard Yoder, *The Politics of Jesus* (Grand Rapids, Mich.: Eerdmans, 1972); Stanley Hauerwas, *The Peaceable Kingdom: A Primer in Christian Ethics* (Notre Dame, Ind., and London: University of Notre Dame Press, 1983); and Stanley Hauerwas, "Epilogue: A Pacifist Response to the Bishops," in Paul Ramsey, *Speak Up for Just War or Pacifism: A Critique of the United Methodist Bishops' Pastoral Letter "In Defense of Creation"* (University Park and London: Pennsylvania State University Press, 1988).
14. See Robert Holmes in the introduction to Chapter 23 below.
15. The entailment of the principles of discrimination and proportionality by that of right intention is also recognized by the Confucian philosopher Mengzi (see Philip Ivanhoe in Chapter 14 below, under "Punitive Wars": "Ching has quoted passages like *Mengzi* 1B11 and 7B4 . . . last more than a season"). On this point, I find myself aligned with Robert Holmes in his contradiction of Michael Walzer's thesis that the criteria of *jus ad bellum* are logically independent of those of *jus in bello* (see Robert Holmes in Chapter 23 below, under "Sources and Principles": "Some just war theorists might object . . . the independence thesis is false").
16. This Christian concern for right intention finds equivalents in other religious traditions, for example, Confucianism (see Julia Ching in Chapter 13 below, under "Sources and Principles: Just and Unjust Wars").
17. The connection between right intention and proportion is made explicit by Aquinas in *Summa theologiae*, IIaIIae, Q.64, a.7.
18. Richard Shelly Hartigan, *The Forgotten Victim: A History of the Civilian* (Chicago: Precedent, 1982), 31.
19. See ibid., 43.
20. I rely here on Robert Regout's interpretation of Vitoria (*La doctrine de la guerre juste de Saint Augustin á nos jours*), as endorsed and reported by Hartigan, *Forgotten Victims*, 82, 142 n. 6.

21. Francisco de Vitoria, *Commentary on the* Summa theologiae *of St. Thomas Aquinas, IIa IIae*, Q.40, a.1.10 (quoted by Hartigan in *Forgotten Victim*, 84); *On the Law of War*, Q.1, a.3.4 (quoted by Hartigan in *Forgotten Victim*, 87).

22. Vitoria, *On the Law of War*, Q.3, a.1.1 (quoted by Hartigan in *Forgotten Victim*, 84).

23. Vitoria, *Commentary on the* Summa, Q.40, a.1.10: "Thirdly, I hold that it is not permissible to slay any of the enemy, after victory has been won, in cases in which they were fighting licitly, *provided that there is no longer any danger threatened from them.* " The emphasis is mine.

24. The notion of restorative justice has been developed to explicate the rationale for dealing with gross violations of human rights in South Africa's civil war by way of a Truth and Reconciliation Commission, rather than Nuremberg-style trials.

25. Augustine, *City of God*, trans. Henry Bettenson (Harmondsworth: Penguin, 1972), XIX.6.

26. For some famous examples, see the Gospel of Luke, 15.11–32 (Parable of the Prodigal Son) and 23.34 (Jesus prays God to forgive his murderers); the Gospel of Matthew, 18.23–35 (Parable of the Unmerciful Servant) and 6.12 (the Lord's Prayer); and the Epistle of St. Paul to the Romans, 12.14–21 (love for the enemy is enjoined).

27. Aquinas, *Summa*, IIaIIae, Q.64, a.7. John Kelsay observes the operation of a version of the double effect principle in Islamic thought (see John Kelsay in Chapter 18 below, under "Discrimination": "Thus we have texts . . . but not intended").

28. In the light of the possibility of *incapacitating* enemy combatants by means of certain chemical weapons, rather than killing them, Paul Ramsey doubts whether just war theory needs this exception: "As long as an enemy combatant had to be and was done to death it seemed nonsense to say that this was not what was wanted. [Hence the requirement of reference to the public good.] . . . Now that what is done in war might be the combatant's incapacitation and not his death, it again makes some palpable sense to say that what was wanted (as a *means*) even in killing him is his incapacitation and not his death." Ramsey, "Incapacitating Gases," *The Just War: Force and Political Responsibility* (Lanham, Md.: Rowman & Littlefield, 1968, 1983), 471.

29. Vitoria, *Commentary on the* Summa, Q.40, a.1.10.

30. Gospel of Mark, 12.28–31.

31. Augustine, *Letters*, 47 (to Publico); *De libero arbitrio*, bk. I, ch. 5.12.

32. Augustine, *Letters*, 138 (to Marcellinus).

33. This two-fold affirmation is made at the very beginning of the Hebrew Scriptures, and so of the Christian Bible, in the first creation story (Genesis 1).

34. Augustine, *City of God*, bk. V, chs. 24–25. Mengzi urged a similar point on Confucians (see Philip Ivanhoe in Chapter 14 below, under "Punitive Wars": "A ruler who could not liberate . . . and follow him"). In contrast, it seems that the weight given in Islamic thought to "the argument from necessity" – especially the necessity of a Muslim victory – tends to let the requirements of military success trump moral constraints on the conduct of war (see Sohail Hashmi in Chapter 17 below, under "Sources and Principles"). Intriguingly, John Rawls's invocation of "the supreme emergency exemption" appears, on this point, to align liberalism with Islam and against Christianity

(see Henry Shue in Chapter 7 above, under "Liberalism and Weapons of Mass Destruction": "Thanks to Michael Walzer's . . . excused by supreme emergency").

35. Nevertheless, some kinds of nuclear weapons are inherently more discriminate and proportionate than others. For example, neutron warheads are radioactively "cleaner" and leave property relatively undamaged – which is "significant for protecting the rights of non-combatants, who must have buildings in which to live, work, and shop, means of transportation, land to farm, and so on." James Turner Johnson, *Can Modern War Be Just?* (New Haven, Conn., and London: Yale University Press, 1984), 47.

36. Paul Ramsey (1913–88), the American Methodist theologian, was responsible for incorporating the rigor of Roman Catholic casuistry into Protestant ethics.

37. Paul Ramsey, *War and the Christian Conscience* (Durham, N.C.: Duke University Press, 1961), chap. 8, esp. pp. 182–83.

38. Ibid., 187–88.

39. Johnson, *Can Modern War Be Just?*, 121.

40. See, for example, Johnson's discussion in ibid., 40–47.

41. Whether Ramsey did or did not countenance the possibility of a morally legitimate (and therefore proportionate) counterforce use of nuclear weapons depends on how one interprets his position on nuclear deterrence. Richard Miller, however, is in no doubt that Ramsey "is quite clear about the fact that his notion of a *just* fight-the-war policy may include some nuclear weapons." Richard B. Miller, "Love, Intention, and Proportion: Paul Ramsey on the Morality of Nuclear Deterrence," *Journal of Religious Ethics* 16:2 (Fall 1988): 212.

42. The Pentagon was reported in April 2001 to be examining the feasibility of producing a low-yield nuclear warhead for just such use. *The Guardian*, London, April 18, 2001. In the early days of the American and British campaign against al-Qa'ida in Afghanistan, it seems that nonnuclear munitions were considered sufficient for attacking heavily armored subterranean bunkers (*The Independent* [London], October 12, 2001). Presumably, this was because these bunkers were not thought to contain biological or chemical weapons.

43. As Robert Sherman, head of the nuclear security project of the Federation of American Scientists, has argued: "We have gone 56 years without a nuclear weapon being used anywhere. There is universal recognition that once you use the first nuclear weapon it becomes a great deal easier for someone to use the second." *The Guardian*, April 18, 2001.

44. Paul Ramsey, "Incapacitating Gases," 466. Among those who have leapt to premature conclusions about chemical weapons are the U.S. Catholic bishops, who in their 1983 pastoral letter, *The Challenge of Peace*, write without qualification of "the unspeakable use of gas and other forms of chemical warfare." National Conference of Catholic Bishops, *The Challenge of Peace: God's Promise and Our Response* (Washington, D.C.: United States Catholic Conference, 1983), I.C. 3.102. Likewise, the United Methodist Council of Bishops (USA), in their 1986 pastoral letter, "In Defense of Creation: The Nuclear Crisis and a Just Peace," declare themselves "categorically opposed" to the production, possession, or use of chemical and biological weapons. "In Defense of Creation," in *War in the Twentieth Century: Sources in Theological Ethics*, ed. Richard B. Miller (Louisville, Ky.: Westminster/John Knox Press, 1992), 436.

45. Johnson, *Can Modern War Be Just?*, 94.

46. Ibid., 95.

47. Ibid.

48. Ramsey, "Incapacitating Gases," 466. My emphasis.

49. Ibid., 476.

50. For my account of Temple, I rely entirely on Stephen E. Lammers's research in the archives of Lambeth Palace, as presented in his article, "William Temple and the Bombing of Germany: An Exploration of the Just War Tradition," *Journal of Religious Ethics* 19:1 (Spring 1991): 71–92.

51. John C. Ford, S.J., "The Morality of Obliteration Bombing," *Theological Studies* 5 (September 1944); reprinted in Miller, *War in the Twentieth Century*, 138–77.

52. Lammers reports an interview with Fr. Ford, in which "he stated that he [had] really meant to ask a question about the bombing, not to take a position. In his own mind, the question had yet to be answered." Lammers, "William Temple," 87 n. 1.

53. Oliver O'Donovan, *Peace and Certainty: A Theological Essay on Deterrence* (Oxford: Oxford University Press, 1989), 79; cf. p. 11.

54. Miller, "Love, Intention, and Proportion," 201, 214.

55. See, for example, Ramsey, *Just War*, chaps. 7 ("The Case for Making 'Just War' Possible"), and 8 ("The Hatfields and the Coys").

56. Miller, "Love, Intention, and Proportion," 210.

57. David Attwood, "Threats and Nuclear Deterrence: Paul Ramsey's Account of the Morality of Nuclear Threats," *Studies in Christian Ethics* 4:1 (1999): 46.

58. Ramsey, "More Unsolicited Advice to Vatican Council II," *Just War*, 303.

59. Evidence for such a reading can be found in ibid., 304–5.

60. Ramsey, "Again, the Justice of Deterrence," *Just War*, 358–59.

61. Paul Ramsey, Letter, *Newsweek*, July 5, 1982; reprinted in Paul Ramsey, with Stanley Hauerwas, *Speak Up for Just War or Pacifism*, 206–7.

62. Attwood, "Threats and Nuclear Deterrence," 46–48, 49–51.

63. Ramsey, "The Limits of Nuclear War," *Just War*, 253. Author's emphasis. See also ibid., 330.

64. U.S. Catholic Bishops, *Challenge of Peace*, II.C.2.152.

65. Ibid., II.C.2.150.

66. Ibid., II.C.2.153, 161.

67. Ibid., II.C.3.158.

68. Ibid., II.D.2.180.

69. Ibid., II.D.2.186.

70. Ibid., II.D.2.188.

71. *The Church and the Bomb: Nuclear Weapons and Christian Conscience*, the report of a working party of the Board for Social Responsibility of the General Synod of the Church of England (London: Hodder & Stoughton, 1982), 30, 55.

72. Ibid., 18, 30, 49, 95–96.

73. Ibid., 97.

74. Ibid.

75. Ibid., 98.

76. Ibid., 99, 153.

77. John Finnis, Joseph Boyle, and Germain Grisez, *Nuclear Deterrence, Morality, and Realism* (Oxford: Clarendon, 1987), V.4, 5.

78. Robert Song, review in *Studies in Christian Ethics* 2:1 (1989): 124.

79. The authors take *The Challenge of Peace* to task for attaching too much signifi-
    cance to targeting policy as such. The fact that U.S. weapons are directly aimed
    only at military targets is of no moral consequence, if the collateral damage
    done by hitting them is an essential part of the threat and is therefore an
    immorally intended means. Finnis et al., *Nuclear Deterrence*, 160–61.
80. Finnis et al., *Nuclear Deterrence*, 136–39, 147–49.
81. As Robert Song has noted, the principle of proportionality "has a surprisingly
    shadowy existence" in the analysis conducted in *Nuclear Deterrence*. Song, review,
    127.
82. Finnis et al., *Nuclear Deterrence*, V.2.
83. Song, review, 130.
84. Finnis et al., *Nuclear Deterrence*, 109–10.
85. Ibid., 147–48. The authors do consider the morality of a victory-denying strat-
    egy but return a negative verdict because, once defeat is inevitable, there is no
    longer any justification for continuing to fight and the enemy's forces are no
    longer legitimate targets (ibid., 134–36).
86. Ibid., 134.
87. Ibid., 147.
88. Ibid., 150.
89. Ibid., 150–52.
90. Ibid., VI.3.
91. O'Donovan, *Peace and Certainty*, 6–7.
92. Ibid., 25 n. 13.
93. Ibid., chap. 2. An element of the modern project of pursuing absolute peace
    by totalizing war, according to O'Donovan, is the doctrine that war is "essen-
    tially" without moral constraint. One root of this notion, he speculates, lies in
    the Old Testament's concept of holy war, at whose heart is the idea that war is
    theophany – that is, the manifestation of the providence of God in human activ-
    ity (for details, see Joseph David, Chapter 20 below, under "Total Destruction
    and the Idea of the Day of the Lord"). This O'Donovan judges to be heretical
    from the viewpoint of New Testament faith, since there the theophanic expec-
    tations built around war in the conquest narratives of the Old Testament have
    been transferred to the suffering of Jesus and its vindication in his resurrec-
    tion. O'Donovan, *Peace and Certainty*, 45–47. Here lies the germ of a line of
    theological criticism of the Christian apocalypticism Martin Cook describes in
    Chapter 10, insofar as that looks forward to nuclear conflagration as the means
    by which God's purposes will be achieved. Indeed, there is a curious and ironic
    parallel between this pseudo-Christian apocalypticism and the titanic modern
    project, as O'Donovan describes it: both look kindly on the totalizing of war as
    the means to absolute peace.
94. O'Donovan, *Peace and Certainty*, 26, 28, 61, 92, 121.
95. Ibid., 21, 33, 36, 58, 65.
96. Ibid., 20–21, 83–84.
97. Ibid., 81–85.
98. Ibid., 68.
99. *The Church and the Bomb*, 63–64.
100. Finnis et al., *Nuclear Deterrence*, 213.
101. Johnson, *Can Modern War Be Just?*, 97–101.

102. *The Church and the Bomb*, 161.
103. Ibid., 64.
104. Ibid., 160–61.
105. *Challenge of Peace*, III.A.1.208.
106. Strictly speaking, the word "unfair" is preferable here, since there is nothing wrong as such with discrimination.
107. Sydney D. Bailey, *War and Conscience in the Nuclear Age* (London: Macmillan, 1987), 146.
108. Johnson, *Can Modern War Be Just?*, 101–2.
109. Ibid., 103–4.
110. *Challenge of Peace*, III.201.
111. Ibid., III.A.1.205.
112. *The Church and the Bomb*, 134.
113. Ibid., 160.
114. *The Church and the Bomb* finds more – and solid – ground for hope in the history of arms control: "Some of the agreements relating to different types of armament are significant achievements. Biological weapons have been forsworn. Nuclear weapons have been banned from outer space, the seabed and Antarctica. There have also been the partial test bans, the Non-Proliferation Treaty, and the Treaty of Tlatelolco of 1967 aimed to keep Latin America free of nuclear weapons" (p. 130).
115. Finnis et al., *Nuclear Deterrence*, 324, 369.
116. Ibid., 326.
117. Ibid., 326, 335–37.
118. Ibid., 333–34.
119. Ibid., 68–74.
120. Ibid., 379–81.
121. Ibid., 381–82.
122. Ibid., 371–72.
123. Ibid., 382.
124. Ibid.
125. O'Donovan, *Peace and Certainty*, 63–64.
126. Ibid., 65, 74, 87–88.
127. Ibid., 66–67.
128. Ibid., 69–70.
129. Ibid., 93–95.
130. Ibid., 106–7.
131. Ibid., 107.
132. Ibid.
133. Ibid., 109–12.
134. See n. 48 above.
135. See Paul Szasz in Chapter 2 above, under "Nuclear Weapons."
136. Ibid., in the introduction.
137. Such published Christian opinion as there is about attempts to build a nuclear missile defense system is universally negative. See, for example, the views of Finnis and company discussed in this chapter under "Nuclear Deterrence." Their concern about the destabilizing effects of attempting such a system is shared by James Turner Johnson: "The results of such a defensive scheme

might be morally worthwhile, but getting there poses such risks as to be seri-
ously questionable both morally and politically" (*Can Modern War Be Just?*, 93).
It is also shared by the Church of England's working party (*The Church and the
Bomb*, 17), and by the United Methodist bishops: "We support an unequivocal
reaffirmation of both the purposes and provisions of the ABM Treaty of 1972.
Such action would help to curb the costly, provocative, and illusory development of new 'defensive' missile systems, whether ground-based or space-based"
(*In Defense of Creation*, 435). All of these judgments, however, presuppose a cold
war context.

138. See Sverre Lodgaard, "European Views of the US NMD Programme," Pugwash
Occasional Papers, II:ii, March 2001, at www.pugwash.org/reports/nw/op2_2/
opv2n2_6.htm (November 24, 2003), under "Russia"; also Jeffrey Boutwell,
Pugwash Workshop on Nuclear Stability and Missile Defense, Sigtuna,
Sweden, October 26–28, 2000, at www.pugwash.org/reports/nw/nw12.htm
(November 24, 2003), under "Russia."

139. "China, Fearing a Bolder U.S. Military, Takes Aim on Proposed National Missile
Shield," *New York Times*, April 29, 2001, p. 10.

140. In September 1999, China was believed to have about twenty ICBMs that
could reach targets throughout the United States – according to the National Intelligence Council in its report on "Foreign Missile Developments
and the Ballistic Missile Threat to the United States through 2015," at
www.cia.gov/cia/publications/nie/nie99msl.html (November 24, 2003), under "Potential ICBM Threats to the United States."

141. "Any substantial American effort to build a missile defense may have the effect
of neutralizing China's small force. . . ." "China, Fearing a Bolder U.S. Military,"
p. 10.

142. Among these "rogue states" – or, to give them their more recent, politically
correct title, "states of special concern" – are North Korea and Iran. Iraq,
presumably, is now no longer among them.

143. This is implied by the National Intelligence Council when it writes of the countries that are developing longer-range missiles (including China) that they
probably view their limited strategic forces "more as weapons of deterrence
and coercive diplomacy than as weapons of war" and that "the *threat* of their
use would complicate American decision-making during crises" and would "increase the cost of a U.S. victory and potentially deter Washington from pursuing
certain objectives." National Intelligence Council, "Foreign Missile Developments," under, respectively, "Potential ICBM Threats to the United States" and
"Classification of Ballistic Missiles by Range." It is acknowledged by the Federation of American Scientists, when they write that "Russia (and China) are
concerned, not simply with the potential impact of American NMD on their
own deterrent postures, but more generally with the projection of American
diplomacy backed by force." See "National Missile Defense: Rushing to Failure,"
Journal of the Federation of American Scientists 52:6 (November/December 1999),
at http://fas.org/faspir/v52m6a.htm (November 24, 2003), under "Trouble-
some Components of the NMD System." Sverre Lodgaard makes the same
point when he notes that NMD would widen U.S. military options in East Asia,
and that "[a]ccordingly, many observers believe that China is in fact the main

rationale for NMD, so it is no surprise that the stiffest opposition to the programme comes from Beijing." Lodgaard, "European Views of the US NMD Programme," under "China."

144. See the report of statements by Sha Zukang, in ibid., and in "China, Fearing a Bolder U.S. Military," p. 10.

145. Ivan Safranchuk, "Russian Views on Missile Defenses," Pugwash Occasional Paper, II.ii, March 2001, at www.pugwash.org/reports/nw/op2_2/ opv2n2_4.tm (November 24, 2003), under "Putin's Deep Cuts Initiative."

146. Boutwell, "Pugwash Workshop on Nuclear Stability and Missile Defense," under "Russia"; John Rhinelander, foreword to Pugwash Occasional Papers, II.ii, March 2001, at www.pugwash.org/reports/nw/op2_2/opv2n2.htm (November 24, 2003), under "Offensive Reductions"; Safranchuk, "Russian Views on Missile Defenses," under "Official Russian Policy on ABM and NMD."

147. "China, Fearing a Bolder U.S. Military," p. 10: "Mr. Sha suggested that instead of engaging in a large and costly build-up, China would concentrate on a range of relatively low-cost responses, such as developing plans to attack the vulnerable radar network and communication nodes that would form the nervous system of America's defense. 'We will do whatever possible to ensure that our security will not be compromised, and we are confident that we can succeed without an arms race,' he said." See also Julia Ching's discussion in Chapter 13 below, in the conclusion.

148. See Professor Jack Harris, FRS, "Star Wars II," letter to the editor, *Daily Telegraph*, July 7, 2001, at www.pugwash.org/reports/pim/pim39.htm (November 24, 2003).

149. As several commentators have pointed out, it is possible for "rogue" leopards to change their spots. For example, Sverre Lodgaard writes that "the list of countries posing possible missile threats has not only changed, it has become *shorter*." Lodgaard, "European Views of the US NMD Programme," under "States of Special Concern." George N. Lewis suggests that "improved relations with North Korea and Iran...are *possible*." Lewis, "U.S. National Missile Defense Options," Pugwash Occasional Papers, II.ii, March 2001, at www.pugwash.org/reports/nw/op2_2/opv2n2_3.htm (November 24, 2003), under "Is NMD Deployment Inevitable?"

150. See, for example, Anatol Lieven, "Strategy for Terror," *Prospect* (London), October 2001, pp. 16, 17.

10

Christian Apocalypticism and Weapons
of Mass Destruction

Martin L. Cook

Nigel Biggar has done an excellent job in the previous chapter of summarizing the long history of Christian thought about war and weapons of mass destruction. He has skillfully analyzed the contributions of major thinkers within the Christian tradition to the moral evaluation of nuclear and other weapons of mass destruction in this century. I dispute none of what he said and could offer only further elaboration on the points he made if I attempted to deal with the history, traditions, and thinkers he addressed.

Instead, I wish to augment his treatment by adding a modern Christian perspective radically different from those he considers. Biggar's treatment dealt with the major traditions of the Christian past – Roman Catholic and so-called mainline Protestant. I wish to turn to those movements within Christianity that are now growing most rapidly and spreading most broadly, and which are most likely to shape at least popular Christianity's future.

These are Evangelical Protestantism and the Pentecostal/Charismatic traditions of Christianity and, in particular, the view of history and interpretation of biblical prophecy known as "dispensationalist" within those communities. While the number of adherents to Roman Catholicism and mainline Protestantism is generally declining in North America and Western Europe, the newer traditions are aggressive in their missionary activities and highly effective in spreading their message throughout the world.[1]

Furthermore, at least in the United States, these strands of Christianity have moved since the 1960s from the periphery of American cultural and political life to near its center, if not the center itself. At least at the level of political symbolism, current American political leaders associate themselves visibly with the leaders, and often with the rhetoric, of Evangelical Christianity. It was, after all, the Southern Baptist Billy Graham (author of his own dispensationalist tome, *The World Aflame*) who was called on to lead the memorial service at the National Cathedral in Washington, D.C., for the victims of September 11, 2001, and not a Catholic or "mainline" Protestant leader. George W. Bush received "84 percent of votes cast by observant evangelical Christians" and "[e]vangelicals supplied 40 percent of all Bush votes."[2] Ronald Reagan similarly received strong electoral support from the same groups. The influential televangelist Jerry Falwell published newspaper advertisements on the eve of the 1984 campaign endorsing the Reagan presidency with the following claim: "We have a President who wants to build up our military strength. . . . He and loyal members of Congress need to know that you are with them."[3]

I hasten to note that I do not understand the beliefs I am about to describe as normatively Christian, for two reasons. First, as a movement of little more than 100 years in age, surely it cannot claim to speak for the much longer and more carefully elaborated Christian traditions. Of course, there has been a millennialist element in Christianity from its beginning, but after the apocalyptic cast of the very earliest Christian communities abated, it has not been a central element of normative Christianity since that time. In most Christian traditions, to be sure, there remain elements of future expectation of "the last things" in the official creeds of the church and in official doctrine. But in practice and in the piety of the ordinary believer these are elements rarely, if ever, made central to the faith. Indeed, the expectation of a general "end of the world" tends to be supplanted in practice by questions of personal mortality and afterlife. Dispensationalism is distinctive among modern Christian movements for its linkage of biblical interpretation and the expectation of literal historical developments in the near future.

Second, I consider the fundamental assumptions (about the nature of the biblical text and its responsible interpretation) on which these views rest to be not merely mistaken but indefensible. Modern historical critical reading of biblical texts and a theologically defensible view of the relationship between biblical text and historical events make the hermeneutical assumptions undergirding dispensationalist views intellectually indefensible in my judgment. Nevertheless, no full descriptive account of the Christian tradition's attitudes toward weapons of mass destruction would be complete without including dispensationalist concepts and expectations.

THE DISPENSATIONALIST WORLD-VIEW

Dispensationalist views are extremely widespread, even among American Christians who formally belong to denominations and traditions that do not endorse the dispensationalist world-view – indeed, among churches that condemn and reject it: "66 percent of Americans, including a third of those who say they never attend church, say they believe that Jesus Christ will return to Earth some day,"[4] and "one in four adult Christians expects Christ to return very soon, or certainly in his or her lifetime."[5]

The elements I discuss below are not centrally or denominationally organized (although some denominations, such as the Assemblies of God and Southern Baptists, are completely identified with the dispensationalist world-view). Rather, they are transmitted and inculcated by means of magazines, books, films, para-church agencies, and television and radio evangelists, almost all without official sanction of any Christian body. The most famous recent manifestation of this phenomenon are the novels in the Left Behind Series, now experiencing a great popularity well beyond Evangelical and Pentecostal Christian circles. Even the large chain bookstores have whole sections devoted to the series and its many product spin-offs.[6] Daniel Wojcik writes:

Today in the United States, belief in apocalyptic prophecy is integral to the world-views of many evangelical Christians, such as the Southern Baptist Convention (with an estimated fifteen million members) and various Pentecostal and charismatic denominations (roughly eight million members), including the Assemblies of God Church, the Church of the Nazarene, and thousands of independent evangelical "Bible churches."...Premillennial dispensationalism...is espoused by the majority of televangelists...many of whom have stated...that nuclear weapons and the prospect of nuclear war are a fulfillment of biblical prophecy. According to a Nielsen survey of television views conducted in October 1985, approximately 61 million Americans (40 percent of all viewers) regularly listen to preachers who tell them nothing can be done to prevent nuclear war in our lifetime.[7]

This view of history is known as "dispensationalism," because the core idea is that God has foreordained the development of human history and divided it into seven distinct ways of dealing with human beings known as "dispensations." A classic representation of dispensationalist history is the chart shown in Figure 10.1, widely available in Evangelical bookstores and prominently displayed in many churches.[8]

What the chart displays is the whole of human history, keyed to one of seven divinely ordained periods, or "dispensations." Dispensationalists view the course of history as completely foreordained by God. They look forward to the literal and bodily return of Christ in the near future. The central text of this belief system is from Paul's epistle, I Thessalonians, Chapter 4, in the New Testament:

But we do not want you to be uninformed, brothers and sisters, about those who have died, so that you may not grieve as others do who have no hope. For since we believe that Jesus died and rose again, even so, through Jesus, God will bring with him those who have died. For this we declare to you by the word of the Lord, that we who are alive, who are left until the coming of the Lord, will by no means precede those who have died. For the Lord himself, with a cry of command, with the archangel's call and with the sound of God's trumpet, will descend from heaven, and the dead in Christ will rise first. Then we who are alive, who are left, will be caught up in the clouds together with them to meet the Lord in the air; and so we will be with the Lord forever. Therefore encourage one another with these words.

All dispensationalist traditions make a literal interpretation of this passage central to their belief system. They imagine that in the not-too-distant

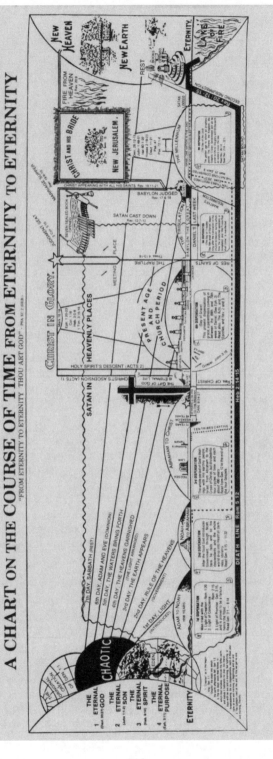

FIGURE 10.1: A. E. Booth, "The Course of Time from Eternity to Eternity" (Neptune, N.J.: Loizeaux Bros., 1999).

future Jesus will return "on the clouds of heaven," as the passage says, and that faithful Christians still living will physically rise to meet Jesus's return. Deceased faithful Christians will likewise be resurrected and will similarly fly away.

Those human beings not caught up in this "Rapture" will experience a time of war, pestilence, and suffering. The details of the chronology of this suffering, or "Great Tribulation," in relation to the Rapture are questions of endless dispute among writers who share the broad perspective. A favorite biblical passage to fill in these details is found in Ezekiel 38, which envisions an attack by a nation referred to as Gog on the nation of Israel. God promises to intervene in that attack in apocalyptic language:

For in my jealousy and in my blazing wrath I declare: On that day there shall be a great shaking in the land of Israel; the fish of the sea, and the birds of the air, and the animals of the field, and all creeping things that creep on the ground, and all human beings that are on the face of the earth, shall quake at my presence, and the mountains shall be thrown down, and the cliffs shall fall, and every wall shall tumble to the ground. I will summon the sword against Gog in all my mountains, says the Lord God; the swords of all will be against their comrades. With pestilence and bloodshed I will enter into judgment with him; and I will pour down torrential rains and hailstones, fire and sulfur, upon him and his troops and the many peoples that are with him. So I will display my greatness and my holiness and make myself known in the eyes of many nations. Then they shall know that I am the Lord.

Further imagery is supplied by the apocalyptic visions of the book of Revelation:

When he opened the sixth seal, I looked, and there came a great earthquake; the sun became black as sackcloth, the full moon became like blood, and the stars of the sky fell to the earth as the fig tree drops its winter fruit when shaken by a gale. The sky vanished like a scroll rolling itself up, and every mountain and island was removed from its place. Then the kings of the earth and the magnates and the generals and the rich and the powerful, and everyone, slave and free, hid in the caves and among the rocks of the mountains, calling to the mountains and rocks, "Fall on us and hide us from the face of the one seated on the throne and from the wrath of the Lamb; for the great day of their wrath has come, and who is able to stand?"

The main shared assumptions of virtually all Evangelical and Pentecostal Christianity are the following: The return of Jesus on the clouds of heaven and the Rapture are literal and imminent events. There will be a period of suffering, death, and natural disaster without precedent in human history (the Tribulation) either just before or just after that Rapture. There will be a major and horrific war fought by all major powers in and over the land of Israel in which God will intervene – and this war is an absolutely necessary precursor to the culmination of history in the desired culmination of God's plan. "God's plan for mankind, established before the world began, is unalterable."[9] All share the assumption that the apocalyptic books of

Daniel, Revelation, the section of Ezekiel just referred to, and parts of the Gospels provide to the reader who can properly interpret them a detailed blueprint of the human future and the culmination of history in the decisive intervention of God to establish the New Jerusalem.

Lest one think these views are "fringe," I would stress that several American presidents (Carter, Reagan, and George W. Bush, at least) explicitly embraced this interpretation of history. Reagan's secretary of the interior, James Watt, was famous for suggesting there was no point in conservation because the end of the world was at hand.[10] I would note anecdotally that virtually all of my American students at the United States Army War College (lieutenant colonel and colonel in rank) who are religiously committed Protestants hold views along these lines. Hal Lindsey, the author of *The Late Great Planet Earth*, has spoken to various military audiences. "When he spoke at the American Air War College, [Lindsey reports] 'virtually the entire school turned out, including many officers accompanied by their wives.' When he spoke at the Pentagon, [Lindsey similarly reports] 'hundreds jam[med] the room.'"[11] And I reiterate, if present demographic trends continue, the growth of Christianity in the coming century all over the world will come from traditions that make these beliefs central.

For an observer who knows the "code" of this belief system, the evidence of its widespread appeal is pervasive in American society. The bumper stickers are probably the most immediately visible of the symbols of dispensationalist belief, visible on a short drive through almost any American town. A visit to any Evangelical bookstore, however, will reveal the full range of dispensationalist paraphernalia available to attest to the buyer's convictions:

Rapture believers may proclaim their views through bumper stickers with slogans ("The Rapture – What A Way To Go!"; "Warning – driver will abandon car in case of Rapture"; "Beam me up, Jesus!") and by purchasing framed paintings, postcards, watches, and other items depicting the Rapture . . . such as laminated Rapture dinner place mats which depict an open-armed Christ returning above the skyscrapers of an urban center as raptured Christians float out of automobiles crashing on a freeway and dead Christians rise from their graves in a cemetery.[12]

IMPLICATIONS

What are the implications of such beliefs for attitudes toward WMD? At a minimum, such Christian believers *expect* destruction and death on a global scale – and the biblical descriptions of the nature of the Tribulation resonate with descriptions of the use of nuclear, chemical, and biological weapons. Since the Tribulation is a completely necessary and inevitable element in the apocalyptic timetable, there is a sense in which they are welcomed as signs of the fulfillment of God's purpose: "One writer put it exuberantly in 1967: 'Thank God, I will get a view of the Battle of Armageddon from the grandstand seats of the heavens. All who are born again will see the Battle of Armageddon, but it will be from the skies.'"[13]

Furthermore, the Rapture functions to transform horrific visions of destruction into welcome harbingers of escape: "The belief in the Rapture . . . with its promise of planetary escape prior to nuclear cataclysms and other disasters, offers a compelling scenario by which fears of inevitable doom are transformed into expectations of salvation."[14] Paul Boyer's observations on this point are worth quoting in full:

[P]rophecy writers viewed nuclear holocaust from a unique vantage point. They described its horror as graphically as any antinuclear activist, but not as a *possible* historical outcome to be avoided at all costs. For them it was the *probable* form of Earth's divinely ordained end. *Escape* had an individual meaning, but not a corporate, social meaning: hope lay only in accepting Christ and holding oneself in readiness for the Rapture. In the secular world, the possibility of thermonuclear war tended to be either psychologically numbing or politically energizing, as people transformed anxiety into action. For prophecy writers it served different functions: spurring missionary effort, promising future judgment, and validating the premillennial belief system and the Bible itself.[15]

But not only does it reduce fear, it completely eliminates responsibility. At a minimum, passively awaiting Armageddon is evidence of faithfulness; human action to forestall disaster might easily be viewed as opposition to the divinely foreordained plan: "[B]elievers watch the workings of the United Nations with particular suspicion and revile every peace initiative."[16] Grace Halsell has studied extensively the connection between dispensationalist ideas and American foreign policy in the Middle East, especially attitudes toward the Arab-Israeli conflict. She reports:

[N]umerous individuals with political and financial power in the United States assert that the Battle of Armageddon is foreordained and that any attempt to prevent a nuclear scenario in the Middle East is heretical. For instance, television evangelist Jim Robinson, who was invited by Ronald Reagan to deliver the opening prayer at the 1984 Republican National Convention, states, "There'll be no peace until Jesus comes. Any preaching of peace prior to this return is heresy; it's against the word of God; it's anti-Christ.[17]

Clearly, if this is one's view of history and the future, there is no incentive whatsoever for attempting to eliminate WMD from the world, or even from working aggressively to restrain the use of WMD. WMD will be used; it is inevitable and desirable that they be used. God's purposes and timetable require their use.

On this "passive" interpretation of the consequences of dispensationalism, in which human beings are merely pawns in a divine plan, one might reasonably ask whether it is an ethic at all. If ethics is meant to inform action based on some notion of independent human agency, in what way is a counsel of passive expectation an ethic?

The answer is, I believe, that dispensationalism provides a world-view that has very real-world implications for action and for political conviction. Typically, dispensationalists are (as Halsell demonstrates) completely uncritical of Israeli policy and unhesitatingly favor all means of support for the Israeli state. Given the volatility of the region and the possession of WMD by numerous states in it, these attitudes have serious implications for the development and possible use of WMD regionally, which in turn of course have global repercussions.

The normal human response of fear of the threat posed by WMD and urgency to gain control over that threat is similarly overridden for the dispensationalist. As Jim Robinson's comment above indicates, dispensationalism easily shades into the view that any effort to work for peace and disarmament here and now is "heresy" – the deliberate attempt to subvert God's plan by forestalling the inevitable Armageddon. In practice this means support for large military budgets, unquestioning acceptance of the development of new and more destructive weapons systems, and a calm acceptance of the inevitability of large-scale conflict among nations.

Besides passivity and faithful waiting, however, it is but a short additional step from passively waiting for apocalyptic events to occur as part of God's timetable to thinking one might be assisting the Divine Plan by initiating destruction on that scale. One need not look far in the literature of dispensationalism for hints of such ideas as well. One reads periodically of Christians of this persuasion being captured by Israeli police for plotting the bombing of the Dome of the Rock in Jerusalem – an act intended to start the apocalyptic stopwatch. Mark Juergensmeyer's recent *Terror in the Mind of God: The Global Rise of Religious Violence* is a thorough and carefully documented cross-cultural analysis of the psychology and logic of that transformation.[18]

While the move from passivity in the face of providentially ordained catastrophe to seeing oneself and one's group as the divinely ordained trigger or agent of apocalyptic events makes intuitive sense, the precise circumstances and environment in which that is probable is difficult to predict with precision. Events in the United States, such as the burning of the Branch Davidian compound in Waco, Texas, the Heaven's Gate cult mass suicide in a suburb of San Diego, California, and the standoff and shooting engagement with the Montana Freemen, have generated some attention within the American law enforcement community to developing profiles of personalities and groups likely to make such a transition. Although none of these groups is in the mainstream of Christian thinking (or, in the case of Heaven's Gate, of Christianity at all), examination of their evolution is still instructive. Like dispensationalists, they all imagined they were about to pass through a period of earthly turmoil from which they would emerge and be delivered to their version of the Kingdom of God. Like dispensationalists, these groups share a belief that they alone possess the key to the proper interpretation of contemporary history; they alone understand the fundamental historical forces working to bring about inevitable ends. Under certain conditions, these beliefs can inform communities with distinctive characteristics that sociologist Colin Campbell has dubbed "the cultic milieu."[19] Bradley C. Whitsel writes:

This means of looking at the world approximates a reverse image of accepted knowledge and its sources, upon which the general society relies. Whereas conventional religion, the state, media, and institutions of higher learning "produce" information and ideas that are received and accepted by the society at large, these courses are rejected in the cultic milieu as corrupted and misleading. In such a thoughtworld the norms for orthodox knowledge are displaced by the conviction that "the truth" resides in more remote and secretive places.[20]

Whitsel has attempted to "profile" the circumstances in which such views can congeal into a form likely to produce violent action and, perhaps, deliberate use of WMD as a means to bring about desired ends. Although it is not germane to the topic at hand to go too deeply into this sociological analysis, the most important aspect of the formation of potentially violent groups is their withdrawal from their ambient society. They may live within it but be psychologically divorced from it. They may even relocate physically to remote places, further emphasizing their separation. They form close-knit communities, reinforcing their belief system and insulating them from challenges to it. Such withdrawal provides a crucial, though not always sufficient, preliminary step in the willingness to perpetrate violence in the society that "rejects" them.[21]

The establishment of the cultic milieu poses serious challenges to law enforcement. "The cultural underground of the cultic milieu provides violence-prone millenarians with a virtually impenetrable shield behind which their radically dualistic and heterodox interpretations of reality can flourish."[22]

What one would ideally like (that is, from a law enforcement, public order perspective) is a means of "seeing the world" from the group's perspective with sufficient clarity to anticipate the event or events likely to trigger the community's sudden shift from patient anticipation to millenarian activism."[23] Naturally, the very isolation of fully developed cults makes acquisition of such knowledge (and therefore prediction and control of their behavior) difficult if not impossible.

CONCLUSION

As dispensationalist views of history gain hold more broadly throughout the Christian world and as circles of real political and military power hold these views, one may reasonably wonder whether the traditions Nigel Biggar so accurately reviews will not be supplanted by apocalyptic visions. This admittedly alarming prospect can hardly be ruled out.[24] Further, if dispensationalist views predominate in a group or culture possessing WMD, it is difficult to predict whether and how long the group will remain content with the mere possession, awaiting God's inevitable timetable, or will use such weapons as agents of God's plan.

Clearly, however, understanding the internal logic, pervasiveness, and growth of this particular interpretation of Christianity is just as important in our post–September 11 world as is grasping al-Qa'ida's or other Islamic radical groups' search for means to inflict mass casualties. The same recipe and ingredients for religiously inspired acts of violence and use of WMD exist in American political culture and, through the effective and aggressive missionary efforts of American Evangelicals, increasingly in world Christian culture as well.

Notes

The views expressed in this chapter are those of the author and do not necessarily reflect the official policy or position of the United States Air Force, Department of Defense, or the U.S. Government.

1. See Philip Jenkins, *The Next Christendom: The Coming of Global Christianity* (Oxford: Oxford University Press, 2002), for a detailed analysis of the global spread and diversity of the newly emerging patterns of Christianity.

2. Gill Donovan, "Report Details Religious Vote of Presidential Election," *National Catholic Reporter*, February 9, 2001, p. 8.

3. Cited in Janice Love, "From Pacifism to Apocalyptic Visions: Religious Perspectives on Nuclear Deterrence," in *After the Cold War: Questioning the Morality of Nuclear Deterrence*, ed. Charles W. Kegley, Jr., and Kenneth L. Schwab (Boulder, Colo.: Westview, 1991), 170.

4. Jeffery L. Sheler and Mike Tharp, "Dark Prophecies," *U.S. News and World Report*, December 15, 1997, pp. 62–63.

5. David S. Dockery, "Is Revelation Prophecy or History?" *Christianity Today*, 43:12 (1999): 86. The definitive study of dispensationalism in American religious life is Paul Boyer, *When Time Shall Be No More: Prophecy Belief in Modern American Culture* (Cambridge: Harvard University Press, 1992).

6. "The spread of [dispensationalist] ideas about the end of the world can . . . be seen in the sale of books. The Left Behind Series, a sequence of thrillers by Jerry Jenkins and Tim LaHaye that follow premillenial dispensationalist lines, has sold ten million copies (and a major film based on it has now been released). Still more spectacularly, Hal Lindsey's *The Late Great Planet Earth* (1970), another treatment of the 'endtimes' and the return of Jesus, has sold some 34 million copies in 54 languages and may be the biggest selling book of the late 20th century." Daniel Pipes, "Holy Ground," *Commentary*, April 2001, p. 69. It is worth noting that the on-line bookstore Amazon.com maintains its own separate on-line "store" devoted exclusively to Left Behind products.

7. Daniel Wojcik, *The End of the World as We Know It: Faith, Fatalism, and Apocalypse in America* (New York: New York University Press, 1997), 7.

8. "The Course of Time from Eternity to Eternity" was published by A. E. Booth in 1896. After three printings, a revised and more detailed chart in full color

took its place. This version has been continuously in print ever since, with thirty-eight printings selling nearly 500,000 copies of the chart and more than 100,000 copies of the accompanying guide. It may be the most popular prophetic chart in use around the world.

9. Boyer, *When Time Shall Be No More*, 135.

10. Watt testified during his Senate confirmation hearing regarding conservation of the environment for future generations: "I do not know how many future generations we can count on before the Lord returns." Quoted in ibid., 141.

11. Ibid., 141.

12. Wojcik, *End of the World as We Know It*, 43.

13. Boyer, *When Time Shall Be No More*, 136.

14. Wojcik, *End of the World as We Know It*, 57.

15. Boyer, *When Time Shall Be No More*, 136–37.

16. Ted Daniels, ed., *A Doomsday Reader: Prophets, Predictors, and Hucksters of Salvation* (New York: New York University Press, 1999), 122.

17. Quoted in Wojcik, *End of the World as We Know It*, 41.

18. Mark Juergensmeyer, *Terror in the Mind of God: The Global Rise of Religious Violence* (Berkeley: University of California Press, 2000).

19. Colin Campbell, as cited in Bradley C. Whitsel, "Ideological Mutation and Millennial Belief in the American Neo-Nazi Movement," *Studies in Conflict and Terrorism* 24 (2001): 89–106.

20. Bradley C. Whitsel, "Catastrophic New Age Groups and Public Order," *Studies in Conflict and Terrorism* 23 (2000): 23.

21. Ibid., 21–36.

22. Ibid., 25.

23. Ibid. See also Whitsel's *"The Turner Diaries* and Cosmotheism: William Pierce's Theology of Revolution," *Nova Religio* 1:2 (April 1998): 183–97, for a detailed analysis of the function of a single apocalyptic novel within the cultural near-underground of white supremacy movements in the United States.

24. "Read against the background of martyrdom and exile, it is not surprising that so many Christians look for promises that their sufferings are only temporary, and that God will intervene directly to save the situation. In this context, the book of Revelation looks like true prophecy on an epic scale. . . . In the South [Southern Hemisphere], Revelation simply makes sense, in its description of a world ruled by monstrous demonic powers. These forces might be literal servants of Satan, or symbols for evil social sources, but in either case, they are indisputably real." Jenkins, *Next Christendom*, 219.

PART TWO

EXPANDING THE CONVERSATION

11

Buddhist Perspectives on Weapons
of Mass Destruction

David W. Chappell

Contrary to popular views of Buddhist pacifism, this chapter holds that Buddhist laity have sometimes advocated violence or the threat of violence for specific social roles and in extreme historical situations. Like other political leaders, Buddhist rulers traditionally used physical force to protect their countries. Although governments with large Buddhist populations (such as Japan, Sri Lanka, Bhutan, Mongolia, and Thailand) reject the use of weapons of mass destruction, and the Tibetan government-in-exile has advocated a nuclear-free zone, Buddhist organizations in France, England, and the United States have largely acquiesced in national policies of nuclear deterrence. While this chapter acknowledges that the acceptance of WMD as a deterrent by some Buddhists during the cold war was not an anomaly in Buddhist history, the main point to emphasize is that neither practical arguments nor Buddhist principles can support the deployment of WMD today, and they should be rejected based on the ultimate Buddhist goals of nonviolence and the protection of all living beings.

Most Buddhists do not advocate the use of violence except as a last resort, if at all, and the thrust of lay Buddhist ethics is toward pacifism. Although I argue here that, in the light of modern history and Buddhist political experience, the deployment WMD might have been justified during the cold war, this policy should have been supported by efforts to build greater cross-cultural awareness, economic fairness, and political inclusiveness in the global community. Greater efforts should have been made toward strengthening international agencies that implemented universal agreements on the control and ultimate elimination of WMD. Since the cold war is now ended and the world is increasingly open economically, socially, and politically, more aggressive peacework is now possible. Based on Buddhist values of personal virtue, compassion for others, and the need for political inclusiveness, the Buddhist consensus today is to actively reject WMD in order to counter the powerful military-industrial complex and to rechannel resources into global community building.

The traditional goals of Buddhism were to attain peace and freedom, goals that initially were seen not in political or social terms but as a victory over personal addictions, fears, hatred, and ignorance. However, these individual achievements were never unrelated to society, and in later Mahayana Buddhism individual salvation became inseparable from the peace of others. So most Buddhists have a commitment not just to inner peace but to world peace.[1]

The guide for Buddhist ethical action is *dharma* (in Sanskrit [Skt.]; *dhamma* in Pali), variously translated as "law," "duty," "righteousness," or "truth."[2] Even though the Buddhist tradition has many streams and is not a centrally organized community that speaks with a single voice, there is a clear emphasis on pacifism and nonviolence (Skt., *ahimsa*). In particular, Buddhist spiritual goals and practices (to dissolve ego attachments and cultivate calm mindfulness of the interdependence of all things) are opposed to perceiving anyone as an enemy, to dividing the world into false dichotomies of "us versus them." Instead, they are aimed at dissolving the fear, hatred, and hostility that spring from this divisive and false perception. Buddhist values are strongly opposed to keeping weapons, to say nothing of fueling an arms race that uses energy and resources that should go to support life.

The ethics for monastics – those who have left the world of family and social responsibilities – are distinct from the ethics for laity. But for most of Buddhist history, monastic morality was seen as the ideal and goal, so nonviolence was the norm. However, there were exceptions, especially for those with the responsibilities of rulers and modern forms of state Buddhism. Also, monastic practice has sometimes been stretched to include political responsibilities, as vividly demonstrated by the monk rulers of Tibet. But scripture never legitimated this political role for monastics, nor has scripture foreseen the rise of WMD.

Killing is the single most important prohibition in Buddhism. At first glance, Buddhism is opposed to the development and deployment of WMD. This conviction is strengthened by the fact that most of the victims of WMD have also been Buddhist, namely, the citizens of Hiroshima and Nagasaki. For Japanese Buddhists, this topic is not just a theoretical issue but an experiential one, and they have strongly supported the abolition of WMD. Not only have Buddhist rulers rejected WMD, but Buddhist peace activists such as the Buddhist Peace Fellowship and the Nipponzan Myohoji constantly work to eliminate WMD and to diminish all physical violence.[3]

In spite of the strong Buddhist opposition to violence and WMD, Buddhist practice always tries to be grounded in compassion and mindful awareness of the interrelatedness of things. These weapons are part of our world, our community, and ourselves. They are interconnected in many complex ways with social values and institutions meant to protect some life, even as they are designed to destroy other life. Buddhists have always existed in a world with weapons and war, and warriors have sometimes been Buddhists, and some Buddhist texts have allowed killing. A major section of this chapter is devoted to showing the range of Buddhist relationships to weapons and killing as a context for discussing WMD. While nonviolence has been emphasized by Buddhist scriptures and monastics as the Buddhist norm, this chapter proposes that during the cold war Buddhists with social responsibility for the welfare of others could have supported the possession of WMD as a deterrent. However, the cold war was an extreme historical situation, while in today's increasingly integrated world, Buddhist principles reject the possession of WMD as a threat to human civilization and instead emphasize education and mindfulness training to guide economic and political policies to safely eliminate them.

WHAT ARE THE SOURCES AND PRINCIPLES GOVERNING THE USE OF WEAPONS IN WAR?

Some theorists, such as Johan Galtung, have outlined points where Buddhism is strong and weak in support of peace.[4] Instead of generalizing about Buddhism as a whole, and in order to provide a foundation for discussing Buddhist views of WMD, I review four ethical frameworks: monastic ethics, the ethics of lay supporters of monastics, lay ethics for those who do not consider monastic ethics as the ultimate norm, and the ethics of Buddhist rulers in relation to the use of weapons in conducting war. Views on pacifism vary among these four Buddhist social groups and provide a range of Buddhist attitudes on the use of weapons and the conduct of war.

Monastic Ethics

Buddhist rules for monastics are included as a major section of Buddhist scriptures called the *vinaya*.[5] The primary guide is a list of over 200 prohibitions that are recited twice a month and that have seven categories of severity. The four prohibitions that are the most stringent and that require expulsion from the monastic order are killing, stealing, lying about spiritual attainments, and sexual misconduct. The prohibition against killing includes prohibition against keeping weapons and prevents monastics from advocating the development or deployment of WMD.

Because Buddhism is not centrally organized, the monastic tradition has served as the chief institutional form and is very consistent in its rules and procedures for personal morality across Buddhism, with some notable exceptions. Although there are cases of armed monks in Japan during the Kamakura period (1185–1333), and Korean monks who fought against Japanese invaders in the early seventeenth century, the most sustained violation of monastic nonviolence has been the political responsibility accepted by Tibetan monks at the instigation of the Mongols in 1642. While these monk-rulers have delegated political responsibilities for war to laity, they have on occasion taken up arms themselves.[6] There is no scriptural support for this deviation, however, and the present Dalai Lama, the political ruler of the Tibetan government in exile, is famous for trying to follow a path of nonviolence in his foreign policy toward the Chinese occupation of Tibet. Furthermore, in his acceptance speech for the Nobel Peace Prize in 1989, he proposed making Tibet a nuclear-free zone.[7]

The other sustained exception to the monastic rules has been Japanese Buddhism, which began to liberalize the monastic rules beginning in the ninth century based on the thought of Saicho (766–822). Celibacy ceased to be the pattern for the popular devotional movement inspired by Shinran (1173–1262), but this break became pervasive in 1872 when the government lifted the ban on celibacy for everyone, so that the pattern today in Japan is married priests. Regarding military issues, in the Kamakura period (1185–1333) monk-soldiers engaged in intermonastic fighting and burned rival monasteries, although no Buddhist writing supported this violence nor did any justify Japanese militarism. However, almost all Buddhist priests gave support to government aggression in Asia during the Second World War. But this trend has not gained approval among other Buddhists and is now an issue for reevaluation by Japanese Buddhists.[8]

After reviewing the scriptural norms and the historical record, we can safely conclude that the overwhelming view of Buddhist monasticism is to reject the possession of weapons, the use of war, and violence. Even though some monastics skirted this norm at certain times in history, no new norm was established: The possession of weapons and engaging in violence and war are strictly prohibited.

Lay Supporters of Monastics

Unlike the special *vinaya* scriptures to guide monastic morality, there is no separate section dealing with lay ethics. Still, five precepts – no killing, stealing, lying, sexual misconduct, nor intoxication – applied to all laity, as well as right speech and livelihood as found in the Eightfold Noble Path. In this regard we read that "one should abstain from making one's living through a profession that brings harm to others, such as trading in arms and lethal weapons, intoxicating drinks, poisons, killing animals, cheating, etc., and one should live by a profession which is honorable, blameless and innocent of harm to others."[9] As a result, early Buddhism advises against serving as a butcher or a soldier.

While general lay ethics are expressed in the morality tales presented as Jataka stories of the Buddha's former lifetimes, some specific advice is given in the *Sigalaka sutta*,[10] which the eminent fifth-century commentator Buddhaghosa called the layman's code of conduct. This text gives a series of guidelines that includes not killing, stealing, lying, nor sexual misconduct, as well as not acting out of hatred, desire, delusion, or fear – the last being the main motivation for building WMD. Next comes advice against squandering wealth – such as through addictions, roaming the streets late at night, attending shows, gambling, bad companions, and idleness. The *Sigalaka sutta* next lists cultivating good habits, including the fourfold basis for social harmony: giving, kindly words, a life of service, and impartial treatment and participation with others.

None of these addresses the use of weapons in war, but the obligation to provide for primary kinship relationships does serve as a basis for strategic defense. In addition, the guidelines for social harmony provide advice on how to avoid developing enemies, obviously a vital teaching with respect to national security concerns and for deescalating the nuclear buildup (to be discussed below).

Early Buddhist ethics is often summarized as "Avoid evil, cultivate good, and purify the mind." What is distinctively Buddhist is the emphasis on transforming our mind, to change our understanding of good and evil based on purifying our mental awareness. If we have a heightened view of our own importance and permanence, then we will be egotistical and selfish, and our sense of goodness can become self-righteousness, self-serving, and destructive to the happiness of others and ourselves. On the other hand, if we develop a clear awareness that our own nature is diverse, changing, and interdependent with others, then we will be more flexible, less likely to demonize others, more supportive of others, and better able to find common ground. Not having this understanding of interdependence and impermanence breeds recurring feelings of insecurity, fear, anger, and war with the inevitable vicissitudes of life. The goal of Buddhists is to clear our minds and to find inner security as a precondition to national security. This transformation of consciousness is a crucial ingredient for all Buddhist peace proposals. But this alternative consciousness requires systematic education and training, the details of which are discussed below.

Independent Lay Social Ethics

Several centuries after the death of the Buddha, a major new movement became visible in Buddhism called Mahayana. The foundation of ethics in Mahayana Buddhism differs from earlier Buddhism by emphasizing the obligation to save others, and that one's one salvation was not complete until everyone had been liberated. As a result, the earlier summary of Buddhist ethics was changed to read: "Avoid evil, cultivate good, and save all beings." This obligation toward others, based on our interdependence with others, means that Mahayana ethics cannot be isolated from the welfare of all living things. Based on these assumptions, Mahayana Buddhists cannot withdraw from the WMD dilemma by individually avoiding weapons and killing, but must assume that they are culpable as long as any WMD exist.

Mahayana ethical virtues straddle the monastic-lay divide, and classically are listed as the six perfections: charity, morality, patience, zeal, meditation, and wisdom.[11] While these are foundational, more than 200 other Mahayana Buddhist ethical scriptures exist, but to date no collaborative study has been done to develop a comprehensive Mahayana social ethic.[12] Most of the texts exist only in Chinese, but the state control of Buddhist social activities in East Asia has restricted the development of Buddhist social theory and practice. Only recently have Buddhists worked cross-culturally to seek social princi- ples for modern times,[13] especially among socially engaged Buddhists in periodicals such as the *Journal of Buddhist Ethics, Seeds of Peace,* and *Turning Wheel* (the journal of the Buddhist Peace Fellowship). Opinions in these publications have almost[14] unanimously supported nonviolence, including a rejection of WMD.

The most frequently used ethical text in Mahayana is the *Fanwang jing* (Jp., *Bommokyo; Brahma-net Scripture*) that has ten major (A) precepts and forty-eight minor (B) ones. Besides forbidding killing (A1), it also rejects serving as a military envoy (B11) and dealing in weapons (B32). In other words, it reflects the monastic ethics discussed above. However, among Chinese Buddhists in Taiwan, a different Mahayana ethical text is used specif- ically for laity, the *Youposaijie jing* (Skt., *Upasakasila-sutra*).[15] This text explic- itly connects itself to the *Sigalaka sutta* discussed above by using Sigalaka as an interlocutor, but is about twenty times longer and has only a few traces from the earlier text. Also, unlike the *Fanwang jing,* the text acknowledges the dilemmas of lay life and elevates lay practice above monastic practice by saying that monks can give only teachings, whereas laity can offer practical help for the relief of suffering.

Commitment to social activism and social responsibility in the *Youposaijie jing* expands the tradition by adding the obligation to care for sick strangers encountered along the road.[16] Here the circle of relations for whom we have responsibility has changed from those who have close kinship and familiarity to us to include anyone who has need of help. The virtue of selfless giving (Skt., *dana*) is the major topic in the *Youposaijie jing,* and practitioners are told if they have little wealth, they should give first to the poor, and second to the Buddhist community.[17] Moreover, the benefits of giving to animals out of compassion are equal to making offerings to the Buddha.[18] This is a dramatic reversal of conventional Buddhist values.

A basis for this radical departure is offered by many heroic illustrations from stories of the previous lives of the Buddha where he used his vows to seek rebirth in difficult circumstances to help others. Some stories show him reborn as a fish, beast, or medicine tree, or sacrificing himself for others, such as when the Buddha gave his body to save the life of a pigeon. This elevation of compassionate actions to mythic proportions in these tales is applied to the religious life in chapter 10 of the *Youposaijie jing* by equating the path to enlightenment with enlightenment itself.[19] This claim has the effect of raising compassionate and ethical behavior to a supreme level over traditional practices of monastic recluses as a new form of soteriology: Since benefiting others is the bodhisattva path, which is equal to enlightenment, "to benefit others is to benefit oneself."[20]

The theme of "self-benefit, benefit-others" in chapter 10 is expanded in chapter 11 by emphasizing correct speech and the task of reconciliation, especially by having compassion for one's enemies:

[The bodhisattva] always shows kindness to his foes. When friends and foes are suffering, he first saves his foes. He is compassionate to those who scold him. Seeing someone steal his things, he keeps silent and unmoved. He has compassion for those who come to beat him. He sees sentient beings as his parents. . . . When harm befalls him, he returns it with good. . . . He is willing to make others happy through his own suffering.[21]

In chapter 8 the *Youposaijie jing* says that a true Buddhist has equanimity with both friends and foes. In chapter 12 we learn that not making a distinction between friend and foe is the perfection of wisdom.[22] Consistent with the teachings of early Buddhism, the text teaches that a bodhisattva should develop an inner attitude that accepts foes without feelings of ill-will and sees "all foes as dear friends."[23] Beyond this inner goodwill, however, the *Youposaijie jing* urges bodhisattvas to actively "benefit one's foes"[24] with a willingness to transform them.[25] At this point, the *Youposaijie jing* goes beyond traditional Buddhism by urging bodhisattvas to take responsibility for one's foes and even give them preferential treatment over one's friends.

For a layperson in the world, having equanimity and compassion for one's enemies, seeing them as intimate family members ("dear ones"), and favoring them has economic and legal dimensions, such as not reporting robbers who steal from you and refusing to defend yourself against those who physically fight and attack you. This must raise serious questions when we consider women who suffer sexual aggression or those, like modern Tibetans, who have been conquered militarily. Even though the Dalai Lama has received the Nobel Peace Prize for not supporting terrorism toward China and has demonstrated remarkable freedom from hatred and vengeance, the concept of loving one's enemies is not without many ethical problems.[26]

A practical consequence of recognizing the value of one's enemies for Buddhists is the instruction in the *Youposaijie jing* to study secular writings and to honor non-Buddhist teachings. In chapter 13 the lay disciple is taught to increase positive thoughts and "to make offerings indiscriminately to all Buddhist and non-Buddhist practitioners as far as he can."[27] "Although secular studies are not beneficial, he learns them for the sake of sentient beings. What he learns should be the best in the world."[28] In chapter 12 this theme is repeated as part of the five *dharmas* to be practiced: faith, compassion, courage, "reading secular texts without becoming weary," and "learning all secular business without becoming tired."[29] The study of non-Buddhist writings is significant in being primarily aimed not at making others into Buddhists but in helping others, for developing positive attitudes in others, and for removing greed and hatred from others.[30]

In chapter 27 of the *Youposaijie jing*, the two-character phrase for compassion (Ch., *ci-bei*) is broken into two parts: *ci* increases a sense of affinity, kinship, or kindness, such as being able to see enemies as members of one's own family. On the other hand, *bei* involves both awareness and action: It not only increases affinity, but also relieves suffering of others. At this point, it involves the practice of giving: "Good son, if a person can see even one hair's breadth of goodness in one's foes rather than their unwholesomeness, you should know that he is practicing kindness. When his foes are suffering from illness and if he goes visiting, takes care of them, and gives them what they need, you should know that he is cultivating compassion."[31] This ethic is a profound challenge to Western strategies for peace and security (to be discussed below).[32]

We should carefully distinguish between the obligation to care for sick strangers and the proposal to treat enemies as kin. The first provides a clear goal of trying to heal those in physical distress, and it rests on the power of universal sympathy to override our normal in-group priorities based on family-friends-teacher first. Treating enemies as kin, however, does not have universal sympathy as its foundation, nor does it mandate a specific action like medical care, nor does it provide a clear goal such as relieving suffering. The injunction does not invoke any action beyond a new interpretation, namely, seeing enemies as kin. Loving enemies "as dear ones" need not involve chaos or total self-sacrifice by laying down one's arms. Being a lay bodhisattva need not mean total indulgence of the whims of others and inattention to the consequences of their actions. It demands only that enemies be seen as kin, as members of our family, as being connected to us, so that they are no longer estranged and objectified as "them." Their suffering becomes our suffering. Etymologically, the word "kindness" is not first of all an emotion but the recognition that others are the same kind as us. Similarly, according to the *Youposaijie jing* interpretation of *ci-bei* discussed above, *ci* is not first a "feeling with the other" (com-passion), but a "recognition of affinity." Later *bei* arises, namely, helpful actions to relieve suffering. Compassion as *ci-bei* first involves an enlargement of our self-identity to include a sense of connectedness with the fate of others. The primary basis for this action is enhancing not our own individuation, but instead our relations with others. This implies a strong criticism of nationalistic chauvinism that is the primary basis for present American (as well as other states') policies supporting the possible use of some WMD.

Early Buddhism gave many vivid exhortations to avoid treating enemies with hostility, especially in passages that taught the four immeasurable minds: "Bhikkhus [monks], explain even if bandits were to sever you savagely limb by limb with a two-handled saw, he who gave rise to a mind of hate towards them would not be carrying out my teaching."[33] To avoid hostile feelings, early Buddhism emphasized a constellation of factors: insight into oneself (Skt., *anatman*), impermanence, suffering, and interdependence. By comparison, the *Youposaijie jing* emphasizes activism based on a sense of kinship with others, even sick strangers and enemies, as foundational for its ethics. Because we do not normally see our enemies as members of our own family, the *Youposaijie jing* recommends the necessity of mindfulness and wisdom as supports to compassionate activity, and therefore as essential aspects of its ethical platform.

Ethics of Buddhist Rulers and Citizens

The major Buddhist writings about political responsibility are Buddhist teachings for kings. Most Buddhist instruction deals with inner intentions and personal behavior and only briefly touches on the use of force and violence. According to the leading Thai monk-scholar of our generation, Phra Dhammapitika (Rajavaramuni),[34] the king is guided by four sets of virtues. The set most emphasized by Thai Buddhists is the Ten Virtues of the King (Pali, *dasa rajadhamma*): charity, high moral character, self-sacrifice, integrity, gentleness, nonindulgence, nonanger, nonoppression, tolerance, and nondeviation from the norm. This list focuses on inner attitudes, not on military responsibility.

The second set is the Twelve Duties of a Universal Monarch (Pali, *cakkavattivatta*) that deals explicitly with security issues. The duties are right oversight and protection for one's own family and the armed forces, for the nobility, for the royal dependents, for brahmins and householders, for townspeople and villagers, for monks and priests, for animals and birds, prevention and suppression of unrighteous deeds, distribution of wealth to the poor, frequently seeking counsels from monks and religious leaders, abstention from unlawful sexual desire, and abstention from unjustly coveting the property of others.[35]

The third is the Fourfold Royal Acts for Social Integration (Pali, *rajasanghavatthu*), namely: shrewdness in agricultural promotion, shrewdness in encouragement of government officials, binding the people's hearts by vocational promotion, and kindly beneficial words. The fourth set consists of the Fivefold Strengths of a Monarch (Pali, *khattiyabala*), namely, strength of arms, wealth, ministers, royal ancestry, and wisdom. The most important for our purposes is the duty of kings to have strong armed forces.[36]

Phra Dhammapitika comments that what is "especially noteworthy about these virtues and duties is the emphasis on the absence of poverty. Poverty is regarded as the main source of crime and disorder as well as greed,[37] whereas economic sufficiency is a prerequisite for a happy, secure, and stable society, favorable to individual development and perfection. Economics is especially important in today's world as a major foreign policy tool along with military force.

For Buddhists, the ancient Indian king Asoka (r. c. 273–232 B.C.E.) is the most influential model of an ideal king. Following the conquests of his grandfather and father, Asoka unified India by a bloody conquest of Kalinga (c. 261 B.C.E.), but after becoming remorseful of the suffering he had caused, he converted to Buddhism and proclaimed an ethic of non-violence (*ahimsa*). His edicts show that he promoted the renunciation of war, advocated religious tolerance, medical services, and social relief for the poor and elderly, instituted restrictions on killing animals, and softened the harsh laws of his predecessors.[38] Stanley Tambiah compares these edicts of toleration with the Hindu duties of kings to give divine punishment to those who deviate from their caste duties. As a result, he argues that Asokan edicts were distinctively Buddhist in place of a Hindu model of righteousness.[39]

There are several other treatments of ethics for rulers, such as *The Precious Garland of Advice for the King*, written by Nagarjuna.[40] However, theory is not always practice, and Buddhist ethics has been based more on the Asoka of legend than of history.[41] Tambiah observes how early Buddhism evolved a theory of cosmic law (*dharma*) as the basis for the concept of a universal monarch (Pali, *cakkavatti*), but this new "rhetoric of kingship" neglected the practical wisdom of power and administration. Asoka manifested Buddhist tolerance and moderation only after his conquests, but his successors failed to hold his territories, and under Hindu kings Buddhism gradually disappeared from India. Buddhism gave a noble ideal for integrating a newly conquered territory but was ineffective for either conquering or controlling territory.

While much has been made of the "two wheels of *dhamma*" – a dialectical model of the spiritual sage versus the temporal king[42] – Tambiah argues that Buddhism evolved a galactic model in which virtue was essential for a universal monarch who was supposed to radiate his righteous influence universally. Nevertheless, this cosmic model of concentric circles of influence contained few practical guidelines, and Buddhist kings and emperors in Asia have exercised absolute power as often as they have provided benevolent social welfare. The tragic recent history of Myanmar (Burma), Cambodia, and Tibet – arguably among the most Buddhist cultures on earth – also forces us to question the adequacy of Buddhist norms to evolve fair and effective governance structures.

The complex relationships between Buddhism and politics is evident in other modern states that have adopted Buddhism as their state religion, such as Thailand. At the coronation of King Rama VI in 1910, the chief Buddhist patriarch[43] gave a sermon that approved of nations organizing armies to fight against enemies. "Wars must be prepared for even in times of peace, otherwise . . . one would be in a disadvantageous position towards one's foe." The preface to the printed edition stated that it is "an erroneous idea to suppose that the Buddha condemned all wars and people whose business it was to wage war."[44] Chaiwat Satha-Anand discovered that in 1915 a monk, Phra Thep Moli, published a sermon criticizing military expertise as bad knowledge that inevitably led to harm. As a result, Chaiwat notes that "King Rama VI punished Phra Thep Moli . . . because to preach something against the state policy is a challenge to the power of that state. In an absolute monarchical state . . . [a]ny challenge cannot be tolerated."[45]

Many Buddhist teachers in Sri Lanka have also accepted state violence in recent years. Although the idea that Buddhism is pacifistic is widespread and can be supported by Buddhist scriptures, there are other texts that allow for war. In the summers of 1997 and 1998 Tessa Bartholomeusz interviewed approximately fifty Buddhist monks and laity who support the government's effort to eradicate the Liberation Tigers of Tamil Eelam (LTTE), a group fighting for a Tamil homeland in the northern part of Sri Lanka. Some argue that this is not a defensive war for the Sinhalese, but a Sinhalese-Tamil conflict over territory. But Buddhist supporters see the government in the role of a righteous Buddhist king fighting to defend Buddhism against the predominantly Hindu Tamils. This war, which has claimed about 50,000 lives since 1983, demonstrates that Buddhists can support the idea of a "just war," since appeal is often made to the *Cakkavatti sihanada* Buddhist scripture that describes a Buddhist king with a fourfold army (consisting of units of elephants, cavalry, chariots, and infantry).[46]

Narratives such as the *Mahavamsa* that legitimate the identification of the island of Sri Lanka with Buddhism are rare, and so is Buddhist militancy. On the whole Buddhism focuses less on social and national life than on the fate of individuals. Buddhists emphasize that culture is primarily developed by one's own mind and not by society, and this mental culture is the prime source of good and evil, not society. Based on this view, Buddhists in China, such as the Falun Gong movement begun in 1992, cannot act violently to defend themselves and their reputation, since by doing so they would be killing their own culture, not defending it. Having been outlawed in July 1999 for peaceful demonstrations, the Falun Gong members are providing a contemporary testimony to the strong Buddhist tradition of self-sacrifice for the ideal of nonviolence, even when it means their torture and death.

There are many ways for Buddhists to understand and interpret their tradition,[47] and we must be careful not to generalize about Buddhist ethics based only on monastic models, on doctrinal grounds, or on regional examples. Buddhism offers many ethical models, monastic and lay, for citizens and for rulers, who all use the rhetoric of peace and nonviolence as a goal, but who do not always embody it as a practice.

WHEN IS IT MORALLY PERMISSIBLE TO USE WMD IN WAR?

Buddhists are unique in being the main victims of weapons of mass destruction, with an estimated 200,000 dying in Hiroshima and Nagasaki in 1945. It is interesting that the issues under discussion in the present volume are framed, generally, from the perspective of those (theoretically) using WMD, not those on the receiving end. For many Japanese Buddhists, this topic is not a theoretical issue, but an experiential one. Stanley Hauerwas questioned the validity of the Gulf War by asking "Whose justice? Which peace?" and similar questions can be asked about the use of WMD. From the point of view of those who died or were displaced, there is no peace and no justice. And those Buddhists who were in contact with the victims of the atomic bomb in Japan do not accept their use under any circumstance. A recent book by Daisaku Ikeda, president of Soka Gakkai International, a postwar lay Buddhist organization of about ten million members, lists seven paths to world peace, the last path being renunciation of nuclear arms.[48] However, one does not have to be a Japanese Buddhist to see that nuclear war is the "ultimate immorality," as Linus Pauling once said to Ikeda.[49]

The indiscriminate nature of weapons of mass destruction implies not just killing to protect one's own group but being willing to kill any number of other individuals because they are representing another group that is deemed unworthy and dangerous to life. The role of the individual on both sides is overshadowed by the fate of one group in contrast to another group. The moral mathematics – based on killing the few to save the many – fades away because of the indiscriminate nature of weapons of mass destruction. Instead of making decisions based on quantifying the greater good, WMD are developed and deployed to defend a system of government, a way of life, a society, and a culture, as more beneficial to life than its opposing society and culture.

The existence of WMD offers a moral challenge to Buddhists who live in countries that possess WMD. The cold war was justified ideologically as a competition between communism and democracy. Today critics can assert that the real issue was the defense of territory and national power, since the Russian and American nuclear missiles are still pointed at each other. Ironically, some of the former military commanders of these missiles apparently believed the ideology, for the collapse of the Iron Curtain in the 1990s led them to embark on friendship campaigns and to seek the elimination of the missiles. However, political leaders have not adopted this view, and the report submitted to the president and Congress on February 15, 2001, by the U.S. Commission on National Security based itself on safeguarding U.S. territory. This report is the first extensive national security review in fifty years. It took two years to complete, was bipartisan in nature, and reported that security experts were unanimous in saying that it is inevitable that the United States will receive an attack by WMD in the next decade or so. Even though the cold war has ended, the consensus was not whether WMD would be used, but when and under what circumstances. The overriding concern was to defend U.S. territory against WMD, and potential enemies included Russia, China, and terrorists supported by Usama bin Ladin's network or by Iran.[50]

Buddhists always reflect on how things arise, so the source of threats to the United States must be examined. The Dalai Lama repeatedly asserts that our enemies are precious not only because we share so many connections with them, but also because they can teach us things that we cannot learn from our friends.[51] Discussion of enemies must raise questions about the causes and conditions that produce enemies, as well as methods of defense, mediation, and reconciliation. In addition to the strategic issues raised by WMD, Buddhists focus on the mindset that is involved and the related institutional causes and conditions. To treat WMD simply as a strategic issue is to oversimplify and to falsify the living situation. Oversimplification is an act of ignorance, and ignorance is the primary enemy of Buddhism.

The two prime motives for using WMD are the defense of territory or the defense of a way of life, and sometimes both, as in the Second World War. But most modern nuclear arms provide a new context for war since they cause indiscriminate and uncontrolled slaughter. Buddhists consider territory and a way of life as limited and subject to change, and not adequate to justify killing indiscriminately. Based on the unlimited destruction from WMD in the name of very limited and historically conditioned goals (national territory and a way of life), Buddhists in good conscience can never actually use WMD.

Instead, Buddhism is famous for the willing self-immolation of Buddhist monks, such as Thich Quang Duc on June 11, 1963, in Vietnam, as protest against the abuse of power. The Jataka stories told to Buddhist children in Southeast Asia are fables about the past lives of the Buddha, often involving self-sacrifice that later reaped positive benefits. While such sacrifice cannot be asked of others, many Buddhists willingly sacrifice themselves for the benefit of others, comforted by belief in a moral universe that extends through many lifetimes, ensuring that their sacrifice will not be in vain.

The opposite situation also holds. If a Buddhist kills someone else in the name of a greater good, such as the protection of a larger number of others, the group may benefit, but the Buddhist killer himself is not safe. He must suffer karmic consequences in future lifetimes. Of course, as in all religious traditions, a major consideration is whether one's intentions were for self-gain or to serve the needs of others. Killing has been justified in some rare Buddhist texts, such as in the *Upaya sutra*, for the protection of a greater number,[52] or in stories of the Buddha's previous lifetimes as a universal monarch.[53] But Tambiah argues that the violence initially used by a universal monarch is to be supplanted with moral force, and that moral force is superior.[54]

The nuclear threat far outweighs other risks, so it is the main focus of Buddhist opposition. One caveat is that to the degree that nuclear, biological, or chemical weapons become controllable, their tactical uses may then be considered. But ancillary systems that may limit destruction by making targeting more precise or defensive measures more accurate – such as missile delivery methods, detection, tracking and interception devices, and the sophistication of radar-blocking technology – are still unproven. If destruction could be limited and not involve mass destruction, then Buddhist views would revert to just war arguments, and, as in Sri Lanka, Buddhists may differ on this question.

IS DEVELOPMENT OR DEPLOYMENT FOR DETERRENCE MORALLY ACCEPTABLE?

It is claimed that the threat of these weapons has already been used to stem the tide of communism. Further, it is said, the nuclear standoff of the cold war prevented outright aggression against the "free" world. In this sense, WMD already have been used in the balance of power to preserve life and peace. These claims raise moral questions on the development and deployment of WMD as a deterrent. The unusual experience of the past half-century when both the United States and the USSR developed and deployed WMD, especially nuclear missiles, for the sake of deterrence demonstrates that this action in itself need not cause death, although it greatly magnifies the risk of total destruction.

Because so much is at stake when we discuss WMD, it is imperative that we remember the historical failure of Buddhists to preserve or extend their ideals in practical power politics. The holocaust in Cambodia in the 1970s and the military dictatorship in Myanmar (Burma) in the 1990s both arose in cultures dominated by Buddhism. As a consequence, in giving a Buddhist response to the challenge of WMD, after reviewing Buddhist values and norms, the historical failure of Buddhist political theory to protect life and to cultivate cultures of peace and tolerance necessitates that we break new ground.

What has convinced me that traditional Buddhist commitments to nonviolence cannot be normative when dealing with social and political responsibility is the Jewish experience of the Holocaust. Not the moral force of righteous Jews, nor their belief in the goodness of humanity, nor their trust in the metaphysical goodness and power of God were sufficient to prevent the indiscriminate killing of the innocent.[55] I fear that not the moral force of Buddhist saints (such as the Dalai Lama), nor their belief that all people have a Buddha nature and are good at heart, nor their trust in the moral authority of the universe as expressed in the doctrine of *karma* is sufficient to prevent a future holocaust. The Buddhist ideal of nonviolence and the avoidance of weapons of any kind must be weighed against the wide range of Buddhist political practices. Based on the apparent effectiveness of WMD as a deterrent during the cold war, and the duty of Buddhist rulers to protect their population, I would argue that Buddhists in good conscience could have supported the development of WMD as a deterrent during the cold war. Did any do so? Not publicly or in writing, to my knowledge, but only through silent support of American, British, and French government policies.

Buddhists teach that the three poisons of hatred, greed, and ignorance are the cause of suffering, and I would suggest that the fight against ignorance includes the responsibility to learn the lessons of Buddhist history. Being aware of Buddhist political ineffectiveness in the past must serve as a clear warning against advocating unilateral disarmament as a state policy, even though individual Buddhists may choose this path for themselves. Instead, for those who bear social responsibility for the welfare of others, Buddhists must support some minimal weapon and defensive development, while working strenuously for a mutually negotiated end of WMD.

The basis for the justification for developing a strong defense, including development and deployment of WMD, can draw on already existing Buddhist principles. First, Buddhist laity have always had material responsibilities, among them the duty to protect their families (*Sigalaka sutta*). Second, Buddhists with political responsibility – and in a democracy this means everyone who votes – are obliged to build wealth and strength of arms (*Cakkavatti sutta*). If the primary goal is to relieve suffering, then the use of physical deterrents and violence against brutality may sometimes be required.

The present moral irresponsibility lies in the careless and mindless way in which governments currently maintain WMD without erecting aggressive programs of education to sensitize the population to the enormous risks and precise details of these weapons. The veil of secrecy over their development and deployment that is maintained by the military neither serves the role of deterrence by warning an enemy nor does it arouse its citizens to the necessity of building cultural bridges and political reconciliation. What is morally unacceptable is keeping the population ignorant and unprepared to deal with these horrendous tools.

Warning signs are placed on cigarette packages, instructions are put on medicine bottles for individual protection, and flashing warning bells sound when nuclear plants have potential meltdowns to warn the work force. However, no comparable alarm has been sounded, nor preparation given, in the past forty years by governments who possess WMD. Now that WMD are spreading around the globe, this lack of alarm and education amounts to increasing sharply the risk of death without a proportionate emphasis on warning, education, and safeguards. This is not responsible.

Death comes to us all, and people are able to deal responsibly with death not by avoiding the subject but by learning about it so that they can make appropriate choices in action and attitude. The government is exercising god-like responsibilities in not including citizens in its circle of knowledge, and this hubris is planting seeds of potential disaster.

The Buddhist teaching of mindfulness systematically ensures that practitioners face both the pleasant and unpleasant aspects of reality in a clear, calm manner in order to be free of delusion, fear, desire, and hatred. This process is classically presented in the *Satipatthana sutta*, which includes visits to the charnel grounds where practitioners can contemplate dead bodies in various states of decomposition in order to become familiar with their own bodies and the processes of death.[56] Having WMD necessitates not just theoretical knowledge but similar kinds of experiential education. For example, the Youth Division of Soka Gakkai in Japan organized oral history projects for their youth to interview survivors of the atomic bomb attacks on Hiroshima and Nagasaki. As they wrote, "There are many young people today who have never experienced the fires and death of actual war. One way to ensure that they never do is to reveal to them the face of war unmasked in the hellish experiences of the victims."[57] In addition, the Soka Gakkai Women's Division Peace Committee compiled a twelve-volume series called *Heiwa e o negai o komete* (With hopes of peace) consisting of Japanese women's testimonials about their war experiences as a way to give young people "a true picture of the war as witnessed by women who actually lived through it." A one-volume set of selections is also available in English.[58]

Today the immediate moral problem is not the development and deployment of WMD but ignorance about WMD. Without greater knowledge, citizens will not be prepared to evaluate and deal with WMD except as a vague unknown. This ignorance can breed paralysis, hysteria, or warped ideological wrangling. It certainly fails to mobilize efforts to overcome social divisions and to build shared values and mutual agreements for handling the WMD problem. Wisdom and compassion cannot evolve effectively in a fog of ignorance, and ignorance needlessly compounds the risks of WMD. For me, this is the main moral issue surrounding WMD.

IS IT JUSTIFIABLE TO DENY WMD TO OTHERS?

Buddhists are basically against the possession of weapons of any kind, always support the idea of limiting weapons, whether handguns or WMD, and are against proliferation. Fewer weapons mean fewer opportunities and temptations to use weapons, which means less violence. The first guide of Buddhist ethics is against killing, so to limit weapons of any kind to others is a Buddhist imperative. The only exception to this principle is that stated earlier: when the possession of weapons might save lives.

IS DISARMAMENT A MORAL IMPERATIVE?

Reduction and elimination of WMD and, finally, of all weapons is a social and moral imperative for Buddhists. However, the issue of unilateral disarmament versus a negotiated, universal disarmament is an issue of timing and tactics about which Buddhists may disagree. What is clear is that disarmament will never happen without the development of massive campaigns for education, social justice, cross-cultural understanding and reconciliation, and internal psychological growth and transformation. These actions can be done unilaterally and should be.

CONCRETE OPTIONS: EDUCATION, ECONOMICS, AND ENEMIES

Reduction of WMD will require an integrated and universal agreement involving arms reduction by all eight nuclear powers (Britain, France, China, India, Israel, Pakistan, Russia, and the United States) with a larger percentage of reduction by the great powers, especially the United States. This will probably not happen without a drastic reduction in global tension and the strengthening of globally recognized international agencies that could monitor and administer the political and legal process (such as the International Criminal Court, UN peace-keeping forces, and an enlarged Security Council). It is not likely that these international agencies will be strengthened until there is greater equity economically and technologically. Obviously, more parity is not the goal of the United States, or other members of the G-7, such as France, Germany, Japan, and the United Kingdom, who wish to develop global markets but not increase global competition, since that means less profit. Certainly, Buddhist morality based on noninjury to all life should support human and environmental rights and international agencies to maintain them.[59] However, global culture needs to be changed before these international agencies will be effective, and from a Buddhist perspective, three areas might be emphasized: education, economics, and enemies.

Education

Treaty negotiation for phased and complete elimination of WMD is a specialized area, but it has become clear that no matter how good or valid the treaties may be, popular support and political will are needed for them to become law. A major moral responsibility for religious communities and governments is to develop societies and people who are informed, aroused, and committed to the goals of the treaties. In spite of the gigantic expense and horrendous risk involved in developing and maintaining WMD, there has not been a proportionate level of public education to evolve moral and political sensibilities to the horrible threat of nuclear holocaust, as well as to the fragile and decaying safety mechanisms that restrain their use.

Education is not simple. First, the government must be more aggressive in communicating the kinds of damage that WMD can inflict based on its best estimates and tests. Information needs to be communicated in a variety of formats for different age groups: videos, cartoon features, and publications. Second, civil society groups need to use this information to raise ethical questions to inform our political discussions so that an aroused and informed public can develop political will. Third, Buddhists must integrate this information into mindfulness practices.

Among the hundreds of early Buddhist scriptures, perhaps the most important is the Foundation of Mindfulness Scripture (*Satipatthana sutta*).[60] To gain liberation and inner peace, a Buddhist dwells on contemplating in great detail the body, feelings, the mind, and mental images. For our modern era, we should also introduce mindfulness of our "society as society," to notice its structures and institutions, its different processes, and the rise and fall of its virtues and flaws, because today wars are fought in the name of societies. As such, part of our mindfulness practice should include the experience of wars, the havoc wreaked by our wars, and the forces that lead into these wars. Information about life and death needs to be internalized, not just studied, if we are to find balance and inner peace as a preparation for world peace.

Economics

Early Buddhist scriptures teach that the leading cause of strife in the world is poverty. In the *Cakkavatti sutta*, the Buddha instructed a universal monarch: "Let no crime prevail in your kingdom, and to those who are in need, give property." The text shows how stealing, lying, killing, and all social ills inevitably arose for those who were reluctant to follow this advice.[61]

It is often claimed that global business will enforce global peace for the sake of profit. While there may be some hope in these claims, the World Trade Organization has not moved in that direction, and the World Bank is weakly trying to nurture institutional development in poorer countries,[62] while national debts have increased and complicated international cooperation. Regional and/or universal peace-keeping forces are still in their infancy and need enormous support from business and the general public to become a reality. Furthermore, the military-industrial complex stands in the way of arms reduction, and the permanent members of the UN Security Council make most of the world's arms.

Calling for a moratorium on arms trade would be a major step not only to reduce violence, but also to free money for human services. Greater public and political criticism of the economics that drive global and regional conflict is necessary. Economics have positive and negative conditions that need to be discussed more publicly and regulated more cooperatively. The secret deliberations of the WTO are undemocratic and are intolerable from a Buddhist view because they work against social mindfulness and global reconciliation.

Enemies

Suicide bombers are the most unpredictable source of violence against the United States, and terrorism is the most likely source for unleashing a WMD attack. But it is amazing that the overwhelming reaction of the United States to terrorist attacks is outrage, defiance, and bolstered defenses. No one seems to ask publicly and in a sustained way what is so wrong with American society that people are willing to kill themselves in a suicide attack in order to challenge the United States. What impact has the United States made that provokes people to go to such extremes? What is the Buddhist analysis of the motivating factors for terrorists? Can the United States learn from Buddhists something that may shed light on the harmful consequences of American policies abroad, policies that might be changed to lessen, if not neutralize, the threat of terrorism?

Abraham Lincoln said that the quickest way to get rid of an enemy is to make him your friend. While friendship is not something that anyone can control, our attitudes toward our enemies are within our control. As discussed earlier, a major teaching of the *Youposaijie jing* is that Buddhists should view their enemies as members of their own family, as "dear ones," in order to relieve suffering. Although much expense is committed to identifying and keeping under surveillance suspected enemies of the United States, currently there is little public effort by the American government to cultivate understanding and appreciation of its enemies, or a concern to relieve their suffering.

Threats from others should raise questions about the nature of the enemy's society, and one's own, especially about global structural violence, the links between politicians and the weapons industry, and the misinformation and bias that is perpetrated by the news media with the support of major corporations who profit from the war industry. Every society is imperfect, and Buddhist mindfulness practice encourages looking at all aspects of society equally. Open appreciation of the causes of enemy hostility, and self-criticism of one's own flaws, is a third requirement that Buddhist ethics would suggest as a necessary condition for the success of global treaties and international agencies.

To avoid doing violence to others, Buddhists have a tradition of self-immolation, as exemplified by Thich Quang Duc on the streets of Saigon during the Vietnam War. Also in Vietnam in the 1960s, the Buddhist leader Thich Nhat Hanh insisted that the School of Youth for Social Service (SYSS) should not be aligned with any political group because they cared for the suffering of all people. But in refusing to join either side, government officials and the communists saw the SYSS as disloyal to their cause, and SYSS volunteers were killed. In 1967, after a four-month period in which six SYSS members died and others were wounded, Sr. Chan Khong wrote in her eulogy: "We cannot hate you, you who have thrown grenades and killed our friends, because we know that men are not our enemies. Our only enemies are the misunderstanding, hatred, jealousy, and ignorance that lead to such acts of violence. Please allow us to remove all misunderstanding so we can work together for the happiness of the Vietnamese people."[63]

Buddhists continue to be willing to die rather than to be violent against those who attack them. In the public pledge made by members of the SYSS at a funeral of their colleagues, they said: "Now, once again, we solemnly promise never to hate those who kill us, above all never to use violence to answer violence, even if the antagonists see us as enemies and kill until they annihilate us. We recall our pledge that people, no matter what their origins, never are our enemies. . . . Help us to keep steadily this non-violent mind in our social work by love that asks nothing in return."[64]

This chapter proposes that some Buddhists with political responsibility – and in democracies everyone has political responsibility – might have maintained WMD as a deterrent during the cold war in order to protect innocent populations. However, today the world is becoming increasingly integrated, and now both for practical reasons and foundational principles Buddhists should oppose WMD and advocate the elimination of WMD universally. But there is little hope that removal of WMD will happen until major cultural changes take place globally, and these changes depend on reforms in the areas of education, economics, and enemies. Rather than calling for a sacrifice by self-immolation, the call today is sacrifice by constructively working in these three areas. As Sr. Chan Khong wrote at the death of her friends: "Social change must start in our hearts with the will to transform our own egotism, greed, and lust into understanding, love, commitment, and sharing responsibility for the poverty and injustice in our country."[65]

In sum, we are left with two major models of Buddhist ethics. One involves political responsibility based on the galactic model of the universal monarch who marshals military strength and moral influence to control and channel disruptive elements in society. This model will use force when necessary for the greater good, guided by utilitarian ethics and motivated by compassion. The other model separates religious and political roles into the two wheels of the *dharma*, the sage and the ruler. The Buddha left his father's palace and political responsibility to find a way to end individual suffering and attain peace based on virtue ethics. Under this model, Buddhists relinquish power politics as beyond their control and counterproductive. As Jesus accepted arrest and execution, practitioners on this path are willing to die, and let others die, rather than to kill. The first model may justify WMD as a deterrent in an extreme emergency, but not their use under any circumstances. The second model rejects WMD, not only because of the risk to the planet, but also because all weapons destroy the root causes of peace at both the individual and communal level. Today, both models of Buddhist ethics reject the deployment of WMD. Instead, energy should be given to transforming the sources of conflict – including changing the ruthlessness of economic and national ambition into a community of interdependence through more inclusive institutions of global governance.

In other words, the need is to develop not the arms race but the human race.

Notes

1. See Kenneth Kraft, ed., *Inner Peace, World Peace: Essays on Buddhism and Nonviolence* (Albany: State University of New York Press, 1992).

2. See John Ross Carter, *Dhamma: Western Academic and Sinhalese Buddhist Interpretations: A Study of a Religious Concept* (Tokyo: Hokusido Press, 1978) for studies of various levels of meaning for Buddhist *dharma/dhamma*.

3. See Judith Simmer-Brown, "Speaking Truth to Power: The Buddhist Peace Fellowship," and Paula Green, "Walking for Peace: Nipponzan Myohoji," in Christopher Queen, ed., *Engaged Buddhism in the West* (Boston: Wisdom, 2000), 67–94 and 128–56.

4. Johan Galtung found twenty points where Buddhism was strong in support of peace, and six weak points. See Johan Galtung, "Peace and Buddhism," in *Buddhism and Leadership for Peace* (Tokyo: Soka University Peace Research Institute, 1986), 16–28.

5. See Charles S. Prebish, *A Survey of Vinaya Literature* (London: Curzon, 1996).

6. Tsepon W. D. Shakabpa, *Tibet: A Political History* (New Haven, Conn.: Yale University Press, 1967), 111ff.

7. The Dalai Lama, "The Nobel Peace Prize Lecture," in Sidney Piburn, ed., *The Dalai Lama: A Policy of Kindness* (Ithaca, N.Y.: Snow Lion, 1990), 23–24.

8. See Brian Victoria, *Zen at War* (New York: Weatherhill, 1997), and James Heisig and John Maraldo, eds., *Rude Awakenings: Zen, the Kyoto School, and the Question of Nationalism* (Honolulu: University of Hawaii Press, 1995). The iconoclastic impact of the Buddhist idea that all things lack permanent identity is seen often in Zen actions, including a famous *koan* of Nansen killing a cat (Mumonkan Case no. 14). See James Whitehall, "Is There a Zen Ethic?" in Charles Prebish, *Buddhist Ethics: A Cross-Cultural Approach* (Dubuque, Iowa: Kendall/Hunt, 1992), 195–215, and Peter Hershock, *Liberating Intimacy: Enlightenment and Social Virtuosity in Ch'an Buddhism* (Albany: State University of New York Press, 1996).

9. Walpola Rahula, *What the Buddha Taught* (Bedford, U.K.: G. Fraser, 1959), 47.

10. For an English translation of this early Buddhist scripture, see Maurice Walshe, trans., *Thus Have I Heard: The Long Discourses of the Buddha* (London: Wisdom, 1987), 461–69.

11. See Har Dayal, *The Bodhisattva Doctrine in Buddhist Sanskrit Literature* (London: K. Paul, Trench, Trubner, 1937), 165–269.

12. David Chappell, "Are There 17 Mahayana Ethics?" *Journal of Buddhist Ethics* 3 (1996), at http://jbe.la.psu.edu/3/chappell (January 11, 2001).

13. For example, several conferences have recently met to consider the message of Buddhism in the modern social and cultural context. In November 1999 Rissho University in Tokyo sponsored a conference, and in July 2000 and January 2001 Ariya-Vinaya conferences were held in Thailand. But no discussion arose concerning Buddhist attitudes toward war and WMD.

14. One exception is the view of Ken Jones, a leading socially engaged Buddhist in England and writer for the journal *Indra's Network*, who wrote that the Buddhist commitment to relieve suffering may sometimes require armed intervention in situations such as Rwanda and Kosovo, so Buddhists should not hold the precept against killing as an absolute (personal correspondence).

15. *Taisho Shinshu Daizokyo* (Tokyo: 1914–1922), 24:1034–75. For an English translation, see Heng-ching Shih, trans., *The Sutra on Upasaka Precepts* (Tokyo and Berkeley, Calif.: Bukkyo Dendo Kyokai, 1991).

16. Ibid., 75.

17. Ibid., 35–36.

18. Ibid., 114.

19. Ibid., 41.

20. Ibid., 43.

21. Ibid., 52–53.

22. Ibid., 56, 81, and 90.

23. Ibid., 95.

24. Ibid., 76.

25. Ibid., 57.

26. These issues are discussed at length by Stephen J. Pope, *The Evolution of Altruism and the Ordering of Love* (Washington, D.C.: Georgetown University Press, 1994), and by Donald W. Shriver, Jr., *An Ethic for Enemies: Forgiveness in Politics* (Oxford: Oxford University Press, 1995).

27. Shih Heng-ching, trans., *Sutra on Upasaka Precepts*, 61.

28. Ibid., 53.

29. Ibid., 56.

30. Ibid., 47.

31. Ibid., 187.

32. Chapter 19 ends with an extended description of various social welfare projects that a lay bodhisattva should undertake, including learning medicine, building hospitals, repairing roads, building guest houses, digging wells, planting fruit trees, building bridges, maintaining canals, protecting animals, massaging tired travelers, making shade with umbrellas, providing people with ear picks, and consoling the grieving. Although similar examples can be found in early Buddhist literature, the difference is the higher priority given to works of compassion in the *Youposaijie jing*. This is based on the simple argument that a Buddhist is defined as one who is committed to seeking enlightenment, and that works of compassion constitute the necessary path to achieve enlightenment.

33. *The Middle Length Discourses of the Buddha*, trans. Bhikkhu Nyanamoli and Bhikkhu Bodhi (Boston: Wisdom, 1995), 223.

34. Ven. Phra Dhammapitika is the official title recognized by the government for the scholar-monk Phra Maha Prayudh Payutto, the name given at his ordination and used by the Buddhist sangha. He was born January 12, 1939, as Prayudh Aryankura. The title that he received from the state from 1973 to 1987 was Phra Rajavaramuni, the name he used as the author for an article, "Foundations of Buddhist Social Ethics," in Prebish, ed., *Buddhist Ethics*, 30–55.

35. See the Buddhist scripture, *Cakkavatti-sihanada sutta* (The lion's roar on the turning of the wheel), in Walshe, trans., *Thus Have I Heard*, 395–405.

36. These five strengths of a ruler serve as an analogy in the Buddhist scriptures for the qualities that a monk should cultivate. See the Pali scripture *Atthakatha* V.120, trans. E. M. Hare, *The Book of Gradual Sayings (Anguttara-Nikaya)*, vol. 3 (London: Luzac, 1961), 113–24.

37. *Cakkavatti-sihanada sutta* and the *Agganna sutta* (On knowledge of the beginnings), in Walshe, trans., *Thus Have I Heard*, 398–99 and 412–13.

38. See N. A. Nikam and Richard McKeon, eds. and trans., *The Edicts of Asoka* (Chicago: University of Chicago Press, 1959).

39. Stanley Tambiah, *World Conqueror and World Renouncer* (Cambridge: Cambridge University Press, 1976), 23–27.

40. See Robert Thurman, "Guidelines for Buddhist Social Activities Based on Nagarjuna's *Jewel Garland of Royal Counsels*," *The Eastern Buddhist* 16:1 (Spring 1983): 19–51. For a complete translation, see Jeffrey Hopkins, *The Buddhism of Tibet* (London: George Allen & Unwin, 1975), 105–206.

41. See John S. Strong, *The Legend of King Asoka: A Study and Translation of the Asokavadana* (Princeton, N.J.: Princeton University Press, 1983).

42. Frank Reynolds, "The Two Wheels of Dhamma: A Study of Early Buddhism," in *The Two Wheels of Dhamma*, AAR Studies in Religion, no. 3, ed. Gananath Obeyesekere et al. (Chambersburg, Penn.: American Academy of Religion, 1972).

43. The Sangharaja, or "ruler of the Buddhist community," the leader of the hierarchical monastic structure established by the Thai government.

44. Trevor Ling, *Buddhism, Imperialism and War* (London: George Allen & Unwin, 1979), 136–37; quoted in Chaiwat Satha-Anand, "The Leaders, the Lotus and the Shadow of the Dove: The Case of Thai Society," in *Buddhism and Leadership for Peace* (Tokyo: Soka University Peace Research Institute, 1986), 66–67.

45. Chaiwat, "Leaders, Lotus, and Dove," 66.

46. Venerable Athuraliya Rathana, the coordinating secretary of the National Sangha Council, told Bartholomeusz in 1998 that "there are many stories in the canon that depict the Buddha as an advocate of force and violence if there is a just cause." See Tessa Bartholomeusz, "In Defense of the Dharma: Just-War Ideology in Buddhist Sri Lanka," *Journal of Buddhist Ethics* 6 (1999): 3; http://jbe.la.psu.edu/6/bartho991.htm (January 11, 2001).

47. For example, Andrew Huxley shows how a *jataka* tale of ethical instruction about the five precepts has been used in medieval Thailand as an organizing platform for describing the duties of eleven different palace functionaries. See Andrew Huxley, "The Kurudhamma: From Ethics to Statecraft," *Journal of Buddhist Ethics* 2 (1995): 191–203; http://jbe.la.psu.edu/2/huxley.html (January 11, 2001).

48. Daisaku Ikeda, *For the Sake of Peace: Seven Paths to Global Harmony* (Santa Monica: Middleway Press, 2001).

49. Linus Pauling and Daisaku Ikeda, *A Lifelong Quest for Peace: A Dialogue* (Boston: Jones and Bartlett, 1992), 94.

50. The full report entitled "Roadmap for National Security: Imperative for Change" can be found at http://www.nssg.gov/PhaseIIIFR.pdf (December 29, 2003).

51. The Dalai Lama, "Living Sanely," in *The Dalai Lama: A Policy of Kindness*, ed. Sidney Piburn (Ithaca, N.Y.: Snow Lion, 1990), 105–106.

52. See the *Upaya sutra* translation, "On the Paramita of Ingenuity," in *A Treasury of Mahayana Sutras: Selections from the Maharatnakuta Sutra*, ed. Garma

C. C. Chang (University Park and London: Pennsylvania State University Press, 1983), 427–68.

53. Hare, trans., *Book of Gradual Sayings*, IV:54.

54. Tambiah, *World Conqueror and World Renouncer*, 45–53.

55. See especially the article by Irving Greenberg, "The Dialectics of Power: Reflections in the Light of the Holocaust," in *Confronting Omnicide: Jewish Reflections on Weapons of Mass Destruction*, ed. Daniel Landes (London and Narthvale, N.J.: Jason Aronson, 1991), 12–35.

56. See the *Satipatthana sutta*, The Middle Length Discourses of the Buddha (*Majjhima-nikaya* no. 10), which has been translated with extensive commentary by Nyanaponika Thera, *The Heart of Buddhist Meditation* (New York: Samuel Weiser, 1965).

57. After sending young people among families who had experienced the atomic bombs, they collected the interviews and published them in fifty volumes entitled *Senso o shiranai sedai e* (To the generations who do not know war). A one-volume set of selections is also available. See Youth Division of Soka Gakkai, *Cries for Peace: Experiences of Japanese Victims of World War II* (Tokyo: Japan Times, 1978).

58. Soka Gakkai Women's Division Peace Committee, *Women against War: Personal Accounts of Forty Japanese Women* (Tokyo: Kodansha, 1986).

59. At least that is my argument in my "Buddhist Peace Principles," in *Buddhist Peacework: Creating Cultures of Peace*, ed. David W. Chappell (Boston: Wisdom, 1999), 199–231.

60. This text is found in two places in the Pali canon, namely, the *Digha-nikaya* no. 22 and the *Majjhima-nikaya* no. 10. It has been the focus of many publications, such as Nyanaponika, *Heart of Buddhist Meditation*.

61. For an English translation, see Walshe, trans., *Thus Have I Heard*, 395–405.

62. See the statement by the chief economist of the World Bank, Nicholas Stern, "Overcoming Poverty: A Vision of Good Government," presented at the Second Annual Bank Conference on Development Economics (ABCDE) Europe in July 2000, available in his book, *A Strategy for Development* (Washington D.C.: World Bank, 2002).

63. Chan Khong (Cao Ngoc Phuong), *Learning True Love: How I Learned and Practiced Social Change in Vietnam* (Berkeley: Parallax Press, 1993), 92–93.

64. James H. Forest, *The Unified Buddhist Church of Vietnam: Fifteen Years of Reconciliation* (Hof van Sonoy, The Netherlands: International Fellowship of Reconciliation, 1987), 7.

65. Chan Khong (Cao Ngoc Phuong), *Learning True Love*, 93.

12

Buddhism and Weapons of Mass Destruction

An Oxymoron?

Donald K. Swearer

TAKING STOCK OF A DILEMMA

One of the most enduring principles of Buddhist ethics is the teaching of nonviolence (*ahimsa*), and the first of the five basic moral precepts is not to take the life of a sentient being. In the light of these teachings, is a conversation about Buddhist perspectives on weapons with the capacity for large-scale death and destruction not a contradiction in terms? David Chappell describes the tensions in the tradition between the normative Buddhist principles of peace and nonviolence and the actual behaviors of Buddhists both past and present, for example, rulers who have promoted war in defense of nation and religion and clergy who supported militarist regimes. In the light of this tension, Gananath Obeyesekere holds that Buddhism's noble principles are inevitably compromised by history and politics, a point of view that can be applied to other religious traditions, as well.[1] To situate the Buddhist ethical principles of peace, nonviolence, and nonkilling beyond history, however, obviates any capacity they might have to challenge and, it is hoped, to transform violence in any form, including violence associated with weapons of mass destruction. Whether Buddhism and the other world religions have anything uniquely distinctive to contribute to the specific policy decisions related to debates about WMD, such as utilization, deterrence, and proliferation, is moot. What the world's religions, including Buddhism, do have to offer, however, is a vision of hope where the values of peace, nonviolence, compassion, and the opportunity for human beings to flourish cooperatively are uppermost. These values should not be consigned to an ahistorical utopia. They must be calibrated not only to challenge the possession and use of WMD but to broaden the range of policy considerations to include long-term concerns for the well-being of the increasingly interconnected populations of the world and the natural environment on which we all depend. Buddhism teaches that all life forms are causally interconnected.

The destructive potential of WMD poses the greatest of threats to the world as Buddhists have understood it.

At issue in regard to the applicability of the world's religions to matters of contemporary urgency, such as terrorism and WMD, is what I call the "ethics of retrieval." Classical religious texts depict the issues of violence, murder, war, and so forth in a context vastly different from our own. Antisocial modes of behaviors were addressed on interpersonal and political levels in ways that could not have envisioned the potential for global crises caused by nuclear or biochemical attacks with the capacity for massive destruction to life, property, and environmental degradation. However, the fact that today's world is so radically different from that of classical Buddhist texts does not invalidate the applicability of their ideals, values, and principles. Nor does it vitiate the power of their narratives and metaphors to bring a crucial ethical and spiritual critique to bear on contemporary policy debates and decisions. This modern application calls for an imaginative retrieval, perhaps nothing short of the creativity that launched the tradition originally and marked its major turning points. At issue is survival, not merely the survival of Buddhism, the other world religions, or even nation-states as we have known them in the modern period but the very survival of the planet.

BUDDHIST ETHICS, PEACE, AND NONVIOLENCE

David Chappell claims correctly that the sources and principles of Buddhist ethics in general, and the ethics of weapons and war in particular, are to be found not only in text and world-view but in the Buddhist understanding of community. Consequently, he organizes his analysis in terms of four ethical frameworks: monastic ethics, the ethics of lay supporters of monks and nuns, lay ethics independent of monastic norms, and the ethics of Buddhist rulers in relationship to weapons and war. In each of these contexts, nonviolence and nonkilling are basic to the Buddhist moral life. In the case of monks and nuns (*bhikkhu/bhikkhuni*), taking human life may lead to expulsion from the monastic order. But destroying other life forms – animal, insect, and plant – also has disciplinary consequences. *Intention* figures prominently in the moral calculus of monastic ethics in terms of both karmic consequences and disciplinary action within the *sangha*. Equally important is the nature of the *result* of an action. Thus, with respect to the prohibition against murder, the legal or disciplinary consequence is less if the intended victim does not die or if the intended victim does not die and also does not suffer any pain or injury.

Additionally, it should be pointed out that while "a blow" delivered in anger is a monastic offense, a blow in *self-defense* does not entail punishment, "even if anger or displeasure arises in one's mind."[2] The rule prohibiting a monk from intentionally going to see an army on active duty (*Pacittiya* 48 of the Buddhist monastic code) accepts the presence of standing armies as a matter of course and also indicates the nature of warfare in early Buddhist history.

Armies in those times consisted mainly of what we would call reserve units. These were organized into four divisions: elephant units, cavalry units, chariot units, and infantry units. The soldiers for the most part were citizens who would live at home until called up on active duty to engage in actual warfare or to practice maneuvers, activities that always took place outside the city. Battles, both actual and practice, were fought according to rules . . . and it was possible for non-military citizens to watch . . . much as people at present watch football games.[3]

A monk was allowed to visit an army on duty only for good reason. He was not allowed to stay for more than two or three nights and was also prohibited from viewing the army in battle or even battle formation.

Thus, while monastic ethics do not support the possession of weapons or engaging in violence, warfare was clearly accepted as a fact of life in society at large. But based on these same sources, we may draw the following inference relevant to WMD debates: Because of the extent of death, injury, and destruction caused by weapons of mass destruction, any first strike or *offensive* use of WMD is not justifiable regardless of how noble the intention is – even though, in Buddhist terms, noble intention would mitigate the karmic consequence.

The ethics of devout lay Buddhists (*upasaka/upasika*) lacks the legal, de-tailed, prescriptive nature of monastic ethics but embodies many of the same ethical principles. At the opening of Buddhist rituals and ceremonies the participants "take" the five precepts (*panca sila*) beginning with the prohi-bition against taking the life of sentient beings. The Eightfold Noble Path, included in the Buddha's first teaching after his enlightenment, valorizes life work that, as Walpola Rahula states, does not bring harm to others and promotes the conditions of mutual human flourishing.[4] Even more impor-tant than the specific elements of the Eightfold Noble Path, such as "right action" and "right vocation," is the basic intention of this ethical catechism, namely, to confront and resolve motives and drives responsible for nega-tive, destructive behavior that brings suffering to self and other – the "poi-sons" or "cankers" stipulated as hatred, greed, and delusion. For this reason, Buddhist social ethics necessarily includes mental cultivation, epitomized by the term "mindful awareness." Right action depends on understanding that nothing – atom, individual, nation-state – exists in isolation; everything is causally intertwined. In this regard, the Buddhist-path ethic has been sum-marized not only as "avoid evil and do good," but also "purify the mind." The prohibition against taking life is coupled with the positive virtues of generosity and compassion, and both are linked to "understanding things as they really are."

The connection between mindful awareness and compassionate action is beautifully expressed in the poem, "Please Call Me by My True Names," written by Thich Nhat Hanh, the Vietnamese Zen monk and founder of the Tiep Hien Order of Interbeing. Nhat Hanh, who worked tirelessly for peace during the Vietnam War and to assist Vietnamese refugees fleeing the country by boat after the war, wrote the poem after being told that pirates had pillaged a refugee boat in the Gulf of Siam. The excerpt below refers to the pirates' rape of a young girl, who subsequently jumped overboard and drowned:

> I am the twelve-year-old girl, refugee
>   on a small boat,
> who throws herself into the ocean after
>   being raped by a sea pirate,
> and I am the pirate, my heart not yet capable
>   of seeing and loving.
>   . . .
> Please call me by my true names,
>   so I can wake up,
> and so the door of my heart can be left open,
>   the door of compassion.[5]

The Buddhist-path ethic necessarily entails a view of human nature and the conditions for the realization of a state of human flourishing.[6] It de-centers the autonomous self, placing human agency in a series of interconnected webs – social, natural, and cosmic. The *Sigalaka sutta,* to which Chappell refers, stipulates a social web of mutual responsibilities. Other Buddhist sources, including the contemporary Thai monk Buddhadasa Bhikkhu, expand this web of social interconnectedness to a broad vision of a universal moral commonwealth.[7] Citing Mahayana texts, Chappell asserts that other-regarding action based on a realization of a common kinship with all beings – including enemies – would not mean a total self-sacrifice or the laying down of one's arms. It would simply mean that by acknowledging a universal kinship with all beings, they are not objectified as "the other." Hence, in any action, such as armed conflict, their suffering becomes our suffering.

Does such an idealistic vision have any relevance to the ethics of weapons and war? In general terms, it challenges the viability of any international policy based on narrowly construed national self-interest. More specifically, it would certainly support treaty agreements that limit the proliferation of WMD and promote their elimination. Contemporary Buddhists, for example, were signatories to the Global Ethic declaration produced by the Council for a Parliament of the World's Religions in 1993. And Buddhists support the NGO Abolition 2000 Statement: "A world free of nuclear weapons is a shared aspiration of humanity. This goal cannot be achieved in a non-proliferation regime that authorizes the possession of nuclear weapons by a small group of states. Our common security requires the complete elimination of nuclear weapons. Our object is definite and unconditional abolition of nuclear weapons."[8]

Options: Deterrence, Disarmament, Negotiated Settlement, Just War

Not surprisingly, the ethics of Buddhist rulers and citizens provide examples most directly relevant to the topic of weapons and the conduct of war. Buddhist texts adopt a rather ambivalent attitude toward rulers. After all, though they may patronize the *sangha*, they can also act arbitrarily and capriciously. Nevertheless, the texts assume that kings are necessary to maintain and protect the social and political order. To do so, the rulers need weapons, armies, competent generals, and able advisors. In what follows, I briefly examine four war stories that offer different solutions to military engagement, at least as I choose to interpret them: military forces as a *deterrent* to war; *disarmament* as the best deterrent to war; a peaceful resolution to armed conflict through *negotiated settlement*; and minimal conditions for a *just war*. They offer, I believe, relevant perspectives on the modern questions relating to weapons of mass destruction being considered in this volume.

In the *Three Worlds of King Ruang*, a thirteenth-century Thai Buddhist cosmological treatise, the mythic Buddhist world-ruler/world-conqueror (*cakkavattin*) negotiates peace with the help of a large, standing army. He travels to the four quarters of the world led by a gem wheel and followed by the four divisions of his armed forces. He establishes his rule, presumably with such great force that none dares to challenge him:

None of the rulers, neither the great ones nor the small ones, are able to bring their weapons to do battle with the great Cakkavatti king.... Instead they are drawn ... [to him] by love and adoration ... they come to pay their respects to him ... and gather around to pay him homage. Neither the ogres, nor the evil spirits, nor any kind of beasts that can kill and bring death to human beings harbor any evil intentions against the great Cakkavatti King.[9]

The mythic war waged by the Cakkavatti king may thus be viewed as an argument for maintaining overwhelming military force as a deterrent to violent conflict. Under the righteous rule of the king, not only all classes of people, but also all manner of animals will find shelter and protection.

A second legendary story – which itself has come down to us in two versions – provides the basis for an alternative perspective that suggests disarmament as a more rational alternative to the vagaries of war. According to one version, King Ajatasattu of Magadha mobilizes a fourfold army to attack King Pasenadi of Kosala. Pasenadi, in turn, mobilizes his fourfold army and launches a counterattack. In the ensuing battle, King Pasenadi is defeated and retreats to his capital. The following morning a group of

Buddhist monks returning from their alms round reports the events to the Buddha, who, in turn, replies: "Monks, King Ajatasattu . . . has evil friends, evil companions, evil comrades. King Pasenadi of Kosala has good friends, good companions, good comrades. Yet, for this day, monks, King Pasenadi, having been defeated, will sleep badly tonight."[10] The opening line of the capstone stanzas concludes, "Victory breeds enmity." In the second version of the battle, King Pasenadi captures Ajatasattu, but instead of killing him he merely confiscates his army, that is, his power to wage war. The monks who report these events to the Buddha are then instructed with the following verse: "A man will go on plundering/So long as it serves his ends/But when others plunder him/The plunderer is plundered//The fool thinks fortune is on his side/So long as his evil does not ripen/But when the evil ripens/The fool incurs suffering."[11] This and other stories of armed conflict in Buddhist texts make clear that today's victor is tomorrow's vanquished and vice versa and that karmic justice dictates there is no absolute victory or final solution brought about by armed conflict regardless of the scale of the weaponry. The moral of these stories seems to be that armed conflict may or may not bring a short-term benefit, but that there is no such thing as an absolute victory, a war "to end all wars."

The third illustration comes from the commentary on the *Dhammapada* (Dhp.A. iii.254–56). It relates the story of hostilities between the Sakyas and Koliyas over water rights from a dammed river that ran between their territories. As the two republics prepared for war, the Buddha by his meditative powers perceived the situation and flew over the area, hovering above the river. In the ensuing events, the Buddha acts as a negotiator, convincing both sides that they were about to sacrifice something of great value – the lives of warrior nobles – for something of much less value.[12] In this story, a negotiated compromise is reached because the parties to the conflict are made to realize the human tragedy caused by war, that the results achieved would not be commensurate with the cost.

The final story of kingship has become quite well known even beyond Buddhist circles because it has been cited so often in the context of the ethnic conflict in Sri Lanka between Sinhalese Buddhists and Tamil Hindus. It is the story of King Dutugemunu told in the *Mahavamsa,* the sixth-century Pali chronicle that relates the fate of Buddhism in Sri Lanka. The climax of the narrative is Dutugemunu's defeat of the Tamil king, Elara, who ruled over part of the island. The story has figured in various ways in the development of Sinhalese Buddhist nationalism from the 1950s to the contemporary conflict in Sri Lanka and is the focus of Tessa Bartholomeusz's analysis of Buddhist just war theory.[13] As background to the Dutugemunu story, she describes the tension found in Pali *sutta* texts: On the one hand, they portray the righteous Buddhist monarch as adhering to the principle of nonviolence, and on the other, they establish his duty to guarantee the peace and protect the citizenry. The king maintains a standing army both as a deterrent and as a course of last resort. In the story of Dutugemunu, the *Mahavamsa* provides the following justifications for the king's actions: First, the cause was just, that is, in defense of Buddhism and to establish a "dharmic" or just order ("Not for the joy of sovereignty is this toil mine, my striving [has been] ever to establish the doctrine of the Buddha");[14] second, the king did not act with false intentions, namely, personal ambition or hatred; third, he felt deep remorse and honored the king he had defeated and killed; fourth, the enemy was treated justly in defeat.

Bartholomeusz concludes that Dutugemunu's sacrifice of his prima facie duty of nonviolence – one of the stipulated virtues of the just king – is judged in the text as proportional to the goal of creating a just realm. Yet from the standpoint of the limits of war, the *Mahavamsa* does not stint in describing the violence of the conflict: The king conquered seven mighty Tamil princes in one day and gave the booty to his troops; sitting on his horse he slew the Tamils in great numbers; the water in a reservoir was dyed red with the blood of the slain; and so on. This description seems to challenge the proportionality of the act and might be read as a surreptitious criticism of excessive violence. A modern interpretation might see it as a critique of the wanton destruction associated with WMD. Furthermore, in stepping back from the text, we might also observe that while its monk-authors ascribed noble motives to Dutugemunu, their own motives may have been more self-serving. Rather than justifying a defensive war as a last resort, they may have been seeking to legitimate a conflict that protected their monastic property.

In conclusion, it will be instructive to look briefly at the Buddhist response to the events of September 11, 2001, a national tragedy that has been construed as an attack of mass destruction. The Buddhist Peace Fellowship website includes remarks by several internationally distinguished leaders, including the Dalai Lama and Thich Nhat Hanh. The predominant theme is the often quoted phrase from the *Dhammapada* that hatred should not be answered with hatred but with nonhatred and compassion. The Dalai Lama expresses his shock and personal sadness at the terrorist attacks, but then goes on to caution President Bush, "I personally believe we need to think seriously whether a violent reaction is the right thing to do and in the greater interest of the nation and the people in the long run."[15] Nhat Hanh comments, "All violence is injustice. Responding to violence with violence is injustice, not only to the other person but also to oneself."[16] In a typically Buddhist manner, he then addresses the issue of the causal matrix of this violence:

The violence and hatred we presently face has been created by misunderstanding, injustice, discrimination, and despair. We are all co-responsible for the making of violence and despair in the world by our way of living, of consuming and handling the problems of the world. Understanding why this violence has been created, we will then know what to do and what not to do in order to decrease the level of violence in ourselves and in the world to create and foster understanding, reconciliation, and forgiveness.[17]

Other voices worry that identifying terrorists as evil-doers perpetuates a simplistic dualism that "keeps us from looking deeper [and] from trying to discover causes. Once something has been identified as evil, there is no more need to explain it; it is time to focus on fighting against it."[18] These representative responses to September 11 do not speak directly to the issue of weapons of mass destruction, but Buddhist responses to a potential WMD attack may be extrapolated from them. The Buddhist call is for nonviolent action, one that is not motivated by hatred or revenge but directed instead toward addressing the complex matrix of causes that lead to violence and destruction. This call is joined with a cautionary warning that in the long term answering violence with violence will lead only to a cycle of increasing violence. On the level of policy, Buddhists would favor treaties that restrict, limit, and eventually eliminate weapons of mass destruction. But a Buddhist perspective insists that in a more fundamental sense, policy options and defense strategies calculated to defend national self-interest are ultimately insufficient without a more inclusive vision of human flourishing.

Notes

1. Gananath Obeyesekere, "Buddhism, Nationhood, and Cultural Identity: A Question of Fundamentals," in *Fundamentalisms Comprehended*, ed. Martin E. Marty and R. Scott Appleby (Chicago: University of Chicago Press, 1995), 233.
2. Thanissaro Bhikkhu (Geoffrey DeGraff), *The Buddhist Monastic Code* (Valley Center, Calif.: Metta Forest Monastery, 1994), 448.
3. Ibid., 398.
4. Walpola Rahula, *What the Buddha Taught*, 2nd ed. (New York: Grove Press, 1974), 47.
5. Thich Nhat Hanh, *Call Me by My True Names: The Collected Poems of Thich Nhat Hanh* (Berkeley: Parallax Press, 1993), 72–73.
6. Damien Keown, *The Nature of Buddhist Ethics* (New York: St. Martin's Press, 1992), chap. 8.
7. Buddhadasa Bhikkhu, "Democratic Socialism," in *Me and Mine: Selected Essays of Bhikkhu Buddhadasa*, ed. Donald K. Swearer (Albany: State University of New York Press, 1989), 167–81.
8. http://prop1.org/2000/abolstat.htm (February 15, 2001).
9. Frank E. Reynolds and Mani Reynolds, *The Three Worlds of King Ruang* (Berkeley: Asian Humanities Press, 1981), 146.
10. Bhikkhu Nanamoli and Bhikkhu Bodhi, *The Middle Length Discourses of the Buddha* (Boston: Wisdom, 1995), 177.
11. Ibid., 178.
12. Peter Harvey, *An Introduction to Buddhist Ethics: Foundations, Values, and Issues* (Cambridge: Cambridge University Press, 2000), 241.

13. Tessa Bartholomeusz, "In Defense of Dharma: Just-War Ideology in Buddhist Sri Lanka," *Journal of Buddhist Ethics* 6 (1999): 1–16.

14. Wilhelm Geiger, *The Mahavamsa or the Great Chronicle of Ceylon* (Colombo: Government Information Office, 1960), 171.

15. http://www.bpf.org/hhdl/html (February 15, 2001).

16. http://www.bpf.org/tnh.html (February 15, 2001).

17. Ibid.

18. http://www.bpf.org/Loy-war.html (February 15, 2001).

13

Confucianism and Weapons of Mass Destruction

Julia Ching

INTRODUCTION: CHINA AS A WORLD TO ITSELF

We are now looking at a civilization – the Chinese – that, for geopolitical reasons, looked at itself for the longest time as *the world*, a world of culture surrounded by groups of "barbarians." It dealt with these from a superior position, expecting tributes, while ready to share certain cultural benefits, including the teachings of Confucius.[1] In this sense, China was unaccustomed to regarding itself as an equal partner interacting with others. It was outraged and humiliated by military losses under superior firepower, followed by the imposition by Western powers and Japan of "unequal treaties" during the late nineteenth and early twentieth centuries.[2]

But the Chinese were not arrogant conquerors. On the contrary, their influence was a civilizing one. The Chinese people trace their origin to the mythical Yellow Emperor, to whom is attributed the invention, among many other things, of the compass – which helped to direct his war chariot. He brought order out of chaos after winning a cosmic battle against the arch-villain Zhiyou, the enemy of civilization. It is said that Zhiyou built many kinds of heavy, metal weapons as he prepared for the war with the Yellow Emperor. This myth discloses the cultural disdain for so-called superior weapons and supports the belief that the values of civilization will always triumph. It explains in part the society's preference for civil rather than military virtues, and the consequent inferior status given to the military for most of its known history.

This does not mean that the Chinese neglected weaponry. They are known to have invented gunpowder – ironically, a product of accident in the ninth century, invented by Daoist recluses experimenting with alchemy for the sake of finding something to prolong life! Its accidental discovery reveals a lack of strong interest in weapons as such, which is confirmed by history. But the Chinese also put it to military use and went on to invent rockets and land mines in the thirteenth century and sea mines during the fourteenth century, apparently all before the Europeans.[3] Nevertheless, the Chinese state tended to prefer having a good civil administration to maintaining a strong military. The popular saying goes: "A good piece of iron is not wasted on nails; a good boy does not become a soldier." This situation remained unchanged as China entered the late nineteenth and early twentieth centuries, to face tremendous challenges from the West.

While traditional China did not invent weapons of mass destruction as we know them today, it did make use of certain means that led to "mass destruction," whether war by water, poison, or fire. The instance that comes to mind is the use of flooding by building and breaking river dikes, documented early during the Warring States period in the years 455–453 B.C.E.[4] Planned flooding continued to cause massive civilian disaster, even in the twentieth century, during the war with the Japanese. Other war measures involved the use of "chemicals," such as placing poison on arrows or trapping soldiers underground and causing death by gas, whether in offensive or, more commonly, in defensive wars. Ditches and wells were blocked or poisoned to prevent the enemy from having access to drinking water. A scorched-earth policy, sometimes on a large scale, was often applied – and also in the twentieth century – to prevent the enemy from acquiring needed resources.

Even without weapons of high technology, early warfare entailed much inhumanity. An early military text, the *Weiliaozi*, while short on the subject of weapons, discusses in detail the problem of deserters and encourages massive cruelty on the part of the generals: "I have heard that the generals of old who handled their troops well were ready to kill half their own men, the next were ready to kill three out of ten, the next one out of ten. . . ."[5]

Another war measure involved the mass killing of enemy soldiers, sometimes of an entire army, presumably those who were cornered, defeated, or surrendered. In one case, reportedly, the state of Qin buried alive 400,000 men from the state of Zhao at Changping, an event that was long remembered. But the twelfth-century neo-Confucian philosopher Zhu Xi expressed his doubt at the account's credibility, saying that it was not possible for so many to be killed without their fighting back.[6] Here his undertone is moral, even without an explicit condemnation of such practices.

The disintegration of feudal society, which was going on in Confucius's time (sixth century B.C.E.), was accompanied by changes in the conduct of war – from that governed by a gentlemen's code, with feudal lords riding chariots supported by foot soldiers, to open aggression aided by new weaponry, a professional cavalry of mounted archers, and the increasing use of iron and steel in arms and armor. The seven "great powers" of the Warring States period (fifth to third centuries B.C.E.) competed with one another for superior moral prestige and military power and to become the "superpower" or hegemon (*ba*). From that period on came the struggle for absolute victory – come what cost – until the semi-barbarian state of Qin emerged in the west. Qin unified China (third century B.C.E.) and established a new system, a monolithic empire, imposing a uniform script while "burning books and burying scholars," ridding the country of its many philosophical schools, except the Legalist, which assured the state's dominance by manipulation of power and strategy.

WHAT IS CONFUCIANISM?

Confucianism is represented by the Chinese term *ru*, literally, the tradition of scholars. *Ru* was the mainstream intellectual and ethical tradition in China, until modern times. The *ru* tradition was identified as "Confucianism" by Western missionaries. This was not entirely a misnomer, since the Chinese themselves often refer to *ru* as *Kongxue*, or the teaching of Master Kong – Confucius. But I should emphasize that Confucianism is a complex tradition, whose history and development began with the early sage philosophers Confucius (551–479 B.C.E.), Mencius (c. 390–c. 305 B.C.E.), and Xunzi (c. 310–c. 219 B.C.E.) and was further and more systematically elaborated by medieval philosophers, often influenced by Buddhist ideas. Prominent among the so-called neo-Confucian scholars are Zhu Xi (1130–1200), sometimes called China's greatest philosopher because of the comprehensive and architectonic system he created, and the idealist Wang Yangming (1472–1529), who challenged Zhu Xi's teachings but did not break from the tradition. In the seventeenth century and afterward, speculative Confucian thinking declined while more positivist philologists took over the task of interpreting the old tradition. However, in the late nineteenth and early twentieth centuries, other Confucian philosophers arose, men such as Kang Youwei (1858–1927) and Liang Qichao (1873–1929), who were challenged by the introduction of Western ideas. They in turn were succeeded by the "New Confucians" of the twentieth century, thinkers such as Tang Junyi (1907–78) and Mou Zongsan (1909–95), both of whom have by now become cultural icons.

Confucianism is not a governing ideology in China today, as is Hinduism in India or Islam in some contemporary Muslim countries. Therefore, today's China should not be labeled as Confucian, since the mainland has been under a Communist government for the past fifty years. Besides, Legalism, the amoral, realist philosophy of power, influenced state-approved Confucianism and, even more, today's Communism. For these reasons, it is useful to look at Confucianism in a broad sense and to refer occasionally to other traditions such as Mohism (which is sometimes regarded as a by-product of early Confucianism) and Legalism. Each of these currents of thought has interacted with Confucianism and so must be considered here in order to give an accurate and full account of Confucian thinking. I am omitting Buddhism, which has also interacted extensively with Confucianism, because it is discussed by David Chappell and Donald Swearer in the preceding two chapters of this book.

SOURCES AND PRINCIPLES GOVERNING WARS AND WEAPONS

Although the historical Chinese civilization was rich and complex, weapons of mass destruction, as understood in this volume, were not really known until very recently, that is, until the United States first developed its atom bomb. Popular or even elite reactions to the advent of WMD are hard to gauge. As is well known, the present Chinese state does not tolerate much dissent, for which reason there has been no reported protest of nuclear bomb tests within the country, in spite of the widely suspected harm to local populations near the test sites. To the contrary – and aside from government manipulation – evidence indicates that China's status as a nuclear power is a cause for genuine pride among many of its people, as is the case also in India and Pakistan, which developed their nuclear programs much later. After all, possession of nuclear power has meant for China inclusion in the exclusive "nuclear club" as recognized by the Nonproliferation Treaty – the only Asian country to have this distinction.

In the absence of a well-developed Confucian discourse on weapons of mass destruction, I am faced with a largely constructivist task. The sources from which I derive the ethical principles regarding war and weapons are mainly from the early Confucian tradition; the texts are Confucius's *Analects*, *Mencius*, and *Xunzi*, all dating to before the second century B.C.E. I also refer to the neo-Confucian philosophers Zhu Xi, Wang Yangming, and Huang Zongxi, and some of their followers of the late nineteenth and early twentieth centuries, especially Kang Youwei and Liang Qichao. I also use other sources, including the more specifically military treatises and encyclopedias, of which there are many. But other than Tang Junyi and Mou Zongsan, who worked mainly in Hong Kong and Taiwan, I have found no major ethical thinker of the contemporary period who has talked directly of weapons of mass destruction.

The Mandate of Heaven Theory and the Virtue of Humaneness

Before discussing specific ideas, I should refer to the more general principles governing political and military affairs. The problem is that Chinese philosophy tends to be an organic whole, difficult to separate into parts, just as the various schools of thought are often interrelated, in spite of internecine disagreements and conflicts. It was generally accepted that the universe is constituted by *qi* (air, breath, matter-energy), and all living beings participate in this *qi*. With it, we are alive; without it, we die. This belief was articulated more clearly by Daoists and the so-called eclectic schools, although Confucians appear also to share it. Mencius thinks that *qi* can be directed by the human will when he says: "The will is the leader of *qi*. Qi pervades and fills the body." And also: "I nourish my vast, overflowing *qi*" (*Mencius* 2A:2). I shall refer to *qi* later in the context of war.

Confucian classics speak more of a supreme and just Heaven, which oversees the world or "all under Heaven" (*tianxia*), a belief that does not necessarily clash with that of *qi*. Heaven gives the mandate to rule to a worthy man and removes it from tyrants, thereby permitting armed rebellions or revolutions. The "Mandate of Heaven" (*tianming*) represents an early theory of government that emerged out of dynastic changes. In this sense, the theory also helps to define certain wars as just. It lends legitimacy to the status quo, while the ruler grants legitimacy to his wars. Those who fight for him are presumed to be fighting a just war. The Mandate of Heaven is often presumed to be a Confucian idea, as it stems from classical texts associated with that tradition.[7]

The Mandate of Heaven theory deals with the legitimation of authority, including the authority's right to pursue war. A much more important and inspiring ethical idea is the principle of humaneness (*ren*). Confucius taught this universal virtue of humaneness, which underlies the practice of all particular virtues. In plain words, the humane person "loves others" (*Analects* 12:22; *Mencius* 4B:28). In every tradition, love would preclude injury and harm. Confucius also articulated what has been called the *negative* Golden Rule: "Do not do unto others what you would not want them to do unto you" (*Analects* 15:23). In this one sentence, he reveals his disposition toward war, conflict, and, should he have known such, weapons of mass destruction. This kind of teaching tends to mark his followers as well – a general, universalized message underlying a quest for the highest perfection, rather than arguments about particular virtues and situations. It means, however, that they did not leave behind a systematic doctrine about the ethics of war and weapons.

But Confucius and those who followed him all knew war. If anything, Confucius accepted military preparedness as a necessary evil. When asked about how to govern a state, he gave three things as necessary: enough food, enough arms, and the trust of the people. When asked what priority he would give to each, he said weapons are to be placed last, food next, but the people's trust is essential (*Analects* 7:7).[8] This underlines his teaching of humane governance, which includes attention to economic security and political well-being, with moral education as the base.

Mencius was the second most important name of the early Confucian school. He advocated the same kind of humane governance, which permits agriculture to flourish and moral education to develop, with the state imposing light taxation and other burdens on the people. Mencius recognized the importance of military training but did not place much store in weapons. He condemned flooding one's neighboring state in an effort to save one's own (*Mencius* 6B:11), not in a military context but to emphasize his ethical position against harming others to help oneself. He was fond of saying, "The humane person has no enemies" (*Mencius* 1A:5). And he insisted that it would be wrong to do one unjust deed or kill one innocent person even if that could win an empire.[9] In his teachings we find the highest ideal set by the Confucian school, embracing all the principles that ought to govern war and weapons: "When the ruler practices humaneness, the state is without enemies in the world. If he does battle in the south, the inhabitants in the north (*di*) would complain. If he fights in the east, the people of the west (*yi*) would complain" (*Mencius* 7B:4).[10]

The philosopher Xunzi has often been considered as a rival to Mencius, with whom he did not always agree. But he echoes Mencius in this regard: "A true king carries out punitive expeditions, but does not make war. . . . He does not massacre the defenders of a city; . . . he does not keep his forces long in the field; he does not let a campaign last more than a season."[11]

On the use of arms, Xunzi says:

If the bow and arrow are not properly adjusted, even the famous archer . . . cannot hit the mark. . . . If the six horses of the team are not trained, even the famous carriage driver . . . could not go far. If the people and their officers are not devoted to their leaders, even the sages . . . cannot win a war. He who is *good at winning the people's support* [emphasis mine] will be good at using arms. [This] is . . . essential in military undertakings.[12]

Some challenged the sage's moral tone. One critic says: "When you talk about the use of arms, you speak of humaneness and righteousness. . . . But those who take up arms only do so to contend with others and seize spoils."[13] Xunzi's answer explicates his understanding of humaneness: "The humane person takes up arms in order to put an end to violence and do away with harm, not to contend with others for spoils."[14]

These moral philosophers did not explicitly speak out against weapons of mass destruction, even as they may have understood them in their own times, but it is obvious that their humane philosophy would oppose the use of such in any war. We note the high moral ground of the early Confucians on questions of war and peace. But its effects have not been to stimulate moral discussions in contemporary society about issues like weapons of mass destruction.

Just and Unjust Wars

We also find in the early sources a distinction between just and unjust wars. Among the philosophical schools, Confucians and Mohists are especially careful in distinguishing a just from an unjust war. Mozi (or Mo Di), who lived in the fifth century B.C.E., was allegedly influenced by the school of Confucius. But he also started his own school, teaching belief in a supreme Heaven and in spirits, universal love, and a pacifism supported by militant action. The text *Mozi* contains a chapter, "Against Aggression." Here, an aggressive war is defined as *gong*:

If a man today enters another's orchard, and steals his peaches and pears, he would be attacked by all who hear of it, and punished by the authorities who get him. . . . Now when a large state attacks a small state, people no longer know that as wrong, and

even praise [such action]. . . . We say that killing one man is not right, and deserves
death as punishment. Then we go on and say that killing ten people would be ten
times as bad, . . . killing one hundred would be a hundred times as bad. . . . Why is
it that when there is an [aggression] which is a huge transgression of rightness, like
an attack on a state, such [condemnation] is not voiced?[15]

Mozi and others follow principles already laid out in the classical and
historical texts: A just war is a punitive expedition (*zhu*), as in the case of the
sage king Yu punishing the Miao tribes, and other sage kings overcoming
tyrants, such as King Jie of Xia and King Zhou of Shang. The Confucians
also use the same term, as well as *zheng*, to define a punitive expedition.[16]
As Mencius puts it, "To punish [*zheng*] is to correct." A good king takes up
war to free the oppressed peoples:

When [King] Tang began his just war [*zheng*], all under Heaven trusted him. When
he fought in the east, the western tribes complained; when he fought in the south, the
northern tribes complained. They were saying: Why are we last [on the list]? People
looked to him, as those in a great drought looked for clouds and rainbows. . . . While
he punished [*zhu*] their rulers, he consoled their peoples. (*Mencius* 1B11)[17]

Early Chinese discussions of a just war also frequently involved the idea
of a just rebellion. Such theorizing was done both within the context of
the Mandate of Heaven theory and possibly to render ideas of legitimacy
more flexible. In the early records, we have instances of dynastic rulers being overthrown and replaced by armed rebels – thought today to be leaders
of other ethnic groups. The record-keepers take pains to justify these rebellions or mini-revolutions. They assert that the leader of such an uprising
was usually a virtuous man, to whom was given the Mandate of Heaven – to
govern the world. Out of compassion for the suffering populace, he fought
to replace the tyrant of the time and won. Examples are the founders of
the Shang and Zhou dynasties. At the time of Mencius, the state of Qi over-
came another state of equal status, Yan. The victor asked whether he might
annex the territory. Mencius replied: "[Yes,] if this will please Yan's people.
Among the ancients, King Wu [of Zhou] did so [when he attacked the Shang
ruler]."[18]

The victor, however, was not pleasing to the conquered population, and
he in turn was threatened by other states with war. When asked about it,
Mencius advised:

The Yan [ruler] was cruel to his people, who thought your war would save
them. . . . But you responded by killing their fathers and brothers, confining their
sons and younger brothers, destroying their ancestral temple, and removing their
precious vessels. . . . If you would quickly order the return of the captives, stop the
removal of precious vessels, and depart after entrusting [the state] to a new ruler
chosen after consulting its people, you may yet avert the war threats.[19]

To use the language of Robert Holmes on pacifism (Chapter 23 below), Confucians (and Mohists) tend to be principled, "just war pacifists," that is, they do not rule out war, but their criteria for a just war effectively limit (immediate or frequent) recourse to it. This position is well illustrated in the following report: In the twelfth century C.E., the philosopher Zhu Xi lived in the south when the Jurchens (a Manchurian people) were occupying northern China, having captured in war two Chinese emperors, father and son. Southern China under the Song Dynasty remained a relatively great state, its size and prosperity exceeding that of western Europe at the time. The humiliation of conquest and the loss of northern territories was hard to bear, while the threat of being overrun was always present. So self-defense meant military alertness. At his time, the "hawks" wanted to recover the north, and the "doves" preferred to appease the north. Zhu was a hawk, although he opposed the then prime minister, Han Tuozhou, also a hawk, as incompetent in military matters. He argued for greater flexibility:

At court today, the talk is either of war or peace. . . . People no longer know that the ancients knew how to contend with each other between war and peace. In these fifty or sixty years, those [in power] preferred peace and have not trained soldiers. . . . In this case, the talk of military recovery is nonsense.[20]

"How to contend with each other *between war and peace*" – Zhu appears to be thinking of some forms of preparedness, at least for deterrence purposes, possibly even for the recovery of lost land. For a just war, a government should be ready to consider a variety of options. We turn, therefore, to the issue of application, to the legitimate use of weapons in war.

USE

To understand the applied ethics of war and weapons, we must refer to the Chinese inclination to integrate theory with practice in philosophical discussions. This is especially true for warfare. Theirs is a preference for harmony, which warfare presumably destroys but which must be preserved even in war as much as possible. As the world is constituted by *qi* or energy, war is to be directed by a sage-general in such a way that the energy on his own side will be maintained while that of his enemy will be dissipated. As a microcosm of the macrocosm, the human being strives for a victory that will harmonize with cosmic events and yield a reconciliation of the conflicting energies. So the path of war is not lightly chosen, and in battle, destruction is to be limited.[21] All this helps to explain a relative disregard by the philosophers for the development of the most effective and fearsome weapons. In addition, while "discrimination" and "proportionality" in war were never spelled out as clearly as in Europe, they were presumed and implied not only by the moralists, but also by the writers of the best military treatises.

Although not all works have survived, China's famous treatise, *The Art of War*, attributed to the sixth-century-B.C.E. Sun Wu (or Sunzi, Sun Tzu), is usually assigned to the Legalist school, even though the school became dominant only much later. This is because the tone of the work clearly supports the Legalists' emphasis on power and political manipulation, as opposed to moral values. Interestingly, the value of the text has grown, not only in the old country, where it was the favorite reading of Chairman Mao, but also as a textbook in today's American military academies.[22] One reason for this durability is its focused discussion on intelligence and strategy, rather than on military technology. Everything depends on information and advance planning. To win a war, one needs to know thoroughly one's own position as well as the enemy's. After all, wars are sometimes lost or won in the heads of the planners, long before they are taken to the battlefield. To quote the text: "The best military policy is to attack strategies; the next to attack alliances; the next to attack soldiers; and the worst to assault walled cities."[23]

In the art of war, intelligence means – among other things – having access to secret information regarding the enemy. The exercise of intelligence also includes deceiving the enemy. Mao Zedong famously cherished the following advice: "Warfare is the art of deceit. And so: when able, appear unable; when ready, appear unready; when nearby, appear distant; when distant, appear nearby. If the enemy seeks an advantage, entice him; if he is in disorder, attack and overcome him. If he is formidable, prepare against him; if he is strong, avoid him."[24]

War is about winning. Presumably, no restrictions are acceptable, whether imposed by moral code or custom. Still, Sun says little about arms, and is silent about anything resembling WMD. He is not for war as such, only for *winning*. If a war could be won without fighting, so be it: "It is best to keep one's own state intact; to crush the enemy's state is only a second best. . . . So to win a hundred victories . . . is not the highest excellence. The highest excellence is to subdue the enemy's army without fighting at all."[25]

The text's alleged author was a contemporary of Confucius, the great moralist. Each is regarded as rationalist, since Confucius seldom discusses questions of religion or the afterlife. Each appears ignorant of the other. But Sun's was not the only voice during this period. Another military treatise was composed by Wu Qi, a fifth-century-B.C.E. warrior and follower of Confucius. He puts the task of instructing and loving the people as first. One does not make war except when all else has been tried:

The moral ruler first tries to keep peace to do great things, and always before using his people. He will not believe in intrigues, but will first announce things to
the ancestral temple, seek divination through the great tortoises, consulting with
the conditions of nature and time. Only when all is propitious would war begin.

The people should know the ruler values their lives and regrets their deaths. In that case, they would face conflict together with the ruler, and officers will take glory in dying, and be ashamed if they survive.[26]

He respects the role of weapons but does not dwell on them. For he knows that victory depends as much on morale, good organization, and flexibility in the face of change. "The short ones should use spears, the tall ones use bows and arrows, the strong ones hold on to the banners, the strong ones hold the golden drums, the weak ones take care of provisions, the wise ones decide on strategy."[27]

It is clear from the preceding discussion that the great sages and ethicists never relied on wars and weapons, and even the great strategists did not give military technology much thought. The ancients preferred using their brains to technology. They of course knew nothing of our modern WMD. But given the ethical teachings of the tradition, it is unthinkable for a Confucian to use weapons of mass destruction as we know them today, whether they are nuclear, chemical, or biological.

DETERRENCE AND PROLIFERATION

Through most of its history, China saw itself as *the* global order, surrounded on its borders by subordinate neighbors. To find in Chinese history a context somewhat analogous to the international situation today, we need to go back to the ancient Zhou dynasty, straddling the two periods called "Spring and Autumn" (722–481 B.C.E.) and the "Warring States" (481–221 B.C.E.). At this time, different sovereign states shared a common culture of sorts, and a Zhou suzerain, called "king" (*wang*), relied on harmony between these feudal states for his own dynastic survival. It was a time of alliances and counteralliances, of warfare governed by recognized norms of ritual and political behavior. By consensus, these norms included respect for covenants and state envoys, refraining from attacks on states in mourning for deceased rulers, protection of the elderly or "white-haired," and good treatment of war captives.[28]

Living during the Warring States period, Mozi had much to say *against* wars but *for* the deterrent value of weapons. Mo was a strategist, emphasizing in his teachings the prevention of war. He was also an arms specialist; he and his disciples are credited with inventing the trebuchet for hurling stones and hanging signals. The last two chapters of the text *Mozi* deal extensively with defense weaponry.

One story about Mozi illustrates his dual roles of strategist and inventor: A large state was preparing to invade a small state, having manufactured scaling ladders to mount the city walls. Hearing of this, Mo walked ten days and nights to reach the large state, tearing up his clothes to bandage his sore feet as he went. He got an audience with its ruler and chief minister.

Together, they played a "war game" in pantomime, with Mo using his belt as a wall and a stick as a weapon, while the other side set up nine different attack machines. Mo repelled the attacker nine times. Embarrassed, the chief minister declared that the war could still be won. Mo answered that he too knew what his opponent was thinking: that they had to kill him. But he informed them that he had already sent his disciples to the small state, with his defense strategy. The ruler then decided to cancel the invasion.[29]

The Mohist school stands for qualified pacifism. It would prefer to outlaw war and abolish weapons. It holds *universal* disarmament to be a moral imperative. Short of that, it was ready to deter war with advanced weapons.[30] Such would not include WMD, however. If deterrence implies the possibility of mutual destruction, it is difficult to envisage Mohist approval, as it was in the case of Confucians. After all, both Confucians and Mohists refer to Heaven, the higher power that gives and engenders life. Belief in this power brings with it a distaste for permitting humans to risk the large-scale destruction of life.

This is not to say that all ancient Chinese writers would necessarily agree with this position. The third-century-B.C.E. eclectic text *Lüshi chunqiu* criticizes the Mohist position on the abolition of wars and weapons. It recalls that ancient sage kings had just wars and righteous armies. It reasons that physical force is also natural: "To forbid people to eat because someone choked to death is against nature. . . . To abolish war and weapons because someone lost his state is also against nature. The military cannot be abolished. Take water and fire: Using them well is good; using them ill is disaster. The same is true of medicine. Good medicine saves lives; bad medicine kills."[31]

The argument here is to act according to nature. Yet we could hardly qualify the nuclear, chemical, and biological weapons of today as "natural." And it is once again unnecessary as well as impossible to draw distinctions among nuclear, biological, or chemical weapons. The traditional works have not left us enough clues to permit the drawing of distinctions on the use or proliferation of such weapons. If we must speculate today, in this world of asymmetrical defense systems, we must consider the question of costs. Chemical and biological weapons are more feared than nuclear weapons because they are less costly and therefore easier for poorer states to acquire. If the ancients were alive today, they would have lively debates on the ethical issues raised by asymmetrical military systems, rather than on how a superpower could defend itself against so-called rogue states. Indeed, the Confucian tradition insists on the correct use of language, that only the virtuous may use "correct names." A hegemon or superpower, therefore, has no right to call others "rogues." Might ought not to define right, anywhere, anytime.

As I have indicated, our world resembles the Warring States period in early China, when hegemony was sought by military might. Nonproliferation of WMD can be achieved only when those states possessing nuclear, chemical, and biological weapons are willing and ready to limit and even give up their arsenals, first by adhering to those treaties and conventions they have already signed, and then by going on to total elimination of WMD of any type. From April 24 to May 20, 2000, some 187 states that are parties to the Nonproliferation Treaty met for the Sixth Review of the NPT. The final document issued by the conference presented a genuine consensus. Its central element was: "An unequivocal undertaking by the nuclear-weapon States to accomplish the total elimination of their nuclear arsenals leading to nuclear disarmament to which all States parties are committed under Article VI."[32]

The obligation to end proliferation and move to disarmament is on the states as parties to the NPT and other international agreements. But the increasing sophistication in weapons technology, the widespread dissemination of technical expertise, and the dangers of terrorism may also require special efforts to prevent individuals or groups – anywhere in the world – from producing, possessing, or using WMD.[33] Only a *total* nuclear/ chemical/biological disarmament will rule out proliferation and the use of WMD in war or for deterrence. I believe that WMD disarmament is a moral imperative, faced as we are otherwise with the threat of catastrophe.

DISARMAMENT

Ancient China knew about disarmament (*mibing*) through various but scattered writings. "Should the sage king abolish his weapons and not use them, the world would be at peace."[34] The Confucian classic, the Book of History (or Historical Documents), records that King Wu, founder of the Zhou dynasty (1122–256 B.C.E.), ceased military affairs after his conquest of Shang. He ordered that battle horses be set free south of a mountain, and cattle outside a forest, to signify that wars were at an end.[35] It is even said that he created the position of war minister only to teach people hunting.[36] The Confucian classic, the Book of Poetry, describes the dawn of peace:

> Spears and shields are stored away,
> Bows and arrows are hidden.
> I seek the virtuous man,
> To write a good song,
> In praise of King Wu.[37]

Confucius himself had disciples who glorified military valor. Zilu, for example, announced his readiness to fight to the end, even against wild tigers, in order to overcome the enemy. Confucius, however, preferred another disciple, Yan Hui, who advocated good government, so that "[all the parties] will *voluntarily* [my emphasis] give up their weapons . . . and the people in the entire world will enjoy peace. . . . [The ruler] would execute those who promote warfare."[38]

As the Zhou dynasty lost its power, small feudal states competed for a stronger position. Though war begot war, the people still desired peace. We have the record of an early covenant among three states: Song, Jin, and Chu. The initiative came from the smallest state, Song. The parties tried in vain to include more major states. Negotiations were long and arduous, but resulted eventually in agreement to disarm. And the resultant peace lasted for forty years, from 546 to 506 B.C.E.[39] This event is faithfully recorded in the Spring/Autumn Annals, a chronicle attributed to Confucius, which Mencius characterizes as "never [describing] a war as righteous" (*Mencius* 7B:2).[40]

Since its early political unification, China knew mostly *defensive* wars.[41] It usually reacted to others' aggressions, the Great Wall being a salient example. The country was overrun by nomadic invaders – Mongols in the thirteenth century and Manchus in the seventeenth. Commentators attribute these defeats more to internal political disunity than to inferior military technology. Nevertheless, it could be said that the country relied principally on good political administration and economic structures – not on advanced weaponry – for its defense. The Mongols did not rule long, while the Manchus became culturally assimilated and lost their martial spirit, to be eventually defeated by the mightier Westerners. In more recent times, China became known as the "sick man of Asia," unable to defend itself from outside military intrusions. In these circumstances, reformers emerged who advocated a stronger military – but not necessarily more bloodshed.

The reformer Liang Qichao witnessed the weakness of the Manchu court in the face of Western military threats. He wrote first about reviving a martial spirit among the Chinese, as he praised the Japanese for their samurai spirit, or *bushido*. But an older Liang, abandoning his hopes for unending progress after his visit to war-torn Europe in 1918, was eager to find peace through universal disarmament: "Are we speaking of peace? This can be decided by one talk. . . . Should we abolish the military, what disturbance would take place? Such an easily resolved question is taking too much time. . . ."[42]

He proposed that the League of Nations form its own international peace-keeping force:

Whether we are for absolute disarmament, or for a relative but enforced ideology of peace, we need an international force belonging to the League of Nations that is stronger than any national army. . . . A League of Nations . . . without force . . . [would be like] the Zhou suzerain watching [impotently the warring] states of Qi, Jin, Qin and Chu. So the great powers, should they really want world peace, must give over all or most of their own military forces to the League . . . , sending soldiers to defend [peace in] the worst trouble spots in the world.[43]

Kang Youwei, Liang's former mentor, went even further. Pushed by Buddhist and Confucian ideals and influenced by developments in the West, he published in 1913 his utopian ideas in the *Datong shu* (On the "Great Unity"), named after the early Confucian vision of a past Golden Age. He declared himself in favor of a "One World" where happiness would replace suffering. He wanted the abolition of all national, class, racial, economic, and even family boundaries, advocating the sharing of all goods and services, and even of spouses. To cancel national boundaries, one must begin with universal disarmament, proceed to founding a world parliament, and establish a world government:

When among the people of the world there is no inhumanity of warfare, no calamity of soldiers pillaging and burning, no knowledge as to what things shields and spears, guns and canons are, . . . the preservation of human lives in all the states will be incalculable. . . . When we shift over from the work of [producing implements with which] to kill and produce the implements of civilization . . . this will also be benevolence and benefit incalculable.[44]

A generation of "New Confucian" philosophers came to maturity in the interwar period, witnessed firsthand the horrors of the Second World War, and sought to apply Confucian ethics to the problems of the postwar period. Tang Junyi and Mou Zongsan, two of the most important thinkers of this group, sought to assimilate Western thought, including that of Hegel and Kant, into their own moral philosophy. But Tang strongly opposed the Hegelian tendency to make the state supreme. He was also against using military power to establish world peace, since such use stems from the will to power, which he condemned as the first step toward the oppression of the conquered.[45] He discerned this will to power in the nations of the West, "especially those with very short cultural histories."[46] In a third world war, Tang remarked, several dozen atom bombs would destroy the whole human race: "The destruction of the human race is not impossible, as humanity is experiencing everywhere the sentiment of such collective death. And materialist thinking sees people as things, with the necessary conclusion that it does not matter if the human race is to suffer destruction."[47]

Tang also did not place much faith in the ability of international organizations to bring about world peace. He held the spirit behind such institutions to be far more important. He feared that the spirit animating all politics was to regard human beings merely as instruments, as machines to be used and maintained. To counter this, he called for the renewal of a humanist spirit in politics and economics and the revival of the letters and arts, moral philosophy and religion.

Mou Zongsan also wrote specifically about weapons of mass destruction, presumably in the context of the talks that led to the Anti-Ballistic Missile (ABM) Treaty in 1972:

In our times everyone is talking peace. First, the U.S. is talking peace with the USSR. Haven't they been doing this every day for years? No one really wants to fight, yet no one really wants to enter negotiations with sincerity. The U.S. and the USSR are only talking about how to limit each side's nuclear arsenal, without touching on freedom or totalitarianism. . . . Such talks are superficial . . . for which reason they remain inconclusive.[48]

Mou's wish for dialogues deeper than negotiations over strategic disarmament does not appear as naive today as it sounded then. The mid-1980s saw the ascendance of Mikhail Gorbachev to the Soviet helm, leading to *glasnost*, to a conversation about freedom and totalitarianism, and eventually to the dissolution of the Soviet Union itself by 1991.

Tang and Mou were idealist philosophers, more interested in metaphysical and religious questions than in the applied ethics of war and peace. Still, in their works the Confucian distaste for war comes through clearly. I believe that a sufficient array of Confucian voices from the past and present can be mobilized to support a move to universal disarmament, especially, but not exclusively, for WMD.

CURRENT OPTIONS: A BETTER GLOBAL GOVERNANCE

A classical Confucian text, the *Great Learning*, offers its advice for becoming a "great man," that is, one fit to be a ruler. He is to begin by extending his knowledge, following up with making his intentions sincere, rendering his mind and heart correct, cultivating his person, bringing order to his family, governing his state, and then, as a climax, *bringing peace to the world* (chap. 1). So the entire process begins with knowledge and sincerity. Although this text is sometimes regarded as issuing from a more "tender-minded" group, we note that even the "tough-minded" Confucian thinker Xunzi expresses his disdain for weaponry and his preference for good government:

In ancient times the only weapons were spears, lances, bows and arrows, and yet enemy states submitted without waiting for these to be used. Men did not build walls and battlements, ditches and moats, defences and watch stations or war machines, and yet the state was safe and secure from fear of aggression. . . . The only reason for this is that the rulers . . . sincerely loved the people. . . . "Let your authority inspire awe, but do not wield it; set up penalties but do not apply them."[49]

Similarly, Wang Yangming, a military commander and philosopher of the early sixteenth century, taught the "unity of knowledge and action." According to his own account, his philosophy of *liangzhi* was discovered in the midst of a thousand difficulties.[50] He learned from this experience how legitimate rulers could make life miserable for their subjects, especially by imposing unreasonable taxation on a peasantry plagued by droughts and wars. He understood that some peasants were forced to turn to banditry. So he appealed to the bandits to surrender before the battle:

You are accustomed to evil habits, including killing others, and have many suspicions. You don't know that . . . my heart would not tolerate killing a chicken or a dog for no reason, and how much more a human life, which is Heaven's concern! Should one kill others casually, there will be retribution in the after-life. . . . Alas, people are all brothers. . . . What a pity that is if I cannot comfort you, but have to kill you. What a pity! With these words, my tears are flowing.[51]

Wang understood that problems relating to the people's livelihood have to be resolved first, in order to prevent restiveness and rebellions. In a memorial addressed to the throne, he wrote: "Wealth is what the people want. When wealth is given to the people, they will live together [in peace]. The people make up the foundation of the state. When the foundation is secure, the state will be in peace."[52]

A later figure, Huang Zongxi (1610–95), left behind *Mingyi daifang lu*, a critique of premodern despotism as well as a blueprint for political reform. He emphasized the importance of a sound and fair legal system (so much neglected in China), advocating good schools and military service to prepare candidates for official service. His book was written in the wake of the Manchu conquest of China, which stimulated painful reflections among scholars.[53] Huang's treatise, which was published well after the author's death, was widely read two centuries later in the circle of reformers surrounding Kang Youwei and Liang Qichao. All this is to reiterate a point made earlier: The Confucian tradition generally regards good administration as more important to a people's security than developing weapons systems.

Neo-Confucian thinkers have a message for us as we seek solutions to the arms race. I am thinking of good global governance, including protection of the environment, of all sentient beings, including wildlife. This idea underlies Kang Youwei's seemingly naive utopian proposals for "One World." Having witnessed the demise of the League of Nations, and now through the experience of the United Nations, we know the difficulties of working with international organizations and the reluctance of individual states to surrender, even in part, their sovereignty. But a *negotiated global order* appears to remain as the only option currently available to those of us who desire lasting peace without the threat of WMD. This is the option Confucius and Mencius would have chosen, I think, were they living today. This is also the teaching left behind by their followers throughout the centuries. Through its wise Confucian advisors, traditional China, regarding itself as the one world, was forever seeking a better "global order," where the distribution of wealth would not threaten those who have less, attention would always be given to finding more equity, and basic moral education would prevail over increasing armaments in the interests of lasting peace.[54]

Is it possible to be more specific about a negotiated global order? Chinese history teaches us that all types of conventions should be tried, whether between several states on their own initiatives or through an international organization. Today, there are many states with nuclear arsenals, and proliferation among other states remains a possibility. In the name of self-defense and just wars, a nation's search for some form of deterrence cannot be condemned outright, even if that nation's political system is not exactly a democracy. Democracies take time to evolve. In the meantime, many peoples are tolerant of various forms of so-called benevolent despotism.

The quest for deterrence and the risks of proliferation are intrinsically linked. Proliferation of weapons of mass destruction cannot be outlawed unless the world's remaining superpower and its allies observe the same rules. Otherwise, the deterrence policy of the powerful nations cannot but lead to the proliferation of WMD among the weaker nations.

We should work toward universal disarmament, although the great powers are obliged morally to consider the option of unilateral disarmament – at least in drastically reducing the contents of their strategic arsenals – to make the world a safer place and as a confidence-building measure for less militarily advanced nations.

Today's NATO, seeking a raison d'être now that the cold war is over, speaks increasingly of its new mission to maintain the peace and punish trouble-makers. It seems in many ways to be preparing itself to engage in "corrective strikes" similar to those the ancient Chinese philosophers supported. But we should remember that the ancients attributed such punitive wars to semi-legendary sage kings. I do not think the Confucian tradition would support today's world powers in arrogating such prerogatives to themselves.

Finally, I would urge that we as individuals need to look at disarmament as our own personal responsibility, rather than leaving it to politicians and international leaders. Building peace, in small ways and big, is everyone's mission. This has always been the message of Confucian thinkers. They would agree heartily with Nobel peace laureate Joseph Rotblat, a cofounder of the Pugwash Conference group that promotes peace and opposes war, who is now asking for a Hippocratic Oath for scientists. He is urging that just as physicians have to swear to do no harm, scientists should seek to prevent misuse of science, especially in its applications. At the very least, they should forswear scientific efforts that can lead only to the harm of others:

Nowadays there is much talk about human rights but much less about human responsibilities. The ever-growing interdependence of the world community (largely arising from the application of science) offers great benefits to individuals, but by the same token it imposes responsibilities on them. Every citizen must be accountable for his or her deeds. This applies particularly to scientists. . . . It is also in their own interest, because the public holds scientists responsible for any misuse of science.[55]

We are not all scientists. But even those of us in the humanities and social sciences work alongside our scientist colleagues. We are often coresponsible for the effects of their work as well – either as collaborators or as silent supporters. We too must remember our responsibility to know what is going on in the scientific-military arena and to do something about it. I am now speaking of education, for ourselves and for others. This is surely the essence of the Confucian legacy, which places a humanistic and moral education before everything else.

CONCLUSION

We have extant an argument between the third-century B.C.E. Confucian thinker Xunzi and his disciple Li Si, who left him to become chief minister in Qin, the state destined to conquer the world that was China. Li says: "Qin has won victory for four generations. Its armies are the strongest in the world. . . . It did not attain this by means of benevolence and righteousness."[56]

Xun's response is: "But Qin has lived in constant terror and apprehension lest the rest of the world someday unite and trample it. . . . Stout armour and sharp weapons are not enough to assure victory. High walls and deep moats are not enough to assure defence."[57]

Is it worth being a superpower, even conquering the world, and yet living in "constant terror" that the rest of the world might turn around and overcome the oppressor? Moralists delight in pointing out that the Qin dynasty lasted barely two generations, evidently an example that "might" did not make "right."[58] Are the moralists right, though? What insights do they hold for Communist China today, as it enters its sixth decade with increasing prosperity, possessing an arsenal of nuclear and other weapons of mass destruction, but still insecure in its relations with other world powers, especially the United States? Has the Communist party turned its back on Chinese culture, so that the study of Chinese history and values cannot be used to understand its behavior and intentions? I would say: not entirely. While Confucian vestiges remain, the Chinese state today should be more correctly called Legalist rather than Confucian.[59] Legalism here refers to the use of harsh laws to support the government's policies. But even the Legalist tradition, as reflected in *The Art of War*, understands the needs of self-preservation and would not, unwisely, support an arms race. It too would oppose mutual deterrence if deterrence's failure spells mutual destruction. As Chinese history shows, when the country is unified, the government's task has been to build and consolidate its authority, not to launch new wars.

During recent decades, China's military actions were undertaken mainly to defend itself from perceived threats to its sovereignty and in the periphery of its own domain – such as with the United States in Korea in the 1950s, with Vietnam during the 1970s, and with Taiwan in the "war games" incident of 1996. The government has time and again reiterated its lack of interest in becoming a hegemon or "superpower," if only because of its commitment to building the economy of a vast country, where, despite some prosperity, most of the rural population still lives in third-world conditions. Many observers conclude that the Soviet Union fell apart economically before it did so politically, drained by the cost of the arms race. China's leaders may have learned the lesson; its very high defense budget was drastically cut in recent decades when a new policy of economic openness was introduced.

Critics of China point to its recent, alleged "expansion." They refer to the reversion of Hong Kong to China in 1997 and the country's long-stated intent to absorb Taiwan. Let me set the record straight: Hong Kong was Chinese territory taken by Britain after the infamous Opium Wars of the mid-nineteenth century. Taiwan was taken from China by Japan several decades later. Following its reversion to China at the end of the Pacific War, it became the seat of the Chinese Nationalist government in 1949 after the Nationalists were defeated on the mainland by the Communists. China's experience of "being robbed" by the Great Powers has powerfully conditioned its national psyche, leaving a legacy of victimhood. The real issue before us is not "expansion" but "reversion." However, there is an important additional dimension to this issue, that of populations living under a measure of freedom or democracy who fear being dragged into a communist state. For that reason, the people in Taiwan – who are overwhelmingly of Chinese background – assert that they would be ready for some form of "reversion" once China democratizes.

I believe it politically unwise to make China a potential enemy, just because of its different governing system. Today's China is not yesterday's Soviet Union, and we should not try to make it such. China does not have the militaristic traditions and ambitions of either Germany or Japan. Before the normalization of diplomatic relations between the United States and China, the Communists did have a guerrilla mentality – out of fear of both the United States and the USSR. We should by no means encourage them to revert to such a paranoid posture.

Today's China appears to accept a polycentric power system in the world at large, as well as in the Asia-Pacific region. Its nuclear arsenal consists of sixteen DF-9 missiles, old, liquid-fueled weapons maintained at a low level of alert, while warheads are stored separately. Everything is strictly for deterrence – what arms control specialists call a "minimal deterrent." China is, however, developing the DF-31, a solid-fuel mobile missile with a range to strike Alaska and the northwestern United States, as well as a long-range follow-up, the DF-41. China has no intercontinental-range bomber force, and its lone strategic submarine rarely leaves port. Unsurprisingly, China has unilaterally declared a "no first strike" policy. It says it will not use nuclear weapons to attack states not possessing such, and it wishes ultimately – when deterrence is no longer necessary – to destroy all nuclear weapons. It strongly opposes U.S. plans to move forward with a National Missile Defense (NMD) system, which would theoretically negate China's modest strategic capability and force the country to enter a renewed arms race.[60] As a Chinese official commented: "Once the United States has both a strong spear and a strong shield, it could lead them to conclude that nobody can harm the United States and they can harm anyone they like anywhere in the world."[61]

It is reported that when President George W. Bush assumed office, he was stunned to learn of the extent of the U.S. strategic nuclear arsenal, with its

5,400 warheads on intercontinental ballistic missiles, 1,750 nuclear bombs and cruise missiles ready for launching from B-2 and B-52 bombers, 1,670 "tactical" nuclear weapons, and another 10,000 warheads in bunkers around the United States. "What do we need them for?" he is quoted as saying.

The American force is so large that even deep cuts would leave the country with an overwhelming advantage over the rest of the world, including China. Yet the Bush administration has announced its intention to implement the National Missile Defense system, allegedly aimed at defending the United States from "rogue nations" armed with WMD. But it is actually part of the Star Wars project, supported by unbridled corporate greed. The United States is seeking unilaterally to promote the NMD, over its allies' objections and with no proof that the technology will ever work. America's pursuit of NMD is succeeding in driving China and Russia back into each other's arms – as did NATO's air war in Yugoslavia in 1999. In July 2001 the two countries signed a friendship treaty. If China and Russia step up their efforts to counter America's NMD, they will unleash a domino effect, as other powers in Asia and the world seek to increase their military forces, including perhaps their nuclear arsenals. Thus, America's "defensive" shield will erode respect for international law and may threaten world stability, while neglecting the real causes of conflict among nations.[62]

In the realm of chemical weapons proliferation, China is actively working to abide by international standards. The country signed the Chemical Weapons Convention on April 25, 1997, the same day as the United States. As for biological weapons, China was a victim during the Second World War when Japan used Chinese civilians for experiments. China acceded to the Biological Weapons Convention in 1984, although U.S. intelligence reports suspect China of expanding its biological weapons program.[63] If that is so, I would presume the purpose again to be deterrence, at minimal costs. It should also be pointed out that, as of this writing, the United States under the Bush administration is backing away from the Biological Weapons Convention, as it is from many other international commitments.

Notes

In transliterating Chinese, I have used the *pinyin* system, but retained whatever style (e.g., Wade-Giles) is given in quotations, including in book titles (e.g., Hsün Tzu for Xunzi, Chu Hsi for Zhu Xi). As translations of Chinese texts vary, I adapt these according to my reading of the original whenever necessary.

1. Confucianism spread to Korea, Vietnam, and Japan, each of which developed the tradition in its own way. For the purposes of this study, I deal only with China.

2. Zhaojie Li, "International Law in China: Legal Aspects of the Chinese Perspective of World Order," S.J.D. thesis, University of Toronto, 1996, chap. 1.

3. Joseph Needham and Robin D. S. Yates, *Science and Civilisation in China* (Cambridge: Cambridge University Press, 1994), vol. 5, pt. 6, p. 40.

4. Ibid., 455–56. The account is given in *Han Feizi*; see especially section 10. The problem of flooding is discussed in detail by Gu Yanwu in *Rizhi lu*, Sibu beiyao ed., 12:28–38.

5. See *Weiliaozi*, sec. 24, in *Binshu sizhong* (Four kinds of military texts), ed. D. C. Lau and the Institute of Chinese Studies, Chinese University of Hong Kong (Hong Kong: Commercial Press, 1992), 35.

6. *Zhuzi yülei* (Classified conversations of Zhu Xi), 1473 ed. (reprint; Taipei: Zhengzhon, 1973), 134:10b-11a. The event probably took place in the third century B.C.E.

7. With this theory, the Zhou government justifies its overthrow of the Shang dynasty, just as the latter can justify its earlier, successful uprising against the Xia. So it is recorded in the ancient classics, such as the Book of Historical Documents and the Book of Poetry. These texts were later appropriated by the Confucian school. But the theory predated Confucius.

8. Confucius was also against random capital punishment: "To put people to death without having first instructed them is called cruelty" (*Analects* 20:2).

9. See *Mencius* 2A:24. It calls to mind the New Testament saying: "What will it profit a man if he gains the whole world, and forfeits his life?" (The Bible, Revised Standard Version, Matthew 16:26). In comparison, Mencius appears much more altruistic.

10. He meant that a humane ruler is loved by people everywhere, including outside his state's boundaries. See also *Mencius* 4A7.

11. English translation adapted from Burton Watson, *Hsün Tzu: Basic Writings* (New York: Columbia University Press, 1963), sec. 15, p. 68.

12. Ibid., 56.

13. Ibid., 69.

14. Ibid.

15. See *Mozi*, chap. 5, sec. 17, 1a-b; the English translation is my own. Consult Burton Watson, trans., *Mo Tzu: Basic Writings* (New York: Columbia University Press, 1963), 56–58; Robin D. S. Yates, "The Mohists on Warfare: Technology, Technique, and Justification," *Journal of the American Academy of Religion*, special issue: "Studies in Classical Chinese Thought," ed. Henry Rosemont, Jr., and Benjamin J. Schwartz, 47 (September 1979): 550–615.

16. For the Confucian classics, see *The Shoo King or Book of Historical Documents*, in James Legge, trans., *The Chinese Classics* (Oxford: Clarendon, 1893–95; reprint, Hong Kong, 1960), vol. 3, esp. p. 162.

17. English translation adapted from Legge, *Chinese Classics*, 1:170–71.

18. *Mencius* 1B10, in Legge, *Chinese Classics*, 169.

19. *Mencius* 1B11, in Legge, *Chinese Classics*, 171–72.

20. *Zhuzi yulei*, 132:12a. Consult Julia Ching, *The Religious Thought of Chu Hsi* (New York: Oxford University Press, 2000), chap. 1.

21. Consult Christopher C. Rand, "The Role of Military Thought in Early Chinese Intellectual History," Ph.D. dissertation, Harvard University, 1977.

22. There was another Master Sun, his descendant, called Sun Bin. Extant versions of Sun Wu's text date back only to the second century B.C.E. Of these, the most complete version was unearthed only in 1972, on inscribed bamboo slips, including both Sun Wu's work and that of Sun Bin. I use and adapt the English translation by Roger T. Ames, *Sun-tzu: The Art of War*

(New York: Ballantine, 1993). This incorporates recently discovered Yin-ch'ueh shan texts.

23. Ibid., chap. 3, p. 111. See also p. 113: "He who knows himself and the enemy, will win every battle."

24. Ibid., chap. 1, pp. 104–5. Consult Julia Ching, *Mysticism and Kingship in China: The Heart of Chinese Wisdom* (Cambridge: Cambridge University Press, 1997), chap. 8.

25. Ames, trans., *Art of War*, chap. 3, p. 111.

26. *Wuzi*, in *Binshu sizhong*, 36.

27. Ibid., 40. It is said that as a result of following Wu Qi's advice, the ruler of Wei, with 500 chariots and 3,000 cavalry, was victorious over a Qin force of 500,000 men. See p. 44. Another Confucian treatise, the *Simafa*, echoes the same sentiments.

28. The humane treatment of war captives is counseled in Sunzi's *Art of War*. Indeed, a time-honored practice was to extend extreme courtesy and generosity to the enemy – capturing and imprisoning them during the fight, but releasing them soon afterward, showered with gifts and kindnesses. The reason? To decrease their will to fight or their desire for vengeance.

29. See *Mozi*, Sibu beiyao ed., chap. 13, sec. 50, pp. 9a-10b. Consult Y. P. Mei, *The Ethical and Political Writings of Mo-tzu* (London: Probsthain, 1929; reprint, 1973), 257–59.

30. Consult Needham and Yates, *Science and Civilisation in China*, 457–85.

31. Ibid.

32. See Senator Douglas Roche and Ernie Regehr, "Canada, NATO and Nuclear Weapons," paper presented for Canadian Pugwash/Science for Peace Seminar, Toronto, March 17, 2001.

33. See Paul Szasz in Chapter 2 above on attempts to broaden international law on WMD to include individuals.

34. *Yi zhuanshuo yin* (Introduction to the explications of the Book of Changes), quoted in Fang Lizhong, ed., *Binjia zhimou quanshu* (A complete book on military wisdom) (Beijing: Xueyuan, 1996), 2:2004.

35. Legge, trans., *Chinese Classics*, 3:308.

36. *Shangshu Zengzhu* (Book of historical documents with Zheng Xuan's commentary), quoted in Fang Lizhong, ed., *Binjia zhimou quanshu*, 2:2005.

37. My own English translation. Consult Legge, trans., *Chinese Classics*, 4:578.

38. *Hanshi waizhuan*, chap. 7; see Fang Lizhong, ed., *Binjia zhimou quanshu*, 2:2009–10. This is a later source than the *Analects*.

39. See Legge, trans., *Chinese Classics*, vol. 5, pt. 2: *The Ch'un Ts'ew, with the Tso Chuen*, Duke Seang, 27th year, pp. 528–36, esp. p. 530. These are bilingual texts. But the details of demilitarization are not given.

40. The word for "war" here is *zhan*. Mencius does add, though, that some wars are "better" than others and that there are differences between wars and "corrective strikes" (*zheng*).

41. One reason may be that the sedentary population of China had little desire to expand into the frozen north of Siberia, the steppes and deserts of Central Asia, the tropical south with its known "savages and sicknesses," and the forbidding waters of the east, from which came seasonal typhoons and marauding pirates.

42. *Liang Rengong jinzhu diyiji* (Recent works by Liang Qichao) (Shanghai: Commercial Press, 1922), 1:265. Consult Philip C. Huang, *Liang Ch'i-ch'ao and Modern Chinese Liberalism* (Seattle: University of Washington Press, 1972), 142–43.

43. *Liang Rengong jinzhu diyiji*, 266–67.

44. K'ang Yu-wei, *Ta T'ung shu: The One World Philosophy of K'ang Yu-wei*, trans. Laurence G. Thompson (London: George Allen & Unwin, 1958), 98.

45. Tang Junyi, *Wenhua yishi yu daode lixing* (The consciousness of culture and the rationality of morality) (Taipei: Students Bookstore, 1975), 1:267–74; see Liu Guoqiang, "Tang Junyi de zhengzhi zhexue," in Liu Shu-hsien et al., *Dangdai xin ruxue lunwen ji: waiwang ji* (Collected essays on contemporary New Confucianism: Politics), vol. 12 of *Ohu xuexu congkan* (Goose Lake Collection of Scholarly Writing) (Taipei: Wenjing Publications, 1991), 68–70.

46. Tang Junyi, *Renwen jingsheng zhi chongjian* (The reconstruction of the humanist spirit), in *Tang Junyi quanji* (Taipei: Student Bookstore, 1989 ed.; reprint, 2000), 5:38.

47. Ibid., 36.

48. Mou Zongsan, "Pianzhi, lixing yu tantu" (Obstinence, rationality, and the straight path), in *Shidai yu gangshou* (Taipei: Ohu Publications, 1986), 98.

49. Watson, trans., *Hsün Tzu: Basic Writings*, 73.

50. He was involved with battles against internal rebels rather than fighting aggressors from the outside.

51. Wang Yangming, *Wang Yangming quanji* (Complete writings of Wang Yangming), ed. Wu Guang et al. (Shanghai: Guji chubanshe, 1992), 2:1244–45.

52. Ibid. Consult Julia Ching, *To Acquire Wisdom: The Way of Wang Yang-ming* (New York: Columbia University Press, 1976), 134.

53. See English translation in W. T. de Bary, *Waiting for the Dawn: Plan for a Prince* (New York: Columbia University Press, 1993), 132–33. But Huang Zongxi did not discuss weapons.

54. The neo-Confucians frequently discussed economic problems, which, for want of space, I cannot always include here.

55. Sir Joseph Rotblat, "A Hippocratic Oath for Scientists," *Science* 286:19 (November 1999): 1475.

56. Watson, trans., *Hsün Tzu: Basic Writings*, 70.

57. Ibid., 71.

58. I hesitate to compare the United States with a despotic state like the Qin. However, in arms building, the comparison is not without merit.

59. I disagree here with Samuel Huntington, *The Clash of Civilizations and the Making of World Order* (New York: Simon & Schuster, 1996), where he confuses Communist China with traditional, Confucian China. However, even with democratization, Taiwan, South Korea, and Singapore may still be called Confucian states, to the extent that they are still inspired by certain Confucian principles.

60. See report by Michael R. Gordon, "China, Fearing a Bolder U.S. Military, Takes Aim on Proposed National Missile Shield," *New York Times*, April 29, 2001, p. 10. Japan already has a large defense budget, second only to the U.S. budget (in 1999), whereas China's is smaller than all the G-7 nations.

61. See ibid.

62. Frank Ching, "Scrap the National Missile Shield," *Far Eastern Economic Review*, June 8, 2000, p. 36. Consult Wu Xinbo, "U.S. Security Policy in Asia: Implications for China-U.S. Relations," Foreign Policy Studies, Working Papers Series, Brookings Institution, Washington, D.C., October 2000; at http://www.brook.edu/fp/cnaps/papers/2000_wu.htm (August 10, 2001).

63. See Center for Defense Information: http://www.cdi.org/issues/cbw/china.html (August 10, 2001).

14

"Heaven's Mandate" and the Concept of War in Early Confucianism

Philip J. Ivanhoe

In the previous chapter, Julia Ching offers us an informative introduction to various Chinese views about war, its proper conduct, justification, and goals. She notes that in traditional China, armies did employ tactics, such as flooding, that resulted in indiscriminate and massive death, including the death of noncombatants. In contrast to such practices, she describes a number of themes in the Confucian tradition that seem deeply opposed to such conduct, for example, the central place that the notion of *ren* ("benevolence" or "humaneness") occupies within the tradition. Several of the themes that she discusses directly concern normative conceptions of war and the state, and I believe that with a little more analysis and further argument we can see in these ideas a clear and respectable philosophical justification for rejecting any use of weapons of mass destruction. This is the main focus of my remarks.

Before turning to this task, however, I would like to endorse and elaborate a bit more on another issue that Ching raises early on in her chapter. She notes that her chapter describes the views of "Confucianism" but that one should not take this as exhausting what Chinese thinkers have thought about this or related issues. In the course of Chinese history, and especially during the so-called classical period, the 500 years or so prior to the unification of China in 221 B.C.E., there was a wide variety of different philosophical schools and thinkers offering a broad range of distinctive views. Venerable traditions such as Confucianism absorbed many ideas from such competitors, and in at least some cases, this borrowing dramatically affected the form, content, and style of what Confucian thinkers had to say. Perhaps the most dramatic example of such influence is the effect that Buddhism had on Confucian thought after it established itself in China sometime in the first century C.E.

While it is true to say that Buddhism was never the same after it arrived in China and that it was transformed as it blended with and responded to indigenous Chinese culture, it is equally true to say that China was never the same as well. In particular, the Confucian tradition was profoundly affected by Buddhist thought and practice. Confucian views on a wide range of issues changed in the course of their interaction. For example, the so-called Neo-Confucians, who lived and worked after the tenth century C.E., tended to rely on comprehensive metaphysical beliefs about the fundamental identity of the self and the world in arguing for their views about how the cultivated person should feel concern for all the world. This belief in the fundamental identity of the self and the world is quite alien to early Confucianism and is clearly the result of Buddhist influence.

The interaction with Buddhism changed not only the form and style of Confucian views but their content as well. For example, prominent thinkers such as Wang Yangming (1472–1529) insisted that the cultivated person feels concern not only for people and other creatures but for plants and tiles as well.[1] One of the founders of the Neo-Confucian movement, Zhou Dunyi (1017–73), refused to cut the grass in front of his house, citing the fact that it contained the same principle as was found within himself.[2] This general line of thinking is well represented in a quote from Cheng Hao (1032–85):

In medical books a paralyzed arm or leg is said to be "unfeeling" or "not benevolent" (*buren*). This expression is perfect for describing the situation. The benevolent person or "one with feeling" (*ren*) regards all things in the universe as one body. There is nothing that is not [a part of] him. If he regards all things as [parts of] himself, to where will [his feelings] not extend? However, if he does not see them [as parts of] himself, why would he feel any concern for them? It is like the case of a paralyzed arm or leg. The "ether" (*qi*) does not circulate through them and so they are not regarded as parts of oneself.[3]

Anyone who embraces anything resembling the view expressed in such passages could not possibly condone what we might call the clear-eyed use of weapons of mass destruction. For harming any aspect of the world is inflicting a wound on oneself. Only someone deeply deluded – a state akin to being massively self-deceived – would pursue such a course.

As moving as such a view of the world surely is, it relies on heroic metaphysical assumptions that many no longer find compelling or even plausible. However, at earlier stages of the tradition, Confucian thinkers did not invoke such complex metaphysical justifications for their ethical views. They appealed to much more low-flying beliefs about human nature and human anthropology. My point then is that even within the purview of the Confucian tradition, we need to distinguish distinctive philosophical movements and approaches. I would separate a discussion of Neo-Confucians more clearly from any account of the early tradition.[4] In the rest of my remarks, I rely only on material from pre-Buddhist China.

I focus on two ideas that Ching discusses in her essay: the notion of "Heaven's Mandate" (*tianming*) and the notion of a "punitive expedition" (*zheng*). Both of these ideas find very early precedents in Chinese history and can be found throughout the writings of the early Confucian tradition. The former is used as a way of distinguishing legitimate states from those of despots, describing when the subjects of a morally bad king have ethical warrants to overthrow him, and explaining the succession of ruling dynasties. The latter is one of several terms used to distinguish justified military action from aggressive, often expansionist, campaigns.

HEAVEN'S MANDATE

The basic idea behind the notion of Heaven's Mandate is that a ruler occupies his position as ruler only so long as he is worthy of and attentive to his role-specific responsibilities. In the earliest written records, gaining and maintaining Heaven's Mandate was primarily a matter of conducting proper sacrifices to ancestral and nature spirits with the appropriate reverence and humility. This idea developed into the notion that legitimate rulers gain and maintain the support of their people because they are morally good rulers. Such rulers possess a special kind of authoritative charisma called "virtue" (*de*) that arises out of their ethically exemplary characters. People naturally defer to a person with such moral charisma and freely offer him their support and loyalty. This enables such a ruler to reign and not just rule, and he will do so as long as he enjoys the support of Heaven, which takes the welfare of the people as its primary and overriding concern.

A ruler who fails to care for his people will lose Heaven's Mandate, and as Mencius (c. 390–c. 305 B.C.E.) made explicit on several occasions, there is no ethical warrant prohibiting the overthrow of such a ruler. These aspects of Mencius's philosophy did not always find favor among later Chinese rulers. The founder of the Ming Dynasty, Emperor Hong Wu (1368–98) was so displeased with this aspect of the sage's philosophy that he commissioned a special board of scholars to excise those passages that implied a lack of devotion to the ruler. A total of eighty-five passages were deleted.

In Japan, "Heaven" was found in the person of the emperor, and his pronouncements themselves constituted "Heaven's Mandate" (*tianming*). The notion that there could ever be a "stripping of the mandate" (*geming*, a term that later came to mean "revolution") – never mind a *legitimate* case of such change – was thought abhorrent and grotesque. Mencius's advocacy of this idea was ignored, criticized, or interpreted away in Japan. This aspect of his philosophy also gave rise to the story that a "divine wind" (*kamikaze*) sank the first ships that tried to bring the *Mencius* to Japan, a manifestation of the displeasure of Japan's native spirits.

The lesson I want to take away from this all-too-brief discussion of the idea of Heaven's Mandate is that the ruler of a state is considered legitimate only if he takes the welfare of his people as his primary responsibility. This precludes the possibility that a legitimate ruler could exploit or harm – much less bring about the death – of his people, for such actions would violate his primary role-specific duty to protect and nurture them. We might extrapolate from this to the view that any such ruler would not engage in actions or policies that would place his people at risk from states or individuals outside his realm. Even in the defense of his people, a proper ruler would always employ those methods and policies that posed a minimal threat to the well-being of his people. This offers a prima facie reason for believing that such a ruler would avoid pursuing the development and deployment of weapons of mass destruction on the belief that such a policy would encourage other states to develop and deploy the same weapons and direct them toward his people. It would seem that an ideal Confucian ruler could not even be persuaded to develop such weapons in light of considerations about deterrence. The Confucian ruler would prefer to step down from his throne, surrender, and even leave his own kingdom rather than be forced to develop weapons with such devastating potential. He would do so in the belief that *over time* the kind of inhumane attitudes, character, and attendant policies that spawn such weapons would prove incapable of providing the people with happy and satisfying lives. In the end, they would turn away from the logic of mutual assured destruction and toward the more humane path of the Confucian Way. When we turn to the notion of a "punitive expedition," we find further and stronger evidence to support such an interpretation of the early Confucian tradition.

PUNITIVE WARS

As Professor Ching has shown, early Confucians such as Mencius and Xunzi (c. 310–c. 219 B.C.E.) employ a distinction between a "punitive expedition" (*zheng*) or "righteous war" (*yi zhan*) and "war" (*zhan*) or "attack" (*fa*) simpliciter. The gist of this idea is to distinguish what Heaven deems as legitimate and warranted conflicts from those that are not. In the same way that a conflict within a state can be distinguished as a case of a "stripping of the Mandate" (*geming*), as opposed to an unjustified "rebellion" (*luan*), conflicts between states are differentiated as "punitive expeditions" and wars.[5] Punitive expeditions are military campaigns that are motivated and justified by the good they are designed to bring about. A legitimate ruler engages in such campaigns in order to relieve the suffering of those unfortunate enough to be subjects of morally corrupt states. The idea is akin to a certain conception of a war of liberation.

Ching has quoted passages such as *Mencius* 1B11 and 7B4 that describe how the people in such benighted states yearn for the day when such military actions will liberate them from the oppression they suffer. Such campaigns are designed to increase the well-being of the oppressed, and this justification would preclude deploying weapons or tactics that involved extensive and indiscriminate harm to the people one sought to liberate. This is why

Mencius was opposed to the use of flooding as a military tactic. In another important passage, 7B3, he rejects the idea that in carrying out a punitive expedition against the tyrant Zhou, King Wu caused so much blood to be shed that the "pestels of the grain mortars floated [upon it]."[6] According to Mencius, this could not possibly have happened because the justification and motivation of punitive expeditions prevents them from employing large-scale slaughter. In more contemporary terms, you can't "liberate" the village from the enemy by bombing it out of existence. Xunzi adds the further point that such campaigns cannot be pursued at extreme costs to either the defenders of the enemy state or the ruler's own soldiers and civilians. A proper ruler "does not massacre the defenders of a city . . . he does not keep his forces in the field; he does not let a campaign last more than a season."[7] Long campaigns disrupt agricultural production and too deeply undermine the well-being of one's people.

The concept of a punitive expedition employed by these early Confucians places fairly strong constraints on the nature of legitimate interstate conflicts. The strong emphasis on preserving the well-being of both the people and soldiers of an enemy state and the well-being of one's own people offers a strong and respectable warrant against developing or deploying weapons of mass destruction. A ruler who could not liberate the people of another state without inflicting great harm on them would not engage in military action against them, and one who could not defend his own people without putting them at severe risk of grave injury would abdicate rather than enter into such a conflict. Such a scenario is described in another passage in the *Mencius*, 1B15. A king who could find no way to appease the barbarian tribe that was harassing his borders assembled the elders of his state and announced to them, "What the barbarians want is my territory. I have heard this – that the ruler does not injure his people with that wherewith he nourishes them. My children, why should you be troubled about having no prince? I will leave this [place]."[8] The king then travels to a distant place, but his people are so moved by his benevolence that they stream after him and declare their support for him.

There is a developed line of thought in early Confucian writings arguing that the ultimate and trumping concern of the ruler of a state is the welfare of his people. This idea is expressed in the notion of Heaven's Mandate and used to explain how a good ruler is able to reign over his people through the power of his moral authority. It also provides an account of when the people of a morally corrupt ruler have the warrant – and Mencius believes some even have the obligation – to overthrow their ruler and strip him of Heaven's Mandate.

The same concern for the well-being of the people informs and shapes early Confucian views about the nature and proper conduct of interstate armed conflict. No proper ruler will engage in campaigns that are too costly to either the civilians or soldiers of a hostile neighbor or to his own people.

Given the very nature of weapons of mass destruction, their development, deployment, and use would seem to be precluded by this cluster of beliefs shared by early Confucian thinkers.

As a postscript to what I have said, I want to note that while I believe a study of traditional cultures, Chinese as well as others, can often help us to think about many important issues of contemporary relevance, I have concerns about a certain kind of approach to traditional ethical views. What I doubt and to some extent worry about is the approach that seeks to find, within the ethical writings of traditional cultures, well-formed and ready-made answers to complex, contemporary problems, such as the development, deployment, and use of weapons of mass destruction. I seriously doubt that such an approach will prove productive, for important parts of what is most daunting and perplexing about these modern problems inheres in the new challenges they make us face. I have the same concern in regard to issues such as cloning or when to terminate someone's life when it is being sustained through massive technological intervention. The ancients never thought about these problems for the simple reason that they were not *problems* for them. They could not clone people nor could they sustain or annihilate human life in the ways we can today.

If we try to find clear precedents for these modern problems in classical texts, we often will be led to produce rather strained analogies that can obscure the really tough issues. For example, consider Professor Ching's innovative use of the case of flooding as a weapon in early China. As I noted earlier, there are some significant similarities between flooding and modern weapons of mass destruction. Both can cause widespread and indiscriminate death and damage. However, the scope, level, and persistence of such effects are dramatically different in the two cases. Nuclear war can escalate into a conflagration that risks ending the possibility of life itself. Even a "local" nuclear conflict will ravage all life across a wide area, down to the molecular level, and leave the area inhospitable to life for generations to come. A massive intentional flood may indeed kill a large number of people and other creatures, but it lacks the scope, does not affect organisms across such a broad spectrum of levels, and after passing, presents no lasting harm. Even the most massive of floods leaves an area wet, not radioactive.

My concern should not be construed as implying that the ancients have nothing important to tell us about such modern problems. To the contrary, I believe that the form of ethics practiced by Confucians and by many other traditional cultures may well point the way toward the most fruitful approach to such problems. For I take the early Confucians as representatives of virtue ethics, an approach that insists that the task of ethics should be focused on what kinds of lives are – all things considered – most satisfying for creatures such as ourselves. For only in light of some general conception of what we can be and would like to be can we begin to decide between dignified and degrading ways to prolong human life, whether replicating ourselves is an advantage or an abomination, and whether developing, deploying, and using weapons of one sort or another will promote or destroy our individual or collective well-being. While the ancients do not provide us with ready answers to such questions, unlike many modern moral theories or models of rational choice, they do point the way toward answers by providing an example of the way to think about an important range of ethical problems.

Notes

1. See Wing-tsit Chan, trans., *Instructions for Practical Living and Other Neo-Confucian Writings of Wang Yang-ming* (New York: Columbia University Press, 1963), sec. 179.
2. This episode is recorded by one of the Cheng brothers (probably Cheng Hao) in *Henan Chengshi yishu* (*SBBY* ed.), 3:2a.
3. *Henan Chengshi yishu* (*SBBY* ed.), 2A:2a,b. (Cf. 2A:15b).
4. I describe some of the important differences that one can find among prominent Confucian thinkers at different historical stages of the tradition in P. J. Ivanhoe, *Confucian Moral Self Cultivation*, rev. 2nd ed. (Indianapolis: Hackett, 2000). I offer a more sustained and thorough comparison of Mencius and Wang in P. J. Ivanhoe, *Ethics in the Confucian Tradition: The Thought of Mencius and Wang Yang-ming*, rev. 2nd ed. (Indianapolis: Hackett, 2002).
5. *Mencius* offers a succinct description of these basic differences in 7B2. "During the Spring and Autumn Period [722–481 B.C.E.] there were no righteous wars (*yi zhan*), though there were cases of one being better than another. A 'punitive expedition' (*zheng*) is when the supreme [state] attacks one of its subordinates. Hostile states cannot launch punitive expeditions against one another."
6. Xunzi also argues that King Wu's defeat of the tyrant Zhou was relatively bloodless. He specifically states that prisoners were not executed nor were rash charges into the enemy line rewarded. Xunzi also claims that Zhou's own troops turned against and killed him in the thick of battle, allowing King Wu and his men to achieve victory without having to engage in wide-scale slaughter. See John Knoblock, trans., *Xunzi: A Translation and Study of the Complete Works* (Stanford, Calif.: Stanford University Press, 1990), 2:77–78. Thanks to Eric L. Hutton for pointing out this passage to me.
7. Quoting Julia Ching's adapted translation of Burton Watson, trans., *Hsün Tzu: Basic Writings* (New York: Columbia University Press, 1963), 68.
8. James Legge, trans. *The Chinese Classics*, vol. 2: *The Works of Mencius* (Hong Kong: Hong Kong University Press, 1970), 176. The story also appears, with minor variations, in chap. 28 of the *Zhuangzi* and chap. 21 of the *Lushi chunqiu*. My thanks to T. C. Kline for pointing out these other occurrences of this passage.

15

Hinduism and the Ethics of Weapons of Mass Destruction

Katherine K. Young

In the Western imagination, Mahatma Gandhi (1869–1948) has been the icon of nonviolence (*ahimsa*) and pacifism. Because Gandhi was Hindu, people assumed that Hinduism and modern India (which is about 80 percent Hindu) were also nonviolent and pacifist. This idea was reinforced by India's policy of nonalignment under Jawaharlal Nehru and by a general image of Hinduism as the religion of peace (*santi*) and tolerance (*tulyatva*) promoted by philosopher-statesmen such as Sarvepalli Radhakrishnan (1888–1975). This stereotype of Hindu nonviolence was shattered in May 1998 when India detonated five nuclear bombs. An act that shocked the rest of the world, it was far from shocking to Indians themselves – at least those who know Indian history.

When the first atomic bomb was tested in New Mexico, Robert Oppenheimer quoted from the Hindu scripture, the *Bhagavad Gita*: "Now I am become Death, the destroyer of worlds."[1] Gandhi said, "Unless now the world adopts non-violence, it will spell certain suicide for mankind."[2] Several months later, he said to an interviewer: "Oh, on that point you can proclaim to the whole world without hesitation that I am beyond repair. I regard the employment of the atom bomb for the wholesale destruction of men, women and children as the most diabolical use of science."[3] He was then asked, "What is the antidote? Has it antiquated non-violence?" and answered, "No. It is the only thing the atom bomb cannot destroy. I did not move a muscle when I first heard that the atom bomb had wiped out Hiroshima. On the contrary, I said to myself, 'Unless now the world adopts non-violence, it will spell certain suicide for mankind.'"[4]

Jawaharlal Nehru, too, was appalled by the destruction of the atomic bomb. In 1954, he became the first world statesman to plead for universal disarmament: "If anything, he was more deeply wounded by the act, for his faith in the practice and philosophy of science had been all the greater. For Nehru, the generation of 'atoms for peace' could help redeem the promise of science and rid it of the ugly stain of Hiroshima. So he supported his friend Homi Bhabha and the Atomic Energy Commission to the hilt."[5]

From 1948, India started to develop capacity for atomic energy with help from Canada and the United States. The death of Nehru in 1962 marked a shift from acceptance of Gandhian nonviolence to greater acceptance of force for national security. The continuing conflict with Pakistan over Kashmir and the 1962 border crisis with China – among other factors – had undermined confidence in Nehru's Gandhian-style politics. In 1965, Prime Minister Lal Bahadur Shastri approved the idea of a subterranean nuclear test, and Indira Gandhi endorsed the program again in 1971. A twelve- to fifteen-kiloton nuclear device was tested at Pokhran on May 18, 1974 – what India called a "peaceful nuclear explosion." In the aftermath, Canada halted its nuclear cooperation with India, and the United States stopped supplying fuel. The Soviet Union, however, continued supplying heavy water. In the late 1970s and 1980s, India developed more nuclear technology[6] while its neighbor Pakistan was pursuing its own nuclear program and developing a surface-to-surface ballistic missile. India claimed that China was providing technical assistance and selling missiles to Pakistan, a charge supported by Western observers.[7] The dynamics of this three-party nuclear rivalry kept India and Pakistan suspended in a state of nuclear ambiguity for two decades, while both refused to sign the Nonproliferation Treaty.

At the same time, India was also suspected of developing chemical weapons and experimenting with biological warfare agents. Even less information on these activities was publicly available than on the highly secretive nuclear program, but it was always clear that India's military planners considered chemical and biological weapons of only secondary concern compared with nuclear weapons. India ratified the Biological Weapons Convention in July 1974, and analysts concur that its research in biological warfare has been limited to defensive countermeasures. In June 1997, following India's ratification of the Chemical Weapons Convention the previous year, government leaders acknowledged that the country had a chemical weapons production program, one that would have to be dismantled under the terms of the convention.[8]

During these decades, Hindu intellectuals were beginning to make a case for legitimate violence based on the need for self-defense. Arvind Sharma, a professor of Hinduism, wrote in 1993, for instance, that India must maintain "military *preparedness of a strictly defensive nature.*"[9]

HINDU VIEWS ON THE 1998 NUCLEAR TESTS

The nuclear tests at Pokhran in 1998 elicited very few public comments from an explicitly Hindu perspective and none that could be considered an ethical analysis.[10] This is partly because India is a secular state, and national defense is considered a secular matter. The ensuing debate referred to Hinduism, however. The Bharatiya Janata Party (BJP), a party with pro-Hindu sympathies (considered by its critics to be a Hindu fundamentalist party[11]) was in power at the time under the leadership of Atal Behari Vajpayee.

The BJP (and the Jan Sangh, its antecedent) had long been hawkish on national security. In the 1980s, it had promoted a "Hindu bomb" as opposed to the "Islamic bomb,"[12] a reference to the fear that Pakistan was developing nuclear weapons. In its election manifestos of 1996 and 1998, the BJP supported the long-range goal of a weapons-free world but argued for the right to have nuclear weapons in the meantime. As a result, it opposed the Comprehensive Test Ban Treaty (CTBT), the Fissile Material Control Regime (FMCR), and the Missile Technology Control Regime (MTCR) on the grounds that these treaties were discriminatory (permitting only some countries to have nuclear weapons). During the 1998 election campaign, Brajesh Mishra, the BJP's foreign policy spokesman, declared that India would produce a nuclear bomb if the BJP were elected. That year, the party's manifesto advocated development of the Agni series of intermediate-range ballistic missiles that would carry nuclear warheads.

One critical article, which appeared after the May 1998 nuclear tests, was titled "Saffron Bomb," alluding to the fact that saffron is the sacred color of ascetics' robes, and militant Hindu ascetics had been associated with the BJP:[13] "It would seem that sections of the saffron establishment fail to understand the logic of nuclear deterrence and irresponsibly consider it to be just another, if more lethal, kind of weapon."[14] But Rajnikanta Verma, then the Indian High Commissioner in Ottawa, Canada, argued that "nobody has been able to point to any action taken by the Government which could be described as 'Hindu fundamentalism.' . . . Every Government, at least since the Chinese nuclear test in 1964, has been engaged in developing this capability, and indeed, but for the preparations made over these past decades, the BJP Government, which assumed office only in March 1998, could not have carried out the tests less than two months later in May."[15]

Be that as it may, protest demonstrations followed the tests. One year later, for example, there was a massive antinuclear rally sponsored by leftist political organizations and groups such as Greenpeace International, Friends of the Earth, Association for India's Development, Global Initiative, and Pakistani peace groups. The protest took the form of a long march from the test site near Pokhran, beginning on May 11, 1999, and ending in Sarnath (Varanasi) on August 6, 1999, Hiroshima Day. The purpose was "to highlight the perils of the nuclear arms race and the Indian government's 'twisted' logic behind conducting nuclear blasts in 1998."[16] This strategy was ostensibly in the Gandhian tradition of marches to educate and mobilize people. These, in turn, had been derived from the pan-Indic tradition of pilgrimage (*yatra*). The choice of Sarnath is striking because it is a famous Buddhist site (where Buddha first began to teach after achieving enlightenment) rather than a Hindu pilgrimage site.

The main ethical argument made by this coalition of leftists, minorities, and (mostly secular) Gandhians was a social justice and economic one. India could ill-afford "illusions of grandeur," intended only to confuse the masses by making them forget about the stark reality of poverty.[17] The subtext drew on an Indian tradition of nonviolence but avoided a specifically Hindu connection because of the BJP's links with Hinduism. The marchers protested not only India's nuclear tests, in short, but also the ruling BJP's use of Hinduism partly to justify them. One person wrote that "unless the link between the bomb and Hindutva is recognised and all secular and democratic forces are rallied along with the Left, the aggressive chauvinism sought to be fostered by the nuclear weapons will provide the thrust for an authoritarian state."[18]

On the other side of the debate, some supporters of the nuclear tests looked for lessons from history. One commentator pointed out that even the Buddha was pessimistic that peace was possible when military inequality existed: "When Buddha heard of Ajatshatru of Magadha attacking the Licchavi confederacy led by Vaishali, he was dismayed that his disciples of Magadha should have attacked his Sakya kinsmen. He sighed and said that perfect peace would never come until all the nations of the earth were equally mighty."[19]

The controversy was not limited to India or Indians. David Frawley, director of the American Institute of Vedic Studies, often defends Hindu causes. He pointed to the hypocrisy of Western commentators who decry how the nuclear tests have destroyed Gandhi's legacy in India, yet do not call for Gandhian-style nonviolence from their own Western governments acting against terrorists and "rogue" regimes. The real reason for the rebuke to India's tests, he suggested, was the fear of a strong, assertive India with its large population. In addition, he noted the erroneous perception that Hinduism has a basic premise of nonviolence by calling attention to the "classical Hindu teachings that always honoured a defensive war."[20] The *Mahabharata* and *Ramayana*, India's great classical epics, center on battles, for example. Historically, Frawley added, Hindus have used force for self-defense, though not for invasion beyond the subcontinent or for conversion.[21] He observed, moreover, that many Hindus today feel that Mahatma Gandhi's use of nonviolence in the Indian independence movement was a temporary politicization of a spiritual principle traditionally confined to monks and ascetics. With independence, Indians realized that "total non-violence does not work very well as a national or international policy."[22]

For many Indians, news of the tests occasioned much more than sobering reflections on the need for self-defense. It brought a feeling of jubilation that India was now coming of age and taking its place among the powerful nations of the world. "Atalji [the prime minister] has released a flood of pent-up energy and generated a mood of heady triumphalism. He has kick-started India's revival of faith in itself. To the West, the five explosions are evidence of Hindu nationalism on a Viagra high. To Indians, it is conclusive evidence that we count, that there is nothing to fear but fear itself. The Pokhran tests are only tangentially about security. Their significance is emotional. The target is not China and Pakistan. It is the soul of India."[23]

HINDU CONCEPTS OF ETHICS (*DHARMA*)

Underlying the preceding comments in the wake of the 1998 tests is a deep conflict of values: Violence is ethically acceptable under certain conditions or it is ethically unacceptable. Any attempt to characterize a Hindu ethic on WMD must be situated in the general context of Hindu notions of ethics (*dharma*), and these two contradictory positions must be examined systematically. The first position is represented by the Hindu just war tradition (though it must be pointed out that its sources and principles can be used both to justify and to prohibit the use of WMD). The Hindu ascetic tradition, its extension into general cultural values, and its politicization by Mahatma Gandhi during the Indian independence movement represent the second position. As Sharma points out: "It should be clearly realized that, apart from the specifics of the situation, the Hindu ethos, as distinguished from the Buddhist and the Jain, provides for both options. The saying of the Great Epic *ahimsa paramo dharmah* or that non-violence is the same supreme *dharma*, is often quoted; but it is also supplemented by the saying: *dharmya himsa tathaiva ca* – that dharmic violence is equally so. The million-dollar question, of course, is: What is *dharmya?*"[24]

The key term for ethics in Hinduism is *dharma* (from the verbal root *dhr*, meaning "to hold firm" or "sustain"). It is based on specific religious actions (*karma*) – in the form of undertaking vows, offering gifts, chanting the names of God, renunciation of something, and so forth – that create a positive power (*bhavana*). This will come into manifestation as a good effect (*phala*) in the future, thereby making a firm (and positive) connection between this life and a future one (alternatively, this world and another, such as heaven). *Dharma* has a range of traditional meanings, including ethics (custom, good works, prescribed conduct, duty, virtue), cosmic order (human action sustaining the universe), religion, justice, and law. *Dharma* begins the classical list of human goals: *dharma*, *artha* (governance, politics, economics), *kama* (leisure, pleasure), and *moksa* (liberation). It is in the first position because it establishes the ethical constraints for *artha* and *kama*[25] (whereas *moksa* is beyond this worldly realm altogether). In theory, these constraints belong to the inherent order of the universe; in praxis, they indicate that brahmins were the authors of texts because they privileged ethics over the political power of the *ksatriyas*.[26]

Beginning in approximately the fifth century B.C.E., genres known as the Dharma-sutras, Dharma-sastras, and Itihasa elaborate on *dharma*. *Dharma* has been divided into two types: *samanya* and *visesa*. *Samanya* refers to the general or common moral virtues.[27] This category is also known as *sadharana-dharma* (the *dharma* resting on the same support) or *sanatana-dharma* (the eternal *dharma*, which is universal and unconditional). By contrast, *visesa-dharma* refers to the particular duties defined by one's sex, caste, stage of life, region, occupation, and so forth.

The four sources of *dharma* are arranged in descending order of importance: (1) transcendent, eternal "heard" scripture (*sruti*), (2) human, "remembered" scripture (*smrti*), (3) the behavior of the good people (*sadacara*), and (4) knowledge based on personal experience (*anubhava*) or conscience (*atmatusti*). Each source of authority amplifies or makes explicit the preceding one (and therefore is anchored ultimately in transcendental authority, which is manifested in the most ancient scripture of the tradition, the Vedas).

As a result, appeal to authority is ostensibly traditional and conservative.[28] Hindus recognize differing interpretations of texts, however, and admit that *dharma* is hard to understand. This point is captured in two well-known sayings. According to one, it is difficult to fathom the very subtle ways of *dharma*.[29] According to the other, the truth of *dharma* lies in the dark cave.[30]

Because of this ambiguity, Hindus recognize that real moral dilemmas arise when people disagree on the order of listed items or if two or more virtues such as truth and nonviolence conflict. Such a conflict occurs, for example, when telling the truth causes someone's death. Moral dilemmas (*dharma-pasa*) might arise because of the ways in which *samanya* virtues are understood. They have been described as common virtues, which implies that they should govern the behavior of everyone. But the list appears first in the Upanisads (and is further developed in the Yoga-sutras), which suggests that they originally defined the behavior only of renunciates and ascetics (*sannyasins* and *tapasvins*). Later, in the *Artha-sastra* and *Manu*, they were viewed as common virtues (especially *ahimsa*). This view may have developed to allow Hindus to compete with Buddhists and Jains, who were criticizing the brahminical tradition for its legitimation of violence in animal sacrifice.

The Hindu ethical scheme introduces ambiguities of other types. The highest authority for Hinduism (*sruti*) contains texts such as the *Rg-veda* that celebrate war and warrior deities (e.g., Indra), but also ones that promote nonviolence, such as the Upanisads. In other words, there is a conflict of values at the heart of the supreme authority. As a result, there is tension between *visesa-* and *samanya-dharma*. *Visesa-dharma* makes killing (*himsa*) a duty for warriors (*ksatriyas*)[31] under specific conditions, but many *samanya* lists begin with *ahimsa*. Is the violence of warriors an exception to the general principle of *ahimsa*? If so, why is *artha* (which includes the theory and practice of war[32]) one of the four goals of human life (*purusartha*) in Hindu axiology? And if warriors find a fundamental conflict between *himsa* and *ahimsa*, why is it said that "a person attains happiness when there is no clash between *dharma* and *artha*, *dharma* and *kama*, and *kama* and *artha*"?[33]

SOURCES AND PRINCIPLES: WAR AND JUST WAR

One strand of Hinduism acknowledges that sheer power can determine the course of events. This insight is captured in the maxim, "Big fish eat little fish," in statements suggestive of anarchy (captured in this phrase: "Relative or no relative, crush the foes: conquer those who attack, conquer others by attacking"[34]), and in the heroic literatures (such as Tamil *cankam* poetry from the first century B.C.E.) that celebrate chiefs and kings as bloodthirsty, powerful, even cruel rulers who strike terror into their subjects. Gradually, this power, which developed as chiefdoms and early states emerged by force from tribal societies, was tamed by classical concepts of the just king who brings peace and harmony to his realm. Now *artha* (governance) was to be controlled or at least constrained by *dharma* (ethics).

So important was the topic of warfare that passages relating to it (scattered through many genres of texts, such as the Dharma-sastras and Itihasas) were given the designation Dhanur-veda, the Veda of Warfare (Veda being the category of scripture par excellence), and war itself was sacralized and considered a religious ritual (*yajna*). Death in battle, as in many other traditions, gave warriors heaven. Hindu tradition has acknowledged both defensive and offensive wars. The latter has been theoretically represented by the *cakravartin* (literally, a ruler whose wheels roll everywhere without obstruction), an emperor or sovereign of the world.

In addition, Hinduism has distinguished two types of war: just and unjust. A war is just if both its cause and means are just. The following principles of just war (both cause and means) have been extracted from various key sources.

Legitimate reasons for war. Texts on traditional warfare make a distinction between war that is righteous or just (*dharma-yuddha*) – because the reason for war is to maintain or establish justice according to public standards and the means are regulated by recognized rules of warfare, and are therefore also just[35] – and unrighteous war (*kuta-yuddha*), which has an unjust cause and is secretive and unregulated.[36]

Clarity. As for the battle itself, opposing sides should meet before the fighting starts and discuss procedures. There should be no secrecy about battle; it is to be an open fight (*prakasa-yuddha*) between equals equipped with proper armor and without stratagem or artifice.

Discrimination. According to the ethical code of righteous war compiled from the scriptures, war must take place only in restricted places, at restricted times, and with restricted people (i.e., war should be fought only by warriors of the *ksatriya* caste). Battles must not take place, for instance, in gardens or near temples. They must occur at announced times. People in some categories, moreover, must not be harmed by war: brahmins (priests and teachers), the aged, women, children, peaceful citizens walking along the road, the mentally ill, and the support staff for battle (such as quartermasters, menials, and guards).[37]

Containment: Hinduism has not tried to do away with war altogether. In theory, at least, it has tried to regulate and limit war by confining it to a particular caste and a special place and time, and by making it a duty performed stoically without ego and greed or a duel involving only two people.

Prudence: Because the backdrop to Hindu ethics is long historical experience with warfare, it has a well-established tradition of prudence.[38] Ethics is grounded in realism and closely related to the preceding principle of containment. At the same time, the scriptures sometimes celebrate war. Although this may seem a contradiction, the war epics no doubt functioned as societal propaganda to appreciate the warrior caste's role of protecting society (which often necessitated putting life on the line) and drew from the heroic literatures of martial bravery. The concept of *dharma* was also used to keep Hinduism allied with the sources of political power. The intent was to prevent kings from becoming Buddhist or Jain, which carried the threat that Hinduism might not be honored and the state might even be used against it, as had occurred under the Buddhist king Asoka (c. 273–232 B.C.E.), who discouraged brahmanical sacrifice.

Fairness and equality: Battles should be between equals in physique, armor, and psychology. Soldiers are required to stop fighting if their enemy counterparts become panic-stricken, are scattered, go into hiding, succumb to fatigue, fall asleep, are thirsty, become disabled, have no sons, use broken weapons, or give the sign of unconditional surrender (a piece of straw between the lips). They should stop, moreover, if a brahmin enters the battlefield (a method by which the battle can be stopped by a third party).

Reciprocity or the Hindu golden rule: "One should not do unto others that which is unpleasant to oneself"[39] or its variant, "Whatever one desires for oneself one should desire the same for others."[40]

Self-defense: Hindu ethics has recognized violence for the purpose of self-defense as a basic ethical principle. It can be at an individual level (saving the life of a mother over a fetus, say) or at the societal level (warfare to defend the community) and therefore, by extension in modern times, at the national level. Most of those Hindus who have viewed nonviolence as the basic ethical principle have made self-defense an exception. Gandhi's refusal to acknowledge this exception was unusual in the history of Indian ethics.

Reconciliation after victory: A defeated king would be reinstated on the throne (or his son or kin if he had died in battle) and permitted to maintain his own customs and laws as long as he accepted the victor's suzerainty. Because of this, victors should offer help to defeated kings, hold their hands with affection, and show tears of sympathetic identification with their plight in order to facilitate the transition and solicit their loyalty.

These principles on which the Hindu concept of just war was based do not, of course, resolve the basic tension with the competing ethical orientation premised on nonviolence. If nonviolence were to be practiced by everyone, did this not contradict the warrior caste's duty to fight just wars? But if violence destroyed every one, did not this defeat the purpose of war in the first place, which is justice?

The moral dilemma created by the conflict between nonviolence and violence for *ksatriyas* is explored in the *Mahabharata* (an epic that pivots on the great war between two sides of a family, the Kauravas and the Pandavas) – especially in its most famous section, the *Bhagavad Gita*.[41] The latter was composed around the first century B.C.E.

On the eve of a great battle, the warrior Arjuna does not want to fight. The battle would cause the destruction of his whole family, even though it is about justice (the Pandavas' rightful succession to the throne) according to the prevailing rules of just war. The moral dilemma is also the conflict between protection of the family and protection of the state (loyalty to kin or polity). The two are closely connected in the royal or dynastic family, which must preserve its own lineage but also the kingdom.

The traumatized Arjuna, as if a modern conscientious objector, argues that war is caused by greed, which is morally wrong. The suffering created by war, moreover, is absurd and leads to hell. Far better to renounce action in this world altogether and become an ascetic. Lord Krishna, who is his charioteer, disapproves. He calls Arjuna ignoble (*anarya*), womanly (*kliba*), engaged in unprofitable action (*ajusta*), and dishonorable (*akirtikarana*). Arjuna denies that he wants victory, kingship, pleasures, enjoyments, or sovereignty of the three worlds if any of these things requires the killing of his extended family, the elimination of ancient family laws (*kula-dharma sanatana*), and the ascendancy of unrighteousness (*adharma*). He would be better off killed.[42] Krishna still disagrees, arguing now on a more philosophical note that life is characterized by birth and death; there will always be another rebirth.[43] This cycle, moreover, belongs to the ordinary level of existence. Ultimate reality is beyond this opposition altogether, with neither killing nor being killed.[44]

The Gita's solution for the conflict between *ahimsa* and *himsa* is to insist that warriors do their military duty but with a new yogic perspective. This is called "renunciation in action" (*nais-kamya-karma-yoga*). God himself both manifests violence (*himsa*) and nonviolence (*ahimsa*) in the cosmic cycles, but also transcends them.[45] Arjuna is instructed to find the same kind of equilibrium in the midst of action, to act without wanting the results of action, and to experience mental peace in the midst of battle. Only by developing spiritually beyond illusion and greed can he work for the ideal society (*ramrajya*) based on moral values and justice.[46]

A second major problem for the Hindu theory of just war is whether the epics themselves were models of behavior according to their own criteria. One study of the *Mahabharata* has analyzed it from the perspective of a war-crimes tribunal. Were there really legitimate reasons for the war? Was it fought according to the rules?[47] In other words, were both the reason and the means dharmic, which would be necessary for it to be a just war (*dharma-yuddha*)? After careful scrutiny of all the battles, M. A. Mehendale concludes that it was not a *dharma-yuddha*, because it did not maintain the principle of equality, especially in large battles.[48] In this context it is important to remember that everything in the epic is more extreme than it would be in real life because there is another level of the *Mahabharata* narrative. This war initiates the change from the *dvapara-yuga* to the *kali-yuga*, one cosmic period of time to another (curiously, the epic presents this change of the *yugas* like the change of the *kalpas* on an even more cosmic scale when the universe is destroyed), and this occurs at the level of *daiva* or fate, not *purusakara* or human effort. "The Mahabharata war has been dramatized by the epic author as a cosmic sacrifice analogous to the destruction of the worlds at the 'end of the yuga' (*yuganta*). The weapons of war are compared to the fire at the end of a yuga. . . . This destruction is represented as a gigantic funeral pyre in which the old order of the world, Pandavas and Kauravas alike, must perish to give way to a new order established with the assistance of the divine incarnation Krsna [Krishna] from the remnant represented by Pariksit, the perfect monarch embodying the qualities of both Arjuna and Krsna."[49]

By contrast, Mehendale points out, there are fewer rules mentioned in the other great epic of the Hindu tradition, the *Ramayana*, and no instances of unjust stratagems or a change of the *yugas*.[50] Mehendale's observation might be explained as follows: This epic pits good (the god-king Rama) versus evil (the demon Ravana) in a kind of *dharma-yuddha*. In this head-on struggle, there is little moral ambiguity involved, no need for discussions of subtle rules. The battle is over the fact that Ravana has abducted Sita, Rama's wife, which is an obvious moral wrong. It is assumed that Rama, the embodiment of *dharma*, must answer such an obvious affront. Moreover, the scale of violence in this epic is limited. The battle is mainly between Rama and Ravana, and it is fought in the terrestrial realm, although extraordinarily powerful weapons are at times used, as in the *Mahabharata*.[51]

SOURCES AND PRINCIPLES: THE ETHICS OF NONVIOLENCE

The Hindu tradition has another kind of deontology altogether: one captured in the basic principle of nonviolence. The word *ahimsa* (nonviolence) is a compound consisting of *himsa*, a feminine noun from the verbal root *han* (to kill or injure), with the negative prefix *a*. The resulting word means to not kill or injure and (because it is a desiderative) to not even want to do so. The compound can connote positive meanings as well, so *ahimsa* can be understood as benevolence, protection, and compassion.

The principle of nonviolence is found in the Upanisads and other sources that extended it under the rubric of *samanya* or common *dharma*. Depending on the source, there is minor variation in the list of *samanya-dharmas*. According to *Yoga-sutra* 2:20–31, it includes nonviolence, truthfulness, nonstealing, celibacy, renunciation of possessions, and self-control; according to *Kautilya Arthasastra* 1:3:13, nonviolence, truthfulness, purity, absence of envy, and forbearance; and according to *Manu* 10:63, nonviolence, truthfulness, nonstealing, purity, and restraint of sense organs. Some traditional lists, however, put truth (*satya*) first.

Ksatriyas were exempt from this principle; in fact, they were not allowed to be ascetics[52] because this would provide an opportunity for them to avoid war and justify it by claim of superior spirituality. Other groups of householders (nonascetics), however, based their identity on this principle (the brahmin caste, for example, and some sectarian groups such as the Vaisnavas). The practice of *ahimsa* by elite castes and some sects encouraged its imitation by other upwardly mobile groups. The principle of nonviolence thus had a solid basis in Hindu society (not to mention among Jains as well) that Gandhi could tap.

Ironically, according to Mehendale, the most important Hindu source for Gandhi was the *Bhagavad Gita*. Gandhi admitted that the *Gita* was not written as a treatise on nonviolence but argued that its meaning could be "extended" by interpreting it as an allegory – the eternal duel between the "forces of darkness and of light"[53] – because Hinduism is always evolving as a living religion. His own interpretation, Gandhi said, emerged from his study of Hindu texts, other religions, and his own experience. Gandhi focused his commentary[54] on the second chapter, which is about disinterested action (*nais-kamya-karma-yoga*), but limited his understanding of action to nonviolent action.

Gandhi's basic values were closely allied to the *samanya* principles,[55] but he politicized and modernized them. Gandhi followed those traditional lists in which truth (*satya*) comes first. He often mentioned his experiments with truth through self-effacement. He saw truth not only as the means and goal of human existence but as the very nature of God,[56] saying, "What then is Truth? A difficult question, but I have solved it for myself by saying that it is what the voice within tells you."[57] In this way, Gandhi equated truth with conscience, thereby elevating conscience from last on the traditional list of dharmic authorities to first. Once again, he justified such changes by saying that a religion is allowed to progress.

Gandhi was ostensibly a principled pacifist. His opposition to war was rooted in the more general principle of *ahimsa*. He made no distinctions among types of war (defensive vs. offensive, just vs. unjust) or types of person (ascetic vs. nonascetic). Killing, he often argued, is inherently wrong for anyone in any situation. He ostensibly acknowledged no permissible recourse to war (but see below) and therefore no permissible conduct of war or type of weapons. *Ahimsa*, for Gandhi, seemed to mean not only nonkilling, noncooperation, and civil disobedience, but also active love. Moreover, he connected *ahimsa* with self-purification, fasting, and abstinence (from drugs, drink, tobacco), which correspond to purity (*asauca*) in some *samanya* lists, as well as with nonstealing (*asteya*), nonpossession (*aparigraha*), and sexual abstinence (*brahmacarya*), also *samanya* virtues.

For Gandhi, *satyagraha* was closely related to both the *Gita* and the *samanya* principle. He understood *satyagraha* as purification and penance. *Satyagraha* literally means grasping and insisting on truth as well as acting in the knowledge that truth is on one's side. He coined the term in South Africa, when he called for passive resistance to a new law requiring Indians to be registered and fingerprinted.

Possibly because he perceived his position in religious terms, Gandhi ostensibly permitted no compromises, not even for self-defense. In this sense, his position was more extreme than traditional Hindu ethics, which permitted it. According to him, "It can certainly be said that to experiment with *ahimsa* in face of a murderer is to seek self-destruction. But this is the real test of *ahimsa*. He who gets himself killed out of sheer helplessness, however, can in no wise be said to have passed the test."[58]

In this context, it is intriguing to examine Gandhi's understanding of Adolf Hitler. On December 24, 1940, Gandhi wrote to him:

That I address you as a friend is no formality. I own no foes. My business in life has been for the past 33 years to enlist the friendship of the whole of humanity by befriending mankind, irrespective of race, color or creed. I hope you will have the time and desire to know how a good portion of humanity who have been living under the influence of that doctrine of universal friendship view your action. We have no doubt about your bravery or devotion to your fatherland, nor do we believe that you are the monster described by your opponents. But your own writings and pronouncements and those of your friends and admirers leave no room for doubt that many of your acts are monstrous and unbecoming of human dignity, especially in the estimation of men like me who believe in universal friendliness. . . . Hence we cannot possibly wish success to your arms.[59]

It might strike the reader as curious that Gandhi addressed Hitler as a friend. This, however, was a common approach that Gandhi took with his political foes. With the British, too, he made a distinction between the person and the act. Although many historians have claimed that Hitler and the Nazis represented a unique evil, Gandhi's premise is that there is no intrinsic human evil. All human beings are capable of change for the good, theoretically even Hitler. Gandhi went on to point out that the difference between the British and the Germans is only one of degree, not kind, because both resort to violence. By contrast, India is unique in its moral politics of nonviolence.

Gandhi concluded: "It is a marvel to me that you do not see that it [violence] is nobody's monopoly. If not the British, some other power will certainly improve upon your method and beat you with your own weapon. You are leaving no legacy to your people of which they would feel proud. . . . I, therefore, appeal to you in the name of humanity to stop the war."[60]

Besides upholding his confidence in the moral and political superiority of nonviolence, Gandhi is here also replying to those who argued that if India joined Hitler in the war effort, a victory would give India her freedom from Britain. But for Gandhi, this would necessitate using immoral means to achieve a moral goal, and that would be unethical.

For Gandhi, *ahimsa* had to be based on courage. If someone lacked courage, however, then violence was preferable to nonviolence:

Supposing in the presence of superior brute force one feels helpless, would he be justified in using just enough force to prevent the perpetration of wrong?" Gandhi was once asked. He answered: "Yes, but there need not be that feeling of helplessness if there is real non-violence in you. To feel helpless in the presence of violence is not non-violence but cowardice. Cowardice must not be confused with non-violence.[61]

This position seems to create a "permissible" use of violence for Gandhi, but in fact its purpose was to distinguish two very different phenomena: running away from or avoiding a problem because of fear or indifference and facing a problem nonviolently with courage. It could even be argued that these two types of nonviolence are ethically opposed – the first position is not a moral one, the second is – based on a distinction between psychological states or motives. Remember, fear was Krishna's diagnosis of Arjuna's prebattle qualms in the *Gita*, and his main task was to transform Arjuna's fear into courage. Gandhi was using hyperbole – better violence than passivity born out of fear – to underscore his distinction between "no violence" and nonviolence (such hyperbole, called "praise," or *arthavada*, was common in Hindu texts and was distinguished from "command," or *vidhi*).

More confusing is the fact that Gandhi himself supported the British war effort in World War I, arguing then that he was opposed to war, but if there had to be war, then it should be on the side of justice. Later, in 1929–30, he did not oppose violence to quell the Malabar Moplah uprising in India. And he backed Sardar Vallabhbhai Patel's deployment of troops to Kashmir in 1948.[62] How is this support for violence to be explained? Some have argued that Gandhi was foremost a politician, not a *mahatma* (a saint). If so, then this would make his ethic of nonviolence not absolute but rather pragmatic, contextual, and instrumental (even though Gandhi himself had accused the Indian National Congress Party of being instrumentalists and had distanced himself from it for this reason). Alternatively, it could be argued that these few situations in which Gandhi condoned violence were the exceptions that proved the rule. Or, instead, the few instances in which Gandhi accepted the use of violence could be understood within his broader hermeneutic for negotiating an end to the opposition between nonviolence and violence. One must not use nonviolence as an excuse for weakness. Violence is better than that. But true nonviolence born out of courage is better than violence. One with such courage must be absolutely nonviolent, even risking his or her own life if need be. One acting out of nonviolence should try to change the hearts of those willing to use violence by all nonviolent means possible. When such conversion is not possible, one should support (nonviolently) those who use violence for just causes over those who use it for unjust ones. And one should continue to work toward the goal of justice and nonviolence within one's own society rather than opting out if others do not abide by the principle of nonviolence.

THE MORAL DILEMMA OF NONVIOLENCE
AND VIOLENCE REVISITED

A famous critique of Gandhi's position was that of Martin Buber in 1939. Buber poignantly replied to an article in which Gandhi had drawn a parallel between the treatment of Hindus in South Africa and that of Jews in Nazi Germany. He began by telling Gandhi that there was no comparison between the problems experienced by Indians in South Africa (a denial of rights, a life in ghettos, a few fires set to Indian shops, and arrests for being out after curfew) and what Jews were experiencing in Germany (the destruction of thousands and thousands of shops, the burning of synagogues and scrolls of the Torah, and torture and death in concentration camps):

> Do you know of the torments in the concentration camp, of its methods of slow and quick slaughter? I cannot assume that you know of this; for then this tragic-comic utterance "almost of the same type" could scarcely have crossed your lips. . . . It does not seem to me convincing when you base your advice to us to practise *satyagraha* in Germany on these similarities of circumstance. . . . An effective stand may be taken in the form of non-violence against unfeeling human beings in the hope of gradually bringing them thereby to their senses; but a diabolic universal steam-roller cannot thus be withstood. . . . "*Satyagraha*" means testimony. Testimony without acknowledgement, ineffective, unobserved martyrdom, a martyrdom cast to the winds – that is the fate of innumerable Jews in Germany. God alone accepts their testimony, and God "seals" it, as is said in our prayers. But no maxim for suitable behaviour can be deduced therefrom. Such martyrdom is a deed – but who would venture to demand it?[63]

In short, Buber argued for just war in the face of the Holocaust, not absolute nonviolence. Many Jews, he said, had tried passive resistance, to no avail. He based his ethical reasoning on the principle of self-defense, adding that he did not want to use force but would do so as a last resort to prevent the evil from destroying the good: "If I am to confess what is truth to me, I must say: There is nothing better for a man than to deal justly – unless it be to love; we should be able even to fight for justice – but to fight lovingly. I have been very slow in writing this letter to you, Mahatma. I made repeated pauses – sometimes days elapsing between short paragraphs – in order to test my knowledge and my way of thinking."[64]

Several decades after the time of Gandhi, one of the foremost modern gurus of Hinduism, the Sankaracarya of Kanci, Pujyasri Candrasekharendra Sarasvatisvami,[65] argued a position similar to that of Buber. This is found in the posthumous collection of his essays called *Hindu Dharma*.[66] Although the essays were written before the 1998 nuclear tests, it was as if he had in mind the need to give modern Hindus moral license once again – after Gandhi – to wage wars for national defense. He uses several hermeneutical strategies to create scope for the general concept of a just war. First, he calls just war (and animal sacrifice[67]) an exception to the general principle of *ahimsa*. Second, he places emphasis on the intention rather than the act. If violence is intended for the welfare of society and there is no hostility, it is permissible. Third, he argues that *samanya-dharma* is really required only for formal renunciates and functions merely as an ideal for the ordinary person. *Ahimsa* as a common value, moreover, should be understood as the absence of ill-feeling in all action. As such, it is optional. Fourth, he implies that violence in the context of a just war is no longer confined to the *ksatriya* caste and therefore acknowledges the modern reality of conscription. Fifth, he concludes that acts that "apparently cause pain to others may have to be committed for the good of the world and there is no sin in them."[68]

This discussion shows how a contemporary, highly respected Hindu leader has reaffirmed the tradition of just war and accommodated it to modern political realities. He integrates the two types of *dharma*: *samanya*, which makes *ahimsa* central, and *visesa*, which allows violence in several circumstances by calling such violence a legitimate exception to the general rule of nonviolence. Finally, he suggests that Hinduism has taken a "realistic" view of the issue of violence and nonviolence and that this pragmatism has a greater chance of limiting violence than promotion of an absolute principle that people will find too difficult to uphold. Thus, he bypasses Gandhi's position, which extended the nonviolent ethics of specific groups to everyone, and returns to the just war tradition.

USE OF WMD IN WAR

It should be noted that the concept of weapons of mass destruction was already imagined[69] when the Hindu epics were written (around the fourth century B.C.E. to the fourth century C.E.). They were extraordinarily powerful weapons (*astra*) of the gods (called *brahmastra*, *narayanastra*, and so forth). In the *Ramayana*, for instance, Rama sets the *brahmastra* in his bow. The mountains shake, the sky darkens in all four directions (even though the sun is scorching), trees fall, comets dart about in the sky, the earth cracks, heavy clouds form, the heat of lightning increases, animals cry and tremble, and huge tidal waves hit the shore.[70] The *Mahabharata*, which has similar descriptions,[71] also mentions a category of divine weapon, *sakti*, which always hits and destroys its target. And the texts refer to a third type of war as *mantra-yuddha* (extraordinary means),[72] premised on the belief that utterance of a *mantra* (a sacred syllable, word, phrase, or stanza) by powerful brahmins, ascetics, or other holy persons creates enormous power. Because brahmins were generally the authors of the religious texts, they may have exploited this idea to promote the view that religious power is greater than military power, and therefore their power is greater than even that of the *ksatriyas* – a one-upmanship of sorts, more suitable for the literary arena, of course, than the battlefield.

On the basis of their sources and ethical principles, Hindus could argue that the use of WMD of the modern and human-made variety is never permissible or that it is permissible under certain circumstances. Possible arguments *against* WMD include the following.

First, Hindus could argue that WMD must never be used because violence is prohibited by all the four traditional authorities for *dharma* (*sruti, smrti, sadacara,* and *atmatusti*). The Upanisads, which emphasize the ethic of nonviolence, belong to *sruti,* or the Vedas, the most authoritative scripture. In addition, there are texts belonging to the second category of scriptural authority (*smrti*), such as the Yoga-sutras that prohibit any violence. Moreover, there are holy people whose behavior exemplified good (here understood as nonviolent) behavior (*sadacara*). Finally, conscience (*atmatusti*), the fourth authority, can support the other three. The latter position could be underscored by the argument that in the modern age, *dharma* has been interiorized through meditation, notions of individual conscience, and social responsibility to others so that virtues such as nonviolence, selflessness, compassion, and peace that were once mainly within the domain of asceticism or certain castes and religious sects are now important for the ordinary person. This shift of emphasis could be justified by the argument that emphasis changes with the age, because social conditions change with the *yugas*. This change could also be rationalized by the traditional idea that conscience makes explicit what is implicit in the prior sources of authority (which is sufficiently contradictory or vague that new ideas can be introduced). Nonviolence is now, it might be said, part of the "collective conscience" of Indians, intrinsic to their identity, community, and civilization.

Second, they could deny any use of WMD that seeks authority from supposed precedents in the Hindu epics. Because the epics are literature, the discussion of WMD there must be understood as mere fiction, they would argue. Or, like Gandhi, they might argue that to facilitate a religion's progress, allegorical interpretations (in this case of war) should supplant literal ones. Moreover, because analogies have limited applications according to Indian philosophy, ethicists cannot make an extension from the epics to modern political situations to legitimate WMD.

Third, they could deploy a range of arguments based on traditional Hindu notions of just war. For example, they could argue that WMD are not acceptable because even the traditional rules of just warfare forbid the use of "cruel, poisoned, or treacherous weapons,"[73] which today's WMD are in full measure. A first strike using WMD would not be permissible by traditional criteria because WMD involve secrecy (contravening the rule that combatants must meet before battle and agree on the procedures). Because WMD allow no flexibility once released, the battle cannot be stopped for ethical reasons mandated by tradition, such as in the case of a rout or the surrender of the enemy.

Hindus could argue from the existing principle of discrimination that WMD are inadmissible because they do not allow citizens to be protected and because they would seriously damage the earth.[74] In this context, those who are inclined to cite the traditional sources for precedents might turn to the *Mahabharata* story of Asvatthaman. When Asvatthaman heard that his father had been killed, he hurled with fury his "weapon of mass destruction," his powerful *narayanastra*, against the Pandavas, who had killed his father. Krishna intervened to save them from being reduced to ashes, but everything else was burned and there was no rain.[75]

Hindus could turn to the notion of reciprocity and appeal to the two versions of the Hindu golden rule mentioned earlier. That is to say, one should not use WMD against others if one does not want others to use them against one; put otherwise, because one desires a world without the threat of WMD, one desires the same world for others.

They could also resort to the principle of proportionality and refer to the following two episodes. The first is found in the *Mahabharata*, where, on one occasion, Drona begins a mass slaughter of the Pandava army. To counter this, Krishna tells Arjuna: "Having set aside *dharma*, take recourse to a stratagem (*yoga*) for victory, O Pandava."[76] The Pandavas then falsely report in a loud voice, so Drona could hear, that Asvatthaman (Drona's son) had been killed, hoping that Drona would become disheartened and withdraw from battle. To lessen the unrighteousness (*adharma*) of telling a lie, they then say in a soft voice, so that Drona could not hear, that Asvatthaman is really an elephant. But instead of withdrawing from the battle, Drona becomes enraged and unleashes his weapon of mass destruction, his *brahmastra*, on ordinary soldiers. This causes such massive destruction that sages such as Visvamitra, Vasistha, and Bharadvaja appear in the sky to demand that he stop. Even when Drona is finally told the truth – that Asvatthaman is alive – he continues to fight. Bhima rebukes him for killing thousands of *ksatriyas* because he is a brahmin and brahmins are supposed to be nonviolent. He also rebukes him for breaking other rules of warfare, such as killing many for the sake of one person.[77]

The second episode is in the other famous Hindu epic, the *Ramayana*, where Rama must dissuade his brother Laksmana from using a *brahmastra* against Indrajit (the demon Ravana's warrior son). Doing so, we are told, would involve killing many demons and thus break the rule against killing many to kill one, as well as the rule against fighting those who are weaker.[78]

On the other hand, the following arguments might be made in *support* of the use of WMD.

To begin with, Hindus could argue that on the basis of all four traditional sources of authority (*sruti*, *smrti*, *sadacara*, and *atmatusti*), WMD can be legitimated because war is acknowledged and sacralized in *sruti* and *smrti*. Because the sources often contain both the violent and nonviolent positions, either in the same text or in the same genre, the arguments based on authority overlap. Moreover, many great sages of the past have been advisors in the art of warfare (*dhanur-veda*), which sets the example of good behavior, and Hindus across the political spectrum today are advocating support of the atomic bomb on the basis of conscience.

In addition, they could argue that the *samanya* principles such as *ahimsa* are really just for special groups (ascetics, women, and children) who are pursuing the path to liberation and therefore are not relevant for others, especially in modern India because caste (*ksatriya*) protection has been replaced by modern conscription. Hindus could also draw on the well-established fact that self-defense has traditionally been viewed as an exception to the principle of nonviolence.

Second, Hindus could argue that a hypothetical supposition (*arthapatti*) is one of the valid means of knowledge. Because the epics give us literary examples of WMD and the ethical issues involved, they can provide guidance as hypothetical suppositions to be applied toward an ethics of WMD today.

Third, they may interpret Hindu just war principles to legitimate WMD. On the basis of the following line, "For Krishna *dharma* is at least sometimes dictated by the constraints or the contingency of the situation,"[79] they could argue that there is a new contingency – India's enemies now have nuclear, chemical, and biological weapons – and this fact permits India to develop and possibly to use WMD.

Support for WMD could be derived from the concept of *apad-dharma* (literally, the *dharma* for times of difficulty, *apatti*).[80] This concept refers to exceptions to normal rules necessitated by natural disasters (such as famine) or by political anarchy (when no king is in power). When "big fish are allowed to eat little fish," one can use any means for survival or to restore well-being.[81] Therefore, Hindus today might argue that the boundaries created by *dharma* can be renegotiated in these exceptional circumstances (India's neighbors having WMD), though once normalcy is restored, these weapons must not be used.

In addition, the use of WMD in war could be justified ethically as a last resort, referring again to the *Mahabharata* story of Asvatthaman. When Asvatthaman out of rage hurled his divine, all-powerful weapon (capable of causing severe damage to the environment and the massive loss of life),

Krishna instructs Arjuna to set aside ethics as a last resort to ensure victory. In other words, illicit means may be used for a licit goal in extremis. In another context, *mantra-yuddha* (battle employing the extraordinary means of powerful mantras) is said to be "permissible only for purposes of defense, and that too only as a last resort."[82]

Short of a last resort, there is Hindu precedent for arguing that these weapons can be directed against rogue states that use unrighteous strategies or resort to war for unrighteous reasons[83] according to the distinction of *dharma-yuddha* and *kuta-yuddha*. To be prepared for all situations, therefore, warriors traditionally are to be taught both *dharma-yuddha* and *kuta-yuddha*. Kautilya's *Artha-sastra* says that *kuta-yuddha* might involve attacking when enemies are vulnerable, attacking after feigning retreats, and other stratagems.[84] Krishna admits that the strategy he used against Drona was unrighteous but claims that it was necessary. The strategy is permissible if used for the sake of justice and if its use is minimized. The *Gita* concludes that "wherever there is Krishna, the master of strategies, and Arjuna, the archer, there will be splendor, wealth, and lasting morality (*dhruva-nitih*)."[85] By contrast, the epic presents a very harsh judgment on Drona's use of the *brahmastra* on ordinary soldiers; his behavior is considered serious *adharma* because it was motivated by rage, not a sense of justice.[86]

Although poisonous weapons were forbidden according to the traditional rules of warfare, they could be used if the enemy used them first. The *kuta-yuddha* "permitted the use of deadly and poisoned weapons which would slay thousands of men."[87] This could arguably give precedents for biological and chemical weapons.

Finally, we should note that the permission for using extraordinary weapons in the above cases comes in the midst of battle, once the war has already begun. Because traditional rules of righteous warfare exclude fighting those who have not announced their intention to fight, there are Hindu precedents for arguing against any preemptive attack.[88]

DETERRENCE

The logic of deterrence is the fear of massive retaliation created in the mind of the enemy. The Gandhian position rules out the development of weapons for deterrence because this would mean that illicit means were being used for a licit goal, and this is immoral.

By contrast, other Hindus could argue that the divine weapons mentioned in the epics (*brahmastra* and so forth) that are analogous to nuclear weapons should be used only for deterrence. These weapons are so powerful that using them in war would mean breaking all the rules of traditional warfare and destroying the environment. In some *samanya* lists truth/reality (*sat*) comes before *ahimsa*. They could argue, therefore, that truth (in the sense of the legitimate act of self-defense) coupled with the new nuclear reality means that nations such as India should have nuclear weapons for deterrence, but that they should not be used because the principle of *ahimsa* comes second in the list. In addition, stratagems are allowed against rogue states, and fear can be used as a stratagem for a lasting peace.

One supporter of the 1998 nuclear tests used the following parable to argue for the legitimacy of WMD as a deterrent:

In the outskirts of the village, in the dense forest, lived a poisonous cobra. It posed a danger to all travelers passing by the village. One day a saint happened to take that route. The cobra tried to bite him but was transformed by his loving touch. The saint taught the cobra about love, compassion and non-violence. In a few days the villagers noticed that the cobra didn't pursue them any more. They went closer and closer to it, out of curiosity. They even pelted it with stones and beat it with sticks. The snake simply sat still and took it all.... The saint returned to the village in a few days. He noticed the snake lying by the side of the road, bleeding and bruised. Going near it, he caressed it and asked, "Why did you let this happen to yourself?" The snake replied, "Holy One, you taught me love and non-violence. I wouldn't retaliate or harm those who beat me." The saint smiled sadly, "Dear child, I asked you not to bite. But I never forbade you from hissing."[89]

PROLIFERATION

Again, there are Hindu positions on both sides of this debate. The strict non-violent ethic is against proliferation for all the reasons having to do with the immorality of using WMD either in war or for deterrence. Hindu opponents of proliferation might also appeal to broader utilitarian concerns of the sort made by secular opponents of India's nuclear tests. Again, along the lines of Gandhi, they could argue that just as religion's progress requires embracing new ideas of social justice and democracy, so does religion's progress require the rejection of such costly and fruitless ventures as an arms race while many people in a poor nation lack basic health and education. Said one critic of the 1998 nuclear tests: "And what about deterrence? How far do we go to satisfy ourselves that it is adequate or significant? The doctrine puts the onus on other countries. This means that the need will expand on the basis of perceived threats.... It is tragic that we are becoming jingoistic when the international community is realising that destructive weapons do not solve any problem."[90]

Not everyone thinks this way. Many Hindus, though not necessarily speaking from a religious perspective, have pointed to a double standard. Countries advocating nonproliferation are often the very ones that either have nuclear weapons or are protected by treaties with countries that do have them. If every country were to give up nuclear weapons, India would not want them: "What we said was: For your security, for international security, and most important, for our security, let us eliminate nuclear weapons. If you don't, then there are no restraints on us. And therefore we test. For

25 years, we adopted a moral argument because we still adhered to the concepts of Mahatma Gandhi and our reactions against Hiroshima-Nagasaki. Our foreign policy was based on the principle that our independence was a moral victory, not just a political one. We found that moral suasion did not work in a world of moral chicanery."[91] For former colonial powers to maintain their own nuclear weapons but forbid these to their former colonies is unacceptable to many Hindus.[92]

Let us return to our thought experiment on what a Hindu ethic on proliferation derived from the just war (*dharma-yuddha*) tradition might be. The traditional rules stipulated that wars must be between equals in age, preparedness, strength, and energy.[93] Extrapolating from this idea, modern Hindus could argue that India's neighbors (China and Pakistan) created an unequal situation by developing nuclear bombs and missiles capable of delivering them, amounting to preparation for unrighteous war. Under these circumstances, the rules of war could be ignored until new ways to deal with the threat are evolved. Hindus could draw on the *realpolitik* of the *Artha-sastra* tradition (which also belongs to a category of scripture) to affirm that the state has to be preserved at all costs, and this takes precedence over all else.[94] Thus, India's nuclear program is a legitimate defensive move to equalize power between it and the enemies on its borders. This argument is bolstered by another rule: "'Fight between equals' also meant that the weaponry used by opposing combatants be of the same kind."[95]

Hindus could argue, moreover, that because they worked for several decades in the international context for disarmament, but to no avail, those nuclear powers that have refused to sign treaties or to comply with the terms of treaties they have signed are in fact rogue states. In this situation, Hindu ethics permits Hindus to use the same means as an exception to the normal rules of just war. Because realism, power, and prudence – not ethics or law – seem to be driving the policies of nuclear powers, India too should operate on the realist principle of containment. Containment here requires that the chances for war be minimized by maintaining an arsenal just large enough to be effective, thereby preventing an arms race. R. P. Kangle draws this conclusion based on an assessment of the *Artha-sastra*:

It is in the sphere of foreign policy that the *sastra* may be said to have lost much of its validity at the present time. Yet it would be quite possible to maintain that what it says in this connection is still largely true in the wider field of world politics. We have still the same distrust of one nation by another, the same pursuit of its own interest by every nation tempered only by considerations of expediency, the same efforts to secure alliances with the same cynical disregard of them in self-interests, the same kind of intelligence service maintained by one nation in the territory of another which we find referred to in the *Artha-sastra*. The present day cold war tactics are not essentially different from what the text recommends to the *vijigisu* [one who desires victory] when placed in similar situations. . . . It is difficult to see how rivalry and the struggle for supremacy between the nations can be avoided and the teaching of this *sastra* which is based on these basic facts rendered altogether superfluous until some sort of a one world government or an effective supra-national authority is established. The arrival of the nuclear age might hasten the advent of such an authority by the strengthening of the United Nations. But until that happens, the teaching of the *sastra* would in actual practice be followed by the nations, though it may be unknown to them and though it may be openly condemned by those that know it.[96]

DISARMAMENT

For Gandhians (at least those who understand nonviolence as an absolute principle), both universal and unilateral disarmament would be required. We have already noted that for Gandhi the lesson of Hiroshima was either universal disarmament or suicide. After independence, Indian policy followed (in this regard) the Gandhian path. In 1986, India participated in the Five-Continent Six-Nation Initiative for Nuclear Disarmament and followed this up with the Rajiv Gandhi Plan for the elimination of nuclear weapons in the United Nations. As late as March 1996, India stated to the Conference on Disarmament that "we are . . . convinced that the existence of nuclear weapons diminishes international security. We, therefore, seek their complete elimination."[97]

But for just war–oriented Hindus, universal disarmament would be a universal moral imperative, whereas unilateral disarmament would be morally objectionable. An example of this position is Rajnikanta Verma's argument that India refrained from developing nuclear weapons for many years because it supported universal disarmament, but that doing so only encouraged countries with weapons to keep them. Those countries lacked any motivation for disarmament. They found it advantageous to encourage nonproliferation among nonnuclear countries. As a result, India had to choose between being at the mercy of nuclear countries, including ones in its own region, or its independence.[98]

One ingenious approach creates scope for having nuclear technology and at the same time working actively for disarmament. In *Nuclear Menace: The Satyagraha Approach*, Eric A. Vas, Keshav S. Pendse, and Anil A. Athale discuss the problems of nuclear proliferation and disarmament on the eve of the 1998 tests. The three retired military officers begin this way: "That there are many Indians . . . who would want India to be totally at the mercy of the Big Five, is an uncomfortable fact that one has to live with. Partly these Indians take shelter behind the Gandhian concept of nonviolence, deliberately distorting the Mahatma's legacy. Gandhi advocated *satyagraha* from a position of strength and moral conviction and not fear of 'economic sanctions' as some of the present day 'followers' of his want."[99] The authors use Gandhi's idea that violence is better than inaction based on fear to give the semblance of Gandhian legitimacy for the development of nuclear weapons. A policy of abstaining from nuclear weapons, they aver, can be based only on the fear of economic reprisals by the superpowers.

Once they legitimate the acquisition of these weapons through their questionable logic, they take the moral high road. Declaring that nuclear weapons are weapons for genocide and crimes against humanity, they call on the UN Security Council to act as trustee by providing nuclear protection for countries that lack nuclear weapons. The United Nations would have to provide some way of accounting for and controlling production of fissile material. Finally, it would have to ban the use of nuclear weapons and ballistic missiles.[100] The authors would allow nations to maintain nuclear weapons (because terrorists could always develop them secretly) but not to use them, even for self-defense, unless doing so were cleared through the United Nations. They argue that Indians should use Gandhi's method of *satyagraha* to create a nuclear weapon–free world. India should declare a policy forbidding preemptive strikes and help an international body (such as the United Nations) make other countries adopt the same policy.

This would be in the Gandhian tradition requiring that both the means and the goal be moral (assuming that having weapons for deterrence is moral). Because the goal of disarmament is moral and just, they add, *satyagraha* should be used to mobilize the masses and wear down the resistance of adversaries, while maintaining openness and control over the movement. They admit that "harmonising all these factors and spreading the movement globally may well need another Gandhi. The basic point here is that India on its own cannot win this battle. Indians will have to be much more proactive and create public opinion worldwide in favour of sane policies."[101] That is, they will have to convert people to nonviolence.

INTERNATIONAL AGREEMENTS

Hindus have a premodern tradition of treaties to limit types of warfare. On the eve of war, for instance, both sides would sign a contract (*samaya*) with specific rules.[102] The importance of the virtue of telling the truth (*sat*) supports the principle of keeping faith with agreements in Hindu ethics. Hindus, therefore, have long been innovators in attempts to limit the devastating effects of war. But these treaties have always been based on fairness and equality. This is not the case, many Hindus argue, with contemporary treaties on nuclear weapons.[103]

According to Vas, Pendse, and Athale, the NPT, CTBT, and the treaty under discussion for fissile material production discriminate against non-nuclear powers. Therefore, they have no moral force and are doomed to fail.[104] The three writers express the opposition felt in India to the hypocrisy underlying international agreements noted earlier. India could not and still should not in good faith sign the NPT and CTBT.

Verma notes that India's refusal to sign has subjected it to much international criticism – based supposedly on the fiction of an international "will" – including calls for sanctions. He points out that India's case is different from those of many other countries. "India's position is unique in that it is surrounded by nuclear weapons, it does not have a credible nuclear umbrella provided by a military ally, and it has the capacity to develop its own nuclear deterrent. Surely, it would be highly irresponsible in these circumstances for any Government in India not to develop a nuclear deterrent."[105]

The nuclear states are even more devious, according to Verma, because they developed new measures (such as the Nuclear Suppliers Guidelines, Missile Technology Control Regime, and the Fissile Material Cut-Off Treaty) that would make it impossible for India to have nuclear weapons. India was forced to do nuclear testing in 1998 because that was the only way it could keep open its nuclear possibilities.[106] Verma concludes by arguing that India will pursue its own course toward disarmament, one that is compatible with the right of the democratically elected government to decide how to maintain India's security.

CONCLUSION

Because of its long history spanning some four millennia and moving from small-scale societies into states and empires, the Indian subcontinent has seen its fair share of wars – but not religious wars, thanks to a common rule that kings must support all the religions within their realm. It has also experienced a reaction to such warfare in the form of asceticism within both Hinduism and the other Indic religions. Aware of the dangers of these two extremes, Hindus have sought a middle path that recognizes the importance of defense for both the individual and the state. In the past, Hinduism encouraged the *ksatriya* caste to perform this duty for society in a contained and regulated manner. At the same time, Hinduism honored the nonviolent ethics of the ascetics, which was extended as an ideal to all other castes except *ksatriyas* under the aegis of *samanya-dharma*. As a result, the large scriptural tradition and its even larger commentarial tradition have become home to both an ethics of just war and an ethics of nonviolence.

Gandhi, in the name of still further religious progress, tried to extend the ethics of *ahimsa* to everyone (thereby including the old *ksatriya* warriors, which theoretically eliminated any military). Not all Hindus agreed with him (there were also violent revolutionaries in the fight for independence), and even more did not follow his course after Indian independence, when the reality of governing a state (with its need for police and military) once again assumed critical importance. The religion, after all, had already faced the experience of what happens to a state when it cannot defend itself, first in the classical age and later under Muslim and British rule.

It might appear surprising that Hindus have not offered a sustained ethical commentary on WMD, either pro or con, in the wake of the 1998 nuclear tests. Yet this should not be misunderstood. The lack of principled Hindu positions in the immediate wake of the tests is best explained by the fact that ethics is not a separate branch of knowledge in Indian philosophy, and so it is unlikely that scholars would write from within a specifically ethical framework. In addition, the Indian intelligentsia – centered in influential English-medium universities – is largely socialist/Marxist and concerned about what is perceived as a Hindu threat to the secular state and a growing Hindu fundamentalism (what Kanti Bajpai calls "political Hinduism" in the next chapter).

Still, even in the absence of much systematic moral debate, it is possible to discern two emerging positions among Hindus. One is the realist tradition of the *Artha-sastra*: Self-defense is absolutely necessary for the state, dictated by the policies of others. Arvind Sharma observes:

The manner in which a tradition chooses to interpret its scripture, or the option it adopts in terms of conflict-resolution is not done in a vacuum. At the moment the issue of power, force and nonviolence both within India and in relation to powers outside India cannot be assessed independently of the other powers involved. The other parties involved in India are the Sikhs and the Muslims, both of whom favour militancy.[107]

A second perspective, perhaps the one that will prevail in the long run, is a modern version of the just war tradition, with emphasis on nuclear weapons for deterrence. It is important to remember that Hindu thinkers have had a long history of reflection on the ethics of violence and nonviolence, and we can rest assured that principled Hindu positions (and there could be several) will be forthcoming.

Notes

1. I have tried to trace Oppenheimer's interest in the *Bhagavad Gita*. He may have been introduced to this work at the Ethical Culture School in New York, which he attended from the second grade. This school promoted nonsectarian ethical principles, especially in its Sunday-morning meetings. It is also possible, given Oppenheimer's literary and philosophical interests, that he encountered the *Gita* during his Harvard years. A few months before Hiroshima, Oppenheimer quoted from it in his remarks at a memorial service for President Franklin D. Roosevelt (Los Alamos, April 15, 1945): "In the Hindu Scripture, in the Bhagavad-Gita, it says, 'Man is a creature whose substance is faith. What his faith is, he is.'" Alice Kimball Smith and Charles Weiner, *Robert Oppenheimer: Letters and Recollections* (Cambridge: Harvard University Press, 1980), 288. Robert Jungk, *Brighter Than a Thousand Suns: The Moral and Political History of the Atomic Scientists* (London: Victor Gollancz, 1958), 198, recounts the popularized version of events in the early morning hours of July 16, 1945: "People were transfixed at the power of the explosion. Oppenheimer was clinging to one of the uprights in the

control room. A passage from the *Bhagavad Gita*, the sacred epic of the Hindus, flashed into his mind: If the radiance of a thousand suns were to burst into the sky, that would be like the splendour of the mighty One . . . Yet, when the sinister and gigantic cloud rose up in the far distance over Point Zero, he was reminded of another line from the same source: I am become Death, the shatterer of worlds. Sri Krishna, the Exalted One, lord of the fate of mortals, had uttered the phrase." Oppenheimer also quoted this line from the *Gita* in a speech that was filmed after the test. The film was edited so that only the last part of the quotation "I am become Death . . ." is heard.

2. Raghavan Iyer, ed., *The Moral and Political Writings of Mahatma Gandhi*, vol. 2: *Truth and Non-violence* (Oxford: Clarendon, 1986), 13.

3. Ibid., 455.

4. Ibid., 455. See also ibid., 503, citing *Harijan*, February 10, 1946; ibid., 120, citing *Biharni Komi Agman*, 216–17; and ibid., 457, citing *Biharni Komi Agman*, 253–54.

5. Ramachandra Guha, "An Incomplete Iconography," *Indian Express*, June 1, 1998.

6. For this history, see George Perkovich, *India's Nuclear Bomb: The Impact on Global Proliferation* (Oxford: Oxford University Press, 1999).

7. Alison Barr and Erik Jorgensen, "Chronology of Pakistani Missile Development" (Monterey, Calif.: Center for Nonproliferation Studies, Monterey Institute of International Studies), 1998, at http://cns.miis.edu/research/india/pakchron.htm (December 3, 2003). See also "Chronology of Indian Missile Development" by the same source at http://cns.miis.edu/research/india/indiach2.htm (December 3, 2003).

8. See Joseph Cirincione et al., *Deadly Arsenals: Tracking Weapons of Mass Destruction* (Washington, D.C.: Carnegie Endowment for International Peace, 2002), 191–99.

9. Arvind Sharma, "Gandhi or Godse? Power, Force and Non-violence," in *Ethical and Political Dilemmas of Modern India*, ed. Ninian Smart and Shivesh Thakur (New York: St. Martin's, 1993), 26.

10. I thank Ashok Chowgle for making available to me his files of newspaper clippings on this topic and for facilitating interviews with supporters of the BJP's position when I was doing research for this article in Mumbai (December 2000). My conclusions on Hindu views in the wake of the 1998 tests are based on the content analysis of more than 100 articles and editorials in the years 1998–2000. Page numbers were not recorded for all these articles in Chowgle's files; as a result, I have not provided them in my citations.

11. See Katherine K. Young, "The Indian Secular State under Hindu Attack: A New Perspective on the Crisis of Legitimation," in Smart and Thakur, eds., *Ethical and Political Dilemmas of Modern India*, 194–234.

12. John Cherian, "The BJP and the Bomb," *Frontline* 15:8 (April 11–24, 1998).

13. Ascetics are believed to have extraordinary power from yogic discipline and self-denial (the word for asceticism is *tapas*; it denotes heat or energy and connotes power). Some orders of ascetics have been warriors. A recent expression of this militancy was the participation of ascetics in the destruction of the Babri Mosque in Ayodhya, which was widely perceived by Hindus as an act of restoring Hindu power after centuries of domination.

14. "Saffron Bomb," *Telegraph* 17:347 (June 24, 1999).

15. Rajnikanta Verma, "A Credible Nuclear Deterrent," in *India's Crisis Resolution: The Nuclear Issue*, ed. Ajit Jain and N. K. Wagle, South Asian Studies Occasional Series No. 4 (Toronto: Centre for South Asian Studies, University of Toronto, 1998).

16. "Anti-nuke Rally from Pokhran to Sarnath to Begin on May 11," *Asian Age*, May 5–6, 1999.

17. Ibid.

18. Prakash Karat, "A Lethal Link," *Frontline*, June 19, 1998.

19. K. R. Malkani, "India, China and the Bomb," *Hindustan Times*, June 3, 1998.

20. David Frawley, "India's Nuclear Tests, Gandhi and Non-violence" (published in the *Organizer* and *BJP Today*); see www.vedanet.com/India.htm (December 3, 2003).

21. Ibid. It is important to point out that although there were no invasions outside the subcontinent, there were many aggressive wars within it, for dynasties were constantly vying for power and land. Stephen Rosen, a modern historian of India's military, argues that brahmin control over the warrior class prevented it from making military decisions and was thus partly responsible for the ineffectiveness of Indian armies. He argues that war was common throughout Indian history. This was partly because armies tended to replicate the general social structure (caste), making it difficult to unify the various castes and control the locally dominant ones. The resulting problems included fission, rebellions, and lack of trust needed to coordinate military maneuvers. In addition, military weakness occurred because brahmanical control over the military (symbolized by the idea that *dharma* regulates *artha*) meant the army could never develop an independent view based on military knowledge. In modern times, the civilian government has controlled the army and made decisions about nuclear weapons. Stephen Peter Rosen, *Societies and Military Power: India and Its Armies* (Ithaca, N.Y.: Cornell University Press, 1996).

22. Ibid.

23. Swapan Dasgupta, "Character-Building Nukes," *India Today*, May 25, 1998.

24. Sharma, "Gandhi or Godse?" 24.

25. The fact that *dharma* places moral constraints on *artha* reflects the relation between two major elite groups in India: the *brahmana* (i.e., brahmin, or priestly and intellectual) caste, whose domain traditionally was *dharma*; and the *ksatriya* (warrior) caste, whose domain traditionally was political rule and protection of the state. Warfare was therefore related only indirectly to religion; there were no religious wars per se in India, because the king was supposed to protect all religions within his realm.

26. The *Atharva-veda* brahmins were closely connected to the kings. The *Atharva-veda* describes the role of the king as leader in battle. He receives tribute from those he has conquered and ensures agricultural success, general prosperity, and peace. The *Atharva-veda* brahmins performed rituals and advised the king to ensure these goals.

27. The fact that these have been listed as both virtues and principles can be explained by the fact that classical Sanskrit developed a lingistic preference for

nominalization, thereby transforming the earlier injunctions (derived from imperatives of ritual action) into nouns and therefore virtues.

28. Hindus also classify authority as follows: valid means of knowledge (*pramana*), sense perception (*pratyaksa*), inference (*anumana*), scripture (*sabda*), analogy (*upamana*), hypothetical supposition (*arthapatti*), and nonperception (*abhava*).

29. *Dharmanam gatim suksmam duranvayam. Mahabharata* 8.49.28.

30. *Dharmasya tatvam nihitam guhayam.* Cited by B. K. Matilal, "Moral Dilemmas: Insights from Indian Epics," in *Moral Dilemmas in the Mahabharata*, ed. Bimal Krishna Matilal (Delhi: Motilal Banarsidass, 1989), 17.

31. One of the four Hindu *varnas* (castes) is the *ksatriya*. It formed the military core, although the *Artha-sastra* says that *vaisyas* and *sudras* may form fighting units. *Artha-sastra* 9.2.21–24.

32. *Artha* denotes aim or purpose and connotes livelihood or occupation, as well as the acquisition and protection of the state.

33. *Dharmarthau dharmakamau ca kamarthau capyapidayan*, in *Mahabharata* 9:59.18; cited by Y. Krishan, "The Meaning of the Purusarthas in the *Mahabharata*," in Matilal, ed., *Moral Dilemmas in the Mahabharata*, 55.

34. *Kausitaki-brahmana* XX.8.6.

35. See *Mahabharata* 8.49.22, 8.66.62–63, 7.118.7–8, 7.131.3, and the discussion in V. R. Ramachandra Dikshitar, *War in Ancient India*, 2nd ed. (Delhi: Motilal Banarsidass, 1948).

36. Dikshitar, *War in Ancient India*, 61.

37. Megasthenes, a Greek ambassador to India in the fourth century B.C.E., observed: "Whereas among other nations it is usual in the contests of war to ravage the soil and thus reduce it to an uncultivated waste, among the Indians, on the contrary, by whom husbandmen are regarded as a class that is sacred and inviolable, the tillers of the soil, even when battle is raging in their neighbourhood, are undisturbed by any sense of danger, for the combatants on either side in waging the conflict make carnage of each other, but allow those engaged in husbandry to remain quite unmolested. Besides, they neither ravage an enemy's land with fire, nor cut down its trees. Nor would an enemy coming upon a husbandman at work on land do him harm, for men of this class, being regarded as public benefactors, are protected from all injury." Cited in Dikshitar, *War in Ancient India*, 71–72.

38. I thank Kanti Bajpai (see Chapter 16 below) for characterizing this type of Hindu ethics as prudential and inspiring me to think about this principle.

39. *Na tatparesu kurvita janannapriyamatmanah. Mahabharata* 12.251.19; cited by Y. Krishnan, "Meaning of the Purusarthas in the *Mahabharata*," 55.

40. *Yadyadatmani iccheta tatparasyapi cintayeta. Mahabharata* 12.251.21; cited by Y. Krishnan, "Meaning of the Purusarthas in the *Mahabharata*," 55.

41. The *Bhagavad Gita* is found in the *Mahabharata*, Bhismaparvan 23–40.

42. *Bhagavad Gita* 1.46.

43. Ibid., 2.27.

44. Ibid., 2:19.

45. Hindu art, for instance, reveals a deep (yogic) passivity (the contemplative visage), yet expresses action, even violent action within the world (represented in some forms by many arms with hands holding weapons).

46. M. M. Agarawal, "Arjuna's Moral Predicament," in Matilal, ed., *Moral Dilemmas in the Mahabharata*, 136–37.

47. M. A. Mehendale, *Reflections on the Mahabharata War* (Shimla: Indian Institute of Advanced Study, 1995).

48. "Some of the rules, like throwing a challenge, fighting words with words, engaging an equal in a duel, not killing the spectators and opponents under certain conditions, were scrupulously observed by both parties. But it becomes immediately evident that some of the above rules were not followed with regard to ordinary soldiers. These soldiers were attacked by heroes superior to them in every respect and were also killed even when fleeing for life. It must also be observed that charioteers and horses – who were not supposed to be attacked at all – were ruthlessly attacked and even killed by all the major heroes from both sides. . . . The conclusion, therefore, can only be that from the point of view of the observance of the rules of war, the *Mahabharata* war cannot be called a *dharma-yuddha*, the heroes on both sides having to share the responsibility for this." Mehendale, *Reflections on the Mahabharata War*, 23.

49. Julian F. Woods, *Destiny and Human Initiative in the Mahabharata* (Albany: State University of New York Press, 2001), 12.

50. Mehendale, *Reflections on the Mahabharata War*, 65.

51. I would like to thank my colleague, Arvind Sharma, for providing these comparative insights on the two epics.

52. In his commentary on *Bhagavad Gita* 3:20, Sankara suggests that some *ksatriyas* have attained "right knowledge" without being *sannyasins*. But they abide in perfection accompanied by action (in other words, even though they are liberated, they continue to act). Needed to rule the world, they continue to act within the world (*loka-sangraha*) because of their past *karma* (*parabdha-karma*).

53. Mahatma Gandhi, *Harijan* (October 3, 1936), 265.

54. See Mahadev Desai, *The Gita According to Gandhi* (Ahmedabad: Navajivan, 1946). This is a translation and interpretation by Gandhi's secretary, which grew out of Gandhi's many discussions of the *Bhagavad Gita*.

55. There have been many debates over the origins of Gandhi's ethics. Paul Hacker sees Gandhi's source for *ahimsa* primarily in Tolstoy and only secondarily in Hinduism. See the discussion of Hacker's views in Wilhelm Halbfass, ed., *Philology and Confrontation: Paul Hacker on Traditional and Modern Vedanta* (Albany: State University of New York Press, 1995), 308. Hacker's assessment is a product of his thesis that neo-Hinduism is largely derived from Christianity.

56. See Klaus K. Klostermaier, *A Survey of Hindism* (Albany: State University of New York Press, 1994), 453–54.

57. M. K. Gandhi, *Truth Is God* (Ahmedabad: Navajivan, 1955), 14.

58. *Harijan* (April 28, 1946), 106; cited in M. K. Gandhi, *In Search of the Supreme* (Ahmedabad: Navajivan, 1961), 36.

59. M. K. Gandhi, "Letter to Adolf Hitler (Wardha 24 December 1940)," in the *Collected Works of Mahatma Gandhi*, vol. 73 (12 September 1940–15 April 1941) (Delhi: Government of India: Ministry of Information and Broadcasting, 1978), 253–55.

60. Ibid.

61. See Pyarelal [Nair], *Mahatma Gandhi: The Last Phase* (Ahmedabad: Navajivan, 1956), 2:506.

62. See ibid., 2:502.

63. Martin Buber, "A Letter to Gandhi (1939)," in *Nonviolence: A Reader in the Ethics of Action*, ed. George F. Estey and Doris A. Hunter (Waltham, Mass.: Xerox College Publishers, 1971), 146–47.

64. Ibid., 152.

65. The *sankaracaryas* are the heads of monastic orders that were supposedly founded by the famous Advaitin Sankara in the eighth century C.E.

66. Pujyasri Candrasekharandra Sarasvatisvami, *Hindu Dharma: The Universal Way of Life* (Mumbai: Bharatiya Vidya Bhavan, 2000), 704.

67. Ibid.

68. Ibid., 694.

69. There are some Hindu fundamentalists today who argue that the epic examples of WMD are not products of literary and ethical imagination but concrete evidence that India had this technology in the past.

70. *Ramayana*, Dvavimsah 5–16.

71. There are thirty-seven references in the *Mahabharata* to *brahmastra*. Considering all the other weapons causing mass destruction as well, the epic is a rich source that I plan to examine in further research.

72. Dikshitar, *War in Ancient India*, 59.

73. Ibid., 80.

74. *Mahabharata*, Aranyakaparvan 13–21.

75. Mehendale, *Reflections on the Mahabharata War*, 34–35.

76. *Asthiyatam jaye yogo dharmam utsrjya pandava. Mahabharata* 7.164.68.

77. Asvatthaman then had to apologize, admitting that it was a sin because his mind was full of rage. Asvatthaman's punishment for using the weapon was to roam the world for 3,000 years without companions and be inferior to all beings.

78. *Ramayana* 6.67.38.

79. Matilal, "Moral Dilemmas: Insights from Indian Epics," 10; citing *Mahabharata* 12.36.2.

80. This idea is developed in *Mahabharata*, Santiparvan, sec. 2.

81. T. S. Rukmani, "Moral Dilemmas in the *Mahabharata*," in Matilal, ed., *Moral Dilemmas in the Mahabharata*, 29–30.

82. Dikshitar, *War in Ancient India*, 59.

83. Ibid., 61.

84. R. P. Kangle, ed., *The Kautiliya Arthasastra* (Delhi: Motilal Banarsidass, 1988), 3:260–61. Otherwise, Kautilya upholds *samanya-dharmas* such as *ahimsa*. He "regards them as obligatory on individuals with as much sincerity as does Asoka [the Buddhist emperor who renounced all violence]. The only thing is that he does not agree that the conduct of public life should be guided by rules of individual morality. . . . [T]he preservation of the state at all costs is the foremost duty of the ruler and the interests of the state have to take precedence over all other considerations." Ibid., 3:281–82.

85. *Bhagavad Gita* 18.78.

86. *Mahabharata* 7.164.79.

87. Dikshitar, *War in Ancient India*, 87.

88. *Samabhasya prharatavyam. Mahabharata* 6.1.30; cited by Mehendale, *Reflections on the Mahabharata War,* 6.
89. Barun Sengupta, "Left Out of Security Debate," *The Pioneer,* June 4, 1998.
90. Kuldip Nayar, "Between Welfare and Weapons," *Indian Express,* August 31, 1999.
91. Arundhati Ghose, quoted in Abhijit Sinha, "If Clinton Comes with Respect, He Will Be Welcome," *Sunday Observer,* June 7–13, 1998.
92. This point was made many times in my interviews with Hindus in India during December 2000–January 2001.
93. *Yathayogam yathaviryam yathotsaham yathavayah prahartavyam. Mahabharata* 6.1.30.
94. Kangle, *Kautiliya Arthasastra,* 3:281–82.
95. Mehendale, *Reflections on the Mahabharata War,* 10.
96. Kangle, *Kautiliya Arthasastra,* 3:283.
97. Praful Bidwai, "Nuclear India: A Short History," in *Out of Nuclear Darkness: The Indian Case for Disarmament* (New Delhi: Colour Prints for MIND, Movement in India for Nuclear Disarmament, n.d.), 14.
98. Verma, "Credible Nuclear Deterrent," 9–10.
99. Eric A. Vas, Keshav S. Pendse, and Anil A. Athale, "Editor's Note," in *Nuclear Menace: The Satyagraha Approach* (Pune: Pune Initiative, Peace and Disarmament, 1997), 1.
100. Ibid., 141.
101. Ibid., 138–40.
102. *Tatas te samayam cakruh* and *dharmans ca samsthapayam asuh. Mahabharata* 6.1.26.33; cited by Mehendale, *Reflections on the Mahabharata War,* 6.
103. It was noted earlier that India has ratified both the Biological Weapons Convention and the Chemical Weapons Convention. These treaties created little controversy inside the country, perhaps because there were no perceived inequalities in them, as is the case with the Nonproliferation Treaty.
104. Vas et al., *Nuclear Menace,* 139.
105. Verma, "Credible Nuclear Deterrent," 10.
106. Ibid., 7–9.
107. Sharma, "Gandhi or Godse?" 24.

16

Hinduism and Weapons of Mass Destruction

Pacifist, Prudential, and Political

Kanti Bajpai

What kind of ethical stance do Hindus adopt toward weapons of mass destruction, especially nuclear weapons? Katherine Young's illuminating chapter suggests that, broadly speaking, Hinduism has two traditions of thought that speak to this question: a *pacifist*, Gandhian viewpoint that is repulsed by violence in virtually any form, including that perpetrated by nuclear weapons; and a more *prudential*, existential viewpoint that accepts the necessity of violence and nuclear weapons but seeks to constrain both. Young bases her analysis largely on classical Hindu texts as well as on the statements of Mahatma Gandhi and contemporary Indian officials and analysts.

Is there anything that one could add to her fine, path-breaking analysis? The sources of Hindu thought and practice are many, and Young would admit that there are other classical texts from which one could extrapolate Hindu stances toward nuclear weapons and organized violence.[1] In this chapter, I argue that there is a third source of Hindu thinking on nuclear weapons, namely, contemporary *political* Hinduism, or Hindutva. I use "political Hinduism" or "Hindutva" to refer to the pronouncements and writings associated with the conglomerate of political groups known as the Sangh Parivar.[2] Young gestures at some of its perceptions. This chapter attempts to describe the historiography within which political Hinduism thinks about nuclear weapons and to analyze an influential text of political Hinduism for what it says about international relations and the problem of war and peace. It suggests that there is a nuclear "third way" among Hindus, and it is certainly not pacifist nor particularly prudential. It arises from a highly political stance that draws not on classical Hindu texts but rather on a narrative about the past, present, and future of the Hindu community that is a quite different "text."

ETHICS AND NUCLEAR WEAPONS IN INDIA AFTER
THE MAY 1998 TESTS

By way of preface, it should be said that the Sangh Parivar and its growing band of supporters clearly endorse India's acquisition of nuclear weapons.[3] The BJP had long promised to give India nuclear weapons, and its supporters took jubilantly to the streets when India tested in May 1998. This is unique in global nuclear history. It is hard to think of any other society, except neighboring Pakistan, that had such a public and popular display of *jouissance* over the testing of nuclear weapons.[4] Young, mostly Hindu, men danced in the streets, distributed *laddus* to passers-by, and held noisy rallies under banners inscribed in English that were evidently addressed to an international television audience (judging by the nature of the defiant slogans on display).[5] It should be said that these demonstrations were largely spontaneous and were not orchestrated by the ruling National Democratic Alliance (NDA) led by the Hindu nationalist Bharatiya Janata Party (BJP).[6]

Nearly five years after the tests, political Hinduism has not advanced any explicit and self-consciously ethical reflections on nuclear weapons. Young notes that there is a dilemma at the heart of Hindu ethics in terms of the tension between the pacifist and prudential tradition. The theoreticians of political Hinduism do not appear to see nuclear weapons as posing any very serious ethical dilemmas or challenges. The utility of nuclear weapons for India is regarded as self-evident in a world where others have them. India's earlier opposition to nuclear weapons, its strategic, political, and legal objection to them, and the principled Gandhian rejection of them as an abomination are cited as evidence that India went nuclear only in extremis.[7] To this extent, political Hinduism shares something with the prudential Hindu view of nuclear weapons, namely, that nuclear weapons were forced on India.

Critics of the nuclear tests, who could have used ethical arguments in support of their objections, have not done so. There was some discomfiture among Gandhians in May 1998, but few criticized the tests, and fewer still, if any, have written about the ethical unacceptability of nuclear weapons.[8] To the extent that an ethical argument against nuclear weapons has been advanced, it has come from secular-minded critics, most prominently the novelist and activist Arundhati Roy and two well-known journalists-cum-activists, Praful Bidwai and Achin Vanaik.[9] Needless to say, the secular critique, as Young rightly notes, does not base itself on Hindu ethics. The Movement in India for Nuclear Disarmament (MIND), representing a coalition of activists and nongovernmental organizations, has also opposed the tests and nuclearization, but its objections are absent ethical arguments.[10]

In sum, political Hinduism has avoided any very serious engagement with the ethics of weapons of mass destruction, at least ethics in the sense that we have come to think of it in the academy in relation to the usability of nuclear weapons, the morality of deterrence, and the imperatives as well as limits of violence. Critics of nuclearization too have based their arguments on "pragmatic" considerations and, with the exception noted above, have avoided ethical/moral statements.

POLITICAL HINDUISM, HISTORY, AND NUCLEAR WEAPONS: A THOUGHT EXPERIMENT

Is there not an ethics concealed within political Hinduism's view of nuclear weapons? Is the advocacy of nuclear weapons not itself based on some kind of ethical stance? Imagine a theoretician of political Hinduism and how she or he would state the argument for India's nuclearization. It would go something like the following:

Hindu civilization was a glorious historical project. Beginning with the Muslim invasions of about 1100 C.E., it fell on hard times. Internal dissension among Hindus allowed Muslim invaders to defeat much stronger Hindu rulers. Superior technology, ruthlessness, and trickery allowed the Muslims gradually to conquer most of India. They used the force of arms to convert Hindus and to destroy their cultural artifacts. Hindus not only converted but also in many cases collaborated with the ruling Muslims out of self-interest. Hinduism went into decline. Hindus lost confidence in their own abilities and culture and developed a servile and fatalistic mentality.

In the seventeenth century, the Europeans arrived in India, and within a century the British wiped out Muslim rule. Superior technology, ruthlessness, and trickery once again were the undoing of the rulers of India, this time the Muslims. The British played a dual role. On the one hand, they conquered India and thus denied the Hindus, once again, the opportunity to take control. On the other hand, they defeated Muslim power and gave Hindus a chance to escape the domination of the Muslims. Even as Hindus escaped Muslim rule, though, they continued to play the slavish role they had become used to under Muslim rule. Some converted to Christianity, many took to Western education and culture, but more importantly, large numbers of Hindus collaborated with British rule. With Westernization and modernization, their civilizational memory continued to wane and their confidence in Hindu culture dissipated and declined.

Beginning sometime in the nineteenth century, however, a Hindu renaissance of sorts began. Hindus embarked on a voyage of rediscovery. The nationalist movement had some positive elements in this respect. However, its insistence on a secular, liberal nationalism was dangerous because it played down the interests of the Hindu majority. The nationalist movement should have been a great awakening for Hindu culture and power. Unfortunately, the Congress Party under Gandhi and Nehru took the wrong path. More than the British, it was the Congress that appeased the Muslims and allowed Muslim power once again to assert itself in India. The result was Partition and the vivisection of the sacred space of India.

With Partition, Hindus had a chance to come into their own. India was finally independent, and Hindus were the largest community in the new nation. However, the pseudosecular Hindus in the Congress, along with their leftist collaborators, continued to appease Muslims. They did so by being soft on Pakistan and by ignoring the interests and feelings of the majority Hindus while catering to the demands of the Muslim community (as well as other minorities), who combined with the secularists to stop political Hinduism from coming to power. Independence should have resulted in the emancipation of Hindus and the flowering of their once great civilization under the auspices of the Indian state. Instead, Hindus once again languished. Externally, China and Pakistan, individually and in combination, humiliated India in a variety of ways, as India refused to develop its military power. The West, which could have been an ally, turned against India in reaction to Nehru's policy of nonalignment. With time, the West developed contempt for a weak and vacillating India spellbound by nonalignment and Nehruvian idealism. Internally, schisms grew under the pseudo-secularist Congress, in Kashmir, Punjab, and the northeast of India. China, then Pakistan, and even the West took advantage of India's internal troubles to advance their own interests and keep India weak.

Finally, tired of the mess created by the Congress and its leftist allies, Hindus and others in India turned to political Hinduism to restore dignity and order to India and to the majority Hindu community, which is the mainstay of a stable, strong, and united India. Nuclear testing, which the BJP's precursor, the Jana Sangh, had argued for since the 1950s, was a turning point, not so much because it strengthened India militarily against China and Pakistan but rather because it represented a new Hindu confidence, a willingness to sacrifice for a larger cause, and a sign that Hinduism would not be cowed by anyone.[11]

This historiography has several underlying general themes. The first is that of a glorious civilization gone astray under the weight of its own fallibilities and the exploitation of those fallibilities by ruthless, powerful outsiders. The second relates to a defeated civilization's repeated loss of coherence and confidence as a result of its military and political defeat and its intellectual and cultural subordination to its conquerors. The third theme is of periodic opportunities for emancipation and redemption that came the way of a wounded civilization, opportunities that were squandered by the continuing mental enslavement and material backwardness of its people. The fourth theme is a more triumphalist one that describes the growing assertion and anger of this subordinated civilization, which finally casts off its own disunity, apathy, and weakness to ascend to its rightful position in the conclave of great cultures.

Together these four themes make up a momentous narrative – of decline, fall, and redemption, of chance, circumstance, and choice, of serendipitous happenings and repetitious cycles, and of tragedy and triumph. How political Hinduism sees nuclear weapons has to be seen within this epic-like historiography.

Arguments about the strategic utility of nuclear weapons (and other WMD) and the ethical dilemmas posed by these weapons will have to confront our Hindu theoretician's likely response:

We Hindus know that nuclear weapons may not solve all our military and diplomatic problems. We know also that nuclear weapons are terrible instruments and that their use would be devastating. We recognize that as long as nuclear weapons exist they may be used – accidentally or by unauthorized and irrational personnel. Our own tradition has principles by which the possession of nuclear weapons must be judged unethical. It also has traditions by which nuclear weapons can at best be seen as a regrettable necessity. However, we must weigh all these concerns and points of view against the terrible dispossession, loss, and humiliation of a great people that is struggling to recover its place in the world, a people that even now is under threat. History has given us the opportunity to develop and deploy a technology that will allow us to recover militarily. It has also given us the opportunity to redeem ourselves morally by giving us the chance to resist those who would deny us this technology and our place in the sun. It would be irresponsible and in the end unethical for our rulers not to join the fight for military equality and give our civilization a chance at material and moral revival. Nuclear ethics is a small thing compared with the ethical imperatives of a great human struggle for emancipation and resurgence over one thousand years.

Our imaginary Hindu theoretician, steeped in the historiography we have sketched in here, would answer the various questions considered in this volume in the following terms. The possession of nuclear weapons is a necessity for the Hindu/Indian people who have been dispossessed materially and psychologically. Nuclear weapons should be "used" primarily as a deterrent, but they may also have to be used in actual fact as a means of defense.[12] If others have nuclear weapons, India must have them too, especially since those who have them or are developing them (Pakistan, China, and the West) threaten Indian independence and culture. Disarmament may be feasible, but its desirability depends on whether or not individual groups and nations are made more secure, materially and culturally, by giving up these weapons. Inequalities of power and the ability to coerce others are not necessarily abolished by disarmament; indeed, they may be increased in some cases.[13] Treaties and agreements (as in arms control) are legitimate methods of restraining the spread and use of nuclear weaponry, but those who propose such accords have a history of manipulation and deceit (namely, the Western powers) going back 500 years when they came ostensibly in search of trade and commerce and stayed on to conquer and plunder.[14] In short, for our theoretician, nuclear weapons have to be seen in the *longue durée* of history. Given the travails of Hindus over the past thousand years, the dubious behavior of others in the past (e.g., using subterfuge and manipulation to defeat Hindus on and off the battlefield), and the present threats to India, the Indian state is free to use any methods to protect itself, including the development and use of nuclear weapons.

However, for our theoretician, the questions being asked in this volume are in large part the wrong questions. Nuclear weapons are not primarily about the harnessing of a technology for military purposes. They are a vital symbol in a political and cultural contest going back a thousand years and going forward who knows how long. They encapsulate an attitude toward the

Self and the Other that Hindus perforce must adopt, given the hard knocks of history. This is an ethics, if a hard-bitten one. Nuclear weapons signify an ethics of opposed and unalterable forces pitted against each other, unable to change, forgive, and reconcile. There is little here of the Gandhian pacifism or the tragic existentialism that Young portrays.

M. S. GOLWALKER AND THE ETHICS OF POLITICAL HINDUISM: A TEXT

Are there any writings in the tradition of political Hinduism that we could use to substantiate our suggestion that its ethics is a rather hard-bitten one? The most extensive writings available in English are those of M. S. Golwalker, who succeeded K. S. Hegdewar as head of the Rashtriya Swayamsevak Sangh (RSS). The RSS is the organizational center of contemporary political Hinduism, and Golwalker remains its most important theoretician, at least in terms of his writings. In particular, *A Bunch of Thoughts*, a compilation of his best-known essays, deals fairly extensively with international relations and the problems of war and peace.

Golwalker's basic view of international relations is an extremely Hobbesian/Darwinian one that any arch-realist would recognize. Thus, he writes:

> We find in this wide world that there is never any real peace. In fact it is always in a state of intermittent strife. And peace is only an interval between two wars. Conflict is in the very nature of mankind as it is constituted today.... [D]eath and destruction are in the very nature of this world.... Whatever the strategy the basic rule of relations between nations is the law of the jungle – the strong feeding upon the weak and getting stronger.... the big fish devouring the small fish and becoming bigger at the cost of the smaller.[15]

In such a world, Golwalker argues that the Palmerstonian dictum holds all too well: There are no permanent friends, only permanent interests.[16] How then should nations behave? What are their strategic choices in such a remorseless world?

For Golwalker, the answer is clear. History shows that the only way to protect oneself is through strength, including military strength. Pacifism is either cowardice or foolishness, in the absence of strength.[17] Rules and institutions favor the great nations and will not protect the interests of the weaker ones.[18] Allying with stronger powers can only be enslavement.[19] Nations must therefore be strong and self-reliant: "The only basis for our free and prosperous national life is invincible national strength – a strength that will strike terror into the hearts of aggressive powers and make other nations seek our friendship. Strength is the very elixir of national life."[20] To be weak, Golwalker intones, "is the most heinous sin in this world, as that would destroy oneself and also incite feelings of violence in others."[21]

What is national strength? What does it consist of? National strength is "the consolidated, dedicated and disciplined life of the people as a whole. After all, the various spheres of national life are only so many manifestations of the innate strength of the people. Political power is one such manifestation. Military power is the well-disciplined, intensely patriotic and heroic attitude of the people."[22] A massive mobilization of society is the surest source of national strength: "All our efforts have therefore to be concentrated in the direction of generating invincible national strength by making our people nationally conscious and moulding them all for a well-disciplined, co-ordinated and invincibly powerful national entity...."[23] Golwalker understands of course that real, material, economic and military power must be available in dealing with one's adversaries and protecting oneself, but he notes, "it is not the gun but the heart behind it that fights."[24]

If war comes, how should one fight? Golwalker's view is that war should be prosecuted coldly and calculatedly in the service of complete victory. When threatened by wicked, adharmic forces, the response must be rational, bold, and total. This is evident in many places in Golwalker's text. For instance, Golwalker suggests that reaction and self-sacrifice as a strategic response is one of the main failings of the Hindu approach to life. Hindus look to great men to save and protect them. Confronted by calamity and challenges, they turn to self-sacrifice, as the heroic Rajputs did against superior opponents.[25] However, according to Golwalker, Hindu philosophy, as distinct from the actual historical practices of Hindus, does not hold martyrdom to be the supreme value: "In our Bharatiya tradition, ... immolation is not considered as the highest ideal. We have not looked upon ... martyrdom as the highest point of greatness to which man should aspire."[26] Martyrdom is "suicidal" and "a sad chapter" in the "Bharatiya tradition."[27] Why? Because looking to great men and choosing martyrdom is symptomatic of a reactive view of life: "Intelligent and mature men do not merely react to circumstances. They boldly act with a will to make circumstances their slave."[28] In war, then, as in all spheres of social life, one must be coldly calculative and bold, and always keep in mind that the goal is victory. Everything must be subordinated to victory in the service of survival and righteousness. That is "true *dharma*."[29]

Not surprisingly, Golwalker questions the idea that dharmic restraints on fighting are always applicable. Contingencies and circumstances matter, and in particular the ultimate goal of victory over wickedness must be uppermost in guiding behavior: The ends can justify the means. Killing a woman during a fight, Golwalker notes, is "supposed to be against our *kshatra dharma*." *Kshatra dharma* also enjoins one "to fight the enemy in the open" rather than by covert means. It is also adharmic to attack an "unarmed and chariotless adversary."[30] But surely, Golwalker reasons, the injunction against killing a woman does not apply to a "demoness." Thus, Rama killed the demoness, Tataka, and shot Vali from behind a tree.[31] And Krishna urged Arjun to slay his opponent Karna when Karna dismounted his chariot that was stuck in the mud. What justifies Krishna's arguments is his understanding that "his [Krishna's] ultimate duty [is] ... establishing the rule of righteousness by destroying the wicked."[32] Those who are wicked or adharmic cannot expect the protection of dharmic, that is, restrained, behavior.[33]

Who are the wicked and thus undeserving of restraint? India, if not the world, confronts a number of wicked-minded forces. There are "demoniac forces of evil [that] are strutting about the world stage, armed with world-destructive weapons and threatening the very future of humanity."[34] This presumably refers to all the nuclear and great powers. However, Golwalker's reference to these powers is *en passant*. The real enemies, in his strategic cosmology, are Communist China and Pakistan, as they are particularly perfidious and dangerous. China is the "yellow peril," "expansionist," and "a grave peril to humanity." It is also communist, which is an "intensely aggressive, expansionist and imperialistic ideology." The Chinese "do not possess even normal human qualities like kindness, pity or respect for human life." Thus, "the technique used against a civilized people like the British is of no use in dealing with the Chinese."[35]

As for Pakistan, it is the "green danger." Pakistanis are dangerous because they are Muslims, and Muslims are dangerous because they are aggressive and violent. Thus, Golwalker notes that "it is always the Muslim who strikes first and it is the Hindu who bears the brunt."[36] Like China, Pakistan infiltrates and subverts India and uses Indians for their own ends. Whereas the Chinese use the communists and other malcontents within India, the Pakistanis use the Muslims of India as a "fifth column."[37] Pakistanis, in addition, are insatiable. "History" reveals that "countless were the experiments made to 'win their hearts' by patting their backs and showering concessions upon them. Finally we even gave them parts of our motherland. Even then they were not satisfied. They attacked Kashmir."[38] Before long, Golwalker warns, they will covet Assam and Bengal as well.[39]

How does one fight such wickedness? With boldness and unstinting perseverance. The best defense, Golwalker quotes approvingly, is offense. If necessary, one should be prepared to cross international frontiers and take the fight to the enemy, deep into its territory.[40] One should also be prepared to give refuge to the internal opponents of one's adversaries and urge and equip them to fight.[41] Above all, war should be total, with no holding back until complete victory is achieved. Reacting to the war with China in 1962, Golwalker urged, "Let all persons physically fit be ready for military service. And let their mothers bless and send forth their sons at this hour of trial."[42] Elsewhere, he writes: "In order that we may mobilize our entire internal resources and liquidate all types of internal forces of subversion and fight till the enemy is completely vanquished and the yellow scourge [i.e., China] erased from the face of the earth, the one great and inexhaustible storehouse of power that we have to build up is the sterling national character of the people."[43]

With respect to Pakistan, Golwalker suggests that those who argued in the 1965 war that India should simply destroy Pakistan's war-making capacity were grievously wrong. Instead, India should have liberated the Pakistani-occupied part of Kashmir and captured all its major cities. The root of the problem in Pakistan's case is not armaments but rather an "evil propensity." To cut out this root, it is "inevitable to annihilate the support [of the propensity] – the evil persons." This means that Pakistan – or at least those parts of Pakistan that are restive under Punjabi domination – should be liberated and brought back into India.[44] India should not be lulled by the end of hostilities. It should prepare for and indeed initiate war as soon as possible given that "warmongering nations have always utilized the recess after a war to prepare for a much bigger further war."[45] Pakistan occupies Indian territory and continues to harass India militarily in various ways even after the cease-fire. "This," Golwalker holds, "is a situation insulting to us in the extreme. It is intolerable. It should not be allowed to hang on like this for long. There should be some finality about it. The issue should be decided once and for all."[46] Golwalker not only seems to be proposing a final reckoning of some kind but also, apparently, justifying preventive war. Later in the text, he writes: "It would be futile – nay, it would be only inviting further and bigger troubles – if we merely take up a defensive posture and somehow try to save our skins; we should, on the contrary, vanquish such an evil enemy completely; not because we harbor any territorial ambitions but to put an end, once for all, to his capacity to indulge in his anti-human crimes.... Such a total victory ought to be our aim." Golwalker goes on to justify this view in terms of ancient Hindu teachings that say of enemies, "Even their smallest traces will have to eliminated."[47]

Golwalker's interest in total war is not just as a military instrument that is unavoidable in the modern world. It is, in addition, as a psychological and political instrument. Total war is total in terms of its war aims but also in the way that it involves the entire population of a country. For a country that is used to being passive and divided, though, total war is much more: It is an opportunity to restore its honor and pride and to consolidate itself politically. Thus, Golwalker writes of the war with China in 1962: "It is a fact that foreign aggression affords a golden opportunity for a nation to purge itself of corroding tendencies like selfishness, internecine feuds, separatist pulls, etc., and to recast itself into a single unified and purified entity."[48] So also the war with Pakistan was an opportunity for total war and nation building:

Such a total war, unlike the present limited one [i.e., the 1965 war] would have involved every one of our countrymen in active participation in an all-out war effort and that would have been a great chastener of the national mind. The long spell of slavery and submissive living under the British has bred many a vice of indolence, selfishness, parochialism, etc. All these vices and weaknesses would have been completely burnt in the fire of a long-drawn war and the pure gold of a united and heroic nationhood would have emerged ever more resplendent.[49]

In short, Golwalker's view of righteous war is that it should be total, redemptive, and cathartic. This is not just a long way from Gandhian pacifism; it is also a considerable distance from the prudential tradition of realist statecraft represented by Kautilya or a discriminating, defensive just war tradition.

Our reading of one of political Hinduism's "prophet voices" suggests that Hindutva's ethical stance on international relations and the use of violence is not a particularly prudential one. Admittedly, Golwalker's views are not the only ones worth consulting, but they are probably the most widely read by the more energetic, committed followers of political Hinduism. Clearly, also, much more could be done in terms of interpreting Golwalker's and Hindutva's views of international relations and war. For instance, to read everything he says literally would probably be unwise. Finally, Golwalker does not address the issue of nuclear weapons (and other WMD) and how they should be used. We are forced therefore to extrapolate from Golwalker's more general comments on international relations and war. India's possession of nuclear weapons and an understanding of the terrible devastation they would cause might well have modified political Hinduism's view of conflict and war. As things stand, though, there is little to go on: As far as one can see, there are no contemporary, postnuclear Golwalkers who are revisiting and moderating political Hinduism's views of external relations and the uses of violence.

CONCLUSION

Nuclear weapons are seen by many Westerners as a tragic necessity. Sitting triumphally atop the international system and in the vanguard of global history, those at the apex of power may not view nuclear weapons as much of an adornment and may, ultimately, consider them dispensable. Classical Hinduism, of the kind that Katherine Young abstracts from, also has an ambivalent view of nuclear weapons.

For the political Hinduism of today, there is nothing very troubling about nuclear weapons. In the eyes of Hindutva supporters, at this time and given the history of the past thousand years, nuclear weapons are necessary – for deterrence, for defense, but above all, for the moral rearmament of the Hindu community. Nuclear weapons may represent an old technology for the West, but it is one of the few technological areas where contemporary Hindus are at the forefront. And, for a people who have sat at the bottom of the international hierarchy for hundreds of years and have been marginalized historically for a thousand years, nuclear weapons appear as a vital talisman of power and status.

Critics may say that Hindu interests could be better protected and their cultural pride better served by other instruments and accomplishments. Political Hinduism, drawing on the historiography outlined here, would reply: A thousand years ago, Hindu economic and cultural attainments did not stop the Muslim invasions. Six hundred years ago, they did not stop the

European conquest. Military power is vital. Nuclear weapons give Hindus that power. From that sense of power will flow economic and cultural resurgence. Nuclear weapons are both materially and symbolically indispensable.

Whether one likes it or not, this view of nuclear weapons and other weapons of mass destruction is a powerful one in India, principally among the votaries of political Hinduism. I suggest that political Hinduism's attitude to nuclear weapons is at some distance from the pacifist Gandhian and more prudential, existential Hindu view so well documented for us by Katherine Young. Pacifist Gandhians deplore nuclear weapons. Prudential existentialists ruefully accept them. Political Hinduism embraces them.

Notes

1. Whether or not these other sources would measurably alter the picture that emerges from Young's already detailed analysis is a matter for further analysis.
2. The Sangh Parivar consists of the Rashtriya Swayamsevak Sangh (RSS) and various related groups including the Bharatiya Janata Party (BJP), Vishwa Hindu Parishad (VHP), Bajrang Dal, and the Swadeshi Jagran Manch. The "prophet voices" are K. S. Hegdewar, the founder of the RSS; M. S. Golwalker, *A Bunch of Thoughts*, 3rd ed. (Bangalore: Sahitya Sindhu Prakashana, 1996), and *We, or Our Nationhood Defined* (Nagpur: Bharat Publications, 1939); V. D. Savarkar, *Hindutva: Who Is a Hindu?* (Mumbai: Swatantryaveer Savarkar Rashtriya Smarak, 1999); Balraj Madhok, *Indianization: What, Why, and How?* (Delhi: S. Chand, 1970). Deendayal Upadhyaya's views are in C. P. Bishikar, *Pandit Deendayal Upadhyaya, Ideology and Perception*, vol. 5: *Concept of the Rashtra*, (New Delhi: Suruchi Prakashan, 1991).
3. The Congress Party, of course, was the first to test a nuclear device in 1974 and has at various times considered additional tests, as late as 1995–96. The left-of-center political coalition known as the National Front also toyed with the idea of nuclear testing in 1996–97. See George Perkovich, *India's Nuclear Bomb: The Impact on Global Proliferation* (New Delhi: Oxford University Press, 2000), 353–403. Neither the Congress nor the National Front chose to go nuclear outright in the sense of publicly stating the intention of building up an arsenal and actually deploying nuclear weapons. The BJP has done both. In its election manifesto of 1996, it promised that it would test and make India a nuclear weapons power (it was more equivocal in its 1998 election manifesto). The earlier incarnation of the BJP, the Bharatiya Jana Sangh, had, in 1962 – just six weeks after the end of the 1962 war with China – urged the Indian government to go nuclear. It was the first major political party to do so. See G. G. Mirchandani, *India's Nuclear Dilemma* (New Delhi: Popular Book Services, 1968), 21.
4. Nuclear weapons in popular American culture in the 1950s had their moment, as it were. My image of American attitudes toward the bomb, though, is one of fascination and quiet pride at best, not of spontaneous public celebration. A thoughtful account of American attitudes is Paul S. Boyer, *By the Bomb's Early Light: American Thought and Culture at the Dawn of the Atomic Age* (New York: Pantheon, 1985).

5. *Laddus* are sweets that are traditionally shared on festive occasions. The word *laddu* is metonymic for celebration and success.

6. The Western media has used the adjectives "Hindu nationalist" to describe the BJP. Some Indians are uncomfortable with this description. I think it is perfectly accurate judging by the party's statements and actions over the past decade of its existence.

7. For this view, see Jaswant Singh, *Defending India* (Chennai: Macmillan India, 1999). Jaswant Singh has served as India's minister for external affairs, defense, and finance.

8. The parlous state of Gandhians in India is one of the great mysteries of postindependence Indian political life. It would be fair to say that Gandhianism is nearly dead in the land of its prophet.

9. Arundhati Roy, "The End of Imagination," in Arundhati Roy, *The Algebra of Infinite Justice* (New Delhi: Penguin India, 2001); Praful Bidwai and Achin Vanaik, *South Asia on a Short Fuse: Nuclear Politics and the Future of Disarmament* (New Delhi: Oxford University Press, 1999). Other well-known opponents of the bomb in India are Ashis Nandy and N. Ram. See Ashis Nandy, "The Epidemic of Nuclearism: Clinical Profile of the Genocidal Mentality," in *The Nuclear Debate: Ironies and Immoralities*, ed. Zia Mian and Ashis Nandy (Colombo: Regional Center for Strategic Studies, July 1998); and N. Ram, *Riding the Nuclear Tiger* (Delhi: Leftword Books, 1999). Other antinuclear books include Itty Abraham, *The Making of the Indian Atomic Bomb: Science, Secrecy and the Postcolonial State* (New Delhi: Orient Longman, 1998), and Amitav Ghosh, *Countdown* (New Delhi: Ravi Dayal, 1999). My own views on nuclear weapons are "Abstaining: The Nonnuclear Option," in *India and the Bomb: Public Opinion and Nuclear Choices*, ed. David Cortright and Amitabh Mattoo (Notre Dame, Ind.: University of Notre Dame Press, 1996), 23–52, and "The Fallacy of an Indian Nuclear Deterrent," in *India's Nuclear Deterrent after Pokhran II*, ed. Amitabh Mattoo (New Delhi: Har Anand, 1998), 150–90. For an excellent collection of antinuclear views from a range of South Asian intellectuals, see Zia Mian and Smitu Kothari, eds., *Out of the Nuclear Shadow* (Delhi: Lokayan and Rainbow and London: Zed Books, 2001).

10. See Movement in India for Nuclear Disarmament (MIND), *Out of Darkness: The Indian Case for Disarmament* (New Delhi: Movement in India for Nuclear Disarmament, n.d.). MIND was formed after the nuclear tests of May 1998. The booklet was probably published later that year.

11. This kind of view can be reconstructed from a number of texts. See, for instance, Jaswant Singh, *Defending India*, chap. 1, on India's strategic culture. See also Golwalker, *Bunch of Thoughts* and *We, or Our Nationhood Defined*.

12. Deterrence and defense are not the same thing in strategic studies. Deterrence is the use of threats to prevent someone from doing something that you do not want them to do, in particular, to attack you. Defense is to limit an action against you that has already begun and eventually to undo it altogether in order to restore the status quo ante. Defense is what you do when deterrence has broken down. For the conceptual distinction and further refinements, see Glenn H. Snyder, *Deterrence and Defense: Towards a Theory of National Security* (Princeton, N.J.: Princeton University Press, 1961).

13. For instance, the much-vaunted Revolution in Military Affairs (RMA) may well cause the United States to someday argue for complete nuclear disarmament

in the confidence that it has alternative military technologies with superior, more usable capabilities than nuclear weapons. For an Indian view that this is in fact a possibility, see C. Raja Mohan, "Post-Pokhran II: Nuclear Defiance and Reconciliation," in *Post-Pokhran II: The National Way Ahead* (New Delhi: India Habitat Center, 1999), 22. Raja Mohan is not a Hindutva supporter.

14. Golwalker, *Bunch of Thoughts*, 3–4, on how the UN is a tool of the great powers, is indicative of political Hinduism's distrust of international rules and institutions. It should be noted that most Indian thinking on treaties and agreements is wary of the role of great powers in manipulating negotiations to suit their own ends.
15. Ibid., 257–58.
16. Ibid., 260.
17. Ibid., 272–76.
18. See ibid., 265–69, on why India should be skeptical of "internationalism" as it is only a cover for the wishes and interests of the powerful.
19. Ibid., 261–62.
20. Ibid., 262.
21. Ibid., 271.
22. Ibid., 277.
23. Ibid.
24. Ibid.
25. Ibid., 278–83.
26. Ibid., 283.
27. Ibid., 285.
28. Ibid., 286.
29. Ibid.
30. Ibid., 286–87.
31. Ibid., 286.
32. Ibid.
33. Ibid., 287.
34. Ibid.
35. Ibid., 289–91.
36. Ibid., 277.
37. Ibid., 298–99.
38. Ibid., 300.
39. Ibid.
40. Ibid., 302, 316–17.
41. Ibid., 302.
42. Ibid., 290.
43. Ibid., 303.
44. Ibid., 319–22.
45. Ibid., 325.
46. Ibid.
47. Ibid., 341.
48. Ibid., 313.
49. Ibid., 326.

17

Islamic Ethics and Weapons of Mass Destruction

An Argument for Nonproliferation

Sohail H. Hashmi

Since the early 1960s, several Muslim states have figured prominently in international concerns on proliferation of weapons of mass destruction. The Comprehensive Test Ban Treaty lists seven Muslim-majority states among the forty-four "nuclear-capable" states whose ratification is necessary for the treaty to enter into force: Algeria, Bangladesh, Egypt, Indonesia, Iran, Pakistan, and Turkey. Pakistan, of course, became a confirmed nuclear power in May 1998. Not included in this list are three other states that are known to have sought nuclear capability: Iraq, Libya, and Syria. Iraq not only came close to developing nuclear weapons during the 1980s, but it was also a leading developer of chemical and biological weapons. Its repeated use of chemical weapons against Iranians and Kurds during the Iran-Iraq War is one of the most egregious violations of international agreements banning the use of such weapons. Iraq is, however, not alone among Muslim states in having stockpiled and used chemical weapons, nor in developing biological weapons.

Aside from these states, the threat posed by Muslim terrorist groups has steadily increased over the past decade. Because of its financial resources, its network of affiliated organizations around the world, and the technical sophistication of its recruits, al-Qa'ida is justifiably perceived as the principal WMD terrorist threat today. Documents and crude laboratories uncovered by coalition forces in Afghanistan indicate that the network led by Usama bin Ladin tried actively to develop or acquire chemical, biological, and nuclear weapons.[1] The September 11 attack on the United States represents a quantum leap in the ability and willingness of such terrorist groups to use weapons of mass destruction.

Yet despite the development, stockpiling, threats to use, and even the actual use of WMD by Muslim states and nonstate actors, the morality of such weapons has not elicited significant discussion from Islamic ethicists. In contrast to the medieval Islamic literature on war, in which concerns for the proper conduct of war loomed large, the modern Islamic discourse focuses mainly on the legitimate grounds (*jus ad bellum*) for war and largely neglects legitimate means (*jus in bello*).[2] Within the sparse discussion of legitimate means, Muslim scholars have yet to explore in a detailed and systematic fashion how nuclear, chemical, and biological weapons relate to the Islamic ethics of war.

The paucity of Muslim discussion of this topic may in part be the result of the relatively recent advent of weapons of mass destruction and the even shorter time in which such weapons have become directly relevant to Muslims. Another factor is the repressive political atmosphere in which the majority of Muslim intellectuals write and work. Open consideration – let alone debate – of state policies can hardly be expected under military dictatorships, such as those in Iraq, Libya, or Syria. Even in relatively more open, and sometimes democratic regimes, such as those in Egypt, Iran, and Pakistan, challenges to the official line are unlikely when support for "national defense" policies is equated with patriotism. In such states, it is not only or even primarily the military censors who squelch dissenting voices; a societal consensus promoted by the media and civilian politicians performs this censorship quite effectively without direct military intervention.[3]

The slow response to the advent of WMD also conforms to the historical pattern of Muslim ethical discourse on new methods of warfare. Long after Muslim armies had resorted to tactics and weapons that had no precedents in the classical legal treatises on jihad, Muslim scholars were still debating whether they were compatible with Islamic ethics.

Contemporary Islamic views on the ethics of WMD may be divided into three broad categories, mirroring those found in other religious traditions.[4] First, the WMD jihadists argue for the acquisition and possible use – given the right circumstances – of weapons of mass destruction. Theorists of this group acknowledge that WMD push the moral limits of Islamic injunctions on fighting properly, but they argue that with the appropriate caveats, such weapons may be incorporated into the framework of traditional Islamic thinking on the proper conduct of jihad.

An even greater embrace of WMD occurs with the second group, a group that may be labeled the Muslim WMD terrorists. Proponents of this view not only argue that it is morally and pragmatically necessary for Muslims to acquire WMD, they also justify and, more importantly, seem prepared to employ WMD as a weapon of first resort. Moreover, they place little value in the mainstream jihad tradition's distinctions between combatants and noncombatants, arguing that all non-Muslims – and even so-called nominal Muslims or Muslims who choose to live among non-Muslims – are legitimate targets.

The last group may be identified as the Muslim WMD pacifists. These theorists renounce the acquisition and any possible use of WMD as contrary to Islamic ethics. Muslim WMD pacifism should be distinguished from the total pacifism that renounces all recourse to violence in the settlement of political disputes. A pure pacifist ethic is difficult to sustain within the Islamic tradition because of numerous qur'anic injunctions to the contrary, including most pointedly verse 2:216: "Fighting is prescribed for you, though you dislike it. But it may be that you dislike something that is good for you, and like something that is bad for you. God knows, and you do not." This is not to say that an ethic of nonviolent resistance is alien to Islam; indeed, the prophet Muhammad's statecraft provides many important examples of such a policy.[5] But the Qur'an and *hadith*, the authoritative traditions of the Prophet, provide so many justifications for the resort to force when nonviolent measures fail to provide for justice or security that outright pacifism is virtually nonexistent in Islamic intellectual history. Muslim WMD pacifists are not an exception to this generalization. They accept that jihad may require the resort to violence under certain circumstances, but they reject any conceivable set of circumstances in which nuclear, chemical, or biological weapons may be properly used.

Of these three positions, the WMD jihadists comprise by far the majority of Muslim scholars who deal with this issue. By comparison, Muslim WMD terrorists and Muslim WMD pacifists constitute fringe elements. None of these three positions is well articulated, so any attempt to delineate the salient points of difference among them is inherently an exercise in inference from the scarce sources. And there is nothing, to my knowledge, that can be identified as sustained discussion or debate among the different groups or even between two scholars.

So, in addition to presenting the range of Islamic opinion on the ethics of WMD, I hope in this chapter to open a debate. I argue the Muslim WMD pacifist position, partly because this position has been drowned out by other voices, especially in the wake of the Pakistani nuclear tests and the post–September 11 concerns over Muslim terrorism. But I do so mainly out of conviction. Muslims should reject the proliferation and hence the possibility of any use of WMD, I believe, for the following reasons.

First, nuclear, chemical, and biological weapons do not permit a level of discrimination between combatants and noncombatants that is required by Islamic rules of war.

Second, even if WMD could be employed strictly against military targets, they kill or maim in such horrible ways that they violate Islamic teachings on fighting humanely.

Third, they wreak lasting damage on the natural environment, a result that must be considered in Islamic moral evaluations because all life has worth as God's creation quite apart from any utility derived by humans. "There is not an animal on earth, nor a bird that flies on its wings, but they are communities like you" (Qur'an 6:38). Destroying or damaging the natural habitat of species unable to defend themselves against human attack constitutes the height of what the Qur'an labels *fasad fi al-ard* (corruption in the land).[6]

Fourth, because WMD cannot be used for any morally defensible purpose, any expenditure to develop and stockpile them, any resources diverted
from other, constructive purposes, amounts to what the Qur'an and *hadith*
condemn as *israf* (waste).[7]

In arguing against the use of nuclear, biological, and chemical weapons,
Muslim WMD pacifists do not and should not accept the use of other types of
weapons traditionally considered "conventional" weapons, including cluster bombs, antipersonnel land mines, or firebombs. These weapons are
also objectionable on the grounds that they make discrimination between
combatants and noncombatants difficult or that they kill and wound in particularly brutal fashion. But the Muslim WMD pacifist position rests on the
argument that nuclear, biological, and chemical weapons deserve particular
attention because they are qualitatively different and in a class by themselves
in the extent and the longevity of the harm they produce – not just to human
beings, but to the natural environment as well. Indeed, all three Muslim positions seem to agree that there is no morally significant distinction among
nuclear, biological, and chemical weapons.

SOURCES AND PRINCIPLES

Much of the specifically Islamic ethical discourse on WMD draws on the
work of the early jurists who first elaborated rules for the proper conduct
of war, including permissible targets, weapons, and tactics. These scholars
relied first on the two basic sources for Islamic law and ethics, the Qur'an
and *sunna* (exemplary sayings and actions of the prophet Muhammad).[8]
But on many specific points, the Qur'an and *sunna* provided limited or apparently contradictory guidance. They therefore stipulated regulations on
what Muslim armies may and may not do in the chapters on jihad, which
invariably formed an important part of their legal corpus, through their own
independent interpretive activity. Sometimes the conclusions were drawn by
analogy from verses in the Qur'an or examples from the life of the Prophet.
But quite often the conclusions reflected ex post facto rationalizations of the
commands of Muslim rulers or the practice of Muslim armies. The ethical
reasoning in these cases seems to have been a rather straightforward tele-
ological concern for the welfare of Muslim armies or the state and society,
rather than any claims of divine command. Still, this legal theory (*fiqh*) of
war, based on the conclusions of men working in the eighth through the
fourteenth centuries, came to be identified over time as an intrinsic part of
the broader set of divine moral-legal guidance called *shari'a*.

Three basic questions underlie the juristic discussions on war: Against
whom is it permitted (or obligatory) to wage war? What type of harm (if any)
may be inflicted on different categories of persons? What type of damage
may be inflicted on the enemy's property? Most of the moral issues germane
to a discussion of the ethics of WMD fall under the last two questions, those

dealing with legitimate means in war (*jus in bello*). I therefore address only briefly the early jurists' answers to the first question dealing with legitimate grounds for war (*jus ad bellum*).[9]

Legitimate Wars

Sunni jurists distinguished wars against non-Muslims from those against other Muslims. The first type was generally the one to which the term *jihad* was applied in a formal sense. One form of jihad was defensive war to repulse the aggression of unbelievers. On the basis of many qur'anic verses (e.g., 2:190–91, 4:74–76, 22:39–40), the jurists commonly assumed that such a war was not only permissible to Muslims but an obligation of all able-bodied Muslims, male and female (*fard 'ayn*).

The more widely discussed form of jihad was to expand the territory in which Islamic sovereignty prevailed (*dar al-Islam*) by reducing the domain of unbelievers (*dar al-harb*). While this type of jihad was considered obligatory for the head of the Islamic state (imam) if doing so would not jeopardize the security and stability of the Muslim community, participation in it was obligatory only for those able-bodied, adult, free males who were capable financially of engaging in such an activity (*fard kifaya*). The enemy was to be fought only after it rejected two other options, either that it accept the Islamic faith or that it accept Islamic sovereignty and agree to live as an "autonomous" community within the Islamic state.

Because *dar al-Islam* was theoretically a unified entity in the Sunni view, wars against Muslims were regarded as police actions undertaken by the imam against three main categories: renegade apostates (*murtadun*), brigands and highway robbers (*muharibun*), and Muslim rebels (*bughat*). Shi'ite doctrine departed slightly from the majority Sunni view on this matter by classifying all opponents of the true imams ('Ali and his descendants) – whether Muslim or not – as legitimate targets of jihad. But this point of difference was largely academic when the Shi'ite theory was being developed because another point of difference with the Sunni theory held that the obligation to wage jihad against unbelievers had lapsed with the disappearance of the twelfth imam in the ninth century C.E. Only defensive wars could be sanctioned by the imam's agents, the 'ulama, until the imam returns.[10]

A similar, if belated consensus disavowing the classical theory of the expansionist jihad seems to have emerged over the past two centuries in Sunni circles. Most Muslim theorists today (even the WMD terrorists) answer the first question on the legitimate grounds for war by speaking of defensive war – defense of Muslims against aggression by non-Muslims, defense of "true" Muslims against the corruption and repression of nominal Muslim governments. The medieval jurists' conception of jihad as a military struggle to propagate Islamic sovereignty and Islamic faith worldwide is generally viewed as contrary to a comprehensive understanding of the Qur'an and historically anachronistic. Only a few of the most radical Muslim groups still invoke the early juristic notion of the unified territory of Islam (*dar al-Islam*) locked in an incessant struggle to reduce the territory of the infidels (*dar al-harb*) – and even they seem to give this jihad less importance than their immediate goal of seizing power in whatever Muslim country they happen to be based.

Damage to Persons

The goal of jihad against unbelievers for the early jurists was to incorporate them into *dar al-Islam*, not to annihilate them. Thus, Muslim armies needed rules of war that facilitated the absorption of non-Muslims into the *pax Islamica* once the fighting ended. The guiding qur'anic principle was "Fight those who fight against you, but do not transgress limits, for God loves not the transgressors" (2:190). From an early date, the "limits" mentioned in this verse were interpreted as requiring rules to regulate not only who could be attacked and killed, but also the weapons that may be used in the process.

Discrimination in targeting was a principle clearly established by several prophetic *hadiths*.[11] The jurists agreed on the basis of these reports that women and children should not be deliberately killed. The reason for the prohibition, according to most jurists, is found in the words of the Prophet, who, on seeing a slain woman during a campaign, said, "She is not one who would have fought," before ordering his troops not to kill women, children, and peasants. As Ibn Taymiyya (d. 1328) elaborates:

As for those who cannot offer resistance or cannot fight, such as women, children, monks, old people, the blind, handicapped and their likes, they shall not be killed, unless they actually fight with words [e.g., by propaganda] and acts [e.g., by spying or otherwise assisting in the warfare]. Some [jurists] are of the opinion that all of them may be killed, on the mere ground that they are unbelievers, but they make an exception for women and children since they constitute property for Muslims. However, the first opinion is the correct one, because we may only fight those who fight us when we want to make God's religion victorious.[12]

In other words, the majority opinion was that capacity to fight, not belief in or rejection of Islam, was the criterion for determining liability to damage in war. This view, of course, is not equivalent to modern conceptions of noncombatant immunity; adult, able-bodied males, fighting or not, are not immune from harm, nor are women and children immune from enslavement, even in the majority view.

The consensus among Sunni and Shi'ite jurists was challenged by extremist interpreters of the Qur'an throughout the early centuries. The best known is Nafi' ibn al-Azraq (d. 685), who gave his name to the most belligerent faction of the Kharijite movement, the Azariqa. This group practiced a form of terrorism known as *isti'rad*, in which all Muslims and polytheists – including women and children – who refused to join their cause were dubbed infidels and were therefore liable to be killed.[13]

Echoes of such extremist views are heard among Muslim terrorist groups today. Because these latter-day Kharijites consider themselves as the only authentic Muslims, they feel no compunction about waging an indiscriminate war against all others, whether they are civilians in their own country, as is the case with the Armed Islamic Group in Algeria, or foreign civilians, as is the case with Hamas or Palestininan Islamic Jihad in Israel or the Jama'at Islamiyya in Egypt.[14] Al-Qa'ida justified its terrorist actions in a 1998 statement by declaring:

The ruling to kill the Americans and their allies – civilians and military – is an individual duty for every Muslim who can do it, in order to liberate the al-Aqsa Mosque and the holy mosque [in Mecca] from their grip, and in order for their armies to move out of all the lands of Islam, defeated and unable to threaten any Muslim. This is in accordance with the words of Almighty God, "and fight the pagans all together as they fight you all together.... "[15]

Yet despite the attention that such radical groups garner, they represent a fringe element and their tactics have been widely condemned by most scholars. The consensus among Muslim scholars today is that the modern principles of international humanitarian law are in no way incompatible with Islamic ethical principles and that they are a logical extension and development of the classical *shari'a* rules.[16] The work of the influential Syrian scholar Wahba al-Zuhayli is representative of this argument. Not only does al-Zuhayli adopt the combatant/noncombatant terminology in his work (in Arabic, *muharibun/ghayr muharibun*), he declares explicitly that

Islamic law does not characterize all of the enemy population as combatants. The combatants include all those who prepare themselves for fighting, either directly or indirectly.... As for the civilians who are at peace and devote themselves to work that is neutral in terms of assisting the enemy ... none of these are termed as combatants whose blood may be shed with impunity. On this point, Islamic law and international law converge.[17]

Permissible Weapons and Tactics

The classical theory held that women, children, the old, and the infirm should not be directly targeted by Muslim forces. But the nature of ancient warfare inevitably placed such categories of persons in harm's way, particularly when the enemy retreated to a fortified settlement. The early jurists responded generally in what can only be termed a keenly pragmatic way to this problem: In vanquishing the enemy, Muslim forces had to be able to resort to weapons and tactics that had the potential to kill indiscriminately and possibly on a mass scale. If the enemy made discrimination difficult by mixing their fighters with their civilians, then the responsibility for the deaths of civilians lay with the enemy, not Muslim forces.

The precedent for this principle comes from one of the final campaigns of the Prophet, the siege of Ta'if in 630 C.E. Ta'if was a fortified settlement in the mountains just east of Mecca inhabited primarily by the Thaqif tribe and was one of the last remaining pagan holdouts in the Hijaz. When Thaqif fighters were defeated by Muslim forces in the valley below Ta'if, they retreated behind the walls of their city. For twenty days, Ta'if resisted the siege laid by the Muslim forces. Finally, the Prophet authorized the use of siege engines against the city walls. Ibn Hisham writes: "The apostle shot at them with catapults. One I can trust told me that the apostle was the first to use a catapult in Islam when he fired at the men of Ta'if."[18] Then, as narrated by Ibn Ishaq, "when the day of storming came at the wall of al-Ta'if a number of his companions went under a testudo and advanced up to the wall to breach it. Thaqif let loose on them scraps of hot iron so they came out from under it and Thaqif shot them with arrows and killed some of them."[19] Thus, even though Ta'if eventually capitulated, the first and only use of "unconventional" weapons by the Prophet appears to have been rather brief and disastrous.

Muslim armies would employ such catapults (known as *manjaniq*, or mangonels) in later battles. 'Amr ibn al-'As reportedly used several mangonels to effective use in the siege of Alexandria in 645.[20] On the basis of these historical precedents, jurists generally permitted the use of mangonels and other forms of siege engines and ballista.

The projectiles fired by mangonels were frequently incendiary devices, such as naphta, or "Greek fire," a weapon borrowed from the Byzantines. Ships mounted with naphta-hurling catapults were used against the Byzantine navy during the second Arab siege of Constantinople in 715–17. Muhammad ibn al-Qasim is reported to have employed similar devices on land in his campaign in Sind.[21]

The use of such incendiary devices raised some serious moral qualms among the early jurists. According to a well-known *hadith*, Muhammad proscribed the use of fire against opponents with the words: "Do not punish creatures of God with the punishment of God."[22] On the basis of this *hadith*, jurists of three of the four principal law schools in Sunni Islam, the Hanbalis, Malikis, and Shafi'is, expressed various reservations regarding the use of incendiary weapons. The general rule adopted seems to be that the deliberate burning of persons, either to overcome them in the midst of battle or to punish them after capture, is forbidden. But the use of incendiary devices to overcome enemy installations or armaments was permissible, if required by military necessity or in reciprocation of enemy provocation. The Hanafis, who tended to be the least stringent regarding weapons and tactics, permitted the use of fire in attacking the enemy with few reservations.[23]

Classical jurisprudence evinces fewer moral qualms about other types of indiscriminate weapons. Muhammad Hamidullah cites an unpublished, early-thirteenth-century manuscript of Hanafi law that permits the use of "smokes, prepared liquids, and ill-smelling deadly odours (gases?), for causing damage to forts and castles and horrifying the enemy."[24] Most jurists also permitted the use of poison-tipped weapons as well as the poisoning of water supplies. The Malikis, however, dissented from the majority on this point. Some in their ranks prohibited poison-tipped arrows on prudential grounds, fearing that the enemy would retaliate in kind against the Muslims, while others considered such weapons reprehensible but permissible if the enemy resorted to them first.[25]

Finally, the early jurists condoned one other tactic with the potential for mass destruction: flooding. As is the case with poison, their rationale comes not so much from the Qur'an or traditions of the Prophet but from pragmatic military considerations.[26] Because this tactic was employed by the Muslims' adversaries, the jurists legitimated it on the grounds of military necessity or reciprocity.[27] Numerous records of its use as a battlefield tactic by Muslim armies are available. The Almohad ruler 'Abd al-Mu'min dammed a stream running through the city of Fez in 1146, and when enough water had accumulated, broke the dam, allowing the tide to sweep away the city fortifications. The same tactic was employed in another region by the Khwarizm-Shah 'Ala' al-Din when attacking Herat in 1206.[28] The indiscriminate nature of the destruction wreaked by this tactic is evident from the many instances in which it backfired against its perpetrator, sweeping away his own besieging troops along with his enemies.[29]

Damage to Property

The early jurists had to balance two considerations: First, they understood that war inevitably requires some destruction of the enemy's property, not just his inanimate property, such as forts and other buildings, but also his living property, both animals and plants. No precedents may be found in the Prophet's campaigns of the large-scale killing of animals.[30] But there are at least two instances in which he ordered the destruction of the enemy's orchards in order to diminish their will to resist: when he had the palm trees of the Banu Nadir cut down during the siege of this Jewish tribe in Medina (625 C.E.), and when he ordered the grape vines of the Banu Thaqif uprooted during the siege of Ta'if mentioned earlier.[31]

Yet a second consideration for the jurists was the general condemnation of corruption, waste, or unnecessary destruction – all encapsulated in the term *fasad* – that runs throughout the Qur'an and the *hadith*.[32] In addition, there were the famous ten commands to the Muslim army given by the first caliph, Abu Bakr, including: "You shall not fell palm trees or burn them; you shall not cut down [any] fruit-bearing tree; you shall not slaughter a sheep or a cow or a camel except for food."[33] The scholars who relied on these orders as the basis for their rulings argued that Abu Bakr would not have contravened the practice of the Prophet had he not known that the Prophet's earlier actions were either abrogated by the Prophet himself or the Qur'an or limited in their ethical and legal import to their particular occurrences.[34]

The attempt to reconcile these two considerations produced a range of opinions among the early scholars. The Hanafis again seem to have been the most liberal in permitting rather destructive methods in order to disrupt the enemy's economy. The Hanbalis, Malikis, and Shafi'is advised against the cutting of fruit trees and the slaughter of animals but allowed such actions if necessary to overcome the enemy.[35]

The Argument from Necessity

As the foregoing discussion demonstrates, classical jurisprudence tended to allow Muslim commanders wide latitude on the grounds of military necessity, even if this resulted in large-scale death of noncombatants and wholesale destruction of their property. The argument from necessity (*darura*) was further divided into two categories. First, the jurists cited the principle of *maslaha mursala*, or the general welfare of the Muslim community. I consider the best-known philosophical discussion of *maslaha mursala*, that of the twelfth-century sage al-Ghazali, in the next section. As we see below, al-Ghazali imposed a rather high threshold for invoking necessity as a justification for suspending normal moral prohibitions – the utter destruction of the Muslim community. But it should be noted here that *maslaha* was discussed in most juristic treatises on war in the context of far less dire circumstances. It often meant simply that all means ordinarily considered reprehensible but not expressly prohibited could be employed if necessary to ensure a Muslim victory – not just to prevent a Muslim defeat.

The second principle was *muqabala bi al-mithl*, or reciprocity. Qur'anic justifications for reciprocity were found in such verses as "If then anyone transgresses the prohibition against you, transgress you likewise against him" (2:194) and "Fight the polytheists all together (*kaffatan*) as they fight you all together" (9:36–37). By combining them with earlier qur'anic injunctions on retaliating no worse than the original affront (16:126–27; 22:60), jurists adduced the general principle that reciprocity not only permitted but required Muslims to resort to rather indiscriminate and destructive methods if the enemy initiated their use. Unfortunately, the moral or legal basis for such permission is developed no further than the invocation of necessity, meaning, again, to prevent a Muslim defeat or a loss of Muslim honor.[36] And as the famous adage goes, *al-darurat tubih al-mahzurat* (necessities make permissible the forbidden).

Given the general outlook of classical jurisprudence that all means should be developed to match the enemy's resources, it is ironic that the centuries following the codification of medieval law saw the entrenchment of an intellectual conservatism in Sunni Islam that made reform of law – even in so practical a sphere as military regulations – difficult. The failure of Muslim rulers to match the technological innovations of the West was the result, of course, of numerous factors, but one among them must be the sheer inertia of tradition. As late as the mid-nineteenth century, the Ottoman state found it necessary to issue declarations from its 'ulama authorizing the military reforms that figured importantly in the modernization effort known as the Tanzimat. To counter the claims of conservative religious elements that reform constituted illicit innovation (*bid'a*), the 'ulama resorted to the doctrine of reciprocity. Military reforms in training, strategy, and tactics were required, they argued, in order to fight an increasingly powerful and threatening enemy with his own weapons.[37]

Twentieth-century Muslim states have faced fewer obstacles from conservative religious opinion in modernizing their militaries. The anticolonial struggles and postcolonial disputes, such as the Arab-Israeli conflict and the Indo-Pakistani wars, have shaped a consensus that Muslims cannot afford to lag behind others in military technology. As noted earlier, this consensus has been slow to incorporate weapons of mass destruction, but it is reflected today in the prevalence of the WMD jihadist position. The following sections of this chapter challenge some of the fundamental assumptions of this consensus.

USE IN WAR

Chemical weapons have been used in at least two conflicts involving Muslim states. The first was the Yemeni civil war of 1963–67, in which Egypt is alleged to have bombed Yemeni royalist forces with munitions carrying phosgene and mustard gas. More than 1,000 people are believed to have died as a result, but details of this chemical warfare are scarce.[38]

The second conflict was the Iran-Iraq War of 1980–88. Within weeks of the outbreak of the war on September 22, 1980, the Iranian government alleged that Iraq was employing chemical weapons in its offensive. The charges, like the war itself, were received with general apathy in much of the international community. It was not until March of 1984 that a UN commission confirmed Iranian charges of repeated chemical weapons use by Iraq during the past few months. Its report was supported by the International Committee of the Red Cross, which announced on March 7, 1984, that it had found 160 cases of wounded combatants in Tehran hospitals whose injuries led "to the presumption of the recent use of substances prohibited by international law."[39]

On the basis of this evidence, the UN Security Council issued a resolution on March 30, 1984, condemning the use of chemical weapons
in the Iran-Iraq War. The resolution did not identify Iraq as the instiga-
tor of chemical warfare nor did it single Iraq out for special sanctions.
Given this tepid international response, Iraq continued to use chemical
weapons against Iranian troops and against Shi'ite rebels in the southern
marshes.

The Iranians could not retaliate against Iraq's chemical attacks because
at the outset of the war Iran had no stock of chemical weapons. The shah's
military, it seems, had seen no use for chemical weapons, possibly intending
to offset any chemical warfare threat by developing nuclear weapons. In
Chapter 3, Scott Sagan recounts the initial Iranian reluctance to develop
and use chemical weapons against Iraq, to a large extent because of the
moral qualms about such weapons held by Ayatollah Khomeini and other
senior 'ulama. By 1984, however, Iranian troops had begun using captured
stocks of Iraqi chemicals against the Iraqis. Whether this reflected an official
change of government policy is still unclear, but it was also during this same
time period that the Islamic republic's attitude toward nuclear weapons began to change as well (discussed below under "Disarmament"). Clearly, by
the mid-1980s, Khomeini had begun to relent to pressures from the revolutionary guards and younger clerics. By 1987, Iran was manufacturing and
using its own chemical agents, apparently with Khomeini's acquiescence.
By this time, however, Khomeini was in ill health, and the extent to which
he was still functioning as commander-in-chief of the Iranian military is
uncertain.[40]

Analyses of the chemical warfare during the Iran-Iraq War conclude that
it yielded some tactical military success for the Iraqis, but only when Iranian
troops were inadequately trained and equipped to defend against the chemical agents.[41] Its most effective use was to terrorize civilian populations with
the prospect that they might be gassed, as Iraq threatened repeatedly.[42] The
most devastating and notorious single use of chemical weapons took place
in fact against Kurdish civilians in the town of Halabja on March 16, 1988,
when an estimated 5,000 people were killed and 10,000 more injured after they were subjected to mustard gas, sarin gas, and other asphyxiating
chemical agents.[43] Recent investigations by a British physician, Christine
Gosden, indicate that the effects of the attacks continue until the present.
Gosden has documented not only the expected cases of continuing neuro-
logical and other damage to the direct victims of the attack, but also genetic
mutations that were passed on to a second generation. She observes that
mustard gas is considered radiomimetic in the scientific literature, that is,
its effects are similar to those of ionizing radiation. Furthermore, Gosden
and others observe that the chemicals used in the attack leached into the
groundwater around the village and subsequently destroyed much of the
plant and animal life in a large area.[44]

Halabja was the culmination of a genocidal war pursued by the Ba'thist regime against Iraqi Kurds throughout the 1980s. The code name for this internal war was "al-Anfal." The term was carefully selected for its Islamic connotations; it is the title of the eighth chapter of the Qur'an. The title comes from one of the main subjects of this chapter, namely, the dispensation of the "spoils of war" taken by Muslims during their fighting with their polytheist enemies. No Muslim could mistake the significance of this code name. The Kurds, by rising up against Baghdad and in some cases supporting the Iranians, were beyond the pale of the true Muslim community. Their rebellion could be suppressed as a jihad against infidels.

The self-serving application of the qur'anic term *anfal* by the secular Ba'thist dictatorship of Saddam Hussein was transparent to most Muslims. Certainly, very few Islamic scholars or organizations lent unequivocal support to the way the Iraqis were prosecuting the war. Whatever defense of Iraq was mounted on religious grounds tended to be a reflection of the official conservative Arab line that Iraq was holding the line against fanatical Shi'ite Iranians who refused to end the fighting once Iraqi troops had been pushed back across their border. Yet if there was little enthusiasm for the way the war was being fought, there was also very little condemnation for the distortion of Islamic rules regarding the treatment of rebel soldiers and the general proscription against targeting noncombatant populations, whether Muslim or non-Muslim. Outside of Iran and its few supporters in the Muslim world, the use of chemical weapons went largely unremarked in Islamic legal and scholarly circles.[45] The crime of Halabja was met with deafening silence.

The absence of serious moral evaluation of what is in many ways the most terrible conflict of the twentieth century involving Muslims is at the very least a tragically missed opportunity. But regrettably, there is nothing unusual about this case. Even in the very few works that do treat the morality of weapons of mass destruction, the question of when such weapons may be used, if ever, is rarely discussed.

The majority of Muslim theorists who have expressed an opinion on the topic of WMD use fall within the category of WMD jihadists. They agree that Muslims should acquire WMD only for defensive purposes and that resort to such weapons is permissible only after the enemy has resorted to them first. Under such circumstances, the principle of reciprocity that was often invoked by classical jurists permits, according to most modern scholars, the resort to such weapons. For such theorists, weapons of mass destruction do not seem to pose qualitatively new problems for the Islamic ethics of war.

The work of Wahba al-Zuhayli is representative of this position. His treatise *Athar al-harb fi al-fiqh al-Islami* (The influences of war upon Islamic law) and a shorter work, *al-'Alaqat al-duwaliyya fi al-Islam: Muqarana bi al-qanun al-duwali al-hadith* (International relations in Islam: A comparison with modern international law), are premised on the need for Islamic theory to respond to changed international circumstances. Yet in his consideration of weapons of mass destruction, he mentions only in passing that Islamic principles do not obviate the possibility of using such weapons but that they "do not accord with the principle of compassion, which is the basis of Islamic law, or requirements of fairness in battle."[46] Muslims may acquire such weapons as a deterrent against their enemies, but they should refrain from using them first, for, as he writes, "they cause the destruction and death of those whom it is not permissible to kill, such as those not fighting, women, and the like."[47] Their use is conceivable only if deterrence fails, and the enemy employs them first. Muslims may retaliate with such deadly force as a final and necessary recourse (*akhir al-dawa' al-kai*, literally, "the remedy that cauterizes" the wound).[48]

The justification for WMD use in self-defense appears also in the statements of WMD terrorists. In an interview on December 22, 1998, Rahimullah Yousafsai of ABC News asked Usama bin Ladin about U.S. government charges that al-Qa'ida was "in a position to develop chemical weapons and try to purchase nuclear material for weapons. How would such weapons be used?" Bin Ladin answered: "Acquiring weapons for the defense of Muslims is a religious duty. . . . It would be a sin for Muslims not to try to possess the weapons that would prevent the infidels from inflicting harm on Muslims. But how we could use these weapons if we possess them is up to us."[49]

Bin Ladin was asked again about the WMD aspirations of al-Qa'ida by the Pakistani journalist Hamid Mir in an interview given on November 8, 2001, in the midst of the U.S. campaign in Afghanistan. He responded: "We have these weapons as a deterrent; they are not for attacking. We do not wish to use these weapons for barbaric purposes. But if these weapons are used against us, then we will respond. We do not wish the destruction of human beings. Our mission is to spread the call to Islam. But if these weapons are used against us, then we have the right to retaliate."[50]

U.S. investigators in Afghanistan concluded that al-Qa'ida had not succeeded in developing or acquiring chemical, biological, or radiological weapons (let alone a nuclear bomb) up to the time of the American military action.[51] But as Bin Ladin's statements confirm, al-Qa'ida considers the acquisition of WMD to be an important part of its military mission. And once it acquires WMD – Bin Ladin's disavowal of any first use notwithstanding – the chances are quite high that it will use them. This is true not only for all the various reasons that WMD are attractive to terrorists in general,[52] but because al-Qa'ida in particular has perfected and frequently justified methods of mass killing. Bin Ladin sees his war as a defensive jihad against a vastly more powerful and unscrupulous superpower and its minions. As such, normal strictures on how and under whose leadership Muslims may fight may be relaxed, according to classical notions of defensive jihad, in order to meet the aggression of the enemy. In the interview with Hamid

Mir quoted above, Bin Ladin defended the killing of American civilians on September 11, 2001, thus: "The American people pay taxes to their government, they elect the president, and they support the government's foreign policy. . . . The American Congress passes measures designed to thwart our aims. Since the Congress has the support of the American people, we cannot say that the people are innocent."[53] Given Bin Ladin's conception of collective responsibility, it is entirely conceivable that one day he or one of his lieutenants would justify the first use of WMD against civilians as an emergency measure.

Assuming for the moment that the classical legal rules on permissible weapons are applicable to weapons of mass destruction, then I suppose a limited number of modern chemical weapons could be judged according to the medieval criteria. It is possible (under a plausible set of conditions) to direct their use to the battlefield and thereby observe the strictures against willfully targeting noncombatants or to design them in such a way that they incapacitate rather than seriously maim or kill their victims. The problem with the analogy, of course, lies in the fact that most chemical weapons are far more lethal than their crude medieval precursors, the ones classical Muslim scholars had in mind, and the types of injuries they cause are much more severe and longer lasting, extending, as in the case of those attacked at Halabja, to unborn generations. Modern chemical weapons, as a class of weapon, cannot be evaluated according to medieval strictures on the use of poisons or "noxious odors." They, like nuclear and biological weapons, should be treated by Muslim lawyers and ethicists as new types of weapons posing new and qualitatively different challenges to Islamic ethics.

The use in war of any WMD should be rejected by Muslims, even as purely second-strike weapons. Retaliating with chemical, biological, and nuclear weapons against an unscrupulous enemy who initiates their use is not likely to deter the enemy from further use; instead, it may spur an escalation of WMD use, as happened in the Iran-Iraq War. Their use in retaliation can only be seen as an inhumane punishment of some unprotected front-line troops, most likely those with little responsibility for the initial attacks. Chemical and biological weapons are most effective as weapons of terror, against civilian populations who are the least protected from their dangers. Tactical nuclear weapons remain as yet a chimera. As in the cold war, so in any potential nuclear war in the Middle East or South Asia, it is difficult to imagine nuclear weapons being confined to the battlefield. Large civilian populations will be targeted and destroyed, particularly in a retaliatory second strike.[54] No Islamic state, no Islamic military force can pursue jihad while intentionally targeting the civilian population, even if the enemy is doing so. The attitude commonplace among early Muslim theorists that the responsibility for the death of enemy noncombatants lies with the enemy commanders who refused to remove them from harm's way cannot be validly applied in the age of WMD.

A second point requiring consideration in an Islamic framework is that any use of nuclear, biological, or even chemical weapons by a Muslim state in the Middle East or South Asia will assuredly result in the death of large numbers of Muslims living in the territory of the opponent or maybe in the Muslim state itself. Given the close geographical proximity of targets, how feasible is it to wage nuclear war (to focus on just this weapon for the moment) that will not, like the flooding of medieval armies, backfire on the attacker as radioactive fallout is deposited in neighboring countries?

An answer to this question is provided, for some contemporary theorists, in the doctrine of the general Muslim welfare that was closely allied with reciprocity in the early jurists' arguments from necessity. The best known and most coherent justification for suspending normal prohibitions because of the need to realize the general welfare of the Muslim community in extremis is that of al-Ghazali (d. 1111) in *al-Mustasfa min 'ilm al-usul* (Selected [topics] from the science of the sources [of jurisprudence]). Al-Ghazali is illustrating a general principle of jurisprudence, but conveniently for Muslim theorists of jihad, he uses a military hypothetical: When a dangerous non-Muslim enemy that threatens to overwhelm the territory of Islam and kill all Muslims uses Muslim captives as shields, it is permissible for Muslim troops to kill the Muslim captives as part of their attack on the enemy. The killing of the Muslim hostages violates clear qur'anic prohibitions on taking innocent life (Q. 4:93, 6:151), but in this case their deaths do not incur moral culpability because (1) it is a matter of vital necessity (*darura*), that is, there is no other way to stop the enemy attack; (2) the harm the enemy would inflict on the Muslims is a case of clear-cut certainty (*qat'iyya*); and (3) its importance is universal (*kulliya*) to all Muslims, because they would all be adversely affected by an enemy victory.[55]

In the Islamic tradition, al-Ghazali's argument comes closest to the notion of "supreme emergency" as formulated by Michael Walzer and as critiqued by Henry Shue in Chapter 7 of this book. We can only wonder what al-Ghazali would have argued with reference to weapons of mass destruction. Yet I have heard al-Ghazali's example invoked to sanction a possible nuclear attack by Pakistan against India, in spite of the fact that millions of Indian Muslims would certainly perish at the hands of their Pakistani coreligionists. The argument asks us to equate Muslim citizens of India with hostages being manipulated by the non-Muslim government of India as shields in its nuclear strategy. Leaving this strain in the analogy aside, it must be pointed out that al-Ghazali's invocation of necessity in this example involves the welfare of all or nearly all Muslims facing extinction; he clearly rules out the application of the same principle when a majority, even a large majority, confronts a similar situation.[56]

One could argue that the prospect of the annihilation of a Muslim nation, Pakistan, by Indian nuclear weapons meets the standard established by al-Ghazali. In this case, reasoning along the lines al-Ghazali establishes, does not the inexorable logic of the situation lead to a first, preemptive use of nuclear weapons by Pakistan? For what use would Pakistan's defensive arsenal be if it had failed to deter the enemy and the enemy had already destroyed much of its population? If the Indian nuclear attack is limited to the battlefield, then an all-out Pakistani response cannot be justified according to al-Ghazali's criteria nor even according to less strict notions of reciprocity. If the Indian attack is a massive assault using only conventional weapons that nevertheless threatens to destroy Pakistan, Pakistan's resort to nuclear weapons would be a case of first use, an escalation by it to weapons of mass destruction. Few Muslim theorists seem prepared to embrace this scenario.

DETERRENCE

For the first two decades of the nuclear age, Muslim states generally demonstrated very little interest in acquiring nuclear weapons. Zulfikar 'Ali Bhutto reports that in 1963 as a young counselor to Pakistan's military ruler, Muhammad Ayyub Khan, he had urged the start of a "peaceful nuclear program" to counter any nuclear threat arising from India. Ayyub Khan, Bhutto claims, showed no interest in such advice, saying: "If India went nuclear we would buy a weapon off the shelf somewhere."[57]

The logic of nuclear abstinence in the Indian subcontinent changed during the mid-1960s when India, threatened by China, moved steadily toward a nuclear capability. When India's "peaceful nuclear explosion" occurred on May 18, 1974, less than three years after the latest Indo-Pakistani war, a Pakistani response was assured. Bhutto, now the prime minister of the country, pledged not to succumb to India's "nuclear blackmail," which he linked directly to the continuing dispute over Kashmir and what he saw as India's desire to fragment further what was left of Pakistan in the wake of the secession of Bangladesh. By the time of Bhutto's overthrow in July 1977, Pakistan had advanced further than any other Muslim state toward the goal of acquiring nuclear weapons. From his prison cell, Bhutto penned lines intended to seal his legacy as the man who brought the atom bomb to Pakistan: "We know that Israel and South Africa have full nuclear capability. The Christian, Jewish, and Hindu civilizations have this capability. The communist powers also possess it. Only the Islamic civilization was without it, but that position was about to change."[58] From this bit of vague, self promoting grandiloquence would spring a double irony: first, that the secular Bhutto would be remembered as the man who coined the phrase "Islamic bomb," and second, that the idea of the Islamic bomb would serve well the interests of the regime that executed him. As part of its general resort to religion for legitimacy, the government of Zia al-Haq encouraged the grand illusion that

Pakistan's nuclear program was indeed serving not narrow national interests but the greater good of the entire Muslim nation, or *umma*.[59]

Throughout the two decades of nuclear ambiguity, Pakistani officials insisted that their nuclear program served only to deter the Indian threat, both conventional and nuclear. Haider Nizamani observes: "Zia's version of Pakistan was based upon a militarily strong, politically and socially homogenized Pakistan with 'Islamic ideology' as the ultimate test of patriotism, and the nuclear option as the best available sword to deter India. . . . "[60] The elite consensus on the necessity to match India's nuclear capabilities continued intact into the post-Zia period.

Thus, when India under a Hindu-nationalist government resumed nuclear testing on May 11, 1998, a Pakistani response was inevitable. In his address to the nation announcing the successful Pakistani tests, Prime Minister Nawaz Sharif declared, "Today we have fully settled the account of the nuclear tests conducted by India recently and have carried out five successful nuclear tests. Millions of thanks to God that he gave us the ability to carry out the retaliatory tests."[61] The Pakistani tests, the prime minister claimed, had restored the "power equilibrium" in the subcontinent.

The fact that Pakistan's tests came a mere seventeen days after the Indian explosions attests to strong pressures from not just the military but the public as well. Pakistan's principal Islamic party, the Jama'at-i Islami, had mobilized mass demonstrations throughout the country demanding that the government respond to the Indian "provocation." The Jama'at's leading spokesman on this issue and also a senator in the National Assembly was Khurshid Ahmad. In a 1995 seminar on "Pakistan's Security and the Nuclear Option," Ahmad maintained that "it was because of the nuclear deterrence that India and Pakistan did not go to war during the last eight years."[62] Six months after the Indian and Pakistani tests, he argued that Pakistan's goal should not be nuclear parity with India but "competitive capability." In practical terms, this meant that Pakistan must continue its testing in the face of international pressures to declare a moratorium. The Islamic justification Ahmad provides is the following: "The Qur'anic command is . . . very clear. 'Make ready for an encounter against them all the forces and wellreadied horses you can muster that you may overawe the enemies of Allah and your own enemies and others besides them of whom you are unaware, but of whom Allah is aware. Whatever you may spend in the cause of Allah shall be fully repaid to you, and you shall not be wronged' (al-Anfal 8:60). This principle of deterrent power is a dynamic concept and must not be compromised if we want to protect our honour, faith and national security."[63]

The qur'anic verse Ahmad cites (8:60) is invariably cited by Muslim scholars who express an opinion on the subject of nuclear proliferation. For them, the verse not only permits but requires Muslim states to acquire whatever means are necessary to defend themselves. The verse frames the issue of military preparedness in terms of deterrence, and the consensus of Muslim opinion is that nuclear and other weapons of mass destruction serve primarily as a deterrent.

Unfortunately, beyond this rather superficial level, the Muslim discussion has yet to advance much further. The legitimation of nuclear weapons as a deterrent raises of course some very difficult moral issues. Does nuclear deterrence promote stability or instability in a hostile environment? Which deterrence strategy is the most effective, counterforce or countervalue? If counterforce targeting is adopted, can escalation be prevented? If countervalue targeting is adopted, is it morally acceptable to threaten the extinction of civilian populations?

Stable deterrence requires the confidence by the belligerents that both sides are capable of surviving a first strike with enough weapons intact to launch a second strike. Thus a credible deterrence strategy inevitably fuels an arms race. Such costly ventures are financially disastrous and morally unjustifiable for impoverished third world states. The security returns are dubious at best while the opportunity costs of resources diverted are staggering.

The counterargument is sometimes made that in fact nuclear weapons reduce defense expenditures. In a July 1998 interview, Pakistan's foreign minister, Gawhar Ayyub Khan, stated: "The cost of the nuclear program and the production of the missiles is much less than the cost of tanks and aircraft. The costs of the nuclear program and missiles are the cheapest costs for a most effective system of weapons." This is a disingenuous claim; because nuclear weapons serve primarily political and not military purposes, their very "unusability" does not permit a concomitant decrease in conventional weapons spending. When the journalist interviewing Gawhar Ayyub Khan pressed him on this issue by asking whether Pakistan would rely on nuclear weapons to provide the security heretofore provided by conventional weapons, the foreign minister responded predictably: "We can never dispense with the need for tanks and artillery, which are weapons with varied objectives."[64]

Finally, to consider the question of threatening evil in order to forestall evil, which lies at the heart of nuclear deterrence: According to one of the foundational prophetic *hadiths* in Islamic ethics, "Actions are judged by intentions."[65] The intent (*niyya*) behind nuclear deterrence may, to some Muslims, be the praiseworthy goals of averting war, especially nuclear war, or of defending one's nation. But behind the strategy of nuclear deterrence, whether it is counterforce or countervalue, lies the assured killing of large numbers of innocents, the ravaging of the natural environment, and the injuring of generations yet unborn. These actions cannot be justified by any intent, not even the intent of averting some "supreme emergency" such as the feared death of large numbers of Muslims, as I argued in the previous section.

To this some may respond that nuclear deterrence can rely on the intent merely to deceive the enemy, to keep the enemy guessing whether such weapons will actually be used in war or not. After all, didn't the Prophet say, "War is deception"?[66] The problem with this line of reasoning is that nuclear deterrence, unlike conventional deterrence of the sort that the Prophet may have had in mind in the last *hadith* or that the Qur'an discusses in verse 8:60, has catastrophe awaiting both the would-be deterrer and deterred should deterrence fail. Nuclear deterrence works only when there is the conviction on the part of one's opponent that one intends to use nuclear weapons. The more money and energy one expends on convincing the other side of the sincerity of one's intentions, the more blurry the intentions become, and the more likely one is to cross the threshold.

PROLIFERATION

The majority view in Islamic intellectual circles, as I have been able to discern it, is that proliferation is both inevitable and morally acceptable, if not desirable. The responsibility for proliferation lies not with Muslims, the claim is frequently made, but with their enemies – Israel in the Middle East and India in South Asia – who introduced weapons of mass destruction into their respective conflicts.

Egypt, Iran, Libya, Pakistan, Sudan, and Syria are believed to have chemical and biological weapons programs.[67] As for nuclear weapons, in spite of the dominant discourse favoring nuclear proliferation during the past thirty years, the cases of nonproliferation are as prominent as those of proliferation. Algeria, Egypt, and Syria, three Arab states that during the 1970s and 1980s seemed poised to develop a nuclear-weapons program, today appear to have given up such ambitions. Given the United States's inability to uncover Saddam Hussein's alleged WMD arsenal, it would seem that Iraq's WMD program was dealt a crippling blow by the UN inspections regime after the Gulf War. Libya announced in December 2003 that it would dismantle its WMD research and development programs and allow UN inspectors to verify its compliance with international agreements. The Iranian case is considered in detail in the following section.

Only Pakistan to date has taken the final step in violation of the nuclear nonproliferation regime. Having acquired nuclear weapons, the question now is, will it abide by the nonproliferation regime in the future?

The notion of an "Islamic bomb" is central to answering this question. In the aftermath of the Pakistani tests, Jama'at-i Islami supporters dragged through the streets of Islamabad models of missiles with the words "Islamic bomb" stenciled down their side. It is clear from the statements of Jama'at leaders that the phrase carries more than merely rhetorical value. Khurshid Ahmad has repeatedly emphasized that while Pakistan's nuclear deterrent is aimed at countering India, Pakistan as an Islamic state has responsibilities to the broader Muslim *umma.* No matter how much Pakistani officials disavow any military role in the continuing Palestinian-Israeli conflict, he states, Pakistan's nuclear weapons will inevitably be seen as a threat by Israel, and therefore Pakistan must include Israel in its defense planning. In spite of their tremendous oil wealth, the Arabs "figure nowhere by way of either conventional or nuclear defence capability. Their freedom and security hangs by a 'thread,' which the U.S. and/or Israel can sever any moment. Under the circumstances, the future of the Muslim world depends on Pakistan. That is exactly why the whole political, economic and technological pressure is exerted against Pakistan."[68] It is unclear from Ahmad's statements what he considers to be morally required of Pakistan in its defense of the *umma.* Should Pakistan actively assist in the proliferation of nuclear weapons by providing technical expertise and fissionable material to other states? Or should its nuclear arsenal provide eventually a type of extended deterrence to other Muslim countries?

The official Pakistani stance under both Nawaz Sharif and Pervez Musharraf is to deny categorically any pan-Islamic nuclear ambitions. In July 1998, Nawaz Sharif castigated Pakistanis who provided "grist to [the] propaganda mill by their irresponsible statements." The propaganda he was referring to originated, he alleged, in the pro-Israel and pro-India lobbies in the West, which were assiduously "trying to give a religious colour to our nuclear accomplishment. . . . What they are aiming at is to persuade the Western publics into believing that what Pakistan has produced is actually an 'Islamic bomb' that would soon be in the hands of countries like Iran, Libya, and Sudan. . . . " Pakistanis who claimed "that this accomplishment has ensured the security of the Muslim world, particularly of our Arab brethren against a nuclear Israel . . . are in fact unwittingly playing into the hands of the anti-Pakistan lobbies. . . . "[69]

In an earlier statement, Gawhar Ayyub Khan had even more pointedly rejected the idea of an Islamic bomb: "We must not call it 'Islamic Bomb,' for there is nothing called a Christian bomb, a Jewish bomb, or a Communist bomb." The fact that a former prime minister of Pakistan had authored these terms seems to be conveniently forgotten in official Pakistani circles. "The West is trying to brand our bomb the 'Islamic Bomb' when it was the result of the efforts of Pakistani scientists and so it is a 'Pakistani bomb' and our missiles are Pakistani missiles. We would like to keep things in this framework so that the West does not use them to detract from the Islamic countries."[70]

As the Pakistani debate indicates, nuclear proliferation has already become firmly entangled in the rhetorical appeals to Islamic cooperation. But there is little indication, despite the sloganeering of Islamists and the fears of various security analysts, that Pakistan or any other Muslim state will depart from the pattern of pursuing its own national interests for the sake of Islamic solidarity.

DISARMAMENT

When the Soviet Union fragmented in 1991, Kazakhstan became the first state with a predominantly Muslim population to possess nuclear weapons. Its subsequent decision to repatriate nuclear warheads to Russia is the first and only case so far of nuclear disarmament by a Muslim-majority state. Islam probably did not figure in any way in the Kazakh decision.

The clearest and yet most enigmatic case of Islamic ethical concerns leading to the abandonment of a nuclear program comes from postrevolutionary Iran. The Islamic republic inherited from the shah one of the most ambitious and active nuclear technology programs of that time. Launched in the 1960s, the shah's $30 billion project envisioned the construction of twenty nuclear plants by the year 2000. A central, though unstated component of the nuclear project was the acquisition of nuclear weapons capability by the 1980s.

In March 1979, within months of coming to power, the revolutionary government completely halted work at the Bushehr and Darkhuin reactors, the country's two most developed nuclear facilities. At the time the nuclear project was abandoned, the two Bushehr reactors being constructed by a German consortium had reached 90 percent completion; the Darkhuin reactor being built by a French company had reached 30 percent completion. German ships waiting to unload equipment at Bushehr returned with their cargoes after sitting idly in port for months.

The reasons for the sudden abandonment of Iran's nuclear program remain unclear, but reports from Iranian scientists discharged after the decision was made point to moral and ideological qualms expressed by Khomeini. One scientist was advised to join the revolutionary guards because there would be no further use for his skills in nuclear engineering. Khomeini, he was told, considered projects to make Iran a nuclear power or an industrial giant like Japan to be "idolatrous projects."[71]

Ebrahim Yazdi, who served as foreign minister from April to November 1979, emphasizes the role of the provisional government led by Mehdi Bazargan, not Khomeini, in stopping Iran's nuclear program. The government decided, Yazdi states, that for a country with such large petroleum and natural gas reserves, development of nuclear energy was an unnecessary cost. As for the acquisition of nuclear weapons, Yazdi recalls that moral qualms factored into the decision to abandon any such plans:

There is no way to justify the use of nuclear weapons against any target, if one considers the qur'anic teachings. We considered developing nuclear weapons as a deterrent factor, but decided it also was not acceptable. The point here was this: Why should a third world, developing country such as Iran, or a country as poor as India and Pakistan with more urgent economic and educational priorities, invest a large amount of its resources in developing nuclear energy – or even worse, spend those resources for nuclear weapons? So we were against it.[72]

Even after the beginning of the Iran-Iraq War, Iran waited several years before making any moves to revive its nuclear program. In 1984, 'Ali Khamenei, then the country's president, created a committee of experts led by one of the few remaining nuclear scientists in Iran, Reza Amrollahi, to plan for the resumption of the Bushehr and Darkhuin projects. After several months of deliberation, the committee declared that the government's initial policy of abandonment had been misguided and had significantly harmed Iran's national interests. One committee member wrote: "They (Revolution Command Council members) betrayed our people with their March 1979 decision to abolish the reactor project."[73]

Resumption of the unfinished projects proved much more difficult than the committee envisaged in 1984 because of the political isolation of Iran during the war. From 1985 to 1992, Iranian officials tried unsuccessfully to conclude agreements with the original German and French firms, and when these negotiations failed, turned to Italian, Austrian, Japanese, and South Korean companies. Under strong pressure from the United States, all these negotiations ended unsuccessfully. In 1991, reports of Chinese sales of nuclear technology to Iran led to renewed concerns from Western governments, despite Chinese and Iranian assurances that the sale had involved equipment necessary for the peaceful exploitation of nuclear power. When the supply from China proved inadequate, Iranian officials concluded an agreement with Russia for the training of nuclear technicians as well as for assistance in completing the two Bushehr reactors. The Western boycott of necessary equipment, however, has hampered progress toward completion of the reactors.

The revival of Iran's nuclear program has been accompanied by persistent denials from Iranian officials that they seek nuclear weapons. Iran's representative to the International Atomic Energy Agency (IAEA), Muhammad Sadiq Ayatollahi, stated in June 1995: "Ideologically, it is not appropriate for us to develop any nuclear weapons and weapons of mass destruction.... There is no reason for Iran to seek nuclear weapons. If we are going to make any progress, it must be because of our principles, and to reach our goals we do not need nuclear weapons. The Islamic revolution was victorious without even having any rifles or other arms."[74]

Yet the Iranian position has not been entirely consistent on this issue. Former President 'Ali Akbar Hashemi Rafsanjani was quoted as calling for both the outright prohibition and destruction of nuclear weapons as well as for Iran's right to develop them and other weapons of mass destruction. In a speech made in 1988 to the revolutionary guards, he declared: "We should fully equip ourselves both in the offensive and defensive use of chemical, bacteriological, and radiological weapons. From now on you should make use of the opportunity and perform the task."[75] The present government of Muhammad Khatami has continued to develop what it insists is the peaceful use of nuclear technology, but in May 1998 it was one of the first governments to congratulate Pakistan on its successful nuclear tests. The strongest evidence thus far that Iran's civilian nuclear program may be cloaking research into military applications came in November 2003, when Iran admitted to IAEA investigators that it had produced small amounts of low-enriched uranium and plutonium, both of which are elements used in nuclear bombs. The IAEA report on Iran's disclosures concluded: "To date, there is no evidence that the previously undeclared nuclear material and activities . . . were related to a nuclear weapons programme. However, given Iran's past pattern of concealment, it will take some time before the Agency is able to conclude that Iran's nuclear programme is exclusively for peaceful purposes."[76] Iran subsequently signed a protocol that allows stricter IAEA inspections of its nuclear facilities.

Regional and universal nuclear disarmament have been championed not only by a number of Muslim states but by Muslim organizations as well. In March 1984, the Mu'tamar-i 'Alam-i Islami (World Muslim Congress), a nongovernmental organization, convened a seminar at the University of Karachi in Pakistan titled "Nuclear Arms Race and Nuclear Disarmament: The Muslim Perspective." Unfortunately, the proceedings of the conference were not published, and so the conference did little to advance Muslim discourse on this topic. Nevertheless, the conference's final communiqué contains several points on which discussion could proceed. It called for Muslim states to continue developing peaceful uses of nuclear technology, but concluded with regard to nuclear weapons:

1. the teachings of Islam, as contained in the Qur'an and *sunna*, command Muslims "to uncompromisingly oppose the use of any such barbaric instruments of death as there is no room in Islam for indiscriminate killings and destruction";
2. nuclear weapon states have a "moral obligation" to renounce the use of nuclear weapons;
3. the development of nuclear weapons in all forms should be frozen and the nuclear weapons already in stockpile progressively dismantled and nuclear materials so recovered put to peaceful purposes only;
4. all efforts be made to heighten awareness of the enormous resources committed to the development of nuclear weapons, resources that could be better spent on tackling "the problems of hunger, disease, ignorance, lack of shelter and poverty in general which afflict a large part of humanity today, particularly in the Third World countries";
5. all efforts be made by states to establish nuclear-free-zones in Africa, the Middle East, and South Asia.[77]

Yet in the aftermath of the Indian tests of 1998, voices for disarmament have been virtually silenced by the clamor for a Pakistani response. The logic of tit-for-tat that dominates Pakistani military planning and is widely supported by the public obviates any possibility of unilateral disarmament in the foreseeable future. Khurshid Ahmad expresses well the national consensus: "Pakistan is a de facto nuclear power, exactly as India is. Now it is not going to revert to be a non-nuclear state or a nuclear threshold country. If the world is not accepting our position, we accept not the position the world wishes to accord us."[78]

CONCRETE OPTIONS

The vast majority of Muslim states are signatories to the various international agreements regulating the proliferation and use of weapons of mass destruction. Of the fifty-six current member-states of the Organization of the Islamic Conference (OIC), forty-four have signed the Biological and Toxin Weapons Convention, fifty have signed the Chemical Weapons Convention,[79] fifty-five have signed the Nonproliferation Treaty, and forty-nine have signed the Comprehensive Test Ban Treaty. Of the seven OIC members whose ratification is necessary for the CTBT to enter into force (listed at the beginning of this chapter), six have signed the treaty, but only three – Algeria, Bangladesh, and Turkey – have to date ratified it.

Pakistan is the most notable nonsignatory to the Nonproliferation Treaty (NPT) and the Comprehensive Test Ban Treaty (CTBT). Its official reason for refusing to sign these agreements is not opposition to their terms but the fact that India refuses to sign. This policy has been endorsed by most of the Islamic parties in the country as well. Khurshid Ahmad, for example, has led the charge in the Pakistani parliament to prevent Pakistani compliance with either the NPT or the CTBT. His objections focus not simply on the Indian noncompliance but on what he considers to be problems inherent in the "Global Nuclear Regime." The regime is "discriminatory and a means of exploitation, which has been formulated to safeguard the interests and supremacy of the big powers."[80]

Ahmad's comments highlight the fact that much of the Muslim critique of international agreements on weapons of mass destruction derives not from Islamic concerns per se but from the broader third world critique of the double standards applied by Western powers.[81] This became quite clear during the 1995 debate on the renewal of the NPT. In an attempt to spur the Egyptian government's increasingly vocal criticism of Israeli noncompliance with the NPT, several prominent 'ulama ventured into an area they had rarely addressed before. Muhammad al-Ghazali wondered how the Egyptian government could sign an agreement banning a weapon that it did not possess and called for an international boycott of Israel should it fail to sign the treaty. He declared that Muslims should develop a nuclear capability that surpassed Israel's because the Israeli arsenal posed a clear threat to the Muslim countries.[82]

In short, the Islamic critique calls not for the overthrow of the existing international regime, but for its fair and consistent application. Such a basic demand is no doubt justified. But the more fundamental question is what policies Muslim states should pursue given the present realities of unfair and uneven application and the continuing proliferation of weapons of mass destruction. Charges of hypocrisy and double standards are a weak ethical foundation on which to ground action. Such a foundation yields reactive policies that demonstrate a lack of moral vision and abnegation of moral responsibility.

If Muslims are to act on the basis of Islamic ethics, then they cannot, I believe, contemplate any use of weapons of mass destruction. If WMD are not to be used in war, then their development for deterrence (or worse yet, for national prestige) alone is morally, economically, and militarily unjustifiable. As history has shown, they do not deter conventional or unconventional (that is, guerrilla or low-intensity) wars. Whether or not they deter the escalation to WMD is disputed, but the risks of catastrophe from only one failure of deterrence are certain. And alas, threats to Muslims today come not only from foreign states or their own repressive states but from Muslim terrorist organizations operating within Muslim states. The terrorists have demonstrated that they are as ready to kill large numbers of innocent Muslims as they are innocent non-Muslims. The only real way to assure that such people cannot enact mass murder is for states to eschew the weapons that make it all too easy.

Notes

I wish to thank the scores of Muslim scholars and activists in more than seven countries who during the past fifteen years have shared with me their views on Islamic ethics and WMD. Though I cannot mention each by name, and I often disagreed with their positions, my thinking on this issue owes much to them. I am particularly grateful to Dr. Ebrahim Yazdi, whose generous responses to my questions on the Islamic Republic of Iran's nuclear policies greatly contributed to this chapter.

1. Bob Woodward, Robert G. Kaiser, and David B. Ottaway, "U.S. Fears Bin Laden Made Nuclear Strides," *Washington Post*, December 4, 2001, p. A01. Anthony Lloyd, "Scientists Confirm Bin Laden Weapons Tests," *The Times* (London), December 29, 2001, pp. 4–5. An al-Qaʻida training manual on war allegedly contains a "Book 11" on chemical and biological warfare. See Mike Boettcher, "Evidence Suggests al Qaeda Pursuit of Biological, Chemical Weapons," at http://www.cnn.com/2001/WORLD/asiapcf/central/11/14/chemical.bio (August 10, 2003). The U.S. Department of Justice has posted brief excerpts from other sections of the manual at http://www.usdoj.gov/ag/trainingmanual.htm (August 10, 2003).

2. I have suggested possible reasons for the contemporary focus on *jus ad bellum* over *jus in bello* in Sohail H. Hashmi, "Saving and Taking Life in War: Three

Modern Muslim Views," in *Islamic Ethics of Life: Abortion, War, and Euthanasia*, ed. Jonathan E. Brockopp (Columbia: University of South Carolina Press, 2003), 129–54.

3. Samina Ahmed and David Cortright observed in the case of Pakistan before the 1998 tests: "There is little or no input on nuclear policy making from senior political leaders and no involvement from the wider public.... In the absence of informed opinion among elected representatives, public opinion in Pakistan has generally accepted official rhetoric. This internalization of established policy is assisted by prolonged exposure to governmental propaganda conducted via the officially controlled electronic media or through the aegis of sympathetic academics, media personalities, or retired civil and military bureaucrats." "Pakistani Public Opinion and Nuclear Weapons Policy," in *Pakistan and the Bomb: Public Opinion and Nuclear Options*, ed. Samina Ahmed and David Cortright (Notre Dame, Ind.: University of Notre Dame Press, 1998), 7.

4. I have adapted to the Islamic context the categories outlined by Janice Love for the Christian discourse on nuclear weapons: nuclear just war, nuclear pacifism, and apocalypticism. Janice Love, "From Pacifism to Apocalyptic Visions: Religious Perspectives on Nuclear Deterrence," in *After the Cold War: Questioning the Morality of Nuclear Deterrence*, ed. Charles W. Kegley, Jr., and Kenneth L. Schwab (Boulder, Colo.: Westview, 1991), 157–76.

5. See Ralph E. Crow, Philip Grant, and Saad E. Ibrahim, eds., *Arab Nonviolent Political Struggle in the Middle East* (Boulder, Colo.: Lynne Rienner, 1990).

6. For a concise treatment of Islamic environmental ethics, see Mawil Y. Izzi Deen (Samarrai), "Islamic Environmental Ethics: Law and Society," in *Ethics of Environment and Development: Global Challenge, International Response*, ed. J. Ronald Engel and Joan Gibb Engel (Tucson: University of Arizona Press, 1990), 189–98.

7. The general qur'anic command is "Do not waste, for truly he [God] does not love the wasteful" (Q. 6:141, 7:31). According to one prophetic *hadith*: "God hates three things: (1) vain, useless talk, or that you talk too much about others, (2) to ask too many questions (in disputed religious matters), and (3) to waste wealth (extravagance)." Muhammad b. Isma'il al-Bukhari, *Sahih al-Bukhari*, trans. Muhammad Muhsin Khan (Beirut: Dar al-Arabia, 1985), 3:348–49.

8. Sunni writers sometimes included the practice of the Prophet's first four successors, the "rightly guided" caliphs within the scope of *sunna*, and Shi'ite writers did likewise with the imams, most notably 'Ali b. Abu Talib. Nevertheless, such broadening of the concept did not significantly expand the range of normative precedents available on many issues relating to war.

9. For surveys of the classical Islamic literature on war, see Muhammad Hamidullah, *Muslim Conduct of State*, 7th ed. (Lahore: Shaykh Muhammad Ashraf, 1961); John Kelsay, *Islam and War* (Louisville, Ky.: Westminster/John Knox Press, 1993); Majid Khadduri, *War and Peace in the Law of Islam* (Baltimore, Md.: Johns Hopkins University Press, 1955); Alfred Morabia, *Le Gihad dans l'Islam médiéval: Le "combat sacré" des origines au XIIe siècle* (Paris: Albin Michel, 1993). A more concise overview is available in Sohail H. Hashmi, "Interpreting the Islamic Ethics of War and Peace," in *The Ethics of War and Peace: Religious and Secular Perspectives*, ed. Terry Nardin (Princeton, N.J.: Princeton University Press, 1996).

10. See Etan Kohlberg, "The Development of the Imami Shi'i Doctrine of *Jihad*," *Zeitschrift der Morgenländischen Gesellschaft* 126:1 (1976): 64–86.

11. For a sample, see Muhammad b. 'Abdallah, Khatib al-Tabrizi, *Mishkat al-Masabih*, trans. Mawlana Fazlul Karim (New Delhi: Islamic Book Service, 1998), 2:387–89.

12. Ibn Taymiyya, *al-Siyasa al-shar'iyya*, excerpt trans. Rudolph Peters, *Jihad in Classical and Modern Islam: A Reader* (Princeton, N.J.: Markus Wiener, 1996), 49.

13. The Azariqa did in fact perpetrate a number of atrocities, during the lifetime of Nafi' b. al-Azraq and after his death, in which they killed whole villages who refused to join their camp. Curiously, Jews, Christians, and Zoroastrians were treated with much greater tolerance than Muslims in the Azariqa creed. As "people of the book," they were to be granted the protection of *dhimmi* status conferred on them by Q. 9:29. See *Encyclopaedia of Islam*, new ed., s.v. Azarika, Isti'rad, Kharidjites, Nafi' b. al-Azrak.

14. Borrowing from the writings of Mawdudi and Sayyid Qutb, the ideologues of these radical groups view contemporary Muslim societies as being in a state of *jahiliyya* (lit., "ignorance") akin to that prevailing in Arabia before Islam. They are fundamentally un-Islamic in their laws and mores; the Muslims living in them are only nominal Muslims, if not outright apostates. Thus, it is incumbent on the true Muslims to fight and kill the infidels if they resist the establishment of an authentic Islamic order. The Armed Islamic Group is alleged to have killed entire villages in its campaign against the secular Algerian government, in a civil war that has cost 100,000 lives. Hamas and Palestinian Islamic Jihad have orchestrated suicide bombings and other types of attacks that have killed hundreds of Israeli civilians, in retaliation, they claim, for Israeli killings of Palestinian civilians. Among other attacks, the Jama'at Islamiyya killed fifty-eight foreign tourists in Luxor in November 1997.

15. World Islamic Front Statement, "Jihad against Jews and Crusaders," issued February 23, 1998. Text at http://www.washingtonpost.com/ac2/wp_dyn/A4993/2001Sep21 (October 5, 2001). The qur'anic reference is to 9:36.

16. For other Muslim statements on the compatibility of international humanitarian law and Islamic principles, see the following: Yadh ben Ashoor, *Islam and International Humanitarian Law* (Geneva: International Committee of the Red Cross, 1980); and the survey of Muslim doctrine and contemporary practice by Karima Bennoune, "As-Salamu 'Alaykum? Humanitarian Law in Islamic Jurisprudence," *Michigan Journal of International Law* 15 (Winter 1994): 605–43. Ann Elizabeth Mayer, "War and Peace in the Islamic Tradition and International Law," in *Just War and Jihad*, ed. John Kelsay and James Turner Johnson (New York: Greenwood, 1991), 198, sums up the state of the current Muslim discourse quite accurately: "In the absence of updated versions of the premodern *shari'a* rules regulating the conduct of war, the international legal standards have become the operative norms." At least one prominent Muslim jurist has called explicitly for the systematic "updating" of Islamic international law; see Mohammed Bedjaoui, "The Gulf War of 1980–1988 and the Islamic Conception of International Law," in *The Gulf War of 1980–1988: The Iran-Iraq War in International Legal Perspective*, ed. Ige F. Dekker and Harry H. G. Post (The Hague:

Martinus Nijhoff, 1992), 296. The Organization of the Islamic Conference took a step in this direction in 1980 by voting to create an International Islamic Law Commission, but so far this body has yet to convene.

17. Wahba al-Zuhayli, *Athar al-harb fi al-fiqh al-Islami: Dirasa muqarana* (Damascus: Dar al-Fikr, 1981), 503. For more details on contemporary Islamic views on noncombatant immunity, see Hashmi, "Saving and Taking Life in War."

18. Ibn Hisham's notes, in Ibn Ishaq, *The Life of Muhammad*, trans. Alfred Guillaume (Karachi: Oxford University Press, 1990), 779 n. 840.

19. Ibid., 589.

20. Ahmad ibn Yahya al-Baladhuri, *Kitab futuh al-buldan (The Origins of the Islamic State)*, trans. Philip Hitti (Beirut: Khayats, 1966), 348.

21. *Encyclopaedia of Islam*, new ed., s.v. "Naft."

22. Narrated by al-Bukhari, *Sahih al-Bukhari*, 4:127.

23. Wahba al-Zuhayli, *al-'Alaqat al-duwaliyya fi al-Islam: Muqarana bi al-qanun al-duwali al-hadith* (Beirut: Mu'assasat al-Risala, 1981), 45–55; Muhammad Khayr Haykal, *al-Jihad wa al-qital fi al-siyasa al-shar'iyya* (Beirut: Dar al-Bayariq, 1996), 2:1348–53.

24. Hamidullah, *Muslim Conduct of State*, 226.

25. See al-Zuhayli, *al-'Alaqat al-duwaliyya fi al-Islam*, 50.

26. Muhammad ibn al-Hasan al-Shaybani, *Kitab al-siyar al-kabir (The Islamic Law of Nations: Shaybani's Siyar)*, trans. Majid Khadduri (Baltimore, Md.: Johns Hopkins University Press, 1966), 101–2.

27. Al-Zuhayli, *al-'Alaqat al-duwaliyya*, 50–55.

28. *Encyclopaedia of Islam*, new ed., s.v. "Hisn."

29. Ibid., s.v. "Harb."

30. Ibn Rushd, *Bidayat al-mujtahid*, trans. Peters, *Jihad in Classical and Modern Islam*, 37.

31. See Ibn Ishaq, *Life of Muhammad*, 437, 589. The Qur'an speaks approvingly of the cutting down of the Banu Nadir's palm trees in 59:5.

32. For example, Q. 2:205 reads: "When he [the hypocrite] turns his back, his aim everywhere is to spread mischief throughout the earth and destroy crops and cattle, but God loves not mischief [*fasad*]."

33. Abu Ja'far Muhammad b. Jarir al-Tabari, *Ta'rikh al-rusul wa'l-muluk (The History of al-Tabari)*, vol. 10: *The Conquest of Arabia*, trans. Fred M. Donner (Albany: State University of New York Press, 1993), 16.

34. Ibn Rushd, *Bidayat al-mujtahid*, 36–37.

35. Ibid.; al-Zuhayli, *al-'Alaqat al-duwaliyya*, 50–55.

36. Appeals to necessity in classical sources on war are summarized in 'Arif Abu 'Id, *al-'Alaqat al-kharijiyya fi dawlat al-khilafa* (Birmingham, U.K.: Dar al-Arqam, 1990), 191–226.

37. See Uriel Heyd, "The Ottoman 'Ulema and Westernization," in *Studies in Islamic History and Civilization*, ed. Uriel Heyd (Jerusalem: Hebrew University Press, 1961), 74–75.

38. E. J. Hogendoorn, "A Chemical Weapons Atlas," *Bulletin of the Atomic Scientists* 53:5 (September–October 1997) at http://www.bullatomsci.org/issues/1997/so97/so97hogendoom.html (August 10, 2003). Federation of American Scientists, "Egypt: Chemical Weapons Program," at http://www.fas.org/nuke/

guide/egypt/cw (August 10, 2003). Richard M. Price, *The Chemical Weapons Taboo* (Ithaca, N.Y., and London: Cornell University Press, 1997), 134.

39. Cited in Julian Perry Robinson and Jozef Goldblat, "Chemical Warfare in the Iran-Iraq War," Stockholm International Peace Research Fact Sheet (May 1984) at www.sipri.se/cbw/research/factsheet-1984.html (March 21, 2001).

40. See Gregory F. Giles, "The Islamic Republic of Iran and Nuclear, Biological, and Chemical Weapons," in *Planning the Unthinkable: How New Powers Will Use Nuclear, Biological, and Chemical Weapons*, ed. Peter R. Lavoy, Scott D. Sagan, and James J. Wirtz (Ithaca, N.Y., and London: Cornell University Press, 2000), 79–103.

41. A CIA report written during the war states: "Whenever the Iraqis used good delivery techniques, weather conditions, *and the Iranians were not adequately prepared or trained*, the use of chemical weapons has been effective" (emphasis added). "Impact and Implications of Chemical Weapons Use in the Iran-Iraq War," at http://www.fas.org/ irp/gulf/cia/960702/72566/01.htm (August 10, 2003). See also Javed Ali, "Chemical Weapons and the Iran-Iraq War: A Case Study in Noncompliance," *Nonproliferation Review* 8:1 (Spring 2001): 43–58.

42. Giles, "Iran and Nuclear, Biological, and Chemical Weapons," 92.

43. Estimates of the casualties at Halabja vary widely; the figures cited here are those most widely used. The identity of the attackers at Halabja has also been the subject of much controversy since the attack took place. The controversy was reinvigorated when the George W. Bush administration frequently cited Saddam Hussein's gassing of "his own people" as a primary justification for attacking Iraq. Stephen Pelletiere, a CIA officer stationed in Baghdad during the Iran-Iraq War, responded in an op-ed titled "A War Crime or an Act of War?" *New York Times*, January 31, 2003, p. A29, by reiterating claims made in his previous publications that the civilians of Halabja were the unintentional victims of a gas attack by both Iraqi and Iranian fighters against each other. This suggestion is countered by eyewitness accounts of villagers who testified that clearly marked Iraqi military airplanes made repeated runs over Halabja as they sprayed their chemical munitions. In addition, a tremendous amount of documentary evidence has been gathered that consistently holds Iraq responsible for not only this attack but others against Kurdish civilians as part of the Anfal campaign. See George Black, *Genocide in Iraq: The Anfal Campaign against the Kurds* (New York: Human Rights Watch, 1993). For the sake of my argument here, whether the Iraqis or the Iranians or both were responsible for the chemical attack on Halabja is immaterial; the essential point is that unprotected civilians, in or near a conflict zone, are the most likely victims of chemical weapons, even if they are not the direct targets.

44. Transcript of "Halabja: 14 Years Later," *60 Minutes* (CBS News), May 12, 2002. See also Dr. Gosden's testimony before two U.S. Senate subcommittees on April 22, 1998, at http://www.fas.org/irp/congress/1998_hr/s980422-cg.htm (May 12, 2002).

45. One pro-Iranian collection of essays contains a brief, general survey of some of the moral-legal issues relevant to the Iran-Iraq War, but doesn't address the war itself. See Hamid Algar, "The Problem of Retaliation in Modern Warfare from the Point of View of *Fiqh*," in *The Iran-Iraq War: The Politics of Aggression*, ed. Farhang Rajaee (Gainesville: University Press of Florida, 1993), 191–97.

46. Al-Zuhayli, *al-'Alaqat al-duwaliyya*, 48.

47. Al-Zuhayli, *Athar al-harb fi al-fiqh al-Islami*, 789.

48. Author's interview with Wahba al-Zuhayli, Damascus, Syria, January 2, 1991.

49. Rahimullah Yousafsai, "Terror Suspect: An Interview with Osama bin Laden," December 22, 1998, at http://abcnews.go.com/sections/world/DailyNews/transcript_ binladen1_981228.html (August 17, 2003).

50. Hamid Mir, "Interview with Usama bin Ladin," *Daily Ausaf* (Islamabad), November 9, 2001 (in Urdu).

51. David Johnston and James Risen, "U.S. Concludes Al Qaeda Lacked a Chemical or Biological Stockpile," *New York Times*, March 20, 2002, p. A14.

52. Four particularly useful studies are A. R. Norton and M. H. Greenberg, eds., *Studies in Nuclear Terrorism* (Boston: G. K. Hall, 1979); Bruce Hoffman, *Inside Terrorism* (New York: Columbia University Press, 1998); Jessica Stern, *The Ultimate Terrorists* (Cambridge: Harvard University Press, 1999); and Nadine Gurr and Benjamin Cole, *The New Face of Terrorism: Threats from Weapons of Mass Destruction* (London: I. B. Tauris, 2000).

53. Mir, "Interview with Bin Ladin."

54. Estimates of the casualties resulting from one Hiroshima-type nuclear bomb dropped on each of India's and Pakistan's five largest cities are 2.9 million killed and 1.5 million severely injured. Cities are likely to be targeted even in a counterforce strategy because large military bases are invariably situated near them. See Matthew McKinzie, Zia Mian, A. H. Nayyar, and M. V. Ramana, "The Risks and Consequences of Nuclear War in South Asia," in *Out of the Nuclear Shadow*, ed. Smitu Kothari and Zia Mian (Delhi: Lokayan, 2001), 185–96.

55. Abu Hamid Muhammad al-Ghazali, *al-Mustasfa min 'ilm al-usul*, ed. Muhammad Sulayman al-Ashqar (Beirut: Mu'assasat al-Risala, 1997), 1: 420–21. See also Malcolm Kerr, *Islamic Reform: The Political and Legal Theories of Muhammad 'Abduh and Rashid Rida* (Berkeley: University of California Press, 1966), 93–94.

56. Al-Ghazali, *al-Mustasfa*, 1: 421; Kerr, *Islamic Reform*, 93–94.

57. Haider K. Nizamani, *The Roots of Rhetoric: Politics of Nuclear Weapons in India and Pakistan* (Westport, Conn.: Praeger, 2000), 86–87.

58. Zulfikar Ali Bhutto, *If I Am Assassinated* (Delhi: Vikas, 1979), 138.

59. The following statement of Zia al-Haq from 1986 is typical of the ambiguity promoted by his government on this point: "Why must they call Pakistan's bomb, supposing we have it, an Islamic bomb? . . . You can see the mentality. They are fearful that if an Islamic country such as Pakistan acquires this technology they will spread it. In fact, if the Islamic world possessed this technology, it means that 900 million Muslims possess advanced technology. Hence comes the aggressive campaign against Pakistan and the aggressive talk about the Pakistani nuclear bomb. It is our right to obtain the technology. And when we acquire this technology, the entire Islamic world will possess it with us." Quoted in Elaine Sciolino, "Who's Afraid of the Islamic Bomb?" *New York Times*, June 7, 1998, sec. 4, p. 1.

60. Nizamani, *Roots of Rhetoric*, 104.

61. "Pakistan: Sharif Addresses Nation on Nuclear Tests," Foreign Broadcast Information Service (FBIS) -NES-98-148, May 28, 1998.

62. Khurshid Ahmad, "Capping the Nation," *Pakistan's Security and the Nuclear Option* (Islamabad: Institute of Policy Studies, 1995), 147.

63. Khurshid Ahmad, "Nuclear Deterrence, CTBT, IMF Bail-outs and Debt Dependence," *Tarjuman al-Qur'an* (December 1998).

64. "Pakistan: Ayub Khan on Pakistani, Indian N-Tests," FBIS-TAC-98–152, June 1, 1998. In fact, according to data published by the Stockholm International Peace Research Institute (SIPRI) at http://first.sipri.org/non/first/result_milex.php?send (August 5, 2003), Pakistan's overall military expenditures have increased from U.S. $2.83 billion in 1998 to $3.18 billion in 2002 (adjusted to the year 2000 costs and exchange rates).

65. *Mishkat al-Masabih*, 1:84.

66. Ibid., 2:380.

67. Joseph Cirincione et al., *Deadly Arsenals: Tracking Weapons of Mass Destruction* (Washington, D.C.: Carnegie Endowment for International Peace, 2002), 3–23.

68. Ahmad, *Tarjuman al-Qur'an* (December 1998).

69. "Pakistan: Beware Indian, Israeli Propaganda on 'Islamic Bomb,'" FBIS-NES-98–167, June 16, 1998.

70. FBIS-TAC-98–152, June 1, 1998.

71. "Article Views Quest for Nuclear Power," FBIS-NES-95–111, June 9, 1995, pp. 65–66.

72. Author's interview with Ebrahim Yazdi, October 7, 2001, Princeton, N.J.

73. FBIS-NES-95–111, June 9, 1995, p. 66.

74. "Iran to Hand over Nuclear Waste to Suppliers," *Iran Business Monitor*, June 1995, pp. 1, 7.

75. Quoted in Elaine Sciolino, "Report Says Iran Seeks Atomic Arms," *New York Times*, October 31, 1991, p. A7.

76. International Atomic Energy Agency, "Implementation of the NPT Safeguards Agreement in the Islamic Republic of Iran," November 10, 2003, at http://www.ocnus.net/cgi-bin/exec/view.cgi?archive=35&num=8472 (December 16, 2003).

77. Resolution of the seminar on "Nuclear Arms Race and Nuclear Disarmament: The Muslim Perspective," University of Karachi, March 10, 1984. Text provided by the World Muslim Congress secretariat, Karachi, Pakistan.

78. Khurshid Ahmad, "Nuclear Deterrent and the C.T.B.T.: The Moment of Truth for Pakistan" (Lahore: Jama'at-i Islami Pakistan, n.d.).

79. For a review of Muslim attitudes toward the Chemical Weapons Convention, see Frances V. Harbour, "Islamic Principles and the Chemical Weapons Convention of 1993," *Journal of Religious Ethics* 23:1 (Spring 1995): 69–72.

80. Ahmad, "Nuclear Deterrent and the C.T.B.T."

81. Katherine Young reports on similar Indian concerns, for example. See her discussion in Chapter 15 above, under "Proliferation."

82. "Nuclear Armament Seen as 'Sacred Duty,'" FBIS-NES-95–040, March 1, 1995, pp. 3–4.

18

"Do Not Violate the Limit"

Three Issues in Islamic Thinking on Weapons of Mass Destruction

John Kelsay

It is a pleasure to respond to Sohail Hashmi's thoughtful and thorough chapter. I agree with Hashmi that the debate among Muslims on weapons of mass destruction is not particularly well developed. Indeed, at certain points an analysis of Islamic approaches to WMD must have more the character of a thought experiment than of a descriptive analysis. This being the case, much of what we must do involves exploring the framework within which Muslims can (and sometimes do) discuss WMD. I thus develop my remarks in terms of three points at which the relation between Islamic political thought and the debate over weapons of mass destruction deserves elaboration. These are, first, the place of discrimination or noncombatant immunity in historic and especially contemporary Islamic discourse; second, the distinction between use of WMD and possession for purposes of deterrence (with attendant consequences for questions about nonproliferation and disarmament); and third, the importance of the dialectic between universal and particular in Islamic political thought.

DISCRIMINATION

As developed by classical jurists, the Islamic tradition proposes strictures on resort to and conduct of war. Consider the following report of the Prophet's practice, which is cited almost universally as a starting point for discussion:

Whenever the Apostle of God sent forth an army or a detachment, he charged its commander personally to fear God, the Most High, and he enjoined the Muslims who were with him to do good. And he said: Fight in the name of God and in the path of God. Combat those who disbelieve in God. Do not cheat or commit treachery, nor should you mutilate anyone or kill children. Whenever you meet your polytheist enemies, invite them to adopt Islam. If they do so, accept it, and let them alone. You should then invite them to move from their territory to the territory of *emigres*. If they do so, accept it and let them alone. Otherwise, they should be informed that they would be like the Muslim nomads in that they are subject to God's orders as

Muslims, but that they will receive no share in the spoil of war. If they refuse, then call upon them to pay the poll tax; if they do, accept it and leave them alone. If you besiege the inhabitants of a fortress or a town and they try to get you to let them surrender on the basis of God's judgment, do not do so, since you do not know what God's judgment is, but make them surrender to your judgment and then decide their case according to your own views. But if the besieged inhabitants of a fortress of a town asked you to give them a pledge of security in God's name or in the name of God's Apostle, you should not do so, but give the pledge in your names or in the names of your fathers; for, if you should ever break it, it would be an easier matter if it were in the names of you or your fathers.[1]

Of special interest to us are the limitations suggested by the phrase "do not cheat or commit treachery, nor should you mutilate anyone or kill children." Indeed, when joined with other reports, a picture of fighting governed by something like a criterion of discrimination or noncombatant immunity begins to emerge. Thus,

One who has reached puberty should be killed, but one who has not should be spared.

The Apostle of God prohibited the killing of women.

The Apostle of God said: "You may kill the adults of the unbelievers, but spare their minors – their youth."[2]

For classical jurists, these reports constitute one of two foundational sources for developing judgments about the ways Muslim fighters should conduct themselves (the other being the Qur'an). One may ask many questions about them, not least concerning the pre- or extra-Islamic source of the limitations they express. My own view, for what it is worth, is that the Arab tribes who first heard the message of Islam had some similar notions about the targeting of women, children, and other noncombatant classes, largely based on notions of chivalry – the code of honor observed by men of virtue. In that connection, restrictions on harming noncombatants were related to the glory of a warrior. One obtains glory by fighting one's equals (i.e., other soldiers); correlatively, there is no glory to be obtained by killing noncombatants. In ways we still do not understand very well, the version of ethical monotheism practiced by the early Muslims and instantiated in the Qur'an transformed such notions into duties. In short, one no longer abstains from targeting noncombatants for the sake of glory (at least, not solely), but because these are people who do not deserve to die.

More important for our purposes are the ways classical Muslim jurists thought about the conduct of war, based on these reports. What is the force of the prophetic sayings relative to noncombatants? Are these stipulations of an absolute norm? A norm to be respected, except when important values (e.g., survival of the community) hang in the balance? Or do they point to a rule of thumb – a good thing to follow, though hardly binding in the context of war, especially when Muslim victory is at stake? The weight of evidence suggests an absolute norm, though not surprisingly, there is evidence for other interpretations.

Thus we have texts in which the prohibitions on targeting noncombatants are reiterated, with attendant arguments that the only way protected classes can become targets is through behavior that in effect "renounces" noncombatant status – for example, if women take up arms, they are no longer protected. Again, there are texts in which commanders are said to have a duty relative to noncombatants that goes beyond avoidance of harm to actual protection. Women and children captives, for example, deserve protection and transport to a place of safety, even if a commander's resources are depleted.[3] The prohibition is absolute, in the sense that no exceptions to the rule against direct and intentional killing of noncombatants are envisioned, at least as far as women and children are concerned.

In cases where noncombatants are killed, jurists either envision excusing conditions or employ a kind of double effect reasoning, by which killing is foreseen but not intended, and thus those who bring it about may be excused. For example, in the circumstance of a night raid, we are told that companions of the Prophet brought him the news that, in the Muslim pursuit of victory, women and children had been killed. "They are not from us," he is supposed to have said.[4] As jurists took it, this report established a set of excusing conditions, by which blame for the deaths of noncombatants falls to the enemy leadership that, in resisting Islam, placed them in harm's way. Or again, in an instance where the inhabitants of a besieged city place Muslim children on the walls as a way of deterring archers firing into their midst, jurists held that the attack should continue, with the proviso that the archers not fire directly at the children. In such a case, the deaths of the children would be foreseen, but not intended.[5]

In other cases, however, the force of noncombatant immunity seems less potent. Here, what is really important is the victory of Muslim forces, and the principle of discrimination takes on the air of a rule of thumb. For example, the great Hanafi jurist al-Shaybani (d. 804 C.E.) responds to an inquiry as follows:

Do you believe that it is objectionable for the believers to destroy whatever towns of the territory of war that they may encounter?

No. Rather do I hold that this would be commendable. For do you not think that it is in accordance with God's saying, in God's Book: "Whatever palm trees you have cut down or left standing upon their roots, has been by God's permission, in order that the ungodly ones might be humiliated." So, I am in favor of whatever they did to deceive and anger the enemy.[6]

Or in another context, where various modes of attack during siege warfare are in question, al-Shaybani approves the use of arrows, lances, flooding, burning with fire, and mangonels. This is so, even though the issue is specifically framed to indicate the presence of noncombatants in the city. "Even if they had among them [Muslims], there would be no harm to do all of that to them.... If the Muslims stopped attacking the inhabitants of the territory of war for any of the reasons that you have stated, they would be unable to go to war at all, for there is no city in the territory of war in which there is no one at all of these [women, children, Muslim traders, etc.] you have mentioned."[7] The norm of discrimination is thus an important aspect of classical juridical thinking about war, though its nature as a rule or principle is unclear.

For contemporary writers, discrimination remains a significant aspect of an Islamic approach to war. In one of the more striking examples of this, the late Ayatollah Murtaza Mutahhari comments on Qur'an 2:190, which reads, "And fight in the path of God those who are fighting you, but do not transgress limits. For God loves not those who transgress":

What does this mean, not to violate the limit? Not to be the transgressor? Naturally its obvious meaning is that it is those who are fighting us that we are to fight and not anyone else, and that it is on the battleground that we are to fight, meaning that we are to fight with a certain group of people and that group is the soldiers that the other side have sent, the men of war whom they prepared for war with us and who are fighting us.... But with people who are not men of war, who are not soldiers, who are not in a state of combat, such as old men, old women – in fact all women, whether they are old or not – and children, we must not interfere and we must not do any of these other things that are counted as transgression.[8]

In other passages, Mutahhari ties this concern to notions of human rights, so that the highest form of fighting is in defense of those deprived of basic freedoms. In his case, the general importance of the principle of discrimination is clear.

When it comes to more particular applications, however, Mutahhari is less useful. And one must agree with Hashmi: Concern with discrimination or other aspects of *jus in bello* is not a signal characteristic of contemporary Muslim writing about war. The focus is rather on *jus ad bellum* and, in particular, on issues of right or competent authority.[9] The reason for this is very clear and points to a serious problem for Muslim discussion of WMD. The focus on right authority reflects larger questions about the legitimacy of governments in countries where Muslims are the majority. Much of the most interesting thinking about the issue comes out of resistance movements, where the issue at hand is determining precisely who has the right to initiate lethal force in the interests of the Muslim community. The argument of these "irregulars" develops as a rebuttal to the presumption that established governments have a monopoly on the legitimate use of violence.

Right authority in the Islamic case, it is argued, belongs ultimately to God and is delegated to the leader(s) of the Muslims. Such delegation depends, however, on the commitment to establish and maintain a just social order. Where established governments fail in this regard, the entire Muslim community becomes God's legate. And whoever hears and responds to God's challenge has the right to serve.

Is it not high time for those who have believed to humble their hearts to the Reminder of God and to the truth which God has sent down; and that they should not be like those to whom the Book was formerly given, and for whom the time was long, so that their hearts became hard, and many of them are reprobates? (Qur'an 57:16)

This text, cited at the outset of one of the most famous "irregular" treatises, the manifesto of Anwar Sadat's assassins, begins a well-developed argument in which the author justifies irregular military action, inclusive of assassinations. These are, from the point of view of the text, executions of reprobates and tyrants.[10]

With respect to WMD, the role of irregulars in contemporary Islam surely constitutes one of the most important concerns. We have little to go on, by way of explicit pronouncements regarding WMD. We have more considerable evidence regarding notions of discrimination. I do not think it unjust to say that the current and presumptive opinion of Islam as a tradition that promotes "holy" or "total" and indiscriminate warfare rests largely on a number of notorious instances (not least, of course, the attacks on targets in the United States on September 11, 2001) in which irregulars claim the mantle of Islam as a way of justifying acts that violate the war convention. The World Islamic Front's famous *fatwa* justifying acts that strike at Americans without discriminating between combatants and noncombatants provides one example. Suggesting that all Americans, regardless of occupation, participate in a system of oppression, the authors argue that there are no noncombatants on the enemy's side. All are guilty, all aggressors, all deserving of death.[11]

In the great tradition of Islamic thought, Usama bin Ladin, his colleagues in the World Islamic Front and al-Qa'ida, and other irregulars are clearly in the minority. Yet their opinions raise interesting questions. Bin Ladin's argument is that indiscriminate tactics are in accord with justice – all deserve to die and all are thus legitimate targets for attack. Others speak in a different way. Muhammad Husayn Fadlallah, at one time identified as the spiritual leader of the Lebanese Hizballah, does not appeal to justice when he speaks about indiscriminate acts. He does, however, speak about the conditions under which irregulars labor. Convicted of the need for a vigorous (including violent) response to oppression, irregular forces find themselves at a distinct disadvantage. They cannot fight their enemies "straight up." If the irregulars' cause is to have any chance of success, they must employ unconventional tactics. Indiscriminate acts are unjust, and those in leadership should call the irregulars back to the principles of just conduct in war. Nevertheless, those who perpetrate such acts may be excused, given the extremity of conditions.[12]

If Fadlallah speaks of excusing conditions, still others speak of the situation in which irregulars labor in the language of emergency. Hashmi's citation of al-Ghazali in this regard indicates the classical precedent for such language. Classical jurists spoke, most of the time, about wars in which the justifying cause had to do with such things as extending the influence of Islam, protecting its borders, or quelling civil strife. In connection with this type of war, the production of an army adequate to the task was a "collective duty" (*fard kifaya*). So long as sufficient resources were available for this task, individual Muslims might carry on with their lives, not worrying about participating in military activity. In another kind of context, however, fighting in war could become an "individual duty" (*fard 'ayn*). Here, every individual Muslim has the obligation to do whatever possible in order to protect the interests of Islam. The paradigm case from the juridical point of view was an invasion of Islamic territory.

Contemporary irregulars tend to speak in the language of emergency. In this connection, ordinary obligations may be suspended because of the overriding nature of the values at stake. For example:

With regard to the lands of Islam, the enemy lives right in the middle of them. The enemy even has got hold of the reins of power, for this enemy is (none other than) these rulers who have (illegally) seized the leadership of the Muslims. Therefore, waging *jihad* against them is an individual duty, in addition to the fact that Islamic *jihad* today requires a drop of sweat from every Muslim.

Know that when *jihad* is an individual duty, there is no (need to) ask permission of (your) parents to leave to wage *jihad*, as the jurists have said; it is thus similar to prayer and fasting.[13]

Or again:

There is not a higher peak in nationalism or depth in devotion than, if an enemy lands on the Muslim territories then struggle and fighting the enemy becomes an individual obligation on every Muslim and Muslimah [female Muslim]. *The woman is allowed to go fight without permission of her husband and the slave without the permission of his master.*[14]

I hasten to reiterate that we do not have explicit pronouncements that would indicate an application of these notions to WMD. What we do have are groups of irregulars, convicted of the justice of their cause, who often employ tactics that are indiscriminate. While we are largely in the realm of a thought experiment with respect to WMD, it is interesting to consider questions raised by the rhetoric of irregulars. Are indiscriminate acts justified in the conduct of their war, as Bin Ladin implies? Alternatively, are the acts unjust, but the agents nevertheless excused, as with Fadlallah? Or do irregulars fight in the context of a state of emergency, in which ordinary norms are temporarily suspended?

All this is to say that the criterion of discrimination, so clearly a part of the great tradition of Islamic political thought, is clearly susceptible to interpretation. In some contexts, it seems absolute, or nearly so, and one must either find ways to say that noncombatant casualties are "not from us" (as in the night raid) or that they are foreseen but not directly intended. In other contexts, however, the norm seems to function more like a rule of thumb. And in the hands of contemporary irregulars, there appear to be several ways of delimiting the force of discrimination, in view of the justice of the cause or the extremity of conditions.

USE OR POSSESSION OF WMD

With respect to the actions of Muslim states, I take Hashmi's analysis as largely correct. That is, in terms of the use of WMD for deterrence (or, one might add, for projection of power) such actions are governed by considerations of equity and status within the international community. These considerations carry over into discussions of proliferation and disarmament. The Islamic values at stake thus have to do with the security and status of Muslim-majority states.

There are juridical issues to be discussed in this connection. For example, insofar as the prophetic directive forbids cheating or committing treachery, one might wonder about the moral status of policies involving bluffing, since deterrence may involve convincing an enemy of one's willingness to do something that would, under most circumstances, be immoral (as, for example, the use of indiscriminate weaponry). For the most part, however, the discussion does not seem to rise to this point. Most jurists, as most policy makers, seem to agree that possession of WMD is a necessary prelude to commanding respect in the international community.

With respect to use, the situation is somewhat different. Hashmi writes about the use of chemicals during the Iran-Iraq War. Although many questions linger about this aspect of the war, there is no dispute that the use of chemical weapons was initiated by the Iraqis early in the conflict. Such use was part of a pattern of indiscriminate warfare on the part of Iraq. From the Iranian standpoint, it was simply confirmation of the moral degeneracy of Ba'thist ideology. Khomeini characterized the war as "an invasion by an Iraqi non-Muslim Ba'thist against an Islamic country; and . . . a rebellion by blasphemy against Islam."[15] It seems that Iran did eventually respond with chemical weapons against Iraqi troops. Moreover, it engaged in several brief campaigns of countercity bombing and of striking at oil tankers in response to Iraqi practice. Iran's actions had the character of reprisals intended to indicate to the Iraqis the high cost of indiscriminate tactics. As Chubin and Tripp put it, "Iran's policy was to respond to Iraq's attacks at sea or on the cities to show that it was capable of doing so, and in order not to relinquish its right to do so or to acquiesce in Iraq's unilateral aims."[16] Iranian reprisals were temporarily effective. Following bombing raids on Basra and Baghdad, the Iraqi bombardment of Iranian cities ceased for a time, then was later renewed.

The Iranian response is suggestive of al-Zuhayli's metaphor of "cauterizing the wound," as cited by Hashmi.[17] More generally, it suggests that reprisals may, under certain circumstances, be Islamically appropriate. It is interesting that the Iranian use of chemical weapons and the other acts of reprisal came late in the war and only after Khomeini's earlier objections were overcome by the regular military.[18] These facts underscore that the Iranian approach in the war laid heavy emphasis on the Muslim identity of the people (as opposed to the government) of Iraq. Leaders expressed again and again their hope that the war might provide an occasion for the Iraqi people to rid themselves of Saddam Hussein and to choose a new political destiny for themselves. In that context, it is probable that Khomeini's reluctance to authorize the use of chemical weapons was a choice governed as much by issues of Muslim solidarity as by concerns about the principle of discrimination. The point requiring emphasis, however, is that the actual use of WMD, as of indiscriminate tactics generally, poses moral issues of a different sort than holding such weapons for purposes of deterrence. While bluffing involves deception, violations of the criterion of discrimination seem to be of a different order.

UNIVERSAL AND PARTICULAR

My final point concerns the nature of Islamic political thinking, an issue that may in the end affect one's sense of the possibilities for Muslim participation in international society. Much of the debate concerning nonproliferation and disarmament, as Hashmi shows, has to do with concerns about state security and status. A number of the states involved claim Islamic identity, establish the *shari'a* as the law or guide for law making, invoke Islamic values, and so on. In this regard, their focus seems to be on the protection of territories within which Islam may be preserved.

Such protection is an important part of the historic tradition of Islamic political thought. It is easy, however, to lose sight of some of the rationale for this. In effect, the creation and preservation of an Islamic territory was historically seen as providing a power base for Muslims to carry out a universal mission, namely, the creation of a just social order. One of the more creative debates within contemporary Muslim political writing has to do with the ways such an order is constituted and also with the description of justice characteristic of an Islamic territory. North American Muslims are important in this discussion, with some advancing quite distinctive criticisms of the historic assumption that "Islamic territory" and "Muslims holding power" are interchangeable expressions.

Others hold to a judgment more consistent with traditional models, by which "Islamic territory" at least means "the territory where Islam is the established religion." For both, however, it is critical that one realize that Islam is to be understood in universal terms and that the Muslim community realize that it has a universal mission. In that sense, Islam is the "natural" religion of humanity, and the Muslim community is constituted as a means by which the Creator calls human beings to order life in ways that accord with their true nature. Islam is not "just" about the protection of Muslims and their interests. It is interested in the possibilities for a just social order for all human beings.

In that sense, Islamic discussions of the rules of war as applied to WMD or other issues ought not "just" or "simply" be seen as an intra-Muslim example of a broader phenomenon. They are a "site" at which Muslims are debating about the nature of human or universal political order. As Ayatollah Khomeini put it, the creation and preservation of an Islamic state is not an end in itself. The state exists to facilitate the development of "true human beings" who understand life in terms of the Qur'anic dialectic: All things come from God, and to God all things will return.[19] With respect to WMD, then, the proper question from an Islamic point of view must be, "What kind of political order is necessary for human beings to live in peace and justice?" Correlatively, one may ask, "What kind of political order is consistent with the will of the Creator?" It is in the context of these large questions that one can assess the place of WMD, as constitutive of one factor to be considered in discussing the means by which a just political order may be created and maintained.

Notes

1. This is given in various collections. Here I use the translation of Majid Khadduri, *The Islamic Law of Nations: Shaybani's Siyar* (Baltimore, Md.: Johns Hopkins University Press, 1966). The citation is given as section 1 of Khadduri's translation of Shaybani.
2. These also are taken from Khadduri, *Islamic Law of Nations*, secs. 28–30.
3. This is not held by all jurists; indeed, there are complicated issues in the classical perspective on discrimination in war that need sorting out, not least regarding the role of religious identity in assessing the force of norms prohibiting direct attacks on noncombatants. My attempt to sort these out is found in *Islam and War* (Louisville, Ky.: Westminster/John Knox Press, 1993). James Turner Johnson, *The Holy War Idea in Western and Islamic Traditions* (University Park: Pennsylvania State University, 1997), and Khaled Abou El Fadl, "The Rules of Killing at War: An Inquiry into Classical Sources," *Muslim World* 89:2 (April 1999): 144–50, offer different interpretations.
4. See, among others, *Sahih Muslim*, being one of the canonical collections of *hadith*. Here the translation is that of Abdul Hamid Siddiqi (Lahore: Sh. Muhammad Ashraf, 1981), *hadith* no. 4321.
5. See secs. 117–23 of al-Shaybani's text in *Islamic Law of Nations*.

6. Ibid., secs. 88–89. Qur'an citation is 59:5.

7. Ibid., sec. 117.

8. Murtaza Mutahhari, *Jihad: The Holy War of Islam and Its Legitimacy in the Qur'an*, trans. M. S. Tawheedi (Albany, Calif.: Moslem Student Association [Persian Speaking Group], n.d.), 35. Cited in Bruce Lawrence, "Holy War (*Jihad*) in Islamic Religion and Nation-State Ideologies," in *Just War and Jihad*, ed. John Kelsay and James Turner Johnson (Westport, Conn.: Greenwood, 1991), 153.

9. See Kelsay, *Islam and War*, esp. 69–74; idem, "Bosnia and the Muslim Critique of Modernity," in *Religion and Justice in the War over Bosnia*, ed. G. Scott Davis (New York: Routledge, 1996), 117–41.

10. See *The Neglected Duty*, trans. Johannes J. G. Jansen (New York: Macmillan, 1986).

11. One wants to employ the term *fatwa* here in quotation marks. One of the issues that must be explored in Islamic juridical thinking has to do with authority to issue a legal opinion (which is the import of the term *fatwa*). Islam's basically democratic tendencies, whereby any adult Muslim has the right to interpret authoritative texts, were mitigated for much of the tradition's history by the role of 'ulama as religious authorities. The proliferation of media channels, inclusive of the Internet, helps to create a context in which it is no longer clear who is promulgating such opinions, what his or her credentials might be, and so on. On this issue, Khaled Abou El Fadl, *The Authoritative and the Authoritarian in Islamic Discourses*, 2nd ed. (Austin, Texas: Dar Taiba, 1997), is most interesting.

12. See the interview published as "To Avoid a World War of Terror," in the *Washington Post*, April 6, 1986, p. C5.

13. Jansen, trans., *Neglected Duty*, 200.

14. *Charter of the Islamic Resistance Movement (Hamas) of Palestine*, trans. M. Maqdsi (Dallas: Islamic Association for Palestine, 1990), article 15, p. 22. Emphasis of Maqdsi.

15. See Shahram Chubin and Charles Tripp, *Iran and Iraq at War* (London: I. B. Tauris, 1988), 38.

16. Ibid., 55.

17. See Sohail Hashmi, Chap. 17 above, under "Use in War."

18. See ibid.

19. See John Kelsay, "Spirituality and Social Struggle: Islam and the West," *International Quarterly* 1:3 (Summer 1994): 135–51. A longer version of this essay appeared in Betty Rogers Rubenstein and Michael Berenbaum, eds., *What Kind of God? Essays in Honor of Richard L. Rubenstein* (Lanham, Md.: University Press of America, 1995).

19

Judaism, War, and Weapons of Mass Destruction

Reuven Kimelman

This study of the Jewish attitude toward weapons of mass destruction presents the classical sources and principles on war and its conduct,[1] followed by contemporary applications on the subject of WMD in America and Israel.

SOURCES AND PRINCIPLES

Types of Wars

The Jewish ethics of war focuses on two issues: its legitimation and its conduct. The Talmud classifies wars according to their source of legitimation. Biblically commanded wars are termed mandatory (*mitzvah*). Wars undertaken with the approval of the Sanhedrin are termed discretionary (*reshut*). There are three types of mandatory wars: Joshua's war of conquest against the seven biblical Canaanite nations, the war against the biblical Amalek, and defensive wars against an attack in progress. Discretionary wars are usually expansionary efforts undertaken to enhance the political prestige of the government or to secure economic gain.[2]

The first type of mandatory war is only of historical interest, as the Canaanite nations lost their national identity already in ancient times. This conclusion, which appears repeatedly in rabbinic literature,[3] is part of a tendency to blunt the impact of the seven-nations policy. The Bible points out that these policies were not implemented even during the zenith of ancient Israel's power.[4] Indeed, a pronouncement in the biblical exegetical literature of late antiquity known as *Midrash* explicitly excludes the possibility of transferring the seven-nations ruling to other non-Jewish residents of the land of Israel.[5] The Spanish-Egyptian legal scholar of the twelfth century, Moses Maimonides, is just as explicit in emphasizing that all trace of them has vanished.[6] By limiting the jurisdiction of the seven-nations ruling to the conditions of ancient Canaan, it was effectively removed from the post-biblical ethical agenda and vitiated as a precedent for contemporary practice.

The second category of mandatory war, against Amalek, has also been rendered operationally defunct by comparing them with the Canaanites,[7] by postponing the battle to the immediate premessianic struggle, or by viewing them as a metaphor for genocidal evil.[8]

The two remaining categories, reactive defensive wars (which are classified as mandatory) and expansionary wars (which are classified as discretionary) remain intact. So, for example, King David's response to the Philistine attack is designated mandatory,[9] whereas his wars "to expand the border of Israel" are designated discretionary.[10] Intermediate wars, such as preventive, anticipatory, or preemptive, defy so neat a classification. Not only are the classifications debated in the Talmud itself,[11] but commentators disagree on the categorization of the differing positions in the Talmud.

The major clash occurs between the eleventh-century Franco-German scholar Rashi and the thirteenth-century Franco-Provençal scholar Menachem Meiri. According to Rashi (ad loc.), the majority position considers preemptive action to be discretionary, whereas the minority position expounded by the second-century Palestinian authority Rabbi Judah considers it to be mandatory.

According to Meiri, a preemptive strike against an enemy who, it is feared, might attack or who is already known to be preparing for war is deemed mandatory by the majority of the rabbis but discretionary by Rabbi Judah. Accordingly, Rabbi Judah defines a counterattack as mandatory only in response to an already launched attack.[12] A similar reading of Maimonides also limits the mandatory classification to a defensive war launched in response to an attack.[13]

Who Declares War?

Discretionary war, as opposed to mandatory war, requires the involvement of the Sanhedrin. Among the reasons for involving the Sanhedrin in the decision-making process is its role as the legal embodiment of popular sovereignty, the *edah* in biblical terms.[14] Understanding this to imply that the high court was the legal equivalent of "the community of Israel as a whole,"[15] Maimonides uses interchangeably the expressions "according to the majority of Israel" and "according to the high court."[16] Similarly, the former chief rabbi of Israel, Shlomo Goren, explained that the requirement to secure the Sanhedrin's approval in a discretionary war derives from its representative authority.[17] The involvement of the Sanhedrin in a discretionary war safeguards the citizenry from being endangered without the approval of their representative body.

The Sanhedrin is also involved because of its role as the authoritative interpreter of the Torah-constitution. Since the judicial interpretation for the law is structurally separate from its executive enforcement, the Sanhedrin serves as a check on executive power.

The involvement of the Sanhedrin in discretionary wars helps to explain the obligation of citizens to participate. Military obligation is anchored in the biblical perspective that considers the people and the monarch to be bound by a covenant, each with its own obligations.[18] Presumably, statehood involves a pact of mutuality. On the one hand, the people commit themselves to the support of the state and its ruler. On the other hand, the ruler is forsworn to uphold the constitution and not to risk unnecessarily the people's lives.[19] Allocating some war-making authority to the Sanhedrin guarantees the presence of a countervailing force to the ruler, thereby safeguarding the inviolability of the social contract.

Before granting authorization to wage war, the Sanhedrin must weigh the probable losses, consider the chances of success, and assess the will of the people. As David Bleich writes, "The Sanhedrin is charged with assessing the military, political and economic reality and determining whether a proposed war is indeed necessary and whether it will be successful in achieving its objectives."[20] Since wars are always costly in lives, the losses have to be measured against the chance of success.[21] Preventive warfare is unwarranted if the number of lives saved does not significantly exceed the number of lives jeopardized. Calculations of victory alone are not determinative; the price of victory must be considered. The great third-century Babylonian talmudic authority, Mar Samuel, deemed a government liable to charges of misconduct if losses exceed one-sixth of the fighting force, which some interpret as applying to its own forces, and others to the enemy's.[22] Thus, in addition to projecting future losses, a government is required to take precautions to limit them.

Nonetheless, as is well known, precision in military projections is wellnigh impossible. The gap between plan and execution characterizes the best of military calculations. Linear plans almost always fail to deal with the nonlinear world that rules strategy and war. Rabbi Eleazar in talmudic times noted, "Any war that involves more than sixty thousand is necessarily chaotic."[23] Modern warfare has not significantly changed the equation. In the words of Prussian Field Marshal Helmuth von Moltke, "No plan can survive contact with the battle."[24]

The Conduct of War

The estimation of one's own losses and one's own interest is insufficient for validating discretionary war. The total destruction ratio required for victory must be considered. This assessment involves a "double intention," that is, the "good" must appear achievable and the "evil" reducible. For example, before laying siege to a city, a determination must be made as to whether it can be captured without destroying it.²⁵ There is no warrant for destroying a town under the guise of "saving" it.

The other rules for sieges follow similar lines of thought: Indefensible villages may not be subjected to siege. Negotiations with the enemy must precede subjecting a city to hunger, thirst, or disease for the purpose of exacting a settlement. Emissaries of peace must be sent to a hostile city for three days. If the terms are accepted, no harm may befall any inhabitants of the city. If the terms are not accepted, the siege is still not to begin until the enemy has commenced hostilities. Even after the siege is laid, no direct cruelties against the inhabitants may be inflicted, and a side must be left open as an escape route.²⁶

Already in the first century B.C.E., Philo warned against national vendettas becoming justifications for wars. If a city under siege sues for peace, it is to be granted. Peace, albeit with sacrifices, he says, is preferable to the horrors of war. But peace means peace. "If," he continues, "the adversaries persist in their rashness to the point of madness, they [the besiegers] must proceed to the attack invigorated by enthusiasm and having in the justice of their cause an invincible ally."²⁷ Although the purpose of an army at war is to win, both Philo and the ancient rabbis rejected the claim of military necessity as an excuse for military excess. Despite the goal of victory – indeed, victory with all due haste – aimless violence or wanton destruction is to be eschewed.

Much of the moral discussion of the conduct of war derives from the prohibition in Deuteronomy 20:19–20 against axing fruit-bearing trees in the environs of the besieged city. The principal points deal with the issues of wanton destruction and the immunity of the noncombatant. So, for example, Philo extends the prohibition against axing fruit-bearing trees to include vandalizing the environs of the besieged city: "Indeed, so great a love for justice does the law instill in those who live under its constitution that it does not even permit the fertile soil of a hostile city to be outraged by devastation or by cutting down trees to destroy the fruits."²⁸ In a similar vein, a century later Josephus expands on the prohibition to include the incineration of the enemy's fields and the killing of beasts employed in labor.²⁹ Despoiling the countryside without direct military advantage comes under the proscription of profligate destruction.

According to the eleventh-century Spanish exegete Abraham Ibn Ezra (in Deuteronomy 20:19–20), fruit trees are singled out because they are a source of life for humans in general. War is no license for destroying what is needed for human life. Maimonides, in the twelfth century, takes the next step in extending the prohibition to exclude categorically all wanton destruction: "Also, one who smashes household goods, tears clothes, demolishes a building, stops up a spring, or destroys articles of food with destructive intent, transgresses the command 'You shall not destroy.'"³⁰

Nonetheless, as the thirteenth-century Spanish commentator Moses Nachmanides makes clear, acts of destruction are warranted insofar as they advance the goal of victory.[31] He thus permitted the axing of fruit trees as part of a siege or to prevent the enemy from using them for military purposes. Still, an early-fourteenth-century anonymous author underscored that the prohibition was meant "to teach us to love the good and the purposeful and to cleave to it so that the good will cleave to us and we will distance ourselves from anything evil and destructive."[32]

If the destructive urges provoked by war against nonhuman objects can be controlled, there is a chance of controlling the destructive urges against humans. The link between these two forms the basis of two a fortiori arguments for the immunity of noncombatants. The first argument is grounded in the biblical prohibition against axing fruit trees during a siege. Since the prohibition against their destruction can be formulated in a rhetorical manner, to wit, "Are trees of the field human to withdraw before you under siege?" (Deuteronomy 20:19), it is deduced that just as a tree – had it fled – would not be chopped down, so a person – were he or she to flee – should not be cut down. The logic of the argument is spelled out by the fifteenth-century Spanish-Italian exegete Isaac Arama and the sixteenth-century Safedean exegete Moses Alshikh. After mentioning the prohibition against the wanton destruction of trees, the former notes that, "all the more so should we take care not to injure or destroy human beings."[33] The latter notes, "all the more so it is fitting that He have mercy on His children and on His creatures."[34]

The second argument is rooted in the ruling that a fourth side of a besieged city be left open to allow for escape.[35] Whether this ruling is based on ancient tactics[36] or on humanitarian considerations,[37] the opportunity to escape saps the resolve of the besieged to continue fighting.[38] Otherwise, as the fifteenth-century Spanish-Italian exegete Isaac Abarbanel observes, they will out of desperation take heart "and seek to avenge themselves before they die . . . since one who despairs of life and well-being will risk his life to strike his enemy a great blow."[39] Thus, it is important to take measures to ensure that the chance to flee not be exploited for the sake of regrouping to mount rear attacks.[40]

Now, if (unarmed) soldiers have the chance of becoming refugees, then surely noncombatants and other neutrals do too. The principle may be stated as "no harm to those who intend no harm." Thus, Abarbanel says with regard to the immunity of women and children, "Since they are not making war, they do not deserve to die in it."[41] Similarly, the *Midrash* explains that the fear of Abraham noted in Genesis 15:1 was due to him saying, "Perhaps it is the case that among those troops whom I killed there was a righteous man or a God-fearer."[42] As noted, the principle of the immunity of noncombatants discriminates in favor of those who have done no harm. Even this principle that those who intend no harm should not be harmed is derived, according to Philo, from the case of the fruit tree: "Does a tree, I ask you, show ill will to the human enemy that it should be pulled up roots and all, to punish it for ill which it has done or is ready to do to you?"[43] Obviously, the immunity of noncombatants cannot be sacrificed on the altar of military necessity.[44] As Philo notes: "The Jewish nation . . . when it takes up arms, distinguishes between those whose life is one of hostility and the reverse. For to breathe slaughter against all, even those who have done very little or nothing amiss, shows what I should call a savage and brutal soul."[45]

On the one hand, weapons calculated to produce suffering disproportionate to the military advantage are not countenanced. On the other hand, excessive concern with moral niceties can be morally counterproductive. When moral compunction appears as timidity and moral fastidiousness as squeamishness, they invite aggression. To ensure that moral preparedness be perceived from a position of strength, it must be coupled with military preparedness. Philo, reflecting this concern for the military ambiguity of moral scruples, sounds a note of caution in his summary of the biblical doctrine of defense: "All this shows clearly that the Jewish nation is ready for agreement and friendship with all like-minded nations whose intentions are peaceful, yet is not of the contemptible kind which surrenders through cowardice to wrongful aggression."[46]

CONTEMPORARY RESPONSES TO WEAPONS OF MASS DESTRUCTION

The modern Jewish discussion of WMD has two foci: among the superpowers, and among Israel and her neighboring enemies. What combines the two is the perception that the Jewish experience ominously foreshadows the human experience. As Samuel Pisar stated in his book *Of Blood and Hope*: "Standing in the shadow of the crematoria, I wish to give witness to humanity that it is possible to turn the whole world into a crematorium by the use of nuclear weapons."[47] The one event that ties both together is the Holocaust. The common lesson is "never again." With regard to the superpower conflict, "never again" means: Let not genocide become the model for omnicide. With regard to Israel it means: Let not the Holocaust happen again.

Opinions of Authorities

In 1991, a book entitled *Confronting Omnicide: Jewish Reflections on Weapons of Mass Destruction* published the responses of a group of Jewish thinkers on the legitimacy of WMD.[48] Among the respondents were several contemporary rabbis who directly addressed the issue of WMD.[49] Their responses, along with several others published elsewhere, follow.

One of the central issues in the application of traditional teachings to the reality of WMD is the awareness that the exponential growth in human power has upset the balance between its constructive and destructive use. Whereas the crowning achievement of human power – civilization – takes a concerted effort of multitudes over many generations, its destruction can be perpetrated by a few in an instant. This is a modern phenomenon. In the past, it took many people a considerable period of time to bring about mass evil; now, a few can bring about unlimited evil almost instantaneously.

According to Rabbi Irving Greenberg, this new reality has to lead to the "demythologization" of power. He writes:

the glorification of power and the deification of human sovereignty must be reversed. When one glorifies power one makes it absolute. Humanity must grasp the extraordinary attraction and danger of absolute power. In the Holocaust, that power positioned the Jews as the victim. It would destroy the Jews first, but it would not have stopped with the Jews.

In the absence of a moral framework that restricts the heroic claims of power, the exercisers of power inevitably are seduced into arrogant use of the force at their command. The loss of the sense of divine partnership and of being accountable to a covenantal standard has intensified the tendency to be corrupted by power. . . . The environment of unlimited power allowed the special enmity for Jews to be acted out to the ultimate level of evil. But once in place, such concentrations of power are available and tempting to use for evil purpose against others.[50]

For Greenberg, it is wrong – indeed, evil – for good people to appear to lack power. The weakness of the good tempts bullies, especially in the international scene. Even a balance of terror among the superpowers is preferable. Indeed, it may have already saved millions of lives. Jews, in particular, he argues, have a moral obligation not to tempt anti-Semites to attempt genocide again. For him, Jewish weakness invites them to live out their fantasy. Thus Jewish power is not only an imperative for Jewish existence, but also a damper to prevent anti-Semites from running morally amuck. One of the lessons of the Holocaust for Jews is to use their strength to encourage the moral behavior of their enemies. They must therefore be engaged in the punishing of enemies and the rewarding of friends. In this sense, Greenberg uses the Holocaust to come to a conclusion that others would come to based on the Jewish rule that one should seek to prevent a would-be assailant from killing oneself. Letting oneself be killed when an alternative exists is a culpable offense. As taking another's life to save one's own is wrong, so is forgoing one's life. The forgoing of one's life is wrong because no life can be shunted aside for another since all life is of equal value.[51]

Greenberg also learned from the Holocaust that the Nazis were most successful in implementing their murderous policy on the Jews when the local population stood by because they saw the Jews as outside their moral universe. When the populations of Europe experienced a dichotomy between Jews and them, they would not risk themselves to save Jews. It is imperative thus that no power claiming a moral basis place any foreign population outside that power's moral universe. Indeed, as our power for destruction grows, so must grow our efforts to maintain our sense of universal humanity. Just as the Exodus is used by the Bible to demand of the liberated Jews that they not oppress society's most vulnerable, having experienced the vulnerability of the slave in Egypt, so must the Holocaust teach Jews never to inflict on others what was inflicted on them.

Since the genie of nuclear power is already out, Greenberg concludes that "a restrained use of nuclear defense is within the range of legitimate policy judgment."[52] Whatever the case, the lesson of the Holocaust is that no one should have access to unlimited power. All power must be subject to checks. This can be derived from the experience of the biblical flood. Post-Holocaust humanity is like post-deluvian God. After the flood, even the divine realized that unleashing the power to destroy humanity was unacceptable. Thus God initiated a covenant with creation to limit His destructive power.

If God had to learn how to retreat from brinkmanship, all the more so should human beings. This means that we should distinguish between weapons of mass destruction (nuclear, biological, and chemical) and conventional arms. Greenberg allows for the building up of conventional weapons in order to minimize, if not eliminate, the reliance on WMD. Miscalculation could be minimized by replacing a nuclear balance with a conventional arms equilibrium. Such a change should be coordinated. That is, as WMD is reduced, so should conventional weapons be allowed to increase. He further argues that just as discretionary wars are subject to more limits than defensive wars, so could one adopt a policy "of tactical nuclear forces combined with a pledge of no first-strike use of nuclear arms."[53] Whatever policy is adopted, concludes Greenberg, any worthy response to the Holocaust has to include working for the elimination of WMD.

Rabbi David Novak's opposition to any use of nuclear weapons is based on the prohibition against wanton destruction. He follows the interpretation of Abraham Ibn Ezra, who argues that fruit trees are emblematic of what is humanly necessary. Thus there is a prohibition against destruction of what is necessary to human survival. Anything like a scorched-earth policy would be prohibited, regardless of its military advantage. A war that could bring on a "nuclear winter" is all the more unacceptable. On the contrary, he argues that Jews

should participate with those who work to publicly expose these dangerous delusions of nuclear victory.... [Indeed,] universal disarmament must be pursued to lessen the likelihood of nuclear aggression. For Americans, especially, this means working to eliminate the bellicose rhetoric too often used by our leaders, rhetoric which exacerbates international tensions and makes disarmament ever more remote.[54]

Whereas all decry the use of nuclear weapons, most find advantages in their possession. Rabbi Lord Immanuel Jakobovits, former chief rabbi of the

British Commonwealth, lists five nuclear paradoxes, each of them consisting of two parts that appear mutually contradictory and yet are equally true:

1. Nuclear weapons pose the greatest menace to human survival in history; yet they have ensured the longest spell of peace between the great powers in modern times.
2. Enough nuclear arms exist to kill every human being twenty times over; yet not a single life has been lost through them since the Second World War, while over 10 million have died in some 150 conventional wars in these forty-five years.
3. The agitation for nuclear disarmament is the most universally supported campaign in history; yet even if it were to succeed the world would hardly be safer, since enough weapons would still be left to wipe out all human life many times over.
4. Nuclear arms are the largest nonproductive drain on the world's economy; yet starvation faces hundreds of millions because of expenditure not on nuclear but on conventional arms, particularly in the Third World.
5. The betrayal of secrets that enabled the Soviet Union to become the second nuclear power was regarded by many as the crime of the century, yet the only occasion on which nuclear weapons were used in earnest was when they were possessed by only one power.[55]

Based on these observations, he concludes that nuclear weapons are permissible as a deterrent but not for use. They function as a deterrent in the same manner that "robberies do not take place if the criminal knows that the house is booby-trapped against any intruder, liable to kill him together with the owner on any forced entry."[56] The biblical verse (Exodus 22:1) that legitimates self-defense and spawned the rabbinic adage, "If a man comes to slay you, pre-empt him by slaying him first,"[57] applies only if the victim can save his own life. The victim would not be allowed to frustrate the attack by blowing up his house and thus killing both himself and his assailant. "Presumably, the victim would then have to submit to the robbery and even [possibly] to death by violence at the hands of the attacker rather than take 'preventive' action, which would be sure to cause two deaths."[58]

Rabbi Walter Wurzberger has weighed in precisely on the dilemma of having a nonusable deterrent. The dilemma is that the nuclear arsenal is an effective deterrent only if the adversary is persuaded that it will be used in retaliation, but a strategy of mutual assured destruction (MAD) cannot be countenanced in Judaism. He states:

On the one hand, the actual use of nuclear weapons must be ruled out, for it is inconceivable to sanction the very extinction of the human species. On the other hand, a total ban on the use of nuclear weapons would be tantamount to unconditional surrender, not only of a national self-interest, but of our entire values system.[59]

For the deterrent to be effective, there must be the "immoral" intent to use them:

Under such conditions, our only option is to choose the lesser evil. Perfectionism will not do. Given our predicament it appears that no matter how unpalatable, deterrence with the intent to retaliate with nuclear weapons is preferable to the otherwise unavoidable sacrifice of our value system in the face of nuclear blackmail.[60]

Wurzberger admits that such a position cannot be legitimated in Jewish law, but argues that this is a time for "*hora'at sha'ah* (temporary suspension of laws enabling society to cope with extraordinary situations) or *lemigdar milta* (recourse to extraordinary measures by communal authorities for the protection of the common good)."[61]

Wurzberger's position appears to be rebutted by Rabbi Bradley Artson, who argues that Judaism presents

a flat refusal to countenance the use of nuclear weapons even as tools of defense. The scope of their devastation, the inability to provide for the immunity of noncombatants, and the meaninglessness of dividing defense from offense in a nuclear war propels this weapon beyond the pale of acceptability.[62]

He goes on to argue that a nuclear holocaust would represent a rejection of a divinely created order, for the prophet Isaiah says: "The Creator of heaven Who alone is God, Who formed the earth and made it, Who alone established it, did not create it for a waste, but formed it for habitation" (Isaiah 45:18). As the divinely appointed stewards of earth, humanity is mandated to maintain it as a life-sustaining place. As the *Midrash* says,

When the Holy One encountered the first human being, He took it before all the trees in the garden of Eden and said: "See how lovely and excellent My works are. All that I have created, I have created for you. Consider this carefully, do not corrupt or desolate My world. For if you corrupt or desolate it, there is no one to set it aright after you." (*Ecclesiastes Rabbah* 7:13)

The point is that God's covenant is not just with humanity but with all life on earth, as Genesis says at the end of the first worldwide destruction through water: "I now establish My covenant with you and your offspring to come, and with every living thing that is with you. . . . That [the rainbow] shall be the sign of the covenant that I have established between Me and all flesh that is on the earth" (Genesis 9:8–17). Since the rainbow serves as a reminder of the covenant of life, it has been adopted as the emblem of the Jewish nuclear freeze movement.

Just as humanity has the duty to prevent the earth from becoming desolate, so will humanity be rewarded for enhancing it. As the third-century code known as the *Mishnah* states,

The world was created by ten divine pronouncements. What was the reason for this? Could it not have been created by one pronouncement? It is to make grave the judgment that is to fall on the wicked who injure the world that was created by ten pronouncements, and to merit a goodly reward for the righteous who sustain the world that was created by ten pronouncements. (*Avot* 5:1)

About which Artson comments: "Because God created the world through ten decrees rather than through one, the merit of someone who works to preserve the world is increased tenfold. Similarly, someone who contributes to the destruction of the world commits an especially grave offense."[63]

Nonetheless, Artson does not question the morality of possessing nuclear weapons as deterrence, as long as it is seen as "a crisis-management response," a term not unlike Wurtzberger's "recourse to extraordinary measures." Recognizing it as a temporary stop-gap measure means that military spending must be limited to "only what is absolutely necessary to maintain a credible deterrence," implying the immorality of every weapon beyond necessity. Moreover, since the Bible says, "Seek peace and pursue it" (Psalm 34:15), the quest for peace and the effort to reduce dependence on nuclear weapons must be unremitting. None of this entails unilateral disarmament, since in an unredeemed world, we are commanded to protect ourselves from evil and defend ourselves from attack. After all, as the *Midrash* says, "One who is compassionate toward the cruel will end up being cruel to the compassionate" (*Ecclesiastes Rabbah* 7:16). To avert the evil of resolving national conflict by resorting to violence, Artson also advocates the type of repentance called *teshuvah*. Such repentance involves a return to God and a desisting from evil. The turning to God in this case demands turning away from weapons that destroys God's world.[64] Similarly, Rabbi Joseph Polak argues that it is "immoral to use the knowledge of the power of the atom for the construction of megabombs which can end history."[65] As he poignantly asks, "Is it really given to man to cancel the Messiah?"[66]

Resolutions of Jewish Organizations

In response to the Reagan nuclear buildup, almost every national Jewish organization took a position on nuclear weapons during the years 1981 and 1982.[67] Many of the ethical considerations discussed above were incorporated into these resolutions. For example, the Central Conference of American Rabbis stated:

Our tradition speaks to us of *Sakanat Nefesh*, the danger of exposing ourselves to health hazards; *Ba'al Tashkit*, the abhorrence of willful destruction of the environment; and *Yishuv Ha'aretz*, the betterment and guardianship of the earth. Inspired by the prophets, we raise our voices to call upon the United States government and the Union of Soviet Socialist Republics to adopt a mutual freeze on the testing, production and deployment of nuclear weapons and new delivery systems for nuclear weapons and weapons-grade material, and to commit themselves to reducing their present levels of nuclear weapons and weapons-grade material.[68]

The Holocaust also figured prominently. The Council of Jewish Federations and Welfare Funds resolved:

We declare that there is a consensus that there is a special Jewish viewpoint on this issue. For us, discussion of a "nuclear holocaust" is more than a metaphor. Our history demonstrates that man is capable of perpetrating unspeakable acts on other men and further, that silence in the face of inhumanity is equivalent to complicity. . . . We appeal for an immediate and verifiable world-wide freeze on the testing, production and development of all nuclear weapons.[69]

The Women's League for Conservative Judaism stated:

We, as Jews, having experienced the horrors of mass destruction, must be witnesses to survival. We must feel a special sense of responsibility to speak out against the nuclear armaments proliferation in the United States, the Soviet Union and all nations aspiring to nuclear arms capability.[70]

The biblical flood also came into play. The Federation of Reconstructionist Congregations and Havurot stated:

We should not try to judge the issue of thermonuclear world catastrophe as if it belonged under the category of "war." Wars, however terrible, are lost or won, lead to political and economic results, are just or unjust. A thermonuclear world catastrophe could lead to the wreckage of all human societies, to the destruction of human life or even all life on earth. It would be more akin to the Biblical Flood than to any war. No one would "lose" or "win"; there would be no "justice" or "injustice" because no human society capable of being just or unjust would survive. For these reasons, we join in urging all American Jews to develop new approaches of mind and spirit in addressing the issues of thermonuclear world disaster and the need for controlling and reversing the nuclear arms race. We suggest that synagogues and other Jewish institutions serve the great command of the Torah: "Choose life that you may live" (Deuteronomy 30:19).[71]

Similarly, the Rabbinic Council of America stated: "We affirm the responsibility of mankind to preserve life on earth. We call upon the leaders of our government to strive for bilateral programs leading to a nuclear freeze as a step toward the alleviation of tensions and hostilities and the redirection of our priorities."[72]

Some extended their concern to chemical and biological weapons. The National Council of Jewish Women resolved to urge the United States

To support national and international efforts which advance the cause of world peace and human welfare including:

a. Strict control of sale of weapons, technology and material which can be used in warfare, while working toward the goal of general disarmament.
b. Effective control of the sale of nuclear technology and material in order to prevent the proliferation of nuclear weapons.
c. Banning chemical, biological and nuclear warfare.[73]

All advocated a reduction of nuclear weapons. The American Jewish Congress resolved: "The foremost political priority of the United States must be to achieve an agreement with the U.S.S.R. on the control, limitation, and destruction of nuclear weapons, beginning with the mutual cessation of nuclear weapons development."[74] B'nai Brith International called "for a strengthening of the safeguards system so that nuclear non-proliferation might become a reality."[75] The National Federation of Temple Brotherhoods passed a resolution that

1. Commends President Reagan for his strong statement calling for the mutual reduction of nuclear weapons.
2. Urges the United States and the USSR to renew, with utmost urgency, negotiations for a new SALT or START agreement aimed at significant cutbacks of intercontinental nuclear weapons in a phased and verifiable pattern of arms control.
3. Calls on the US and USSR to agree mutually to cut their existing nuclear stockpiles.
4. Appeals to all nuclear powers and especially the US and USSR to mutually agree upon a reduction in the testing, production and deployment of nuclear weapons.
5. Calls upon the US to take vigorous world leadership in the achievement of effective non-proliferation treaties. We support legislative proposals which would impose a moratorium on the transfer of nuclear technology to those nations which have not demonstrated the ability or intention to use that technology responsibly, until such time as genuine safeguards can be established.[76]

In sum, the bent of contemporary Jewish thinking seems to be that just as there are unacceptable targets, there are also unacceptable weapons. From the limitations on sieges in the classical sources, it can be extrapolated that weapons directed primarily at civilian targets would be proscribed. As such the military option of counterpeople warfare in conventional war as well as a policy of mutual assured destruction in nuclear warfare would be precluded. Multimegaton weapons whose primary goal is civilian slaughter and only secondarily military targets would be totally proscribed, which is not the case with weapons that may be used in a discriminate fashion on military targets.[77]

THE ISRAELI SITUATION

Napalm

The distinction between acceptable and unacceptable targets informs Israeli military thinking. I recall an event at Yale University in the early 1970s where Prime Minister Yitzhak Rabin, who was then the Israeli ambassador to the United States, was asked to relate the most difficult question he had encountered on a university campus. He responded by mentioning that after delivering a talk at the University of Wisconsin, at the height of the anti–Vietnam War protests, he was asked by an Egyptian student: "General Rabin, as chief of staff of the Israeli Defense Forces during the Six-Day War, will you tell this audience whether Israel used napalm?" Rabin answered that there was no international convention against the use of napalm, and that it was used by Israel in the war, for Israeli policy focuses more on the target than on the weapon. As long as napalm has not been outlawed and the target is military, its use is considered legitimate. Having answered the Egyptian's question, Rabin asked him why Egypt had used biological and possibly chemical weapons in Yemen, both of which had been condemned by international convention and the Red Cross. The Egyptian retorted that it was none of his business what Arabs do to each other.

Rabin's response suggests that for some Israeli leaders the moral assessment is on the target as opposed to the weapon as long as international convention has not prohibited it.[78]

Purity of Arms

The concern for the moral quotient of the soldier and the life of the enemy constitutes the "purity of arms" doctrine of the Israeli Defense Forces. The doctrine limits killing to necessary and unavoidable situations.[79] The former prime minister of Israel, David Ben-Gurion, made it a fundamental principle of the Israeli military.[80] Some claim that Israel has maintained these standards even under war conditions.[81]

Nuclear Weapons

The moral issue of Israel's development and possession of WMD, especially nuclear weapons, has not received much public attention in Israel. This is probably due to two factors. The first is the widespread belief in Israel that its neighbors would destroy it if they could. Most Israelis cannot imagine the Arabs treating them with more consideration than they do their own people. So when Israelis see how the Iraqi government gassed its own citizens, how Syria wiped out a large section of one of its own cities, or how Sudan massacred its Christians to the south, they have little doubt about the fate that would await them were they to lose a war.

The second factor is Israel's policy of nuclear opacity, a policy – much like that of Pakistan until recently – that is intended to minimize the visibility of its nuclear program and thus minimize the pressure on Arab governments to acquire a nuclear option. Still, there exists an extensive discussion of Israel's development of its nuclear deterrent by Avner Cohen[82] and a helpful recent article by Louis Beres.[83] Cohen describes how the policy of nuclear opacity allowed Israel to move from being an ambiguous nuclear power to an undeclared one. "By 1969 Israel committed itself not to reveal its nuclear capability by conducting a test or by declaration. With these new understandings both the United States and Israel moved from the era of nuclear ambiguity to the era of nuclear opacity."[84]

Because of this policy of opacity there has not been a public discussion of its utility or its utilization. Noteworthy is the fact that it did not deter Syria and Egypt in 1973 from going to war against Israel in the Yom Kippur War. Israel did not even put its nuclear capacity on alert even though no other war had so threatened it. According to Cohen:

From the outset, Israeli thinking about the unthinkable has been linked with the concept of last resort. That is, the defense of Israel must not rely on the threat or use of nuclear weapons as long as its enemies have no nuclear weapons, except in cases of extreme national emergency when the survival of the state as a political entity is threatened.

Cohen goes on to claim that "the 1973 war provided Israel a great lesson in what constituted a last resort, and the extent to which Israeli leaders were committed to the principle of nonuse and were aware of the nuclear taboo."[85] He concludes that Prime Minister Golda Meir's "reluctance to consider use of nuclear weapons raised the bar of what constitutes a true dire moment in which the use of nuclear weapons is justified."[86] Indeed, he generalizes: "The instinctive reluctance of Israeli leaders to consider seriously the use of nuclear weapons in these two crises [the Six-Day War and the Yom Kippur War] is rooted in a *double* sense of prohibition: the evolving global normative prohibition against the use of nuclear weapons and Israel's own code and culture of nuclear opacity."[87]

This raises the question of its utility as a weapon of last resort. If a successful Syrian-Egyptian two-pronged attack in which the supply of planes, tanks, and ammunition was rapidly being depleted was not considered a dire moment, what would constitute a last-resort threat to Israel? Apparently, a last resort would be only if the enemy had encroached on its major urban areas. But by then it would be too late to use nuclear weapons, for if the enemy were already entrenched inside Israeli territory, Israel would never incinerate its own population centers, and it would be too late to use nuclear weapons against the enemy's cities if the function is deterrence and not revenge. Thus it would seem that nuclear weapons may prove to be irrelevant in a war between Israel and its neighbors. Such, however, is not the case with, say, Iran, where, as Beres notes:

Israel's conventional and nuclear deterrents are interrelated. For the foreseeable future, any enemy states that would launch an exclusively conventional attack upon Israel would almost surely have multiple unconventional weapons capabilities in reserve. This means that even if Israel can rely upon conventional deterrence as a "first line" of protection, that line will necessarily be augmented by Israeli nuclear deterrence to prevent escalation that might be initiated by certain enemy states after the start of hostilities.[88]

Is there a Jewish justification for Israel's possession of nuclear weapons? Among the respondents in *Confronting Omnicide,* the only rabbi who mentions Israel is the Israeli rabbi Pinchas Peli. Peli guardedly uses the Holocaust to justify Israel's possession of nuclear weapons:

If anyone has the right to possess nuclear weapons in order to deter murderous aggression, Israel is the country that irrefutably should have such a right. It is, after all, the only state in the world that is threatened openly and constantly with total destruction. . . . Auschwitz and Treblinka are still with us. To the Jewish people "Final Solutions" through annihilation are not a nightmarish fairy tale.[89]

Peli does not endorse outright Israel's possession of weapons of mass destruction. Rather, he states that if anyone has the right, it is Israel, and then only in order to deter murderous aggression. Knowing the danger of such a policy, he offers two safeguards: Explaining the requirement that new houses have parapets on the roofs lest one fall from them, the Bible says, "Do not bring blood on the house" (Deuteronomy 22:8). The Talmud (*B. Ketubot* 41b) expands the prohibition of bringing blood upon the house to keeping a vicious dog, because, as Maimonides says in his Code of Jewish Law, its harm is considerable and frequent.[90] Nonetheless, the Talmud (*B. Babba Kamma* 83a) does permit such a dog for security in a border town at night, provided that it is properly chained during the day. Applying this to WMD, Peli concludes:

Possession of dangerous materials could easily "bring blood upon thy house"; one should therefore not have them in the house. If however, they have to be in one's possession, one must take the necessary precautions and make sure to have the proper "chain" and lock in order to curb escalation from "possession" of the dreadful stuff to its "use."[91]

Apparently, Peli allows the possession of nuclear weapons with the proper safeguards, but not their use. He concludes his analysis with a version of the following comment from the *Midrash*: "When iron was created, the trees began to tremble. Said God to them: 'Why do you tremble? Let none of your wood enter it (as a handle), and not one of you shall be harmed'" (*Genesis Rabbah* 5:7). This would seem to be the ancient equivalent of the modern saying, "Guns don't kill people. People kill people." Whether such thinking is adequate to the risk of nuclear miscalculation is open to question.

CONCLUSIONS

Utilization: From a contemporary Jewish perspective, America and Israel are conceived as the guarantors of the security of the Jewish people in particular and of humanity in general. Thus their security is valorized above others. Nonetheless, the consensus of Jewish thought is against their using weapons of mass destruction. Indiscriminate conventional weapons, such as incendiary bombs and antipersonnel mines, may be used only if they can be significantly limited to military targets.

Deterrence: WMD may be developed as a deterrent, but probably never to be used.

Proliferation: Since the more countries that have nuclear weapons, the greater the possibility of intentional or mistaken use, no nonnuclear country should be allowed to acquire them. On the principle that you stop what is stoppable, no country should be allowed to develop biological and chemical weapons. Indeed, the present nuclear club should join forces and bully other countries into compliance with the Chemical Weapons Convention, the Biological Weapons Convention, the Nuclear Nonproliferation Treaty, and the Comprehensive Test Ban Treaty.

Once all the countries that have sought the destruction of Israel complied, then should Israel also be bullied into compliance? The difficulty of such a policy with regard to nuclear weapons is that Israel could not legitimately be asked to forgo its nuclear capability without Iran and Pakistan forgoing theirs. But it is unlikely that Pakistan would comply without the compliance of its nuclear neighbor, India, which in turn would probably not comply without the compliance of its nuclear neighbor, China, which of course would require the compliance of Russia, which of course would need the compliance of the United States. Yet nothing could be more salutary for the Jewish vision of a nuclear-free world as the first step to world peace than to have the elimination of Israel's nuclear weapons be the trigger for the worldwide elimination of nuclear weapons.

Disarmament: Unilateral disarmament is immoral for countries such as Israel or the United States, who have declared enemies with the capacity to destroy them. Still, universal disarmament has always been a Jewish vision, a vision, however, not bereft of a modicum of realpolitik. Thus before the prophet Isaiah envisages nations beating their swords into plowshares and their spears into pruning hooks, he says,

In the days to come ... many people shall come and say: "Come, let us go up to the mountain of the Lord ... that He may teach us His ways ... for out of Zion shall go forth teaching and the word of the Lord from Jerusalem. He shall judge between the nations, and shall arbitrate for many peoples." (Isaiah 2:3–4)

Isaiah's vision of universal disarmament is predicated on the existence of a universal house of prayer that will function both as a locus of moral instruction and as a court for the arbitration of national conflict. When national conflicts can be adjudicated properly by an international tribunal, there are grounds to envision a world where "nation shall not lift up sword against nation, neither shall they learn war any more" (Isaiah 2:4).

For Isaiah, it is not enough to desist from going to war; nations must also cease the education for war. Training for war itself may make war irresistible. The Isaianic policy of swords into plowshares, however, entails not just the replacement of the sword with the plowshare but the beating of the sword into a plowshare, that is, the conversion of the means of destruction into the means of construction. Creating an economic alternative to the arms industry is thus an imperative of realistic disarmament.

Notes

1. The section is adapted from my "War," in *Frontiers of Jewish Thought*, ed. Steven Katz (Washington, D.C.: B'nai Brith Books, 1992), 309–32.

2. See *Jerusalem Talmud* (hereafter J.) *Sotah* 9:10, 23a, *Babylonian Talmud* (hereafter B.) *Berakhot* 3b, *B. Sotah* 44b, *B. Sanhedrin* 16a, and Maimonides, *Mishneh Torah* (hereafter MT) "Laws of Kings and Their Wars," 5:1, along with Chanoch Albeck, *Mishnah, Seder Nashim* (Tel Aviv: Bialik Institute, 1958), 390f.

3. *Mishnah* (hereafter M.) *Yadayim* 4:4; *B. Berakhot* 28a, *B. Yoma* 54a, cf. *Tosefta* (hereafter T.) *Yadayim* 2:17.

4. 1 Kings 9:20–21; 2 Chronicles 8:7–9. Cf. Joshua 13:13, 16:10, 17:12–13; Judges 1:21–35; 3:5–6; and Psalms 106:34.

5. Following David Hoffmann, ed., *Midrash Tannaim* to Deuteronomy 20:15, p. 121, n. 10. On the nontransferability of the seven-nation rulings, see Joseph Babad, *Minhat Hinukh* to *Sefer Ha-Hinukh*, commandment no. 527, s.v. *ve-im* (Jerusalem: Machon Yerushalayim, 1991), 3:307b.

6. Maimonides, *MT*, "Laws of Kings and their Wars," 5:4; idem, *Book of the Commandments*, commandment no. 187.

7. *Sefer Ha-Hinukh*, commandment no. 425 with *Minhat Hinukh*, ibid. (3:126), and end of commandment no. 604 (3:425).

8. See Moses b. Jacob of Coucy, *Sefer Mitsvot Gadol* (SeMaG), negative commandment no. 226; R. David b. Zimra (RaDBaZ) with *Maimonidean Glosses* to "Laws of Kings and their Wars," 5:5; and Menahem Kasher, *Torah Shelemah*, 42 vols. (Jerusalem: Beth Torah Shelamah, 1949–91), 14:340.

9. *Midrash Samuel* 22:2, ed. S. Buber, p. 110.

10. *Midrash Lekah Tov*, ed. S. Buber, Deuteronomy, p. 35a. *Leviticus Rabbah* 1:4 draws the distinction between David's wars "for Israel" and those "for himself." Cf. Rashi to *B. Gittin* 8b, and 47a, s.v., *kibush yahid*, and *B. Avodah Zarah* 20b, s.v., *suria*.

11. *B. Sotah* 44b, and *J. Sotah* 8:10; 23a.

12. Menachem Meiri, *Beit Ha-Behirah* to *B. Sotah* 42a. R. Isaac of Vienna in his *Or Zaru'a*, as cited in the gloss to the *Shulkhan Arukh, Orakh Hayyim* 329:6, also permits a preemptive strike against a hostile intention, as does the eighteenth-century German rabbi Naphtali Fraenkel (*Sheyarei Korban* to *J. Sotah* 8:10). According to the sixteenth-century Bohemian-Polish rabbi Mordecai Yafeh, this ruling applies especially to the defense of strategically vulnerable areas; see his *Levush Ha-Tekhelet Ve-Ha-Hur* (New York, 1966) to *Orakh Hayyim* 329:6.

13. Maimonides, *MT*, "Laws of Kings and Their Wars," 5:1, according to Avraham Karelitz, *Hazon Ish Al Ha-Ramban* (B'nei B'rak, 5729), 841. Maimonides's

Commentary, however, on *M. Sotah* 8:7 agrees with Rashi. For a clear statement of Maimonides's method, see Zvi Kaplan, '*Al Gedot Yam Ha-Talmud* (Jerusalem: Ariel, 1990), 120f.

14. *B. Sanhedrin* 16a. For the biblical material, see Abraham Malamat, "Organs of Statecraft in the Israelite Monarchy," in *The Biblical Archaeologist Reader,* vol. 3, ed. E. F. Campbell, Jr., and D. N. Freedman (Garden City, N.Y.: Doubleday, 1970), 167f.

15. Maimonides, *Commentary to the Mishnah, Horayot* 1:6, ed. Kafih, *Nazikim,* p. 309; see Gerald J. Blidstein, *Political Concepts in Maimonidean Halakha* (in Hebrew) (Ramat Gan: Bar Ilan University, 2001), 64–67.

16. Following Yosef Dov Soloveitchick, *Kovets Hidushei Torah* (Jerusalem, n.d.), 51–55; and Gerald J. Blidstein, "Individual and Community in the Middle Ages," in *Kinship and Consent: The Jewish Political Tradition and Its Contemporary Uses,* ed. Daniel J. Elazar (Ramat Gan: Turtledove, 1981), 247, n. 62.

17. Shlomo Goren, *Mashiv Milhamah* (Jerusalem: Ha-idra Rabba, 1983), 127–30. See Blidstein, *Political Concepts,* 65, n. 18.

18. 2 Kings 11:17 and 2 Chronicles 23:3 along with 2 Samuel 5:3. On using the term "covenant" for the Israelite polity, see Hayim Tadmor, "'The People' and the Kingship in Ancient Israel: The Role of Political Institutions in the Biblical Period," in *Jewish Society through the Ages,* ed. H. H. Ben-Sasson and S. Ettinger (New York: Schocken, 1971), 59–62; and F. M. Cross, *Canaanite Myth and Hebrew Epic* (Cambridge: Harvard University Press, 1972), 221.

19. See the example in Josephus, *Antiquities* 9.7.4 (153).

20. David J. Bleich, "Preemptive War in Jewish Law," *Tradition* 17 (1983): 25. According to one source, the endorsement of a war policy falls within judicial jurisdiction, whereas the assessment of victory falls within the province of the priestly Urim and Tummin (*B. Eruvin* 45a, see Rashi to *B. Berakhot* end of 3b). In *J. Sabbath* 2:3, 5b = *Midrash Ha-Gadol* to Numbers 27:21, ed. Rabinowitz, p. 483, the judgment of the Urim refers to the judgment of the court on high.

21. Rabbi Girshuni, based on the comment of Gersonides (RaLBaG) to the Book of Judges (6–8), argues that this applies to all wars; see Yehudah Girshuni, "War and Bravery" (in Hebrew), *Techumim* 4 (5743): 58f.

22. *B. Shavuot* 35b, see Samuel Edels (MaHaRSHa), ad loc.; *The Commentary of the Netsiv* to Genesis 9:5–6. *Responsa Hatam Sofer* (Vienna, 1865) to *Shulkhan Arukh, Orakh Hayyim* no. 208, p. 77a; and Joseph Akhituv, "The Wars of Israel and 'the Sanctity of Life'" (in Hebrew), in *Sanctity of Life and Martyrdom: Studies in Memory of Amir Yekutiel,* ed. I. Gafni and A. Ravitsky (Jerusalem: Zalman Shazar Center for Jewish History, 1992), 255–76, 260–63.

23. *Song of Songs Rabbah* 44:4.

24. For the "Clausewitzian friction" that distinguishes the fluid and chaotic nature of real war from war on paper, see Gordon Craig, "The Political Leader as Strategist," in *The Makers of Modern Strategy from Machiavelli to the Nuclear Age,* ed. Peter Paret (Princeton, N.J.: Princeton University Press, 1986), 481–509; and Edward N. Luttwak, *Strategy: The Logic of War and Peace* (Cambridge: Harvard University Press, 1987), 10–15.

25. *Sifre Deuteronomy* 203, ed. Finkelstein, p. 239, with *Midrash Ha-Gadol Deuteronomy* 20:19, ed. Fisch, p. 451.

26. Ibid., and *Midrash Ha-Gadol Numbers* 31:7, ed. Rabinowitz, p. 538, n. 17. See David S. Shapiro, "The Jewish Attitude Towards Peace and War," in *Israel of Tomorrow*, ed. Leo Jung (New York: Herald Square Press, 1946), 239. A more comprehensive and analytic treatment of this material is found in Lawrence K. Milder's unpublished rabbinic thesis, "Laws of War in the Bible and Formative Rabbinic Literature," Hebrew Union College-Jewish Institute of Religion, 1983.

27. Philo, *The Special Laws* IV, 221.

28. Ibid., 226.

29. Josephus, *Contra Apion* II, 212–14.

30. Maimonides, *MT*, "Laws of Kings and Their Wars," 6:10. See also idem, "Book of Commandments," negative commandment no. 57.

31. Nachmanides (RaMBaN), *Commentary* to Deuteronomy 20:19.

32. *Sefer Ha-Hinukh, mitzvah* no. 529 (ed. Chavel, no. 530, p. 647).

33. Arama, *Akedat Yitshak*, no. 81, 105.

34. Alshikh, *Sefer Torat Moshe, parshat shoftim* (Warsaw, 5682), 134a. Cf. 2 Kings 6:22.

35. See Rabbi Nathan, *Sifre Numbers* 157, ed. Horovitz, p. 210; *Midrash Ha-Gadol Deuteronomy*, ed. Fisch, p. 450 with n. 3; Maimonides, *MT*, "Laws of Kings and Their Wars," 6:7; and Yitshak Kaufman, *Ha-Tsava Ke-Halakha* (Jerusalem: Kol Mevaser, 1992), 11–12 n. 20.

36. See Saul Lieberman, *Tosefta Ki-fshutah*, 10 vols. (New York: Jewish Theological Seminary of America, 1955–88), 8:989.

37. There is biblical (2 Kings 6:21–23, according to RaLBaG, ad loc.) and midrashic warrant (*Seder Eliahu Rabbah* 8, ed. Friedmann, p. 39) for promoting the immunity of noncombatants on both ethical and tactical grounds.

38. See the addenda of Nachmanides to Maimonides, *Sefer Ha-Mitzvot*, ed. Chavel (Jerusalem, 1981), the fifth commandment, p. 246.

39. Abarbanel, *Commentary to Deuteronomy* 20:10 (Jerusalem: Benei Arbel, 1964), 193a.

40. Based on *Targum Onqelos, Targum Pseudo-Jonathan*, and *Midrash Leqah Tov* to Numbers 33:55, p. 282.

41. Abarbanel, *Commentary to Deuteronomy*, p. 193b. Philo also argues that women are spared because they are exempt from war service; see *The Special Laws* IV, 224.

42. *Genesis Rabbah* 44:4.

43. Philo, *The Special Laws* IV, 227.

44. The idea of noncombatant immunity expressed by Philo in the first century B.C.E., applied by *Midrash Sifre* in the third century, and codified by Maimonides in the twelfth century reflects some of the earliest thinking on this subject in Western thought.

45. Philo, *The Special Laws* IV, 224–25.

46. Ibid., 224.

47. Samuel Pisar, *Of Blood and Hope* (Boston: Little, Brown, 1980), 306.

48. Daniel Landes, ed., *Confronting Omnicide: Jewish Reflections on Weapons of Mass Destruction* (Northvale, N. J.: Jacob Aronson, 1991).

49. David Ellenson, "A Theology of Fear: The Search for a Liberal Jewish Paradigm," in ibid., 142–63, teased out the positions of past thinkers such as Franz Rosenzweig, Abraham Joshua Heschel, Hermann Cohen, Hans Jonas, and Martin Buber.

50. Irving Greenberg, "The Dialectics of Power: Reflections in the Light of the Holocaust," in *Confronting Omnicide*, 27.

51. See *B. Sanhedrin* 72a, 74a, with Reuven Kimelman, "Terror, Political Murder, and Judaism," *Journal of Jewish Education Review* 62:2 (1996): 6–11.

52. Greenberg, "The Dialectics of Power," 30.

53. Ibid., 31.

54. David Novak, "Nuclear War and the Prohibition of Wanton Destruction," in *Confronting Omnicide*, 115.

55. Immanuel Jakobovits, "Confronting Omnicide," in *Confronting Omnicide*, 201f. In the same vein, Henry Kissinger has noted that "*all* wars in the postwar period have occurred where there were *no* American forces and *no* nuclear weapons, while Europe under American nuclear protection has enjoyed the longest period of peace in its history" (Henry A. Kissinger, *Nuclear Weapons and the Peace Movement* (Washington, D.C.: Ethics and Public Policy Center, 1982), 32.

56. Jakobovits, "Confronting Omnicide," 205f.

57. *B. Sanhedrin* 72a.

58. Jakobovits, "Confronting Omnicide," 204.

59. Walter S. Wurzburger, "Nuclear Deterrence and Nuclear War," in *Confronting Omnicide*, 230.

60. Ibid., 230.

61. Ibid., 231. The former chief rabbi of Palestine, Abraham Hakohen Kook, *Mishpat Kohen* (Jerusalem, 1985), secs. 142–44, allows for such recourse when the nation itself is at risk.

62. Bradley Shavit Artson, *Love Peace and Pursue Peace: A Jewish Response to War and Nuclear Annihilation* (New York: United Synagogue of America, 1988), 221.

63. Ibid., 228.

64. See Samuel H. Dresner, *God, Man and Atomic War* (New York: Living Books, 1966), chap. 6.

65. Joseph Polak, "Torah and Megabombs," *Judaism* 36:3 (Summer 1983): 308.

66. Ibid., 305.

67. The following resolutions are assembled in David Saperstein, ed., *Preventing the Nuclear Holocaust: A Jewish Response* (New York: UAHC, 1983), 49–63.

68. Ibid., 51.

69. Ibid., 52.

70. Ibid., 63.

71. Ibid., 53.

72. Ibid., 59.

73. Ibid., 54.

74. Ibid., 49.

75. Ibid., 50.

76. Ibid., 55.

77. See Marc Gopin, *Between Eden and Armageddon: The Future of World Religions, Violence, and Peacemaking* (New York: Oxford University Press, 2000), 70.

78. Rabbi Shaul Yisraeli also derives from the principle of Jewish law (*halakha*) "the law of the land is the law," the halakhic force of international convention. See Akhituv, "The Wars of Israel and 'the Sanctity of Life,'" 264.

79. See Ehud Luz, "The Moral Price of Sovereignty: The Dispute about the Use of Military Power within Zionism," *Modern Judaism* 7 (1987): 76.

80. See Haim Cohen, "Law and Reality in Israel Today," in *Violence and Defense in the Jewish Experience*, ed. S. Baron and G. Wise (Philadelphia: Jewish Publication Society, 1977), 332.

81. See Meir Pa'il, "The Dynamics of Power: Morality in Armed Conflict after the Six-Day War," *Modern Jewish Ethics: Theory and Practice*, ed. Marvin Fox (Columbus: Ohio State University, 1975), 215; and Avraham Shapira, *The Seventh Day: Soldiers Talk about the Six-Day War* (London: Deutsch, 1970), 132.

82. Avner Cohen, *Israel and the Bomb* (New York: Columbia University Press, 1998).

83. Louis René Beres, "Israeli Nuclear Deterrence," *Midstream* 47:2 (February/March 2001): 10–12.

84. Cohen, *Israel and the Bomb*, 337.

85. Avner Cohen, "Nuclear Arms in Crisis under Secrecy: Israel and the Lessons of the 1967 and 1973 Wars," in *Planning the Unthinkable: How New Powers Will Use Nuclear, Biological, and Chemical Weapons*, ed. Peter R. Lavoy, Scott D. Sagan, and James J. Wirtz (Ithaca, N.Y.: Cornell University Press, 2000), 120.

86. Ibid., 121.

87. Ibid., 123.

88. Beres, "Israeli Nuclear Deterrence," 12b.

89. Pinchas H. Peli, "Torah and Weapons of Mass Destruction: A View from Israel," in *Confronting Omnicide*, 80.

90. Maimonides, *MT*, "Laws of Monetary Damage," 5:9.

91. Peli, "Torah and Weapons of Mass Destruction," 79.

20

Between the Bible and the Holocaust

Three Sources for Jewish Perspectives on Mass Destruction

Joseph E. David

In the previous chapter, Reuven Kimelman offers a broad survey of how Jewish ethical reflection on war, both *halakhic* and modern, relates to weapons of mass destruction.[1] By invoking the traditional halakhic principles on when and how wars may be fought, Kimelman is claiming, so I understand, that moral reasoning relating to conventional wars provides a relevant framework for constructing an ethical position on unconventional wars in which WMD are employed. Such an argument casts doubt on the need to distinguish within Jewish military ethics between conventional and unconventional wars. The prohibition against the possession and use of WMD or restrictions on their use would, in this view, be derived from the same ethical principles that apply to the use of military power of any kind.

If my reading of Kimelman's position is correct, then I disagree with his approach. My premise in this chapter is that the ethical basis on which questions of possession and use of WMD must be examined is significantly different from the ethics of conventional warfare.[2] Conventional war ethics, which Kimelman uses as a starting point for his discussion, is devoted to examining the morality of war at two stages: before the war, when the legitimacy of declaring war is considered (*jus ad bellum*), and during the war, when the proper methods of fighting are evaluated (*jus in bello*). Yet the principal ethical concerns in a war in which WMD are employed arise, in my opinion, neither before nor during the fighting but in the aftermath of such a war. More precisely, the major moral issue is the likelihood that in a war in which WMD are used, the outcome of even a just war (as defined by the two traditional sets of criteria) is likely to be catastrophic. The ethics of WMD therefore lie beyond the regular ethics of war. The principal questions are not, What is a just war? or What behavior is justified during battle? Rather, the relevant question is, Is there any conflict that justifies the threatened or actual use of weapons of mass destruction?

In attempting to answer this question, I broaden Kimelman's presentation by elucidating perspectives from three traditional Jewish sources that emerged parallel to the halakhic tradition.[3] Clearly, the prospect of mass destruction perpetrated by human hands was not a real possibility for the halakhic authorities.[4] Accordingly, I suggest that we redirect our attention to other sources of Jewish consciousness, to myth, imagination, and living memory – in addition to theology. Bringing in these sources alongside the *halakha* literature allows us to form a more complete Jewish ethics regarding the questions of this book.

The first source I examine is the idea of the Day of the Lord and its related images in the conceptual world of the Bible, including the image of God as warrior and the idea of holy war. Passages relating to the Day of the Lord include descriptions of total annihilation of the enemies of Israel and prompts the question: Do these descriptions provide religious sanction for mass destruction?

The second source that I discuss might be called the rabbinic interpretations of the rainbow covenant, the covenant God makes in the book of Genesis following the mass annihilation of the flood. The rainbow covenant is the first mythical precedent that negates the possibility of mass destruction. I present a number of interpretations associated with the covenant's negating role and with the idea of human responsibility for the continuation of humanity's existence.

The third source is the imprint left on the Jewish people by their experience of genocide during the Holocaust. I explore the extent to which the Holocaust shapes the modern Jewish ethic of war and, in particular, its influence on Jewish thinking on total war.

TOTAL DESTRUCTION AND THE IDEA OF THE DAY OF THE LORD

The literature on war and its justification recognizes a number of well-known distinctions as a basis for ethical conduct: the distinction between combatants and noncombatants, the distinction between those who have the ability to defend themselves and those who do not, the distinction between the front line and civilian areas, and so forth. Yet when one examines the characteristics of war contained in biblical descriptions of the Day of the Lord, it seems that such distinctions are irrelevant to this type of war. Indeed, in this type of war, total annihilation and destruction are not only not disqualified, they are enjoined.

Biblical passages relating to the Day of the Lord suggest a point of time in the future when God is expected to punish the wicked and justice will triumph. The term "Day of the Lord" occurs as a key phrase in nine prophetic passages,[5] and in others it appears in some slightly varied form.[6]

The notion of a future war that will take place on the Day of the Lord must be considered first and foremost in the context of the intrabiblical tension between two distinct political yearnings. Two approaches regarding the nature and identity of the governmental rule expected at the end of days appear in the Jewish Bible, the rule of the House of David and, alternatively, the rule of the Lord himself. The differences between these political aspirations stem, in effect, from two messianic conceptions that may be derived from the Bible: restorative messianism and utopian messianism.[7] Restorative messianism is founded on the biblical assertion that King David and his successors were selected by God to reign over Israel until the end of generations,[8] hence they have a right to rule and to maintain this rule.[9]

In contrast, the idea of the Day of the Lord produces in the utopian messianic framework a longing for the tangible appearance of the deity in history. The term "Day of the Lord" is the figurative designation for the date on which the omnipotent deity will literally display his unparalleled grandeur and power. On that day he will demonstrate his dominion over the earth through heroic and powerful deeds, beginning by overcoming his enemies.[10] Accordingly, the prophets describe it in dismal terms: "The day of the Lord is one of darkness and not light."[11] It will be a day of war, calamity, and the Lord's revenge over his enemies.[12] From that point on will begin the Lord's rule on earth.

Scholars suggest a number of possible origins for the idea of the Day of the Lord. The most widely accepted explanation is that it derives from preprophetic ideas of holy war dating back to the appearance of the ancient Israelites in Canaan at the end of the thirteenth century B.C.E.[13] The cataclysmic destruction wreaked by God on the world at the end times, according to this view, is closely related to the idea that God commanded the Israelites of that period to annihilate their enemies in wars of conquest and vengeance.[14] God was believed to reveal his will in battle, and therefore the battle itself was called a "Day of the Lord." All of the activities and operations relating to the battle were acts of holiness. The rally to battle required sanctification by the priestly class; integral to conducting the war was the taking out of the Ark of the Covenant, accompanied by fasts, public gatherings, sacrifices, and other rituals.[15] The descriptions of war that accompany the references to the Day of the Lord are therefore grounded in and themselves lend support to a national belief that the Lord goes to war along with the Israelites, that their war is his war, and therefore the enemies of Israel are also enemies of the Lord himself.

If God is perceived as a "warrior," then war becomes an arena of divine revelation. Battle maneuvers become not only political moves between rival parties but evidence of divine presence and power. Military victory or defeat assume religious significance and are understood as proofs of divine intercession in human affairs. The end of war entails not just the vanquishing of the enemy and the destruction of his power, but also the elimination of "unholy" ideas and practices. Such total war can be justified as reflecting the complete and omnipotent rule of God.[16]

Perceiving war as theophanous also explains the apparent absence of ethical considerations and limits in many biblical passages describing the wars of the ancient Israelites. Human actions committed at the behest of God transcend discernible ethical limits.

Likewise, the descriptions of the future war on the Day of the Lord are descriptions of total destruction and calamity. The anger of the deity (in Hebrew, *Haron-apo*, literally, "the anger of his nose"[17]) is devoid of mercy and subject to no constraints:

> And I will requite to the world its evil. . . . All who remain shall be pierced through, all who are caught shall fall by the sword. And their babes shall be dashed to pieces in their sight, their homes shall be plundered. . . . Their bows shall shatter the young; they shall show no pity to infants, they shall not spare the children.[18]

The stroke of divine annihilation does not distinguish between warrior and child, between attacks on natural resources and human beings.[19] In fact, a theophanous conception of war removes the necessity to provide an ethical accounting of military actions, since theophany is beyond the normative and the ethical.

Indeed, "God's wars" as described by the Bible pose some obvious challenges to ethical intuition. For this reason, perhaps, the theophanous concept of war underwent an ideational metamorphosis in the world of Jewish rabbinical thought after the destruction of the Second Temple (70 C.E.) and was effectively rejected as a paradigmatic model of postbiblical war ethics.

Kimelman's overview of the early Jewish sources makes clear at the outset that the rabbinic discussions treated war not as an expression of divine power but as a political phenomenon subject to normative evaluation. The very categorization of wars into *mitzvah* (commanded), *reshut* (permitted), and *asurah* (prohibited)[20] in fact subjects all justifications and acts of war to the authority of earthly halakhic institutions, the king (the political authority) and the Sanhedrin (the spiritual-religious authority).[21] The total and indiscriminate destruction of holy war was suppressed in favor of Deuteronomic concepts of limited war, such as the prohibition against axing fruit trees during a siege,[22] or later ideas, such as the halakhic requirement that the population of a besieged town be allowed an escape route.[23]

Did the "halakhization" of war root out the theophanic conception of war from traditional Jewish consciousness? Not entirely, because remnants of the holy war concept are evident in a number of streams of Jewish thought considered relatively marginal to the rabbinic mainstream. For example, there are many theophanic expressions of war among the cultic and apocalyptic movements of the Second Temple period,[24] in the writings of the Judean desert cult,[25] or in later eschatological writings such as the *Book of Zerubbabel*.[26] An expectation that the Day of the Lord may not be far off links these disparate elements.

A conceptual analysis of these writings is beyond the scope of this chapter, but it is important to mention that they all adopt, to some extent, a dualistic approach: All of humanity is divided into two opposing camps, "us" versus "them," or in the terminology of the Qumeran texts, the "children of light," who are the faithful, versus the "children of darkness," who belong to the kingdom of evil.[27] It can thus be said that while the theophanic concept of war was rejected by the rabbinic mainstream, it remained current in the world-view of counterparties and messianic trends espousing a dualistic view that drew clear lines between those protected by the deity's compassion and the "others" sentenced to total annihilation.

A dualistic view by nature tends to emphasize existing differences through the amplification of such differences and the creation of a typology based on the contrast between them. For example, from a dualistic standpoint, the distinction between body and soul is understood as representing a series of religious differences of far-reaching significance. The body is external, material, bestial, sinful, and mortal. In contrast, the soul is internal, spiritual, divine, sublime, and eternal.[28] A similar phenomenon occurs when the dualistic approach is applied in the ethical realm. Here the tendency to identify the differences between "us" and "them" with the basic opposition between good and bad, justice and evil, children of light and children of darkness is readily apparent.

This tendency toward opposing and significant typology has indeed proven seductive and convincing time and again. The moral vocabulary of dualism has frequently transformed political conflicts into something "greater" or "higher," into struggles for "our survival" that require "their destruction." Once this binary logic is adopted, all the distinctions that really matter, those that paradoxically illuminate our common humanity, are set aside. It is then but a short step to set aside the ethical intuition that says in war we must distinguish between soldiers and civilians, between those who can defend themselves and the helpless.

Messianic expectations and dualistic approaches may be identified in marginal strands of Jewish thinking throughout the centuries of exile. Since the nineteenth century, the Zionist movement has encompassed a few ideologies that were inspired, to some extent, by versions of traditional messianic world-views. Most of them did not claim that reestablishing the state of Israel necessarily involves reviving the biblical obligation to conquer the land associated with concepts of holy war. Nevertheless, there are some radical nationalist groups today, such as Gush Emunim, who are inspired by the analogy between the Zionist project and the conquest of Canaan by the ancient Israelites. Dualistic views about the Israeli-Arab conflicts and calls to adopt the Bible and the biblical concepts of war as grounds for military action are prominent in the ideology of such groups. They identify themselves with the soldiers of Joshua and David and claim that the Israeli Defense Forces are indeed God's army on earth.[29]

To summarize this section, the possibility of mass destruction is not entirely absent from the Jewish consciousness. Conceptions of war embodied in biblical descriptions of the Day of the Lord not only confirm the possibility of total destruction, but also view it as an expected historical goal. The sources that describe this idea and enumerate its details may therefore even encourage this expectation. The biblical strand that conceives war as a theophany raises it above ethical limitations. Although this concept was blatantly rejected in halakhic tradition, dualistic approaches that ignore the individuality of people preserved both this conception of war and its related descriptions of total destruction.

THE FLOOD EPIC: SYMBOLIC MEANINGS OF THE RAINBOW COVENANT

In contrast to the Day of the Lord, the biblical epic of the flood may be used as a symbol or ideational paradigm for the formulation of a Jewish stance against the development and possession of WMD and in favor of a commitment to prevent mass destruction. Indeed, as Kimelman notes, the rainbow is the symbol of the Jewish nuclear-freeze movement.

The biblical flood story was unique – in contrast to the flood stories familiar to us from the ancient Near East[30] – in its emphasis of two motifs: first, the representation of the flood as divine recompense for human evil, and second, the divine covenant promising that total destruction of human beings and other living things will not occur again.[31] A significant portion of the ethical readings of the flood story in fact emphasizes the first point, that God purified the earth from human corruption but saved Noah and his family because of their righteousness. At the same time, in medieval biblical commentary, we find another ethical reading of the flood story, one that sees it as constituting a normative source of human obligation to prevent mass extinction.

As is well known, the biblical narrative ends with the revelation of divine insight that mass destruction such as the flood ought not to be repeated:

And the Lord said to Himself: "Never again will I doom the earth because of man, since the devising of man's mind is evil from his youth; nor will I ever again destroy every living being, as I have done. . . ."[32]

This insight is then formalized in the eternal covenant made by God, symbolized by the rainbow in the sky, which serves as a periodic reminder of the covenant's validity:

I will maintain My covenant with you: never again shall all flesh be cut off by the waters of a flood, and never again shall there be a flood to destroy the earth. . . . I have set My bow in the clouds, and it shall serve as a sign of the covenant between Me and the earth. . . . When the bow is in the clouds, I will see it and remember the everlasting covenant between God and all living creatures, all flesh that is on earth.[33]

The medieval commentators on this passage grappled with a number of questions stemming from it: Who is bound by this obligation? What is its content? And how does the rainbow symbolize this obligation? They offered at least two symbolic understandings of the rainbow covenant that bear on human responsibility for preserving life: the rainbow as a symbol of reconciliation and self-limitation of power, and the covenant itself as a mutual obligation of God and humankind to ensure the existence of the world and the continuation of all life on earth.

The shape of the rainbow is reminiscent of an ancient weapon, the warrior's bow. Because of this, it has frequently served as a symbol of battle and armament or as an indicator of power and victory. Indeed, in ancient Near Eastern mythology, the rainbow represented the weapon of the gods, and its appearance in the heavens was understood as signifying victory of the gods in their cosmic battles.[34] In a similar fashion, in the world of biblical images, the bow appears as the deity's weapon of war, by means of which he punishes humans for their sins.[35] Yet its signification of a covenant here, at the end of the biblical story, evokes not victory or surrender, but instead peace, reconciliation, and abdication of the power of destruction.[36]

In this spirit, rabbinic commentaries from the Middle Ages developed an intriguing interpretive tradition for this symbol, which retains the martial connections of the rainbow image while reworking them into a message of peace and reconciliation embodied in the rainbow covenant. One such example is that of the thirteenth-century writer Nachmanides:

Now, commentators have said concerning the meaning of this sign that He has not made the rainbow with its feet bent upward because it might have appeared that arrows were being shot from heaven, as in the verse, And He sent out his arrows and scattered them on the earth.[37] Instead He made it the opposite of this [with the feet bent downward] in order to show that they are not shooting at the earth from the heavens. It is indeed the way of warriors to invert the instruments of war, which they hold in their hands when calling for peace from their opponents. Moreover, [with the feet of the bow being turned downward towards the earth, it can be seen] that the bow has no rope upon which to bend the arrows.[38]

Nachmanides thus specifies two ways the rainbow symbolizes God's reconciliation with his creation.[39] First, just as human fighters indicate their intent to cease war by inverting their bows in a way that no longer threatens the enemy, so God promises humanity peace by suspending the rainbow in the sky upside-down relative to the earth. Second, because the feet of the rainbow are planted in the earth, it lacks the string to shoot arrows and is therefore a useless weapon. Again, the symbolism is that God has relinquished both the intent and the means to war against humanity. He is disarmed forever.[40]

According to such interpretations, the deity's promise after the flood illuminates an ethic of peace distinct from the usual warrior's code. God's will is manifest not only in the destruction-filled arena of battle, but also in the call to peace and reconciliation. The deity as warrior not only takes revenge on his enemies with anger and terror, but also calls them to peace, dismantles his weapon, and vows that his omnipotent strength will never again be directed toward his creation. Thus, the rainbow covenant opens the doors to a theology of omnipotent power limiting itself.

Can this theology be transferred to the human realm? Can human beings likewise derive an ethic of reconciliation and disarmament while holding in their hands the awesome destructive power they have acquired?

Clearly, a theology of reconciliation and self-limitation can give rise to an ethical obligation through the basic religious norm of *imitatio dei*. It is this kind of claim that stands at the base of the positions referred to by Kimelman. For example, when Rabbi Irving Greenberg claims that the flood story teaches us that even God rejects the power to destroy humanity, he is implicitly stating that the religious obligation of *imitatio dei* requires human beings also to abjure the means of annihilation.[41]

Alongside the reading that views the rainbow as a theological symbol of reconciliation, another rabbinical reading may be found that holds the rainbow covenant to be a direct and binding source for human obligations. The author of this interpretation, Solomon Astruc, was a rather obscure Barcelonian scholar from the second half of the fourteenth century.[42] But his novel reading of the rainbow covenant not only extricates its symbolic meaning from the system of military images, but also interprets the obligation to prevent additional destruction as a mutual obligation of God and human beings:

> The intention is that if they sin and merit annihilation, I will remember the covenant between Myself and you, to protect the world in its entirety, and this is the rainbow that points to the upholding of the house that is built upon it. Alternatively, the rainbow being half a wheel is symbolic of the continued existence of the world. When a covenant is made [Heb., krt, lit., "cut"], the object is cut into two, and he, the Blessed One, took half the wheel – i.e., half the world – and gave the other half to mankind. And just as the half in his hand shall continue to exist, so shall that in the hand of man continue to exist. . . .[43]

Here also two interpretations of the symbolic meaning of the bow are offered. The first interpretation identifies the convex shape of the rainbow with an arch that supports a building. The appearance of the rainbow symbolizes that God's covenant is intact and thus the integrity of his creation is assured.

The second interpretation of the rainbow is related to the symbolic meaning of the circle as representing completeness and harmony. The complete circle, composed of two half-circles or bows whose ends touch, represents the complete structure of the universe. As such, its division into two bows signifies that the rainbow covenant is not only a unilateral commitment of the deity[44] but a delegation and recognition by God of humanity's equal responsibility to protect the world. God directly endows humanity with joint responsibility for preserving life, according to this interpretation, by giving it one-half of the full circle.

These interpretations broaden the theological meaning of the flood story and view it as a basis for the human obligation to uphold the world and protect it from annihilation. This interpretive line corresponds, of course, with other standpoints presented by Kimelman, such as that of Rabbi Bradley Artson, who opposes the very possession of WMD, even for purposes of deterrence, based on what he sees as the biblical conception of humanity's mission – the preservation of creation.

MASS DESTRUCTION AND LESSONS OF THE HOLOCAUST

No survey of sources informing Jewish consciousness on the ethics of WMD would be complete without a consideration of the mass killing of six million European Jews (one-third of the Jewish population in prewar Europe) during the Holocaust. As can be seen in Kimelman's overview, the experience of the Holocaust can operate in two opposite directions. On the one hand, there are those who view the Holocaust as a living and tangible reminder of the catastrophic results of the possession and use of the means of mass destruction. On the other hand, the terror of such an experience may lend support for justifications of nuclear armament as a means of deterring and preventing the recurrence of this event.

I would add to Kimelman's discussion the observation that a national experience such as the Holocaust not only raises new ethical considerations and claims, but also creates an ethical context quite different from a purely hypothetical position. The central considerations of the ethics of war in the philosophical literature pertain to defense and attack, and the standard applied is that of fairness. The Jewish experience with mass destruction during the Holocaust introduced an additional aspect to the system of moral evaluation. This element produces a fundamental change in the nature of ethical logic as a whole and in the morality of the use and possession of WMD in particular. This consideration is that of survival. It is based on the distinction between defending the group's interests versus defending its very existence. In this moral universe, questions of fairness in the use of force give way to the basic necessity of ensuring continued existence.

I am not claiming that the logic of survival exists today only in Jewish consciousness. Survival mechanisms exist in all groups with a collective identity, and they are certainly more active among political groups that face a real threat to their existence or their identity. However, I believe that the experience of the Holocaust sharpened Jewish national sensitivity to survival mechanisms and created a survival instinct grounded in the sense that threats to Jewish national existence are quite real. This consciousness has been intensified and solidified among many Israelis (and among many non-Israeli Jews) by the prolonged Israeli-Arab conflict. The plan for the destruction of the Jewish people devised and implemented under the Third Reich and the goal of destroying the Jewish state expressed by many Arabs are viewed as part of the same continuum.

The heightened sense of insecurity among Israelis explains not only Israel's arsenal of WMD, but also the complete public silence (and the support or acceptance that this silence conveys) surrounding this development. An examination of the moral issues raised by the absence of public debate or the silencing of such a debate are beyond the aims of this chapter. I would only note that in a political situation of violent military confrontation, such as the Israeli-Palestinian conflict, the lack of a public debate on WMD could actually remove the option to use WMD as a military response. In the minds of many Israelis, mass killing using chemical, biological, or nuclear devices is not that different in result from mass killing through crude terrorist attacks. WMD and terrorist attacks both employ unconventional combative means aimed indiscriminately at innocent civilian populations. In both cases, the roles of front line and home front are inverted, and in both instances, ethical intuition rejects this type of attack as a legitimate means for achieving political ends. While WMD may normally be viewed as supraconventional and terrorist attacks as subconventional, for those with an increased consciousness of survival, the similarities between them make them part of a continuum that ranges from the death camps of Europe to the feeling of vulnerability and random death in Israel today.

It could be argued then that if Israelis were to open a public debate on WMD at a time of actual and threatened mass terror attacks, some political groups would probably demand that the Israeli government respond to such terrorism using WMD. The fact that such demands are not being made today is largely attributable to the societal consensus that all discussion of WMD lies outside the boundaries of public discourse in Israel. So, at a time when Israeli (and not only Jewish) society is vulnerable to terrorist attacks, the absence of a public discourse regarding WMD serves to restrain their use. This conclusion will come as a paradox to those who argue that democracies may be trusted not to employ such terrible weapons.

Finally, I end my observations by briefly discussing the ideas of one of the most important Jewish thinkers of the post-Holocaust period, the French philosopher Emmanuel Levinas (1906–95).[45] Levinas's thought places the concepts of the "other" and of "responsibility" at the foundation of ethics, and ethics itself at the foundation of ontology and epistemology.[46] Interpreters of Levinas identify a relationship between his placing of ethics above any other realm of consciousness and his personal experience as a Holocaust survivor.

With regard to the ethicality of WMD, one of the foundations of Levinas's ethics, the "phenomenology of the face," should be noted.[47] This idea relates to the ancient Jewish concept of human dignity (Heb., *kvod ha-adam*).

Levinas's concept constitutes an improvement on and expansion of the biblical theme of man's creation "in God's image,"[48] the basis for the interpretive claim of some kind of likeness between man and the deity (*imagio dei*).[49] This idea, developed in the first centuries of the common era in rabbinic circles, made the similarity between humans and God into a guiding principle for a number of halakhic norms.[50] For example, the explanations for the prohibition on murder maintained that an attack on a human being, the iconic representation of the deity, constitutes an attack on the divine presence.[51]

In this spirit, Levinas seeks to direct our attention to the primordial and familiar situation of seeing the face of the other. Seeing the other's face, Levinas suggests, creates a situation in which our shared humanity bursts forth and supersedes any other identity. Gazing into the face is first and foremost to stand opposite the humanity of the other. "[T]he relation to the face is straightaway ethical. The face is what one cannot kill, or at least it is that whose meaning consists in saying: 'thou shalt not kill.'"[52]

The face is what one cannot kill. Symbolic of this perception is the custom in some cultures and countries to cover the faces of both the executioner and the condemned, so that the natural aversion to killing that emanates from beholding the human countenance may not impede the execution:

The first word of the face is "Thou shalt not kill." It is an order. There is a commandment in the appearance of the face, as if a master spoke to me. However, at the same time, the face of the Other is destitute; it is the poor for whom I can do all and to whom I owe all. And me [*sic*], whoever I may be, but as a "first person," I am he who finds the resources to respond to the call.[53]

In the spirit of Levinas's thought, I would argue that any suggestion of the possible use of WMD arises from the impersonalization of the battlefield – from the avoidance of the face of the other – that steady technological advances have made possible over the past two centuries. The grave ethical flaw inherent in rationalizing the firing of missiles with unconventional warheads stems, according to this perspective, from the very attempt to ignore the face of the enemy, to ignore the prohibition on murder glaringly obvious when one stops to see that the enemy has a face.

CONCLUSION

From the three sources I have examined above, we see possibilities for both accepting and rejecting human control over the means of mass destruction. The biblical passages regarding the idea of holy war seem to offer divine sanction for annihilation, but traditional rabbinic understanding limits such destruction to a past whose repetition is forever foreclosed. The memory of the Holocaust creates a strong Jewish aversion toward even contemplation of mass destruction, but at the same time it lends acceptance to the acquisition of WMD as a deterrent – so that "never again" will Jews be defenseless in the face of genocide.

But on the whole, and as demonstrated best in readings of the rainbow covenant, the thrust of Jewish interpretations of these sources seems to point toward the rejection of the means to cause mass destruction and the archaic identification of the deity's power with military force. The Jewish tradition offers no single or conclusive answer to the question, Is there any conflict that justifies the threatened or actual use of weapons of mass destruction? Yet I would suggest that the religious background reinforces the basic, intuitive obligation we feel to prevent or remove hazards to the continuation of human existence.

The march of reason and progress has transferred to human hands many capabilities that were once considered the exclusive domain of the divine. Technological evolution has given us the power of mass destruction. We have no choice but to assume the responsibility that comes with the power. The responsibility to ensure the preservation of human life, once considered God's prerogative, is now truly our own.

Notes

The author thanks Jessica Bonn for her help in translating this paper from Hebrew.

1. For the most part Kimelman presents the positions of religious authorities living and working in the United States and the United Kingdom. The silence of Israeli halakhic authorities on this subject is typical of the silence of Israeli society as a whole, a matter that I address below.

2. This is also the position of Michael Walzer: "Nuclear weapons explode the theory of just war. They are the first of mankind's technological innovations that are simply not encompassable within the familiar moral world." Michael Walzer, *Just and Unjust Wars* (New York: Basic Books, 1977), 282.

3. By the terms *halakha* and "halakhic," I refer to the mainstream of rabbinical Judaism since the destruction of the Second Temple (70 C.E.) until today. The basic character of this stream is its legalistic attitude toward the religion, namely, the identification of the religious commandments as legal duties and of worship as fulfillment of those duties. The basic canonical compositions of the halakhic tradition are the Mishnah (edited around 220 C.E.) and the two Talmudim – the Palestinian Talmud (edited around 400 C.E.) and the Babylonian Talmud (edited around 500 C.E.).

4. The possibility of mass destruction was never an actual option that the halakhic authorities had to allow or forbid. Closely related biblical precedents, like the case of a town condemned for idolatry (*ir hanidachat*; see Deuteronomy 13:13–19), were never discussed as actual but only as theoretical and hermeneutic issues. In fact, there is a very early saying that the case of *ir hanidachat* never occurred in the past and will never occur in the future, meaning that it is only a theoretical case (*Tosefta Sanhedrin*, 14:1). For more on this, see Moshe Halbertal, *Interpretive*

Revolutions in the Making: Values as Interpretive Considerations in Midrashei Halakha (Jerusalem: Magnes Press, 1997), 122–44 (in Hebrew, hereafter "H").

5. Isaiah 13:6–13; Joel 1:15, 2:1, 3:4; 4:14; Amos 5:18–20; Obadiah 15; Zephaniah 1:17–18; Malachi 3:23.

6. Isaiah 2:12, Ezekiel 30:3, Zechariah 14:1–9. The Day of the Lord idea continues into the New Testament. See Luke 17:24; 1 Cor. 1:8, 5:5; 2 Cor. 1:14; 1 Thes. 5:2; 2 Peter 3:11–12; Rev. 16:14. Christian interpreters continue to debate the precise chronology and relationship of the Day of the Lord to uniquely Christian end-time events, such as the battle of Armageddon, the Rapture, Tribulation, and the Second Coming of Jesus. See Martin Cook's discussion of Christian dispensationalism in Chapter 10 above.

7. Restorative messianism wishes to restore the glory of the past and utopian messianism hopes for a better future, more perfect than even the glorious past. The former is more rational and desires to bring the present reality to perfection, while the latter expects radical changes with the coming of the messiah. This phenomenology of the tension between two polarized messianic conceptions – restorative and utopian – has been discussed by Gershom Scholem, *The Messianic Idea in Judaism and Other Essays on Jewish Spirituality* (New York: Schocken, 1995).

8. 2 Samuel 7 and 23:3–51.

9. 2 Samuel 22:44–51; Psalms 2 and 18: 44–51. The term "messiah" derives from the act of crowning kings by anointing (Heb., *m-s-h*) them. David is thus called "Messiah" in 2 Samuel 22:51.

10. Scholars of the Bible and the ancient Near East have emphasized the uniqueness of the idea of the Day of the Lord in the prophetic literature and have pointed out that it does not appear in the subsequent literature that is external to it. See Meir Weiss, "The Origin of the 'Day of the Lord' – Reconsideration," *Hebrew Union College Annual* 37 (1966): 29–60.

11. Amos 5:18.

12. Descriptions of the Day of the Lord by the prophets abound. Those that emphasize total annihilation are found in the following verses: Isaiah 13:6–13 and chap. 34; Ezekiel 30:3–6; Obadiah 15; Yoel 3:4, 4:14; Zephania 1:17–18, 2:3.

13. See Gerhard von Rad, "The Origin of the Concept of the 'Day of Y,'" *Journal of Semitic Studies* 4 (1959): 97–108; idem, *Holy War in Ancient Israel*, trans. and ed. Marva J. Dawn (Grand Rapids, Mich.: W. B. Eerdmans, 1991). The different position of Meir Weiss should be noted here. In his opinion, the idea of the Day of the Lord should be seen not with reference to the idea of holy war but as a strictly theological interpretation of the understanding of the deity espoused by the prophet Amos. See Weiss, "Origin of the 'Day of the Lord.'"

14. See Numbers 31, Deuteronomy 20, Joshua 8–12, 1 Samuel 15.

15. See, for example, Judges 5:26–27.

16. Exodus 15:21. See also Patrick D. Miller, "God the Warrior: A Problem in Biblical Interpretation Apologetics," *Semeia* 61 (1993): 135–65; Marc Brettler, "Images of YHWH the Warrior in the Psalms," *Interpretation* 19 (1965): 39–46.

17. This expression, incidentally, is used to convey religious fanaticism in the Bible and in the literature of the Hasmonean period (second century B.C.E.). See the act of Pinhas (Numbers 25:1–9); descriptions of Mattithias as defusing the divine anger (Heb., *Mesaleq-haron-af; Hasmoneans* I 2:15 and onward); and even

the mishnaic description of the town condemned for idolatry (*Mishnah San-hedrin* 10:6).

18. Isaiah 13:11–19.

19. "And on the day of the Lord's sacrifice . . . their wealth shall be plundered and their homes laid waste. They shall build houses and not dwell in them, plant vineyards and not drink their wine. . . . That day shall be a day of wrath, a day of trouble and distress, a day of calamity and desolation, a day of darkness and deep gloom, a day of densest clouds. . . . Their blood shall be spilled like dust, and their fat like dung. . . . In the fire of his passion the whole land shall be consumed; for He will make a terrible end of all who dwell in the land" (Zephaniah 1:8–18). All biblical quotations are from *A New Translation of the Holy Scriptures according to the Traditional Hebrew Text* (Philadelphia: Jewish Publication Society, 1985).

20. See Aviezer Ravitzky, "Prohibited Wars in the Jewish Tradition," in *The Ethics of War and Peace: Religious and Secular Perspectives*, ed. Terry Nardin (Princeton, N.J.: Princeton University Press), 115–27.

21. This displacement is also evident in the types of spiritualization of biblical war descriptions found in the Midrash and the Talmud. For example, the means of battle were interpreted as prayers and supplications (*Onkelos translation of Genesis* 48:22; *Tanhuma Beshalah*, chap. 9). Descriptions of the biblical warriors were interpreted as descriptions of the sages "discussing the war of Torah" (*Babylonian Talmud Hagigah* 14a; *Babylonian Talmud Megila* 16b). Military commanders were likened to sages and heads of the Sanhedrin; see Aviezer Ravitzky, "Peace: Historical versus Utopian Models in Jewish Thought," in *History and Faith: Studies in Jewish Philosophy* (Amsterdam: J. C. Gieben, 1996), 31–32.

22. Deuteronomy 20:19–20. On the other biblical conception of war, see Michael Walzer, "The Idea of Holy War in Ancient Israel," *Journal of Religious Ethics* 20:2 (Fall 1992): 215–28.

23. See Kimelman's discussion in Chapter 19 above, under "The Conduct of War."

24. This approach first appears in the book of Daniel 12:1 and in the sources that follow in its path: *Sibylline Oracles* 3, 652–795; *1 Enoch* 90:15–38; *Ascension of Moses*, chap. 10; *Jubilees* 23:27–31, 31:18–20, 32:18–19.

25. For example, the *War Scroll* (from the Dead Sea Scrolls) teaches us that the cult members were expected to take an active part in upcoming battles, which would lead to the "end of days" period. Characterizations of these battles' results are astoundingly similar to the descriptions of the biblical Day of the Lord. The evil forces will be driven to extinction and the victory of the cult members will be absolute, confirming them to be the true Israelites. See Philip R. Davies, "War of the Sons of Light against the Sons of Darkness," in *Encyclopedia of the Dead Sea Scrolls*, ed. Lawrence H. Schiffman and James C. VanderKam (Oxford: Oxford University Press, 2000), 965–68.

26. This book is dated to the first half of the seventh century. It expresses the messianic expectation of the Jews in the land of Israel at the end of the Persian kingdom and on the eve of the Islamic conquest (638 C.E.).

27. On the great affinity between the dualistic approach of members of the Judean desert cult and early Christians, see David Flusser, *Judaism and the Origins of Christianity* (Jerusalem: Magnes Press, 1988), 23–74. In the *Book of Zerubbabel*, descriptions of the future war are based on a dualistic division between the faithful and those primed for entry into the religion, on the one hand, and

those fated for doom, on the other: "Now the folk that will be assembled about him will be divided into two categories, one consisting of notorious sinners marked out for perdition, the other of people who have mended their ways in order to enter the faith." Quoted in Saadia Gaon, *The Book of Beliefs and Opinions*, 7:6, trans. Samuel Rosenblatt (New Haven, Conn.: Yale University Press, 1948), 305–306.

28. See David Flusser, "Body-Soul Dualism in the Judean Desert Scrolls and in the New Testament," *Tarbitz* 27 (1957): 158–65 (H).

29. See Yosef Achitov, "State and Army According to the Torah: Realism and Mysticism in 'Merkaz Harav' Circles," in *Religion and State in Twentieth-Century Jewish Thought* (Jerusalem: IDI Press, forthcoming).

30. See A. S. Yahuda, *The Accuracy of the Bible* (New York: E. P. Dutton, 1935), 188–207.

31. Indeed, in various versions of the Babylonian epic, the flood is not a punishment for the sins of humanity but the response of the god Analil to the noise of humans, which disturbed his rest. In addition, it lacks the motif of the covenant and the symbol of the rainbow. See Shin Shifra and Jacob Klein, *In Those Distant Days: Anthology of Mesopotamian Literature in Hebrew* (Tel Aviv: Am Oved, 1996), 88–130 (H).

32. Genesis 8:21.

33. Genesis 9:11–16.

34. For example, in Babylonian tradition, it is told that the god Marduk hung his bow in the sky after he conquered Theimat, goddess of the seas, in battle.

35. "Are you wroth, O Lord . . . that you are driving your steeds, your victorious chariot? All bared and ready is your bow" (Habakkuk 3:8–9). "The sun and the moon stood still in their habitation at the light of your arrows as they sped, at the flash of your glittering spear. You tread the earth in rage, you trample nations in fury. You have come forth to deliver your people, to deliver your anointed. You will smash the roof of the villain's house, raze it from foundation to top" (Habakkuk 3:11–13). See also Abarbanel commentary on these verses: "All the ancients call the sparks of the sun arrows, and the sun, God's bow, since the sparks are emitted by the sun as an arrow from the hero's bow, and in them will cause the existence and the non-existence on earth." Yitzhak Abarbanel, *The Complete Abarbanel Commentary* (Warsaw, 1862), 32 (H).

36. See the interpretation of Genesis 9:13 by Shmuel David Luzzatto, who claimed that the symbolic meaning of the rainbow in the Bible is quite different from its meanings in the ancient Mesopotamian world: "The ancient nations believed that it [the rainbow] is the messenger of the gods (Iris), and spewed excessive nonsense on the matter. The Torah purified the matter from spoil, defect, and damage, and repaired it in a manner that would be useful and not damaging. It also appears to me that it is likely that the ancients divined and second-guessed by the rainbow, i.e., that it hinted at the future and functioned as the gods' messenger. The Torah set aside all this by saying that it is only a sign that there will not be another flood. We also found that the ancient poet Homer said that the rainbow symbolized war and storm, and here the divine Torah shows these distortions to be false by saying the rainbow is the sign of a covenant of peace." Shmuel David Luzzatto, *Commentary on the Pentateuch*, trans. into Hebrew by Pinchas Schlesinger (Tel Aviv: Dvir, 1965), 50 (H).

37. Psalms 18:15.
38. Nachmanides, *Commentary on the Torah*, trans. Charles. B. Chavel (New York: Shilo, 1971), 136–37.
39. On Nachmanides's tendency toward symbolic exegesis, see Amos Funkenstein, *Perceptions of Jewish History* (Berkeley: University of California Press, 1993), 98–121.
40. This symbolic interpretation was prevalent among thirteenth-century Jewish scholars. For Germany, see Hezekiah Ben Manoah (Hezkuni), *Commentary on the Pentateuch* (Jerusalem: Rav-Kook Institute, 1994), 121 (H). For Spain, see Bahya Ben Asher, *Commentary on the Pentateuch* (Jerusalem: Rav-Kook Institute, 1981), 46 (H).
41. See Kimelman, Chapter 19 above, under "Opinions of Authorities."
42. Other than the fact that he authored two biblical commentaries, we know very little about Astruc. See *Encyclopaedia Judaica*, 7:336.
43. En-Solomon Astruc, *Midrashei ha-Torah*, ed. Simon Eppenstein (Berlin: Mekizei Nirdamim, 1899), 13 (H).
44. In the world of the Bible and in ancient Mesopotamia, there were two types of covenant. One type is of an obligatory nature, such as the Sinaitic covenant, and the other is a covenant of promise, such as those promises given to Abraham and David. See M. Weinfeld, "The Covenant of Grant in the Old Testament and in the Ancient Near East," *Journal of the American Oriental Society* 90 (1970): 184–203.
45. Levinas's influence on French philosophers, such as Jacques Derrida, is considerable. Although during most of his life he was virtually unknown in Israel, his impact on Jewish intellectual circles in the United States and Israel has become clearer in recent years.
46. See Ze'ev Levi, "The Concepts of 'The Other' and 'Responsibility' in Levinas' Ethics," *Da'at* 30 (1993): 21–40 (H).
47. Levinas himself was skeptical of the term "phenomenology of the face," which was applied by others to his thought. He objected to it because "phenomenology describes that which is visible," while his idea of seeing the face transcends any sensory experience or perception. Emmanuel Levinas, *Ethics and Infinity: Conversations with Philippe Nemo*, trans. Richard A. Cohen (Pittsburgh, Pa.: Duquesne University Press, 1985), 67. For a more detailed exposition, see Emmanuel Levinas, *Totality and Infinity*, trans. Alphonso Lingis (Pittsburgh, Pa.: Duquesne University Press, 1969), 187–247.
48. Genesis 1:27.
49. "In the access to the face, there is certainly also an access to the idea of God." Levinas, *Ethics and Infinity*, 92.
50. The connection of God's likeness to human likeness is not an anthropomorphic conception of God, but rather a theomorphic conception of humans. On this point, see Yair Lorberbaum, *The Image of God: God and Man in Rabbinic Law and Philosophy* (Los Angeles: UCLA Press, forthcoming).
51. For example, see the homiletic interpretation on the arrangement of the heavenly tablets delivered to Moses: "How were the Ten Commandments arranged? Five on the one tablet and five on the other. On the one tablet was written: 'I am the Lord thy God.' And opposite it on the other tablet was written: 'Thou shalt not murder.' This tells that if one sheds blood, it is accounted to him as

though he diminished the divine image. To give a parable: A king of flesh and blood entered a province and the people set up portraits of him, made images of him, and struck coins in his honor. Later on, they upset his portraits, broke his images, and defaced his coins, thus diminishing the likenesses of the king. So also if one sheds blood it is accounted to him as though he had diminished the divine image. For it is said: 'Whoso sheddeth man's blood . . . for in the image of God made He man'" (Genesis 9:6). *Mekilta de-Rabbi Ishmael*, trans. Jacob Z. Lauterbach (Philadelphia: Jewish Publication Society of America, 1933), 2:262.

52. Levinas, *Ethics and Infinity*, 81.
53. Ibid., 89.

PART THREE

CRITICAL PERSPECTIVES

21

A Feminist Ethical Perspective on Weapons
of Mass Destruction

Carol Cohn and Sara Ruddick

> The world will note that the first atomic bomb was dropped on Hiroshima, a
> military base. That was because we wished in this first attack to avoid, insofar
> as possible, the killing of civilians.
>
> President Harry Truman, August 9, 1945[1]

> I heard her voice calling "Mother, Mother." I went towards the sound. She
> was completely burned. The skin had come off her head altogether, leaving a
> twisted knot at the top. My daughter said, "Mother, you're late, please take me
> back quickly." She said it was hurting a lot. But there were no doctors. There
> was nothing I could do. So I covered up her naked body and held her in my
> arms for nine hours. At about eleven o'clock that night she cried out again
> "Mother," and put her hand around my neck. It was already ice-cold. I said,
> "Please say Mother again." But that was the last time.
>
> A Hiroshima survivor[2]

We are reporting on a feminist tradition that we label antiwar feminism. We
consider ourselves inheritors of this tradition and draw on it to formulate
a position on weapons of mass destruction. To put our position briefly:
Antiwar feminism rejects both the military and political use of weapons
of mass destruction in warfare or for deterrence. It is also deeply critical
of the discourses that have framed public discussion of weapons of mass
destruction. It calls for ways of thinking that reveal the complicated effects on
possessor societies of developing and deploying these weapons, that portray
the terror and potential suffering of target societies, and that grapple with
the moral implications of the willingness to risk such massive destruction.

ANTIWAR FEMINISM

There is no single feminist position on war, armament, and weapons of mass
destruction. Some feminists fight for women's right to fight and command
fighters; some participate in armed nationalist struggles; some are pacifists;

405

some believe that peace and war are not "women's issues." Most feminists do not divorce feminism from national, ethnic, religious, class, or other identities and politics that together create their attitudes toward war.

We report on one particular feminist tradition that opposes war making as a practice and seeks to replace it with practices of nonviolent contest and reconciliation. We call this tradition "antiwar feminism" and see ourselves as its inheritors and continuers; despite disagreements with some of its aspects, we refer to it as "ours."[3] Our tradition is represented by groups as much as by individuals. Among the most venerable is the Women's International League for Peace and Freedom (WILPF), which was founded in 1915 to protest World War I and which today is actively involved in disarmament and nonproliferation issues, as well as in advocacy for gender analysis in security affairs at the United Nations. During the cold war, many women's movements protested nuclear weapons (see note 21). Many other women's protest movements represent some but not all aspects of antiwar feminism. The courageous protest of the Madres of Argentina against a military dictatorship only gradually became antimilitarist and seems never to have been conventionally feminist. Women in Black began in Israel/Palestine and has moved to many conflict-ridden sites around the world; though it nearly everywhere engages in struggles for peace, its members differ about the extent and generality of its antimilitarism. In armed conflict zones around the world, there are many other women's peace initiatives and groups; although many would identify themselves as antiwar, fewer would adopt the label "feminist." An excellent place to start researching these groups is the website www.peacewomen.org, which was started to provide a clearinghouse of information and website links for women's peace groups.

Antiwar feminists' opposition to the practice of war is simultaneously pragmatic and moral. We have an abiding suspicion of the use of violence, even in the best of causes. The ability of violence to achieve its stated aims is routinely overestimated, while the complexity of its costs is overlooked. Our opposition also stems from the perception that the practice of war entails far more than the killing and destroying of armed combat itself. It requires the creation of a "war system," which entails arming, training, and organizing for possible wars; allocating the resources these preparations require; creating a culture in which wars are seen as morally legitimate, even alluring; and shaping and fostering the masculinities and femininities that undergird men's and women's acquiescence to war. Even when it appears to achieve its aims, war is a source of enormous individual suffering and loss. Modern warfare is also predictably destructive to societies, civil liberties and democratic processes, and the nonhuman world. State security may sometimes be served by war, but too often human security is not.

Though they oppose war as a practice – and some individual antiwar feminists are committed to nonviolence – the tradition as a whole is not typically "pacifist" as that term is usually understood. It neither rejects all wars as wrong in principle nor condemns people just because they resort to violence. Some antiwar feminists support particular military campaigns. As a Northern Irish woman explained to Cynthia Cockburn, "We've always given each other a lot of leeway on [violence]." We continue to call these temporary militarists antiwar because they continue to oppose war making as a practice, mourn the suffering of *all* of wars' victims, and, in the midst of war, imagine the details of a future culture of peace. Although they do not reject violence in principle, they are committed to "translating" or "transfiguring violence into creative militant nonviolence." This requires letting go of "dangerous day dreams whether of promised homes of our own or of an apocalyptic demolition of all walls . . . [and replacing these dreams] with the idea of something we could perhaps really have: a careful and a caring struggle in a well lit space."[4]

Nor is the feminist antiwar tradition a version of just war theory. In contrast to antiwar feminists who oppose war as a practice even if they support a particular military campaign, just war theorists implicitly accept war as a practice even when condemning particular wars. Just war theory accepts war only as a defense against serious attacks on one's state or one's people or as intervention on behalf of other states or people who suffer such aggression (*jus ad bellum*). Antiwar feminists may agree that the cause is just, but for us it does not automatically follow that war is therefore justified – for at least two reasons. First, while just war theorists claim that war must be a "last resort" after all nonviolent alternatives have failed, in our view they barely explore nonviolent alternatives once just cause is determined nor seek to return to nonviolent struggle once war has begun. Antiwar feminists continue to explore nonviolent alternatives even after war starts and seek every opportunity to return to nonviolent means of fighting. Second, just war theorists tend to abstract particular wars from the war system on which they rely and which they strengthen, whereas antiwar feminists are acutely critical of the political, economic, social, and moral costs of that system.

However just the cause, just war theorists set moral limits to permissible strategies of war (*jus in bello*). Ideally, only armed combatants or, at most, people contributing directly to combat should be targeted. Weapons must be able to target discriminately and then should cause only the suffering required to render combatants harmless. Antiwar feminists are skeptical of these "rules of war." Some argue that they depend on unworkable abstractions, including, in much contemporary warfare, the central distinction between combatants and noncombatants. Others document the routine, often willful, violation of these rules, beginning with the use of weapons that cannot discriminate. Generally, antiwar feminists, like many pacifists, do not so much argue as point insistently to the facts of suffering and destruction that cannot be limited, in place or time, to battlefield and soldier.[5]

To suggest the distinctive character of our tradition as contrasted with just war and pacifism, we identify four of its constitutive positions.

War Is a Gendered Practice

It is a common perception that war making is an activity primarily engaged in by men and governed by norms of masculinity. Antiwar feminism both asserts and challenges the association of war and masculinity in at least three ways.

First, antiwar feminists insistently underline the gendered character of war, stressing its domination by men and masculinity, thus making visible what has been taken for granted. But they also stress that women's labor has always been central to war making – although it has also consistently been either unacknowledged or represented as tangential in order to protect war's "masculinity."[6]

Second, they challenge the view that war is inherently gendered – in particular, the view that biology renders men "naturally" war-like and war therefore a "natural" male activity. They stress that multiple masculinities (and femininities) are required by the mobilization for war and argue that the simple link of some "innate" male aggression to the conduct of war is belied both by what men actually *do* in war[7] and by many men's reluctance to fight.[8] Whatever the role of biology in gender and gender in war, antiwar feminists identify the association of manliness with militarized violence as the product of specific social processes that they try to analyze and change.[9]

Finally, antiwar feminists not only explore the multiple gendered *identities* needed for and shaped by the practice of war making; they also analyze the ways that warmaking is shaped by a gendered *system of meanings*. We understand gender not just as a characteristic of individuals but as a symbolic system – a central organizing discourse in our culture, a set of ways of thinking, images, categories, and beliefs that not only shape how we experience, understand, and represent ourselves as men and women but that also provide a familiar set of metaphors, dichotomies, and values that structure ways of thinking about other aspects of the world, including war and security. In other words, we see the ways in which human characteristics and endeavors are culturally divided into those seen as "masculine" and those seen as "feminine" (e.g., mind is opposed to body, culture to nature, thought to feeling, logic to intuition, objectivity to subjectivity, aggression to passivity, confrontation to accommodation, war to peace, abstraction to particularity, public to private, political to personal, and realism to moral reflection.), and the terms coded "male" are valued more highly than those coded "female."

Once the gender coding takes place – once certain ways of thinking are marked as masculine and feminine, entwining metaphors of masculinity with judgments of legitimacy and power – then any system of thought or action comes to have gendered positions within it. For example, we see the devaluation and exclusion of "the feminine" as shaping and distorting basic national security paradigms and policies. And once the devaluation-by-association-with-the-feminine takes place, it becomes extremely difficult for anyone, female or male, to take the devalued position, to express concerns or ideas marked as "feminine." What then gets left out is the emotional, the concrete, the particular, human bodies and their vulnerability, human lives and their subjectivity.[10]

The characteristics that are excluded as "feminine" are characteristics of women and men. They are also characteristics that women often ascribe to themselves "as women" and that feminists also sometimes ascribe to women. There is considerable disagreement among feminists, in print and casual conversation, about the degree to which women and men differ from each other, how these differences arise, and whether they are subject to change. Our own understanding of gender has changed over time and is affected by the circumstances in which we reflect and speak. In the circumstances of this discussion, we allude to women's actual differences from men only when describing the distinctive effects of war on women and the particular experiences and insights women themselves say that they would bring to peace negotiations.

Start from Women's Lives

Our second position applies a central tenet of feminist methodology to the particular case of weapons of mass destruction. We attempt to look at war and weapons from the perspective of women's lives, making women's experiences a central rather than marginal concern. In the context of war, "women's lives" has two primary referents: the work women do and the distinctive bodily assaults war inflicts on women.

Women's work traditionally includes life-shaping responsibilities of caring labor: giving birth to and caring for children, protecting and sustaining ill, frail, or other dependents, maintaining households, and fostering and protecting kin, village, and neighborhood relations. Seen from the standpoint of caring labor, war is at least disruptive and usually destructive. In war women often can't get or keep the goods on which they depend, whether medicine, cattle, or food. War threatens the well-being and even existence of the people, relations, and homes that women maintain.[11]

Caring labor may be intertwined with or depend on other labor. In many economies, women "work" to secure the cash to get the goods that "women's work" requires. Whether or not they are responsible for care, women work for wages in jobs that are lower paid and often in the service of others. In war, women's work typically expands to include "comfort" and prostitution, low-skilled workers/servants, secretaries, and many others who keep militaries functioning. Notoriously, war gives some women special job opportunities,

training, and experience unavailable elsewhere. Some survive postwar down-
sizing and the return of men to "their" jobs. But other women are in effect
conscripted for dangerous or demeaning work whose effects may also survive the official end of war.

The practice of war implies a willingness to inflict pain and damage on
bodies, to "out-injure" in pursuit of war's aim.[12] Women are no more or less
embodied than men, but their bodies are differently at risk. There has been a
quantitative shift in the ratio of women to men sufferers as civilian casualties
come to outnumber those of the military. Women also suffer sexually more
than men and distinctly. Rape is the conqueror's reward and taunt. It is a
weapon against "woman" and also against the men and community to whom
she "belongs." The woman who becomes pregnant by rape may be seen by
the rapist or may see herself as forced to join the enemy, to create him. She
may fear and her rapist may hope that she is contributing to the destruction
of her own people.[13]

Given the effects of war on women's work and the multiple ways that war
commits violence against women, it is suspect, at the least, to look for "security" from militaries. Conceptions of security based in the military defense
of state borders and interests often mean greater insecurity for women.

War Is Not Spatially or Temporally Bounded

Antiwar feminism rejects the conception of war as a discrete event, with clear
locations, and a beginning and an end. It is not that we fail to distinguish between war and peace or to make distinctions between kinds of violence, but
in our vision, and in contrast to much just war theory, it is crucial not to separate war either from the preparations made for it (preparations taken in the
widest possible sense, including the social costs of maintaining large standing armies and the machinery of deterrence) or from its long-term physical,
psychological, socio-economic, environmental, and gendered effects. This
conception of war is sometimes explicit in feminist writings, typically implied by the rhetoric and symbols of feminist movements and fundamental
to our response to the questions being asked in this volume.[14]

Women's war and postwar stories underline the unboundedness of war
in at least two different dimensions: cultural and practical. Culturally, war is
understood as a creation and creator of the culture in which it thrives. War's
violence is *not* understood as separate and apart from other social practices.
There is a continuum of violence running from bedroom to boardroom,
factory, stadium, classroom, and battlefield, "traversing our bodies and our
sense of self."[15] Weapons of violence and representations of those weapons
travel through interlocking institutions – economic, political, familial, technological, and ideological. These institutions prepare some people but not
others to believe in the effectiveness of violence, to imagine and acquire
weapons, to use and justify using force to work their will. They prepare

some but not others to renounce, denounce, or passively submit to force, to resist or accept the war plans put before them.

Practically, feminists see war as neither beginning with the first gunfire nor ending when the treaties are signed. Before the first gunfire is the research, development, and deployment of weapons; the maintaining of standing armies; the cultural glorification of the power of armed force; and the social construction of masculinities and femininities that support a militarized state. When the organized violence of war is over, what remains is a ripped social fabric: the devastation of the physical, economic, and social infrastructure through which people provision themselves and their families; the havoc wrought in the lives and psyches of combatants, noncombatants, and children who have grown up in war; the surfeit of arms on the streets and of ex-soldiers trained to kill; citizens who have been schooled and practiced in the methods of violence but not in nonviolent methods of dealing with conflict; "nature" poisoned, burned, made ugly and useless.[16] Typically, "peace" includes official ongoing "punishment" – retribution, reparations, domination, and deprivation. At best, even the most laudable treaty is only the beginning of making peace.

Alternative Epistemology: The Inadequacy of Dominant Ways of Thinking about War

Most Western philosophers have thought that knowledge is more trustworthy when generated by people who have transcended institutional constraints, social identities, gender identifications, and emotion. Many feminists propose an "alternative epistemology" that stresses that all thinkers are "situated" within "epistemic communities" that ask some but not other questions and legitimate some but not other ways of knowing. We are each of us also situated by social identities and personal histories. To take an example at hand: Some of us address this volume's questions as heirs of the "victims" of nuclear weapons or associate ourselves with them.[17] Others are heirs of the attackers. Some address the issue of "proliferation" of nuclear weapons from the situation of a possessor state, others from a situation in which they would find the term "proliferation" inappropriate. None of us speaks from nowhere; there is no phenomenon – including nuclear attack or proliferation – that can be seen independently of the situation of the seers.[18]

Three tenets of this "alternative epistemology" seem especially relevant to our work. Knowing is never wholly separated from feelings. Indeed, in many kinds of inquiry the capacity to feel and to account for one's feelings are both a source and a test of knowledge. Second, as useful as hypothetical thought experiments and imagined scenarios may be, we begin with and return to concrete open-ended questions about actual people in actual situations. Finally, we measure arguments, and ideals of objectivity, partly in terms of the goods that they yield, the pleasures they make possible, and the suffering they prevent.

Grounded in this alternative epistemology, antiwar feminists criticize the dominant political/strategic paradigm for thinking about weapons of mass destruction, which we call "technostrategic discourse."[19] In contrast to just war theory, this discourse is explicitly centered not on the ethics of warfare but on its material and political practicalities. As a tool for thinking about weapons of mass destruction, it essentially restricts the thinker to three issues: the actual use, that is, the detonation, of these weapons in state warfare or by terrorists; the physical and geo-political effects of this use; and the deployment of these weapons to deter attacks involving either conventional weapons or weapons of mass destruction. In other words, the concerns of the dominant strategic discourse are limited to the destructive effects of the weapons when *and only when* they are detonated and to the possible deterrent effects of possessing these weapons. There is scant attention to the potential suffering of targeted societies and no attempt to evaluate complicated effects on possessor societies of deploying and developing these weapons, nor to grapple with the moral significance of willingly risking such massive, total destruction.

When antiwar feminists think about wars, they take into consideration the political, social, economic, psychological, and moral consequences of accepting the practice of war. When assessing weapons, they do not single out or isolate weapons' physical, military, and strategic effects from their embeddedness in and impact on social and political life as a whole nor from the effects of the discourses that constitute "knowledge" about these weapons. Hence, when asked to think about weapons of mass destruction, we strive to consider the totality of the web of social, economic, political, and environmental relationships within which weapons of mass destruction are developed, deployed, used, and disposed of – all the while starting from the perspective of women's lives. It is not possible to do so from within the bounds of "just war" and/or "technostrategic" frameworks – yet those are the very discourses that have shaped the questions we are asked to answer in this volume. Thus, as we respond to the editors' questions, we find we need to both think inside their frame and about the frame itself.

SOURCES AND PRINCIPLES

The first question asks whether our tradition includes general norms governing the use of weapons in war. It does not. If, as it appears, the question assumes the inevitability, perhaps even the acceptability, of war making, we do not. And granted the existence of wars, we are ambivalent about making ethical distinctions between weapons. We recognize that some weapons, and uses of weapons, are worse than others. Some weapons can be sparingly used and carefully aimed to cause minimal damage; others cannot. Some weapons may be deliberately cruel (e.g., dum dum bullets), outlast the occasion that apparently justified them (e.g., land mines), harm indiscriminately (e.g., cluster bombs, land mines again, or poison gas in a crowded subway), or injure massively and painfully (e.g., incendiary bombs). While respecting these distinctions, we nonetheless fear that stressing the horror of some weapons diminishes the horrors that more "acceptable" weapons wreak. For us the crucial question is not "How do we choose among weapons?" but rather, "How can we identify and attend to the specific horrors of any weapon?"

Moreover, it is striking that the criteria by which some weapons are declared less horrible than others do not fare well by feminist antiwar criteria. We consider two kinds: small arms and light weapons, and high-tech weapons aimed precisely from a distance.

"Small arms and light weapons" are weapons light enough to be packed over a mountain on a mule. Among them are stinger missiles, AK47s, machine guns, grenades, assault rifles, small explosives, and hand guns. Far more than weapons of mass destruction (WMD), these weapons can allow for distinguishing attackers and combatants from bystanders. Some, such as hand guns, can be accurately aimed to incapacitate without killing a dangerous attacker. Of course, the weapons may be misused. But if they are carefully aimed by properly trained gunners, they can satisfy conventional moral criteria of doing the least harm commensurate with protection from violence.

If, however, we start looking at weapons from the perspectives of women's lives, small arms and light weapons become visible as the cause of enormous, sustained, and pervasive suffering of very specific kinds. Light weapons are a staple of the arms market, and the principal instrument of violence in armed conflicts throughout the world. They are inexpensive, require little or no training to use, and are easily available, often unregulated by state, military, civic, or even parental authority. They have a long shelf life, travel easily, and therefore can, in the course of time, be traded, turned against various enemies, and brought home.

These weapons are so easy to get that they threaten to turn any conflict violent – whether between peoples, neighbors, or family members. Women can carry them, but they more often remain the property of men and late adolescent boys, increasing the imbalance of power between men and women.

These weapons can wreak havoc among the relationships women have tended and destroy women's capacity to obtain food, water, and other necessary staples or to farm and to keep their animals safe. Thus, it is not surprising that current international feminist attention to war is often focused on ethno-nationalist armed conflicts that are fought with light weapons. These wars, brutal in their effects, often in gender-related ways, are undeterred by – indeed, unaffected by – the existence of weapons of mass destruction.

Ironically, by contrast with small arms and light weapons, nuclear weapons can in some ways seem attractive. They are expensive and difficult to produce, complicated to deploy, require training if they are to be used, and rarely make their way onto main street or into homes, except as waste material. In the lives of women around the world, it is small arms and light weapons, more than weapons of mass destruction, that constitute a clear and daily present danger.[20]

Consider the "virtues" of a quite different class of weapons, precision-guided munitions (PGM). Modern, high-tech PGM can reputedly be precisely aimed at carefully selected targets, a virtue often on verbal and graphic display during the Gulf War – although the degree of precision of both weapons and target selection are sometimes more illusory than real. PGM are typically launched from great distances, the human "targets" invisible to the attacker and the weapons' effects transmuted into unreality by video game–like imagery. Neither the attackers nor civilians at home need to be aware of the destruction they cause. Moreover, PGM on "electronic battlefields" appear to make warfare safer for the warriors who use them.

From our perspective, these virtues, too, become suspect. Critics charge that we – citizens, military, political leaders – are too easily reassured by images of PGM's precision. In fact, PGM are notoriously subject to "mistakes" of judgment, information, and technological control. While we agree with these critics, we emphasize two other moral doubts.

With PGM, not only is the discourse of war abstract, but war fighting itself becomes increasingly abstract and unreal to those who kill, mutilate, and destroy. Antimilitarists have often seen war as a fiction, an Old Lie, that obscures brutality through patriotic rhetoric, euphemistic language, abstract theories, and discourse. To these are now added the abstracted illusion of precision strikes displayed on video screens. By contrast, we consider it a virtue if the brutality of war is evident to the combatants, to those who order them to war, and to the society they represent.

Second, we cannot unambivalently applaud the relative safety that PGM accord those who use them. This safety is purchased by an ignorance of injuries, ultimately an indifference toward "the targets." We understand the military obligation and human desire to save one's own fighters. But we cannot praise a weapon for its ability to save "us" while endangering the lives and destroying the resources of "the enemy" we don't see, whose humanity we never confront. Indeed, people who reject war, including feminists, refuse to construe an enemy as killable.

By calling into question the criteria by which weapons are judged, we do not in any way minimize the horror of weapons of mass destruction. Women and feminists of our tradition have been protesting the development, testing, deployment, and possible use of nuclear weapons, in particular, since Hiroshima.[21] But antiwar feminism urges that we appreciate the specificity of horror and learn to mourn the damage that each kind of weapon inflicts on both its possessor and the injured. This would be both an expression and a development of our tradition.

WMD UTILIZATION

The second question asks us whether it is ever morally permissible to use weapons of mass destruction. We are tempted to answer with only three words: "of course not."

Rather than pondering the question of when, if ever, it is morally justified to use WMD, we move in two directions. First, we note that antiwar feminists' energies have not been focused on when to use these weapons, but rather on attempting to explain why, over many years, there has been widespread acceptance of the deployment of nuclear weapons and of the stated willingness to use them. Second, we move to question the question itself.

Antiwar feminist attention to WMD has largely focused on nuclear weapons – their horrors, the urgency of abolishing them, and the question of how anyone could think it sane to develop and deploy them. In this chapter, we, too, write primarily about nuclear weapons – as a reflection of the tradition on which we report, but also because they are the weapons whose magnitude of destructive power seems distinctive and to best warrant the description "weapons of mass destruction." However, as we learned in the course of our research, many elements of the antiwar feminist critique of nuclear weapons hold for chemical and biological weapons as well.

Rather than seeing acceptance of nuclear weapons as a "realistic" acknowledgment of the "technologically inevitable," antiwar feminists have seen the political and intellectual acceptance of nuclear weapons' deployment as something to be explained. Some feminists have noted the allure of nuclear weapons, particularly the excitement and awe evoked by actual or imagined nuclear explosions. Some have seen the appeal of exploding or launching nuclear weapons as reflecting and reinforcing masculine desires and identities.[22]

Several antiwar feminists have focused less on the weapons themselves and more on the discourse through which the weapons (and their use) are theorized and legitimated. They have written about both the sexual and domestic metaphors that turn the mind's eye toward the pleasant and familiar, rather than toward images of indescribable devastation. They have identified in nuclear discourse techniques of denial and conceptual fragmentation. They have emphasized the ways that the abstraction and euphemism of nuclear discourse protect nuclear planners and politicians from the grisly realities behind their words. Speaking generally, antiwar feminists invite women and men to attend to the identities, emotions, and discourses that allow us to accept the possible use of nuclear weapons.[23]

Perhaps the most general feminist concern is the willingness of intellectuals to talk as usual about nuclear weapons (or about any atrocity). And this brings us back to the issue of the framing of the second question. The question as it is posed seems in some ways similar to the abstract, distancing thinking that we have criticized – but in which we also participate. There is no mention of the horror, let alone a pause to rest with it. We move or are moved quickly to an abstract moral tone: "any circumstances" "might be morally permissible . . . " and then to comparisons.

Abstract language and a penchant for distinctions are typical of philosophy, intrinsically unobjectionable, and often a pleasure. It is continuous abstraction while speaking of actual or imagined horror that disturbs us. Abstract discussion of warfare is both the tool and the privilege of those who imagine themselves as the (potential) users of weapons. The victims, if they can speak at all, speak quite differently.

An account of a nuclear blast's effects by a U.S. defense intellectual:

[You have to have ways to maintain communications in a] nuclear environment, a situation bound to include EMP blackout, brute force damage to systems, a heavy jamming environment, and so on.[24]

An account by a Hiroshima survivor:

Everything was black, had vanished into the black dust, was destroyed. Only the flames that were beginning to lick their way up had any color. From the dust that was like a fog, figures began to loom up, black, hairless, faceless. They screamed with voices that were no longer human. Their screams drowned out the groans rising everywhere from the rubble, groans that seemed to rise from the very earth itself.[25]

It should become apparent then, that our concern about abstract language is not only relevant to the *framing* of the second question, about utilization, but to its *content* – the justifiability of nuclear weapons' use – as well. It is easier to contemplate and "justify" the use of nuclear weapons in the abstract language of defense intellectuals than in the descriptive, emotionally resonant language of the victim; from the perspective of the user rather than the victim. Antiwar feminists note that detailed, focal attention to the human impact of weapons' use is not only considered out of bounds in security professionals' discourse; it is also *delegitimated* by its association with the "feminine," with insufficient masculinity, as is evident in this excerpt of an interview with a physicist:

Several colleagues and I were working on modeling counterforce nuclear attacks, trying to get realistic estimates of the number of immediate fatalities that would result from different deployments. At one point, we re-modeled a particular attack, using slightly different assumptions, and found that instead of there being 36 million immediate fatalities, there would only be 30 million. And everybody was sitting around nodding, saying, "Oh yeh, that's great, only 30 million," when all of a sudden, I heard what we were saying. And I blurted out, "Wait, I've just heard how we're talking – Only 30 million! Only 30 million human beings killed instantly?" Silence fell upon the room. Nobody said a word. They didn't even look at me. It was awful. I felt like a woman.

After telling this story to one of the authors, the physicist added that he was careful to never blurt out anything indicating that he was thinking about the victims again.[26] Fear of feeling like a woman (or being seen as unmanly) silently works to maintain the boundaries of a distanced, abstract discourse and to sustain the tone of the second question – a tone that invites us to think abstractly, "objectively" about WMD use, without pausing to consider human particularities, passions, and suffering.

WMD DETERRENCE

The third question asks whether it is ethical to develop and deploy WMD as deterrents only. That is, it asks the classic question of whether it is ethical to have weapons and threaten to use then, even if it is not ethical to use those weapons militarily. As the question is framed, then, "development" and "deployment" appear not as phenomena subject to ethical scrutiny unto themselves but merely as way-stations, as adjuncts subsumed under what is taken to be the core ethical issue, which is seen as deterrence.

This formulation does not work for us. We need to pause and recognize that there are really several questions enfolded in that one. We must ask not only about the ethical status of deterrence, but also whether its entailments – development and deployment – are themselves ethical.[27]

One of the constitutive positions of antiwar feminism is that in thinking about weapons and wars, we must accord full weight to their daily effects on the lives of women. We then find that the development and deployment of nuclear weapons, even when they are not used in warfare, exacts immense economic costs that particularly affect women. In the recent words of an Indian feminist:

The social costs of nuclear weaponisation in a country where the basic needs of shelter, food and water, electricity, health and education have not been met are obvious. . . . [S]ince patriarchal family norms place the task of looking after the daily needs of the family mainly upon women, scarcity of resources always hits women the hardest. Less food for the family inevitably means an even smaller share for women and female children just as water shortages mean an increase in women's labour who have to spend more time and energy in fetching water from distant places at odd hours of the day.[28]

While the United States is not as poor a nation as India, Pakistan, or Russia, it has remained, throughout the nuclear age, a country in which poverty and hunger are rife, health care is still unaffordable to many, low-cost housing is unavailable, and public schools and infrastructure crumbling, are all while the American nuclear weapons program has come at the cost of $4.5 trillion.[29]

In addition to being economically costly, nuclear weapons development has medical and political costs. In the U.S. program, many people have been exposed to high levels of radiation, including uranium miners, workers at reactors and processing facilities, the quarter of a million military personnel who took part in "atomic battlefield" exercises, "downwinders" from test sites, and Marshall Islanders.[30] Politically, nuclear regimes require a level of secrecy and security measures that excludes the majority of citizens and, in most countries, all women from defense policy and decision making.[31]

From the perspective of women's lives, we see not only the costs of the *development* of nuclear weapons, but also the spiritual, social, and psychological costs of *deployment.* One cost, according to some feminists, is that "Nuclearisation produces social consent for increasing levels of violence.[32] Another cost for many is that nuclear weapons create high levels of tension, insecurity, and fear. As Arundhati Roy puts it, nuclear weapons "[i]nform our dreams. They bury themselves like meat hooks deep in the base of our brains."[33]

Further, feminists are concerned about the effect of nuclear policy on moral thought, on ideas about gender, and how the two intersect. Nuclear development may legitimize male aggression and breed the idea that nuclear explosions give "virility" to the nation, which men as individuals can somehow also share.

[T]he strange character of nuclear policy-making not only sidelines moral and ethical questions, but genders them. This elite gets to be represented as rational, scientific, modern, and of course masculine, while ethical questions, questions about the social and environmental costs are made to seem emotional, effeminate, regressive and not modern. This rather dangerous way of thinking, which suggests that questions about human life and welfare are somehow neither modern nor properly masculine questions, or that men have no capacity and concern for peace and morality, can have disastrous consequences for both men and women.[34]

All in all, we find the daily costs of WMD development and deployment staggeringly high – in and of themselves sufficient to prevent deterrence from being an ethical moral option.

A so-called realist response to this judgment might well pay lip-service to the "moral niceties" it embodies, but then argue that deterrence is worth those costs. Or perhaps to be more accurate, it might argue that the results of a nuclear attack would be so catastrophic that the rest of these considerations are really an irrelevant distraction; deterring a WMD attack on our homeland is the precondition on which political freedom and social life depend, and so it must be thought about in a class by itself.

We make two rejoinders to this claim. First, we note that in the culture of nuclear defense intellectuals, even raising the issue of costs is delegitimized, in large part through its association with "the feminine." It is the kind of thing that "hysterical housewives" do; something done by people not tough and hard enough to look harsh "reality" in the eye, unsentimentally; not strong enough to separate their feelings from theorizing mass death; people who don't have "the stones for war." Feminist analysis rejects the cultural division of meaning that devalues anything associated with women or femininity. It sees in that same cultural valuing of the so-called masculine over the so-called feminine an explanation of why it appears so self-evident to many that what is called "military necessity" should appropriately be prioritized over all other human necessities. And it questions the assumptions that bestow the mantle of "realism" on such a constrained focus on weapons and state power. Rather than simply being an "objective" reflection of political reality, we understand this thought system as (1) a partial and distorted picture of reality and (2) a major contributor to creating the very circumstances it purports to describe and protect against.

Second, just as feminists tend to be skeptical about the efficacy of violence, they might be equally skeptical about the efficacy of deterrence. Or to put it another way, if war is a "lie," so is deterrence. This is not, of course, to say that deterrence *as a phenomenon* never occurs; no doubt, one opponent is sometimes deterred from attacking another by the fear of retaliation. But rather, deterrence *as a theory, a discourse,* and a set of practices underwritten by that discourse is a fiction.

Deterrence theory is an elaborate, abstract conceptual edifice, which posits a hypothetical relation between two different sets of weapons systems – or rather, between abstractions of two different sets of weapons systems, for in fact, as both common sense and military expertise tell us, human error and technological imperfection mean that one could not actually expect real weapons to function in the ways simply assumed in deterrence theory. Because deterrence theory sets in play the hypothetical representations of various weapons systems, rather than assessments of how they would actually perform or fail to perform in warfare, it can be nearly infinitely elaborated, in a never-ending regression of intercontinental ballistic missile gaps and theater warfare gaps and tactical "mini-nuke" gaps, ad infinitum, thus legitimating both massive vertical proliferation and arms racing.

Deterrence theory is also a fiction in that it depends on "rational actors," for whom what counts as "rational" is the same, independent of culture, history, or individual difference. It depends on those "rational actors" perfectly understanding the meaning of "signals" communicated by military actions, despite dependence on technologies that sometimes malfunction, despite cultural difference and the lack of communication that is part of being political enemies, despite the difficulties of ensuring mutual understanding even when best friends make direct face-to-face statements to each other. It depends on those same "rational actors" engaging in a very specific kind of calculus that includes one set of variables (e.g., weapons size, deliverability, survivability, as well as the "credibility" of their and their opponent's threats) and excludes other variables (such as domestic political pressures, economics, or individual subjectivity). What is striking from a feminist perspective is that even while "realists" may worry that some opponents are so "insufficiently rational" as to be undeterrable, this does not lead them to search for a more reliable form of ensuring security or to an approach that is not so weapons-dependent.

Cynthia Cockburn, in her study of women's peace projects in conflict zones, describes one of the women's activities as helping each other give up "dangerous day dreams."[35] From a feminist antiwar perspective, having WMD as deterrents is a dangerous dream. The dream of perfect rationality and control that underwrites deterrence theory is a dangerous dream, since it legitimates constructing a system that could be (relatively) safe only if that perfect rationality and control were actually possible. Deterrence theory itself is a dangerous dream because it justifies producing and deploying WMD, thereby making their accidental or purposive use possible (and far more likely) than if they were not produced at all nor deployed in such numbers. "Realists" are quick to point out the dangers of *not having* WMD for deterrence when other states have them. Feminist perspectives suggest that that danger appears so self-evidently greater than the danger of *having* WMD only if you discount as "soft" serious attention to the costs of development and deployment.

WMD PROLIFERATION

The fourth question asks: "If some nations possess weapons of mass destruction (either licitly or illicitly) for defensive and deterrent purposes, is it proper to deny such possession to others for the same purposes?"

We believe that the rampant proliferation of weapons of *all kinds*, from handguns to nuclear weapons, is a massive tragedy, the direct and indirect source of great human suffering. Given this starting point, we of course oppose the proliferation of weapons of mass destruction. But our opposition does not allow us to give a simple "yes" answer to the fourth question as it is posed. Before turning to proliferation as a *phenomenon*, we must first consider current proliferation *discourse*.

Proliferation as a Discourse

"Proliferation" is not a mere description or mirror of a phenomenon that is "out there," but rather a very specific way of identifying and constructing a problem. "Proliferation," as used in Western political discourse, does not simply refer to the "multiplication" of weapons of mass destruction on the planet. Rather, it constructs some WMD as a problem and others as unproblematic. It does so by assuming preexisting, legitimate possessors of the weapons, implicitly not only entitled to those weapons but to "modernize" and develop new "generations" of them as well. The "problematic" WMD are only those that "spread" into the arsenals of other, formerly nonpossessor states. This is presumably the basis for the "licit/illicit" distinction in the question; it does not refer to the nature of the weapons themselves nor even to the purposes for which they are intended – only, in the case of nuclear weapons, to who the possessor is, where "licitness" is based on the treaty-enshrined "we got there first."

Thus, use of the term "proliferation" tends to locate the person who uses it within a possessor state and aligns him or her with the political stance favoring the hierarchy of state power enshrined in the current distribution of WMD. The framing of the fourth question, "... is it proper to deny [WMD] possession to others for the same purposes?" seems similarly based in a possessor state perspective, as it is presumably the possessor states who must decide whether it is proper to deny possession to others.

As we have already stated, we find WMD themselves intrinsically morally indefensible, no matter who possesses them, and we are concerned about the wide array of costs *to any state* of development and deployment. We therefore reject the discourse's implicit division of "good" and "bad," "safe" and "unsafe" WMD (defined as good or bad depending on who possesses them). Our concern is to understand how some WMD are rendered invisible ("ours") and some visible ("theirs"); some rendered malignant and others benign.

Here, we join others in noting that the language in which the case against "proliferation" is made is ethno-racist and contemptuous. Generally, in Western proliferation discourse as a whole, a distinction is drawn between "the 'Self' (seen as responsible) vs. the non-Western Unruly Other."[36] The United States represents itself as a rational actor, while representing the Unruly Other as emotional, unpredictable, irrational, immature, misbehaving. Not only does this draw on and reconstruct an Orientalist portrayal of third world actors;[37] it does so through the medium of gendered terminology. By drawing the relations between possessors and nonpossessors in gendered terms – the prudential, rational, advanced, mature, restrained, technologically and bureaucratically competent (and thus "masculine") Self versus the emotional, irrational, unpredictable, uncontrolled, immature, primitive, undisciplined, technologically incompetent (and thus "feminine") Unruly Other – the discourse naturalizes and legitimates the Self/possessor states having weapons that the Other does not. By drawing on and evoking gendered imagery and resonances, the discourse naturalizes the idea that "We"/the United States/the responsible father must protect, control, and limit "her," the emotional, out-of-control state, for her own good, as well as for ours.

This Western proliferation discourse has had a function in the wider context of U.S. national security politics. With the end of the "Evil Empire" in the late 1980s, until the attacks of September 11, 2001, the United States appeared to be without an enemy of grand enough proportions to justify maintaining its sprawling military-industrial establishment. This difficulty was forestalled by the construction of the category of "rogue states" – states seen as uncontrollable, irresponsible, irrational, malevolent, and antagonistic to the West.[38] Their unruliness and antagonism were represented as intrinsic to their irrational nature; if it were not in their "nature," the United States would have needed to ask more seriously if actions on the part of the West had had any role in producing that hostility and disorder.

The discourse of WMD proliferation has been one of the principal means of producing these states as major threats. To say this is neither to back away from our position of opposing weapons of mass destruction nor to assess the degree to which WMD in the hands of "Other" states actually do threaten the United States, the "Other" states' regional opponents, or their own population. But it is an assessment of the role of WMD proliferation discourse in naturalizing and legitimating programs and expenditures such as National Missile Defense that are otherwise difficult to make appear rational.[39]

Proliferation as a Phenomenon

Within the logic of deterrence theory and proliferation discourse, the phenomenon of WMD proliferation is understandable in two main ways. States acquire WMD either for purposes of aggression – that is, to use WMD or to threaten their use in acts of aggression, intimidation, and/or coercion against other states or populations within their own state – or to enhance their own security by deterring an opponent's attack. Within a strategic calculus, either is understood as a "rational" motivation for WMD possession, even if not everyone would view these reasons as equally morally defensible.

Some in the security community have argued that this "realist consensus" about states' motivations for development of WMD "is dangerously inadequate." They argue that "nuclear weapons, like other weapons, are more than tools of national security; they are political objects of considerable importance in domestic debates and internal bureaucratic struggles and can also serve as international normative symbols of modernity and identity."[40] We agree, but would add that understanding any of those motivations will be incomplete without gender analysis.

We argue that gendered terms and images are an integral part of the ways national security issues are thought about and represented – and that it matters. During the 1991 Gulf War, for example, the mass media speculated about whether George Bush had finally "beat the wimp factor." When in the spring of 1998, India exploded five nuclear devices, Hindu nationalist leader Balasaheb Thackeray explained, "We had to prove that we are not eunuchs." An Indian newspaper cartoon "depicted Prime Minister Atal Behari

Vajpayee propping up his coalition government with a nuclear bomb. 'Made with Viagra,' the caption read."[41]

Feminists argue that these images are not trivial, but instead deserve analysis. Metaphors that equate political and military power with sexual potency and masculinity serve to both shape and limit the ways in which national security is conceptualized.[42] Political actors incorporate sexual metaphors in their representations of nuclear weapons as a way to mobilize gendered associations and symbols in creating assent, excitement, support for, and identification with the weapons and their own political regime. Moreover, gendered metaphor is not only an integral part of accomplishing domestic power aims. The use of these metaphors also appropriates the test of a nuclear weapon into the occasion for reinforcing patriarchal gender relations.

That a nation wishing to stake a claim to being a world power (or a regional one) should choose nuclear weapons as its medium for doing so is often seen as "natural": The more advanced military destructive capacity you have, the more powerful you are. The "fact" that nuclear weapons would be the coin of the realm in establishing a hierarchy of state power is fundamentally unremarked, unanalyzed, taken for granted by most (non-feminist) analysts. Some antiwar feminists, by contrast, have looked with a historical and postcolonial eye and seen nuclear weapons' enshrinement as the emblem of power not as a natural fact but as a social one, produced by the actions of states. They argue that when the United States, with the most powerful economy and conventional military in the world, acts as though its power and security are guaranteed only by a large nuclear arsenal, it creates a context in which nuclear weapons become the ultimate necessity for and symbol of state security.[43] And when the United States or any other nuclear power works hard to ensure that other states do not obtain nuclear weapons, it is creating a context in which nuclear weapons become the ultimate arbiter of political power.[44]

An Ethical Nonproliferation Politics?

Finally, after our critique of both the framing and political uses of Western proliferation discourse and our questioning of the adequacy of the models through which proliferation as a phenomenon is understood, there remains the question: "If some nations possess weapons of mass destruction (either licitly or illicitly) for defensive and deterrent purposes, is it proper to deny such possession to others for the same purposes?"

We have spoken of the multiple costs of developing and deploying nuclear weapons *to their possessors* (third question) and the immense suffering that weapons of mass destruction would bring. Given what we have said, we should not be indifferent to other states' developing nuclear weapons unless we were indifferent to them. Additionally, as we argue in response to the fifth question, we believe that more WMD in more places would make their "accidental" or purposive use by states, as well as their availability to terrorists, more likely. So we are opposed to the development and deployment of any WMD, by any state or nonstate actor.

Despite this clear opposition to the spread of WMD, we are uneasy simply answering "yes" to the question *as it is posed*. The question assumes that some states already have WMD and asks only whether it is proper to deny WMD to others. Denying WMD to others implies maintaining the current international balance of power, in which the West is privileged, politically and economically. As feminists, we oppose the extreme inequality inherent in the current world order and are troubled by actions that will further enshrine it. But at the same time, we cannot endorse WMD proliferation as a mode of equalization, nor do we see it as an effective form of redress.

Second, we come to the question not only as feminists but as citizens of the most highly armed possessor state. As such, we must ask: Are citizens of possessor states entitled to judge, threaten, allow, or encourage the decisions of nonpossessor states to develop WMD? On what grounds? In what discursive territory? As we have outlined above, we find the existing proliferation discourse too ethno-racist, too focused on horizontal rather than vertical proliferation, and too sanguine about the justifiability of "our" having what "they" are not fit to have.

Our task, then, as antiwar feminists, is to learn how to participate in a constructive conversation,[45] eschewing the vocabulary of "proliferation," learning to listen, perhaps publicizing the warnings that women – and men – are issuing about the multiple costs and risks of WMD in their particular states. As citizens of the most highly armed possessor state, our credibility as participants in this conversation will be contingent on our committed efforts to bring about nuclear disarmament in our own state and our efforts to redress the worldwide inequalities that are underwritten by our military superiority.

WMD DISARMAMENT

Our tradition has advocated and will continue to advocate unilateral reduction in nuclear arms. Our commitment to nuclear disarmament originates in a general understanding of the use and dangers of weapons. We begin by noting that conflict is endemic to human relationships. "Peace" means, among other things, engaging in conflicts, that is, "fighting," without actually injuring or damaging others, without trying to do so, at best without being willing to do so.

There will always be something at hand to use as a weapon and threaten the "peace"; it is impossible to create a weaponless scene of conflict. A child's block, a kitchen knife, a passenger airliner can injure or kill. There is no substitute, then, for learning to fight without resorting to weapons.

But having "real" weapons at hand makes conflict far more dangerous. It makes injuring more likely, whether accidental, deliberate, unwitting, or willing. It also tends to expand the scale of injury; for example, while two airliners hitting the World Trade Center resulted in more than 3,000 deaths, a "small" nuclear warhead dropped on the twin towers would have instantly killed at least 100,000, with another 100,000 deaths in the days that followed. Deliberately relying on weapons – purchasing them, learning to use them, keeping them nearby – makes less likely the development of other strategies of self-protection. Once on the scene, weapons may be used in anger or ignorance, just because they are nearby. Weapons injure; as far as possible they should be cleared out.

Nonetheless, individuals and states continue to keep weapons at hand. States and citizens draw lessons from history that show the dangers of disarmament. We believe that the recourse to weapons underestimates their complex costs and dangers. People equate being armed with being safe, unarmed with being vulnerable. They overlook the risk of guns at hand and exaggerate the protection guns may give. But we understand that the issue of weapons arises from personal experience and collective identities, that it is deeply felt and in no way simple. We would insist only that weapons are never a substitute for negotiation and nonviolent fighting and that they may well hinder the success of nonviolent methods.

When we turn to weapons of mass destruction, we have only three additional comments. First, given the political will, nuclear weapons are among the most easily reduced. The scale of the effort required to produce them, the scientific and technological expertise and financial investment involved, have all militated toward state ownership and control of nuclear weapons. Thus, in contrast to weapons such as small arms – which are unregulated, can travel anywhere, and often become the property of near-children – nuclear weapons are relatively controllable and so can be selectively destroyed.

Second, unilateral disarmament is not an all-or-nothing matter, in which weapons disappear almost overnight. Would that this were possible. In reality, destroying nuclear weapons would be a massively complicated feat, slow and gradual at best. It is often said, rightly, that the United States can never disarm itself completely, can never lose the capacity to develop nuclear weapons. We are saying that the United States would lose *nothing* by beginning to destroy its remaining weapons. It would always have weapons, remain a nuclear "power," even if it wished otherwise. The example of unilateral disarmament might, on the other hand, lend credibility to the stated desire for a more stable world less endangered by nuclear weapons.

Finally, George W. Bush's nuclear missile defense, Reagan's impenetrable shield *redux*, symbolizes the sense of safety and power that nuclear weapons of all kinds appear to bestow. We know that even if such a shield were technologically feasible, it would be porous, "penetrable," not only by nuclear warheads on missiles but by nuclear weapons in suitcases, on boats, and in Piper Cubs; by biological weapons sent through the mail; by chemical weapons sprayed by crop-dusters; by passenger airliners employed as tools of mass destruction. But "giving up" weapons and giving up the promise (no matter how far-fetched) of a means to defend against them makes one feel vulnerable – and, thus, by extension, "feminine." There is nothing shameful – and nothing masculine or feminine – about the desire to be safe and to provide safety for others. But the hope of finding safety in weapons is another "dangerous dream" that nuclear weapons inspire.

CONCRETE OPTIONS

The final question asks us to evaluate current or proposed treaty agreements concerning nuclear, biological, and chemical weapons. We are offered a place at the negotiating table, a position few women, probably fewer feminists, have occupied.

For feminists there are two questions: How should we respond to the invitation? And what should we say about particular treaties if we accept? The second question is not one to which antiwar feminists have a distinctive answer arising from our tradition. It is the first question, whether to come to the table and how to act effectively once there, that traditionally and today preoccupies feminists.

Peace making, like war, has been dominated by men. Few women have been asked to participate in negotiations; when asked, it has usually been late, after the agenda was already set. But women are now claiming their place in negotiations.[46] They have participated in the struggles and have a right to be present; many feel that only they will represent women's distinctive interests.

Getting and accepting an invitation is only the first step in being able to participate effectively. Often women have to overcome outright hostility and ridicule from male participants. When they are treated with courtesy, they may still feel unable to express their concerns and ignored or dismissed when they try. Even when present in large numbers, women may be unable fully to engage. In South Africa women were welcomed to the peace table and occupied half its seats, but no one had contended with the divisions of work and responsibility in their lives. When negotiations lasted well into the night, no one was taking care of their husbands and children; women who stayed became tense and preoccupied.[47]

Women's difficulties participating in peace negotiations may be especially marked when the topic is weapons, a subject that, as we have said, is particularly liable to lend itself to abstraction. A report by a woman participant at biological weapons treaty negotiations sounds familiar themes. What counts as "reason" prevailed, what gets coded as "emotions" were excluded. Disturbing concerns, for example, with the effects of a vaccine on troops or the populace, were labeled "emotional." Speakers engaged in "cool, detached reasoning about the possible uses of weapons against an adversary. . . . 'Useful' in this context means ability to cause serious loss of life." Talking about a vaccine's negative effects was tantamount to "complaining," "whining," "carrying on."[48]

In discussions of biological weapons, as in issues of proliferation, the dichotomous division between reason and emotion is entwined with a similar division between [Western] Self and [unruly] Other, a particular instance of self and other, Us and Enemy typical of peace and arms negotiation. "One test of belonging and being heard in this group was whether one accepted the nature of the source of the BW problem. Did one accept the identity of the adversary?" That identity was often described in racist terms – for example, "[they] don't value human life the way we do" – and these remarks elicited no comment.[49]

"To belong and speak and be heard" would mean ignoring the rules and interrupting the cool detached voice of reason. Again the gender discourse system is at work, frustrating these efforts. An objection that acknowledges emotion, that talks about the fate of bodies or lives, becomes an "outburst." Reason ignores them in order to continue the discussion of weapons and their effects. Outbursts are "feminine"; in the silence that follows an outburst, anyone, male or female, can "feel like a woman." The effect of gender discourse depends on a person's complex personal and social identities. But for a feminist, who aims to speak as herself-who-is-a-woman, the *accusation* of "being a woman" or a wimp has to be poignantly inhibiting.

For feminists struggling to participate effectively, the final insult may be the realization that the negotiations, especially if they are presented as inclusive and democratic, are more ritualistic displays than political action. "In reality, major decisions are made in secret in the capitals, based on calculations that seek military (and increasingly commercial) advantages."[50] In the words of a male political scientist: "Arms control is war by other means." Real power is always already somewhere else by the time a woman takes her place at the table.[51]

Should women then give up the effort to join in negotiations? It seems that many do. They "get intimidated, and don't put up with it, so they step aside."[52] But other women in increasing numbers are resisting ridicule and discrimination in order to make their views known. There are many reasons, personal and social, why some women persevere where others do not. Cultural attitudes toward women vary; women are more easily heard when many women are present, especially if they are linked in alliances that include all parties in conflict.

One reason that some women persevere is their belief that they have a distinctive perspective to bring to negotiation. Women participants in peace negotiations have said that they bring to the table an ability to attest to "the severe human consequences of conflict" and a commitment to expose the "underbelly of war." They stress the importance of speaking openly about pain and fear and loss, of building trust among adversaries, of opening up difficult, divisive issues rather than cloaking them in rhetoric or postponing them. They are apt to "see more clearly the continuum of conflict that stretches from the beating at home to the rape on the street to the killing on the battlefield." "They witness vivid links between violence, poverty and inequality in daily lives." They define peace in terms of "basic universal human needs" and advocate practical solutions to the building of peace, focusing on ordinary safety, housing, education, and child care.[53]

In sum, these women introduce a perspective that satisfies the criteria of the "feminine" as it functions metaphorically in gender discourse. The women only sometimes compare themselves with men, occasionally with some anger, more often speaking quietly of what women are more likely to believe and do. But it would be hard to *accuse* them of acting like women; and if women are present in sufficient numbers, they may be less vulnerable to the silencing power of gendered national security discourse.

Making treaties is only a small part of making peace. There are virtues in treaty making even when individual treaties are seriously flawed. Negotiating requires structured places in which opponents can talk; signed treaties require further conversation and negotiation. Prolonged negotiations create relations that at the least survive post-treaty crises and at best may help to resolve them. But treaties are no substitute for peace-building processes. They are made in formal contexts where participants are apt to cling to their ethno-national political identities and to keep their eye on political boundaries, rewards, and positions.[54] Among treaties, arms control negotiations, which extrapolate weapons from their context of injury and pain, may be the least amenable to the perspectives attributed to and claimed by women.

But if there are to be treaties, if weapons of mass destruction are to be subject to negotiation, then our tradition would encourage the participation of women. This is not because we believe that women offer a perspective "different" from men's – though that may be the case in many cultures at this historical moment. What gets left out of dominant ways of thinking about weapons – the emotional, the concrete, the particular, the human bodies and their vulnerability, human lives and their subjectivity – is neither masculine nor feminine but human. Rather, we would hope that the power of gender discourse to exclude what is now coded as "feminine" would be weakened by the presence of numbers of women for whom "acting and feeling like a woman" were a matter of course, even sometimes a source of strength, and not an occasion for self-doubt and silence.

Notes

We thank Neta Crawford, Barry O'Neill, William Ruddick, and Marilyn Young for helpful comments on earlier drafts of this paper and Felicity Hill for helpful suggestions for resources. We also thank our colleagues at the Mount

Holyoke conference for useful comments and encouragement, especially Duane Cady.

1. From a speech by Harry S. Truman. The full text was published in the *New York Times,* August 10, 1945, p 12.

2. Cited in Bel Mooney, "Beyond the Wasteland," in *Over Our Dead Bodies: Women against the Bomb,* ed. Dorothy Thompson (London: Virago Press, 1983), 7.

3. Certain figures are taken as representatives of antiwar feminism. Images of Kathe Kollwitz's artwork and phrases from Virginia Woolf's writing appear on postcards and T-shirts. On a deeper look, each of these women expresses complexities of antiwar feminism. Kollwitz, who sent her son "off to war" with flowers and a blessing, slowly and with difficulty achieved an antiwar stance. Woolf, whose imagination was fundamentally shaped by her fear and rejection of war, found her antimilitarism tested by Nazi aggression. Woolf explicitly situated her antiwar feminism within a particular class: "daughters of educated men." Yet Cynthia Enloe, who studies the effects of masculinist militarization on women's lives across the globe, finds that Woolf's *Three Guineas* (New York: Harcourt Brace, 1938) sheds "new light on the subtle practices of militarization" with each new group of students from "the United States, Japan, Mali, Korea, Bulgaria." Enloe, *Maneuvers: The International Politics of Militarizing Women's Lives* (Berkeley: University of California Press, 2000). The editors of *Feminist Studies* chose for its post–September 11 cover a photograph of Jane Addams at age seventy "campaigning for peace" with her friend Mary McDowell, who, like Addams, was a pacifist, suffragist, and unionist. Jean Bethke Elshtain, herself an engaged reporter on and ambivalent participant in antiwar feminism, has just produced a biography of Addams and a "reader" that collects Addams's writings. Addams was ostracized for reporting that many soldiers were loath to kill and that they could use a bayonet only after they were given "dope." Were Addams now to become representative, as Kollwitz and Woolf are, she would highlight the typical commitments of antiwar feminism to social justice and to the well-being of men made killers in war.

4. There are principled pacifists among antiwar feminists. One of the clearest secular accounts of nonviolence is Barbara Deming's "Revolution and Equilibrium," in *We Are All Part of One Another* (Philadelphia: New Society, 1984). By contrast, and more typical of antiwar feminists, Virginia Woolf, whose lifelong opposition to war making was central to her thought and imagination, accepted military resistance to Hitler. At the same time, she continued to belittle war making, talked evenly of enemy and English soldiers, and tried to imagine postwar change. See, as one example, her "Thoughts on Peace in an Air-raid," written in August 1940, published in *Collected Essays,* vol. 4 (New York: Harcourt Brace, 1953). On antiwar feminists supporting particular military campaigns while still remaining antiwar, see Sara Ruddick, "'Woman of Peace': A Feminist Construction," in *Synthesis Philosophica* 12 (1997): 265–82. Cynthia Cockburn speaks of "translating" violence and takes the phrase "transforming violence into creative militant non-violence" from Kumar Rupesinghe, ed., *Conflict Transformation* (London: Macmillan, 1995). See Cynthia Cockburn, *The Space between Us: Negotiating Gender and National Identities in Conflict* (London: Zed Books, 1998), 8. "Letting go of dangerous day dreams" comes from ibid., 11; "Giving leeway" from p. 89. In recent years in the United States, many antiwar feminists supported

the military campaigns of the African National Congress and the Sandinistas. Many also advocated military interventions in the former Yugoslavia and in Rwanda.

5. This is of necessity a brief and simplified account of just war theory. In the extensive literature, we recommend particularly Michael Walzer, *Just and Unjust Wars*, 3rd ed. (New York: Basic Books, 2000); and the U.S. Catholic bishops' letter, "The Challenge of Peace: God's Promise and Our Response," *Origins* 13:1 (May 19, 1983). This letter is distinct in its concern for the effects of the war system. For extensive criticism of just war theory, see Robert Holmes, *On War and Morality* (Princeton, N.J.: Princeton University Press, 1981); and Duane Cady, *From Warism to Pacifism: A Moral Continuum* (Philadelphia: Temple University Press, 1989), as well as their chapters in this volume. In respect to *jus ad bellum*, Holmes notes that successive generations respond to perceived threats without regard to the responses' cumulative effect. As a result, societies are transformed into "war systems," geared socially, politically, and economically to the maintenance and celebration of organized violence. In regard to *jus in bello*, Holmes notes that anyone who justifies going to war necessarily justifies the willful injury, maiming, killing, and destruction that are inherent to and intended by war. Holmes, *On War and Morality*, 181. For a feminist critique of the Catholic bishops' letter, see Mary C. Segers, "A Consistent Life Ethic: A Feminist Perspective on the Pro-Peace and Pro-Life Activities of the American Catholic Bishops," in *Women, Militarism and War*, ed. Jean Bethke Elshtain and Sheila Tobias (Savage, Md.: Rowman & Littlefield, 1990). For an example of the feminist argument that just war theory relies on unworkable abstractions, see Sara Ruddick, "Notes Toward a Feminist Peace Politics," in *Gendering War Talk*, ed. Miriam Cooke and Angela Woollacott (Princeton, N.J.: Princeton University Press, 1993). For a clear account and critique of feminists' charge that just war theory depends on inapplicable abstractions, see Lucinda Peach, "An Alternative to Pacifism: Feminism and Just War Theory," *Hypatia* 9:2 (Spring 1994): 152–72, as well as her chapter in this volume.

6. Cynthia Enloe has been a pioneer in this field. See her works, including: *Does Khaki Become You?: The Militarization of Women's Lives* (Boston: South End Press, 1983); *Bananas, Beaches, and Bases: Making Feminist Sense of International Politics* (Berkeley: University of California Press, 1989); *The Morning After: Sexual Politics at the End of the Cold War* (Berkeley: University of California Press, 1993); and *Maneuvers*.

7. The moment that one looks beyond the simple equation of war making with aggression and asks what men actually *do* when they make war, it is apparent that many of the activities involve no aggression at all. And so the equation of militarized masculinity and aggression holds up no better. For some men at war, masculinity must be inextricably linked to having and firing weapons. But for others, it must inhere in cooking for or cleaning up after soldiers; and for others, masculinity will be found in suits and ties and abstract strategizing. For some men, masculinity takes the form of taking risks in order to kill and destroy; for others, it is taking risks for the sake of healing; and for others, masculinity will have little if anything to do with risk taking, as they sit behind desks far from the frontlines. Some men must find masculinity in their physical capacity to slog through miles of jungle or desert terrain; others must find it in their cognitive

capacity to design high-tech armaments. Each of these masculinities, and more, are required for war making. On the multiple masculinities required by war making, see Sara Ruddick, *Maternal Thinking: Toward a Politics of Peace*, 2nd ed. (Boston: Beacon Press, 1995); and Enloe, especially *Bananas, Beaches, and Bases* and *The Morning After*.

8. For men's reluctance to fight, see Joshua S. Goldstein, *War and Gender: How Gender Shapes the War System and Vice Versa* (Berkeley: University of California Press, 2001), esp. chap. 5. The relation among masculinity, aggression, and war remains highly controversial. Goldstein provides a lucid, balanced assessment of this debate.

9. See Enloe, especially *Maneuvers* and *Bananas, Beaches, and Bases*; Jacklyn Cock, *Women and War in South Africa* (Cleveland, Ohio: Pilgrim Press, 1993).

10. Carol Cohn, "War, Wimps and Women," in *Gendering War Talk*, 227–46. See also idem, "Sex and Death in the Rational World of Defense Intellectuals," *Signs* 12:4 (1987): 687–728.

11. For examples of discussions of war's destructive effects on women's work, see Aili Mari Tripp, "Rethinking Difference: Comparative Perspectives from Africa," *Signs* 25:3 (2000): 649–75; Ruddick, *Maternal Thinking*; Radhika Coomaraswamy, "Reinventing International Law: Women's Rights as Human Rights in the International Community," *Bulletin of Concerned Asian Scholars* 28:2 (April–June 1996): 16. Cynthia Cockburn reports: "To the women working in the refugee projects of the Yugoslav successor states . . . it sometimes seems as if the Yugoslav wars of 1992–1995 were wars waged against women. . . . Eighty-four percent of the refugees are women and children. Many have been raped and abused as women by male fighters. All come with stories about the destruction of everything they had nurtured: offspring, homes, fruit trees, cows and sheep, small businesses." Cockburn, *Space between Us*, 156.

12. Elaine Scarry, *The Body in Pain* (Oxford: Oxford University Press, 1985).

13. Among many discussions, see Indai Lourdes Sajor, ed., *Common Grounds: Violence against Women in War and Armed Conflict Situations* (Quezon City, Philippines: Asian Center for Women's Human Rights, 1998); Human Rights Watch/Africa, *Shattered Lives: Sexual Violence during the Rwandan Genocide and Its Aftermath* (New York: Human Rights Watch, 1996); Beverly Allen, *Rape Warfare: The Hidden Genocide in Bosnia-Herzegovina and Croatia* (Minneapolis: University of Minnesota Press, 1996); Anne Llewellyn Barstow, ed., *War's Dirty Secret: Rape, Prostitution and Other Crimes against Women* (Cleveland, Ohio: Pilgrim Press, 2000); Robin Schott, "Philosophical Reflections on War Rape," in *Feminist Ethics and Politics*, ed. Claudia Card (Lawrence: University Press of Kansas, 1999); Claudia Card, "Rape Terrorism," in *The Unnatural Lottery: Character and Moral Luck* (Philadelphia: Temple University Press, 1996), 90–117, and "Rape as a Weapon of War," *Hypatia* 11:4 (Fall 1996): 5–18.

14. For the classic statement of this perspective, see Virginia Woolf, *Three Guineas*. More recently, see Chris J. Cuomo, "War Is Not Just an Event: Reflections on the Significance of Everyday Violence," *Hypatia* 11:4 (Fall 1996): 30–45; and Robin May Schott, "Gender and 'Postmodern War,' " *Hypatia* 11:4 (Fall 1996): 19–29.

15. Cockburn, *Space between Us*, 8.

16. This is primarily a description of after-effects on societies whose territories have been the site of warfare. But even those societies whose soldiers fight in distant

lands suffer related effects. Surviving soldiers may bring home the effects of violence: injured bodies and minds; remorse, rage, and despair; habits of aggression and abuse; syndromes of suffering.

17. See David Chappell, Chapter 11 in this volume.

18. The phrase "Alternative Epistemologies" was used by Charles W. Mills in "Alternative Epistemologies," *Social Theory and Practice* 14:3 (Fall 1988): 237–63. Mills used the phrase to characterize critiques of dominant epistemological ideals by African-American philosophers and Marxist critics as well as by feminists. So far as we know it was Margaret Urban Walker who introduced the phrase to feminist epistemology in her article, "Moral Understandings: Alternative 'Epistemology' for a Feminist Ethics," *Hypatia* 4:4 (1989): 15–28. Also see Walker's *Moral Understandings* (New York: Routledge, 1998). The essays in *Feminist Epistemologies*, ed. Linda Alcoff and Elizabeth Potter (New York: Routledge, 1993), introduce several of the themes of feminist epistemology. Lorraine Code is one of several epistemologists who have explored the connections between gender and knowing. See *What Can She Know?* (Ithaca, N.Y.: Cornell University Press, 1991), and *Rhetorical Spaces* (New York: Routledge, 1995). Among psychologists, this "alternative epistemology" is typically referred to as "connected knowing." See *Knowledge, Difference and Power: Essays Inspired by Women's Ways of Knowing*, ed. Nancy Goldberger, Jill Tarule, Blythe Clinchy, and Mary Belenky (New York: Basic Books, 1996), especially Blythe McKiver Clinchy, "Connected and Separate Knowing: Toward a Marriage of Two Minds," 205–47; and Sara Ruddick, "Reason's 'Femininity': A Case for Connected Knowing," 248–73.

19. Cohn, "Sex and Death," 15–28.

20. Graca Machel makes the same point in the context of talking about war's effects on children. In *The Impact of War on Children: A Review of Progress* (New York: UNICEF, 2001), she titles the tenth chapter "Small Arms, Light Weapons: Mass Destruction" and writes that "the most widely used weapons of mass destruction are not nuclear or biological – they are the estimated 500 million small arms and light weapons that are fueling bloodshed and mayhem around the world" (p. 119). For a gender perspective on small arms, see Wendy Cukier, "Gender and Small Arms," presented to Gender Perspectives on Disarmament, United Nations, New York, March 14, 2001; Ginette Saucier, *Seizing the Advantage: Integrating Gender into Small Arms Proliferation* (Ottawa: Department of Foreign Affairs and International Trade, forthcoming); Magdalene Hsien Chen Pua, ed., "The Devastating Impact of Small Arms and Light Weapons on the Lives of Women: A Collection of Testimonies" (New York: Women's International League for Peace and Freedom, July 2001); and the United Nations Department for Disarmament Affairs, "Gender Perspectives on Disarmament Briefing Notes no. 3: Gender Perspectives on Small Arms" (New York: United Nations, 2001). The best starting place for exploring small arms issues is the website of IANSA (The International Action Network on Small Arms): http://www.iansa.org.

21. In the United States in the early years of the cold war, Women's Strike for Peace protested nuclear testing, taking on both the House Un-American Activities Committee and the defense establishment. In the 1980s, women's protests against nuclear weapons were organized in the Pacific Islands, Australia, Japan, Europe, and North America, with women's peace camps modeled on the one

at Greenham Common in England springing up at numerous military bases. In Hiroshima in August 2000, at the Women's Forum 2000: Away with Nuclear Weapons, women from around the world testified against the testing and use of nuclear weapons and called for nuclear abolition. In preparation for the Nuclear Proliferation Treaty 2000 conference, the Women's International League for Peace and Freedom (WILPF) initiated the Reaching Critical Will campaign to provide information and to stimulate accountability by increasing the transparency of disarmament efforts at the United Nations (see www.reachingcriticalwill.org). India's 1998 nuclear tests provoked antinuclear activity by Indian feminists. See, for example, Madhu Kishwar, "BJP's Wargasm," *Manushi* 106 (May-June 1998): 6–10; Arundhati Roy, "The End of Imagination," in Roy, *The Cost of Living* (New York: Modern Library, 1999), 91–126; Kumkum Sangari et al., "Why Women Must Reject the Bomb," in *Out of Nuclear Darkness: The Indian Case for Disarmament* (New Delhi: Movement in India for Nuclear Disarmament, n.d.), 47–56; Amrita Basu and Rekha Basu, "India: Of Men, Women, and Bombs," *Dissent* (Winter 1999): 39–43.

22. For a classic statement on the sexual allure of nuclear weapons for both men and women, see Helen Caldicott, *Missile Envy: The Arms Race and Nuclear War* (New York: William Morrow, 1984). On the connection between masculine sexuality and nuclear weapons, see Brian Easlea, *Fathering the Unthinkable: Masculinity, Scientists and the Nuclear Arms Race* (London: Pluto Press, 1983); Evelyn Fox Keller, *Secrets of Life, Secrets of Death: Essays on Language, Gender and Science* (New York: Routledge, 1992); Kishwar, "BJP's Wargasm"; Basu and Basu, "India: Of Men, Women, and Bombs."

23. See Cohn, "Wars, Wimps and Women" and "Sex and Death." For a very different presentation of these points, see Susan Griffin, *A Chorus of Stones* (New York: Doubleday, 1992); Christa Wolf, *Cassandra* (New York: Farrar, Straus & Giroux, 1984), and *Accident: A Day's News* (New York: Farrar, Straus & Giroux, 1989).

24. General Robert Rosenberg, formerly on the National Security Council staff during the Carter administration, speaking at the Harvard Seminar on C3I. "The Influence of Policy Making on C3I," in "Incidental Paper: Seminar on Command, Control, Communications and Intelligence," Spring 1980, Center for Information Policy Research, Harvard University, p. 59.

25. Hisako Matsubara, *Cranes at Dusk* (Garden City, N.Y.: Dial Press, 1985). The author was a child in Kyoto at the time the atomic bomb was dropped. Her description is based on the memories of survivors.

26. Cohn, "Wars, Wimps and Women."

27. Feminists are not the only ones who focus on development and deployment as phenomena unto themselves. The U.S. Catholic bishops' letter, for example, explicitly links nuclear weapons spending and poverty.

28. Sangari et al., "Why Women Must Reject," 48. Some defenders of nuclear weapons argue that nuclear weapons are actually economically beneficial, as a form of "defense on the cheap" (in contrast to the costs of conventional weapons and armies). Sangari et al. reject this argument, pointing out that "nuclearisation will not eliminate the necessity for conventional weapons. On the contrary, by provoking neighboring countries severely, it has made the prospect of conventional warfare far more imminent, and has stepped up military investment altogether."

29. In 1995, a study by the Nuclear Weapons Cost Study Project Committee was the first systematic attempt to catalog the comprehensive cost of the U.S. nuclear weapons program from inception in 1940 to 1995. When the committee included the costs to develop, field, and maintain the nuclear arsenal and to defend against attacks from nuclear-armed adversaries, the cost was about four trillion dollars. That figure did not include the cost of disposing of hundreds of tons of uranium and plutonium. It did not include the money spent on the proposed National Missile Defense. Nor did it include the costs of the environmental cleanup necessitated by the "unprecedented legacy of toxic and radioactive pollution at dozens of sites and thousands of facilities across the country," which they estimated would cost at least half a trillion dollars more, where it can be cleaned up at all. Stephen I. Schwartz, ed., "Four Trillion Dollars and Counting," *Bulletin of the Atomic Scientists*, November/December 1995.

30. Schwartz, "Four Trillion Dollars."

31. This point is made by Sangari et al., "Why Women Must Reject," 47.

32. Ibid., 48.

33. Roy, "End of Imagination," 101. She writes: "It is such supreme folly to believe that nuclear weapons are deadly only if they're used. The fact that they exist at all, their very presence in our lives, will wreak more havoc than we can begin to fathom."

34. Sangari et al., "Why Women Must Reject," 48.

35. Cockburn, *Space between Us*, 11.

36. Susan Wright, "Feminist Tales from the Arms Control Front," lecture at University of Michigan, March 24, 2001. Transcript by courtesy of the author.

37. Edward Said, *Orientalism* (New York: Pantheon, 1978); Hugh Gusterson, "Orientalism and the Arms Race: An Analysis of the Neo-colonial Discourse on Nuclear Non-proliferation," working paper no. 47, Center for Transcultural Studies, 1991; Shampa Biswas, "'Nuclear Apartheid' as Political Position: Race as a Postcolonial Resource?" *Alternatives* 26:4 (October–December 2001): 485–522.

38. For "rogue states," see Michael Klare, *Rogue States and Nuclear Outlaws: America's Search for a New Foreign Policy* (New York: Hill and Wang, 1995). See also Wright, "Feminist Tales."

39. Nicholas Berry, "Too Much Hysteria Exists over the Increasing Proliferation of Weapons of Mass Destructions and Ballistic Missile Technology: A More Modest Hysteria Would Be Wiser," *Asia Forum*, January 21, 2000.

40. Scott Sagan, for example, has argued that "nuclear weapons programs also serve other, more parochial and less obvious objectives." Sagan, "Why Do States Build Nuclear Weapons? Three Models in Search of a Bomb," *International Security* 21:3 (Winter 1996/97): 54–86. In our view all three of the models Sagan outlines – the "security model," the "domestic politics model," and the "norms model" – are seriously weakened by their failure to incorporate gender analysis.

41. Basu and Basu, "India: Of Men, Women, and Bombs," 39.

42. Cohn, "Wars, Wimps, and Women."

43. Arundhati Roy put it this way: "But let us pause to give credit where it's due. Whom must we thank for all this? The Men who made it happen. The Masters of the Universe. Ladies and gentlemen, the United States of America! Come on up here, folks, stand up and take a bow. Thank you for doing this to the world.

Thank you for making a difference. Thank you for showing us the way. Thank you for altering the very meaning of life." Roy, "End of Imagination," 100–101.

44. Some Indian feminists have combined this attention to weapons-as-symbols-in-world-power-relations with an analysis of the gendered meanings of power. Basu and Basu argue that the BJP's decision to explode five nuclear bombs was in part an attempt "to shatter stereotypes about the 'effeminate' Indian that date back to the period of British colonialism." The British particularly disparaged "feminized" Hindu masculinity, while seeing Muslims as "robust and brave." Basu and Basu, "India: Of Men, Women, and Bombs," 39.

45. The term "constructive conversation" was introduced to us through a conversation Carol had with Laura Chasin, the director of the Public Conversations Project. Their website, http://www.publicconversations.org, would be a valuable resource for anyone who is trying to think about political conflict.

46. "Women Building Peace: From the Village Council to the Negotiating Table" is a network of grassroots activists and national and international organizations focused on getting women included in peace processes. See their website, www.international-alert.org/women, as well as the website of "Women Waging Peace," www.womenwagingpeace.net, for more information on women's participation in peace-building efforts, including peace negotiations. In October 2000, the UN Security Council passed Resolution 1325 on Women, International Peace and Security, which affirmed the importance of women's role in peace building and stressed the importance of women's equal participation in all efforts for the promotion of peace and security.

47. Sanam Naraghi Anderlini, *Women at the Peace Table: Making a Difference* (New York: UNIFEM, 2000), 30.

48. Wright, "Feminist Tales." For further discussion of the place of what counts as "emotion" in international political discourse, see Neta C. Crawford, "The Passion of World Politics: Propositions on Emotion and Emotional Relationships," *International Security* 24:4 (Spring 2000): 116–56.

49. Wright, "Feminist Tales."

50. Ibid.

51. Ibid. Wright cites Barry Posen, "Military Lessons of the Gulf War – Implications for Middle East Arms Control," in *Arms Control and the New Middle East Security Environment*, ed. Shai Feldman and Ariel Levite (Jerusalem: Jaffee Center for Strategic Studies, 1994), 64.

52. Hanan Ashrawi, cited in Anderlini, *Women at the Peace Table*, 29.

53. Quotes and paraphrases from ibid., 29–36 and passim.

54. Ibid.

22

A Pragmatist Feminist Approach to the Ethics of Weapons of Mass Destruction

Lucinda Joy Peach

The pragmatist feminist perspective that I develop in this chapter is deeply indebted to and affirms in many respects the antiwar feminist approach outlined by Carol Cohn and Sara Ruddick in the preceding chapter, but with some marked differences. These differences, I argue, reveal more completely both the promise and the limitations of antiwar feminism.

At the outset, it is important to note that there is neither a single "feminism" nor a single "pragmatism" with which it might be aligned. Instead, there are multiple feminisms, just as there are multiple pragmatisms. The "pragmatist feminism" developed in this essay draws on several elements from American Pragmatism, a philosophical school developed in the late nineteenth and early twentieth centuries, most prominently by Charles Peirce, William James, John Dewey, and George Herbert Mead.

Despite the many differences among the pragmatists, they tend to share several features. Perhaps most salient to the subject of this volume is their presumption "that human agency in all of its higher manifestations has evolved from . . . concrete circumstances in which a vulnerable organism is confronted, often (if not usually) in concert with other organisms of the same species, with possibilities of both injury and fulfillment."[1] It is the continuous reminder of "human fallibility and finitude"[2] that constrains pragmatists from positions such as foundationalism and dogmatism and thus against ideologies that encourage the use of armed force, and especially of WMD, in all but the most extreme circumstances. It is also a reminder that armed conflicts are composed of embodied human beings, each of whom has the capacity for suffering as well as happiness, a point stressed by feminist analyses of armed conflicts.

There are several significant points of commonality or intersection between pragmatism and feminism.[3] Perhaps most important for thinking about the ethics of weapons of mass destruction is that both are actively engaged in attempting to solve social problems. The early pragmatists viewed the purpose of philosophical reflection to be "the intelligent overcoming of oppressive conditions."[4] Dewey, for example, recommended the criticism of beliefs underlying society that have led to "unsatisfactory conditions in order to radically reconstruct our society according to non-oppressive and cooperative standards."[5]

Feminist goals of liberating women from oppression thus echo pragmatist ones.[6] While most often feminist movements have been focused specifically on ending the male domination and oppression of *women*, a more inclusive feminist vision has as its object the elimination of *all* hierarchical and oppressive relationships, including the oppression of so-called third world or developing nations (especially of the Global South) by those of the so-called first world or industrialized nations (especially of the Global North), of ethnic, cultural, racial, or religious minorities by majorities, homosexuals by heterosexuals, the poor by the wealthy, children by adults, and so on.[7]

In addition, pragmatists advocate the elimination of sharp divisions between theory and practice, reason and experience, and knowing and doing.[8] Pragmatists focus much more on consequences rather than on a priori abstract conceptualizing, captured in the phrase that pragmatists assign value on the basis of "what works" or what provides "emotional satisfaction."[9] From a pragmatist perspective, the most important questions are practical ones.[10]

Pragmatists consider moral agents to be actors within a concrete particular context that both influences what is experienced and is influenced by those experiences. The inextricability of the perceiver from what is perceived means that action, whether in the context of armed conflict and the use of WMD or otherwise, must be situated within the larger context of which it is a part.[11] Since every decision to enter or engage in an armed conflict and every decision to deploy WMD, of whatever type, must be considered within the full context of other relevant actors, agencies, and term strategies or results,[12] a pragmatist perspective is unlikely to result in the kind of abstract thinking that antiwar feminism criticizes in dominant just war and realist approaches.[13]

Feminism also shares pragmatism's rejection of traditional rationalist and empiricist approaches and its commitment to the inseparability of theory and practice.[14] Both believe that reason must be grounded in experience and requires being supplemented, at least in particular circumstances, by emotion.[15] In this respect, feminists also favor a posteriori rather than a priori forms of knowledge, those that develop on the basis of experience rather than those that are posited prior to it.[16]

In sum, both pragmatism and feminism accord a central place to the particular, the concrete, and the factual elements of experience, as opposed to the universal, the generalizable, and the abstract.[17] This opposition to abstraction is apparent, for example, in feminist understandings of women's "different voice" and Dewey's views about the importance of the qualitative background of situations. In contrast to mainstream philosophy, both feminist and pragmatist perspectives focus on everyday life and emphasize respect for others and the constitutiveness of community. The pragmatists' sensitivity to the social embeddedness of persons led them to understand the "I" "only in relation to other selves, so that the autonomy of individual agents needed to be integrated with their status as social beings" existing in community.[18]

This common conception of the "relational self" suggests that both pragmatists and feminists will resist turning others into "the Other," who can then be demonized and made into "the enemy," suitable to be killed. The feminist commitment to the well-being of others, in both the local and the global community, is well illustrated by Carol Cohn's and Sara Ruddick's contribution to this volume. However, this commitment also provides the basis for the pragmatist feminist position articulated here that refuses to categorically rule out the moral legitimacy of any resort to armed force or war, since such resort may be morally imperative to protect innocent others.

In addition to these marked similarities, it is also important to acknowledge how a pragmatist feminism differs significantly from American Pragmatism. Perhaps most important is pragmatist feminism's attention to the gendered character of the social world and gender's impact on the formation and maintenance of male and female identities. These subjects largely were ignored by the American Pragmatists[19] but influence the analysis of the ethics of WMD outlined here. In addition, feminists tend to give greater import to the cognitive aspects of affect than pragmatists, even though, as already discussed, pragmatists recognize the importance of emotions to agency and cognition.

Despite its differences from more mainstream strands of feminism, pragmatist feminism shares the goals of many strands of feminism to make gender a central consideration of the analysis (here of armed force and WMD)[20] and to eradicate (patriarchal) oppression and domination. These goals result in a strong presumption against the use of any weapons, not only WMD, since they are in their very inception designed as tools for domination and suppression of others designated as "the enemy." This opposition to the use of armed force is related to feminist observations of the patriarchal and hierarchical, male-dominated and -controlled character of the military and the oppressive effects of war and militarism around the world, especially on women and children. In addition, the pragmatist feminist view described here affirms much in the "constitutive positions" of antiwar feminism articulated by Cohn and Ruddick,[21] especially its observation of the gendered character of war and militarism, its suspicion of masculinist approaches to war and conflict resolution, and its critique of the dominant tradition for its focus on the physical, military, and strategic effects of these weapons separate from their embeddedness in the rest of social and political life.

With this brief overview in mind, in the following section, I describe how a pragmatist feminist perspective compares with the antiwar feminist position outlined by Cohn and Ruddick in Chapter 21 with respect to the specific issues addressed by this volume.

Although pragmatist feminism itself does not directly provide general norms governing the use of weapons in war, it does so indirectly through its affirmation of elements of just war theory, as described below. Pragmatist feminism does not categorically rule out the use of armed force or engagement in war. Its pragmatist perspective steers in a different direction from the antiwar feminists' "practical" opposition to war. Whereas the realist tradition has been unduly pessimistic in its assumption that war and armed conflict are necessary, certain, and inevitable, on a pragmatist feminist view, antiwar feminist thinking tends to be unduly optimistic about the human capacity to transcend the use of violent methods of resolving disputes, given the consistent and continual resort to such means throughout most of human history.

From a pragmatist feminist perspective, the historical and contemporary experience of the repeated resort to violence and the inability of humanity thus far to develop alternative mechanisms for resolving large-scale disputes suggests the likelihood of future wars and armed conflicts. In light of this history, overcoming the "war culture" that antiwar feminists view so unfavorably can be possible only outside the immediate situation of armed conflict. Once the aggressor has struck or threatens to do so imminently, it is too late to change our societies and ourselves in order to avoid war. Rather, it is then necessary to act in order to avoid annihilation in one form or another.

Given its view that some wars and some opposition to war and armed conflicts are morally necessary to protect ourselves and others from harm, pragmatist feminists seek to impose moral limits on the harm and suffering to the minimum necessary. Despite an awareness of its limitations,[22] a pragmatist feminist perspective considers just war theory to provide a flexible and modifiable set of criteria for attempting to act morally and in accordance with principles of justice, both in entering into an armed conflict (*jus ad bellum*) and in the actual engagement of that conflict (*jus in bello*). In particular, pragmatist feminism shares just war's starting premise of a strong presumption against the legitimacy of the use of armed force and violence to resolve conflicts.

A pragmatist feminist perspective thus rejects Cohn's and Ruddick's contention that just war theorists "implicitly accept war as a practice even when condemning particular wars."[23] Recognizing the historical and global reality of war making and armed force as means of resolving conflicts and adopting strategies to maximize justice and minimize immorality when such means are adopted is not the same as "implicitly accepting the practices of war," at least in the absence of demonstrably effective means of eliminating such conflicts. To ignore the reality of the continuing resort to war and armed force is itself to revert to abstraction rather than offering a practical method for eliminating the human suffering and incalculable damage caused by war and armed conflict.

Here Cohn and Ruddick reveal (intentionally or otherwise) their situatedness as citizens of a war-making state, one that has had the *choice* in many, if not all, instances since the mid-twentieth century, at least, of deciding whether or not to go to war. Just as Cohn and Ruddick criticize just war theory for failing to explore nonviolent alternatives once a just cause is determined or war has begun, their antiwar feminist approach fails to offer concrete suggestions for avoiding armed conflict when a nation or people is confronted with armed aggression or assault by others, the situation where the options boil down to "fight or die." This perspective fails to look at war from the point of view of the aggressed-against, when armed conflict becomes a necessity in order to retain national and/or cultural and/or ethnic identity from subjugation by the aggressor(s). In such circumstances, the moral necessity of armed force looks quite different. And in such circumstances, the threatened use of WMD can be seen as less evil than the alternatives, such as doing nothing and being conquered or fighting a conventional war and faring poorly.

Rather than reverting to abstract thinking about war, pragmatist feminism affirms just war theory's casuistic approach to particular armed conflicts as well as its position that such means are sometimes morally justifiable or even morally obligatory in order to protect oneself (individual or nation) or innocent third parties. Further, pragmatist feminism affirms just war thinking's attention to particular conflicts rather than war in the abstract and its stance of moderation and of imposing the minimal suffering necessary to accomplish the objective of restoring the peace.[24] Thus, with respect to the military response of the United States to the September 11 terrorist attacks, a pragmatist feminist application of just war criteria yields the conclusion that the *jus ad bellum* principles of "last resort" and "proportionality," as well as the *in bello* principles of "proportionality" and "discrimination," were not satisfied.

A second difference in the two feminist perspectives emerges out of the antiwar feminist observation that war and militarism are not separate from everyday life but integral aspects of it.[25] While this is an extremely important insight into the underlying conditions of war and militarism, it needs to be joined with alternative proposals for addressing the "large-scale military conflict." There has been scant attention to this issue in antiwar feminist scholarship. Even if one assumes, as antiwar feminists do, that war is a "presence" in everyday life and not merely a discrete "event" that occasionally "erupts,"[26] it is nonetheless the case that "war" is *more* damaging and harmful, and creates *greater* suffering in a multiplicity of ways, than the absence of war. Pragmatist feminist thinking about the ethics of WMD is attentive to how such differences in consequences differentiate war from "everyday life."

A third significant area of difference between the two types of feminist theories concerns responses to the causes of war. Whereas pragmatist feminists agree with antiwar feminists that wars are *partially* a mutual construction, they also insist that some wars have much more to do with unjust aggression for which opposing sides do not share equal responsibility. Antiwar feminism fails to accept that some wars are not only necessary as a matter of prudence, but also morally justifiable *on feminist grounds*, for example, humanitarian intervention to end the severe oppression of innocent victims.[27]

For a pragmatist feminist, the current state of international affairs unfortunately requires consideration of the circumstances in which the threatened or actual use of such weapons for defensive or deterrent purposes may be morally allowable or even morally necessary. Given these circumstances, pragmatist feminism considers the just war tradition to provide a morally useful source of norms relating to the use of weapons in war.

UTILIZATION

In almost every conceivable circumstance, the use of WMD in a first-strike or offensive deployment is morally illegitimate from the perspective of pragmatist feminism because of its destructiveness of human life and creation of massive amounts of suffering. Under the *jus in bello* principles of just war theory, the principles of proportionality and discrimination make the use of WMD morally illegitimate in almost every conceivable circumstance. The incalculable human suffering generated by the atom bombs dropped on Hiroshima and Nagasaki during World War II, for example, should make the actual use of WMD unthinkable. Pragmatist feminists thus endorse the position of antiwar feminists on this issue as well as that of traditional just war theorists, who argue that any use of WMD would violate the principles of discrimination (noncombatant immunity) and proportionality (between the goal to be achieved and the force necessary to succeed).

Despite this nearly universal rejection of first use, however, pragmatist feminism is critical of the antiwar feminists' opposition to the practice of drawing distinctions among different types of weapons on the grounds that doing so legitimates the use of some weapons as "less bad" than others and disguises the often-hidden costs of the use of "better" weapons, especially the costs for women's lives. Despite these considerations, which complicate any neat categorization between "conventional" weapons and WMD, the very designation and creation of WMD necessarily violate principles of proportionality and discrimination, whereas so-called conventional weapons do not.

Overall, nuclear, biological, and chemical weapons are potentially, and by design, massively more damaging and lethal than conventional weapons.

Among the different categories of WMD, nuclear weapons have thus far been demonstrated to have the most long-lasting effects, given the half-life of their radioactive by-products and capacity to instill genetic defects in unborn generations of humans and other forms of life, and are therefore the most lethal and least legitimate forms of weapons for actual use (as opposed to their deterrent effects, to which I shortly turn). The probability is that the use of WMD will disproportionately escalate suffering and destruction rather than minimize or eliminate it, as well as fail to be discriminating in terms of noncombatants, whereas the use of conventional weapons is far more variable and difficult to assess in advance, and in the absence of specific armed conflicts. The distinction between the two types of weapons makes sense from a pragmatist perspective and should be retained.

DETERRENCE

Antiwar feminists highlight an important consideration often lacking in discussions of the morality of deterrence by emphasizing the unstated costs of the development, deployment, maintenance, and disposal of WMD, including the diversion of funds that otherwise might be available for social welfare programs, the costs of disposing of hazardous wastes, exposure to radiation, and so on. In addition, the effectiveness of nuclear deterrence as an inhibitor of armed aggression is dubious in the post–cold war era, dominated by "internal" armed conflicts that do not directly involve one (nuclear) nation pitted against another, and the growing threat of terrorist tactics such as those used by al-Qa'ida on September 11, 2001. Despite these costs, pragmatist feminist strategy deals with existing actualities, not utopian ideals. Deterrence *has been* "successful," if success can be measured in terms of the lack of the use of nuclear weapons for nearly fifty years.

Looking "pragmatically" at human history – and the scant possibility that nations that have already developed weapons of mass destruction will voluntarily destroy them (all of them, that is) or be deterred from ever using them in the absence of a credible threat that such use would be met by equal or greater force – the possession of WMD for purposes of deterrence may be morally necessary, at least given current geopolitical realities. As military philosopher Malham Wakin suggests:

When we ask whether nuclear deterrence is the only effective way to prevent the use of nuclear weapons in a total war, we must be sure to do so in the context of the actual world situation we now find ourselves in, a situation that includes a very large number of nuclear warheads in the possession of several nations and in at least one of those nations many of those nuclear weapons are aimed at the United States and its NATO allies. In that realistic context is it reasonable to suppose that a nuclear balance is better calculated to deter total war than a nuclear imbalance?[28]

Given the goal of pragmatist feminism to "end oppression," including the domination and control of some nations and peoples by others, and given that the possession and threatened use of WMD have become one of the most effective means by which nations in the world today assert their power, deterrence is morally necessary to help ensure against the oppression of some nations or peoples by others armed with WMD.

However, since the goal of international peace and security can never be fully achieved while nuclear and other WMD exist, whether for defensive, deterrent, or other purposes, pragmatist feminists allow for the interim use of deterrence only in the context of active efforts by nuclear nations to bring about multilateral disarmament, such as that called for by the Nonproliferation Treaty (NPT). Pragmatist feminists thus disagree with the antiwar feminist rejection of any use of nuclear weapons, even for deterrence purposes, arguing for such use as a temporary, interim strategy through the process of mutual disarmament.

Therefore, while pragmatist feminists might agree with antiwar feminists that nuclear weapons never should have been invented or, once invented, never should have been tested or deployed or used as the basis for deterrence, that is not the reality we find ourselves in today. Yes, development and deployment must be factored into the ethical status of deterrence, as antiwar feminists suggest. However, these costs in and of themselves are not too high if viewed from the vantage point of the present, since much of the cost has, in effect, already been spent. The antiwar feminist point about the costs of development and deployment is highly relevant, however, to considering whether to build *additional* WMD for deterrence purposes.

PROLIFERATION

In general, a pragmatist feminist stance on proliferation is in accord with the antiwar feminist position on this issue as articulated by Cohn and Ruddick.[29] Following their distinction between horizontal proliferation (expansion of the number of states possessing nuclear or other WMD), which is the locus of Western concern, and vertical proliferation (expansion of the arsenals of possessor nations), a pragmatist feminist perspective affirms the moral acceptability of denying WMD to nonpossessors (horizontal), but only on the condition that possessor nations also agree to nonproliferation (both vertical and horizontal).

The justification for limiting the proliferation of WMD is because of their potential to create incalculable harm and suffering for both humans and other life forms. The proliferation of WMD in more and more countries risks seriously destabilizing certain regions of the world and increasing the risk that such weapons will be used.[30] In such circumstances, any policy that limits the proliferation of such weapons seems morally desirable, irrespective of differences in particular circumstances. In this post–cold war era of multilateral rather than bipolar politics, both national and international security are better satisfied by a policy of nonproliferation and weapons reductions than they are by proliferation and stockpiling of arms.

It has been suggested that the most effective way to deter nuclear terrorists, for whom rational calculations of the risk of being attacked by nuclear weapons may not be an adequate deterrent, is to "prevent aspiring nations from acquiring nuclear-weapons capability, [and] this involves keeping the sources of nuclear-weapons capability out of the hands of nations without them."[31] National sovereignty and independent satisfaction of national security needs to be deemphasized in the interests of mutual and multilateral security. In this new context, where alternative forms of security are available, the acquisition or development of new WMD can only be presumed to be for immoral purposes.

There remains, however, the issue of fairness to those nations that do not already possess WMD. Antiwar feminists rightly condemn the hypocrisy embedded in the attitudes of moral superiority held by the possessors of nuclear weapons against nonnuclear nations. However, the inequalities resulting from a refusal by the international community to allow an "equal right to annihilate" could be mitigated to a great extent by aggressive enforcement and good-faith implementation of the terms of the NPT discussed below. In addition, developing alliances of nuclear and nonnuclear powers to reduce existing stockpiles of weapons and ensuring no new buildups and establishing agreements that condition the promise of nonnuclear nations to not acquire or develop WMD on promises of further levels of disarmament and guarantees of alternative forms of security by nations that have WMD[32] would even the nuclear playing field to a considerable extent.

In addition, from a pragmatist feminist perspective, some such quid pro quo for an agreement to not acquire or develop WMD by nations that do not yet have them seems morally imperative, given the imbalance of power that exists between the "have" and the "have not" nations, defined not only in terms of WMD, but also with respect to other forms of security and economic well-being. Given pragmatist feminism's larger vision of ending all forms of unjust domination and oppression, the failure by nations with WMD to provide nonnuclear nations with alternative forms of security is grossly unfair and serves to perpetuate the current domination of the third world by the first world, as well as increasing the likelihood of the use of WMD by disaffected "rogue states" or terrorist groups, as witnessed on September 11, 2001, for example. The interest of nonnuclear nations in obtaining WMD is almost certain to diminish once their security, defined broadly, is raised up to the level of nuclear nations.

DISARMAMENT

Since pragmatist feminism is a partialist rather than a universalist approach to ethics, it does not take a categorical stand on the issue of disarmament, such as mandating that disarmament is morally obligatory for all nations in all circumstances to the full extent of their complete stockpiles of either WMD or other weapons. Given the reality of international political relations today, it is highly unlikely that mandatory total disarmament of WMD could be successfully achieved, even if mutually agreed on by most states. However, since pragmatist feminism begins with a strong suspicion of violence and endeavors to find alternative modes of conflict resolution, it thus considers mutual disarmament to be morally the most desirable option. Starting from the current international agreements among a number of nations to disarm, a pragmatist feminist perspective affirms efforts to locate opportunities for encouraging and actualizing mutual disarmament. Active participation by states with the largest WMD arsenals would lend greater credibility to international efforts at reducing overall levels of WMD around the world. A unilateral commitment by the strongest state, the United States, to reduce some of its own stockpiles of WMD might convince other nations to follow suit.

However, contrary to antiwar feminism, pragmatist feminism would oppose any significant or substantial unilateral disarmament (at least radical reduction or complete disarmament) in most cases as destabilizing, potentially suicidal, and contrary to the would-be disarming nation's responsibility to protect its citizens (and perhaps third parties, as well).[33] As Malham Wakin observes, "Ideally, if we wish to remove the threat of a nuclear holocaust entirely, this can only happen if all nuclear weapons in existence are dismantled in parallel and simultaneous fashion. A nuclear freeze as proposed by many will not accomplish this task. A publicly announced 'no first use' policy does not seem likely to bring this about either."[34]

The antiwar feminist view that nonviolent means of resolving conflicts can replace violent ones is not currently a credible alternative, at least with respect to all conflicts. In the short term, in keeping with a pragmatist focus on doing "what works," the retention of some nuclear weapons as a credible threat of retaliation seems necessary for deterrence policy to be effective, at least as an *interim strategy* during the process of mutual disarmament.

CONCRETE OPTIONS

Here, pragmatist feminists are largely in agreement with antiwar feminists that treaties have beneficial but limited uses. On the positive side, there are few if any alternatives that are superior to treaties, with the exception of a negotiated peace among all current or potential future adversaries. Since treaties are designed to limit the development and reduce the spread of

WMD, their implementation (when successful) accrues to everyone's mutual benefit (including women), not only to those included at the negotiating table.

In particular, greater adherence to the Nonproliferation Treaty would achieve several of the goals discussed under "Disarmament" above.[35] The proposal for the creation of a UN nuclear force to help enforce compliance with the NPT and existing or future Security Council resolutions on nonproliferation has promise, but also many problems, including those discussed under the "Proliferation" and "Deterrence" sections above.[36] In addition, tightening the provisions of the Biological Weapons Convention to prohibit explicitly all use as well as acquisition and possession of such weapons and developing more rigorous and comprehensive regulatory mechanisms to monitor potential violations of these prohibitions would forward the goal of eliminating the development or use of biological weapons altogether. Making the use of poisonous weapons a "war crime" in the 1998 Rome Statute of the International Criminal Court is a step in the right direction.

The idea of developing a weapons shield, such as the Strategic Defense Initiative originally promoted by President Reagan and now renewed by President George W. Bush, seems to be a misguided use of vast resources with little assurance of success, either as an effective shield against nuclear attack or as a deterrent to the use of nuclear weapons. Indeed, as some strategists have suggested, the development of such a shield could actually enhance the possibilities of use by WMD by nations protected by the shield, as well as encourage other nations to test the effectiveness of the shield by deploying new weapons.

CONCLUSION

In summary, pragmatist feminism shares many of the views of antiwar feminists regarding the ethics of WMD, especially those concerning the gendered character of both WMD and the discourse that surrounds them. However, there are also significant differences in the two perspectives. These are perhaps most evident in their divergence on the issues of whether war and armed force are ever morally justifiable, whether WMD offers morally legitimate methods of deterrence, and whether unilateral disarmament would be morally legitimate.

In these respects, pragmatist feminism shares more with just war theory than with antiwar feminism and also with realism over pacifism, despite its commitment to the use of nonviolent methods of resolving conflicts whenever possible. Its stance is founded on the belief that it is possible to criticize current policy and practice toward WMD and to advocate for the establishment of nonviolent strategies of conflict resolution, but in ways that do not endanger national and international security, and thus individual women's and others' security and protection from (greater) oppression.

Notes

1. Vincent Colapietro, "Purpose, Power, and Agency," *The Monist* 75:4 (1992): 423–44, at 427.
2. Ibid., 432.
3. Jane Duran suggests that "the cores of the two theories are very similar. They are similar not because any theorist has attempted to make them that way, but . . . because most women are pragmatists. And it is to the experience of women's lived lives that pragmatism and feminism both speak." Jane Duran, "The Intersection of Pragmatism and Feminism," *Hypatia* 8:2 (Spring 1993): 159–71, at 160.
4. Charlene Haddock Seigfried, "Where Are All the Feminist Pragmatists?" *Hypatia* 6:1 (1990): 1–19, at 5.
5. Ibid., 14.
6. See, e.g., Marjorie Miller, "Feminism and Pragmatism: On the Arrival of a 'Ministry of Disturbance; a Regulated Source of Annoyance; a Destroyer of Routine; an Underminer of Complacency,'" *The Monist* 75:4 (1992): 445–57, at 448.
7. bell hooks, "feminism: a transformational politic," in *Talking Back: Thinking Feminist, Thinking Black* (Boston: South End Press, 1989), 19–27.
8. See Colapietro, "Purpose, Power, and Agency," 429–32; Seigfried, "Where Are All the Feminist Pragmatists?" 5. In *Experience and Nature*, Dewey suggests that the value of a philosophy lies in whether it yields conclusions that make ordinary life experiences and problems more significant and clear and our dealings with them more productive. John Dewey, *Experience and Nature* (New York: Dover, 1958), 7.
9. See Duran, "Intersection of Pragmatism and Feminism," 162.
10. Colapietro, "Purpose, Power, and Agency," 429.
11. Thus, both understand truth as contextual and relative to particular interests (what is also known as "standpoint epistemology"). At the same time, both feminists and pragmatists "believe that humanly motivated change is possible, that such change matters, and that philosophy has an important role to play in effecting such change." Phyllis Rooney, "Feminist-Pragmatist Revisionings of Reason, Knowledge, and Philosophy," *Hypatia* 8:2 (Spring 1993): 15–37, at 18.
12. See Colapietro, "Purpose, Power, and Agency," 436.
13. See Cohn and Ruddick in Chapter 21 above, under "Alternative Epistemology."
14. Both pragmatists and feminists are "suspicious of certain forms of theorizing a unitary, ideal, or sovereign Reason and question rigid distinctions and claims to epistemic finality." See Rooney, "Feminist-Pragmatist Revisionings," 21.
15. James, for example, argues that we may, indeed, must, make decisions on the basis of our passions when intellect is unable to supply adequate grounds. See Rooney, "Feminist-Pragmatist Revisionings," 26; Miller, "Feminism and Pragmatism," 448. For example, Rooney observes that "some developments in feminist theory that call for a more critical analysis of the social, political, and cognitive functions of emotion invite comparison with Dewey's views on the significance of feeling and qualitative background in the critical apprehension of situations, the kind of apprehension that propels inquiry and change" (p. 30).

16. See Duran, "Intersection of Pragmatism and Feminism," 160. Thus, both prag-
    matism and feminism have an aversion to foundationalism, the specification of
    principles that are primary, certain, and unassailable, a concern that is central
    to much of mainstream Western philosophy. See Duran, pp. 164–65. Along with
    this, both perspectives suggest that language, including specifically moral lan-
    guage, should not be accepted unreflectively as embodying universal, shared, or
    politically neutral meanings. From these perspectives, language reflects a range
    of meanings, the dominant ones being the (temporary) result of power strug-
    gles. See Chris Weedon, *Feminist Practice and Poststructuralist Theory* (Oxford: Basil
    Blackwell, 1987), 52–53. Consequently, language – including the language used
    to speak about WMD and military responses to terrorist and similar threats –
    needs to be critically interrogated to assess the underlying interests and power
    relations involved.
17. See Miller, "Feminism and Pragmatism" 448; Rooney, "Feminist-Pragmatist
    Revisionings," 17; Margaret Jane Radin, "The Pragmatist and the Feminist,"
    Southern California Law Review 63 (1990): 1699–1726, at 1707; Seigfried, *William
    James' Radical Reconstruction of Philosophy* (Albany: State University of New York
    Press, 1991), 16. Some feminist theorists have explored the potential of pragma-
    tism for feminist theorizing but not, to my knowledge, the specific issues of war
    and conflict resolution. See, e.g., Charlene Haddock Seigfried, "Shared Com-
    munities of Interest: Feminism and Pragmatism," *Hypatia* 8:2 (Spring 1993):
    1–14; Rooney, "Feminist-Pragmatist Revisionings"; Duran, "The Intersection of
    Pragmatism and Feminism," 160; Seigfried, *Pragmatism and Feminism: Reweav-
    ing the Social Fabric* (Chicago: University of Chicago Press, 1996); Colapietro,
    "Purpose, Power, and Agency," 424–25; Seigfried, "Where Are All the Feminist
    Pragmatists?" 4.
18. Colapietro, "Purpose, Power, and Agency," 438; Seigfried, *Pragmatism and
    Feminism*, 8. For example, Peirce replaces the authority of the intuitive judg-
    ments of the *cogito* ("the infallible intuitions of a solitary, disembodied, and
    theoretical consciousness") with the "authority of an ongoing community of
    inquirers" (Colapietro, "Purpose, Power, and Agency," 433). Similarly, James's
    rejection of the style of philosophical argument that seeks to triumph over an op-
    ponent by superior argumentation in favor of a shared understanding as the goal
    is consistent with feminist understandings that women tend to seek "win-win"
    rather than "win-lose" resolutions to conflicts. See Seigfried, *Pragmatism and
    Feminism*, 11.
19. As Seigfried points out, "notably absent from pragmatist analyses are any system-
    atic discussions of sexism or racism." Seigfried, *Pragmatism and Feminism*, 6. She
    notes: "Feminism differs from pragmatism in that it develops women's special
    angles of vision insofar as they critically engage the conditions of women's lives
    with the intent to expose and eliminate oppression and further an alternate,
    woman-centered perspective." Seigfried, "Shared Communities of Interest," 2.
20. Feminist theorists have detailed the myriad ways that militarism and war are
    male-gendered and have had especially horrendous effects on women, who
    are most often the victims rather than the perpetrators of the threat and use
    of militarized violence. See, e.g., Marguerite R. Waller and Jennifer Rycenga,
    eds., *Frontline Feminisms: Women, War, and Resistance* (New York: Garland Press,
    2000); Cynthia Enloe, *Maneuvers: The International Politics of Militarizing Women's*

Lives (Berkeley: University of California Press, 1997); Enloe, *Bananas, Beaches and Bases: Making Feminist Sense of International Politics* (Berkeley: University of California Press, 1989); Enloe, *Does Khaki Become You? The Militarization of Women's Lives* (London: Pluto Press, 1983); Chris Cuomo, "War Is Not Just an Event: Reflections on the Significance of Everyday Violence," *Hypatia* 11:4 (Fall 1996): 30–45.

21. See Cohn and Ruddick, Chapter 21 above, under "Antiwar Feminism."
22. It should be noted that pragmatist feminism agrees with the antiwar feminist opposition to the realist assumptions pervading much just war thinking that the use of armed conflict will be necessary, despite the "last resort" requirement, and its assessments of just war theory's tendencies to abstraction and to universalism (that its template of criteria apply to all armed conflicts), its blindness to the psychological and social costs of war, especially on those not directly involved in the military, and its failure to factor postwar damage into its assessments. The too-easy resort to the use of force when nonviolent alternatives have not been attempted has rightly earned just war theory criticism from feminist thinkers. Such thinking is evident, for example, in Michael Walzer's according of only "prudential" significance to the "last resort" criteria of just war theory. See Michael Walzer, "Perplexed," *New Republic*, January 28, 1991, pp. 13–15, at 14; *Tikkun* editors, "On Just Wars: An Interview with Michael Walzer," *Tikkun* 6:1 (1991): 40–42; Walzer, *Just and Unjust Wars* (New York: Basic Books, 1977), 329–35. In addition, pragmatist feminists endorse antiwar feminist proposals for including women within the conception of "human nature" that underlies thinking about war and armed conflict. Such an expanded notion of what is "human" would serve to soften the realist outlook and make it possible to consider alternatives to WMD more frequently than has been the case under patriarchal, hierarchical, and male-dominated militaristic thinking.
23. Cohn and Ruddick, Chapter 21 above, under "Antiwar Feminism."
24. I recognize that the term "peace" within a feminist analysis encompasses far more than the absence of war but use that term in the more limited way here.
25. For example, Chris Cuomo, a feminist critic of just war thinking, argues that "feminist ethical questions about war are not reducible to wondering how to avoid large-scale military conflict despite human tendencies toward violence. Instead the central questions concern the omnipresence of militarism, the possibilities of making its presence visible, and the potential for resistance to its physical and hegemonic force." Cuomo, "War Is Not Just an Event," 35.
26. See, e.g., ibid., 37.
27. In her essay, "A Woman of Peace," Sara Ruddick suggests that even in the case of "just causes" – "defending one's own or another people against brutal violence or putting a stop to civil massacre" – where "it *appears* to be impossible to stop aggression non-violently . . . and that certain particular military measures are likely to be effective, one possible, even characteristic, response of the woman of peace . . . is to refuse to enter into discussions of the just use of military force. A woman of peace would not enter into cost benefit analyses of particular military actions. . . . Nor would the woman of peace enter into diplomatic questions [regarding particular conflicts]. . . . Just so, a woman of peace might remain outside the rhetoric of just war theory." Ruddick, "Woman of Peace: A Feminist Construction," *Synthesis Philosophica* 23:1 (1997): 265–82,

at 278. The problem with this stance, from a pragmatist feminist perspective, is that it opts out of the discussion just at the point when the moral dilemma becomes most difficult. It is reminiscent of the "beautiful soul" and "women as protected" images discussed by Jean Bethke Elshtain and Judith Stiehm, images of women evading responsibility for armed conflicts by retreating behind the cloak of innocence and moral superiority. See Judith Stiehm, *Arms and the Enlisted Woman* (Philadelphia: Temple University Press, 1989), 233; Jean Bethke Elshtain, *Women and War* (New York: Basic Books, 1987), 243–44. Although antiwar feminism's observation that wars have historically been and continue to be largely men's affairs, in which women have little to gain and much to lose, from a pragmatist feminist perspective, the reality of being on the cusp of war necessitates women's involvement for their own protection as well as on behalf of innocent others.

28. Malham Wakin, *Integrity First: Reflections of a Military Philosopher* (Lanham, Md.: Lexington Books, 2000), 144.

29. Cohn and Ruddick, Chapter 21 above, under "Proliferation."

30. See Richard Regan, *Just War: Principles and Cases* (Washington, D.C.: Catholic University of America Press, 1996), 111.

31. See ibid., 118.

32. As Regan suggests, "It would be far less dangerous and more practical to try to induce minor nuclear powers to relinquish their nuclear-weapons capability voluntarily in return for adequate security guarantees that would make possession of those weapons unnecessary." Ibid., 116.

33. As Wakin points out: "Unilateral freeze or dismantling would make our nation highly vulnerable to attack or to nuclear blackmail by other nuclear powers, and would be an abdication of the moral obligation our public officials have to provide for our defense against potential external enemies." Wakin, *Integrity First*, 144.

34. Ibid.

35. The five main nuclear powers have agreed to eliminate their nuclear arsenals under article VI of the NPT, but this legal duty does not have an enforceable timetable, as it should. And many of the 182 nonnuclear states have committed themselves to refrain from developing nuclear weapons because of the commitment of the nuclear states to negotiate disarmament.

36. Regan proposes that such a force could provide security to nonnuclear nations and help to persuade nuclear ones to relinquish their weapons. Regan, *Just War: Principles and Cases*, 11–17.

23

Pacifism and Weapons of Mass Destruction

Robert L. Holmes

Pacifism is opposition to war. As such, it is distinguished from nonviolence, since one might oppose war but think that violence is sometimes permissible. Nonetheless, earliest pacifism usually derives from explicit or implicit commitments to nonviolence. This is true of early Christianity,[1] Buddhism, Jainism, Daoism, and the Hinduism espoused by Gandhi in his nonviolentist interpretation of the *Bhagavad Gita.* An exception is Mohism in ancient China, which is expressly pacifistic but does not espouse nonviolence.

Pacifism may be personal, principled, or pragmatic, depending on how it is grounded.

1. Personal pacifism is the refusal to participate in war as a personal commitment not considered binding on others.[2]
2. Principled pacifism is opposition to war on religious, spiritual, and/or moral grounds considered valid for others as well.[3]
3. Pragmatic pacifism is opposition to war on practical grounds, such as that it is an ineffective and inefficient way to pursue one's objectives.[4]

Personal pacifists might agree with pragmatic pacifists that war is impractical and, like principled pacifists, take their renunciation of war to have a moral or religious character. It is just that they do not insist that others are required to make that same commitment (some conscientious objectors, for example, are willing to serve in the military so long as they are not expected to carry or use weapons). Personal commitment, rather than general beliefs about religion, morality, or practicality, is central to their pacifism. Principled pacifists, for their part, can also agree that war is ineffective. That is, they can secondarily be pragmatic pacifists as well. But that is not their main reason for being pacifists. Their main reason is their belief that war is wrong for everyone (moral pacifism) and/or contrary to certain religious or spiritual commitments that everyone should have (religious pacifism). And pragmatic pacifists can agree that war is wrong or contrary to various religious or spiritual outlooks. That is, they can secondarily be principled pacifists. But their main reason for being pacifists is their conviction that war is impractical. Whereas principled pacifists are likely to think of war as wrong or immoral, pragmatic pacifists are likely to think of it as stupid or wasteful. Those who support war, either because they think it is morally or religiously justified or because they believe it is practical, I call, following Duane Cady, "warists."[5]

Because of limitations of space, in what follows I deal primarily with principled pacifism of a moral and secular sort.[6] I do not discuss personal, religious, or pragmatic pacifism.

SOURCES AND PRINCIPLES

Regarding general norms that govern the use of weapons in the conduct of war, and the sources from which those norms derive, I shall take "general norms" to refer to moral norms. To ask whether there are norms governing the use of weapons in war would seem to presume that war can justifiably be conducted and the only question is how and by what means. This begs the central question of concern to pacifists, who deny that war is justified in the first place. On their view, no way of conducting war is permissible. That means that there are no weapons whose use is proper in the conduct of war. Whatever norms render war impermissible render the use of any weapons in war impermissible as well.

To take seriously the question of whether it is legitimate to use weapons of mass destruction in warfare typically presupposes that *some* weapons may justifiably be used. To draw a line between supposedly legitimate and illegitimate uses of weapons legitimizes those on one side of the line while delegitimizing those on the other. This, in turn, legitimizes war. That you may permissibly use, say, guns, tanks, and planes in war would normally imply that the activity in which you are engaged is permissible. For that reason this assumption flies in the face of the pacifist enterprise.

Nuclear pacifists, of course, can take such a question seriously.[7] They have no objection to war per se. Their objection is only to nuclear war. But as this position has little claim to being called genuinely pacifistic, I do not discuss it further in this section. It is relevant, however, to the issues in the next section.

What I call "just war pacifism" (JWP) deserves more serious attention, however. The just war theory (JWT) sets forth moral conditions governing both the recourse to war (*jus ad bellum*) and the conduct of war (*jus in bello*). JWT and pacifism are usually contrasted. But they are not necessarily incompatible. Although just war theorists are virtually all warists, they could be pacifists. They would be pacifists if they believed that the criteria that would render a war just are never in fact met.[8] Odd though it may seem, this is perfectly possible. Nothing in the criteria themselves guarantees that they are met. Since they are obviously sometimes not met (otherwise, all wars would be just), it is possible that they are never met. If that should be true, then while some possible wars would be just, no actual wars would be. Just wars would be a little like unicorns: perfectly conceivable but in fact nonexistent. Such a view would be a form of principled pacifism, since it would oppose war on moral grounds. But the relevant moral grounds would be those of the JWT. Of course, if you've decided in advance that some wars are justified, you can always tailor your account of the JWT to accommodate those wars. But then you haven't used JWT to determine the justice of those wars. You've antecedently appealed to other criteria.

So understood, JWP would allow that some possible wars are permissible, namely, those that satisfy the conditions of JWT. But it would hold that no actual wars in fact satisfy those conditions. Hence JWP implicitly recognizes legitimate and illegitimate uses of weapons.

Now anyone who recognizes moral constraints on the conduct of war will distinguish legitimate from illegitimate uses of weapons. If, for example, it is wrong intentionally to kill civilians, then it is wrong whether you use nuclear weapons or machetes. It is not the weapons that are important but their use (though the character of some weapons makes it difficult to confine them to their intended use). If, however, there are legitimate and illegitimate *weapons* as well as legitimate and illegitimate *uses* of weapons, then illegitimate weapons will be prohibited, whatever their use. We discuss in connection with the next topic whether it is plausible to distinguish legitimate and illegitimate weapons themselves.

Accordingly, JWP allows that there are, in principle, legitimate uses of weapons in war. But (since, in JWP's view, there are no just wars) there are no legitimate uses of weapons in practice. If there were a just war, the just war pacifist will say, then its conduct – hence its use of weapons – would be governed by the principles of the JWT, notably discrimination (prohibiting the targeting of civilians and/or innocents) and proportionality (requiring a proper proportion between the resultant good and bad of operations). So, nuclear pacifists maintain a clear distinction between legitimate and illegitimate weapons (conventional weapons being legitimate, nuclear weapons not). But just war pacifists maintain that, whether or not there's a distinction between legitimate and illegitimate *weapons*, there's in theory a distinction between the legitimate and illegitimate *uses* of weapons – even if no actual wars warrant the legitimate uses.

Some just war theorists might object to the pacifist's denial that there are permissible and impermissible ways to conduct war. On that basis they might then object to the pacifist's denial that there are permissible and impermissible uses of weapons in war. Let us explain.

Some hold that the criteria for the recourse to war are logically independent of the criteria governing the conduct of war.[9] That is, they would say that you can judge whether it's permissible to go to war independently of any judgments about what it is permissible to do when you are in a war, and vice versa. Let's call this the Independence Thesis. If the Independence Thesis should be true, you could assess the justice of the conduct of war independently of whether the war was justly entered into. Even if no actual wars were permissible (as JWP concedes), it would still make sense to inquire about the morality of the conduct of war. If so, it would make sense to inquire about the legitimacy of certain uses of weapons. More importantly, it would make sense to do this in the actual wars (however unjust) waged in the "real" world, not merely in those hypothetical wars that might conceivably be just in theory. If that were the case – according to this reasoning – pacifists of any stripe (and not merely just war pacifists) should take seriously the ethical issues involved in distinguishing legitimate and illegitimate uses of weapons.

But *jus ad bellum* criteria can't plausibly be thought to be logically independent of *jus in bello* criteria. Let us see why. I take the Independence Thesis to mean (1) that no judgment about the morality of going to war entails any judgment about what is permissible in the conduct of war and (2) that no judgment about what is permissible in the conduct of war entails any judgment about the morality of going to war. To show that the Independence Thesis is false, it suffices to show that either (1) or (2) is false.

What does it mean (according to JWT) to say that one is morally justified in going to war? Given that war is the systematic use of violence to cause death and destruction in the pursuit of your ends, it means, at the minimum, that you're justified in using such violence in pursuit of your objectives (such as to right the wrong providing you with a just cause). But to do this is to conduct war. It is to engage in the killing and destruction constitutive of war. That you are justified in doing this entails that you are justified in waging war. It does not mean, however, that you may then do whatever you want. The criteria of *jus ad bellum* also include, for example, right intention (requiring that you intend only the good when both good and bad will result from an act) and proportionality. To be plausible these must hold not only at the moment you decide to go to war but throughout the waging of war as well. There must be some permissible means of conducting a war to give substance to *jus ad bellum*. Otherwise, to say that you are justified in going to war would be vacuous. It would be like saying that you are justified in playing chess but not in moving the pieces, or in playing golf but not in hitting the ball. Given that you can be justified in going to war only if you are justified in waging war, this means that the judgment that you are morally justified in going to war entails the judgment that you are justified in the conduct involved in implementing that judgment. If so, then (1) is false. Therefore, the Independence Thesis is false. If the Independence Thesis is false, then pacifists (excluding nuclear pacifists) will deny that there are any morally permissible ways to conduct war. Hence they can consistently deny that there are any general norms the following of which render the conduct of war permissible.

What pacifists can acknowledge, however, is that although no way of conducting war is permissible, some ways are worse than others. There may be better and worse ways of carrying on any wrongful activity. Robbery is wrong, for example. But it's worse to rob and beat than merely to rob. Or to rape and murder than merely to rape. So, given the pacifist's contention that war is wrong, any manner of conducting a war will be bad. But some ways (e.g., using tanks and planes rather than sticks and stones) will be worse than others.

UTILIZATION

I use a gun if I threaten you with it, throw it at you, or hit you over the head with it. I don't need to fire the gun. Similarly, nuclear weapons are used when deployed with a threat to retaliate with them.[10] Whether it is ever legitimate to use nuclear and other WMD in this sense is dealt with in the next section. I confine my concern here to the detonation of such weapons. Moreover, my concern is not with their detonation, say, on the moon, as was once reportedly proposed by physicist Edward Teller, or to dig canals, or even to demonstrate our destructive power, as was considered prior to Hiroshima. My concern is with their use to cause death and destruction in warfare.

In this sense of the question, the pacifist answer is "no." There are no circumstances under which it is morally permissible to use such weapons. This applies to chemical and biological weapons as well.

Should such weapons be treated differently from unusually destructive conventional weapons? The nuclear pacifist will say they should; that while it is permissible to use conventional weapons, it is impermissible to use nuclear weapons. In this the nuclear pacifist and some warists are in agreement. Some warists maintain that it is permissible to use nuclear weapons for deterrence (call this their use$_1$) but illegitimate to use them in the actual waging of war (call this their use$_2$)

A moral pacifist will say, however, that these weapons should not be treated differently from conventional weapons. If it is wrong to inflict death and destruction on other human beings in pursuit of your objectives, it is just as wrong whether you use conventional weapons or nuclear weapons. This does not mean that nuclear weapons are not so bad after all. It means rather that, morally speaking, conventional weapons are just as bad.

Why draw the line at nuclear weapons? That they are more destructive is an odd reason. The history of weaponry has been a relentless search for ever more destructive weapons. That is part of the logic of war. And even WMD cause mass destruction only when used on a large scale. On a limited scale they cause relatively little destruction compared with the widespread use of conventional weapons. The allied bombing of German cities in World War II, for example, caused more destruction than the atomic bombings of Hiroshima and Nagasaki combined. In a few hours a fleet of B-52s laden with conventional bombs can cause as much destruction as a nuclear bomb. Some of the motivation to limit or prohibit the use of WMD probably owes to squeamishness. Just as advocates of the death penalty once sought more "humane" ways to kill people to counteract the revulsion some had to the methods at hand (too short a rope, and the condemned strangled slowly; too long a rope, and he might be decapitated). Similarly, it may be that keeping the killing of warfare within bounds helps to ease people's minds about war. Drawing a line between conventional weapons and nuclear weapons does that. Labeling weapons "conventional" almost sanctifies them. Yes, they kill people. But look how much worse WMD are. Beyond squeamishness, some of the motivation behind trying to prohibit the use of nuclear weapons probably is to preserve war itself. The use of WMD on a massive scale would be a threat to the very institution of war. It would thrust humankind into a realm for which the previous centuries of warfare had not prepared it. The training, strategy, discipline, customs, honors, pride, parades, and patriotism – all of those elements that warists believe make soldiering an honorable profession – would be out the window. Such Absolute Violence would transcend even Clausewitz's Absolute War.[11] To preserve the institution of war you should avoid this at all costs.

DETERRENCE

The development or deployment of nuclear weapons for the sake of deterrence is not a licit moral option for pacifism. Nor is the development and deployment of chemical and biological weapons. Or, for that matter, the development and deployment of conventional weapons.

Paradoxically, however, if nuclear deterrence actually prevented war, some pacifists might endorse it. After all, if you oppose war, and nuclear deterrence prevents it, why not embrace deterrence? Just as a just war theorist might back into pacifism by being convinced that the just war criteria are never met, so a pacifist might back into accepting nuclear deterrence by being convinced that it prevents war. We might call such a sheep in wolf's clothing a pacifistic MADvocate (MAD as the acronym for mutual assured destruction).[12] Just war pacifists and pacifistic MADvocates could then join hands in supporting a powerful military. However, as there are probably no people who represent themselves as pacifists – other than, perhaps, the late Richard Nixon[13] – who support either nuclear or conventional deterrence as a solution to the problem of war, I consider this position largely theoretical.

Back to development and deployment. The development of nuclear weapons is not of itself either a use_1 or a use_2 of them in the senses identified in the preceding section. Development might nonetheless be thought to suffice for deterrence. It might be thought to suffice for so-called existential deterrence to develop nuclear weapons and store them in warehouses. Adversaries would then know you had them readily available if needed. Overt deterrence, on the other hand, requires actually threatening to use$_2$ them if an adversary misbehaves. To be effective such threats must be credible. And to be credible (it is widely assumed) there must be an intention to carry them out. If there is such an intention, logic would call for actually deploying the weapons and unequivocally threatening to use$_2$ them. For deterrence to work, the combination of development, deployment, and express threat make sense. Development alone would not maximize the chances of deterrence. So let us confine our attention to the development and deployment of nuclear weapons.

Let us begin with that wolf in sheep's clothing, the nuclear pacifist. He is not opposed to sometimes causing death and destruction, even on a large scale (say, that of World War II). He simply opposes using nuclear weapons to that end – presumably because with them the death and destruction might get out of hand. So it makes sense that he would oppose the use$_2$ of nuclear weapons. But why their use$_1$? If deterrence works (conventional wisdom would have it), you will never have to use$_2$ such weapons. So why oppose deployment?

One reason, of course, is that deterrence might fail. Everyone knows that. But not everyone agrees on what to do if that should happen. Some nuclear pacifists might shed their sheep's clothing at this point and say that you then bite the bullet and launch away. But others may demur. They will say that even if deterrence fails it is still wrong to use$_2$ nuclear weapons. Let us call these people No Way Nuclear Pacifists (NWNP). NWNP face a challenge their unadorned compatriots do not. They have to confront the so-called paradoxes of nuclear deterrence. How, they must explain, can it be moral (or rational) to threaten mass destruction but immoral (or irrational) to carry out that threat – particularly if a credible threat presumes an intention to carry it out? This question must be confronted by NWNP as well as by warist supporters of deterrence. Without a satisfactory answer to it, the coherence and rationality – not to mention the morality – of the theory of deterrence itself is cast in doubt.

While we do not have space to examine all of the complexities of this issue, I propose one possible pacifist critique of a common way of thinking about it. This is set forth by philosopher David Lewis, in defending the rationality (and morality) of committing oneself to irrational (and immoral) behavior. He says:

I claim that it may be "rational to commit oneself to irrational behavior" (and also that it may be good to commit oneself to evil behavior). . . . I accept [deterrent] . . . policies as right, I reject the actions they (conditionally) require as wrong. My opposed judgments are consistent because I make them about different things. To form an intention today is one thing. To retaliate tomorrow is something else. If we have a genuine case of paradoxical deterrence, the first is right and the second is wrong.[14]

The thinking behind such reasoning is that to form an intention is one act, to carry out that intention another. And if the first act has as its consequence that the second act does not occur, then it is justified, even though the latter act, *were* it to occur, would be unjustified. In other words, the reasoning is basically consequentialist.

There are several problems with this reasoning, however. First, we don't perform acts of forming intentions. If we did, those acts would themselves have to have intentions, and the acts of forming those intentions would have to have intentions, and so on ad infinitum.[15]

Second, it is misleading to speak, as the above passage seems to assume we should, of the intention to retaliate as a "conditional" intention. All intentions are conditional. They consist of willingness to do something under some set of circumstances, as when you intend to thank someone if you see her or to stop at the grocery store on your way home. They are conditional on those circumstances obtaining (seeing the person or traveling home). The nuclear intention is no different. You intend to retaliate if attacked. True, the conditions under which you would do the act in the nuclear case are ones you hope will not ever be actualized; indeed, the whole point of your threatening to retaliate is to try to ensure that they will not be. But that does not make the intention itself different in kind from others. Nor does the hoped-for causal contribution to the nonoccurrence of the undesired act distinguish the intention from many others. "Do that again and I'll tell Mom," one kid says to another, hoping that the threat will ensure that the other does not do whatever it is again and that he therefore will not have to tell his mom, which he might prefer not to do.

Third, to intend to do something, all things being equal, *is to do it* in the appropriate circumstances. There is, in other words, a necessary connection between intending and doing what you intend. You cannot be said to intend to do something if now is the time to do it and you know it is the time to do it and are able but do not do it. You can, of course, change your mind, forget, or fall and break your leg. But in the first case you then cease intending, in the second you are unaware that this is the time, and in the third you are no longer able. It is logically disconnecting what one intends to do from the doing of it that enables some analysts to maintain the fiction that you can justifiably intend to do the unjustifiable. What you intend to do and your intending to do it are inseparable parts of a psycho-physical complex that does not admit of different moral (or rational) assessments of its parts.

If correct, this means that NWNP do not have an adequate explanation of how it can be moral to threaten massive nuclear retaliation if attacked and yet utterly immoral to actually carry out that threat. Nor do MADvocates in general have an explanation of how MAD can be a rationally coherent policy.

That a satisfactory resolution of the paradox is impossible can, I believe, be shown by means of the following argument. It means to establish that it is irrational to threaten credibly to do the irrational. Let us represent two nations as US and THEM.

1. We threaten credibly to attack THEM if they attack US.
2. To threaten credibly to retaliate if attacked is to intend to retaliate if attacked.
3. Therefore we intend to attack THEM if they attack US.
4. To intend to do something is *to do* it in the appropriate circumstances.
5. Therefore to intend to retaliate against THEM if they attack US is to retaliate against THEM if they attack US.
6. We know (by hypothesis) that it would be irrational to attack THEM if they attack US.
7. Therefore we intend knowingly to do what is irrational if they attack US.
8. To intend knowingly to do what is irrational is irrational.
9. Therefore, to threaten credibly to attack THEM if they attack US is irrational.

Since we can construct a parallel argument substituting "immoral" for "irrational," we may conclude that if it is irrational and/or immoral to launch a massive retaliation in response to a nuclear attack, it is irrational and/or immoral to threaten to do so and to intend to carry out that threat.

PROLIFERATION

The pacifist denies that it is proper for others to acquire WMD just because some have them, whether they acquire them for defensive and deterrent purposes or not. At the same time, he maintains that nations possessing, say, nuclear weapons, cannot consistently deny to nonnuclear nations the right to develop them. That is, the pacifist opposes the proliferation of WMD but contends that it is at best inconsistent, and at worst hypocritical, for nuclear nations to deny them to others. Again, I focus on nuclear weapons.

First with regard to consistency. If the reason that nuclear nations want to deny nuclear weapons to nonnuclear nations is purely self-interest, then there is no inconsistency in their seeking to prevent others from acquiring them. They are simply seeking to maximize their power and advantage over others. But if their reason is intended to be moral – for example, if it is grounded in a claim that they have a right to such weapons but others do not – then their position looks inconsistent. If nuclear weapons provided security, and if the universal possession of them ensured peace, then in principle every nation should have them. Otherwise, some nations would be left vulnerable and the opportunity for peace would be missed. By such reasoning, rather than deplore the nuclearization of India and Pakistan, for example, we should applaud it. Rather than deny Iraq a nuclear capacity, we should encourage it. By such reasoning, nuclear parity between Israel and Iraq would help to bring peace to the Middle East. No one in his right mind believes that, of course. For all of the high-sounding rhetoric about nuclear deterrence, nations want to have nuclear weapons themselves but deny them to others. Why? Because they – the good nations (GNs) – can be trusted with them, and others – the bad nations (BNs) – cannot? If that were true, it would constitute an admission that deterrence cannot be counted on. If BNs will go ahead and use them in the face of threatened retaliation by GNs, then the system does not work. And if the system is not meant to deter BNs – those "rogue" states that cannot be counted on to act civilly – whom is it meant to deter? If nuclear weapons are supposed to deter GNs who would not use them anyway, they are superfluous. You cannot deter someone who would not otherwise do what you seek to deter him from doing. On the other hand, if nuclear weapons are meant to deter conventional military action as well as nuclear attack, then in principle GNs might develop them to deter BNs from working their mischief through nonnuclear violence. By remaining armed to the teeth, GNs could maintain order by deterring BNs from conventional violence. There would then be a rationale for preventing nuclear proliferation.

The problem is that there is little evidence that nuclear weapons deter conventional violence and mounting evidence that it does not. If nonnuclear nations (NNNs) were obliging enough to concentrate their forces in large numbers – perhaps wearing red coats as well – it would work like a charm. Any nuclear nation (NN) could then dispatch any NNN in a military confrontation. But NNNs do not fight this way. Instead of standing up and fighting like men, they engage in guerrilla warfare or, worse yet, terrorism. And against these, nuclear weapons are useless. Even if NNNs were deterred from engaging in conventional war against NNs, they are documentably not deterred from confronting nuclear powers with other forms of violence: Witness China against the United States in Korea, North Vietnam against the United States in Vietnam, Argentina against Great Britain in the Falklands, Iraq against the United States in Kuwait. And if we expand our concern to include peoples, groups, or even individuals confronting nuclear powers, we see that the Mujahideen in Afghanistan were not deterred by the USSR, the Chechens by Russia, the IRA by Great Britain, the Palestinians by Israel, or Usama bin Ladin and even Timothy McVeigh by the United States.

Notice that we have two distinctions operating here: that between NNs and NNNs and that between GNs and BNs. It should not be thought that they align neatly, that is, that all NNs are GNs and all NNNs are BNs. They are not, of course. Sweden, Denmark, Costa Rica, and Canada are all NNNs but can scarcely be called BNs. Who the BNs are depends on whom you ask. India will cite Pakistan, Pakistan India. The United States will cite Iran, North Korea, and Syria; and Iran, North Korea, and Syria will cite the United States. Israel will cite practically all of the Arab states, and practically all of the Arab states will cite Israel. GNs and BNs do not come with labels attached to them. Who they are is a matter of judgment. Such judgment is colored by the bias and self-interest of governments. Given that it is pointless for GNs to develop nuclear weapons for use against other GNs, then nuclear weapons can reasonably be for use only against BNs. This means that the system of deterrence can be expected to work properly only if accompanied by an objective determination of who the BNs are. The premises of nuclear deterrence would seem to point further to the conclusion that GNs who are not NNs ought to be encouraged to become NNs. Their doing so would only strengthen the wall of deterrence against BNs. Some think that Germany should have nuclear weapons, and it is suspected that Japan is poised to develop them speedily if need be.

Suppose, however, that all of the above is mistaken. Suppose that nuclear weapons deterred both nuclear attack and lower levels of violence. By what right would NNs deny to NNNs the very means they proclaim necessary for their own security? If (again, contrary to fact) nuclear weapons deterred both nuclear and nonnuclear violence, and if it were known that they do, the world could only be safer, *ceteris paribus*, if all nations possessed such weapons.

In sum, if NNs were all GNs, and if the point of possessing nuclear weapons were to deter a nuclear attack, then such weapons would be pointless if deployed against other NNs. Those states, by hypothesis, would not need to be deterred, since they would have no inclination to attack other GNs. If, on the other hand, they are meant to deter BNs from nuclear attack, then they cannot, logically, do that, since, by hypothesis, BNs do not have such weapons in the first place. Paradoxically, the only way deterrence could work against them is if they were allowed to have such weapons. If, on the other hand, the possession of nuclear weapons is meant to deter BNs from using other forms of violence in the world, then the evidence is that they do not do that.

For all of this, pacifists deny that it is proper for other nations to develop nuclear weapons just because some possess them. There are three main reasons for this.

The first requires that we recognize a third distinction, between rational nations (RNs) and irrational nations (IRNs). Just as we cannot simply assume that all and only NNs are GNs, so we cannot assume that all and only NNs are RNs. A nation might be bent on evil in the world and yet be fully rational (at least in the limited sense of choosing necessary means to its ends). If so, then one should expect that it would be deterred by nuclear weapons as much as GNs that are rational. If such a nation were not rational, then there is little reason to believe that it would be deterred from using its nuclear weapons even at the cost of inviting retaliation. At the same time, nothing in the nature of a GN dictates that it needs to be an RN, or that if it is, it will remain so or even try to appear so.[16] To the extent that the distinction between RNs and IRNs cross-cuts the distinction between GNs and BNs, one can have little confidence that either GNs or BNs will forever, or even for the foreseeable future, use nuclear weapons wisely. Accordingly, one can have little confidence that NNs will indefinitely use such weapons rationally and that NNNs would do so if they came to possess them. And without that assumption, one cannot assume that nuclear proliferation is justified.

Second, the possession and deployment of nuclear weapons comes at a cost: the risk of accidentally triggering a nuclear war. Pacifists and warists agree that it is important to minimize that risk. The more nations possess nuclear weapons, the higher the probability that some of them will be accidentally detonated, whether through human, mechanical, or electronic error. Where the pacifist and many warists differ, however, is over the latter's contention that the NNs should be allowed to keep their weapons. Pacifists contend that if the aim is to avoid accidental nuclear war, the only foolproof way to accomplish that is by nuclear disarmament. It is unconvincing for warists to argue that *their* countries' security needs require running that risk whereas other countries' security needs do not. If other nations run a greater risk of accident because they do not have the sophisticated technology of the NNs, that could be remedied by providing NNNs with that technology or facilitating its development. If – contrary to the pacifist's contentions – nuclear weapons made the world safer, then means should be found to facilitate their development worldwide.

Third, the pacifist believes that the kind of world that would be created by nuclear proliferation would degrade the quality of life of all persons to such an extent as to make it undesirable from that standpoint alone. Nuclear weapons are meant to instill fear. This is in keeping with the philosophical outlook of Hobbes, swallowed practically whole by American academics, that sees fear as central to the foundation of the state and a psychological egoism operating throughout all of human affairs. Combined with the conviction that the way to get along in the world is to manipulate fear (through government domestically and the military internationally), these two tenets, so at variance with much of Eastern thought, dominate Western and particularly U.S. thought on matters of war and peace. The idea of a nuclear "balance of terror" captures this openly. Nuclear deterrence is a form of interstate terrorism, distinguished from run-of-the-mill terrorism by the fact that it tries to achieve its objectives by threatening death and destruction rather than by actually inflicting it. Neither shows much regard for innocent life. It is the intention to instill fear that makes a policy terroristic, not the means by which that fear is instilled. Pacifists hold that meaningful and enduring peace cannot be founded on terror. If violence begets violence, as Gandhi and King maintained, one reason it does so is because it causes fear. Fear generates anger and hatred, and these – given the right conditions – are easily transmuted into violence. It is arguable that most of the evil in the world is done ultimately from fear – where fear broadly encompasses everything from insecurity, mistrust, and suspicion to outright terror. If this is correct, then in addition to overcoming fear in yourself or in your nation, priority must be given to framing policies toward others that dispel fear in them – fear, in the case of the United States, of our military power as well as, in their eyes, of a cultural imperialism that threatens ruination of their cultures. For the pacifist, neither nuclear weapons nor conventional weapons can ensure peace. Neither can stem the continuing use of violence in the world that obstructs the attainment of peace. Only nonviolence can do that, including nonviolent means of national defense.

For these reasons, pacifists oppose the proliferation of nuclear weapons at the same time that they condemn the hypocrisy of NNs in arrogating to themselves the exclusive right to the possession of such weapons.

DISARMAMENT

Virtually all pacifists, possibly excepting nuclear pacifists, view WMD disarmament as morally imperative. Most hold the same with regard to universal and unilateral disarmament.

Nuclear pacifists, if still wedded to the thinking behind the moral paradox of nuclear deterrence, might believe that retention and deployment of nuclear weapons serves a deterrent function. If the argument in the section on deterrence is correct, that thinking is unpersuasive. But at least one can see how a belief in deterrence might be viewed as a possible component of nuclear pacifism.

For the moral pacifist, however, the commitment to WMD disarmament is unequivocal. If you are opposed to the use of WMD under any circumstances (either for deterrence or war fighting), then there is no reason not to get rid of them. That much is clear for the pacifist. But pacifists, for whom the problem is war itself, do not want to legitimize *any* weapons, conventional or nuclear. And as we saw in the first section, to draw a line between legitimate and illegitimate weapons legitimizes some weapons at the same time it delegitimizes others. This makes the pacifist's situation a little like that of a vegetarian. Confronted with the option of seeing farm animals treated humanely or inhumanely, vegetarians will, of course, prefer that they be treated humanely. But in the end they do not want to see them eaten, regardless of how they have been treated. And death penalty opponents will, of course, favor eliminating racial, ethnic, and class injustices from the criminal justice system. But they oppose the judicial killing of people whether or not they have been treated fairly. So the pacifist will be reluctant to attach great importance to WMD disarmament if that is taken to imply that conventional armament is permissible.

Weapons represent a continuum, from sticks, stones, and clubs, at one end, through knives, spears, bows and arrows, crossbows, catapults, swords, firearms, artillery, machine guns, tanks, planes, land mines, battleships, cruise missiles, and chemical, biological, and nuclear weapons at the other. It is unclear why a line should be drawn at the very end of this continuum, delegitimizing WMD but legitimizing everything that goes before. The point that WMD (by which I henceforth mean nuclear weapons) are more destructive than others is obviously correct. But to conclude from this that WMD disarmament would result in less death and destruction in the world is a non sequitur. Conventional weapons toward the WMD end of the spectrum are of such enormous destructive potential that they can inflict death and destruction on a massive scale themselves; with sustained use, they can do so on a scale comparable to all but the most wanton uses of WMD. The point that WMD tend to be indiscriminate (not distinguishing between combatants and noncombatants and/or innocents and noninnocents) is also obviously correct. If you do not intend to kill civilians/innocents, it will obviously be more difficult to avoid doing so the more destructive the weapons you are using. But this is true not only of the distinction between nuclear and conventional weapons; it is true also of the distinction between bombs and bullets or between bullets and bows and arrows. A conventional bomb (however "smart") dropped from 12,000 feet cannot by itself discriminate between combatants and noncombatants, much less between innocent and noninnocent persons. Nor can a 2,000 pound shell fired from the sixteen-inch guns of a battleship ten miles away, or a land mine planted ten years before. Even without an intention to kill civilians and innocents, an all-out nuclear war between heavily armed nuclear powers would almost certainly kill more of them than would an all-out conventional war. But that near-certainty is no greater than the near-certainty that an all-out conventional war between heavily armed military powers would kill more civilians and innocents than an all-out war with sticks and stones. If the governing concern is not to kill innocents or to minimize the total loss of life, the line between conventional and nuclear weapons, while important, is of no greater importance than any other number of lines one could draw in the weapons continuum.

Moreover, insofar as WMD disarmament alone would tacitly enhance the sense of moral legitimacy in the use of conventional weapons, it might be that such disarmament would actually increase rather than decrease the total amount of death and destruction through war. It might even increase the number of innocents or civilians killed. WMD, of course, could in the worst case destroy civilization, in the very worst case – unlikely but possible – destroy all human life. But if there is a moral obligation to ensure the survival of humankind, that obligation is not met more fully by WMD disarmament alone than by WMD disarmament combined with conventional disarmament, as the pacifist urges. In fact, to whatever extent this consideration weighs in the scales, it weighs equally at any place one draws the line along the continuum. Whatever benefit accrues to eliminating WMD accrues to eliminating other weapons as well. So if one draws the line at swords and spears, the gain is all the lives saved through eliminating WMD plus all those saved by eliminating guns, tanks, planes, and so on as well. Followed to its logical conclusion, the very reasoning that argues for WMD disarmament argues for conventional as well as WMD disarmament.[17]

Warists will bridle at this. Some things are worth fighting for, they say. Some things are worth killing for – even killing tens of millions, as in World War II. It is just that they do not want to kill hundreds of millions, as in a nuclear war. But why? Perhaps there are reasons, but the burden is on the warist to produce them and show why it is permissible to kill tens of millions but not to kill hundreds of millions. What is the moral calculus here? As we have seen, it cannot plausibly be held to lie in the fact that you inevitably kill innocent people with WMD but not with conventional weapons. The twentieth century's wars have increasingly killed larger and larger percentages of civilians. War inevitably kills innocent persons. If *that* is what you want to avoid, you will not wage war. If, however, there are a certain number of innocents that it is permissible to kill, then we need to know what that number is and see an argument to that conclusion as well as to the conclusion that it is permissible to kill so many millions but not so many millions more than that. Absent such arguments, there is no particularly good reason to support WMD disarmament rather than complete disarmament.

Finally, we need to remember that pacifists not only oppose war, they also support the promotion of conditions for a positive and meaningful peace as well. For moral pacifism that means tying any steps toward disarmament to active steps at the same time to provide for nonviolent social and/or national defense. People have a legitimate interest in security. Only if they become convinced that it cannot in the long run be assured by ever-expanding one's capacity to kill other people, and stands a better chance of being assured by developing techniques of nonviolent resistance, does disarmament have the remotest chance of ever being considered acceptable. Contrary to first appearances, this is an empowering notion. When people rely on armies for their security, they become essentially passive. They produce the armaments, of course, and grow the food. But the job of killing and dying is left to a small segment of the population, usually young men. With nonviolent national defense the burden of defending the country is distributed throughout virtually the entire population. The forty- and fifty-year-old men (and women) who are typically deemed unfit for combat can play a central role in nonviolent defense, as can children. A true measure of the value a people attaches to the preservation of the values of their society is their willingness personally to sacrifice for it, not their willingness to send others to sacrifice for it, particularly when those others have been brought to do so through compulsion. Indeed, it is arguable that compelling young people – on pain of fine, imprisonment, or worse for refusal – to kill and be killed in defense of society not only does not preserve the central values of a free, open, and compassionate society but is directly incompatible with those values.

CONCRETE OPTIONS

Pacifists can be expected to support all proposed treaty agreements on WMD. But the moral pacifist will do so half-heartedly. The reason is the conviction that without a radical change in the thinking regarding the use of violence as a matter of policy, expectations of lasting reductions in the killing capacity of governments are naive. Governments are the problem. So agreements among governments are unlikely to provide the solution.

What alternative is preferable? A cross-cultural grassroots movement that bypasses governments and galvanizes those from around the world committed to peace and nonviolence.

The end of the cold war signaled the end of an old world order. That order was based on fear, mistrust, and violence. The best it could offer was a balance of terror through WMD. The end of that order offers the opportunity to begin creating a nonviolent world order. Freed at last from superpower rivalry, the peoples of the world can begin to cultivate openness, trust, and respect. They can begin dismantling war systems, beginning with WMD. They can cease militarizing their youth. They can start devising nonviolent defense strategies. They can redirect their economies to peaceful uses. Such an opportunity may not occur again in a thousand years.

But they need a framework from which to do this. And it must be one not tied to the obsolete thinking of the nuclear age. Violence cannot provide that perspective. Nonviolence can. The time is past for vacuous declarations. Or for piecemeal measures that leave the conditions producing violence unchanged. The time is for something that has never been tried before in history: a worldwide rethinking of social, political, educational, and economic orders from the perspective of nonviolence.

It requires summoning the best minds from every area of human endeavor, from science and technology to economics, education, religion, psychology, and philosophy. And it must engage and challenge the ordinary person in realistic ways. Nothing less has the remotest chance of success. Technology has created previously unimagined possibilities for worldwide communication and collaboration. That technology needs to be put in the service of nonviolence. A community of people of goodwill needs to be created worldwide. This cannot be achieved overnight. Some people will have to lead the way. And they will have to do so without guarantees that others will follow. We could sit back and hope that such people will step forward sometime in the future. And if everyone does that, it will never happen. So why not us? Here and now?

Hence I should call for a Millennium of Nonviolence – a permanent worldwide movement to put the best of human intellectual and moral resources to work, defining and beginning to create a sustainable nonviolent world order.

The only world leader, to my knowledge, to have envisioned anything approximating such an order was Rajiv Gandhi, in a speech to the United Nations Special Session on Disarmament given June 9, 1988. He said in part:

The plan for radical and comprehensive disarmament must be pursued along with efforts to create a new system of comprehensive global security. The components of such a system must be mutually supportive. Participation in it must be universal.

The structure of such a system should be firmly based on non-violence. When we eliminate nuclear weapons and reduce conventional forces to minimum defensive levels, the establishment of a non-violent world order is the only way of not relapsing into the irrationalities of the past. It is the only way of precluding the recommencement of an armaments' spiral. Non-violence in international relations cannot be considered a Utopian goal. It is the only available basis for civilized survival, for the maintenance of peace through peaceful coexistence, for a new, just, equitable and democratic world order. As Mahatma Gandhi said in the aftermath of the first use of nuclear weapons: "The moral to be legitimately drawn from the supreme tragedy of the bomb is that it will not be destroyed by counterbombs, even as violence cannot be destroyed by counter-violence. Mankind has to get out of violence only through non-violence."

The ultimate power to bring about change rests with the people. It is not the power of weapons or economic strength which will determine the shape of the world beyond nuclear weapons. That will be determined in the minds and the hearts of thinking men and women around the world. For, as the Dhammapada of the Buddha teaches us:

> Our life is shaped by our mind;
> We become what we think.
> Suffering follows an evil thought
> As the wheels of a cart follow the oxen that draw it.
> Joy follows a pure thought
> Like a shadow that never leaves.
> For Hatred can never put an end to hatred;
> Love alone can.
> This is the unalterable law.

Notes

I wish to thank Duane Cady for helpful comments on earlier drafts of this chapter.

1. Christian pacifism did not survive long, other than in small sects. By the medieval period it was sometimes even considered heretical. See Richard W. Kaeuper, *War, Justice and Public Order: England and France in the Later Middle Ages* (Oxford: Clarendon, 1988), 338.

2. I have adapted this formulation from a formulation by Eric Reitan in "Personally Committed to Nonviolence: Towards a Vindication of Personal Pacifism," *The Acorn: Journal of the Gandhi-King Society* 10:2 (Spring 2000): 30–42. Reitan's understanding of personal pacifism has to do more directly with the renunciation of violence than the renunciation of war. As I think it important to distinguish nonviolence and pacifism, I focus on the renunciation of war.

3. Duane L. Cady, *From Pacifism to Warism: A Moral Continuum* (Philadelphia: Temple University Press, 1989), understands pacifism to combine opposition to war with a commitment to peace, understood as "commitment to cooperative social conduct based on agreement"(p. 19). While pacifists overwhelmingly share this second commitment, I do not take it to be part of the meaning of pacifism. Notable principled pacifists include Tolstoy, Gandhi, and perhaps Martin Luther King, Jr.

4. This is essentially the position of Stephen King-Hall, *Defense in the Nuclear Age* (Nyack, N.Y.: Fellowship Publications, 1959). It also approximates the position of Gene Sharp, although he does not label himself a pacifist. See particularly his *The Politics of Nonviolent Action* (Boston: Porter Sargent, 1973) and *Civilian-Based Defense: A Post-Military Weapons System* (Princeton, N.J.: Princeton University Press, 1990).

5. See Cady, *From Warism to Pacifism.*

6. Religious pacifism is dealt with in an earlier volume in this series, *The Ethics of War and Peace*, ed. Terry Nardin (Princeton, N.J.: Princeton University Press, 1996).

7. On nuclear pacifism, see Cady, *From Warism to Pacifism,* 69.

8. James P. Sterba comes close to being a just war pacifist in this sense but stops short, allowing that there are a few actual wars that were just. See his *Justice for Here and Now* (Cambridge: Cambridge University Press, 1998), chap. 7.

9. See Michael Walzer, *Just and Unjust Wars* (New York: Basic Books, 1977), 21.

10. This point is made by Daniel Ellsberg, "Call to Mutiny," in *The Deadly Connection: Nuclear War and U.S. Intervention*, ed. Joseph Gerson (Cambridge: American Friends Service Committee, 1983), 17–32.

11. See Carl von Clausewitz, *On War*, ed. and trans. Michael Howard and Peter Paret (Princeton, N.J.: Princeton University Press, 1976), 579–84.

12. The use of the term "MADvocate" owes to Donald Brennan, "When the SALT Hit the Fan," *National Review*, June 23, 1972, pp. 685–92. As cited and used by Steven P. Lee, *Morality, Prudence, and Nuclear Weapons* (Cambridge: Cambridge University Press, 1993), chap. 7.

13. Richard Nixon was raised as a Quaker, which may explain this. Quakers, or members of the Society of Friends, constitute one of the so-called Peace Churches within Christianity, along with Mennonites and Brethren.

14. David Lewis, "Devil's Bargains and the Real World," in *The Security Gamble: Deterrence Dilemmas in the Nuclear Age*, ed. Douglas MacLean (Totowa, N.J.: Rowman & Allanheld, 1984), 143.

15. The assumption, which I do not defend here, is that all actions have intentions.

16. An internal study by the Defense Department's Strategic Command, written in 1995 and disclosed in 1998 under the Freedom of Information Act, says that the United States should try not to appear too rational in its global actions. As quoted by the Associated Press in the Rochester *Democrat and Chronicle* on March 2, 1998, the report says in part: "That the U.S. may become irrational and vindictive if its vital interests are attacked should be a part of the national persona we project to all adversaries."

17. Moral considerations aside, pacifists can agree that WMD disarmament might be less difficult to achieve than total disarmament, and that will be part of their reasons for supporting it.

24

Pacifism and Weapons of Mass Destruction

The Challenge of Peace

Duane L. Cady

It comes as no surprise that pacifism presents an important challenge to major-power policies when we consider ethical issues regarding weapons of mass destruction. In the preceding chapter, Robert L. Holmes has offered clear and careful explanations of a broad range of pacifist objections to the continuing development, proliferation, and use of such weapons. In the process he dispels the myth of deterrence and makes a pacifist case for disarmament. While Holmes and I do not always agree about pacifism, our points of disagreement are few and small; my remarks below in reaction to his chapter more often extend and amplify his arguments than contest them.

It is always a bit awkward for pacifists to participate in a project such as this, since pacifists hold a view that is held by relatively few, and they are typically ignored or even ridiculed by those embracing more conventional values. For this reason it is important to include at least a brief response to some of the more common objections to pacifism at the outset.

Pacifists get used to questions about reacting to a mugger, confronting Hitler, being self-righteous, self-sacrificial, and especially about being unrealistic. Perhaps the most effective forms of refutation of any idea are neglect and ridicule. It is easier to neglect or ridicule a challenging idea than to engage it. Name calling aside, the most common objection to pacifism is a form of "Be realistic." This is usually expressed with statements such as, "I agree in theory but not in practice," "Pacifism sounds good but it just won't work," or "If everyone were a pacifist, things would be different, but they aren't." Since practical objections can be countered only by reference to empirical evidence, I can only point to the long history of nonviolent action. People tend to think pacifism will not work because they are largely ignorant of when and where it has worked – even against Hitler.[1] Understanding the empirical evidence also entails recognizing that pacifism comes in degrees and that very few people are absolute pacifists. So, one can fend off a thug and even support police actions involving restrained use of force without thereby giving up one's moral objections to war.[2]

The most problematic objection to pacifism from the perspective of pacifists is that the view is dismissed out of hand without ever being seriously understood or considered. The word "pacifism" is like a flag, and once encountered, the dominant cultural context – warism – overwhelms almost all thoughtful engagement. War is simply taken for granted, and it seems obvious to most people that pacifism is naive, misguided, and hopelessly idealistic, whereas violence is considered a regrettable but necessary fact of national and international life. Available space is insufficient to meet every objection to pacifism because the dominant context of such discussion presents the issues as already settled. We should remember that not so long ago abolition of slavery was thought naive and idealistic; today slavery is so abhorrent as to be universally condemned. Less than a century ago women could not vote in the United States; now our dominant presumption involves challenging governments around the world for denying women's basic human rights. Fifteen years ago Nelson Mandela was a banned person, jailed in a South Africa persistent in practicing apartheid, and few imagined that system could be dismantled short of a blood-bath; after negotiating his release from prison, Mandela was elected president of a nonracial South Africa. My point is only that notions taken for granted can change dramatically in short order if we can imagine alternatives.

The challenge of pacifism is to imagine a world free of war, to take the necessary conditions seriously, and to do what we must to transform our warist world – step by step, for there is no quick and easy solution. If we genuinely want a more peaceful world in our future, there is no place for weapons of mass destruction. If, on the other hand, we want to defend the status quo and perpetuate the privileges enjoyed by the few and powerful, then we will rationalize any number of horrors. Pacifism calls us to be honest with ourselves about our true aspirations.

What follows falls into two parts. In the first, I review the central features of Holmes's position; here the focus is on what I call "critical pacifism," the range of pacifist arguments against war and against the means by which war is undertaken. Like Holmes, I take moral opposition to war to be central to pacifism. I am inclined to characterize pacifism somewhat more broadly than he does, and I include a second central characteristic of pacifism, the moral commitment to what I call "positive peace." By "positive peace" I mean social order structured from within by collaboration and cooperation of citizens as distinct from what I call "negative peace," social order imposed from the outside by threat or imposition of force.

The second part of this chapter focuses on the positive peace aspect of an ethical consideration of weapons of mass destruction. It is in this second section that I hope to extend and amplify a pacifist position beyond that developed in Robert Holmes's chapter.

CRITICAL PACIFISM: THE CASE AGAINST WEAPONS
OF MASS DESTRUCTION

Holmes rightly opens his discussion by insisting that the burden of proof rests not with pacifists to defend pacifism but with warists to defend their position. Warism is the view that war is both morally justifiable in principle and morally justified in fact.[3] The primary obstacle to taking pacifism seriously is the widespread presumption of warism; the moral acceptability of war seems so obvious to the vast majority of people that they do not realize they are assuming it. They just take it for granted. As a result, pacifism seems hopelessly naive and idealistic. By making clear that war is presumptively wrong, Holmes is putting the burden of proof where it belongs, namely, on those who would justify war.

Once it is clear that war is morally impermissible, it readily follows that there are *no* weapons whose use is morally permissible in war. Asking whether it is morally permissible to use weapons of mass destruction in war typically presupposes that some weapons may be justifiably used and presupposes that war itself is morally permissible, precisely the notion that pacifism rejects. Pacifists reject weapons of mass destruction and in doing so are careful not thereby to legitimate warist presumptions; pacifists reject war itself and with it any and all means of war.

Two Related Parts of Morality in War

In the process of discussing just war pacifism (the view that there are legitimate uses of weapons of war *in principle* but none *in practice*), Holmes dispatches the Independence Thesis (the notion that *jus ad bellum* criteria are logically independent of *jus in bello* criteria). He shows this to be false by showing that to judge one to be morally justified in going to war entails that one is justified in the conduct entailed by implementing that judgment. This is an important feature of the pacifist position because it exposes a logical difficulty of the just war tradition, that of insisting on moral restraint *in* war without seriously asking about the morality *of* war as a central feature of the modern nation state.

"Using" Weapons of Mass Destruction

Holmes rightly notes that although no way of conducting war is morally permissible for the pacifist, still some wars are worse than others. By implication, some weapons may be worse than others. Certainly, this is true. The sheer magnitude of detonating weapons of mass destruction and the "spillage" beyond military targets makes them especially problematic morally.

Although such weapons *are used* when deployed with a threat even if they are never actively detonated, still, detonation seems worse. It should be obvious that pacifism recognizes no circumstances under which it is morally permissible to detonate weapons of mass destruction. Holmes politely asks, "Why draw the line at nuclear weapons?" A less polite pacifist question would be, "Why a book on ethics and weapons of mass destruction?" The more basic question is, "How do so many people within the various religious and secular ethical traditions morally justify war?" or "How do they stand by in silence?" or "How do they tolerate or even support and encourage war?" Pacifists suspect that many do so because they have taken war for granted as simply what nations do; in other words, war is presumed morally justifiable but rarely are the arguments explicitly made. When the vast majorities in most nations and cultures take war for granted, pacifists wonder about the credibility of dominant ethical institutions.

It is here that Holmes is especially sharp in warning us that by condemning weapons of mass destruction we risk legitimating so-called conventional weapons and thereby risk preserving the institution of war. Of course pacifists reject weapons of mass destruction, as do most religious and secular ethical traditions, but let us not kid ourselves about conventional weapons. They are abhorrent as well; given the historical record, one could make the case that they are worse, since they are used – in the detonated sense – so often and on such a large scale.

Deterrence

Holmes is quite right that from a pacifist perspective deterrence is not morally justifiable because it cannot be made coherent. Many are seduced to believe that deterrence is acceptable because they think that threatening great evil will frighten enemies away from actually doing great evil. But is it moral to threaten to do what it would be immoral to do? If so, by what reasoning? If not, deterrence is immoral. And will a threat to do great evil be believed? Each side seems to be in the logically questionable position of thinking the other side to be simultaneously sane and insane; sane enough to know better than to attack, given the inevitable retaliatory attack, and insane enough actually to use their weapons of mass destruction rather than merely bluff their use (it is this sort of insanity that makes the threat credible).[4] And of course there is no evidence that deterrence works. Americans do not believe that the United States has resisted the temptation to use weapons of mass destruction against China, Iraq, Russia, or North Korea because we have been deterred by enemy weapons; we explain our own behavior by reference to other factors. The same could be said for China, Iraq, Russia, and North Korea using their weapons against the United States.

Clearly, we "use" weapons of mass destruction whether we detonate them or not; development, deployment, and threatening use are all uses; making distinctions between them may distance us psychically from the killing that is the purpose of the weapons, but psychic distance does not eliminate the logical relationships or the implications of the weapons. Possession puts us on the road to intentional mass killing.

Proliferation

As Holmes notes, if we really believe that deterrence works, we should favor proliferation. If weapons of mass destruction ensure peace, then every nation should have them. But of course pacifists oppose proliferation because pacifists favor disarmament for all weapons of war and for all nations. Nonetheless, it is hypocritical for nations with weapons of mass destruction to justify them as peacekeepers and then deny them to other nations.

In his discussion of proliferation, Holmes makes a series of distinctions, between nuclear and nonnuclear nations, between good and bad nations, and between rational and irrational nations. In this context he says, "A nation might be bent on evil in the world and yet be fully rational (at least in the sense of choosing necessary means to its ends)." I understand the inclination to distinguish between effective cognitive capacity and operative moral capacity, but I would restrict "rational" to include an operative moral capacity. I cannot imagine a "fully rational" nation "bent on evil." Perhaps nations bent on evil can calculate effectively, but I would regard their evil intent as evidence counting against their full rationality.

Disarmament

Holmes accurately describes the pacifist view that disarmament of weapons of mass destruction is morally imperative and that the pacifist goes on to require conventional disarmament as well. And he is quite right that warists bridle at this. He notes that over the last century, wars have increasingly killed larger and larger percentages of civilians than soldiers, but still those justifying war insist that we must "be realistic" and continue the warist presumption with its subsequent research, development, deployment, and engagement of ever more sophisticated means of killing and destroying. For the pacifist the problem is war itself; all means of fighting war present candidates for disarmament. The pacifist concern is that by stopping disarmament at weapons of mass destruction we are seen as legitimizing other weapons. The reasons favoring disarmament cover conventional as well as mass destruction weapons.

I must confess to being a bit troubled at reading Holmes's suggestion that "only if [people] become convinced that [security] cannot in the long run be assured by ever expanding one's capacity to kill other people, and stands a better chance of being assured by developing techniques of nonviolent resistance, does disarmament have the remotest chance of ever being considered acceptable." This strikes me as too realistic. It seems to me that those of us interested in ethics need to see this argument turn on the moral case and not be dependent on pragmatics. Perhaps Holmes is simply expressing his sense of the depth and breadth of the warist presumption. It seems to me that we have to believe that morality alone is sufficient to turn the tide. Granted, it has not been to date.

By turning the argument on the moral case rather than the practicality, I mean something like what we saw during the civil rights movement in the 1960s. At some point the tide turned not on who had the most force at their command or who had the most votes or who had the legal claim. When Americans saw black demonstrators in Birmingham, Alabama, attacked with fire hoses and by police dogs simply for asking to be included on a racially integrated basis at city lunch counters and on local buses, the power, legality, and politics were displaced by sheer morality: Both the attacks *and* the racial exclusion were wrong. Both participants and observers knew it and could no longer pretend otherwise.

The challenge for those of us with moral concerns about the practice of basing national security on weapons is to make the moral issues so compelling that they take center stage. As things stand, the morality of weapons and war, the question of disarmament, is hardly on the agenda of most of the religious and secular ethical traditions. Pragmatism in its most crass form has trumped ethics across our country in public affairs. The game is economic and to a lesser extent political; ethics has almost nothing to do with it. This is the challenge to be met by those of us who believe morality to be relevant to weapons and war.

Alternatives

In November of 1998 the United Nations passed a resolution calling for 2001–10 to be a decade of nonviolence for the children of the world. Holmes closes his chapter by calling for a millennium of nonviolence, another way of saying that we humans must find our way to replace the general presumption of warism with a general presumption of nonviolence if we are to make our way very far into the new millennium. It is at this point that I move from reviewing Robert Holmes's pacifist case against weapons of mass destruction – critical pacifism – to extending that case by exploring another central feature of pacifism: positive peace.

POSITIVE PACIFISM: THE CHALLENGE OF PEACE

Of course, pacifists will support various proposed treaty agreements on weapons of mass destruction. At the same time, they will do so half-heartedly because they understand the need for radical change in the continuing and persistent use of violence as a matter of government policy. Agreements between governments cannot make the world safe from weapons of mass destruction as long as governments themselves stand on violence as a foundational principle. For pacifists, the problem is that violence is simply taken for granted as a perfectly normal and natural activity, especially in response to injustice; weapons of mass destruction are just one manifestation of that problem. Put bluntly, the core values of dominant culture must change. The de facto motto of the modern nation-state, "In violence we trust," must be replaced. This is where positive peace comes in.

Peace and the Old (Violent) World Order

When we think carefully and critically about our current dependence on violence, it becomes clear that it is a failed means of social order. Violence cannot create and sustain the peaceful, nonviolent world to which we aspire. When we think seriously about what peace is and how we make it, we realize that it is not merely the absence of war (negative peace) but the presence of social order arising from within a group by cooperation and collaboration rather than imposed from outside by force or threat. Contrary to popular opinion, positive peace is common, so common that we hardly notice it:

Whenever channels of discussion remain open; parliamentary bodies genuinely deliberate; courts adjudicate under specified rules of law; citizens are consulted about the formation of public policy; the police use physical force if at all only in a discriminating and non-injurious way; and problems of social justice occupy a central place in political discussion – wherever conditions of this kind obtain, fundamentals of nonviolence, both as means and ends, already exist. Naturally, the exponent of nonviolence will seek to sustain and expand such patterns.[5]

Unfortunately, most pacifist literature is spent almost exclusively raising moral objections to war, the negative side of pacifism. While existing world conditions provide plenty of events that require the antiwar pacifist critique, the positive side of pacifism gets far less attention and development. Pacifism is rarely considered, and when it is, it is often quickly dismissed, not only due to the widespread presumption of warism, but also because of the widespread embrace of realism. Pacifists are dismissed as hopelessly idealistic. In short, realism, the philosophical outlook of Thomas Hobbes that the natural condition of humanity is the war of each against all, takes fear to be at the heart of the basis of the state. Pacifists understand that fear is a poor basis for relationships and cannot sustain nations. While negative peace (absence of war) is often the goal of heads of state and social theorists alike, positive peace (presence of social order from within based on agreement and cooperative conduct rather than imposed from without by threat or force) is what communities and nations (and communities of nations) want and need.

Following the end of the 1991 Gulf War – for more than ten years – U.S./UN economic sanctions were imposed on the civilians of Iraq. According to UNESCO, these sanctions resulted in the deaths of more than 500,000

Iraqi children under the age of five. What has this to do with weapons of mass destruction? From a pacifist perspective, the effects of these sanctions demonstrate the arbitrariness of a focus on ethics and weapons of mass destruction, since a policy not typically considered a weapon of any kind can have such destructive impact; these sanctions show the futility of basing international relations on force, threat, and fear, since they did not achieve their objectives; and the sanctions demonstrate the pacifist point of making the case turn not on pragmatics but on ethics. It is simply wrong for a nation – much less an international body – to maintain a policy that has as its direct result the deaths of more than 5,000 children a month due to preventable diseases caused by the lack of clean water and basic sanitation. This is wrong regardless of the ends sought or the means employed. Are the perpetrators of the sanctions somehow absolved of the implications of their acts because death comes from dysentery rather than immolation? Might these sanctions be considered a biological weapon? How can we abolish or limit one means and not another? Arguably, the sanctions are effective weapons of mass destruction despite their failure to satisfy the technical definitions presented earlier in this volume. Those of us interested in morality and international conflict need to question the ethics of any and all means, including these economic sanctions. And the morality takes center stage over pragmatics when half a million children have died. Why is this not on the agenda regarding ethics and weapons of mass destruction? How convenient it is to define such means out of consideration.

A New (Nonviolent) World Order?

Violence cannot create the peace we want, whether it is the violence of weapons of mass destruction, the violence of "conventional" weapons, or the violence of seemingly benign policies such as economic sanctions. These are simply different means, but all are efforts to coerce certain social arrangements, whether by threat or by actual use of force. But we know that genuine – positive – peace comes not by force at all; it comes by agreement, cooperation, collaboration, by people and nations meeting together, thinking through, talking over, and working out relationships. We can no more use violence to create peace than we can use lies to create truth. Violence can satisfy an urge for revenge and occasionally it can set a temporary negative peace in place, at least for as long as we are willing and able to remain a superior occupying force. But negative peace wrought through violence is at best a begrudging concession of a beaten, resentful, and humiliated enemy, hardly deserving the name "peace" of any sort.

Genuine peace involves willful participation, cooperation, and community. These are created not by violence or threat of violence but by care, trust, respect, and equality. Genuine peace is complex, fragile, and develops slowly; violence is simplistic, insistent, and quick. Powerlessness, frustration, impatience, and injustice all tempt us to seize the means of violence to achieve the ever-elusive quick fix. It is hard to resist the temptation even when we know better. As soon as we are seduced to violence in yet another bad situation where violence is likely only to make things worse, we thereby reinforce the illusion that violence can fix injustice and we reinforce the destructive cycle. Our problem is that virtually all of the effort and resources put to preparing ourselves for dealing with bad situations are focused on the means of violence. Put colloquially, modern nation-states are hooked on violence. Until we imagine nonviolence to be possible and build nonviolent tools for a truly new world order, we will be stuck with the legacy of the failed violent world order.[6]

Missing Voices?

One of my misgivings about getting involved in this project on ethics and weapons of mass destruction was a worry that the conversation would take place on the terms of the dominant culture. What I mean is that the way in which the issues would get raised and what would count as appropriate answers to the various questions raised would reflect the perspectives and interests of powerful elements of the status quo. To my mind, this would "stack the deck" – if you will, set conditions for the discussion that favor the vested interests of those in positions of privilege and power. My concern was not at all about the organizers or participants in this project; they have done an admirable job of including a wider than usual array of perspectives here. My concern was that how we frame and discuss questions about ethics and weapons among modern nations inevitably reflects existing realities of power, privilege, and interest. In an admittedly limited effort to challenge those terms, I want to ask myself – and my readers – a question: Who is not participating in our conversation? It seems that most of the main ethical traditions of various secular and religious perspectives are represented, along with authoritative representatives of dominant institutions, academic, legal, political, religious, and to some extent military. What voices are missing from this discussion? When I press myself on this question, I worry that the bulk of humanity is not represented here. How could that be, given the array of traditions?

As I understand it, roughly 70 percent of the world's people live in what Western Europe, North America, and Japan take to be the "developing" world. During the cold war, the "first world," U.S./NATO industrialized capitalist nations, engaged the "second world," the Soviet-dominated socialist bloc, in a protracted struggle for spheres of influence over the rest of the globe, the "third world." "Development" became a euphemism for more powerful nations encroaching (economically, militarily, and politically) into the "third world" in a first and second world pursuit of resources, markets, and cheap labor. With the collapse of the Soviet Union and the end of the cold war, we see a single, unchecked superpower and a host of multinational corporations for the most part having their way globally. But again, what has this to do with my misgivings about voices left out of our conversations regarding ethics and violence?

In *Blowback: The Costs and Consequences of American Empire,* Chalmers Johnson notes that a decade after the end of the cold war, "hundreds of thousands of American troops, supplied with the world's most advanced weaponry, sometimes including nuclear arms, are stationed on over sixty-one base complexes in nineteen countries world-wide. . . ." Those figures are based on the Department of Defense's narrowest definition of major installation; "if one included every kind of installation that houses representatives of the American military, the number would rise to over eight hundred."[7] Needless to say, no other nation projects its military so widely. The vast majority of nations confine their military within their own borders. What explains this? It is sometimes suggested that U.S. global dominance is the best hope for world peace. Behind this lofty rhetoric are multinational corporate interests in search of resources, markets, and cheap labor for the "global economy," which is actually the economy of North America, Western Europe, and Japan being forced on the rest of the world's regional and subsistence economies.

According to Wolfgang Sachs, there were roughly 5,100 languages spoken around the globe in 1992. "Just under 99 per cent of them are native to Asia, Africa, the Pacific and the American continents, while a mere 1 percent find their homes in Europe."[8] Expectations are that "within a generation or two not many more than 100 of these languages will survive." All of the participants in this project on ethics and weapons of mass destruction speak at least one of these dominant languages. Of course, with the demise of languages, entire cultures vanish. As Sachs puts it, "the homogenization of the world is in full swing. A global monoculture spreads like an oil slick over the entire planet."[9] And, Sachs tells us, if "developing" countries "successfully" follow the model of the United States, Western Europe, and Japan, five or six more planets like ours will be needed to provide resources for such levels of consumption and to serve as waste dumps for the inevitable toxins. These five or six planets like ours are not available.

What has this to do with ethics and weapons of mass destruction? First, it is obvious that the vast majority of those affected by economic globalization, cultural homogenization, military and political dominance, and the like have no role in the decisions leading to these changes. And second, it is evident that the old-world notion that peace rests on justice has been replaced in the past fifty years by a notion of "progress," "development," and "advancement" for people of the world through material improvement.[10] It is the powerful who decide what counts as progress, development, and advancement. This is why I am concerned about missing voices. One effect on our discourse is for issues to be sanitized in a clinical, academic style that insulates us from the human suffering that results from the global weapons system (i.e., the global nation-state structure with weapons amassed, weapons-deal diplomacy, and the myriad implications for ordinary people from toxic waste to land mines left behind for unsuspecting civilians).

CONCLUSION

To concern ourselves with ethics and weapons of mass destruction opens us to rethink not only the various weapons and their characteristics but the full challenge of ethics, and with it the challenge of peace. If we genuinely want a peaceful world in the positive sense of peace – not just the absence of war, but the presence of social order that arises from within through nonforced cooperation – our task goes well beyond a few international treaties regarding selected weapons of a certain scale of destruction. Genuine peace challenges us to reconsider the means/ends thinking characteristic of warism. We cannot justify horrible means with lofty ends. Peace is not an outcome or a result; peace is a way of being, and our world is far from being peaceful.

Regarding ends and means, Gandhi puts it this way: "The means may be likened to a seed, the end to a tree; and there is just the same inviolable connection between the means and the end as there is between the seed and the tree." And again, "If I want to deprive you of your watch, I shall certainly have to fight for it; if I want to buy your watch I shall have to pay for it; and if I want a gift, I shall have to plead for it; and, according to the means I employ, the watch is stolen property, my own property, or a donation."[11]

If we are serious about genuine peace, then we understand that weapons cannot secure it; only good work, collaboration, goodwill, and humility can create and sustain peace. Peace making – literally, "agreement making" – does not mean propping up an oppressive regime with an arms deal to gain a political ally. Genuine peace making means doing the hard work of building communities, engendering cooperative interactions, meeting needs, caring, learning, sharing, doing all of the things characteristic of social justice. This is the challenge of peace, and the challenge is greatest to the privileged and powerful since they have greater resources with which to act.

Notes

I am grateful to Carol Cohn, Robert Holmes, Sara Ruddick, and Richard Werner for their reactions to and encouragement for an earlier draft of this chapter.

1. For the history of nonviolent action, see Peter Brock, *Pacifism in Europe to 1914* (Princeton, N.J.: Princeton University Press, 1972); Brock, *Pacifism in the United States from the Colonial Era to the First World War* (Princeton, N.J.: Princeton University Press, 1968); Brock, *Twentieth-Century Pacifism* (New York: Van Nostrand Reinhold, 1970); *The Quiet Battle*, ed. Mulford Q. Sibley (Boston: Beacon, 1963); Gene Sharp, "Power and Struggle," pt. I of *The Politics of Nonviolent Action* (Boston: Porter Sargent, 1973).

2. Duane L. Cady, *From Warism to Pacifism: A Moral Continuum* (Philadelphia: Temple University Press, 1989), 95–108.

3. Ibid., 3.

4. Ibid., 116.

5. Mulford Q. Sibley, "The Relevance of Nonviolence in Our Day," in Sibley, ed., *Quiet Battle*, 363–64.

6. Duane L. Cady and Robert L. Phillips, *Humanitarian Intervention: Just War vs. Pacifism* (Lanham, Md.: Rowman & Littlefield, 1996), 102–3.

7. Chalmers Johnson, *Blowback: The Costs and Consequences of American Empire* (New York: Henry Holt, 2000), 4.

8. Wolfgang Sachs, "One World," in *The Development Dictionary*, ed. Wolfgang Sachs (London: Zed Books, 1992), 102.

9. Ibid.

10. Ibid., 104.

11. Mohandas K. Gandhi, *Non-Violent Resistance*, ed. Bharatan Kumarappa (New York: Schocken Books, 1951), 10–11.

25

Weapons of Mass Destruction and the Limits of Moral Understanding

A Comparative Essay

Steven P. Lee

Warfare poses difficulties for our moral understanding. It involves, for example, the killing of large numbers of people, something generally morally prohibited. As if warfare in general did not pose a sufficient challenge to ethics, however, developments in the means of warfare are constantly creating new moral difficulties. Any moral consensus reached about warfare is likely to be confounded in time by new military technology. Such is the case with weapons of mass destruction, the ethical implications of which are our subject. The purpose of this volume is to understand whether these weapons can be incorporated into our moral understanding of warfare and, if so, how. The method is to consider these questions from a diversity of ethical perspectives and traditions. This chapter offers a comparative discussion of the preceding essays in the volume on these matters.

The authors considered six questions about how their traditions view WMD. The first question concerns the source within the traditions of the principles and norms governing general conduct in war. The second and third questions are about the moral status of the use of WMD, their use in war (question two), and their use as a deterrent (question three). The fourth and fifth questions consider the moral acceptability of the possession of WMD, including proliferation, the acquisition of the weapons by states without them (question four), and disarmament, the deacquisition of the weapons by states already having them (question five). Finally, question six is about concrete options for change. This question invites the authors to offer or comment on proposals to bring about the changes they earlier argued were morally appropriate or required.

THE TRADITIONS' SOURCES OF MORAL UNDERSTANDING

The first question addressed in the chapters is the sources of the norms and principles of the traditions relevant to the ethical assessment of war. These norms and principles are the basis on which the assessments of WMD are to be made. We begin with a discussion of the four traditions that form the original debate on war in the West, namely, realism, natural law theory, liberalism, and Christianity.

Realism is distinct from the other traditions in that it does not itself offer moral prescriptions.[1] It is a moral tradition only in the negative sense that it sets limits to the applicability of morality. For the realist, international affairs is an arena in which morality does not play a role (the explanatory part of the theory) or should not play a role (the prescriptive part of the theory). The reason is that interstate relations are in a condition of anarchy. Because there is no one to enforce the rules, reciprocity cannot be expected, and reciprocity is a necessary condition for the applicability of morality. The only applicable norms are prudential. Realists argue that leaders should act exclusively on grounds of prudence, but they also argue that that is in fact how they do act. When the behavior of leaders seems to be based on morality, realists seek an alternative prudential explanation. Scott Sagan argues that the appearance that leaders are constrained by moral norms is a mere appearance (p. 75). It has a realist or prudential explanation, part of which is that leaders may be constrained out of fear of setting a harmful precedent. They fear that their lack of constraint would encourage lack of constraint on the part of other states, which would then redound to their own harm. Leaders who appear to follow moral norms do so for purely prudential reasons.

Sagan uses this point to make an important observation about attitudes toward the use of nuclear weapons. Since 1945, the nuclear powers have shown constraint in not using nuclear weapons in conflict. Have they adhered to this norm of nonuse for moral reasons, or have they behaved merely out of prudential concern not to set a precedent potentially harmful to themselves? Sagan refers to the moral norm against nuclear use as the *nuclear taboo* and the corresponding prudential norm the *tradition of nonuse* (p. 76). This is no mere academic distinction because the consequences of a violation of the norm are likely to be quite different in the two cases. If a nuclear taboo is operating, a single violation is likely to strengthen the norm. In contrast, a violation of the tradition of nonuse is, as those who respect the norm fear, likely to make it imprudent to continue to adhere to the norm, thereby leading to further violations and putting an end to the tradition.

Susan Martin supports much of Sagan's discussion of the realist perspective but offers a different understanding of the relation between realism and international morality. Sagan discusses how realism relates to morality understood as a set of specific norms (such as the nuclear taboo). This is a *deontological* understanding of morality, that is, an understanding of morality in terms of duties or rules requiring or prohibiting certain kinds of actions. In contrast, Martin considers how realism relates to a *consequentialist* understanding of morality (p. 96). Moral consequentialism is the view that we should judge an action not in terms of specific norms it may violate but in terms of the likely consequences of that particular action. Realism is already attuned to assessing the consequences of actions, because it is in terms of consequences that one judges whether an action is prudent. Part of Martin's point is that realism can provide an analysis of a state's actions in terms of their likely consequences, and then we may choose to take the moral point of view by focusing on the morally relevant consequences, not just those that affect our own interests.

In the traditional debate in the West over the morality of war, the realist position has been opposed, in one way or another, by the traditions of natural law, liberalism, and Christianity. Each of these three, in different ways, provides support for *just war theory*. Just war theory (JWT), the primary Western approach to the moral examination of military activity, understands war as a morally limited enterprise. JWT provides rules that place limits on *when* a war may be fought (the part of the theory referred to as *jus ad bellum*) and limits on *how* a war may be fought (*jus in bello*). Some wars and some ways of fighting are morally acceptable, and some are not. Speaking generally, under *jus ad bellum*, a state may fight a war only when it is acting defensively, in response to aggression. Under *jus in bello*, the means of waging war must be discriminate (weapons must be aimed at combatants and not at civilians) and proportionate (the likely consequences of military action include at least as much good as harm). These features of *jus in bello* are known as the principles of discrimination and proportionality. The ethics of WMD is mainly a matter of *jus in bello*.[2]

The source of the norms of natural law theory is an appreciation that the universe and the place of humans in it are rationally understandable and that norms for human behavior flow from such an understanding.[3] Part of this understanding, C. A. J. Coady points out, is a notion of human flourishing and of the goods necessary for that flourishing (p. 112). In general, humans should act to promote those goods. In the case of war, then, moral norms would be determined by an understanding of how war relates to the achievement of those goods. The goods that may be achieved by war include security, protection of a community from aggression, special protection of the innocent from harm, and the establishment of a durable peace. It is easy to see how the basic principles of JWT derive from such an understanding. Aggression should not be undertaken, but it may be resisted, leading to the *jus ad bellum* norm that only defensive wars may be fought. In terms of *jus in bello*, the need to establish a durable peace suggests that military efforts should generally be limited and should not do more harm than good, which supports the principle of proportionality. Finally, the good of giving special protection to the innocent supports the principle of discrimination.

In natural law theory, Coady notes, there tends to be a large gap between the goods that, according to the theory, humans should seek and specific prescriptions or obligations regarding individual behavior or public policy (p. 112). John Langan suggests that this gap may be filled by an appreciation of the role of institutions in human society (p. 132). It is through institutions, such as the family, that humans achieve results related to the goods of the theory, so the theory must be sensitive to the role of institutions. This is seen in the criteria of a just war, where a war is justified only if it has been declared by proper authority.

The Christian perspective on war shares much history and content with the natural law perspective.[4] Both have been central in the development of JWT. Christianity supports JWT through the notion that each individual, as a being in the image of God, has value and dignity that must be respected. In addition, Nigel Biggar points out, Aquinas cast Christian theology in an Aristotelian eudaemonistic mode (p. 169). This is similar to the natural law emphasis on human flourishing, and it provides similar support for JWT.

Christianity provides some important refinements to the principle of discrimination, Biggar notes, in particular, a better understanding of the idea of innocence and the formalization of what is called the doctrine of double effect (p. 171). According to the principle of discrimination, civilians, because they are innocent, are not to be attacked in war. But in what sense are they innocent? Not in the sense that they are free of moral culpability, for they may be active supporters of the war effort. Rather, they are innocent in the sense that they, unlike combatants, are not causally responsible in a direct way for the harm posed by the military. Making direct causal responsibility rather than moral culpability the morally relevant factor has theological support in that it represents restorative justice (returning a disrupted situation to a prior just state) rather than retributive justice. The human administration of retributive justice is problematic because it is better left to God, and humans are enjoined to show mercy toward wrongdoers. The doctrine of double effect, developed by Aquinas, posits the moral relevance of the distinction between the intended and the merely foreseen effects of an action. This modifies the principle of discrimination by permitting military actions that kill civilians, so long as these deaths are merely foreseen rather than intended.

A very different Christian perspective is presented by Martin Cook. The apocalyptic tradition, known as dispensationalism, is currently the fastest growing form of Christianity and holds significant political power in the United States (p. 200). According to this tradition, the return of Christ, which is thought to be imminent, will be accompanied by earthly catastrophes, especially in the Middle East. In their biblical description, these catastrophes often sound like the use of weapons of mass destruction. This yields a perspective on WMD that is diametrically opposed to the just war approach of the main Christian tradition.

Liberalism's support for JWT is more equivocal or nuanced than that of the natural law or the Christian traditions. The central source of the principles of liberalism lies in the social contract tradition, which is based on the moral equality of all persons and a respect for individual autonomy.[5] The resulting emphasis on the importance of human choice provides general support for principles of *jus ad bellum* and *jus in bello* along the lines discussed above. But both Henry Shue and Michael Walzer argue, for different reasons, that liberalism is not completely at home with JWT.

For Shue, liberalism's departure from JWT centers on the principle of discrimination (p. 140). The departure is represented by the doctrine of supreme emergency, developed by Michael Walzer in his exposition of JWT.[6] According to this doctrine, the *jus in bello* principle of discrimination may be violated in situations where the survival of a society or its values is imminently threatened by an opponent. This contrasts with the natural law tradition, under which it is likely that any doctrine contravening the principle of discrimination (as modified by the doctrine of double effect) would not be accepted. The doctrine of supreme emergency is of special importance because it has been used to justify the deterrent use of WMD. In any case, Shue argues against the incorporation of supreme emergency into the liberal tradition.

Walzer claims that liberals traditionally have had little interest in war. Instead, they have focused on domestic society as an escape from a Hobbesian state of war (p. 163). When attending to international relations, the liberal project has been to focus not on violent conflict but on cooperation as an extension of domestic principles of order to the international realm. The relevance of JWT is a sign of the failure of this project. In addition, Walzer has pointed out that liberals in power generally act on utilitarian or consequentialist principles, rather than on deontological principles, such as the principle of discrimination. Liberals have in fact been the only ones to use nuclear weapons in war.[7]

It is appropriate now to mention international law, since its development has been largely a liberal project. Paul Szasz observes that international law has resulted mainly from explicit agreements among states, although some of it is customary law (p. 47). It is interesting to compare Szasz's discussion of this process with the realist accounts of Sagan and Martin. States agree, in realist fashion, to provisions of international law based on their perceptions of their own interests. Nonetheless, Szasz claims, there is a moral content to the law, resulting from the influence of a society's moral values on its leaders, especially in democracies, and the consequent tendency over time for the law to reflect these values (pp. 46–8). However, the limited role of the judiciary in international law (a result of the weak role of precedent on international judicial decisions) undercuts one of the main avenues by which, in the domestic case, law develops a strong moral content.

Turning now to the expanded conversation, we consider what other religious traditions have to add to the central Western debate.

In Buddhism, a main goal is mental peace and freedom, a purifying of the mind, referred to as mindful awareness. David Chappell points out that this was originally seen mainly as an individual achievement but was given a social interpretation when, under the influence of Mahayana Buddhism, individual peace came to be understood as inseparable from others' achievement of peace (p. 214). Traditionally, Buddhism recognized four ethical frameworks, one for monastics, one for their lay supporters, one for independent lay persons, and one for citizens and rulers. While monastics, and to a lesser extent lay persons, operate under an ethics of nonviolence, rulers and citizens are allowed to follow principles similar to those of JWT (p. 226). But even then, emphasis remains on individual mental culture. In dealing with violence, Donald Swearer observes, this means confronting and resolving the negative motives that bring suffering to oneself and others (p. 239). Against realism and liberalism, Buddhism emphasizes the decentering of the autonomous self by our recognizing the connections between ourselves and the larger human and cosmic orders. Buddhism opposes narrow self-interest as a principle of action.

Confucianism is a tradition that emphasizes civic virtue over military virtue. Civilization is seen as a more potent force than arms. At the same time, military preparation is seen as a necessary evil (p. 250). One of the most important features of Confucianism, Julia Ching and Philip Ivanhoe observe, is the notion of heaven's mandate, a principle of justified political authority (pp. 250, 272). To have heaven's mandate, a ruler must follow his role-specific responsibilities of promoting the welfare of his people. If these responsibilities are not undertaken by rulers, rebellion is justified. Likewise, a ruler is justified in going to war when this would promote the welfare of people, both his own and the opponent's. Such a war, referred to as a punitive expedition, is regarded as a corrective for the shortcomings of the opponent.

In Hinduism there is a fundamental conflict between a tradition of nonviolence, the ascetic tradition politicized by Gandhi, and a just war–like tradition permitting limited violence. Katherine Young argues that the conflict between these traditions was reconciled in the *Bhagavad Gita* by the prescription that one may fight, but should do so with a proper mind, a state of mental peace and lack of concern about the results (p. 285).[8] Gandhi supported nonviolence by an interpretation and extension of this text. To these two traditions, Kanti Bajpai offers a third, political Hinduism (p. 308). Political Hinduism, a form of extreme realism, is a movement to assert Hindu power and pride after what is perceived as a millennium of Hindu weakness and servility.

The two basic sources of the Islamic tradition, the Qur'an and the *sunna*, provide little by way of a detailed and explicit ethics of war. Rather, Sohail Hashmi notes, Islamic thought on this subject arises mainly from the interpretive work of the early jurists (eighth to fourteenth centuries) (p. 324). These authors often reasoned in support of the existing practices of Islamic states or laid down prescriptions designed to promote the welfare of Muslim communities. The work of the jurists focused on three questions: (1) against whom may one wage war; (2) which persons can be harmed in war; and (3) which property may be damaged in war. In terms of JWT, the first of these is a matter of *jus ad bellum*, and the second and third a matter of *jus in bello*.

Ethical issues surrounding WMD are, of course, a concern of the second and third of these questions, but it is interesting to note some aspects of Islamic thought about the first question, what corresponds to *jus ad bellum*. Hashmi notes that almost all contemporary Islamic thinkers regard defense as the only justification for waging war, abandoning as anachronistic textual justifications for aggressive war (p. 325). At the same time, John Kelsay asserts, Muslims see their religion as universal, as the proper way of life for all humanity (p. 361). So, even if aggression to spread the Muslim faith is not now seen as justified, universalism still colors the discussion of ethical issues. Islam sees itself as prescribing what is necessary for the universal reign of peace and justice. Modern Islamic discourse on the ethics of war, Hashmi observes, is dominated by the justice of waging war rather than the justice of the means of war (p. 321). Kelsay suggests an interesting explanation for this, one relevant to our efforts to understand current Islamic terrorism (p. 357). Much of the recent Islamic writings on military ethics has been authored by "irregulars," those outside government seeking to establish theocratic governments in Muslim countries. They emphasize *jus ad bellum* because they seek to establish themselves as rightful authorities to justify their own use of force to overthrow existing governments in Muslim nations.

In regard to questions of what force may be used against persons and property (*jus in bello*), Hashmi points to commentaries that provide at least qualified support for the use of indiscriminate weapons, such as catapults, fire, poison, and flooding (pp. 327–9). Rules about the use of such weapons are flexible and may be set aside in the face of arguments from military necessity or reciprocity. Kelsay asserts that while the proscription of indiscriminate warfare is sometimes treated flexibly as a kind of rule of thumb, there are also places in the texts where it seems to be regarded more as an absolute, though still subject to the kind of double effect reasoning seen in JWT (p. 355). Regarding the actions of the irregulars in attacking noncombatants, Kelsay points out that these actions are sometimes (1) justified on the grounds that the noncombatants are not innocents, (2) excused on the grounds that the irregulars are unable to confront the military might of their opponents directly, or (3) excused on the grounds that the irregulars are acting under emergency conditions (p. 357). This last rationale brings to mind the notion of supreme emergency.

The Jewish tradition, Reuven Kimelman asserts, is more inductive than deductive, based on historical commentary focusing mainly on particulars. Discussion of military ethics in Judaism is founded on a just war–like distinction between judgments of waging war and judgments of conduct in war. In terms of waging war, wars are either mandatory (when they are reactive wars in self-defense) or discretionary (p. 363). Reactive wars may be authorized by rulers alone, but discretionary wars, which are often expansionary, cannot be authorized solely by the rulers. These wars must be approved by the judiciary, which guarantees a fuller consideration of the goods and harms that would result for both sides. In terms of conduct in war, one of the points in the commentary often cited is the wartime prohibition against the destruction of the opponent's fruit trees (p. 366). This is understood to imply, more generally, a wartime prohibition against destroying what is needed for human life, that is, a just war–like principle of discrimination. However, there is an understanding that an excessive concern for moral niceties is not to be indulged, as this can appear as timidity or squeamishness, encouraging the opponent's aggression (p. 368).

The essay by Joseph David focuses on three aspects of the Jewish tradition that take the ethics of war and WMD beyond the just war–like features discussed by Kimelman. The first of these is the Day of the Lord, a messianic notion leading to a theophanous conception of war (p. 386). With God in the battle against the enemy, war is beyond morality and destruction is total. This holy war notion obviously has some similarities with fundamentalist views in other religions, including Christianity and Islam. The second aspect is the rainbow covenant, the postdeluvian commitment by God never again to bring about such earthly destruction (p. 390). On one interpretation, this covenant also binds humans not to destroy the world. The third aspect is the Jewish experience of the Holocaust, which leads to an ethics of survival beyond just war–like considerations (p. 393). This has obvious connections to the notion of supreme emergency.

Now consider the ethical sources of the two critical perspectives, feminism and pacifism. Each calls into question some fundamental assumptions largely shared by the other perspectives. The critical stance can be seen in the way these perspectives set themselves apart from JWT and raise doubts about the very questions posed for consideration in this volume.

Antiwar feminism, the position presented by Carol Cohn and Sara Ruddick, is not the only feminist approach to military ethics, but it is one widely shared by feminists. Antiwar feminism sets itself apart from JWT in terms of its attitude toward the war system, the set of institutions and conventions representing how we think about and act in international relations (p. 407). JWT (as well as realism) uncritically accepts the war system, while antiwar feminism, along with pacifism, questions it. This critical attitude may be expressed in terms of the notion of *discourses*. The war system is represented by a certain discourse, that is, a certain way of talking and thinking about international relations, and those engaged in the discourse often do not recognize the need either to examine critically what the discourse assumes or to consider the possibility of alternative discourses.[9]

Antiwar feminism criticizes the war system and its discourse in several ways (pp. 408–12). First, the war system is a set of gendered practices, and its discourse a set of gendered meanings, which value the masculine and disvalue the feminine. Second, war is considered from the perspective of men's lives, and the discourse represents this view. War looks very different when seen from women's lives. Third, war is regarded as spatially and temporally bounded in certain ways that do not accurately represent the social consequences of war, especially as these affect women. Fourth, the war system and its discourse embody an epistemology, a certain idea about what counts as knowledge, when there are alternative epistemological perspectives. For example, the discourse enforces a sharp separation between knowledge and feeling, whereas an epistemology that did not recognize the sharpness of this separation might be superior for an understanding of the nature and effects of war.

Antiwar feminism recognizes no general norms permitting the use of weapons in war. The problem with the first question (as with the others), according to Cohn and Ruddick, is that it is cast in terms of and involves the assumptions of the discourse of the war system (p. 412). This discourse assumes the inevitably and acceptability of war. The questions are loaded. They must be as much challenged as answered.

The alternative feminist perspective of pragmatist feminism, represented by Lucinda Peach, assumes the critical stance of feminism regarding military institutions and adds to this the pragmatist opposition to essentializing conflict. In each case, this leads to a presumption against the use of force. But pragmatist feminism shares more with JWT than with antiwar feminism and more with realism than with pacifism (p. 446). While realism is too pessimistic about the possibilities of nonviolence, antiwar feminism and pacifism are too optimistic. Given the fundamental feminist concern to fight oppression, one should recognize that a war fought to end oppression may be justified.

Pacifism opposes all war, though not necessarily all violence. Pacifism can be personal (not binding on others), pragmatic (based on a weighing of outcomes), or principled (binding on all). Robert Holmes presents principled pacifism (p. 451). Due to its principled opposition to war, pacifism, like antiwar feminism, must question the questions themselves. Because the questions assume that some wars and some means of war are justified, they implicitly legitimate war, and war for the pacifist is never legitimate.

Holmes criticizes the view that some means of war are justified by introducing an argument of the just war pacifist (p. 452). The just war pacifist believes that while war may be justified in the abstract, no actual wars are justified, because none of them can satisfy the *jus ad bellum* criteria. But if war can be justified in the abstract, it seems that some means of war could also be justified, and one could thus make distinctions between legitimate and illegitimate uses of weapons, as the second question asks. The problem with this argument is that it assumes the Independence Thesis, which is false. According to the Independence Thesis, judgments of *jus ad bellum* and *jus in bello* are independent of each other. The argument in question assumes the Independence Thesis because it presupposes that one can talk about legitimate uses of weapons even when holding that war itself cannot be legitimate. The Independence Thesis is false because a war cannot be legitimate if there is no legitimate way to fight it, and there can be no legitimate way to fight a war that is itself illegitimate.

Duane Cady adds to our understanding of pacifism and its critical stance in relation to the other traditions. First is the matter of burden of proof (p. 472). Given the general immorality of the sorts of things that go on in war, the justificatory burden of proof is not on the pacifist to show that war is not justified, but rather on the warist (one who believes that war may be legitimate) to show that it is. As the pacifist sees it, of course, this is a burden the warist cannot meet. Second, an important element of pacifism is the idea of positive peace (p. 475). Peace is not simply the absence of violence, but the presence of justice and social accord. To be a pacifist is not only to work against violence but to work for justice.

Cady offers some criticisms of the project of this volume (p. 478). First, he calls into question its content, the scope of its comparative enterprise, arguing that there are many voices (discourses) it leaves out of the discussion, namely, those of the 70 percent of humanity who live in poverty. By leaving out these voices, the volume reinforces existing power and privilege relationships that are closely connected with the war system. Second, he criticizes the volume's form, that is, its focus on the six questions, because pacifists, like antiwar feminists, view the questions as implying that some war is legitimate, which is exactly what they deny. Why, Cady asks, have this volume at all?

Having examined the sources of the traditions' principles, we now consider their answers to the remaining five questions, which directly involve the ethical assessment of WMD. The next section considers the second and third questions on the moral acceptability of the use of WMD, in war and for deterrence. The following section considers the fourth and fifth questions on the moral acceptability of the possession of the weapons, their prospective acquisition (proliferation) and their prospective abandonment (disarmament). Given space constraints, I can, as I have so far, only skim the surface of these rich presentations.

USE OF WMD IN WAR AND FOR DETERRENCE

Like other weapons, WMD may be used in two ways. They may be fired in war or they may be used to deter an opponent's behavior. The second question concerns the ethics of using WMD in war, and the third, the ethics of using WMD for deterrence. Nuclear weapons have been used in both ways. They were used in World War II by the United States against Japan, and they were used for deterrence during the cold war by the United States and the Soviet Union. Likewise, chemical weapons have been used both in war (in World War I and the Iran-Iraq War) and for deterrence (by both the Allied and Axis powers in World War II). It seems that biological weapons have yet to be used either in war or for deterrence.[10] The topic now is whether it is morally permissible to use WMD in either of these ways.

Realism, while not taking explicit moral stands of its own, may, as we have seen, provide explanations for apparently moral behavior on the part of leaders. So, Scott Sagan presents an explanation for the nonuse of nuclear weapons since 1945, an example of apparently moral behavior (pp. 77–83). He argues that the balance of terror provided good prudential reasons for the United States and the Soviet Union not to use nuclear weapons against each other once both had large arsenals and that the United States had good prudential reasons not to use nuclear weapons in a preventative war against the Soviet Union prior to that time. In addition, the United States had good prudential reasons not to use nuclear weapons outside the cold war context, such as in the Gulf War (where the terrain and demographics made discriminate use possible). The United States has an interest in keeping the tradition of nonuse going. One need not appeal to a moral norm, such as the nuclear taboo, to explain the nonuse.

But is a policy of deterrence with nuclear weapons or other WMD prudentially preferable? Is there a realist explanation for states' practicing such deterrence? Susan Martin points out that the preferability of deterrence is a matter of weighing likely consequences, of balancing the advantages of the policy, for example, its ability to prevent deliberate war, against its disadvantages, such as the risk of accidental war that the policy creates (p. 103). Does WMD deterrence work (or did nuclear deterrence work during the cold war)? Realists would generally answer that WMD deterrence does work, but others would disagree. This is a question of interest to ethicists, because, as noted earlier, consequences can be looked at morally as well as prudentially.

The natural law position is opposed to the use of WMD in war, but C. A. J. Coady makes two points about this opposition (p. 120). First, we need to include not only the just war principle of discrimination in making this judgment, but also the principle of proportionality, and, in calculating issues of proportionality, we should not forget to include the effects of nuclear weapons on the environment. Second, any moral criticism arising from this judgment must be impartially delivered. While condemning so-called rogue states in this regard, one should not ignore the roguish behavior of the great powers.

The natural law view of WMD deterrence, Coady claims, is a generalization of its view of nuclear deterrence (p. 121). There are several factors to consider in the moral assessment. First is the complex factual question of whether the deterrence works. Second is the concern about the attitudes and intentions involved in practicing deterrence. This is the *jus in bello* point that WMD deterrence involves the intention to commit murder of the innocent. Third is the fact that deterrence is based on inducing fear. The concern here is that a world order based on fear undermines the prospects for genuine peace. This point echoes Duane Cady's discussion of positive peace.

The mainstream Christian view is generally opposed to the use of WMD in war. Nigel Biggar argues, however, that an isolated, discriminate use of a nuclear weapon may be permissible, now that the end of the cold war has removed the risk of escalation (p. 175). But he qualifies this judgment, noting that breaking the nonuse norm may lead to further nuclear use in war, so that even a well-circumscribed use may not be morally acceptable. Thus, Biggar from a moral perspective would join Sagan from a prudential perspective in having doubts about the acceptability of, for example, using a nuclear weapon in the desolate regions of Kuwait during the Gulf War. In contrast, Martin Cook notes, from the Christian dispensationalist view, the use of WMD, especially nuclear weapons, may be something to welcome, if not actively to promote (p. 205).

Christian perspectives on nuclear deterrence, Biggar notes, spread across the spectrum of possible positions, some theorists endorsing deterrence, others endorsing it conditionally, and still others condemning it outright (pp. 177–82). This disagreement is due to differences over whether nuclear deterrence works and on whether the just war principle of discrimination applies to deterrent use.

Neither Henry Shue nor Michael Walzer views the liberal tradition as supporting the use of WMD in war. The liberal debate, rather, is about deterrence, nuclear deterrence in particular, and the debate turns on the acceptability of the doctrine of supreme emergency.[11] Walzer argued during the cold war that, while nuclear deterrence contravened the principle of discrimination, it may be morally acceptable, given that the United States then faced a condition of supreme emergency.[12] The reason that the liberal debate is about nuclear deterrence, rather than WMD deterrence in general, Shue argues, is that supreme emergency would not apply in the case of a biological and chemical weapons threat (p. 142). The reason is that neither chemical weapons nor (contra Susan Martin's claim [p. 101]) biological weapons make a balance of terror possible. Only when a balance of terror is possible can a society be at imminent risk of destruction, and so the conditions of supreme emergency apply.

Shue argues that supreme emergency does not justify nuclear deterrence (p. 154). He does not argue that supreme emergency *could not* justify nuclear deterrence, but rather that the conditions of supreme emergency were not satisfied during the cold war. Supreme emergency would apply only when there is an imminent threat to the basic rule of law or to a national community's physical survival (as when mass slaughter or enslavement is threatened). Walzer was able to argue that supreme emergency justifies nuclear deterrence only because he interpreted these conditions in a lax way, focusing on the value of political community. Nuclear deterrence does not pass the supreme emergency test, correctly understood.

In the case of international law, there is a clear legal difference between nuclear weapons and other WMD (p. 65). Paul Szasz reports that the possession of biological weapons is prohibited by the 1972 Biological Weapons Convention, and the possession of chemical weapons is prohibited by the 1993 Chemical Weapons Convention. The use of either biological or chemical weapons in war or for deterrence is legally forbidden. There is no corresponding nuclear weapons convention, although there are a number of UN resolutions circumscribing the practice of nuclear deterrence. In 1996, the World Court issued an advisory opinion on nuclear weapons. The opinion held, in part, that the use of nuclear weapons in war or for deterrence is generally contrary to the rules of international law applicable to armed conflict, though their use in extreme circumstances of self-defense might be legally acceptable.

Turning to the other religious traditions and Confucianism, we see a general opposition to the use of WMD in war, but some qualified support for WMD deterrence.

Buddhism, David Chappell observes, is unique among the traditions in that its adherents were victims of a nuclear attack (p. 224). This gives their viewpoint special importance. Given the indiscriminate nature of WMD, Buddhism is opposed to their use in war. In addition, Buddhism finds both oversimplification and falsity in the way WMD deterrence is understood (p. 225). Policy makers consider WMD deterrence merely a strategic issue. As a result, WMD deterrence policy is based on ignorance, which is the main enemy of Buddhism. From the strategic perspective, territory and ways of life are taken as absolutes, and this permits defense at all costs. The truth is that such things are limited and subject to change. The imperative is not simply not to use the weapons but to transform the conflict that would engender their use.

But the four ethical frameworks of Buddhism may differ in their view of WMD deterrence (p. 226). The traditional Buddhist commitment to nonviolence, though it applies to monastics and their lay supporters, is not normative for political leaders. As a result, Buddhism could have supported nuclear deterrence as practiced by political leaders during the cold war, assuming that it was effective. But none of the frameworks would support WMD deterrence since the end of the cold war. The main source of the problem, however, is not the deployment of the weapons themselves but ignorance about them. States possessing WMD have an obligation to educate their citizens about these weapons, because knowledge is required for the operation of wisdom and compassion.

Given the importance of order and harmony and the disorder brought about by war, argues Julia Ching, Confucianism would oppose the use of WMD, since such weapons are the creators of disorder par excellence (p. 255). In addition, while Confucianism is generally favorably disposed toward deterrence, given the importance of organization and intelligence, WMD deterrence would run afoul of the Confucian idea of acting according to nature. Philip Ivanhoe adds that for Confucianism the use of WMD, either in war or for deterrence, would be at odds with the principle of the mandate of heaven and the norm that the only acceptable war is a punitive expedition (p. 273). The purpose of a punitive expedition is to promote the welfare of the people, including the opponent's population, and the use of WMD would run counter to this.

Hinduism, Katherine Young notes, is the only world religion to conceptualize a WMD in its scriptures and to reflect on the ethics of such a weapon as a thought experiment (p. 291). The tradition offers reasons both for and against the use of WMD, whether in war or for deterrence (pp. 292–5). Reasons against use include the general principle of nonviolence and the peculiar cruelty of these weapons. Reasons in favor include that war is allowed in the tradition, that self-defense or national survival allow exceptions to the norm of nonviolence, and that WMD may be used as a last resort or against those who have resorted to war for unrighteous reasons. Kanti Bajpai observes that, though political Hinduism is principally a form of realism, it does contain an implicit moral argument favoring use of WMD (p. 310). Their use may be necessary for the morally important goal of Hindu historical revival and as the only means of escape for Hinduism from a thousand years of weakness and servility.

The morality of the use of WMD is little discussed in Islam, Sohail Hashmi notes (p. 321). Muslim scholars have historically been slow to embrace modern military technology and to assess its implications. In addition, as mentioned earlier, what general contemporary discussion there is in Islam of the ethics of war concerns mostly *jus ad bellum* rather than *jus in bello*. As a result, studying Islamic views on WMD use is "an exercise in inference from scarce sources" (Hashmi, p. 323) or has "more the character of a thought experiment than a descriptive analysis" (John Kelsay, p. 353).

Regarding the use of WMD in war, Hashmi points out that the chemical weapons use by Iraq was little criticized in the Muslim world. One general view among Islamic authors seems to be that WMD may be used in response to their use by one's opponent, based on a justification of reprisal or reciprocity. Such use is referred to by one authority as "the remedy that cauterizes the wound" (p. 334). But Hashmi argues that a second strike with WMD would not be justified, at least in the case of nuclear or biological weapons, given the massive civilian damage that could result. Much Islamic discussion of the deterrent use of WMD has occurred in the context of Pakistan's acquisition of nuclear weapons in its confrontation with India. One issue has been whether the Pakistani nuclear deterrent should be understood as protecting all Islamic nations, that is, whether Pakistan's bomb is an "Islamic bomb" (p. 340). But in fact Pakistan seems to have little interest in sharing its deterrent; it is national rather than religious affiliation that has held sway. Islamic discussion of WMD deterrence, Hashmi notes, has remained at a superficial level, with little attention to the issues of strategy, stability, and costs (p. 339).

Overall, as outlined by Hashmi, there are three positions in Islamic writings regarding the use of WMD (p. 322f.). First are the WMD jihadists, who support the acquisition of WMD for deterrence and their possible use in war under certain circumstances. This group, representing the majority of Islamic scholars, corresponds to the main strand of just war thinking in the West. Second are the WMD terrorists, who argue for the acquisition and use of the weapons in war, paying little heed to the civilian deaths that would result. Third are the WMD pacifists, similar to the nuclear pacifists discussed earlier. Hashmi offers an argument for WMD pacifism (p. 323), which is (1) that WMD are too indiscriminate to satisfy Islamic rules of war, (2) that they kill in horrible ways, placing them at odds with Islamic teachings on fighting humanely, (3) that they produce lasting damage to the environment, thus defiling God's creation, and (4) that resources spent on them are diverted from pressing social needs, thereby representing what the Qur'an condemns as corruption and waste.

In Judaism, the prohibition of wanton destruction and the respect for noncombatant immunity, Reuven Kimelman claims, clearly imply that nuclear weapons are not to be used in war. In addition, God gave man stewardship over the earth and it would be wrong to destroy the earth, as the use of nuclear weapons might. But nuclear deterrence may be acceptable (p. 379). For one thing, it is wrong to appear weak because weakness tempts bullies and so can lead to war. Another reason is that the moral rules prohibiting the kind of intention involved in nuclear deterrence may be temporarily suspended when there is a threat to national survival. We have seen such an argument earlier in the discussion of supreme emergency. A third reason Israeli nuclear policy, in particular, may be morally acceptable, is that it has been shown not to be a policy of use of the weapons in war as a last resort. Instead, it is a policy of pure deterrence, that is, one meant only to deter the use of nuclear weapons against the nation itself. This was shown, Kimelman argues, by Israel's not using its nuclear weapons in the 1973 Middle East war, when its survival was at stake (p. 377).

According to Joseph David, the three special features of Jewish thought he identifies have different implications for the use of WMD (p. 395). The notion of the Day of the Lord may support the use of WMD both in war and for deterrence, though this notion is regarded by authorities as anachronistic. The notion of the rainbow covenant would oppose the use of WMD in war, and perhaps their use for deterrence as well. The experience of the Holocaust may lead to the idea of an ethics of survival beyond an ethics of fairness, which may support the view that WMD deterrence is justified on something like the doctrine of supreme emergency.[13]

The critical perspectives of antiwar feminism and pacifism oppose both kinds of uses of WMD. Carol Cohn and Sara Ruddick, as well as Robert Holmes and Duane Cady, reject the use of WMD by rejecting the very questions that ask them to judge whether use is acceptable.

Cohn and Ruddick argue that the questions are expressed in a discourse that excludes consideration of human suffering (p. 415). In addition, the strategic discourse of nuclear deterrence is about abstractions of weapons, not real weapons, in that it does not consider how the weapons would actually function in war. Also, the discourse is not an objective reflection of political reality, for the rationality that it assumes as a necessary feature of deterrence effectiveness is culturally dependent. Moreover, the question about the legitimacy of deterrence excludes consideration of the moral problems posed by the development and deployment of the weapons shy of deterrence. Such development and deployment has great social costs, especially for women.

Pragmatist feminists agree that the use of WMD in war is unacceptable, Lucinda Peach claims. Like liberalism and natural law theory, pragmatist feminism argues that use of WMD in war would violate the *jus in bello* principles of discrimination and proportionality. But Peach does not dismiss the questions about the acceptability of the weapons nor reject the discourse in which those questions are stated, as the antiwar feminist does (p. 441). Like some of the perspectives discussed earlier, pragmatist feminism might accept WMD deterrence on something like the grounds of supreme emergency. However, consistent with Michael Walzer's understanding of this doctrine, Peach argues that such policies are acceptable only as interim measures.

For Holmes, questions about WMD use imply that the use of conventional weapons is acceptable, which is not the case (p. 455). Weapons have been continuously developed to be more destructive, and WMD are simply part of this process. In fact, conventional weapons can be more destructive than WMD. While it may be true, Cady observes, that some weapons are morally worse than others, this does not imply that the use of the morally better ones is acceptable (p. 472). The use of any weapon in war is unacceptable. What about the nuclear policy of pure deterrence, a policy of threats alone, precluding use in war? Both Holmes and Cady argue that such a policy involves a set of moral and rational paradoxes, and so is condemned by its own incoherence (p. 459). Such a policy seeks logically to separate the intention to threaten from the intention to execute the threat, should it fail, and this separation cannot be made. Short of a bluff, the intention to threaten contains the intention to carry out the threat. The immorality of use in war carries over to the use for deterrence.

PROLIFERATION AND DISARMAMENT

Efforts to deal with the threat posed by WMD over the last several decades have focused on controlling their proliferation to states without them and on convincing states with them of the need for disarmament. It is appropriate to consider these topics together because what nonproliferation is to a state without WMD, disarmament is to a state with WMD. In the one case, it is nonacquisition, and in the other, deacquisition. Paul Szasz points out that there are two forms of proliferation and two forms of disarmament. One form of proliferation, the one usually meant by the term, is horizontal proliferation, which is the spread of the weapons to states that do not have them. The other is vertical proliferation, an increase in the numbers of the weapons on the part of those states that already possess them. One form of disarmament, the one for which the term is usually reserved, is the effort to get rid of all weapons of a certain type, such as WMD, while another form, usually referred to as arms control, is the effort simply to control the numbers of the weapons at levels above zero.

In the case of nuclear proliferation, most of the focus has been on controlling horizontal proliferation, with the chief legal instrument being the 1968 Nonproliferation Treaty (NPT). The NPT, Szasz observes, divides the world into nuclear weapon states and nonnuclear weapon states, obligating the latter signatories not to acquire nuclear weapons (p. 59). While the chief focus of the NPT is thus on horizontal proliferation, it does contain a clause (article VI) concerning vertical proliferation, which obligates the recognized nuclear weapon states to move toward nuclear disarmament. In the case of chemical and biological weapons, concerns about nonproliferation have been superseded by legal instruments of complete disarmament, the Biological and Chemical Weapons Conventions discussed earlier. But there is yet no corresponding convention concerning nuclear weapons. The efforts at controlling nuclear weapons have been represented not by agreements to eliminate the weapons, but by bilateral and multilateral arms control agreements, of which there have been a number since the 1960s (pp. 44–6).

Considering what the different perspectives have to say about proliferation and disarmament, we begin again with the perspectives constituting the traditional debate, realism, natural law, liberalism, and Christianity.

The realist focuses on the prudential aspects of nonproliferation and disarmament proposals. There is a major debate within realism on whether horizontal proliferation is prudentially good or bad. So-called proliferation optimists (such as Kenneth Waltz) argue that the proliferation of nuclear weapons can increase stability and reduce the risk of war by bringing to other states the same kind of cautious behavior that the United States and the Soviet Union learned to practice vis-à-vis each other during the cold war. Scott Sagan argues against optimism, pointing out that nuclear proliferators may have politically weak regimes or be under military control, and they may have difficulty creating the kind of survivable, second-strike capability necessary for stable deterrence (p. 85). In addition, proliferation increases the risk of accidental nuclear war and the theft of nuclear weapons by non-state groups.

The outcome of this debate within realism also determines how nuclear proliferation should be viewed from the perspective of moral consequentialism. If proliferation optimists are correct, the good consequences of nuclear proliferation would make it both prudentially and morally valuable. If proliferation pessimists are correct, nuclear proliferation would be bad on both prudential and moral grounds. The authors of most of the chapters in this volume seem to be proliferation pessimists.

Realists are generally opposed to nuclear disarmament, though they may favor disarmament of other WMD. Sagan argues that nuclear disarmament, contrary to expectation, would make nuclear war more likely, due to the instability of situations in which the number of weapons possessed by each side is small (p. 86). Susan Martin points out that the absence of nuclear weapons would increase the risk of conventional war (p. 104). Partly as a result of such considerations, nuclear weapon states believe that their nuclear weapons have utility for them. Another argument against nuclear disarmament is the dynamic relationship between disarmament and proliferation. Sagan claims that some potential proliferators, such as Japan, are kept from acquiring nuclear weapons by the "nuclear umbrella" of the United States (p. 88). Should the United States disarm, Japan may then be more inclined to acquire nuclear weapons.

These realist arguments about nuclear disarmament, as with the realist arguments about proliferation, make not only a prudential case, but also a moral case, at least from the perspective of moral consequentialism. If disarmament would increase the risk of war, both nuclear and conventional, this is a strong moral reason to oppose it. It seems that many of the remaining chapters, in their support for disarmament, do not consider the issue of stability.

Writing for the natural law tradition, C. A. J. Coady, like some of the other authors, notes an apparent hypocrisy in the antiproliferation stance of the states possessing WMD (p. 123). Their stance, he observes, has "an air of paradox." Possessors of WMD preach against the acquisition of WMD by other states, while refusing to give up their own. A charge of hypocrisy is an important moral criticism, and a defense against it requires showing that there are relevant differences that would justify the double standard alleged in the hypocrisy charge: What is the difference between WMD possessors and nonpossessors that justifies the former being allowed to possess and the latter not? As noted, realists such as Sagan, who in the case of nuclear weapons support a nonproliferation position while opposing disarmament, would seek to rebut the charge of hypocrisy by pointing to the institutional and political differences between possessors and many nonpossessors. Many nonpossessors with politically weak or militarized governing regimes are less likely to keep their WMD safe and secure.

Some critics of proliferation may seek to avoid the charge of hypocrisy by positing a moral difference, rather than institutional or political differences. WMD possessors, they claim, are morally superior to nonpossessors, and this difference justifies the possessors' nonproliferation stance. But Coady claims that WMD possessors are not morally superior (p. 123). The great powers as well as the lesser powers engage in roguish behavior.[14] However, he (along with Sohail Hashmi) points out that a successful charge of hypocrisy against the WMD possessors who preach nonproliferation would not justify such proliferation, if the possession of WMD is itself morally unacceptable (pp. 124, 346). What the charge would then justify, of course, is a call for WMD disarmament on the part of the possessors.

One's view on whether WMD disarmament is morally required is related to one's view about the moral acceptability of WMD deterrence. Recall that, for Coady, three factors are involved in the moral assessment of WMD deterrence: first, the balance of its costs and benefits; second, the morally questionable nature of the intentions it requires; and third, the international regime of fear on which it depends. The last two factors count against deterrence and hence in favor of disarmament, and Coady claims that the first factor may as well. Nuclear or WMD deterrence may have greater costs than benefits (p. 121). Thus, he sees WMD disarmament as morally required. Note that his position on the costs and benefits of deterrence places him on the other side of the issue from the realists, who argue against disarmament. Even assuming that the possession of WMD had the moral drawbacks implied by the second and third factors, if it had a balance of benefits over costs, as the realists believe, an overall moral judgment on disarmament would be more difficult to arrive at. The first factor opposing disarmament would have to be weighed against the other two favoring it. The empirical question of whether WMD deterrence has a balance of costs over benefits is one of the most difficult questions in this debate.

A different natural law perspective on nuclear disarmament is offered by John Langan. Recall Langan's stress on the role of institutions as intermediary between the general moral principles and their policy prescriptions. He suggests that reflection on the apocalyptic nature of nuclear weapons often leads natural law thinkers to call for immediate nuclear disarmament. But a focus on the institutions involved in nuclear weapons policy may lead instead to calls to reduce our nuclear risk by working through the institutions (p. 137). One example he gives is that we should structure the nuclear institutions in a way that ensures a fire break be maintained between the use of nuclear weapons and the use of other weapons, so as to reduce the risk of nuclear use in war. This view may be more supportive of arms control than disarmament.

The liberal position, Henry Shue maintains, opposes nuclear proliferation and favors nuclear disarmament, and the arguments for these two conclusions are the same (p. 158). First, on a strict interpretation of the principle of discrimination, unmediated by the doctrine of double effect, practicing nuclear deterrence requires the immoral intention to kill civilians and is thus prohibited. Second, nuclear weapons are profoundly dangerous, and there is no convincing proof that nuclear deterrence has worked to make the world safer. Thus, liberalism agrees with the natural law position as set out by Coady that states without nuclear weapons should not acquire them and states with them should get rid of them.

Michael Walzer also finds nuclear proliferation to be unacceptable, though his argument relies partly on the claim, which he shares with the realists, that the institutional and political weaknesses of many potential proliferators, especially the rogue states and the failed states, make it very dangerous for them to have nuclear weapons or other WMD (p. 166). In light of these dangers, it is morally acceptable for other states to use force to stop those states from acquiring WMD, at least so long as the states practicing coercion are themselves making efforts to get rid of their own WMD.[15] Walzer, like Shue, favors nuclear disarmament, but on different grounds. It is not because nuclear weapons are so dangerous in the hands of their current possessors, but because the conditions under which the doctrine of supreme emergency justified nuclear deterrence during the cold war have now passed, making the principle of discrimination again determinative of our moral judgment (p. 164). Given his concerns about proliferation, however, he argues that the nuclear powers should not disarm so long as dangerous states are engaging in proliferation.

From the Christian perspective, according to Nigel Bigger, WMD proliferation is not acceptable, but views on WMD disarmament vary, reflecting differing views on the acceptability of WMD (especially nuclear) deterrence (pp. 182–7). Some view WMD disarmament as not required, some see it as required – so long as it can be achieved multilaterally – and some regard it as required even if it can proceed only unilaterally. By contrast, Martin Cook observes, dispensationalists view the invention of WMD as fulfillment of biblical prophecies concerning the future battle of Armageddon, which precedes the Second Coming of Christ (p. 205). Given this world-view, they have little incentive to support disarmament, and many consider WMD proliferation to be divinely ordained.

Buddhism, according to our authors, strongly opposes WMD proliferation and strongly favors WMD disarmament (p. 228). The same is the case for Confucianism. Julia Ching points out that disarmament is often praised in Confucian texts (pp. 257–60). This view follows from the Chinese tendency to rely on nonmilitary means for defense, including good administration and sound economic structure.

The two views within Hinduism, outlined by Katherine Young, give different answers regarding WMD proliferation and disarmament (pp. 296–9). The Hindu tradition of nonviolence would, of course, oppose WMD proliferation and favor WMD disarmament. The just war–like tradition would raise the hypocrisy argument, pointing to the double standard of the nuclear powers, who oppose proliferation in the case of India while retaining their own weapons. This is unacceptable. Nuclear weapons are necessary for Indian security and independence, given the nuclear weapons possessed by that country's neighbors. Thus, this view favors nuclear proliferation, at least for India, so long as other great powers have these weapons. Nuclear disarmament is favored, but only when it is pursued by all states. The tradition of political Hinduism, suggests Kanti Bajpai, holds a similar view (p. 317). Political Hinduism emphasizes that Indian nuclear weapons are necessary to stop stronger nations from exploiting India, as they have done for hundreds of years. India can disarm only when there is equality among nations, so that India would no longer be subject to exploitation. This seems to be a more stringent condition on Indian nuclear disarmament than that stipulated by the Hindu just war tradition, since it appears that the latter requires equality only in the lack of nuclear weapons, while the former requires equality of overall power.

There is a split in Islam similar to the split in Hinduism on the moral problem posed by questions of proliferation and disarmament. On the one hand, Sohail Hashmi notes, there is strong sentiment for regional and universal WMD disarmament (p. 344). On the other hand, there is much support for Pakistan's acquisition of nuclear weapons. One telling episode showing the ambivalence of Islam toward WMD concerns the Iranian efforts to develop nuclear weapons. Under the shah, Hashmi notes, Iran was moving deliberately toward a nuclear weapons capability. But when the 1979 Islamic revolution occurred, this program was abruptly abandoned, reportedly due to the qualms of the leader of the revolution, the Ayatollah Khomeini (p. 342).

Judaism is generally opposed to WMD proliferation, according to Reuven Kimelman, given the danger from the spread of the weapons. (Thus, he, like others, assumes that the proliferation optimists are wrong.) Judaism would also favor universal disarmament of nuclear weapons and other WMD (p. 379). But short of universal disarmament, Israeli nuclear possession would be favored, given the threat that the nation is under from its neighbors. Since the existential threat to Israel is from conventional weapons as well as WMD, the right of Israel to seek military security may override even the call for universal WMD disarmament. Joseph David would support this latter view as well (p. 393). In representing the stringent conditions necessary for Israel to abandon its nuclear weapons, Kimelman argues that Isaiah's prescription to beat swords into plowshares presupposes universal moral instruction, an international judicial institution able to adjudicate conflicts, and an economic alternative to the arms industry (p. 379).

The hypocrisy argument is central to the feminist perspective on proliferation. The hypocrisy lies in the position of the nuclear states that their nuclear weapons are acceptable but those of others are not. According to Carol Cohn and Sara Ruddick, this nonproliferation stance is supported by a discourse that makes some WMD visible (others') and some invisible (the nuclear powers'; p. 421). Lucinda Peach makes a similar point by arguing that vertical as well as horizontal proliferation needs to be addressed

(p. 443). Only by addressing both can the hypocrisy charge be avoided. Cohn and Ruddick argue that the nonproliferation discourse enshrines a hierarchy among states with the nuclear states on top. Also, the discourse is ethno-racist, in its implication that whites can better be trusted with nuclear weapons, and gendered, in that the traits of those allowed to possess nuclear weapons are masculine and those not allowed, feminine. The pressure toward proliferation reflects this gendered understanding, because WMD are symbols of masculine power. While WMD proliferation is clearly a bad thing, how, they ask, can citizens of nuclear states oppose it without being party to the nonproliferation discourse? How can they avoid hypocrisy? Is there an alternative nonproliferation discourse? Perhaps it is the discourse of universal disarmament.

The antiwar feminist perspective, Cohn and Ruddick argue, strongly favors WMD disarmament (p. 424). But, rejecting the implied isolation of WMD from other weapons, they understand the call for WMD disarmament as part of a moral demand for general and complete disarmament. Disarmament should proceed unilaterally if necessary. The pragmatist feminist perspective, on the other hand, is not so committed to WMD disarmament that it should be unilateral (p. 445f.). According to Peach, universal WMD disarmament is the goal, and unilateral initiatives should be attempted in order to stimulate the multilateral process toward that goal. But unilateral WMD disarmament should not be sought for its own sake.

The hypocrisy argument is important for the pacifist as well. WMD proliferation is wrong, Robert Holmes argues, but states possessing WMD cannot consistently deny the right of other states to possess them (p. 461). WMD proliferation is wrong for three reasons. First, WMD proliferators may act irrationally and use the weapons in war. Second, WMD proliferation increases the risk that such weapons will be used accidentally in war. Third, WMD proliferators seek to achieve security and to promote their interests through the manipulation of fear and terror, and this cannot be an adequate foundation for peace. But these reasons apply to all WMD states, whether a current possessor or a potential proliferator. Thus, the standard nonproliferation stance is inconsistent.

The resolution of this inconsistency is a commitment to universal WMD disarmament. But Holmes, like Cohn and Ruddick, makes clear that WMD disarmament is only part of the moral requirement for general and complete disarmament (p. 463). Holmes's argument for this is, in part, a rejection of the morally special character of WMD, a special character argued for (or assumed) by other of the authors, as well as by the editors in the Introduction (p. 10). Weapons represent a spectrum of destructiveness, and drawing a moral line between WMD and conventional weapons is arbitrary. As argued in the Introduction, this line is usually drawn based on the indiscriminateness of WMD. But, Holmes argues, all weapons tend to be indiscriminate in their use.

CONCRETE OPTIONS

Given our moral obligations regarding WMD, how should we fulfill them? What policy options ought we to adopt to bring about the results that morality requires? The authors answer these questions in various ways, recommending a wide range of options. Some of the recommended options are concrete, meaning that they could, assuming it were politically feasible, be quickly adopted and have significant short-term effects. Some are less than concrete.

For the sake of this discussion, I divide the recommended options into four categories. First are the concrete options, which are prescribed to lessen the risk that WMD would be used in war. Second are options that involve a general cooperative stance toward international relations, as this promotes the goal of lessening the danger from WMD and achieving WMD disarmament. Third are options that question the effectiveness or moral appropriateness of a cooperative stance toward international relations. Fourth are options that call for far-reaching change in human social organization, understanding this as a necessary basis for solving the moral problems posed by WMD.

The liberals, Henry Shue and Michael Walzer, offer the most concrete options. Shue argues that the most immediate priority is the de-alerting of their nuclear weapons by the United States and Russia (p. 157). As a holdover from cold war policy, many of the strategic nuclear weapons possessed by these two are set to be fired on short notice, in order to deter a surprise nuclear attack. In Shue's view, this is an accident waiting to happen. The nuclear danger lies not in either nation but in the system of nuclear deterrence itself with the weapons on hair trigger. De-alerting the weapons, taking them off hair trigger, would create a situation in which a much longer time would be required to fire them, thereby greatly decreasing the risk that they will be fired accidentally.

Walzer, too, endorses de-alerting of nuclear weapons, but he is less persuaded that the current danger of accidental war is so great (p. 165). If the risk of accident were great, the nuclear deterrence system would be very unstable, but, he points out, the objections that many liberals have to national missile defense – namely, that it would make nuclear deterrence much less stable – seem to assume that deterrence without the defenses is fairly stable. Other measures endorsed by Walzer include reduction in nuclear stockpiles and changes in the targeting of nuclear weapons. In addition, as mentioned earlier, he argues for the selective use of force against rogue or failed states that are attempting to acquire WMD (p. 166). The justification for this implies that states are not morally equal, a view based on the international and interventionist aspects of liberal thought. Walzer's claim that there is a moral inequality of states puts him at odds with C. A. J. Coady, who rejects such a claim as a basis for a nonproliferation stance. Walzer argues that it may be instrumentally valuable to seek international support, for example, through the United Nations, for such nonproliferation coercion, but that the coercing states are justified in acting unilaterally, if international support is not forthcoming (p. 167). This sets the stage for discussion of the next kind of option.

Options of the other three kinds focus not directly on achieving specific morally desired results but on establishing the conditions necessary to achieve them; that is, they focus on process rather than content. Options of the second kind are a call for internationalism, a focus on the need for international cooperation and agreement. The model and main arena for this cooperation is international law. Paul Szasz presents an array of international agreements that have been adopted regarding WMD, including conventions prohibiting biological and chemical weapons, nuclear test ban treaties (partial in 1963 and complete in 1996), nuclear free zones, and international organizations to control the spread of nuclear materials and technology.

The realists offer strong support for the use of international agreements to control WMD. While a superficial reading of the realist position might suggest that a realist would not support international agreements, Scott Sagan argues that making and abiding by such agreements is very much in the self-interest of individual nations, even the great powers (p. 89). This view not only explains why nations have accepted the constraints of international agreements (without having to suppose that they are acting for moral reasons), but also prescribes that they should accept such constraints. The importance realists place on abiding by international agreements concerning WMD is seen in Sagan's claim that the tradition of the nonuse of nuclear weapons is fragile and unlikely to withstand even a single violation (p. 76). This realist stance is mirrored by those in the long-standing debate about American foreign policy who favor internationalism as against unilateralism. Despite claims about American exceptionalism and the fact of America's inordinate military and economic power, they argue, the nation's interests are best achieved cooperatively.

This view is also taken by the natural law perspective, which has a long history of support for internationalism. C. A. J. Coady argues that internationalism is the only way in which the moral problems raised by WMD can adequately be dealt with (p. 126). Confucianism supports this approach as well. Given the Confucian preference for good government over weapons, Julia Ching argues that global governance is the proper solution (p. 260). WMD need to be outlawed. Sohail Hashmi notes that although Muslim states have overwhelmingly endorsed international agreements on the control of WMD, there is widespread discontent at both the elite and popular levels at what are perceived as great-power double standards and bad faith (p. 345). The United States has a long history, for example, of punishing Muslim states such as Pakistan, Iraq, and Iran for pursuing WMD, while turning a blind eye to Israel. Muslim concerns, Hashmi suggests, should be seen as part of broader third world concerns that international law is enforced by the powerful states only when it suits their interests.

The third kind of option is a rejection of internationalism. This approach, sometimes referred to as the new imperialism, is explained (though not endorsed) by Coady as the belief that a *pax Americana* is the only alternative to internationalism and is preferable to it (p. 125). Coady argues (along with Sagan) that this approach would not solve the problems of WMD and that it has its own moral dangers. Hinduism also tends to reject internationalism, at least under current conditions. While Hinduism has a tradition of treaties limiting warfare, Katherine Young observes, treaties are thought to be appropriate only among equals (p. 299). When nations are not equal in power, treaty making becomes a way for great powers to exploit lesser powers. Because India is a lesser power, Hinduism tends not to support treaties as a solution to the problems of WMD. This is so both for the Hindu just war tradition and (even more) for political Hinduism. This is seen in India's refusal to sign the Nuclear Nonproliferation Treaty.

Options of the fourth kind are the least concrete. They call for fundamental changes in social organization, arguing that the moral problems represented by WMD will not otherwise be solved. In addition, advocates often argue that these options are morally required in their own right, independent of their role in addressing the problems of WMD. The three perspectives most clearly presenting options of this kind are Buddhism, antiwar feminism, and pacifism.

Buddhism maintains that true change must originate with changes in the psychological attitudes of individuals (p. 239). We must, through mindfulness, begin in our own hearts and be willing to address our own imperfections. We must achieve internal psychological growth and transformation. We need, for example, to recognize that our own imperfections may be the basis for the hatred of us by those we regard as our enemies and to seek to reduce conflict by working on correcting those imperfections. (This view has obvious implications for U.S. reactions to the terrorist attacks of September 11, 2001.) As an aid to this process of individual growth, education about WMD and the world situation in general is a top priority, for the practice of mindfulness requires such information and understanding. In addition, we must work to achieve economic and social justice. Being just is necessary for our own growth, and ending poverty is necessary for others having the opportunity to grow.

This idea of transformation is taken up as well by antiwar feminists, although their emphasis is more on social rather than individual transformation. Carol Cohn and Sara Ruddick argue that the most important way to counter the gender bias of the discourse in which international negotiations proceed is to get women to the table (p. 426). But they recognize that once women are there, it is not clear how they should act, for the discourse structures the process so as to make efforts to transcend it irrelevant. For example, women (or men) who bring feelings or emotions into the discussion at the negotiating table are likely to be marginalized and ignored. In addition, it is not clear that the negotiating table is where the real decisions are made. This points to the need for more fundamental changes in society. Making treaties is only a small part of making peace.

Pacifism as well sees at best a limited role for treaty making. According to Robert Holmes, only a radical rethinking of the violence at the foundation of our social order, domestically and internationally, offers the promise of basic change toward genuine peace (p. 466). Governments are part of the problem. The solution must come from a mass, grass-roots, cross-cultural movement for nonviolence that bypasses governments. This movement must organize itself into a force for nonviolent resistance against aggression. This would spread the burden of protection and resistance throughout the entire population. The spread of individual communications technology lays the basis for this. With the end of the cold war, Holmes sees an opportunity for such a movement, a chance that may not come again in a thousand years.

Aside from the desirability of the basic social changes called for by pacifists and antiwar feminists, many would object on the grounds of feasibility, arguing that the large numbers of people that must be involved in such changes could never be mobilized to achieve them. Duane Cady claims that, though people could be motivated to participate on prudential or pragmatic grounds, the moral case for such changes may be what carries the day, as it was the moral case that was so important in other ground-breaking social movements, such as the abolition of slavery, women's suffrage, and the civil rights movement (p. 475). Here we have at the end the antithesis of the realist position with which the discussion began: from the position that morality is not a primary motivator to the view that it can be the most important. Future developments may well hinge on which of these views is closer to the truth.

CONCLUSION

Despite some morally significant differences among chemical, biological, and nuclear weapons, it is appropriate to consider them together under the rubric of WMD. The reason is that most of the kinds of weapons in these categories share the feature that it is difficult or impossible, irrespective of the attacker's intentions, to use them in war without doing great harm to civilians. They are inherently indiscriminate.[16] Given the importance of sparing civilians, which arises in all of the major ethical traditions, WMD are morally problematic.

The chapters in this volume show clearly the struggles of the great ethical traditions, both religious and secular, to come to terms with the moral challenge posed by WMD. At the same time, the chapters reveal the relevance of the traditions to the moral challenge of WMD, despite their often ancient roots.[17] What most of the traditions affirm, more or less strongly, is that, while violent struggle may be endemic among nations, it must be understood to be a morally limited enterprise and that one of the main moral limitations, known as the principle of discrimination in the just war tradition, is that civilians are not to be the target of attack. The combination of that limitation and the inherently indiscriminate nature of WMD shows why virtually all of the traditions come out strongly against the use of WMD in war and why most of them reject the use of WMD for deterrence and call for WMD disarmament.

On the other hand, some of the traditions, especially the critical traditions of antiwar feminism and pacifism, take us in a different direction, emphasizing not the discontinuities between WMD and conventional weapons but the continuities. While other traditions argue that we should not let our acceptance of conventional weapons extend to the acceptance of WMD, the critical traditions argue that we should let our abhorrence of WMD extend to an abhorrence of conventional weapons as well. WMD simply reveal forcefully what is rotten with the whole war system. WMD show the need for a new discourse, but it should be a discourse that shows the unacceptability both of WMD and of war itself.

The moral questions of WMD have a new urgency given the events of 9/11. These events show that substate terrorist groups are willing to kill indiscriminately on a large scale. The actions of the terrorists turned a jet airliner into a WMD. WMD are the tools of terrorists because terrorists are fighting an asymmetric war, their weakness making it impossible for them to confront their opponent in a traditional military manner. Holding no territory, they cannot be deterred. We cannot now doubt the willingness of substate terrorist groups to use chemical, biological, and nuclear weapons, should they get their hands on them. And they may well in the future get their hands on them. WMD may have moved beyond the capacity of states to control them. The generally statist character of our moral discourse about large-scale violence may make that discourse no longer adequate.

Notes

1. Realism might be interpreted as operating under the single moral norm that one's own state is to be preserved and promoted.
2. The claim that the ethics of WMD is a matter of *jus in bello* assumes that the use of WMD is a matter of choices made within a war. But the idea of proportionality also plays a role in *jus ad bellum*, where war is regarded as permissible only if it would bring about more good than harm. If there is good reason to think that a war would escalate to the use of WMD, the proportionality condition of *jus ad bellum* would probably not be satisfied. In this way, the ethics of WMD can also be a matter of *jus ad bellum*.

3. C. A. J. Coady argues that this sort of general understanding of the natural law tradition allows us to see the philosopher Hobbes as a part of it. Because Hobbes is regarded as one of the founders of realism, this suggests that the distinction between realism and natural law is not as sharp as I have suggested it is. This is an illustration of Coady's point that the division into different perspectives on which the study of this volume is based can sharpen lines that in reality are blurred (p. 114).

4. This is the predominant strain of Christian thinking, as Nigel Biggar points out (pp. 169–70). The pacifistic strain, in a secular form, is discussed by Robert Holmes in Chapter 23. The apocalyptic strain is discussed by Martin Cook in Chapter 10.

5. In addition to its source in the social contract tradition of Locke and others, liberalism also has a source in the utilitarian tradition of Bentham and Mill.

6. Walzer develops the doctrine of supreme emergency in *Just and Unjust Wars* (New York: Basic Books, 1977). Shue observes that supreme emergency is taken by our premier liberal political theorist, John Rawls, as a basic part of the liberal perspective on war (p. 140).

7. These remarks of Walzer's about the behavior of liberals in power were made at the conference in which the chapters of this volume were originally presented.

8. It is interesting to compare this Hindu idea of proper frame of mind for the practice of violence with that prescribed by JWT, namely, proper intention.

9. In the conference where the chapters were presented, Donald Swearer strongly endorsed this point about the need to consider alternative discourses, pointing out that this is a way to express the Buddhist point about the need to decenter the self and question the notion of individual autonomy.

10. In Chapter 1, Susan Martin discusses a possible exception to this, namely, the use of smallpox-infected blankets by the British against the Native Americans (p. 40).

11. Nigel Biggar notes that the acceptance of the doctrine of supreme emergency by liberalism would make this tradition closer to Islam than to Christianity (p. 193).

12. Walzer, *Just and Unjust Wars*, chap. 17.

13. One feature of Israeli policy is that nuclear deterrence is opaque, meaning that nuclear weapons are not a matter of public discussion and that nuclear threats are not explicit. David argues that this policy makes it less likely that Israel would ever use its nuclear weapons in war, since to do so would be to destroy the opaque character of the deterrence policy. This feature may also support the moral acceptability of Israeli nuclear policy (p. 394).

14. Coady points out, however, that this claim does not imply the so-called moral equivalency thesis, the position that there is no moral difference between the great powers and many nonnuclear states. He takes this thesis to be a red herring in these debates (p. 123).

15. As an example of this, see Walzer's discussion of the proposed use of force against Iraq in the *New Republic* of September 30, 2002. He argues that though the war for regime change proposed by the United States is not justified, it would be justified to use the threat of force to impose a thorough inspection regime on Iraq to rid it of its WMD. Should Iraq then resist the regime, the use of force itself would be justified. Events have overtaken the debate.

16. As discussed in the Introduction, some weapons in these categories, such as incapacitating gases, may not do serious harm to civilians, but still there is a pragmatic justification for including these exceptional cases in the category of WMD (p. 8). In addition, that this shared feature of inherent indiscriminateness is of great moral importance shows the need to examine WMD from a moral perspective, as undertaken in this volume. Recall another point from the Introduction, that nuclear weapons should be morally examined along with other WMD as well as on their own, since nuclear weapons both share the morally important feature of other WMD (inherent indiscriminateness) and have additional morally important features of their own (p. 11).

17. When nuclear weapons are considered by themselves in terms of the ways in which they differ from other weapons, including other WMD, this statement may not hold. On this point, see the discussion in the Introduction (p. 11). The moral paradoxes posed by nuclear weapons may place them beyond the framework of existing moral traditions. See Steven P. Lee, *Morality, Prudence, and Nuclear Weapons* (Cambridge: Cambridge University Press, 1993), chap. 1.

Contributors

Kanti Bajpai is Headmaster of the Doon School in Dehra Dun, India, and formerly Professor of International Politics at the School of International Studies, Jawaharlal Nehru University. He is the author of *Roots of Terrorism* and coeditor of *Jammu and Kashmir: An Agenda for the Future*. He has been a Visiting Fellow at the Brookings Institution, a Resident Fellow of the Rajiv Gandhi Foundation, and a regular commentator on foreign policy issues in the Indian media.

Nigel Biggar is Professor of Theology at Trinity College, Dublin. He is the author of *Good Life: Reflections on What We Value Today*, *The Hastening That Waits: Karl Barth's Ethics*, and *Theological Politics*. He is also editor of *Burying the Past: Making Peace and Doing Justice after Civil Conflict* and *Reckoning with Barth*.

Duane L. Cady is Professor of Philosophy at Hamline University and author of *From Warism to Pacifism: A Moral Continuum* and coauthor of *Humanitarian Intervention: Just War vs. Pacifism*, *Just War, Nonviolence and Nuclear Deterrence*, and *Bringing Peace Home: Feminism, Violence, and Nature*. He is a past president of Concerned Philosophers for Peace.

David W. Chappell is Professor of Comparative Religion at Soka University and Professor Emeritus at the University of Hawaii. He is editor of *Buddhist and Taoist Studies*, *T'ien-t'ai Buddhism: An Outline of the Fourfold Teachings*, and *Buddhist Peacework: Creating Cultures of Peace*. He is also founding editor of the journal *Buddhist-Christian Studies* and cofounder and past president of the Society of Buddhist-Christian Studies.

Julia Ching was University Professor and Lee Chair Professor Emerita at the University of Toronto and had also taught at Columbia and Yale Universities. She published fifteen books on East Asian philosophy and religion. A member of the Order of Canada and the Canadian Pugwash Group, she received two honorary degrees. She was also a board member of Science for Peace. She died on October 26, 2001.

C. A. J. Coady is Deputy Director (and Head of the University of Melbourne division) of the Centre for Applied Philosophy and Public Ethics. He is the author of *Testimony: A Philosophical Inquiry*. He has published numerous articles on morality and violence and most recently coedited *Terrorism and Justice: Moral Argument in a Threatened World*. He has been a senior fellow at the U.S. Institute of Peace and Laurence Rockefeller visiting fellow in ethics and public affairs at the Princeton Center for Human Values.

Carol Cohn is Senior Research Scholar in the Department of Political Science at Wellesley College. She is the author of *Wars, Wimps, and Women: Gender in the Construction of U.S. National Security*. She has also published articles on defense-related issues in the *Bulletin of the Atomic Scientists* and *Signs: Journal of Women in Culture and Society*. Her current research centers on transnational networks of women peace builders.

Martin L. Cook is Professor of Philosophy at the U.S. Air Force Academy and formerly Elihu Root Professor of Military Studies and Ethics at the U.S. Army War College. He is the author of two books and numerous articles on religious ethics, applied military ethics, and military professionalism. He has served on the editorial board of the *Annual of the Society of Christian Ethics* and currently serves on the boards of *Parameters* and the *Journal of Military Ethics*.

Joseph E. David teaches in the Faculty of Law at the University of Haifa. He is the coauthor of *The State Rabbinate: Appointment, Tasks and Freedom of Expression* and the editor of *The State of Israel: Between Judaism and Democracy* and *Human Dignity or Rights? Between Liberalism and Humanism* (forthcoming).

Sohail H. Hashmi is Alumnae Foundation Associate Professor of International Relations at Mount Holyoke College and serves on the editorial board of the Ethikon Series in Comparative Ethics. He is the editor of *Islamic Political Ethics: Civil Society, Pluralism, and Conflict* and coeditor of *Boundaries and Justice*. He is currently completing a book on the Islamic ethics of war and peace.

Robert L. Holmes is Professor of Philosophy at the University of Rochester, the author of *On War and Morality* and *Basic Moral Philosophy*, and editor of *Nonviolence in Theory and Practice*. A former editor of *Public Affairs Quarterly*, he has served as Senior Fulbright Lecturer in the former USSR and Rajiv Gandhi Professor of Peace and Disarmament at Jawaharlal Nehru University.

Philip J. Ivanhoe is Findlay Visiting Professor of Philosophy at Boston University. He has written and edited numerous books and articles on Chinese philosophy and religion. Among his recent works are *Confucian Moral Self*

Cultivation, Ethics in the Confucian Tradition: The Thought of Mencius and Wang Yang-ming, and a translation and commentary on the *Daodejing.*

John Kelsay is Richard L. Rubenstein Professor of Religion at Florida State University. He is the author of *Islam and War* and coeditor of *Cross, Crescent, and Sword* and *Just War and Jihad.* He has served as coeditor of the *Annual of the Society of Christian Ethics* and is currently coeditor of the *Journal of Religious Ethics.*

Reuven Kimelman is Professor of Rabbinic Literature at Brandeis University. He is the author of *The Mystical Meaning of Lekhah Dodie and Kabbalat Shabbat* and *The Rhetoric of Jewish Prayer: A Literary and Historical Commentary on the Prayerbook* (forthcoming). He is also writing a book on the Jewish ethics of power.

John Langan, S.J., is Joseph Cardinal Bernardin Professor of Catholic Social Thought at Georgetown University. He is the editor of *The Nuclear Dilemma and the Just War Tradition* and *The American Search for Peace* and served as a consultant for the U.S. Catholic Bishops' pastoral letter *The Challenge of Peace.* He is a past board member of the Society of Christian Ethics.

Steven P. Lee is Professor of Philosophy at Hobart and William Smith College. He is the author of *Morality, Prudence, and Nuclear Weapons* and *What Is the Argument? Critical Thinking in the Real World* and coauthor of *The Nuclear Predicament: Nuclear Weapons in the 21st Century.* He also coedited *Nuclear Weapons and the Future of Humanity.*

Susan B. Martin is Lecturer in the Department of War Studies at King's College London, where her work focuses on international relations theory and international security. She is currently completing a book manuscript titled "Deterrence and Proliferation in the Twenty-first Century: How Chemical, Biological, and Nuclear Weapons Shape International Politics." Her work has appeared in the *Journal of Strategic Studies* and *International Security.*

Lucinda Joy Peach is Associate Professor of Philosophy and Religion at American University in Washington, D.C. She is the author of articles on gender and violence, the ethics of women in combat, feminist perspectives on just war theory, the trafficking in women for the sex trade, corporate social responsibility for human rights, and a monograph titled *Legislating Morality: Pluralism and Religious Identity in Lawmaking.* She is the editor of *Women in Culture: An Anthology* and *Women and World Religions.*

Sara Ruddick is Professor Emerita at Eugene Lang College of New School University, the author of *Maternal Thinking: Toward a Politics of Peace,* and coeditor of three anthologies, including *Mother Troubles: Rethinking Contemporary Maternal Dilemmas.* She has written extensively on war, nonviolence, ethics, and feminist theory.

Scott D. Sagan is Professor of Political Science and Codirector of the Center for International Security and Cooperation at Stanford University. He is the author of *Moving Targets: Nuclear Strategy and National Security, The Limits of Safety: Organizations, Accidents and Nuclear Weapons,* and coauthor of *The Spread of Nuclear Weapons: A Debate Renewed.* He has served as a consultant to the U.S. Joint Chiefs of Staff, the Office of the Secretary of Defense, and the Los Alamos and Sandia Laboratories.

Henry Shue is Professor of Politics and International Relations at Oxford University and Senior Research Fellow in Philosophy at Merton College. He is the author of *Basic Rights,* "Torture," "Exporting Hazards," and "Let Whatever Is Smouldering Erupt," and editor of *Nuclear Deterrence and Moral Restraint.* He is the founding director of the Cornell Program on Ethics and Public Life and a founding member of the Institute for Philosophy and Public Policy at the University of Maryland.

Donald K. Swearer is McDowell Professor of Religion at Swarthmore College and author of *Secrets of the Lotus: Studies in Buddhist Meditation, Wealth and Salvation: Studies in Buddhist Social Ethics,* and *For the Sake of the World: The Spirit of Buddhist and Christian Monasticism.* He has been the Numata Distinguished Visiting Professor of Buddhist Studies at the University of Hawaii.

Paul C. Szasz served eighteen years in the United Nations, holding such positions as director of the General Legal Division and legal advisor to the 1979–80 UN Conference on Inhumane Conventional Weapons. After retiring from the United Nations, he taught international law at the New York University School of Law and at other universities. Szasz authored *The Law and Practices of the International Atomic Energy Agency, The Proliferation of Arms Control Organizations, UN Forces and International Humanitarian Law,* and *Environmental Destruction as a Method of Warfare.* He died on April 30, 2002.

Michael Walzer is a permanent member of the Institute for Advanced Study in Princeton. He is the author of *The Revolution of the Saints, Just and Unjust Wars, Spheres of Justice, Toleration,* and other books and coeditor of *The Jewish Political Tradition.* He serves as coeditor of the journal *Dissent,* contributing editor to the *New Republic,* and a member of the editorial board of the Ethikon Series in Comparative Ethics.

Katherine K. Young is James McGill Professor in the Faculty of Religious Studies at McGill University. She has published widely in three fields: Hinduism, gender and religion, and ethics (Hindu ethics, comparative medical ethics, and social ethics). She is the coauthor of *Hindu Ethics: Purity, Abortion, and Euthanasia* and *Spreading Misandry: The Teaching of Contempt for Men in Popular Culture.* She is currently writing a book on the peaceable ideal of manhood in the cultures of Indian Brahmans, Orthodox Jews, Mennonites, and Swedes.

Index